D0846717

NATIVE PEOPLES

THE CANADIAN EXPERIENCE

Fourth Edition | Edited by *C. Roderick Wilson & Christopher Fletcher*

OXFORD
UNIVERSITY PRESS

NATIVE PEOPLES

OXFORD
UNIVERSITY PRESS

Oxford University Press is a department of the University of Oxford.
It furthers the University's objective of excellence in research, scholarship,
and education by publishing worldwide. Oxford is a registered trade mark of
Oxford University Press in the UK and in certain other countries.

Published in Canada by
Oxford University Press
8 Sampson Mews, Suite 204,
Don Mills, Ontario M3C 0H5 Canada

www.oupcanada.com

Copyright © Oxford University Press Canada 2014

The moral rights of the authors have been asserted

Database right Oxford University Press (maker)
First Edition published in 1986
Second Edition published in 1995
Third Edition published in 2004

All rights reserved. No part of this publication may be reproduced, stored in
a retrieval system, or transmitted, in any form or by any means, without the
prior permission in writing of Oxford University Press, or as expressly permitted
by law, by licence, or under terms agreed with the appropriate reprographics
rights organization. Enquiries concerning reproduction outside the scope of the
above should be sent to the Permissions Department at the address above
or through the following url: www.oupcanada.com/permission/permission_request.php

Every effort has been made to determine and contact copyright holders.
In the case of any omissions, the publisher will be pleased to make
suitable acknowledgement in future editions.

Library and Archives Canada Cataloguing in Publication
Native peoples : the Canadian experience / edited by
C. Roderick Wilson and Christopher Fletcher. – 4th ed.

Includes bibliographical references and index.
ISBN 978-0-19-543013-4

1. Native peoples--Canada--History. I. Wilson, C.
Roderick II. Fletcher, Christopher III. Title.

E78.C2N335 2013   971.004'97   C2013-901505-1

Cover image: Matthew Little/Epoch Times

Oxford University Press is committed to our environment.
Wherever possible, our books are printed on paper which comes from
responsible sources.

Printed and bound in the United States of America

1 2 3 4 — 17 16 15 14

CONTENTS

ACKNOWLEDGEMENTS

A scholarly effort reaches completion only with the dedication and co-operation of more people than could possibly be mentioned. So while we mention only a few, our appreciation extends to all who contributed in myriad ways.

The contributors to this volume have endured a great deal of editorial constraint and comment from us. Yet they still managed to produce manuscripts of exceptional quality. We thank them. We particularly appreciated the excellent editorial advice and encouragement offered by Peter Chambers. It sometimes takes longer to get a manuscript together than one anticipates at the beginning. We appreciate his patience as well. We would like to thank Leslie Saffrey for her thoughtful and thorough copyediting. The care she took with the manuscript significantly enhanced the book.

Finally, and of most central importance, the many Aboriginal persons and groups whose co-operation made these chapters possible are gratefully acknowledged.

CONTRIBUTORS

Thomas S. Abler (Ph.D., Toronto) is Professor Emeritus in Anthropology at the University of Waterloo, where he taught for nearly four decades. He conducted fieldwork among the Allegany and Cattaraugus Seneca, but most of his research has focused on ethnohistorical analysis of Haudenosaunee culture. His publications have dealt with the Iroquois creation myth, kinship and social organization, political factionalism, warfare, and missions, among other topics. Two books deal with Iroquois participation as allies to the Crown in the American Revolution and the Handsome Lake revitalization movement which followed those traumatic years: *Chainbreaker: The Revolutionary War Memoirs of Governor Blacksnake* (1989) and *Cornplanter: Chief Warrior of the Allegany Senecas* (2007).

Margaret Seguin Anderson (Ph.D., Michigan) is Professor Emerita of First Nations Studies at the University of Northern British Columbia. She lives and works in UNBC's Northwest Region, in the centre of Tsimshian territory. She continues to work with Tsimshian, Gitksan, and Nisga'a communities to develop resources for language revitalization, including "talking dictionaries," and has also served as an expert witness in several court cases on Tsimshian land and resource rights. She has written and edited three books, the most recent being *Potlatch at Gitsegukla: William Beynon's 1945 Field Notebooks*, co-edited with Marjorie Halpin.

Alestine Andre (M.A., Victoria) is Heritage Researcher for the Gwich'in Social and Cultural Institute. With Alan Fehr, she published *Gwich'in Ethnobotany: Plants Used by the Gwich'in for Food, Medicine, Shelter and Tools* (2nd ed., 2002). In 2007 she was awarded a National Aboriginal Achievement Award in the Culture, Heritage, and Spirituality category. Every August she and her husband return to their Tree River fish camp on the Mackenzie River.

Jennifer S.H. Brown (Ph.D., Chicago) is Professor of History at the University of Winnipeg. As an anthropologist specializing in ethnohistory, her work has focused on the Canadian fur trade. *Strangers in Blood* (1980) dealt with the significance of Native families in the fur trade. More recently she co-edited with Jacqueline Peterson *The New Peoples: Being and Becoming Metis in North America* (1985).

Ernest S. Burch Jr (Ph.D., Chicago) until his death was Research Associate, Arctic Studies Center, Smithsonian Institution. For 40 years he pursued his interest in the structure of hunter–gatherer societies through ethnographic and ethnohistorical research on early contact northern populations. He was author of *The Eskimos* (1988), in addition to other more technical studies.

Sarah A. Carter (Ph.D., Manitoba) is Professor and H.M. Tory Chair in the Department of History and Classics, and Faculty of Native Studies at the University of Alberta . Her publications include: *Lost Harvests: Reserve Farmers and Government Policy* (1990), *Capturing Women: The Manipulation of Cultural Imagery in Canada's Prairie West* (1997), *Aboriginal People and Colonizers of Western Canada to 1900* (1999), and *The Importance of Being Monogamous: Marriage and Nation Building in Western Canada* (2008).

Hugh A. Dempsey (LL.D., Calgary) retired in 1991 as Associate Director of the Glenbow Museum in Calgary after 30 years with the organization. He is the author and editor of several books relating to Indians and western Canadian history, including *Crowfoot: Chief of the Blackfoot* (1972), *Red Crow: Warrior Chief* (1980), and *Big Bear: The End of Freedom* (1984). He was awarded the Order of Canada, and received an honorary doctorate from the University of Calgary in recognition of his work with Native people. He is an honorary chief of the Blood tribe.

L. James Dempsey (Ph.D., East Anglia) is Associate Professor in the Faculty of Native Studies at the University of Alberta. His interests include Blackfoot and Plains history and culture, Native warriors and warfare, treaties, and land claims. Publications include *Warriors of the King: Prairie Indians in World War I* (1999) and *Blackfoot War Art: Pictographs of the Reservation Period, 1880–2000* (2007).

Heather Devine (Ph.D., Alberta) is Associate Professor in the Department of History at the University of Calgary. Her research and teaching specialties include Canadian Native History, American Indian Policy, and Museum and Heritage Studies, with a particular focus on Metis ethnohistory. She has written widely about fur trade ethnohistory, museology, and cultural heritage, in particular *The People Who Own Themselves:*

Aboriginal Ethnogenesis in a Canadian Family, 1660–1900, winner of the Harold Adams Innis Prize for 2004–5 from the Canadian Federation for the Humanities and Social Sciences.

Harvey A. Feit (Ph.D., McGill) is Professor Emeritus of Anthropology at McMaster University. He writes and works regularly with James Bay Crees and often focuses on Cree efforts to reshape their relations to the Canadian and Quebec states and to the other peoples of Canada and Quebec. Through the 1970s he served as senior social science adviser to the James Bay Cree during their court case and the negotiation and implementation of the James Bay and Northern Quebec Agreement. Since, he has continued to collaborate with Crees and with several other Indigenous peoples in Canada, Alaska, and Australia. Recent publications include: "Le peuple cri de la Baie James parle aux gouvernements: développement, gouvernance et co-gouvernance," in *Les Inuit et les Cris du Nord du Québec*, edited by Jacques-Guy Petit, et al. (2010–11:119–32); and *In the Way of Development: Indigenous Peoples, Life Projects and Globalization*, edited with Mario Blaser and Glenn McRae (2004).

Christopher Fletcher (Ph.D., Université de Montréal) is an Associate Professor in the Department of Social and Preventative Medicine at the Université Laval in Quebec City and an adjunct professor of Anthropology at the University of Alberta. He has diverse research interests in medical and ecological anthropology. He has worked in the Canadian North with Inuit and First Nations communities. His research interests focus on Aboriginal health and healing, cultural concepts and practices in social and mental health, cultural landscape, kinship, and cross-cultural dissemination of research results. His publications include: "Healing and Harmony in our Families—Nunavut Case Study," with Aaron Denham, in *Aboriginal Healing in Canada: Studies in Therapeutic Meaning* *and Practice,* Aboriginal Healing Foundation (2008); and *Inuit Piusituqaqtigut Uimanarsijunik Aanniasiurusingit/Premier Soins Traditionnels Inuits/Traditional Inuit First-Aid,* Avataq Cultural Institute, Montreal (2012).

Jean-Guy A. Goulet (Ph.D., Yale) is Professor of Anthropology and Director of the School of Conflict Studies of the Faculty of Human Sciences at Saint Paul University (Ottawa). He has learned from Aboriginal peoples in Latin America and the Canadian Subarctic. His publications include *Ways of Knowing: Experience, Knowledge and Power Among the Dene Tha* (1998). He is co-editor (with David Young) of *Being Changed by Cross-Cultural Encounters* (2nd ed. 1998), and (with Bruce G. Miller) of *Extraordinary Anthropology: Transformations in the Field* (2007). He is also guest editor of a special issue of *Anthropologie et Sociétés,* "La transformation de l'anthropologue par le terrain" (2011).

Douglas Hudson (Ph.D., Alberta) teaches anthropology and archaeology at the University of the Fraser Valley, with a special interest in First Nations cultures, language, Aboriginal rights, resource use and environment issues, social organization, and applied anthropology. He has participated in anthropological and archaeological research and educational projects with a number of First Nations communities in British Columbia.

Marianne Ignace (Ph.D., Simon Fraser) is Professor jointly in First Nations Studies and Anthropology and Director of the First Nations Language Centre at Simon Fraser University. Publications include *The Curtain Within: Haida Social and Symbolic Discourse* (1989), *Handbook on Aboriginal Language Program Planning* (1998), and *Visible Grammar: Sm'algyax Grammar Resources* (2008) with Margaret Anderson. Other writing on Secwépemc and Haida language and culture covers such topics as ethnobotany, language revitalization, ethnography, oratory and stories, ethnohistory, and youth hip-hop culture.

Ronald E. Ignace (Ph.D., Simon Fraser) is a member of the Secwépemc (Shuswap) Nation. He served as elected chief of the Skeetchestn band for over 22 years from the early 1980s. He was also chairman of the Shuswap Nation Tribal Council and other Secwépemc organizations. For many years he served as president of the Secwépemc Cultural Education Society and co-chaired the Aboriginal-university partnership between SCES and Simon Fraser University in Kamloops, BC. He has authored articles on Secwépemc history, traditional ecological knowledge, and language.

Ingrid Kritsch (M.A., McMaster) is Research Director of the Gwich'in Social and Cultural Institute (and was its founding Executive Director). Her research interests include the documentation of Gwich'in traditional knowledge and oral history on topics ranging from traditional land use to the replication of traditional clothing. In 2008 she was named an honorary Gwich'in by the Gwich'in Tribal Council Assembly and in 2012 received the Queen's Diamond Jubilee Award.

Roger Lewis (M.A., Memorial University of Newfoundland) is Curator of Ethnology with the Nova Scotia Museum. His research interests lie in the examination and reconceptualization of Mi'kmaw knowledge-practices tied to land and resource use. He has extensive archaeological survey and research experience and for the past number of years has been working closely with Mi'kmaq communities to record and map invaluable ethnographic information and stories.

Michael Marker (Ph.D., British Columbia) is an Associate Professor in the Department of Educational Studies at the University of British

Columbia and the Director of Ts'kel First Nations Graduate Studies. He has published on the history of Aboriginal education in *Paedagogica Historica, History of Education, History of Education Review, International Journal of Qualitative Studies in Education, Canadian Journal of Native Education,* and *Anthropology & Education Quarterly.* His present research brings to light ecological education and place-based pedagogies in the Coast Salish region. His forthcoming works are focused on Indigenous leadership, traditional knowledge, and modernity.

R. Bruce Morrison (Ph.D., Alberta) is Adjunct Professor of Anthropology at Athabasca University. His applied and scholarly interests have taken him to the Caribbean, southeast Asia, and south Asia. Most recently he has conducted ethnographic and ethnohistorical research in Nepal. He is co-editor with C. Roderick Wilson of *Ethnographic Essays in Cultural Anthropology.*

Brenda Parlee (Ph.D., Manitoba) is Canada Research Chair in Social Responses to Ecological Change, Faculty of Native Studies and Department of Resource Economics and Environmental Sociology, Faculty of Agricultural Life and Environmental Sciences, University of Alberta. Her current research focuses on the knowledge, practices, and institutions important to the resilience of northern communities facing ecological change.

Sylvie Poirier (Ph.D., Laval) is Professor of Anthropology at Université Laval. She has done research among Aboriginal people in the Western Desert of Australia since 1980 and among the Atikamekw, a First Nation in north-central Quebec, since 1990. Her research interests include a comparative perspective (Canada/Australia) on Indigenous issues, Indigenous knowledge, and Indigenous postcolonial territorialities. She is the author of *A World of Relationships: Itineraries,*

Dreams and Events in the Australian Western Desert (2005) and co-editor (with John Clammer and Eric Schwimmer) of *Figured Worlds: Ontological Obstacles in Intercultural Relations* (2004).

Trudy Sable (Ph.D., New Brunswick) is Director of the Office of Aboriginal and Northern Research at the Gorsebrook Research Institute for Atlantic Canada Studies, Saint Mary's University, and an Adjunct Professor of Anthropology. Since 1989, she has worked collaboratively with Aboriginal communities in Canada and internationally, conducting research, developing programs, including place-based educational programs and youth internship programs. She is also the SMU representative to the University of the Arctic. Publications include, with Mi'kmaw linguist Bernie Francis, *The Language of this Land, Mi'kma'ki* (2012).

Carl Urion (Ph.D., Alberta) is Professor Emeritus of Anthropology at the University of Alberta. His research interests are widespread, but have focused on the study of Algonquian languages. Until his retirement he was co-editor of the *Canadian Journal of Native Education.* His major focus as an academic has been working with students.

C. Roderick Wilson (Ph.D., Colorado) is retired from the University of Alberta. He has done anthropological research among Papago and Navaho in the American Southwest, Cree and Metis in Alberta, Waorani in Ecuador, and pastoral nomads in Kenya. He is co-editor with R. Bruce Morrison of *Ethnographic Essays in Cultural Anthropology.* He has a long-term involvement with an international NGO that actively complements his research interests.

Robert Wishart (Ph.D., Alberta) joined the Department of Anthropology at the University of Aberdeen in September 2003 as a postdoctoral researcher, then as an RCUK Fellow, and was appointed lecturer in 2010. His ethnographic work has been on the Gwich'in-Dene of the Mackenzie Delta in Northern Canada, with the Ojibwe of Ontario, and with Scottish fishers. His research is on the political and economic relationships between settlers, development interests and Indigenous peoples of the North and how these relationships have been used in various discourses and (mis)represented in state policy. He is currently a team member of the European Research Council Advanced Grant Arctic Domus.

PART I

Introduction

CHAPTER 1

On the Study of Native Peoples

R. Bruce Morrison, C. Roderick Wilson, and Christopher Fletcher

Canada is a Native land. It is homeland to a great diversity of peoples whose ancestors have occupied its entirety for millennia. Hunters, fishers, farmers, pastoralists, pacifists, warriors, chiefly gods, and slaves . . . all have existed in **Aboriginal** societies somewhere in the country. The First Peoples experience and know the land in the shared history, knowledge, and traditions that spring from their profound engagement with this place as its original human inhabitants. They claim no other place of cultural origin than here.

Canada is a settler country, populated by peoples whose ancestors hailed from around the world. For 400 years now they have progressively shaped and reshaped the landscape, based on the worldviews and practices they carried with them. People arrive here daily, making the global village that is Canada a true source of national pride.

Canada is a hybrid place, formed from a colossal geography with the mixing of peoples, ideas, practices, and labour. Its very name is of Aboriginal origin, coming from Jacques Cartier's original interactions with Iroquoian peoples at what today is Quebec City. The word *Kanata*, or "village," has come to encompass the nation of Canada. Likewise the imprimatur of an Aboriginal history and identity is found in hundreds of place names throughout the country—Quebec, Manitoba, Toronto, Nunavut, Wabush, Niagara, Kananaskis, Okanagan—yet often we do not see a corresponding Aboriginal presence in these places. In some cases the original inhabitants are simply outnumbered by non-Aboriginal peoples; in others they have been pushed aside and excluded. From the point of view of cultural and collective experience we could say that there are several different Canadas. The Canada of an Elder Inuk from Mittimatalik in the High Arctic, for example, is undoubtedly very different from that of a Laotian immigrant to Toronto or a retired Ukrainian farmer in Saskatchewan.

The relationship between peoples and places is at the heart of this book. While we tend to think and speak of Aboriginal people as a singular entity, particularly in their relationship to the state, it is important to keep in mind the number of nations and polities that constitute Canadian aboriginality today. Their plurality of experience with Canada is also a key to how this book is conceptually organized and presents its material. We thus describe Aboriginal communities, groups, **cultures**, and histories in relation to geographic areas and in relation to the broader political geography of the country. As authors and editors we have watched the waxing and waning of political and social attention given to Aboriginal peoples by the government and nation at large, and today we are left wondering if Canada's relationship with the original inhabitants of this land, the First Nations, Inuit, and Metis peoples, is on the edge of some profoundly new arrangement, or do we find ourselves at another point along an incremental journey of relationships? Without doubt Canadians of all origins and persuasions have an interest in understanding the Aboriginal peoples of the country.

National attention in recent years has frequently been given to such issues as Aboriginal land claims, unfulfilled treaty promises, and the constitutional status of **Native peoples**.[1] In 1996 the Royal Commission on Aboriginal Peoples (RCAP) released its comprehensive report, including more than 400 recommendations intended to transform the place of Aboriginal peoples in the social, economic, and political life of the country, addressing the very profound inequities between Aboriginal and non-Aboriginal Canadians. Much to the dismay of those who contributed to the RCAP process, few of these recommendations have been acted on. Nevertheless RCAP did bring national attention to the condition of Aboriginal communities and open our eyes to the historical and ongoing injustices which continue to mark the lives of many. Optimistically, we could consider the RCAP report a form of national conscience to which we refer when considering how to approach and understand issues affecting Aboriginal peoples today. More concretely however, with this book, now in its fourth edition, we hope to contribute to a key tenet of the RCAP findings and an issue that long predates the commission's work; that it is the relationship between the peoples of Canada— Aboriginal and non-Aboriginal—which needs to be transformed so that we may all live better as informed and thoughtful citizens. We have seen a disturbing tendency in the popular media to simplify the discussion of Aboriginal issues,

reinforcing the prevailing stereotypes and notions that somehow Aboriginal people want more and special treatment by the state. In maintaining the analysis at an "us or them" level, the question of how a dynamic and intercultural dialogue may be fostered is avoided. In effect, the recommendations of RCAP concern Canadian society at large. While a few Aboriginal-specific programs and developments may be pointed to as evidence that there has been some response to the commission, what, if anything, has been done to address the relationship in Canadian society at large? We are convinced that most Canadians have some interest in Native peoples, but in the absence of better information, they draw on stereotypes that are not well founded, show little appreciation for the role of Native peoples in our history, and do not understand the basis for Native historical experience and land or other claims. Canadians are not necessarily ill-disposed toward Natives, but there is currently little basis for real understanding.

Many Canadians revel in a national self-image as a mosaic—each ethnic group maintaining its distinctive character while still being essential to the whole. The image has some validity, but it seriously underplays pressures toward cultural conformity, especially at the regional level. Being Ukrainian is marvellous, if it is limited to matters primarily aesthetic: grandmothers dyeing Easter eggs, teenagers folk dancing, and so on. At this level, being Native is fully acceptable, if rather quaint: **totem** poles, soapstone sculpture, and powwow regalia are widely recognized as striking art forms but constitute only a visible edge of a deeper identity. Unlike other groups, Natives are not content simply to be Canadians or even hyphenated Canadians. They generally recognize that they are in Canada and are necessarily Canadians, but they also insist that they are first of all Indian—or Inuit, or Metis. In so doing they place themselves beyond the experience and understanding of most Canadians.

The Book's Approach

This book is based on three assertions. First, an understanding of Native peoples must start from an appreciation of Aboriginal society as it existed and as it continues, on its own terms and not as an appendage to that larger conglomeration of peoples and provinces that we call Canada. It is a fundamental anthropological premise that cultures are best understood within their own frameworks. One cannot comprehend, far less evaluate or judge, behaviour grounded in one cultural system by the standards of another. This is not to say that cultures are mutually unintelligible but rather that we must pay attention to how what we take to be true about the world and our place in it influences how we understand the lives of others. We are all capable of complex understanding but this is far from automatic; it requires work. A perspective that acknowledges cultural differences as inherently rational to those who hold them gives us a way to begin to comprehend. Much that follows is therefore an attempt to understand Canadian Native societies as, first of all, *Native* societies.

Second, any explication of either the objective conditions of contemporary Canadian Native peoples or the perceptions they have of themselves and of their place in the larger Canadian society must also take into account the history of relationships between Indians and Canadian society—particularly in how power has been expressed and denied in the process of encompassing Native society within Canada. Native societies have not existed within the last century simply as Native societies, but more or less have functioned (or been forced to function) as parts of Canadian society: Natives have become tribal peoples encapsulated within a colonial state. Their particular condition has been referred to as the **Fourth World**, a unique social, political, and economic condition in which once-independent nations are encapsulated

FIGURE 1.1 Dr C.M. Barbeau, Quebec's first university-trained anthropologist, transcribing Native folk songs. (© Canadian Museum of Civilization J4840)

within new and larger state societies in the process of colonization. The original nations persist but in radically transformed realities that often result in considerable inequity between groups. A Fourth World[2] condition is normally accompanied by a bureaucratic apparatus that enforces the legalistic framework that organizes how people may live. In Canada the Indian Act—legislation enacted by the federal government without meaningful consultation with Aboriginal peoples—unambiguously indicates that the subjects of the legislation have literally been created by government. From this point of view, status Indians, those people recognized as Indians by the Indian Act, are Canadian in a way that none of the rest of us are. Ironically, the life of non-Inuit Native people declared by the Indian Act not to be Indians (the Metis and non-status Indians) has largely come to be defined by the absence of that legislation. This equally speaks of their embeddedness within Canadian society, of inextricable links and connections.

Third, the scholars who here present their views of Native society and history are not simply recording devices mechanically reproducing data to which they have been exposed. They are people—who happen to be social scientists, who find themselves in interactive situations with other people who happen to be Native. The resulting analysis is in this sense not an objective reality but a product shaped by shared experiences. This interaction is influenced by the nature of the Native community and also by the anthropologist's background. Most immediately, that background includes a particular kind of professional training and an interest in specific kinds of theoretical problems. It also includes a personal, social, and cultural background. An anthropological approach has always emphasized the importance of relationships between the researcher and the people with whom he or she works. Relationships take time to build; hence the anthropological method depends on lots of time in the field. Relationships also need nurturing over time and have periods of up and downs. All these factors affect research and understanding in numerous and subtle ways. Ultimately, anthropological analysis is a creative act. By emphasizing the human elements in the research process, we are not suggesting whimsy or speculation. The point, rather, is that critical rigour is obtained not by mechanizing the fieldwork process but by openly recognizing its interactive nature: greater knowledge of the "subjective" factors tends to increase a study's validity and reliability. Because anthropology is grounded on the quality of relationships, and to varying extents the personalities of the researcher and his or her interlocutors, the authors of each of the chapters were asked to reflect on how they became anthropologists and how they came to work in the communities they did.

This work is not encyclopedic, but it does discuss representative groups[3] from each region of Canada. Not all that is known about each society is presented; each chapter most completely presents that aspect of the culture about which its author feels most competent. Cumulatively, this allows the reader some sense of the richness and complexity of Native life and of the extent of anthropological inquiry. Finally, each author examines Native life from one particular theoretical perspective. Thus, the reader gains a broad knowledge of the current state of Canadian anthropology and related disciplines.

It goes almost without saying that the authors believe that efforts to further the public understanding and awareness of the ways of life of the Native peoples, of the history of relationships between the original inhabitants and later immigrant peoples in Canada, and something of how various anthropological pictures of Aboriginal people are constructed are all worthwhile goals in themselves. At a very practical level, the future of Canada for both Aboriginal and non-Aboriginal peoples alike may hinge on how well we have learned the lessons of our past.

Anthropological Concepts

This book is written for the general reader; it does not assume extensive knowledge either of Aboriginal people or of anthropology. Most concepts are explained as they arise, but some general comments may help. This book uses the notion of culture area as a general organizing principle—and the reader will note that each of the culture areas represented by Parts II to VIII begins with a brief overview chapter. Canada is a very large country, possessing diverse environments, and the Native population exhibits great variety. Nevertheless, within this spectrum of variability are regional similarities, and neighbouring groups tend to have features in common. This regional patterning of Aboriginal societies results from two major factors. First, primary food resources are regionally distributed: salmon is the prime resource in some areas, caribou or moose in others, and so on. Since each resource is taken by techniques that differ in social as well as technological requirements—some require communal activity, while others reward individual effort—regional patterns of subsistence developed. The second factor is that neighbouring groups, especially ones that inhabit essentially the same kind of environment, tend to influence each other. As ideas and techniques spread from one group to another, the regional patterns tend to become intensified: while each group remained unique, areal patterns of life emerged that persisted for millennia.

Although European colonization disrupted Aboriginal patterns, the disruptions themselves were patterned by area. Various regions and cultures experienced first contact with European explorers and settlers at different times, in differing ways, and by varying groups. The first sustained contacts for most Inuit along the northern coast were with whalers, while for the peoples on the west coast they were with traders seeking sea otter pelts and on the east coast with fishermen. Each of these European groups had different economic interests that strongly affected relationships with local Natives. Furthermore, the interests of all three groups on the coasts contrasted strongly with those of Europeans who penetrated the interior of the continent in a fur trade that required major inputs of labour and material goods by the **Indigenous** population. Although colonialism in whatever guise tends to produce parallel patterns of events, and although Canada's recent past has featured numerous national events that affected all Native people, much Native–European interaction has had a decidedly regional quality.

Having argued that it is sensible to think of Indians in regional terms, it is necessary to warn against taking the concept of culture area too literally. "Culture area" is only a generalization, an indication of central tendency; each group also possesses unique practices. Arguments about boundaries are essentially spurious, giving to a

line on the map a specificity that is not present in reality. Organizing the book along the lines of culture areas is a convenient way to give some structure to a very complex reality. In organizing the material this way, however, we are not suggesting that Aboriginal culture is simply the automatic response of people adjusting to a specific environment. New World prehistory was dynamic: populations moved from one region to another; major environmental changes occurred; technological and social innovation emerged. Throughout, regional patterns developed, persisted, and changed. Even within very similar ecological areas people have organized the distribution and consumption of food and resources in quite different patterns. Culture, then, is not a set of activities and objects which appear in response to an environment. It is better seen as a collection of potentials that are realized through human agency and innovation. There are other limitations to the culture-area approach. While the vast majority of Aboriginal people would likely agree that land and relationships to place are fundamental to their sense of identity and culture, people need not be in their homeland to feel its influence. Culture is transportable and transposable. Like people everywhere on the globe, Aboriginal people have become more mobile and urbanized in recent decades. Aboriginal identities are fashioned from cultural histories of great depth and carry forward in these new contexts. It is also important to keep in mind that all people are inventive. New ideas and ways of living come together in fascinating new forms. Culture then is always a process of building, incorporating, and hybridizing new realities that complement the old.

It is fairly clear that culture areas are mental constructs, not visible in the natural world. It is less obvious for seemingly more concrete realities, such as "tribe." At a nineteenth-century Blackfoot Sun Dance, for instance, one could have encountered virtually the entire tribe. Other groups that never gathered together or acted as political units, however, are also customarily spoken of as tribes. Cree and Ojibway, for instance, occupied territories that stretched for thousands of kilometres across the landscape. They clearly are not and never have been singular political units. Each is, however, a political–cultural continuum that links many smaller groups together. What unites them, and what separates them, is primarily degree of linguistic similarity. The concept of tribe is thus quite loose: it can refer to people who think of themselves as a clearly identified political unit and to people who do not. It can refer merely to people designated a tribe by ethnographers essentially on the basis of common language and generally similar behaviour.

In conclusion, the argument here is not that anthropological concepts are deficient. Rather, the world is a complex place where human life does not come pre-packaged. In attempting to explain what people do, how they live and think of themselves, anthropologists have devised various concepts, some of which have proven to be useful, all of which are limited, and none of which provides final answers. They are useful intellectual tools without which we would have no recourse but to return to ethnocentric judgments.

On Doing Anthropology: Agreements and Disagreements

This is a book about Native people; it is necessarily also a book about Canada. Further, it is a book about anthropology, or at least about how some anthropologists work and think, and the analytic frameworks are anthropological. As such, they differ from ones used by sociologists, political scientists, or economists. One should not think of one of these disciplines as right and the others wrong. Rather, they present complementary perspectives, different windows into the complex reality of human life. Similarly, anthropologists have diverse

perspectives. Some anthropologists focus on the words that people use, others on how they make a living, still others on the rise or fall of their numbers. All are potentially useful topics of investigation that add to our knowledge of how societies and cultures survive.

A more troublesome matter arises. At times Native people are in profound disagreement with what has been written about them. Sometimes this is not a matter of differing perspectives but of the researcher's being wrong. This can occur in a number of ways: a linguist analyzing an unwritten language once spent hundreds of hours working with an informant who had a speech impediment. The resultant analysis was correct—but only for that informant. This is a case of sampling error, in principle a simple matter to avoid. But since anthropologists may well have good reasons for working intensively with very few people in a community, it is a recurrent problem. (In a village of 100 people, how many can speak personally of events that took place 60 years ago?) Or what if the anthropologist is the victim of a practical joke but never discovers it, or simply misunderstands what happens? The anthropologist should validate or cross-check all information—but errors can occur.

Error may be difficult to determine. The earliest substantial sources of information on the Denesuline (formerly the Chipewyan), for instance, are the journals of the fur trader Samuel Hearne. In numerous ways he pictures their women as drudges, the victims of abusive and domineering men. Since this seems not to fit what is known of more recent Denesuline society or of other boreal forest people at the time of first contact, what should be made of his account? Was he misinterpreting what he saw because of his European background and his unfamiliarity with the semi-nomadic hunting and trapping life? Or was his account essentially correct, but he happened to be with a small band that, in taking up a fur-trading life, had dropped much of traditional Denesuline values and was now composed of social deviants? Or was Hearne describing behaviour typical for the Denesuline of that time? Contemporary Denesuline, women in particular, may well take umbrage at anthropologists and historians who accept Hearne's account, but the question cannot be definitively resolved.

In other instances where Natives object to anthropological interpretations, it seems parallel to the disagreement between two scholars. A classic case would be those who object to archaeological accounts, particularly to the notion that **Amerindians** ultimately derive from Siberian populations or that there have been relatively recent shifts of Aboriginal peoples from one region to another. These accounts are seen to be in opposition to the traditions of the Elders, to the view that they have occupied this land from the time of creation. At a time when Indians are increasingly turning to the Elders for leadership, an apparent challenge from archaeologists cannot be tolerated. The position taken here is that the two kinds of accounts regarding the past do not confront each other because they cannot. They are different kinds of truth and both can have relevance to contemporary Native people.

A related feature of anthropological writing that Native peoples (and others) frequently find

---

BOX 1.1 Pithouses or Bunkers?

How do anthropologists study representations of Aboriginal peoples? Extensive ethnographic interviews and archival data allowed one anthropologist to analyze the media coverage of the 1995 standoff at Gustafsen Lake, British Columbia, revealing factors promoting media stereotyping. What set the Gustafsen Lake standoff apart from other conflicts involving Natives was that it was the largest Royal Canadian Mounted Police (RCMP) operation in history, with cultural misperceptions and misinformation spread across the country.

The case study of the media coverage of the 1995 Gustafsen Lake standoff demonstrates the depths of understanding attainable with anthropological methods. Many journalistic errors were the result of inadequate cultural knowledge and sensitivity towards Native people. A widely circulated untruth was that the standoff was caused by a spiritual vision. Across Canada, newspaper stories repeated stock phrases providing an oversimplified interpretation about a conflict between Aboriginal spirituality and Euro-Canadian concepts of property ownership. The media used cultural differences to cast the protestors as "the enemy," but could not restrict this characterization to people inside the camp. Several newspapers incorporated perspectives of Sun Dance practitioners and academic sources to explain the Sun Dance, but emphasized its secretive and violent aspects. Others noted the recent introduction of this ritualistic dance at Gustafsen Lake and used this to question the authenticity of protestors' demands. Assumptions about the "barbaric" practices of the Sun Dance and the ulterior motives of those who introduced this Plains ritual into BC exacerbated existing suspicions about those in the camp and Natives in general. One news story written with sensitivity and respect nevertheless served to denigrate a traditional sweat lodge ceremony at Alkali Lake—with the added headline

unsettling is that truth seems to change through time. It seems self-evident that truth, particularly scientific truth, should be immutable. However, new data continuously arise, making necessary the re-evaluation of previous conclusions. Additionally, conclusions are always tentative because they are interpretive. Folk explanations, of course, also change, but not so visibly, nor are the contradictions sudden. We must also keep in mind that writing itself is an act of power. Documenting culture through texts necessarily simplifies a complex reality focusing attention in one direction and away from others. The act of being thus described has been a source of tension between anthropologists and the people about whom they write. In part this reflects the importance of the author as a mediator of broader understanding about people and this in turn lends importance to the outsider. In recent years the older paradigm of the lone anthropologist conceptualizing, undertaking, and writing up research describing the people as if they were unaware of neither their role in his or her work nor their position in the world has given way to collaborative and participatory models of intercultural research. There are many variations on these models, reflecting the different priorities of Native and research communities, but the general principle is that everyone be able to influence what gets researched, how that

"Natives Steamed." The media publicly voiced doubts about a local chief who broadcast a surrender message to the protestors in Shuswap over the radio—simply because they could not understand it!

For the RCMP, Hollywood stereotypes often replaced what they did not know. Some assumed that Natives in the camp had an inherent ability to stalk through heavily wooded areas undetected. Members of the RCMP tactical unit stated that they feared sleeping at night in the bush, lest they be "scalped." After the conflict, the RCMP conducted a media tour of the camp, misidentifying traditional pithouses as "bunkers."

Although the RCMP operation concerned itself with weapons and shooting offences and not with religious practices or the dispute over landownership, nevertheless the media and RCMP co-constructed stereotypes of Native people and their cultures that were mutually reinforcing.

Cultural misperceptions grow out of fear and ignorance, and these prevailed during the standoff. The RCMP frame of reference was that Native **resistance** had become so radicalized that the lives of law-enforcement officers were at risk. Journalists who lacked an understanding of Native cultural traditions were more likely to sensationalize unfamiliar religious practices, make simplistic inferences, and represent Native traditions insensitively. And once these misunderstandings about Native spirituality, Sun Dances, pithouses, and Hollywood myths were transmitted as news, they took on lives of their own. There is little doubt that these misunderstandings could encourage intolerance towards Native people.

Source: Sandra Lambertus, *Wartime Images, Peacetime Wounds: The Media and the Gustafsen Lake Standoff* (Toronto: University of Toronto Press, 2003).

Postscript: the above account is still relevant, but Dr Lambertus notes that the RCMP and other Canadian police appear to have moderated some of their practices since Gustafsen Lake.

happens, and what the outcomes will be. In theory at least, this produces a more just and informed scholarship on Native peoples. Several of the authors here have used anthropology perspectives and methods to consider and intervene in the external relations of the communities in which they work.

Another reason why collaborative and participatory research has gained in importance comes from the criticism that some anthropology has been irrelevant, at best, blind at worst, to the needs of Native communities. For example, Mandelbaum's *The Plains Cree*, the standard work on that group, presents their life during the buffalo-hunting days of the late nineteenth century, as remembered by elderly people in the 1930s. Nowhere does it mention the trauma of everyday life on the reserves of that period. For some, a political and economic analysis of reserve life would seem more to the point. In Mandelbaum's defence it must be noted that his fieldwork could not have been duplicated at a later date and that one's sense of relevance can change. Many contemporary Cree have found the book to be a treasure house of information. Likewise, the work of pioneering anthropologist Franz Boas, who worked first in the Arctic and subsequently in coastal British Columbia Native communities, has helped communities revitalize and reinitiate aspects of material culture and ceremony that were forbidden and suppressed under earlier government policy. More broadly, Boas is

BOX 1.2 On Being a First Nations, Metis, or Inuit Graduate Student

Tansi! My name is Sarah Pocklington (no relation to the famous Peter Pocklington). I am a member of the Aboriginal women's trio Asani, and currently a Ph.D. candidate in Education Policy Studies at the University of Alberta. My area of research is contemporary Aboriginal music in Canada. Recently I have been an Adjunct Professor for the School (Department) of Native Studies and a student advisor for Native Student Services on campus.

My friend Rod Wilson asked me to write about my experiences as an FNMI [First Nations, Metis, or Inuit] student, so I would like to share with you some of what I have learned from the many students and colleagues I have had the privilege to work with over the years as well.

Being an undergraduate or graduate student is really all about the journey—the process—perhaps somewhat like a vision quest (I could have written here, for instance, about how to do well in the course for which you are now reading this, but it seems much more important to write about the process of being a student). There are moments of pain and loneliness where the despair feels like it will swallow you whole (for me this was writing my thesis). But there are also many, many rewards and celebrations along the way (presenting my first international paper in Hawaii certainly did not hurt!). I think, for most of us, the rewards are as great as the challenges and we are grateful, feeling a sense of accomplishment (and very relieved) once the journey is complete. No journey is the same—and while there are similar stages that most of us pass through—- the journey is uniquely our own. This in itself is a gift.

Being a graduate student is challenging on every level: emotional, spiritual, physical, and intellectual. Perseverance, determination,

widely acknowledged for having undermined the powerful idea that culture is hierarchical, a racist notion that has caused untold suffering around the world. Several of our authors have worked on land claims and other legal issues with Native groups for decades. The shifting importance of anthropological research suggests that, ultimately, we do not know what people will make of our research findings down the road. Doing the best we can in our current conditions will have to suffice.

A final criticism is that some ideas propounded by anthropologists have actively undermined and harmed Native people, a charge made both by Native people and by anthropologists. The most obvious examples involve **acculturation** theory practitioners who were interested in how Native society was being changed by its contact with mainstream society. Of particular importance in this era of work was understanding psychological adaptation to changing material and economic conditions: Many Native groups, particularly in northern and remote places, were being encouraged or coerced into new government-sponsored settlements, and optimizing their adaptation to their new circumstances or responding effectively to poor reactions, was of concern. A hidden text in this perspective was that inevitably Native peoples would become culturally indistinct from non-Natives. In focusing so exclusively on how Native culture changes as an accommodation to

commitment, flexibility, adaptability, patience, and a sense of humour definitely come in handy. Initially, many First Nations, Metis, and Inuit students find it difficult to thrive in an education system based on a worldview and educational processes that are often very different from their own experiences and practices. Viewing these challenges as a test within the journey and finding ways to adapt to and explore each new experience definitely helps to make the path less bumpy.

Some advice for each of you:

- Make friends in your department and create a reciprocal support network. Peer support is a wonderful thing and many of your peers will be encountering experiences similar to your own, so you will not feel so isolated.
- You have the right to choose your own supervisor, so make sure that you have chosen a person who can offer you both moral and academic support. This person is VERY important, so choose carefully, and if you find that the relationship is not working, do not hesitate to find another person to take on this role. Changing supervisors should not be taken lightly as any change disrupts your program and every department has definite timelines. On the other hand, you should feel that you have the trust and support of the person you are working with.

- Take time management seriously! If you are a procrastinator like me you need to set personal deadlines for yourself and stick to them.
- Make appointments with the professors of your classes if you have any questions or concerns about assignments. Most will be happy to meet with you, and one-on-one discussions definitely help with understanding course requirements and material.
- Find out where Native Student Services is on your campus. It usually hosts Elders and offers various kinds of support services for FNMI students. This is a great place to meet new friends and offers another avenue of support.

Euro-Canadian culture, anthropologists at least implicitly supported the idea that such change is inevitable. This stance in turn supported policy development designed to do just that, including the now-repudiated residential school system. The issues are complex, but some preliminary comments may be helpful. First, whatever the merits or faults of acculturation theory, its practitioners as a group were actively involved in working with and for Native peoples. Interestingly, good analysis seems to lead to anti-assimilationist conclusions. Second, anthropologists, like nuclear physicists, cannot determine how their work will be taken up, nor can they guarantee that their work will not be misused. A final and more philosophically complex issue concerns how we are all embedded in dominant ways of thinking that seem natural—this is culture at work. Can we really step out of those powerful frames of reference to see clearly beyond them? Intellectual change is closely connected to broader flows of social change at once influencing and being shaped by them. Intellectual orthodoxy cannot exist in this reality of shifting ideas.

This discussion has focused on the anthropologist–Native relationship. The anthropological audience also includes other anthropologists, students, the general public, and, at times, client agencies. The concerns expressed here have also had an impact, in somewhat different forms, on these audiences: the issues are not merely specific to Native peoples but are general. As an example, we mention the treaties that various First Nations have signed. They are centrally of concern to the signatories, and have so been mentioned in a number of chapters. They also impact all other Canadians, but usually this is not noticed. On occasion, however, treaties become front-page news, often in ways that leave many people mystified, because they really have little basis for understanding them.

In summary, anthropologists have always been concerned with accuracy, or more technically, reliability and validity. This has been one of the factors in the search for new methods and new ideas and in the introspective analysis of past problems. Our current understandings are hopefully neither a defence nor a rejection of the past, but a building upon successful parts of the past. Anthropology started with the then startlingly original idea that it was possible, and indeed preferable, to comprehend other cultures from the logic they hold about themselves and that this was possible through objectively recording material gained by the technique of **participant observation**. This involved participating in many activities of the daily life of a community. Like a child, the fieldworker learned the lessons required to be a member of the community, to see the world as they saw it. The insider's viewpoint remains a valid ideal, but we are now more aware of how complex and perhaps ultimately unattainable such a view is. Nevertheless it remains a powerful starting point on which mutual comprehension may be developed. Participant observation is still a basic technique, but we no longer assume that our presence does not alter what happens nor that communities exist as hermetically sealed entities. We are all participants in the global movement of ideas. The community being studied is not simply there as an object but actively and purposively interacts with the researcher. Writing of one's field experiences, including emotional responses to the very demanding task of fieldwork, demands both courage and personal insight, but it creates a more human **ethnography** and allows the reader to judge more fully its merit.

This volume, then, is both a discussion of some current perspectives on Canadian Native peoples and a comment on the scholarly enterprise in itself.

NOTES

1. We have attempted to be consistent and straightforward in our use of terminology. "Native," "Aboriginal," and "Indigenous" are terms that emphasize that the people to whom they are applied, all people tracing their ancestry to the pre-Columbian inhabitants of Canada (and all of North and South America), were here before the arrival of the rest of us. "Amerindian" and an early meaning of "Indian" are almost as broad in scope, excluding only the people of the northernmost land stretching from the tip of Siberia to Greenland. In Canada these northernmost Indigenous people are known as "Inuit." In Alaska and Siberia they are more likely to be "Aleuts," "Yup'ik," or, surprisingly to Canadians, "Eskimos." Collectively, they can be referred to as "Eskaleuts." The usual meaning of "Indian" in Canada refers to those Native people who are recognized by the federal government as having "Indian status" by virtue of the Indian Act. In recent decades such people are more likely to refer to themselves formally as "First Nations." In addition to "Indians" and "Inuit," the Canadian Constitution recognizes "Metis" as a third category of Aboriginal person. A broad definition of "Metis" includes communities of people with mixed Indian and European descent. More narrowly, it can refer specifically to people who trace their ancestry back to the Red River Settlement in present-day Manitoba. We have also resisted the idea that, amidst this welter of terms, one or two should be chosen as being somehow better than the others.

2. The broad division of the globe into first, second, third, and fourth worlds is a not as relevant as it once was. Originally the first world referred to the industrial democratic West, the second to the communist-dominated East, the third to impoverished nations around the world, and the fourth to the world's colonialized Aboriginal peoples. In a post-Soviet era these distinctions are less useful, but the Fourth World nations have in many instances not felt the changes that other places have. We also feel that the term represents a historic first step in analyzing the place of Aboriginals in the modern world.

3. The book covers all culture areas of Canada and two or three societies within each area. Within each area the selected societies are also representative. The basic distinction in the Arctic, for instance, is between maritime and inland societies. On the Northwest Coast it is between northern and southern societies. In both cases we selected one of each. Finally, we chose authors who are recognized for the quality of their work and for their ability to communicate their findings forcefully.

CHAPTER 2

From the Beginning: Canadian Peoples Old and New

C. Roderick Wilson and Carl Urion

Beginnings[1]

If we were to peer through the mists of time to the Age of the Ancestors, the First Americans, what would we see? Probably we would see a small group of people, about 15 or 20. At times they might be joined by people from other bands, but usually that was about the right number of people to live together. Mostly they lived near the sea. They might follow streams to places where it was easy to spear salmon or go inland to hunt deer or bear, or to gather berries on hillsides, but they were seldom far from water. They had spears and baskets, warm clothing and sleeping robes, and, especially in the winter, shelter from the Subarctic storms. But they moved frequently and did not have much else by way of physical possessions.

What they mostly had was not things, but knowledge, the knowledge to find what was needed, that which was provided. Anthropologists for the most part would say that they had environmental knowledge (what do the land and sea provide and how can they be used?) and social knowledge (how do members of the group relate to each other in order to get things done?). Anthropologists might also state that the Ancestors themselves (to judge from their descendants) would have given primacy not to environmental knowledge or to social knowledge but to religious knowledge as being more fundamental.

In our view, however, the Ancestors (again inferring from their descendants' views) would have put it still differently. They would not have thought of **hunting or gathering** or even of knowledge as things unto themselves. They would not have thought of hunting as a specialized skill to be learned so much as an expression of the hunter's spirituality.

In sum, we are suggesting that: (1) just as contemporary Native people are the biological descendants of the Ancestors, and hence we can infer that the Ancestors had straight black hair, skin that tanned easily, and so on, so can we look to the traditional ways of thinking of Native people across the New World to get some sense of what their **world view** was; (2) the Ancestors were real people in time and space about whom we will never know many things but about whom some matters of importance and interest may be said; and (3) Native peoples and anthropologists frequently see things differently and speak about things with different vocabularies, but dialogue on these matters is both possible and important.

Native peoples have their own ways of speaking of beginnings. Tsimshian groups, for instance, consider that they are descended from an ancestress who was carried away and married by one or another supernatural (for example, grizzly or killer whale) in the form of a man, but who eventually returned to her homeland with her children. Such stories, among other things, define the nature of reality and (spiritual) power, the basis for relationships within the group, and the nature of relationships with external groups.

Just as we noted in the first chapter that one should not think of one academic discipline as right and the others wrong, so one should not think of one origin story as right and another wrong. For one thing, each story is told in its own vocabulary; the resulting conflicts in view are more apparent than real. For instance, Native Elders commonly assert that the First Nations have been here forever, since the creation of the world. This view is seen as conflicting with those of archaeologists, some of whom place the original peopling of the New World as recently as 12,000 years ago.[2] How does one relate the archaeological discourse of hypothetical carbon-dated years to the discourse of Aboriginal origin myths? One approach is to ask what even 12,000 years means, not in the scientific language of radiometric dating (where it seems almost as yesterday), but in the language of culture. What does 12,000 years mean in terms of the history of Western culture, the cultural frame for most of us? Two meaningful comparisons, of the many possible, would be to point out that the Judeo-Christian-Islamic tradition is usually seen to begin with Abraham, only some 4,000 years ago, or to point out that the proto-Indo-Europeans, the small horticultural group ancestral to speakers of modern languages ranging from Hindi and Russian in the east to Icelandic and Portuguese in western Europe, began their migrations, as best as we can now reconstruct, some 8,000 years ago. In other words, the most recent suggested date for the inhabiting of North America is far more distant than most ancestral events in Western culture for which there is any glimmering of cultural memory. Thus, the Native Elder and the archaeologist,

in their different ways, seem to be saying much the same thing: 12,000 years ago is, in almost any sense, at the beginning of the world.

Another way of dealing with this apparent contradiction is to note that both the Aboriginal and anthropological/Western narratives are origin myths, but are written in very different modes. Immigrants to the Americas in the last millennium all knew that they were going somewhere new. The Ancestors likely had no such sense. They were not going anywhere, at least in the sense of journeying, and their remembered narratives reflect that. A similar point is that Aboriginal narratives are not primarily about time and space, but about relationships. "The Creator gave us this land and that is why. . . ." The Navajo provide an interesting case. Their oral literature has been extensively translated, so it is easily accessible. It is profoundly rooted in a particular landscape, the land given to the Navajo, between the four sacred peaks. But as archaeologists have shown, the Navajo arrived in their present home, moving south from Canada, not long before the Spanish arrived in the area. That is, their narrative is about the nature of their relationship to the Creator and his provisions, not about what year they arrived there.

In the following sections we will discuss, without making exclusive truth-claims, first, what various kinds of anthropologists have to say about the original settling of the continent and about how Native societies developed in the millennia prior to European discovery, and second, some general issues from the history of Native–Euro-Canadian relationships that will help the reader form a context for the following chapters.

The Settling of the Continent

Viewpoints from Physical Anthropology

All humans are related, forming one species. But some of us are more alike and some are less alike. It is from this perspective that we use the term "Amerindian." It suggests that in general the Aboriginal inhabitants of North and South America are more like each other than they are like people deriving from elsewhere on the globe. This in turn implies that Amerindians have been here for a long time, long enough to become somewhat distinct from other peoples.

The perspective of relatedness also suggests, however, that Amerindians are more like people from eastern Asia than anywhere else. This does not prove that the long-distant ancestors of Native peoples came here from Asia, but it does suggest it as the strongest possibility.

Even to a casual observer, Amerindians and people from eastern Asia share features that link them together and separate them from the rest of the world. People from both areas tend to have straight black hair, a lack of male-pattern baldness, and little facial or body hair; they have skin that tans easily, rarely have blue eyes, and may have epicanthic eye folds ("slanted" eyes). Less visible traits linking these peoples include the Inca bone (the occipital bone at the back of the skull is divided in two, the smaller, upper portion being referred to as the Inca bone, in commemoration of its first being noticed by archaeologists working in Peru) and the Mongolian spot, a purplish spot about the size of a dollar coin on the skin at the base of the spine. Such a list could be expanded at some length. It is not that everyone in these populations has all these characteristics, but these heritable traits are found more or less frequently among these people and are not found among other peoples.

While the relative biological affinity of New World and east Asian peoples is visible to the layperson, we are not limited to the approach of simply listing points of physical connectedness. For instance, large numbers of heritable traits, including non-visible characteristics such as blood proteins, can be treated mathematically to create an index of genetic similarity. While the specific numbers generated in such an approach depend on exactly which characteristics are included, such studies generally attempt to be broadly inclusive and typically conclude both that there are interesting variations within New World peoples and that they are linked more closely to eastern Asia than elsewhere. In fact, the people of the far northwestern part of North America are genetically closer to the people of Siberia than they are to the people of South America.

Ultimately, the question of New World origins must be placed in the context of human evolution generally. The present evidence is that North and South America, like Oceania and Australia, have been inhabited only by fully modern human beings, *Homo sapiens sapiens* (*Hss*). That is, the early evolution of human beings took place primarily in Africa, secondarily in Asia and Europe, and not at all in the rest of the world. While this line of thought categorically concludes that the ancestors of Amerindians must have come here from somewhere, with respect to time it is vague.

The most exciting recent research bearing on this issue is undoubtedly the study of human DNA, with the promise of more detailed studies to come. Looking at the big picture, the most definitive line of research involves Y chromosomes (the study of male lines of descent). The startling conclusion is that all non-African humans are descended from an individual who lived in East Africa about 60,000 years ago (although this view is opposed by the people who think *Hss* evolved in several Eastern Hemisphere locations). Globally, at the most basic level, it is accepted that there are three genetic groups: Africans, Eurasians (which includes natives of Europe and the Middle East, and southwest Asians east to present-day Pakistan), and east Asians, which includes natives of Asia, Japan, Southeast Asia, the Americas, and Oceania. Modern humans reached the Middle East by 100,000 years ago, southern Asia by 50,000, Australia by 40,000, and northwestern Beringia by 28,000.

The study of mitochondrial DNA (mtDNA, inherited through the female line) is revealing a picture that becomes both simpler and more complex as we proceed. The main hypotheses at this time seem to be that: (1) "the Ancestors" emerged from a single-source ancestral population that probably developed in a period of 5,000 to 15,000 years of isolation in Beringia, during which time they became differentiated from their close kin in east Asia and Siberia; (2) this founding population had no more than four major haplotype mtDNAs, which indicates that it was relatively small; (3) the founding haplotypes are uniformly distributed across the Americas, which indicates that the hemisphere was populated relatively quickly, soon reaching even the tip of South America; and (4) there has been some "back migration" of populations from North America to Siberia—that is, some Siberian populations derived from North American groups. In passing, let us note that this research quite explicitly contradicts a "late entry" of as little as 12,000 years ago.

Teeth have played a special role in the study of evolution (human and non-human alike) for two reasons. First, they tend, more often than other parts of animal anatomy, to be preserved. Second, they are evolutionarily conservative; that is, they tend to vary less within populations and to change more slowly over long periods of time than many other anatomical features. This becomes relevant for us in a comparative study of tooth morphology by Christy Turner. He studied the shape of fossil teeth in museum collections around the world and also contemporary teeth. He found a small number of major types, including what he called the **sinodont** pattern, encompassing the prehistoric and contemporary peoples of China, northeastern Asia generally, and the New World. Within the sinodont pattern, he distinguished a number of subtypes. New World peoples divide into three subtypes: the Eskimoan peoples, the Athapaskans and some other Northwest Coast groups, and all other Aboriginal New World peoples. Each of these subtypes in turn is most closely associated with fossil populations coming from distinct areas of northeastern Asia. The implication (not accepted by all) is that there were three separate migratory streams into the New World from that area, with the Eskimoans being the most recent, preceded by the Athapaskans, in turn preceded by the original stream.

In summing up the evidence from the subdiscipline of physical anthropology that relates to the question of the settling of the New World, one can firmly state that the ancestral populations came here from eastern Asia in what seems to any living person a very long time ago but on an evolutionary scale in recent times. It can further be stated, although with less certainty, that they probably came over long periods of time in at least three separate streams of migration.

Viewpoints from Linguistic Anthropology

Language Classification Systems

It has always been clear that some languages are closely related. A shared or similar vocabulary leads easily to the conclusion that there must be a shared past. Reversing this equation, the widespread existence of dialects suggests that contemporary languages might over time evolve into separate languages; the widespread existence of families of related languages suggests that processes of linguistic fission have been going on for a long time.

As early as 1786 Sir William Jones, a British colonial official in India, reported structural similarities between some European languages (by then common knowledge) and the Asian languages Sanskrit and Persian (at the time quite surprising). The idea that peoples who looked quite different and who had very different cultures might nevertheless share, at least in part, a common linguistic ancestry was electrifying.

In North America the first comprehensive attempt at classifying Aboriginal languages was made in 1891 by John Wesley Powell of the Bureau of American **Ethnology**. He classified the Aboriginal languages of North America into 58 (later revised to 51) different stocks. We can now see that his classification was very much a product of the times: there was virtually no information on some of the languages; he assumed that all Amerindian languages represented a single stage of evolutionary development and therefore ignored grammar as a factor in determining relationships; and, because the primary purpose of making the classification was to provide a basis for the placement of tribes on specific reservations, there was no particular interest in the degree of relationship but only in the fact of a relationship. In spite of these rather severe defects it is still regarded as a foundational, if conservative, statement. In the context of this particular discussion, it is a minimalist statement about the past.

In 1921 Edward Sapir constructed a classification that dramatically reduced the number of stocks to six. Although much linguistic work had been done in the intervening 30 years, and Sapir himself had by then worked on 17 Native languages, the difference between the two classifications lies less in the quality of analysis than in the fact that Powell was a "splitter" while Sapir was a "lumper" who was willing to go beyond the hard evidence and who had an eye on the grand sweep of historical processes. For instance, he classified Beothuk, the extinct language of Newfoundland, as Algonquian, largely because its Indian neighbours are. It may well have been, but we will never know. He attempted to link the Na-Dene phylum to Sino-Tibetan. He even suggested that Hokan-Siouan was the basic North American Indian language and implied that an ancestral proto-language might at some point be reconstructed.

This is not to suggest that Sapir was indifferent to the question of to what extent the suggested connections between various languages had been demonstrated. The 1929 version of his classification contains two separate lists (see Table 2.1, compiled by Regna Darnell). The first is the radical 6-unit classification; the second is a more conservative grouping into 23 units. The premise for the second list was that by this date linguistic analysis had proceeded to the point where even the most conservative would now accept some linking of units listed separately by Powell; 12 of the 23 represent this kind of well-substantiated linking.

Until recently the lists of Sapir and Powell more or less defined the parameters of the classificatory discussion. In 1986, Darnell noted that unfortunately linguists usually chose one list or another, but that the field was now generally conservative in that there was growing insistence on thoroughly demonstrating relationships. Table 2.2 is a modified version of her chart showing established linguistic groupings for Canadian languages.

This picture was challenged in 1987 with Joseph H. Greenberg's radical proposal that there are three basic groupings in the New World: Eskimo-Aleut stretching across the Arctic rim from eastern Siberia to Greenland; Na-Dene running from central Alaska to Hudson Bay with outliers as far south as Arizona; and Amerind covering all the rest of North and South America. The first two groupings are not new and are fairly conventional; the proposal of an Amerind macrophylum is startling (as is including Eskimo-Aleut in another macrophylum, Eurasiatic, which also includes stocks as diverse as Chukchi-Kamchatkan, Altaic, Uralic, and Indo-European).

Greenberg's groups are startling for at least two reasons. One is that they link geographically distant peoples whose separation would have taken place well over 20,000 years ago. The other reason is methodological: instead of a painstaking point-by-point analysis of the sound, word, and grammatical subsystems, comparing two languages at a time, repeating the process for possibly numerous dyads, and eventually reconstructing a hypoth-

TABLE 2.1 **North American Linguistic Classifications (after Darnell 1986)**

SAPIR 1929-A	SAPIR-B	POWELL 1891
Eskimo-Aleut	Eskimo	Eskimo
Algonquian-Ritwan	Algonquian-Ritwan*	Algonquian, Beothukan, Wiyot, Yurok
	Mosan*	Wakashan, Chemakuan, Salish
	Kutenai	Kutenai
Na-Dene	Tlingit-Athapaskan*	Haida, Tlingit, Athapaskan Haida
Penutian	California Penutian*	Miwok, Costanoan, Yokuts, Maidu, Wintun
	Oregon Penutian*	Takelma, Coos (-Siuslaw), Yakonan, Kalapuya
	Plateau Penutian*	Waiilatpuan, Lutuamian, Sahaptin
	Chinook	Chinook
	Tsimshian	Tsimshian
	(Mexican Penutian)	—
Hokan-Siouan	Hokan*	Karok, Chimariko, Salinan, Yana, Pomo, Washo, Esselen, Yuman, Chumash
	Coahuiltecan*	Tonkawa, Karankawa, Coahuiltecan
	Tunican*	Tunica, Atakapa, Chitimacha
	Iroquois-Caddoan*	Iroquois, Caddoan
	Yuki	Yuki
	Keres	Keres
	Timucua	Timucua
	Muskhogean	Muskhogean
	Siouan	Siouan, Yuchi
Aztec-Tanoan	Uto-Aztecan*	Nahuatl, Pima, Shoshonean
	Tanoan-Kiowan*	Tanoan, Kiowa
	Zuni	Zuni

*Twelve units that Sapir considered to be accepted by his colleagues. The reduction of Powell's 55 units to 23 reflected the work of a generation of linguists, largely trained by Franz Boas. The further reduction to 6 units Sapir saw as being his own work. Adapted from Darnell (1986).

esized proto-language, Greenberg looks at words only and does so for large numbers of languages at the same time. His work is controversial and points to a far horizon. While the overall picture may turn out to be generally valid, the work itself has serious flaws (some of it is simply sloppy), and the apparent congruence with Turner's model of dental groups is seen by some as superficial. While some recent mitochondrial DNA studies tend to disconfirm the three-wave hypothesis, very recent work studying the entire genome is strongly supportive.

Interestingly, this work also indicates that speakers of second- and third-wave languages may derive the majority of their genes from first-wave sources.

Implications of Typological and Distributional Data

In considering the implications for us of the various classification systems and the distribution of language families across the New World map, let us start with some of the points on which linguists agree.

TABLE 2.2 Languages and Language Families in Canada: Number of Speakers

FAMILY	LANGUAGE	IN CANADA	OUTSIDE CANADA
Algonquian			
Eastern Branch	Abenaki	5	few
	Maliseet	1,100	940
	Mi'kmaq	8,960	330
	Munsee (Delaware)	7	few
	Potawatomi	1,250	50
Central Branch	Cree	97,230	100
	Atikamekw	5,000	
	Innu (Montagnais-Naskapi)	9,657	
	Ojibway	64,400	5,000
	Algonkin	2,430	
	Odawa	7,100	330
	Saulteaux (W. Ojibway)	10,000	
Plains Branch	Blackfoot	4,500	100
Athapaskan			
	Babine	500	
	Dunne-Za (Beaver)	300	
	Carrier	2,060	
	Southern Carrier	2,055	
	Ts'ilqot'in (Chilcotin)	1,140	
	Chipewyan	9,030	
	Dogrib	2,110	
	Gwich'in (Kutchin)	500	300
	Han	7	7
	Kaska	400	
	Tsuu T'ina (Sarsi)	50	
	Sekani	35	
	Northern Slavey	1,030	
	Southern Slavey	2,890	
	Tagish	2	
	Tahltan	35	
	Tutchone	200	
	Upper Tanana	10	14
Eskimo-Aleut	Inuktitut	14,000	47,800
	N. Alaskan Inupiat	1,080	2,420
Haida	Haida	40	15
Iroquoian	Cayuga	50	10
	Mohawk	760	3,000
	Oneida	200	40
	Onondaga	75	25
	Seneca	25	150

TABLE 2.2 *(Continued)*

FAMILY	LANGUAGE	IN CANADA	OUTSIDE CANADA
	Tuscarora	7	4
Ktunaxa	Ktunaxa (Kutenai)	6	6
Salishan			
Interior	Okanagan	400	110
	Ntlakapmuk (Thompson)	720	
	Sepwepemc (Shuswap)	500	
	St'at'imcets (Lillooet)	200	
Coastal	Comox	400	
	Halkomelem	200	
	Nuxalk (Bella Coola)	20	
	Pentlatch	none	
	Sechelt	40	
	Squamish	15	
	Straits	20	few
Siouan	Dakota	3,880	15,300
	Lakota	190	6,200
	Stoney (Assiniboine)	2,300	few
Tlingit	Tlingit	230	1,200
Tsimshian	Gitxsan	1,330	
	Nisga'a (Nishga)	920	
	Tsimshian	750	180
Wakashan			
Northern Branch	Haisla	25	
	Heiltsuk	300	
	Kwak'wala (Kwakiutl)	190	80
Southern Branch	Nuuchahnulth (Nootka)	170	
	Nitinaht	30	

Data from Lewis (2009).

One such point is that the map of Canada is virtually covered by only three language families. The languages of most Canadian Natives, and the vast majority in southern Canada east of the Rockies, are members of the Algonquian family. Cree and Ojibwa are very closely related, implying very recent separation; Blackfoot is more distantly related, implying an earlier independent history. Much of interior northwestern Canada and Alaska is occupied by Athapaskan speakers. The many similarities among Athapaskan languages imply relatively recent division into separate languages. Their greatest linguistic diversity is found on the southeast coast of Alaska; an implication is that they spread from there into the Alaskan interior and thence eastward across northern Canada and that subsequently some groups moved southward, with some (ancestral to the Navajos and Apaches) reaching the American Southwest. The third family is Eskimo-Aleut, represented in Canada by Inupik (Inuktitut). It is an extreme case, a single language continuum spread from northern Alaska across to eastern Greenland. Apart from any archaeological evidence, this is a strong indication of relatively recent occupation of the region.

The British Columbia coast stands out as the one region of Canada characterized by linguistic diversity. On principle, then, one would expect that the BC and Alaskan coasts were inhabited earlier than the other parts of Canada. This is entirely likely *if the continent generally was inhabited prior to the last ice age* (the Pleistocene) when one considers that parts of the coast were virtually the only regions in the country to escape glaciation. At this point we have moved to the controversial.

It should be noted that the controversy here is not really linguistic. It arises because what had been until recently the dominant archaeological model has the New World settled very quickly and very late (post-Pleistocene, about 12,000 years ago). Since for the most part linguists are more concerned with establishing relationships than with determining how old the relationships are, they do not often consider the issue of time.

We have already noted that based on where the most linguistic diversity is to be found within their language family, the Eskimo-Aleut generally are thought to have reached their present distribution from points of origin on the Alaska coast. This is both orthodox linguistics and consistent with the standard archaeological view; it should also be noted that both groups are thought to be relatively late arrivals on the continent and that the point of origin of both would have been on the Beringian side of the ice-age glaciers.

The point here is that the pattern of inferred historic dispersal presented by both the Eskimo-Aleut and the Athapaskans is not exceptional but is very much the general pattern. In plotting the distribution of the likely centres of major Amerindian language families and language isolates, Gruhn (1988) notes that 42 of 47 such centres are to be found in coastal regions, virtually all of them on the Pacific or Gulf of Mexico coasts. In other words, the distributional evidence is that the original settlement of the Americas was along the coastal areas, with interior areas being settled later. The linguistic evidence does not support the notion of people funnelling into an empty North American continent from a northern corridor between mountains of ice, but of people moving eastward from the Pacific and northward from the Caribbean.

Gruhn also argues that the shallow time depth of the standard archaeological model is not sufficient to generate the linguistic diversification found within many language families. It should also be noted that if Greenberg's picture is at all correct, the point is even more nearly valid. If 12,000 years is thought to be inadequate to generate the linguistic diversity found within the Hokan or Penutian groups, for instance, is it sufficient time for the entire Amerind macrophylum—all the diverse languages and language families south of the Athapaskans—to have developed?

The most recent "big news" in Amerindian linguistics is the discovery that the language of the Ket people living on the Yenisei River in central Siberia is related to the Athapaskan languages. The language is dying, with no living monolinguals, fewer than 200 fluent speakers, and none of them younger than 50. So the linguistic analysis indicating that Ket and the Athapaskan languages had a common ancestor is timely; in not many years the work would no longer be possible. In a sense, however, it is also no surprise, confirming what almost everyone thought to be the case (that as relatively recent arrivals from Siberia, Athapaskans likely had close relatives there).

Viewpoints from Archaeological Anthropology

Archaeologists all agree that people have lived in the Americas for at least 12,000 years. That general time frame was established in 1927 when a magnificently crafted stone spear point, to be named Folsom, was found still embedded within the ribs of an extinct form of bison, itself lying in a datable geological formation. That direct association of a human artifact with a datable object in an undisturbed context forever silenced the then-dominant conservative view that people had been here for only some 3,000 years.

When this chapter was first drafted in the mid-1980s, the clearly dominant view at that time was that people had been in the western hemisphere for about 12,000 years. We called this the conservative view or the "Clovis-first view," referring to the proposition that sites identified as belonging to the Clovis culture, widely scattered across North America, were the oldest sites on the continent.

In opposition to this view was the "early-entry view" proposed by radicals who suggested dates on the order of 25,000 years or even older. In recent years the early-entry view has gained ground and has now become dominant.

Let us now take a look at how we arrived at the new consensus.

In the 1980s the late-entry view was that there was no shortage of sites for which claims could be made for earlier dates, but that a careful examination of these sites raised questions that had not been fully answered. Old Crow in the northern Yukon is an example. The most famous Old Crow artifact is a hide flesher made from a caribou leg bone. Originally dated at 27,000 BP, improved technical knowledge has led to it being reassessed at only 1350 BP. Numerous other bones from the area, many of extinct animals, showing unmistak-

able evidence of having been worked on or made into tools are dated from 45,000 to 25,000 BP. The problem for some is that these artifacts have been washed out of their original context by the Old Crow River. Lastly, modified bones have been found in contexts reliably dated at 80,000 BP and earlier, but there is no agreement that the cuts were made by humans.

The view of those advocating an early entry to the Americas is that although some unsubstantiated claims for extreme antiquity were made in a few cases, and although some sites like Old Crow are less than perfect in some regards, there is an ever-growing list of sites in much of North and South America that have been reliably dated as being older than 12,000 BP. Bluefish Cave, for instance, "next door" to Old Crow, has *in situ* mammoth bone cores and flakes dated to 24,000 BP. Meadowcroft Rockshelter in Pennsylvania dates to at least 18,250 BP and contains artifacts similar to those found in Siberia from the same time period. Another of these sites is Monte Verde, in southern Chile. The main site is exceptionally well preserved because of its waterlogged condition and includes a series of wooden hide-covered houses with numerous wooden artifacts, food remains in wooden mortars, and numerous vegetal food sources. Its dwellers were not a small band of mobile hunters. The site is dated to 14,800 BP. Given its far southern location, not just in terms of distance but also in terms of a sequence of major environmental adjustments that people must have made as they made their way south, one can only speculate about what a reasonable starting time would have been.

The excavation of the Buttermilk Creek Complex in central Texas, starting in 2006, has been influential. Dating some 2,500 years before Clovis, it reveals a tool kit characterized as highly portable, but involving stone-working techniques out of which Clovis techniques could naturally have evolved. Significantly, given that a typical Clovis site consists of a handful of blades and other tools, already more than 15,000 Buttermilk artifacts have been catalogued (Waters et al. 2011).

Paisley Caves in central Oregon has also received much attention in the last few years because of its 900 human coprolites dated to over 13,000 years ago. The value of the original find was questioned, since there were no associated tools. Tools have since been found, including points from the Western Stemmed Tradition, previously thought to be younger than Clovis. This finding documents two distinct cultural traditions coexisting at this early time.

The situation with two opposing "camps" of archaeologists (with many, of course, not fully subscribing to either view), has existed for decades. In 1996, however, the situation became newly complicated and lively. The precipitating event was the discovery of a virtually complete human skeleton washing out of the bank of the Columbia River near Kennewick, Washington. Kennewick Man was a middle-aged male about 174 centimetres tall who died about 9,300 BP, and whose long, narrow face and brain case and projecting mid-facial region appear to some archaeologists not to be "typically Amerindian." Relatively little is still known about him, because until 2004 he was immobilized in a series of legal actions. His existence has nevertheless stirred considerable re-examination of the whole field (but not, as reported in the media, a revolution). It turns out that the handful of relatively complete New World skulls of roughly this age share the specific features mentioned but differ in other ways; more importantly, they differ substantially from living Amerindians as a group. The biological history of people in the New World thus seems more complex than previously thought. The most likely explanations involve recognizing that the peopling of America started early enough for genetic changes to take place in local populations. There is at this point no need to conclude that Kennewick Man and his contemporaries were not ancestral to living Amerindians even though they looked quite different.

The controversy generated by the Kennewick discovery need not have led to questions about what route(s) were used in settling the Americas, but it did. As a consequence, the dominance of the conservative position involving a late and mid-continental entry quickly leading to Clovis culture has been substantially weakened and seems now to be the minority position. A glacier-free corridor east of the Rockies apparently did not exist prior to about 11,000 BP, so that a Pacific coast entry, possibly but not necessarily involving boats, seems most likely. In the 1970s Knut Fladmark was the first to propose this idea in print, although as he notes himself, others had discussed the notion. An often unappreciated fact in favour of this route is that during ice age maxima ocean levels were some 120 metres lower than currently. This not only created a large land mass where the Bering Strait now is, so that people could walk to the Americas from Asia, but it meant that a coastal route south was probably feasible. Unfortunately, it also means that direct archaeological evidence supporting this idea is hard to come by, since it is now under water.

There are also serious advocates of other possible routes for people entering the New World. One of the most speculative has the Solutrean culture (a bifacial technology very similar to Clovis) of about 20,000 BP on the north coast of Spain leading to the Clovis culture of America, with Europeans skirting the icefields of the North Atlantic in boats and coming down the coast to what is now the southeastern United States, where the earliest Clovis points to date have been found. Another possible landing site is coastal Brazil, where burials have been discovered that start about 11,000 BP and continue for 3,000 years, and that show what appear to be African morphological characteristics (Neves et al 1999). Still other possibilities can quickly be found on the Internet by curious readers.

One other factor in this controversy must be mentioned, even in such a brief summary. The lifestyle of the oldest "Early Americans" about which archaeologists generally agree, in western North America from about 11,500 to 7500 BP, is often referred to as big-game hunting. The sites giving rise to this designation are characterized by the remains of large animals and the tools to kill and process them. These killing tools are fluted, lanceolate spear points, the earliest being termed Clovis (in use from 11,500 to 11,000 BP). The early-entry advocates think that the late-entry advocates simply project this lifestyle into the older past and assume that the very first Amerinds must also have been big-game hunters and must also have been using the same type of stone hunting tools. There are other forms of tools as well, including bone tools, fire-hardened wood tools, and other types of stone tools. In fact, in South America most of the early people contemporary with Clovis in North America were foragers, and not specialized hunters. The argument is that the "Clovis-first" people are not finding pre-Clovis sites in North America because they are not looking for the right kinds of things.

It is entirely appropriate to end this discussion of the settling of the New World on this note because we need to remind ourselves that the past is not there simply to be dug up; rather, anthropologists are actively reconstructing the past. The patterns upon which reconstructions are based are not only in the data but also in the minds of those doing the reconstruction. Since the radicals and conservatives have largely resolved their differences, perhaps we can start paying more attention to the mental patterns of those who originally provided the data.

The General Archaeological Sequences

The view taken here is that the first people came to this continent from what is now Siberia earlier than was formerly conventionally thought, via a land bridge (or its associated coastal waters) known as Beringia that existed intermittently from 70,000 to 12,000 BP, and first spread down the Pacific coast and then into the continent's interior. Most of what is now Canada either was abandoned when the glaciers came or was not settled at all until they had melted. At that point ancestors of the people now known as Ktunaxa and Salish could move into the BC Interior from the west coast, the Algonquians and then the Siouans and Iroquoians into central and eastern Canada from the south, and the Athapaskans into the interior northwest from the coast. Still later, the Eskimoans[3] moved across the Arctic in a series of west-to-east migrations.

The Paleo-Indian Stage (11,500–7500 BP)

The Paleo-Indians are the earliest people about whom there is relative agreement, both because there is more evidence and because they produced "diagnostic" forms of projectile points. We have already mentioned two of these, Folsom and Clovis. They are both bifacially flaked (worked on both sides), fluted projectile points, a style found widely across the continent. Fluted points have been dated in Canada from the Debert site in central Nova Scotia (10,600 BP), Sibbald Creek near Calgary, Alberta (9570 BP), and Charlie Lake Cave north of Fort St John, BC (10,500 BP). The Debert site yielded 140 artifacts, including spear points, drills, knives, wedges, and scrapers, providing a fuller view of the range of activities and skills of these people than most sites. The distribution of fluted points is most extensive in the United States but extends to western Beringia. One can now state that the base for Paleo-Indian cultures was already established in Siberia by 28,000 BP. It also is significant that Beringia seems culturally complex, with local variations of regional patterns being expressed.

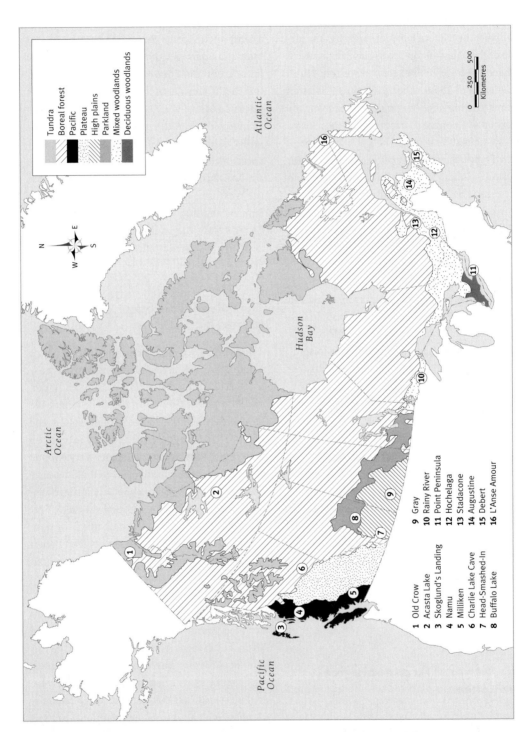

MAP 2.1 Vegetation Zones and Archaeological Sites of Canada

Tundra
Boreal forest
Pacific
Plateau
High plains
Parkland
Mixed woodlands
Deciduous woodlands

Atlantic Ocean

Arctic Ocean

Hudson Bay

Pacific Ocean

1 Old Crow
2 Acasta Lake
3 Skoglund's Landing
4 Namu
5 Milliken
6 Charlie Lake Cave
7 Head-Smashed-In
8 Buffalo Lake
9 Gray
10 Rainy River
11 Point Peninsula
12 Hochelaga
13 Stadacone
14 Augustine
15 Debert
16 L'Anse Amour

0   250   500
Kilometres

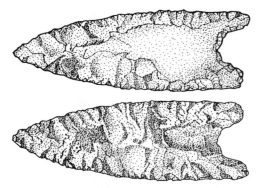

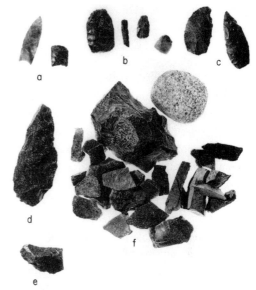

FIGURE 2.1 Fluted projectile point from the Debert site in Nova Scotia. Given what we know of the ecological context, these particular points were most likely used to hunt caribou. (© Canadian Museum of Civilization, image from James A. Tuck, *Maritime Provinces Prehistory*, illustrator Dave Laverie, 1984:5)

FIGURE 2.2 Plano artifacts: (a) projectile points; (b) scrapers used to work various materials such as hide, wood, and bone; (c) knives; (d) roughly shaped "preform," an early step in making projectile points, knives, and other tools; (e) a tool used for slotting bone and wood; (f) hammerstone, core, and flakes (typical of quarry sites where tools were "mass-produced"). (© Canadian Museum of Civilization, from J.V. Wright, *Ontario Prehistory*, 1984:14)

Microblades, very small, unifacial, parallel-sided flakes that presumably were often inset into bone or wood tools, are found in Alaska and the Yukon before 11,000 BP. Part of their interest is that they appear in Siberia about 25,000 BP, and hence they quite directly link peoples on the two continents. They are also of interest because their use persists so long, on the BC coast and Interior until after 4000 BP and in the Arctic (where they are associated with people called Paleo-Eskimos, or the Arctic Small Tool Tradition) until about 2800 BP.

About 10,000 BP, fluted points were replaced on the Plains by stemmed points that are quite thick in cross-section. Collectively called Plano points, they were developed in the US Great Basin around 12,000 BP. They were then used on the Plains, on the northern barren grounds by 8000 BP, and as far east as the Gaspé Peninsula. While they generally seem not to have been used after about 7500 BP, their use persisted in northern Ontario until as recently as 5000 BP. One needs to be cautious in assuming that their persistence in the Subarctic has to do with cultural isolation; Plano style points at Acasta Lake in the Keewatin District dated at 6900 BP have side notches, presumably showing an awareness of a new hafting style developed on the Plains.

Canadian Paleo-Indians east of the Rockies concentrated on hunting big game. In the far West a more diversified economy developed, although from quite early times salmon constituted the primary resource. The productivity of specific locations has led to spectacular archaeological sequences. The Milliken site near Hell's Gate, the narrowest part of the Fraser River and a natural location for fishing, provides an almost continuous record of occupation dating from 9000 BP.

Farther north, the Namu site provides the longest essentially continuous record of occupation, dating from 9700 BP. The deepest level provides the earliest microblades on the coast. Recent work at On Your Knees Cave on Alaska's Prince of Wales Island has revealed human remains and artifacts dating to 10,000 BP made from material that could only have been transported by boat, as well as other tools (not microblades) dating to 10,300 BP. DNA analysis indicates a relationship to about 1 per cent of living Amerindians, but this 1 per cent is restricted to points scattered along the Pacific coast all the way to the tip of South America. (More such work suggesting specific migration routes is much anticipated!) Sites on Haida Gwaii (the Queen Charlotte Islands off the northern British Columbia coast) go back to 10,000 BP and also indicate a strongly developed maritime culture. There are also tantalizing finds of artifacts from underwater beaches that may be even older.

After the Paleo-Indians: Western Canada

Not only are the sequences on the west coast very old, they link at early stages to the area's contemporary residents. That the Haida are a linguistic isolate living on partially unglaciated islands and that sites such as Skoglund's Landing show a growing cultural complexity without significant intrusions suggest that the Haida have occupied the islands for at least the last 10,000 years. The sequence in Prince Rupert harbour begins about 5000 BP and leads directly to the Tsimshian. Because the site was waterlogged, there is remarkable preservation of perishables after 2000 BP, including whole houses and canoes (the large rectangular planked houses typical of the historic period appear on the coast at about this time). Farther south on the coast, Wakashan history can be inferred to extend to at least 4500 BP and Salish to 3500 BP. That is not to say, of course, that these people did not exist earlier as distinct groups.

The history of the Interior Plateau of BC is less well known, partly because people tended to live in the same places as earlier people did, and making a new semi-subterranean pit house often meant digging up an old one. In any case, small villages appear by about 6000 BP, located near good fishing sites (and as salmon re-established themselves on these streams in the post-glacial environment). Houses of much the same style were still used in the nineteenth century.

The Plains appear to have been relatively depopulated from about 7500 to 5000 BP, possibly due to the effects of the hypothesized hotter and drier period known as the Altithermal. If so, this was merely an extreme example of the standard Plains adaptational pattern: both the buffalo and those who lived off them moved from the Plains to the adjacent mountains and parkland during times of stress, including the average winter. Head-Smashed-In, a buffalo jump in southern Alberta, was in use from at least 5700 BP. Such sites, where massive quantities of meat were processed repeatedly, leave an interesting chronology, but of only one aspect of life.

Pottery appeared on the Canadian Plains somewhat before arrowheads. It is found as far northwest as central Alberta and, like burial mounds (found as far northwest as southeastern Saskatchewan) and farming (as far northwest as North Dakota), was derived from the Woodland culture of southern Ontario and the Mississippi Valley and ultimately from the cultures of Mexico or even Colombia.

Eastern Canada: Archaic Period (9500–3000 BP)

"Archaic" is an unfortunate term, but it is thoroughly embedded in the literature. It generally refers to people who have a broadly based foraging lifestyle of hunting, fishing, and gathering.

L'Anse Amour is the earliest known burial mound in North America (7500 BP). Located in southern Labrador, it is associated with the Maritime Archaic culture. It contains the body of a young teenager and numerous grave goods, including points, knives, needles, a flute, and a toggle carved from an antler. Key interpretations are that the grave goods indicate not only a belief system including an afterlife, but: (1) a productive maritime hunting economy (a toggle harpoon head pivots inside the hide of a speared animal after the attached line is pulled, allowing the offshore hunting of sea mammals), and (2) the subsequent development of some degree of social differentiation. By 5000 BP Maritime Archaic people had expanded to Newfoundland, indicating they had seaworthy craft.

The Laurentian Archaic developed in southern Ontario and Quebec, later expanding to New Brunswick and Maine. Few campsites have been found (they moved a lot), but about 6000 BP they started placing grave goods in burial sites. These goods indicate an extensive trade network, including conch shells from the Gulf of Mexico, copper work from west of Lake Superior, and ground slate points from Maritime Archaic people.

Eastern Canada: Woodland Period (3300 BP–Historic Era)

Woodland culture is primarily a culture of the eastern United States, extending into the southern part of eastern Canada. It is a northern extension of a settled, agricultural way of life largely originating in Mexico (although local plants were domesticated before more southerly cultigens were adopted) but achieving a regional cultural focus in the central Mississippi Valley. The archaeological convention (arising out of the incorrect assumption that only agriculturalists made pottery) is to refer to people as Woodland if they made pottery even if they were not actually agriculturalists.

About 3300 BP Laurentian Archaic people started making ceramic beakers with pointed bottoms and cord-marked walls. This marks the begin-

ning of Woodland culture in Canada, although the people continued to be nomadic hunters.

The Point Peninsula phase began about 2750 BP. The pottery marking this phase clearly was strongly influenced by the Adena culture of the Ohio Valley; it also demonstrates local affinities (like cord marking) and influences from northern Ontario ("toothed" markings). As time goes on, the extensive trade in regionally identifiable goods indicates complex and continuing connections spanning half the continent.

Canadian Woodland culture clearly developed in part out of local antecedents generally thought to be associated with the Algonquian language family. Just as clearly, southern Ontario had also been inhabited for some time by Iroquoian speakers. Although there are reasons to think that Iroquoians may have reached the area as early as 3500 BP, only by 1100 BP are there palisaded villages with corn fields and large ossuaries clearly identifiable as Iroquoian. About 700 years ago these people experienced a significant geographic expansion from a southern Ontario base leading to their historically known territories.

From earliest times this has been a region of hunters living in small bands that moved frequently. It is also a region of acidic soils that quickly destroy most of the things that humans leave behind. It is not surprising, then, that we know relatively little about the area.

Boreal Forest and Subarctic Tundra

As noted earlier, Paleo-Indians moved into the Subarctic tundra and boreal forest as the glaciers melted. The lanceolate points characteristic of the Paleo-Indians continued to characterize this region after the side-notched points that archaeologists use to define the Shield Archaic (6000 BP to historic times) were introduced. About 2200 BP Shield Archaic people living in eastern Manitoba and the adjacent Rainy River region of northern Ontario started making pottery associated with

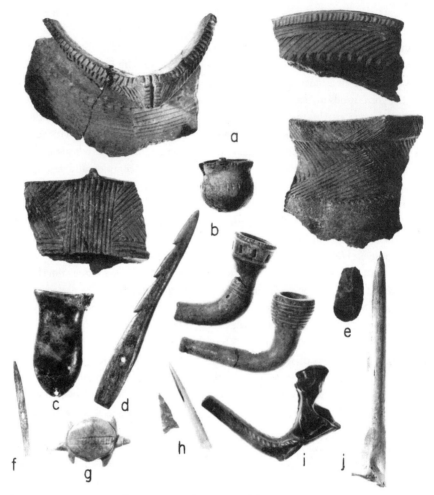

FIGURE 2.3 Iroquoian (Huron-Petun) artifacts: (a) rim fragments from pots; (b) pot, probably made by a small girl; (c) stone pipe bowl; (d) antler harpoon; (e) scraper; (f) netting needle; (g) turtle amulet made of stone; (h) stone and bone arrowheads; (i) clay pipes; (j) dagger made from human bone. (© Canadian Museum of Civilization, from J.V. Wright, *Ontario Prehistory*, 1984:80)

the Laurel culture. The Rainy River region is also known for burial mounds with especially rich grave goods. This is most unusual for boreal forest hunters, but perhaps the point is more that the area is relatively close both to the Great Lakes and to the Plains and, therefore, to people living different lifestyles. Around 700 CE other types of pottery originating in southern Ontario came into use.

The Arctic

The Arctic is the most recently inhabited part of Canada. Only 4,000 years ago did people spread eastward from what is now Alaska, moving quite rapidly across the High Arctic islands to northern Greenland. These first inhabitants of Canada's Arctic are known as Independence I people, from the Greenlandic fjord where they were first identified. They were part of a cultural tradition known both as Paleo-Eskimo and as the Arctic Small Tool Tradition, from their use of microblades as tool components. The use of microblades and a complex of other features link the Paleo-Eskimo both to earlier Alaskan cultures and ultimately to the Diuktai culture of northeastern Siberia. Diuktai, formerly dated to 35,000 BP, is now understood to be only 25,000 years old, making it marginally less interesting but still ancestral to these people. The rapid movement of the first Paleo-Eskimos across previously uninhabited areas seems to require some explanation. One possible factor may be that, although people had been living in the North for some time, their annual cycle had them moving seasonally back and forth between forest and shore; only now had they learned to live throughout the year near the Arctic shoreline.

FIGURE 2.4 These are examples of the kinds of stone tools made by people in Alaska early in the post-glacial period. At lower left is a microblade core from which sharp, parallel-sided blades (lower right) were removed. Microblades could be used as knife blades or further modified to form small points on weapons. Above these artifacts are a larger stone core and a spear point. Few other artifacts have been preserved from this time period. (© Canadian Museum of Civilization, from Robert McGhee, *Canadian Arctic Prehistory*, photographer Don E. Edmond, 1978:11)

Another factor may be that the shore region was now habitable for the first time since the glacial age due to a stabilized sea level and increasing (although still low) stocks of maritime resources. This may be reflected in the apparently greater reliance of the Independence I people on land resources like caribou and muskox than on seals and walrus. Since few land animals live on islands and since these land animals reproduce slowly, an explanation for why the people kept moving from island to island and why they disappeared shortly after reaching the eastern end of the High Arctic island chain may be that they simply ran out of food and in the end literally had nowhere to go.

Only 300 years after the Independence I people, however, a second wave of Paleo-Eskimos, known as Pre-Dorset people, moved eastward out of Alaska. Perhaps because they had a more balanced reliance on land and sea resources, their colonization of the Arctic was successful. In any case, for about 1,000 years small, mobile groups of these people occupied the Far North. This is not to say they occupied all the territory all the time. Richer areas seem to have been used continuously; other areas were occupied or abandoned as local conditions warranted. The cultural variability one would expect under these conditions did in fact arise. In general, we can say that these people lived in skin tents for much of the year. They also used snow houses (they may have invented them) and heated them with oil lamps. They may have used skin-covered boats. They had dogs, but not dog sleds. They used sinew-backed bows much like more modern ones.

Life in the Arctic is never easy, but life for the Pre-Dorset became harder as the decades went by because their entry into the Arctic coincided with a long-term cooling trend. With game becoming scarcer, even good hunters may go hungry. By 3000 BP the Pre-Dorset range seems to have become restricted to Foxe Basin and Hudson Strait.

FIGURE 2.5 These Pre-Dorset artifacts are quite similar to those of the Independence I culture, except for some stylistic features and the two harpoon heads (upper left). Proceeding clockwise, the other items are: what is probably a broken fish spear head, two harpoon or spear points, side blades for insetting into the sides of weapon heads, two burins for working bone or antler, microblades, two scrapers, a bone needle, and a bone pin. (© Canadian Museum of Civilization, photographer Harry Foster, 1978, 77–30)

Given these circumstances, we are not surprised to find that people turned increasingly to hunting sea mammals, particularly those, such as seals and walrus, that are "ice-loving" and hence fairly accessible. With this orientation there is a concomitant decline in the number of dogs, bows and arrows are abandoned, the snow knife is invented, oil lamps are used more, stone cooking pots are used, ice creepers (to strap on the feet while walking on ice) are found, and the kayak is definitely used.

By 2500 BP the cumulative effect of these changes had become transformative; the new society is referred to as Dorset. Dorset culture flourished and recolonized the sea margins of the North from Labrador to Greenland and westward toward Alaska.

While our narrative is focused on the Canadian Arctic, we must now turn to Alaska. The archaeology of Alaska is complex, in part because it was a meeting ground between North Pacific and Arctic peoples. A critical event was the adaptation in the

BOX 2.1 Kwäday Dän Ts'ìnchi—"This is a man, not an experiment"

In August 1999, human remains were discovered melting out of a glacier in Tatshenshini-Alsek Park, located in the extreme northwest corner of British Columbia. Concurrently, a number of artifacts (clothing, tools, food items) made of perishable materials were found in direct association with the remains. Immediately after the discovery was reported to authorities, the site was visited and evaluated by archaeologists and representatives of the Champagne and Aishihik First Nations (CAFN). The discovery was named Kwäday Dän Ts'ìnchi, "Long Ago Person Found." As a recovery and research plan started to evolve, a unique, co-operative, and collaborative relationship, culminating in a formal agreement, was struck between the CAFN and the government of British Columbia (Archaeology Branch). The committee thus formed was responsible for overseeing the recovery and proper handling of the remains and the subsequent proposed research. Priority issues involved quickly planning and coordinating a safe, contamination-free recovery and determining where the remains and artifacts would be housed. They decided that the best location would be specially altered facilities at the Royal BC Museum in Victoria. The preservation protocol was a customized version of the methods used at the University of Innsbruck to protect and preserve the 5,300-year-old Neolithic man found in an Italian glacier in 1991.

During late 1999 and early 2000, the committee evaluated many research proposals submitted by scientists from a number of countries, and selected some to conduct studies. Projects included dating the human remains and artifacts, the forensic evaluation of the body, determination of the individual's diet, and examination of DNA evidence. The needs of these research projects were met by the committee agreeing to the collection and retention of the required samples from the individual and artifacts, and providing access to the discoveries.

Two hundred forty Natives from Alaska, BC, and the Yukon enthusiastically volunteered for DNA testing in hope of establishing a connection to Kwäday Dän Ts'ìnchi. Matching sequences were found and a pool of 17 living relatives has been established, 15 belonging to the Wolf Clan. Dating the remains has been difficult, but currently the time frame is seen as about 1670 to 1850. He was a male between 17 and 22 years old. Isotopic analysis of his remains indicates a strongly marine diet for most of his life with a switch to terrestrial materials in his last year. Analysis of his stomach and intestines reveals that he made his last trip in late summer and that he had eaten meat, seafood, beach asparagus, and berries. Silt grains in his stomach show that he travelled to the glacier up the Chilkat River basin and not the Tatshenshini-Alsek basin. Cause of death is not certain, but likely involved an accident and/or exposure.

Among the items recovered were a robe, a hat, a bag, an iron blade with wooden handle, and a small copper bead. The robe was constructed from 95 Arctic ground squirrel hides. Its existence has sparked renewed interest in this formerly common item. Similarly the hat, skillfully crafted from woven split spruce roots, but known to be of a type used by ordinary people for everyday wear, has sparked serious interest in reviving this traditional craft.

Continued

Another positive outcome has been the continued and growing involvement of the local Native communities. There has, for instance, been an annual visit to the discovery site by a CAFN research team. In 2001 the human remains were returned to the site and interred and the artifacts blessed. In the same year a Tlingit Forty Day Party was held. In 2008 a Southern Tutchone headstone **potlatch** was held.

Many difficult issues and important decisions were made regarding the modern cultural and scientific needs and sensitivities inherent in such a discovery. No perfect solutions exist, but the real possibility that this man could be documented in oral histories highlighted the need to approach the discovery with the same respect and sensitivity that a coroner or medical examiner would show to a recently deceased body. This can be seen to contrast with the need of science to be allowed the unrestricted freedom to pursue the collection of scientific data. Some controversy will always be associated with the natural tension that exists between conflicting needs. But to paraphrase a colleague commenting on these needs, "This is a man, not an experiment." That sentiment has been the guiding philosophy in the research on Kwäday Dän Ts'ìnchi.

—Owen Beattie, Department of Anthropology, University of Alberta

ninth century by northwestern Alaskan peoples of a Japanese innovation—making large floats out of animal skins. By acting as a drag and a marker, the device greatly improved the efficiency of walrus and whale hunting. After this the population expanded greatly and society became more complex. The resultant cultural tradition is referred to by archaeologists as Thule culture. For a variety of reasons, but certainly in part because it was effective both economically and socially, Thule culture spread into southwestern Alaska, into the interior of Alaska, and eastward across Canada to Greenland.

The bearers of Thule culture into Canada were Inupik speakers, ancestral to the modern Inuit. While it is clear that their sweep across the Arctic was rapid, we know very little about the nature of their relationship with the Dorset populations already there. It is easy to envision hostile encounters between bands of armed hunters, but there is no direct evidence of such conflict. Perhaps the Dorset simply retreated. Or, as Hickey (1986) thinks more likely, the Thule incorporated at least some Dorset people (although recent DNA studies suggest little genetic connection between Dorset and Inuit, with the notable exception of the Sadlermiut, who lived on several islands in northern Hudson Bay).

In Hickey's scenario, it would be advantageous to the immigrant Thule to take advantage of the detailed local environmental knowledge of Dorset men. Dorset women would be valued as domestic and procreative assets, but more importantly as a medium for social alliances. Such a process would leave little archaeological evidence. An intriguing line of evidence in favour of Dorset people being incorporated into Thule society is the continued tradition of women in the eastern Arctic making special "dress-up" clothing that is much more complex in construction than are utilitarian garments. This seems more consistent with the ornate Dorset artistic aesthetic than with the generally austere Thule taste. In this view, Dorset women in Thule households would generally have raised their children as Thule, but might well also have passed on special skills and aesthetic judgments that they valued highly. In any case, Thule people prospered and over roughly 1,000 years evolved into the several historic Inuit societies.

As a radical footnote to this discussion, we note that Robert McGhee has proposed that the Inuit traverse to the eastern Arctic was far quicker than previously thought. He suggests that Inuit in Alaska, who were already using and trading iron, heard from Dorset people both about a lode of meteoric iron far to the east and about the Norse, who had new things to trade. In possibly two years they could have travelled the 4,000 kilometres to Ruin Island, between Ellesmere and Greenland, and about 1360 CE established the first Inuit settlement east of Alaska.

In sum, North and South America were inhabited an unimaginably long time ago by people who migrated over the land mass that now constitutes Asia and the Americas. They, of course, did not think of their experiences in those terms, for their frames of reference were different. Nevertheless, they created a series of diverse and successful adaptations to the entire range of environments to be found. And here, in turn, they were "found" by another kind of migrant.

FIGURE 2.6 These are examples of the more "sophisticated" technology of the Dorset people. Clockwise from the upper left: two harpoon heads, a large lance head, a knife utilizing a microblade, a ground burin-like implement with its handle, two flaked stone and one ground stone points, a fish arrow or spear head, a bone needle, and an ivory ice-creeper. (© Canadian Museum of Civilization, photographer Harry Foster, 1978, 77–28)

A Millennium of European Immigration

European immigration began with at least one aborted attempt at settlement by the Norse about 1,000 years ago. There is scant but tantalizing evidence for contact between Europeans and Indigenous Americans over the next 500 years.

European and African immigration to the territory that is now Canada began building in the sixteenth century, accelerated dramatically in the seventeenth century, increased even more dramatically in the eighteenth century, and became overwhelming in the nineteenth century. The human migration from Europe between the early 1600s and 1930 was probably the largest ever, and it changed the face of the Americas. The history of the First Nations of Canada in the face of that massive immigration of Europeans is one of survival. It is first of all a history of physical survival, given the effects that European diseases had on Indigenous populations. An aspect of history that resonates with our

FIGURE 2.7 Illustrating the great difference between Thule and the earlier
Paleo-Eskimo technology, we see clockwise from the right: an adze handle,
an adze head with a ground stone blade, a man's knife with a ground stone
blade, a woman's knife (ulu) with an iron blade, a whalebone snow knife,
a bone scraper for skin working, an engraving tool with an iron point, and
a drill bit with a ground stone point. (© Canadian Museum of Civilization,
photographer Harry Foster, 1978, 77–27)

own era has to do with another kind of survival:
the history of the relations between Indigenous
Canadians and the Europeans, Africans, and Asians
who migrated here after 1600 is one of the struggle for survival of sovereignty within a European
Christian conception of land rights.

The paradox was that during the first century
of sustained contact, it was obvious that Europeans
stayed on at the sufferance of their hosts and trading partners. While explorers could claim a territory for a European crown, in practice control over
the territory was not always coincident with the
claim. Recognition of the reality of Amerindian
control made it necessary to purchase land from
Indians or for Europeans to ally themselves with
Indians for trade and warfare. Europeans professed

dual postures to their Indian allies, trading with
them, even adopting Indigenous forms of negotiation and trade protocols, but claiming European
sovereignty in law. Thus, more than 150 years after
the beginning of sustained contact, the French
could claim to the English that the French presence in Acadia was by right of Indian invitation,
yet in negotiating the Treaty of Utrecht in 1713
they completely ignored consideration of Mi'kmaq
or Maliseet interest or opinion in the French relin-
quishment of Acadia to the English.

In the European conception of things, America
was a wilderness and Natives were part of that
wilderness. That idea could be maintained despite
all the evidence: the obvious concentration of
Indigenous populations, the obvious control and

BOX 2.2 Relations between Norse and Indigenous Peoples of Canada

During the late first millennium CE, northern European venturers, hunters, and farmers explored westward across the North Atlantic islands. Around 1000 CE the Norse established settlements along the fiords of southwestern Greenland, an outpost of Europe that lasted for almost 500 years. Icelandic sagas record voyages of exploration to the west of Greenland during the first decades of the colony's existence, and archaeology confirms that these ventures extended as far as the Gulf of St Lawrence, the Vinland of the sagas. Here, and in Markland, which is thought to have been the forested coast of Labrador, the Norse would have encountered the ancestors of Innu, Beothuk, and Mi'kmaq peoples. The sagas report efforts to trade for furs, but because of fear of Native opposition the Norse abandoned their attempts to establish a settlement in Vinland.

Recently discovered archaeological evidence suggests that a more enduring and complex relationship existed between the Norse and the natives of Helluland, the Norse name for the tundra regions of northern Labrador and Baffin Island. The Norse sailed along these coasts from the time of their early ventures to Vinland, and would have known of the animal resources of the area. The Greenlandic Norse economy depended on exporting local products to Europe, including the tusks and skins of walrus, narwhal ivory, and skins of polar bears and probably other fur-bearing animals. It seems probable that Helluland would have attracted commercial hunters, some of whom would have engaged in trade for ivory and furs with the Dorset Paleo-Eskimo groups that then occupied the region. Dorset archaeological

sites in the region have produced numerous specimens that are either of European origin or derived from European technologies. These include yarn spun from the fur of Arctic hare and other local animals, whetstones of characteristic European forms, notched wooden tally-sticks of the type used by the Norse for recording transactions, and a variety of other artifacts. The nature of relations between the Norse and Dorset people is not yet fully understood, but was likely based on trade that developed over several centuries.

Ancestral Inuit of the Thule culture arrived in the eastern Arctic during the twelfth or thirteenth century, perhaps attracted by the possibility of obtaining metal from the Norse. The earliest known Inuit sites in the eastern Arctic have produced pieces of smelted metal as well as ship rivets, woollen cloth, fragments of chain mail armour, and a portion of a trader's bronze balance. It has been suggested that many of these artifacts came from the salvage of a shipwreck, or perhaps piracy of a small Norse vessel. The eastward expansion of the Inuit brought Europeans into contact with a Native population that had a technology and fighting skills that were at least equivalent to those of the Norse. Although there was probably sporadic contact between Norse and Inuit until the abandonment of the Greenlandic settlements, the archaeological evidence suggests no more than occasional wary encounters.

—Patricia Sutherland, Adjunct Research Professor, Carleton University and Memorial University; Research Fellow, University of Aberdeen

management of unfenced pasture areas in which many Native people harvested mammals for food, the practice of agriculture, the military power and skills of Indigenous groups, and the extensive trade networks. The country was no wilderness, and given the evidence it is a wonder that Europeans could see it as one. It was a European legal and moral convention to assume that land that had not been extensively used and modified by "civilized" peoples was in fact empty, and so could be claimed by Christian, civilized Europeans. That idea may have been a powerful constraint on European understanding of how American Indigenous groups occupied and used land, although willful blindness seems to many more likely.

The period of sustained contact began in Canada in Newfoundland and the Maritimes, and shortly thereafter in the Gaspé and the immediate St Lawrence watershed. During the sixteenth century, European settlement in North America was focused on the subtropical regions, but Europeans had become familiar with the North Atlantic coast through the activity of the Atlantic fishery. Portuguese, Basque, and English exploitation of the Newfoundland fishery accelerated during the 1500s, until every summer saw around 17,000 European males along the northeast coast. Though occasionally some crew members wintered over, there was no really permanent settlement. Trade in furs, at first an adjunct to exploration, began in earnest during this time, with French and English voyages of trade and exploration along the coast and up the St Lawrence River.

The first and lasting effect of sustained contact was disease. No one knows the extent of the first great smallpox epidemic in 1520–4. It began in the West Indies and Mexico and spread northward to affect most of North America. It was followed by a devastating epidemic of measles just seven years later. An epidemic caused by an unknown pathogen affected people of the St Lawrence Valley in 1535, and smallpox struck again in the eastern Great Lakes region in the early 1590s. European diseases took a crushing toll: smallpox, for example, seemed to hit every other generation, as each generation that had gained some immunity was replaced by a new, susceptible one.

The number of people who died or who were permanently disabled by disease is a matter of speculation. Estimates of the population of North America north of the cities of Mexico in the early sixteenth century vary from 4.5 million to as high as 18 million, and one of the difficulties in making the estimate is the incalculably devastating effect of the early epidemics. The cost in human life has been very great: susceptibility to European disease was a major factor in the decline of the Indigenous population until the 1920s, to the extent that by the last part of the nineteenth century the Indigenous population of the United States and Canada dropped to around 300,000. Epidemics of smallpox, measles, influenza, and bubonic plague were the greatest killers, and diphtheria, cholera, typhus, scarlet fever, and typhoid also caused high mortality. The early epidemics preceded initial European settlement in the Northeast, so when that settlement began in earnest in the early 1600s it was among an Indigenous population already seriously affected by European diseases.

Alliances in Trade and Warfare

Acceleration of the trade in furs coincided with the first sustained European settlement in the early seventeenth century in the areas that now form Canada and the United States. European immigration began building in the 1630s, with French, English, Dutch, and Swedish establishment of fur-trading posts and with experiments in agricultural settlement by the French and English. Trade relationships begun during the sixteenth century formed the basis for the initial pattern of European settlement, with the various European nations establishing colonies in territory controlled by the

Indigenous nations with which each European nation had regularly allied itself in trade.

We tend to look at those alliances nowadays in terms of their lasting significance rather than what motivated them at the time. Perhaps we lend too much relevance to those alliances that seem to have endured and to have changed history because of the eventual balance of power between European nations. The seventeenth century was a time of huge increase in trade between Europeans and Amerindians as well as of European encroachment on Indian land. Our discussions cloud a very complex period of competition among the European groups themselves for control of land for expansion and of competition among Indigenous nations, both in economic terms and for favourable terms of survival given the European onslaught.

The alliances built on, exploited, and irrevocably disrupted ancient trade patterns between Indigenous nations. Indigenous trade patterns had been predominantly north and south, but the French inroad had been east to west, from Acadia to Gaspé, the St Lawrence Valley, and then the Great Lakes and south through the Ohio and Mississippi River systems. The French were allied initially in the Maritimes with the Mi'kmaq and Maliseet, then with factions of those groups' occasional enemies, the Eastern Abenaki. Their allies north of the St Lawrence were the Montagnais and, in the interior, the Algonquians and a major group of Huron nations. The Dutch were initially allied with the Algonquian groups around the Hudson River, but sought alliance with the group that became known as the Five Nations Iroquois. England's beachhead was first in New England and then in its settlements south of Chesapeake Bay.

The Iroquois of the Five Nations gained tremendous political power by challenging the French and their allies to control trade on the St Lawrence and then by allying themselves with the British. As the English took over Indian land in New England and along the Hudson River,

groups displaced by British encroachment moved westward, and some former enemies of the Five Nations put themselves under the protection of their erstwhile foes. Five Nations ascendancy was clearly realized when they destroyed the strongest interior trading partners to the north, the Huron allies of the French, during the mid-1600s.

Disease was a continuing major factor in the European expansion of the seventeenth century, with epidemics of bubonic plague in New England in 1612–19, measles in 1633–4 throughout the whole Northeast and again in 1658–9, scarlet fever in 1637 among the Hurons, diphtheria in 1659 in New England and eastern Canada, and smallpox, which racked the entire Northeast at least once during each decade from the 1630s to the 1690s. Military action against Indians was usually along lines consistent with the pattern of European alliance, but in New England there was military action against Indians for control of land. The military action, from the European colonizers' standpoint, was probably not as effective as disease. The effects of disease on Native populations were so obvious that English colonists could interpret the devastation brought by epidemics as divine sanction for European possession and repopulation of the land.

Control over territory and trade was clearly the cause of war. France and England were at war during much of the seventeenth century. The Five Nations Iroquois fought the French for nearly the entire century, the Abenaki fought the English for control of northern New England, and New England Algonquians went to war to attempt to remove the English from their territory.

European Expansion into the Interior during the Eighteenth Century

The eighteenth century was a time of continued conflict between European powers and conflict between England and her American colonies. A significant part of that conflict was played out in America. The Five Nations Iroquois established peace with French colonists in 1701, but their allies the Fox, in the area that is now Wisconsin, continued hostile action against the French and their Dakota allies. The French sought to maintain a continental sphere of influence through the Great Lakes to the Mississippi, and fought with the English over control of trade in Hudson Bay. During the early part of the eighteenth-century French interests were well served by Mi'kmaq military conflict with the English in the Maritimes.

If the focus is on European conflict, the history of relationships between European colonists and the different Indian nations during the seventeenth and eighteenth centuries is one of shifting alliances and unclear national boundaries: for example, during the last era of formal conflict between the French and the Five Nations Iroquois, many Christianized Iroquois settled in villages near Montreal. That illustrates two aspects of Amerindian–European relationship: (1) missionization had become important as a policy of control and pacification; and (2) Amerindian political organization was markedly different from that of Europeans. Indian military strategy, patterns of alliance, social movement, and migration are more clearly explicable if the focus is not on European spheres of influence and power balances but on Amerindian groups' own attempts to control trade and land on their own terms, to adapt to the presence of Europeans, and above all to retain a land base for themselves that they might control. In other words, Indian political alliance was not a matter of less powerful nations aligning with more powerful European partners, but was instead a series of strategic partnerships, negotiations, diplomatic ventures, and armed hostility, all oriented toward maximizing each Amerindian group's interests.

Relationships among Indian nations were oriented to the same end—maximizing the specific national interest of the individual nation. The nations of New England and the American Atlantic seaboard, displaced and decimated by European disease and finding refuge with other groups, were among the first to couch the struggles of the seventeenth and eighteenth centuries in terms of a conflict of a duality, Indians against Europeans. Groups such as the Delaware, formed as a collectivity from Algonquian survivors of groups north of Chesapeake Bay, first moved west to put themselves under the protection of their former antagonists, the Five Nations Iroquois, and then further west to the continental interior and to Upper Canada. Some of their leaders were influential in attempts to bring Indian nations together to fight in common cause against European colonists.

The English Royal Proclamation of 1763, requiring that any alienation of Indian land be negotiated and that the Crown be the sole European agency in negotiation, was a central component of an imperial strategy to ally Indian nations with Britain. When English domination was established in Quebec and the Maritimes during the last half of the eighteenth century, the possibility for Indian nations to play off one power against the other was removed, but during the war between England and the 13 American colonies, Indian nations were fighting on both sides, and they continued to face other Indian nations in battle in alliances with Europeans until the cessation of hostilities between Canada and the United States in 1814.

Patterns of European migration changed as well. Until the establishment of the United States, around two-thirds of the immigrants other than slaves had been indentured labourers. After the American Revolution, European immigration to North America was predominantly by free persons, and there was a large one-time immigration of British Loyalists from the United States to Canada.

The last part of the eighteenth century saw increased direct trade between Europeans and Indians in the interior, building on primarily east–west trade routes that had been established in the fur trade among Indian groups. That trade was extended through the watersheds that led to Hudson Bay.

Trade with the Pacific Northwest began during the last part of the eighteenth century. It was joined by the Russians, who established permanent trading and missionary ventures with their claim to Alaska. English and American trading in the Northwest was initially by ship, and the commodities bought from Indians were primarily maritime products, such as sea otter pelts. By 1821, when the Montreal-based North West Company and the London-based Hudson's Bay Company amalgamated, the fur trade relied primarily on land mammals and was conducted in trading posts, and the HBC had extended its domain to the coast with the amalgamation. The decade of the 1830s saw the beginning of European settlement in the area that is now British Columbia. Though conflict between west coast Indians and individual traders could be bloody, the pattern of alliances and warfare of the east coast was not repeated in the West, except for the battles fought between Tlingits and Russians.

Before any appreciable contact, around 1770, the first of the great smallpox epidemics hit the Northwest Coast. It may have reduced the total population by 30 per cent. Before the introduction of European disease, the area had been the most highly populated of any non-agricultural area in the world, with as many as 180,000 inhabitants. Losses from a single epidemic would claim as much as two-thirds of the population of a single community, and as each succeeding epidemic claimed lives the Native population was reduced to just over 30,000 by the late 1800s.

The eighteenth century was also a time of displacement and migration. In the West, some nations whose way of life and habitation had been primarily in woodlands and parklands saw some of their people move onto the Plains. In the south, adoption of the horse as a central part of the culture facilitated that movement. Some groups whose livelihood had been in agriculture and the harvest of land mammals abandoned agriculture to hunt with horses and to trade for agricultural products and European goods with Indigenous agriculturalists in the river valleys. In the northern Plains, the move was facilitated by a growing market to provision the fur trade with food and other supplies.

A Tide of Immigration and the Beginning of the Reserve Era

The nineteenth century, by contrast to the preceding 200 years, was a period of relative peace between European powers and a period of wholesale change in the Americas. The United States and Canada had used Aboriginal groups as buffers along their common border. When the possibility of war between the two countries diminished after the signing of a formal treaty in 1817, the importance of Indians as military allies decreased and a period of oppressive attempts to control them began. The United States began relocating Indians westward, including groups who had lived near the eastern international border with Canada, and by the 1820s the strategic importance of Indian nations in that area, as military allies of Canada, was diminished.

The intensification of industrialization in Europe displaced many of its own people and created a worldwide demand for agricultural land and agricultural products. Between 1814 and World War I around 50 million people migrated from Europe to the "new Europes" of the Americas and Australasia. Two-thirds of them came to the United States and 4 million to Canada, where the largest tide of immigration was to the West after the 1890s.

The policies of both the United States and Canada were westward expansion and the alienation of ever more Indian land to provide a place for Europeans to farm. Populations of Amerindians continued to decline in the face of repeated epidemics, but the birth rate of new immigrants was one of the highest ever recorded, especially among Caucasians. The African-American population increased as well, through natural increase and the importation of slaves, so that their population in North America rose from 1 million in 1800 to around 12 million by 1930.

Policies that became pre-eminent in the early 1800s seem to have driven Canadian government interaction with Indigenous nations for the next two centuries. It appeared to most non-Native observers that Indigenous groups were dying out. The continuing dramatic toll of disease in Native populations appeared to make their eventual demise inevitable. Social philosophy as it developed during the nineteenth century saw all human groups as developing through inevitably sequenced stages, and Native cultures were thought to be in a stage of "savagery." From that perspective, Euro-Canadian culture was an aspect of western Europe's pre-eminent development to "civilization." During the last half of the nineteenth century the concept of social Darwinism expanded on the assumption that Indian cultures represented less progress and less cultural development than European cultures, and it was assumed that "civilized" cultures were "fittest" to survive in any context of cultural conflict over resources.

Peace between the United States and British North America after 1817 brought an end to the long period of military and political alliance among First Nations and European, colonial, and American governments. No longer needed as political allies, Native people became objects of altruism: European social philosophers saw them as being in need of "advancement" to participate in "civilization." Churches and missionary societies defined Natives as needy in economic, social, moral, and spiritual terms. Indians in areas where Europeans wanted land needed to be protected and, eventually, assimilated. Churches and philanthropic organizations, primarily in Britain but also in the United States, focused on Canadian Indigenous nations as subjects of concerted missionary activity. From the 1820s until mid-century,

British missionary organizations were a powerful lobby in the British Parliament for reorienting colonial policy toward the philanthropic end of Christianizing and civilizing Indians and Eskimos.

Since the Royal Proclamation of 1763, the management of the relationship between Indians and the government had been the responsibility of the British government rather than any colonial government. An imperial policy of "civilization" of Indians as communities began in 1830. It marked the beginning of the reserve period in Canada. Indians were to congregate on land reserved for them, apart from the rest of Canadian society, and, as communities, to adapt to Canada's changing social order by learning to farm. The government encouraged missionary activity, and the nineteenth-century debate over which came first, civilization or Christianization, seems to have had its popular origins in this period. The policy had its greatest impact east of Lake Superior. Rupert's Land was still the domain of the Hudson's Bay Company and the Indigenous nations there were autonomous and relatively self-sufficient through participation in the fur trade and through traditional harvest of food and other resources. They effectively controlled the Plains, the western and northern woodlands and parklands, and the Arctic. European settlement began to increase in BC in the 1840s, and the first reserves in that colony were established during this early period of increased government control of Indians.

In the last few years of 1870s the policy changed from one of **assimilation** by community to one of outright assimilation as individuals: the policy of establishing isolated reserves changed, and it was thought that reserves should be close enough to non-Native communities for individuals to have an incentive to become "enfranchised," that is, to have the same legal status (and way of life) as individuals as non-Native Canadians. Though provision was made for individual enfranchisement, the number of people who opted for it was minuscule.

When Canada took over control of Indian affairs at the time of Confederation, Indigenous nations became internal colonies. Until then, Indian groups had maintained control over their land, financial arrangements, membership, business dealings with outsiders, and internal governance. The first legislation about Indians in post-Confederation Canada, the Indian Act of 1876, effectively removed their control in all those areas and imposed systems of band governance that allowed the federal government exclusive control over Indian national leadership, land, membership, and money. Another challenge to internal band authority and First Nations' community integrity was the policy's manifest orientation toward individual enfranchisement. Canada had no effective control over those matters in the North and West, so at first the policies applied only to those bands east of the Lakehead (the northwestern corner of Lake Superior).

The priority for all Indigenous nations in Canada where they were in contact with Europeans became maintaining the integrity of their individual communities. During the last few years of the 1860s, Native community integrity was at the heart of the conflict surrounding the admission of Manitoba as a province, and it was most surely the issue in the 1885 Rebellion. In the case of Manitoba, an attempt was made to resolve it by negotiating terms for the admission of the province that appeared favourable to retaining Metis community structures. The almost immediate failure of those provisions was one of the origins of the tension that resulted in the 1885 uprising.

During the 1870s pressure to alienate Indian lands in western Ontario and in Manitoba motivated the federal government to enter into formal treaties, as had been done earlier in Ontario with the Robinson Huron and Robinson Superior treaties of 1850. An added federal government impetus as the treaty process moved west was to attempt to extinguish Metis claims. The self-sufficiency of the nations of the prairies and western parklands was threatened during the decade after Confederation because of the dramatic decrease, then absence, of the great buffalo herds upon which they depended. During the 1870s the Plains nations joined treaty negotiations as an alternative to starvation, though some groups of Cree, Assiniboine, and Saulteaux attempted to maintain autonomy through coalition by congregating in the Cypress Hills in Assiniboia, near the intersection of the present boundaries of Alberta, Saskatchewan, and Montana.

In 1871 British Columbia entered Confederation with the federal government assuming responsibility for the administration of Indian affairs, but with a proviso for provincial involvement in any Indian land settlements. (Except for a few early treaties on Vancouver Island and the extension of Treaty No. 8 into the northeastern part of the province, the alienation of Indian land in BC has not involved treaties.)

Thus the establishment of reserves and the policy of wardship of Indians during an anticipated period of assimilation were cornerstones of the policies governing Indigenous nations within Confederation. The policies that characterize the reserve period were begun in the 1830s, were modified in the 1850s and again in the late 1860s, and then were implemented as each area of the country was alienated from effective Native control. A most interesting aspect of the policies was the uniformity with which they were applied. The policies directed governmental relations with groups such as the Mi'kmaq and Iroquois, who had been trading with and fighting alongside Europeans for almost 300 years; with groups such as the Cree and Blackfoot, who had had completely different trading relationships with Europeans; and with groups in the Mackenzie watershed and northern BC, some of whom were entering their first sustained relationships with Europeans.

If we focus on the government's rationale for the institution of such policies, it is possible to accept Tobias's (1991) interpretation that the policies were directed by a concern for the "protection, civilization, and assimilation" of Indigenous people. If, instead, we look at the legislation itself, the way policies were carried out, and the effect of the policies "on the ground," the idea of protection is not an acceptable interpretation. The reserve era was one of control and containment of Indians, primarily under authority provided by the Indian Act. Characteristics of the era are:

- Duplicity in the alienation of even more land, including land previously reserved for Indians;
- Heavy-handedness and arbitrary judgment in the definition of who was an Indian, both through the Indian Act itself and most particularly in the way recognition as being Indian was effected in individual cases;
- Control over internal governance of bands, the election and recognition of leadership, and the definition of band responsibilities;
- Corruption in the provision of goods and services to bands;
- Legal sanctions against the practice of Indigenous religion and spirituality;
- The establishment of industrial schools, then residential schools operated by churches, in which Indian custom was denigrated and in which an attempt was made to wipe out the use of Indigenous languages;
- The institutionalization and structuring of schooling, generally, that made academic success and achievement extremely difficult;
- Control over persons and individual movement and mobility, with the institution of "passes" for leaving reserves;
- Control over the finances of individuals and bands;
- The institution of policies that made early Indian successes at farming impossible to maintain; and

- Legal sanctions against meeting and organizing.

Though the reserve era is characterized by the Indian Act, federal administration of reserves, and oppressive policies, it is in fact simply a name that characterizes oppression over a period of time, whether or not the people affected were resident on reserves. Reserves were not established in the North for either Inuit or northern Dene, and some bands whose treaties provide for reserves have still to see them established, but the Indian Act has applied to all people recognized as Indian under the Act. The constraint and regulation of the reserve era have been as oppressive to off-reserve Indians as to those who live on reserves. Exclusion from identification as Indian under the Act had the effect of socially defining a significant number of "non-status Indians" as "Metis." During the early part of the twentieth century, Inuit were specifically excluded from definition as Indian but nonetheless had their affairs administered by the same department as Indians. The Metis, the large community of mixed-ancestry people who had begun forming Indigenous communities west of the Great Lakes as early as the late 1600s, did not have reserves, as their rights to land were supposed to have been recognized by the issuance to individuals of "scrip," which was to be exchanged for land.

Resistance

The record of First Nations resistance to the measures of the reserve era is a long and detailed one. From the very beginning of the reserve era, individual leaders approached the government with complaints, protests, and constructive suggestions. The kind of control exerted by government agencies over the lives of Indians and whatever Inuit were in the orbit of government influence militated against either economic development or individual achievement. The era between the two world wars was one of particular economic hardship for many Canadians, and particularly so for the many First Nations people whose traditional subsistence base of agriculture and resource harvest had been destroyed.

Pan-Canadian organization of Indians began in 1919 with the efforts of F.O. Loft, a Mohawk army officer who was an organizer of the League of Indians of Canada (Cuthand 1991). Regional coalitions of First Nations groups began organizing in the 1920s and 1930s; one of these in Alberta was responsible for eventual government establishment of Metis settlements in the only province to set such land aside.

After World War II it became increasingly clear to government that the inequities perpetuated in the name of wardship had to change, but change was slow and often apparently in the wrong direction. As after World War I, returning Indian veterans were in the vanguard of organization and protest. For the first time since sustained contact, the rate of increase in the Indigenous population was accelerating, but post-war economic development largely excluded Indians, so the economic distinctions between Euro-Canadians and Indians became more marked. The middle part of the century brought the last relatively isolated groups of Indigenous people into sustained contact with government agencies, and yet another revision of the Indian Act in 1951 reinformed policies of control. The concept of wardship was still firmly entrenched in its provisions. A major change came in 1960 when registered and treaty Indians—quite abruptly and with negligible consultation—were recognized as citizens of Canada. The federal government took over administration of Indian and territorial schools from the missionary groups who had operated them since at least the 1850s, and many of the residential schools were phased out. The courts took on more importance as contentious issues were increasingly being settled there.

In 1969 a major change in governance was proposed in a government White Paper: the Indian Act and reserves were to be phased out and provinces would take over administration of Indian affairs. Echoing the policy changes of the 1850s, Indigenous people were to be dealt with individually by government, not as groups. The government professed the changes to be a movement toward equality and justice.

A very strong Indigenous protest, particularly from the National Indian Brotherhood (later to become the Assembly of First Nations), came in response: the message was that injustice had indeed been perpetuated but that government had not got the main point about the nature of the injustice. Rather than an equality in law as assimilated individuals, Indigenous people—as groups and not as individuals—had rights that derived from their status as Indigenous people. There were rights to land that had never been ceded, rights that derived from treaties, rights that inhered in the nature of Indigenous peoples' relationship with land, and rights to govern themselves. Those rights had not been granted by the government and could not be removed by government: treaty rights had been negotiated and could not be unilaterally changed; other rights were inherent in Aboriginal status in Canada.

In the 1970s, two important court decisions in Canada about land, one brought by the Nisga'a in BC and the other by Cree and Inuit in northern Quebec, made First Nations' claims about land and rights credible to the federal government. For the first time since Confederation there was a government willingness to discuss a remedy for the negative consequences of the policies of the reserve era. The federal government instituted processes whereby claims for compensation and land could be heard, and those claims were to be distinguished as either comprehensive or specific. Comprehensive claims were primarily those where rights to Euro-Canadian use of land had not been negotiated, and specific claims were for cases in which specific obligations had not been met by the government. The claims process continues, but the system set up to deal with claims has been overwhelmed by the several hundred claims brought to it, and should it continue to work at its present pace, claims will not be resolved for centuries.

The policy foundation for a return to First Nations self-government was established in the 1970s, though it was laid piecemeal. The substantive foundation was the persistent will of First Nations leaders and Aboriginal people generally to demonstrate that the right to and responsibility for self-governance had never been relinquished. One of the first government policy objectives was to mandate control of First Nations schools by First Nations peoples. A corollary was the provision of funding for legal treaty research in connection with claims processes, as well as the federal provision of funding for national and regional First Nations organizations to represent Indigenous interests to government.

As a result of those measures, the nature of schooling has changed dramatically since the 1960s. Most schools on reserves, for example, are now run under the authority of band councils; access to post-secondary schooling, while still a problem, has improved dramatically; and there has been a movement to make curricula consistent with First Nations interests and cultures. At this point, however, it must be noted that the actual results of these changes are mixed. Another result of those measures is that Aboriginal organizations have become key players in constitutional issues.

First Nations issues were front and centre in negotiations to patriate the Canadian Constitution in the early 1980s, not because of a priority placed on those issues by government but because of strong and effective First Nations representation to the Canadian public and to the Parliament of the United Kingdom, which was required to pass the measure as a last vestigial act of Canadian colonialism. The constitutional conferences of the mid-1980s between federal, provincial, and territorial

governments and First Nations leadership came to no formal definition of the "existing rights" of Indigenous people—rights that had been codified in the new Constitution—but media attention to those conferences brought the concept of First Nations self-government to public awareness. One of the lasting consequences of those debates is that Aboriginal self-government is now a putative objective of the Department of Indian Affairs.

It is a rocky road. A good example of the complexities of establishing First Nations self-government within Canadian Confederation is the debate over reinstatement of Indians who had been forced to enfranchise at marriage. Bill C-31 was passed in 1985 as a measure that recognized gender equality: Indian women who had married non-Indians had been forced to enfranchise, while Indian men who married non-Indians brought legal recognition as Indian to the spouse. The complex question was whether or not the principle of gender equality was paramount over the principle that First Nations, as all nations, have the right to determine membership and affiliation. Parliament imposed a resolution by passing legislation reinstating large groups of people as Indian and requiring bands to establish clear membership criteria.

When the Meech Lake Accord of 1987 sought to bring Quebec to agreement on constitutional issues, it was couched in terms of recognition of Canada's having been created by "two founding nations," British and French. The response of the Assembly of First Nations and of other Aboriginal groups was to recall a long history of alliance, trade, negotiation, and participation in the establishment of the current Canadian polity. It was more than symbolic that a treaty Indian member of the Manitoba legislature, Elijah Harper, was able in 1990 to delay—and thus obviate—passage of the Accord and its acceptance by the rest of Canada. The subsequent attempt through the Charlottetown Accord of 1992 to reconcile differences between Quebec and the rest of Canada, an effort that included a national referendum, saw First Nations people vote with the majority for rejection, even though national First Nations leadership had been instrumental in fashioning the Accord, and even though it included measures that were supposed to lead to self-government.

The federal government professes a commitment to First Nations self-government but there is no clear agreement among the various levels of government and Canadian First Nations about how to accomplish it. During the first few years of the twenty-first century the federal government attempted to specify legislation that would define the terms of self-government, but all but a few First Nations leaders voiced strong objection to what they said was an inappropriate and unilateral imposition of terms. The discussion is much more complex now than it was 20 years ago. In the first place, Indigenous peoples all over the world are working in concert to effect both international political change and social changes that reflect Indigenous **values**. The United Nations has played an important role in an international and intergovernmental discourse about Indigenous peoples' right to self-government and self-determination. Post-secondary specialization in Native studies has been possible in Canada since the 1970s: now there is an academic and legal specialization focusing specifically on Indigenous governance. Courts are currently playing a large part in redefining the relationship between Canadian Indigenous peoples and others. It is almost impossible to predict how that relationship will evolve, but one generalization that can be made is that the field is very complex. Self-government within the territory of Nunavut, for example, will be realized differently than in urban communities or on reserves.

Self-government is not a right that can be granted by any other government. Thus it is not something for which any formula or policy can apply across the board. It is instead a principle. The long history of First Nations on this part of the continent and the important place that self-directed First Nations have had in the creation of Canada are evidence of the principle that the rights and responsibilities of self-government are inherent and have never been compromised. Except for the most oppressive period of the reserve era, between the 1870s and 1970s, First Nations have in fact been self-governing. In the twenty-first century, individual First Nations will reaffirm self-government in a modern Canadian social context.

In the past 100 years the effects of Europe's diseases have diminished. Physical survival is no longer in question. Survival in terms of community integrity is a continuing struggle, even in the face of federal government commitment to a move to First Nations self-government. Survival as nations honours the Ancestors who established those nations thousands of years ago, as well as those who have struggled to maintain the integrity and autonomy of First Nations communities.

NOTES

1. The first edition of *Native Peoples* had three chapters at this point, one on Canadian Native languages by Regna Darnell, one on the prehistory of Canadian Indians by Alan Bryan, and one on the archaeology of Arctic Canada by Cliff Hickey. The reader wishing a survey of these topics is directed to them; they are thorough and still relevant. We chose to drop them because we realized that the average reader did not require this detailed background. At the same time, we also felt that we had to provide readers with an overview of key issues in Canadian history as they related to Native peoples generally before taking up the stories of specific peoples.

2. This appears to be a straightforward statement, but is not. Like all the other archaeological dates in this

chapter, what it really refers to is radiocarbon years. It is now clear that carbon-dated years in the time range discussed here are younger than calendar years by from about 900 to 2,000 years. Since there is not yet consensus on precisely how to convert radiocarbon years into calendar years, we have left all dates in radiocarbon years.

3. While the Canadian Aboriginals formerly called "Eskimo" are now known by their own term "Inuit," the broader term "Eskimoan," referring to the larger family of related northern peoples, is still in use.

REFERENCES AND RECOMMENDED READINGS

Beattie, Owen, et al. 2000. "The Kwaday Dan Ts'inchi Discovery from a Glacier in British Columbia," *Canadian Journal of Archaeology* 24: 129–47.

Bryan, Alan Lyle. 1986. "The Prehistory of Canadian Indians." In *Native Peoples: The Canadian Experience,* edited by R. Bruce Morrison and C. Roderick Wilson. Toronto: McClelland & Stewart. One of the very few brief synopses on the topic. Written from an early-entry, hemispheric perspective.

Campbell, Lyle. 1997. *American Indian Languages: The Historical Linguistics of Native America.* New York: Oxford University Press. The standard reference on this topic.

Cuthand, Stan. 1991. "The Native Peoples of the Prairie Provinces in the 1920s and 1930s," in Miller (1991).

Darnell, Regna. 1986. "A Linguistic Classification of Canadian Native Peoples: Issues, Problems, and Theoretical Implications." In *Native Peoples: The Canadian Experience,* edited by R. Bruce Morrison and C. Roderick Wilson. Toronto: McClelland & Stewart. A theoretically and historically focused survey.

Dickason, Olive, and David T. McNab. 2009. *Canada's First Nations: A History of Founding Peoples from Earliest Times,* 4th ed. Toronto: Oxford University Press. Now the standard reference for Canadian First Nations history.

Dobyns, Henry F., and William R. Swagerty. 1983. *Their Number Become Thinned: Native American Population Dynamics in Eastern North America.* Native American Historic Demographic Series. Knoxville: University of Tennessee Press in co-operation with the Newberry Library Center for the History of the American Indian. Dobyns is known for his relatively high estimates of pre-contact Aboriginal population levels. This work details the effects of European disease in eastern North America.

Erlandson, Jon M., et al. 2007. "The Kelp Highway Hypothesis: Marine Ecology, the Coastal Migration Theory, and the Peopling of the Americas," *The Journal of Island and Coastal Archaeology* 2, 2: 161–74. An innovative and provocative approach.

Fladmark, K.R. 1979. "Routes: Alternate Migration Corridors for Early Man in North America," *American Antiquity* 44, 1: 55–69. This is not Fladmark's seminal paper on this topic, but a later expansion.

Francis, Daniel. 1992. *The Imaginary Indian: The Image of the Indian in Canadian Culture.* Vancouver: Arsenal Pulp Press. This history of popular and scholarly Euro-Canadian perceptions of First Nations peoples provides a valuable background for contemporary studies.

Grant, Shelagh D. 2002. *Arctic Justice: On Trial for Murder, Pond Inlet, 1923.* Montreal and Kingston: McGill–Queen's University Press. This story of the eastern Arctic's first criminal trial, or, the price paid by a small Indigenous community for Canadian imperial ambitions, reminds the reader of the many narrowly focused histories available.

Greenburg, Joseph H. 1986. *Language in the Americas.* Stanford, CA: Stanford University Press.

Groundbreaking approach emphasizing the big picture, but very controversial.

Gruhn, Ruth. 1988. "Linguistic Evidence in Support of the Coastal Route of Earliest Entry into the New World," *Man* (n.s.) 23: 77–100.

Hickey, Clifford G. 1986. "The Archaeology of Arctic Canada." In *Native Peoples: The Canadian Experience*, edited by R. Bruce Morrison and C. Roderick Wilson. Toronto: McClelland & Stewart. Presents both a cultural history of the region and a regionally focused perspective on the work of archaeology.

Kari, James, and Ben. A. Potter, eds. 2010. "The Dene-Yeniseian Connection." *Anthropological Papers of the University of Alaska*, 5: 1–2. Explaining the Siberian relationship to the North American Dene peoples.

Kehoe, Alice Beck. 2002. *America Before the European Invasions*. London: Longman. Kehoe places Canadian material into a Mexican-centred continentalist context, but this is nevertheless a very useful survey.

Kinkade, M. Dale. 1991. "The Decline of Native Languages in Canada." In *Endangered Languages*, edited by R.H. Robins and E.M. Uhlenbeck. Oxford: Berg. Documents this often-ignored topic.

Lewis, M. Paul, ed. 2009. *Ethnologue: Languages of the World*, 16th ed. Dallas, TX: SIL International.

McGhee, Robert. 2005. *The Last Imaginary Place: A Human History of the Arctic World*. Chicago: University of Chicago Press. The most recent overview by the dean of Canadian Arctic archaeologists.

Maschner, Herbert, Owen Mason, and Robert McGhee, eds. 2009. *The Northern World, AD 900–1400: Anthropology of Pacific North America*. Salt Lake City: University of Utah. An authoritative overview.

Miller, J.R., ed. 1991. *Sweet Promises: A Reader on Indian–White Relations in Canada*. Toronto: University of Toronto Press. Essays explaining government policies in changing social and political contexts through time.

Monsalve, M.V., et al. 2002. "Molecular Analysis of the Kwaday Dan Ts'inchi Ancient Remains Found in a Glacier in Canada," *American Journal of Physical Anthropology* 119: 288–91. Provides key evidence for this case.

Neves, Walter A., et al. 1999. "Lapa Vermelha IV Hominid I: Morphological Affinities of the Earliest Known American," *Genetics and Molecular Biology* 22, 4: 461–9.

Powell, John Wesley. 1891. *Linguistic Families of America North of Mexico*. Washington: Bureau of Ethnology Annual Report for 1885–6: 7–139.

Sapir, Edward. 1929. "Central and North American Languages," *Encyclopaedia Britannica*, 14th ed., 5: 138–41.

Slobodin, Sergei B. 2011. "Late Pleistocene and Early Holocene Cultures of Beingia: The General and the Specific." In *From the Yenisei to the Yukon: Interpreting Lithic Assemblage in Late Pleistocene/Early Holocene Beringia*, edited by Ted Goebel and Ian Buvit. College Station: Texas A&M University Press. Recent authoritative review of both the big picture and key details.

Tamm, E., T. Kivisild, M. Reidla, M. Metspalu, D.G. Smith, et al. 2007. "Beringian Standstill and Spread of Native American Founders," *PLoS ONE* 2, 9: e829. doi:10.1371/journal.pone.0000829. Explicates a recently discovered phase in the peopling of the Americas.

Thomas, David Hurst. 2000. *Skull Wars*. New York: Basic Books. A balanced account of the Kennewick controversy and its underlying issues.

Tobias, John L. 1991. "Protection, Civilization, Assimilation: An Outline History of Canada's Indian Policy," in Miller (1991).

Trigger, Bruce C. 1983. *Natives and Newcomers: Canada's "Heroic Age" Reconsidered*. Montreal and Kingston: McGill–Queen's University Press. A groundbreaking account of Canadian history giving attention to its Native aspects.

Washburn, Wilcomb E., ed. 1986. *History of Indian–White Relations*. Vol. 4, *Handbook of North American Indians*. Washington: Smithsonian Institution. Almost half the articles in this large collection are about Canadian First Nations. Of direct interest also in this series are Vol. 5, *Arctic*; Vol. 6, *Subarctic*; Vol. 7, *Northwest Coast*; and Vol. 15, *Northeast*.

Waters, M.R., et al. 2011. "The Buttermilk Creek Complex and the Origins of Clovis at the Debra L. Friedkin Site, Texas," *Science*, 331: 1599–603.

Wilford, John Noble. 2012. "Spear Heads and DNA Point to a Second Founding Society in North America," *New York Times*, 11 July. Important recent work.

PART II

The Arctic

CHAPTER 3

The Eskaleuts: A Regional Overview

Ernest S. Burch Jr. and Christopher Fletcher

An Aboriginal population known to science as the "Eskaleuts" extended from the western tip of the Aleutian Islands and the Asiatic coast of the Bering Sea around the western portion of Alaska, across northern Canada to the Atlantic Ocean, and farther still to the shores of Greenland. This immense region, some 20,000 kilometres in breadth, was inhabited in the eighteenth century by about 81,000 people speaking at least seven related, but different, languages.

The diversity of Eskaleut peoples in the eighteenth century was much greater than most people realize, but it is not really surprising given their extensive geographic distribution. "Eskaleut," of course, is an artificial word derived from the (also artificial) names of the two major linguistic divisions of the general population, Eskimos and Aleuts.

Aleuts

The Aleuts occupied the Aleutian Islands and a portion of the adjacent Alaska Peninsula. Their natural environment is characterized by a maritime climate noted for its perpetual strong winds, overcast skies, frequent fog, and violent storms. Although the area receives a fair amount of snow in winter, the ocean remains ice-free year-round. Aleutian waters are home to a rich and diverse marine fauna. Whales, sea lions, seals, sea otters, wal-rus, several varieties of fish and shellfish, sea birds, and seaweed provided a reliable resource base for a relatively dense human population. Aleut hunting technology was admirably developed to harvest these resources.

The estimated 14,000 Aleuts of the mid-eighteenth century were divided into three major groups: Eastern Aleuts, numbering some 9,000 people; Central Aleuts, numbering perhaps 4,000; and Western Aleuts, numbering about 1,000.

Rather little is known about the traditional life of the Central and Western Aleuts. The Eastern Aleuts, who have been more thoroughly described, were organized in terms of relatively large-scale (for hunters) societies of up to some 2,000 people, and these societies generally were more complex in structure than any Eskimo society. They were divided into a series of hereditary, ranked classes consisting of chiefs, nobles, commoners, and slaves. Aleut societies were apparently divided into **matrilineal lineages** whose major orientation was toward child-rearing and marriage practices. Girls were raised in their mother's **household**, but boys were brought up by their mother's brother. Residence was **matri-patrilocal**; newly married spouses lived with the wife's parents until a child was born, at which point they joined the household of the husband's parents. Aleut societies were also divided into **patrilineal** lineages, whose

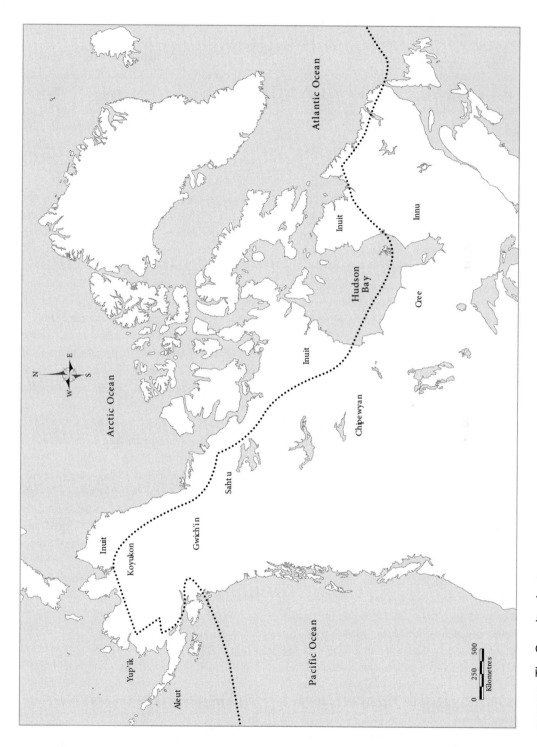

MAP 3.1 The Canadian Arctic

major function was to own land. Ritual, folklore, and art (particularly work with grass) were highly developed among the Aleuts. Inter-societal relations, too, were relatively complex, and included an extensive network of trade, a framework of relatively formal political alliances, and a complementary pattern of active warfare.

Eskimos

The second major branch of the Eskaleut language family is Eskimo. Eskimo-speaking peoples inhabit by far the largest portion of the Eskaleut area and are divided into several language groups. The most fundamental division within the Eskimo language family is between Yup'ik and Inuit. Yup'ik speakers live in south-central and southwestern Alaska, and on portions of the Asiatic shore of the Bering Sea and Bering Strait. Inuit speakers are distributed the whole way across North America, from Bering Strait to Greenland and Labrador.

Linguistic variation is much greater among the Yup'ik Eskimos than among their Inuit cousins. The Inuit language forms a continuum that is divided into a number of dialects among native speakers of the language, all of which share enough similarity that basic comprehension is possible after a brief period of familiarization. Yup'ik, on the other hand, is divided into at least four distinct languages: Pacific, Central Alaskan, Naukanski, and Chaplinski. Sirenikski, formerly thought to have been a fifth branch of Yup'ik, is now considered to have been a distinct non-Yupik and non-Inuit language.

Pacific Yup'ik was spoken in south-central Alaska by perhaps as many as 10,000 people in the mid-eighteenth century. There were two groups of dialects: Chugach and Koniag. Like the Aleuts, Pacific Yup'ik societies had economies oriented to the harvest of marine mammals, although fish were also important. Their societies also were characterized by a system of ranked classes, by relatively elaborate art and ritual, and by complex inter-societal relations. Unlike the Aleuts, they apparently lacked any sort of lineage system.

A second Yup'ik language, Central Alaskan Yup'ik, was spoken in southwest Alaska, along the Bering Sea coast, and for a considerable distance inland along the major river systems. The region includes scattered ranges of hills and mountains, but most of it consists of the immense combined deltas of the Yukon and Kuskokwim Rivers.

The Central Alaskan Yup'ik population of some 14,000 people in the mid eighteenth century was concentrated along the rivers and along portions of the Bering Sea coast. There were three major dialect areas—Bristol Bay, Kuskokwim, and Yukon—and a number of small, local dialect areas. The relatively dense human population was sustained by salmon and several other types of fish, by caribou, by sea mammals along the coast, and by a variety of other plant and animal foods. Unlike the Aleuts and Pacific Yup'ik peoples, the Central Alaskan Yup'ik Eskimos did not have a system of hereditary, ranked classes, and, in most respects, their social system was less complex than that of their southern relatives.

The other two Yup'ik languages are often lumped together under the heading of "Asiatic Yup'ik," although that is strictly a geographic designation, not a linguistic one: The two languages were quite distinct from one another. Sirenikski used to be listed as a third "Asiatic Yup'ik" language, but it is now thought to have been the most divergent of all Eskimo languages.

The more northerly of the two Asiatic Yup'ik languages was Naukanski Yup'ik. In the mid-eighteenth century it was spoken by perhaps 1,000 people living on or near East Cape (on the west side of Bering Strait), and possibly at scattered points along the coast for another 50 kilometres or so on either side of the cape area. Chaplinski Yup'ik was spoken by perhaps 6,000 people who lived on St Lawrence Island and on the adjacent Asiatic mainland.

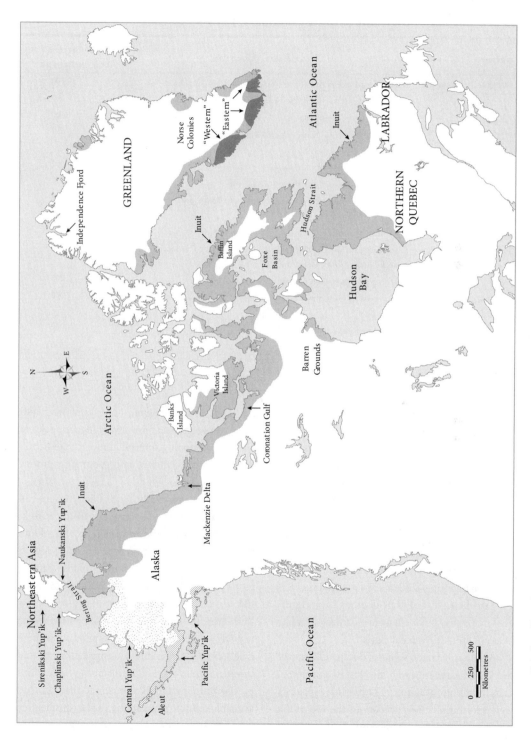

MAP 3.2 Eskaleut Peoples

TABLE 3.1 Major Divisions of Inuit Eskimos, c. 1750

GROUP	GENERAL LOCATION	APPROXIMATE NUMBERS
Northwest Alaska	Bering Strait to the mouth of the Colville River, Alaska	10,000
Mackenzie Delta	Herschel Island to the Baillie Islands	2,000
Copper	Cape Parry to Queen Maud Gulf, including much of Victoria Island	1,300
Netsilik	Adelaide Peninsula, King William Island, Boothia Peninsula, and Pelly Bay	650
Caribou	West central coast of Hudson Bay	400
Satlirmiut	Southern portion of Southampton Island	200
Iglulik	Wager Bay, Repulse Bay, west side of Foxe Basin, and northern Baffin Island	700
Baffin Island	East, south, and west coasts of Baffin Island	2,750
Labrador Peninsula	Coastal area from Great Whale River, on west, to Sandwich Bay, on east, including Ungava Peninsula	4,200
Polar	Extreme northwestern Greenland	200
Southwest Greenland	West coast of Greenland south of Baffin Bay	12,000
East Greenland	Southeast coast of Greenland	1,000
	Total	35,400

Sirenikski was spoken by only 150 to 200 people who lived along the southern shore of the Chukchi Peninsula, just west of the Chaplinski language area. This language is now extinct.

All the Asiatic Eskimo–speaking peoples occupied rugged, barren coastal regions, and their economies were nearly as marine-oriented as those of Aleut societies. They had little access to fish resources, and they acquired virtually all their reindeer (Eurasian caribou) skins and meat through trade with neighbouring Chukchi. Asiatic Eskimo societies are distinguished from all other Eskimo societies in that most of them were organized in terms of **exogamous**, patrilineal **clans**.

All other Eskimos, some 35,000 people, spoke the Inuit language, which also has been referred to as Inupik and as Eastern Eskimo. Inuit speakers were spread the whole way across the top of the continental land mass, many portions of the Arctic Archipelago, and along most of coastal Greenland. They were organized into several dozen societies, which anthropologists have lumped together for descriptive convenience into geographic groups, listed in Table 3.1.

The Inuit generally have been thought of as maritime peoples. In fact, few Inuit were as dependent on marine resources as the Aleuts, the Pacific Yup'ik, or the Asiatic Eskimos. Almost all Inuit relied to a significant extent on caribou as a source of raw materials, and **anadromous fish** were very important in some regions. A few Inuit groups—in northwest Alaska, in the region just west of Hudson Bay, and in parts of northern Quebec—had economies oriented more toward terrestrial than toward maritime resources. The precise combination of animal and plant species available to Inuit populations varied considerably from one section of their vast territory to another,

FIGURE 3.1 Ahiarmiut caribou hunters in their kayaks on the upper Kazan River, 1894. They are taking a break from spearing caribou crossing the river. The man in the foreground is smoking a pipe, a habit the Inuit acquired very early in the historic period. (Courtesy of the Thomas Fisher Rare Book Library, University of Toronto)

as did the climate and the topography. With few exceptions, Inuit economies, yearly cycles of movement, and lifestyles were precisely adjusted to deal with both the assets and the liabilities each local environment had to offer.

Inuit Eskimo culture, in general, was less complex than that of either the Aleuts or the Yup'ik Eskimos. Inuit societies were not divided into ranked classes of any kind, and neither clan nor lineage organizations have been reported for any Inuit group. Art and ritual also were not as well developed among the Inuit as among their Aleut and Yup'ik relatives. On the other hand, Inuit culture was more complex in some areas than most Westerners generally realize, particularly in northwest Alaska and in the Mackenzie River Delta region of Canada.

Contact with Europeans

The first definite encounters between Europeans and Eskaleuts took place about 800 years ago, when Norse settlers encountered Inuit in Greenland. However, there is increasing evidence that encounters may have taken place even earlier, when Norse explorers first visited Greenland, Baffin Island, Labrador, and Newfoundland.

The second period of Eskaleut–European contact also occurred in the east. In the late 1400s, Portuguese and Basque fishermen and whalers began to frequent the waters of the western North Atlantic. They were followed by explorers, and in 1501 Gaspar Corte-Real's expedition encountered Inuit in Labrador and captured several dozen of them to take back to Europe. Other explorers and increasing numbers of whalers and fishermen from several European countries followed. They encountered Inuit in Greenland, Baffin Island, and Labrador with increasing frequency over the course of the fifteenth and sixteenth centuries.

The eighteenth century saw a new phase of Eskaleut–European contacts when permanent European outposts began to be built in Native territory. In the eastern Arctic these outposts were established by missionaries and traders for the most part, and their relations with the Inuit were usually peaceful, if not always friendly. In the West, outposts were first established in the 1740s, when Russians began to move into Alaska. The Russians were bent on conquest and plunder, and Aleuts, Pacific Yup'ik Eskimos, and Tlingit Indians mounted a formidable armed resistance to them. Ultimately the Russians prevailed, and missionaries and traders were able to begin working in the area well before the end of the eighteenth century.

In the eighteenth and nineteenth centuries, explorers, missionaries, traders, and some few other people of European descent gradually pushed forward into Eskimo territory, proceeding from both east and west toward the centre. Despite their generally good intentions toward the Natives, they spread disaster in their wake in the form of diseases for which the Natives had neither immunity nor cure. Smallpox, measles, influenza, mumps, and many other diseases wrought terrible havoc, particularly in the more densely populated areas of Alaska and the Atlantic coast. By the beginning of the twentieth century, the overall Eskaleut population may have been reduced to only half the size it was in 1750.

By about 1920, outposts of non-Natives had been established at key points over the entire length and breadth of Eskaleut country. With few exceptions, each of these tiny settlements included one or two missionaries and traders,

and, in the Canadian North, a detachment of the Royal Canadian Mounted Police. In some areas there were schools as well, typically run by missionaries. In most cases there was also a small resident population of Natives, but the great majority still spent most of the year living "on the land" in small, widely dispersed camps. They made only occasional visits to the mission/trading-post settlements during the winter, but often came in for a month or two in the summer. This general pattern prevailed, particularly in Canadian Inuit territory, until the end of World War II.

World War II and the Cold War that followed it heightened American and Canadian interest in northern regions, leading to the construction of military bases and radar sites all across northern North America. The labour requirements of this work led to the hiring of hundreds of Natives for varying periods of time and to contacts with outsiders of a type and on a scale never before seen in the North. The resulting changes, combined with increasing concern for Native health and welfare and a growing sense of obligation on the part of governments to provide better schooling for Native children, led to still greater government involvement in Native affairs in the 1950s. However, it was impossible to deliver the necessary services to people living in widely dispersed camps, so a systematic effort was made to encourage the Natives to abandon their camps for the administrative centres. This campaign had been largely successful by the late 1960s.

At the end of the twentieth century, there were approximately 2,200 Aleuts in Alaska, another 700 in Russia, 900 Yup'ik Eskimos in Russia, and about 25,100 in Alaska. Of the Inuit, there were some 13,500 in Alaska, 45,000 in Canada, and 48,000 in Greenland. The great majority of these people lived in small, widely dispersed communities in or near their traditional homelands. Although geographically isolated, most villages are connected to the rest of the world by satellite communications (television, telephone, Internet) and are readily reached by scheduled and charter air service. With the advent of full-time community living the growing interdependence of the subsistence and cash economies became a permanent feature of northern community life. Despite the importance of cash and wage labour in Eskaleut life today, hunting, fishing, and trapping by individuals and family groups remain fundamental to cultural identity and provide a considerable portion of the food people consume.

The transition to a mixed economy has brought the legitimacy and sustainability of Eskaleut land-use and subsistence practices into question and has politicized them in the process. For example, animal-rights organizations had a profound impact on the viability of Indigenous subsistence hunting in the 1970s and 1980s. Using sophisticated media portrayals of trapping, which was depicted as cruel to animals, these organizations caused the market for furs to collapse. While well-intentioned, these campaigns failed to consider the devastating financial effects that a loss of the economic viability of trapping would have on Indigenous peoples, the cultural practices designed to reduce animal suffering, and the place of people in the ecosystem generally. If taken to its logical conclusion, the philosophy of some animal-rights groups would stop Indigenous wildlife harvesting altogether.

Similarly, the growing knowledge about the presence of high levels of chemicals in the Arctic food chain has caused widespread concern about the health effects of maintaining a traditional diet. Inuit organizations have supported and sponsored research into these issues as they are critical to traditional practices in the present day.

The impact that people far from the Arctic can have on Eskaleut lives demonstrates how closely tied all peoples are today. For Inuit, Yup'ik, and Aleut peoples these effects are part of a continuum of change imposed from outside of their own political and social structures. In response to these and other events, the Arctic peoples have organized politically at regional, national, and international levels to defend their rights as Indigenous peoples and to protect their traditions from erosion by global events. In Canada, Inuit Tapiriit Kanatami represents the interests of the various Inuit regions within the country. The Inuit Circumpolar Conference encompasses Canadian, Greenlandic, Alaskan, and Russian Eskaleut peoples and represents them internationally.

The continued growth in importance of these organizations stems in part from the successes that Inuit have had in establishing land-claim agreements with national governments. Many of the Arctic peoples have undergone a process of redefining their Indigenous land rights in the countries in which they live. The land-claims process has afforded people renewed control over their territories and new tools to promote and maintain their traditional lifestyles. The first land-claim agreement in the North was the Alaska Native Claims Settlement Act of 1971, under which Eskimos and Aleuts, along with other Alaska Natives, could select nearly 18 million hectares of land and receive a significant cash compensation for surrendering their Aboriginal claims to the land. In 1975 the Inuit of Quebec signed the James Bay and Northern Quebec Agreement establishing the region of Nunavik and beginning a process of increasing Inuit control over municipal and regional matters. In 1978 the Home Rule Act granted a high degree of local autonomy to Greenlanders, and in 1984 the Inuvialuit of the western Canadian Arctic also signed a land-claim agreement. Finally, in 1999 the territory of Nunavut in the eastern Arctic of Canada was created out of the then existing Northwest Territories. It includes an Inuit-dominated system of public government, based on consensus, with full territorial legislative powers. These developments are discussed in greater detail in Chapters 4 and 5 of this volume. In Russia, the Eskimos and Aleuts have not yet signed land-rights agreements. Their situation is quite difficult as their traditions and land base suffered during the Soviet era and now face new challenges in the post-Soviet period as government has largely abandoned the services it once provided and on which people depended.

RECOMMENDED READINGS

Alaska Native Language Center. 1995. Color wall map of the Inuit-Yupik-Aleut world (Inuit Nunait/ Nunangit Yuget). Fairbanks: University of Alaska, Alaska Native Language Center. Map of northern North America and easternmost Asia showing areas and relationships of all Eskaleut languages.

Burch, Ernest S., Jr. 1988. *The Eskimos*, with photographs by Werner Forman. Norman: University of Oklahoma Press. A lavishly illustrated, comprehensive description of Eskaleut ways of life during the early 1800s. Intended for a general audience.

Damas, David, ed. 1984. *Handbook of North American Indians*. Vol. 5, *Arctic*. Washington: Smithsonian Institution. An encyclopedic source of information on Eskaleut peoples.

———. 2002. *Arctic Migrants, Arctic Villagers: The Transformation of Inuit Settlement in the Central Arctic*. Montreal and Kingston: McGill–Queen's University Press. A useful account of the policies and developments leading to the centralization of Inuit settlement in the 1950s and 1960s.

Duffy, R. Quinn. 1988. *The Road to Nunavut*. Montreal and Kingston: McGill–Queen's University Press. A comprehensive and accessible account of the process leading to the creation of Nunavut.

Sontaq, Natascha. 2007. *The Inuit Language in Inuit Communities in Canada/La Langue Inuit dans les Communautés Inuit au Canada/ Inuktitun Inuit Nunanginni Kanatami*. Fairbanks: University of Alaska Press. A very useful combined graphic and written summary of Inuit dialects in Canada.

Wenzel, George. 1991. *Animal Rights, Human Rights: Ecology, Economy and Ideology in the Canadian Arctic*. Toronto: University of Toronto Press. An excellent analysis of the impact of the animal-rights movement on the Inuit of the eastern Canadian Arctic.

CHAPTER 4

Continuity and Change in Inuit Society

Christopher Fletcher

Introduction

The Arctic holds a particular fascination for Canadians. Few of us ever see it, yet everyone is at least dimly aware that it exists as a massive and cold space, "up there" somewhere. The people who live in the Arctic have been the subject of a lot of scrutiny by scientists, writers, artists, explorers, and eccentrics of various kinds. They are objects of fascination to those of us who can barely imagine living in such a place. I am always taken aback by how widespread the stereotypes of Inuit life are. Typically, when I would get into a taxi at the Montreal airport after returning from fieldwork the driver would ask me where I am coming from. When I say, "The Arctic," he asks, "Is it true that they share wives? Or eat raw meat? Or have a thousand words for snow?" It seems everyone knows some ethnographic details about the Inuit. Why is this kind of knowledge about them so widespread?

A good part of the answer comes from the picture that the Arctic conjures in the popular imagination. It is a hostile place and the Inuit ability to survive in such a climate is legendary. How do they do it? The ability of Inuit to live off the land is a source of amazement to us who would have no idea how to do this. The place of Inuit in global popular culture is thus one of admiration, mystery,

and naivety. This background knowledge points to two things: first is the tendency to romanticize the lifestyle of the Inuit in a mythologized "traditional" period and second is the question of the continuity of tradition in the contemporary context. To what extent is an Inuit lifestyle of the past a feature of life today?

An alternative image of Inuit has also become widespread, and is not flattering. A monotony of news and research reports picture a people who are losing their grasp on the value of life. For example, a 2009 front-page photograph in the *Globe and Mail*[1] of two young boys asleep at 6:30 in the morning in front of a store in Iqaluit, the capital of Nunavut, unleashed a torrent of commentary, some informed, some ignorant, about the state of the North and Inuit people. The photograph challenges the reader's ability to understand what is happening in the Arctic. Why are such young children out all night? Where are their parents? What led them to this place to sleep? Do we understand what we are seeing in this image or filling in the meaning with our own prejudices? Clearly social problems including alcohol abuse, sexual abuse, youth suicide, and accidental deaths are major issues in Inuit society today. But we need to keep in mind that this is not the sum of all social interactions.

In contrast to these caricatures of northern life, I have always been struck by the density and quality of Inuit kinship and friendship links and how these serve to create a cohesive and inclusive society. Relatedness and relationships are fundamental to organization of everyday life and the continuation of Inuit culture. My experience in Inuit communities, particularly Kangiqsujuaq, Quebec, is not reflected in the popular accounts, positive or negative. Here, as in all other Inuit communities today, people live in modern dwellings with all the accoutrements of southern Canadian modernity, incorporating these within an Inuit cultural framework. They are remarkably supportive of each other, watchful and mindful of how others are doing and what they need. People have always been stunningly kind to me as well as protective because of my lack of experience with the terrain. In my view, the community works well and the municipal government is involved in the betterment of the people's lives. People volunteer to help on local education, youth, and cultural committees. Children are cherished. People are active on the land. Life in the camps is a source of great pleasure; young and old hunt, eat, sleep, and play together, communicating in their language. Hunting is a full-time occupation for some; everyone enjoys eating food from the bountiful land. Social problems are everyone's concern and people in distress are cared for by friends and family. People participate in a lifestyle that, while clearly different from that of three or four generations ago, is grounded in viable and strong cultural and social principles. It is not surprising, then, that people in the North often ask me why anthropologists and other researchers seem to concentrate only on negative aspects of their lives. This chapter is, in part, a response to this question. What we know about Inuit life and how we know it are influenced by what we consider to be true about ourselves first, and then about them. In my perspective, understanding the Inuit requires that we look at our conceptions of their place in the world and their significance for what they say about our own lives as southerners.

It is important to recognize that persistent characterizations of people as damaged and dysfunctional are powerful forces in themselves that shape the lives of the people being described. There are important implications to these kinds of perceptions about Inuit. They suggest that values of the past have no place in a present where people live in communities, have jobs (or not), and have many of the same preoccupations as southern Canadians. They also suggest that Inuit are not able to manage their own affairs, a discourse that historically has been used to justify Aboriginal disempowerment generally.

But, of course, Inuit are capable of running their affairs and contributing to national and international debates and processes. Canadian Inuit in two territories and two provinces have signed and ratified land rights agreements with the federal and provincial governments, remarkable political achievements that involve jurisdiction over millions of square kilometres of land and administrative control over vast areas of economic and social policy. The Labrador Inuit Land Claims Agreement (LILCA) was the most recent to be struck. It follows on the heels of the Nunavut Agreement (NA), the James Bay and Northern Quebec Agreement (JBNQA), and the Inuvialuit Final Agreement (IFA). Each defines relationships between Inuit and their ancestral territories and provides for Inuit control over sectors of regional economic, justice, environment, education, employment, and cultural policy. As a result of their settled territorial claims (see Map 4.1) and the breadth of experience they have with regional control, Inuit have a unique position as Indigenous people within Canada. Given the enormous changes that have taken place in the North over the span of a single lifetime, it is reasonable to ask how modernity and political development have intersected with Inuit culture and society. Consequently, this chapter focuses on Inuit cultural and social persistence. By looking at the ways people lived in the past and live

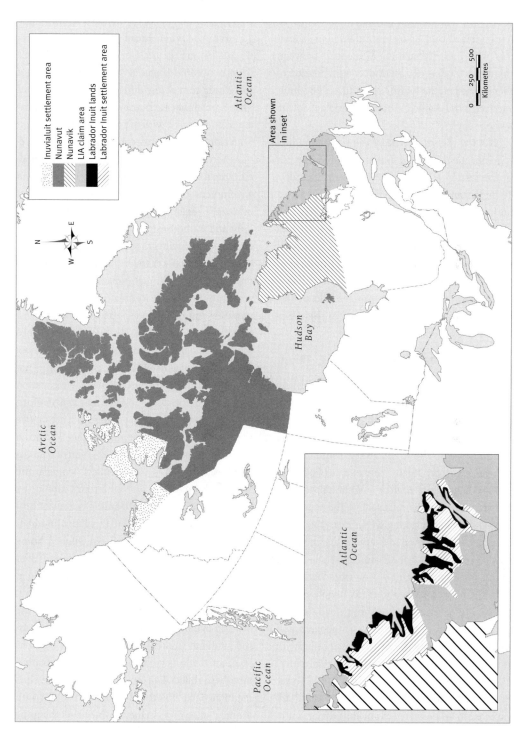

MAP 4.1 Inuit Land-Claims Areas

today, I will address these questions. How does the northern landscape figure in southern understandings of the Inuit? What is the relationship between this understanding and an Inuit comprehension of themselves and the North? How did and do Inuit survive in the Arctic? What is their place in the world today?

Neither the stereotype of the traditional lifestyle nor the rhetoric of modern social decay is a true reflection of the diversity of Inuit life today. To understand Inuit in the Canadian context, we must consider the interaction of their culture and society with others over time and space. We will find a people who are generous to each other and outsiders, confident in their abilities, grounded in tradition, and forward-looking. Inuit have faced challenges in the past and continue to do so. The way they approach these is rooted in their relations with each other and with place.

Becoming an Anthropologist

For those Canadians who grew up in the relatively thin band of densely populated territory hugging the United States, the North represents a wild and "natural" counterbalance to the industrial and political giant to the south. In this sense Canada is suspended perpetually between two states of being: the industrial-modern and natural-timeless. Growing up in southern Canada in the 1960s and 1970s involved navigating these ideas about wilderness and civilization in everyday life. In school we drew pictures of fast cars and igloos, but never in the same frame. Inuit—they were "Eskimos" back then—were stereotyped as people of perpetual winter who lived without need of what we had: houses, record players, skateboards, and TV dinners. There was, and is, a fascination with Inuit that reflects the cultural and geographical difference from our own lives in the South. Today, as a parent, I note that these same ideas are still explored by elementary school children in southern Canada.

The foundations of my interests in anthropology were laid when I read Farley Mowat's *Never Cry Wolf* (1963). In fact, I read this great book three times between the ages of about 8 and 12 and got something completely different from it each time. That I remember each reading demonstrates how much it resonated with me. Likewise, the interests I developed in my professional life—the connections between humans and the environment, modernity in Aboriginal culture, and relations between governmental institutions and the everyday lives of people—were the themes Mowat so successfully and humorously explored. Mowat is one of Canada's most widely read authors and for many people he brought the North to the South for the first time. He had a real impact on the role that government played in creating northern communities and in some respects humanized a distant place and people. Rarely does a writer engage both the imagination and the action of a nation. My experience with *Never Cry Wolf* was thus not uncommon and reflects a broader characterization of the role of the North in Canadian imagination.

After I had finished my undergraduate degree in geography/environmental studies, I found a job in Montreal driving a bus for Native Patients Services. Every day I would collect people at the airport who were coming for tertiary care in the South and take them to boarding houses or hospitals. Over the six years I did this I met hundreds of Inuit and Cree from northern Quebec. Some people came regularly to the hospital and, over time, I made a few friends. I became interested in the relationship between Aboriginal culture and health through my contacts with people in the bus and eventually returned to university to pursue graduate studies. My first fieldwork trip was in 1990, when I went to Kangiqsujuaq for four months to collect data for my master's degree. I had mentioned to a friend that I would like to stay with a family when I was in the North. She set things up with her parents and off I went.

FIGURE 4.1 Kangiqsujuaq, Quebec, 2010. (© Robert Fréchette/Avataq)

When I arrived I found I was miserably unprepared, with little idea of what to do. I had read lots of ethnography that now seemed to be about somewhere else. Unlike the classical ethnographies or the more contemporary **structuralist** approaches that placed Inuit myth and traditional social organization into beautifully rendered analytical frameworks, I landed in a North that appeared resolutely and comfortably modern. Finding the connections between what I was seeing and what I had read would take ages. This is the one of the points of long-term fieldwork in anthropology. It takes a lot of direct experience to get past first appearances and into the realities of how people live, think, talk, and act.

On that first trip I spent a couple of months trying to interview people about kinship. The interviews were awkward and the questions too structured. I had worked too hard on the for-mal aspects of my study and not enough on the observational. I was being much too *Qallunaaq* (European) to understand Inuit. Finally, in early June, the family I was staying with said, "Come with us to the camp." I went, leaving the tape recorder behind, and finally began to learn something. I slept in the family tent, ate food that people captured, watched the ice slowly decay, and was transfixed by the beauty of the landscape. During that time I learned that Inuit are indeed thoroughly and comfortably modern in outlook *and* firmly planted in their culture at the same time. The literature on social problems alluded to earlier tends to portray Inuit between two worlds, making them "stuck" and somehow pathogenic. Others, such as noted Inuktitut linguist Louis-Jacques Dorais, remind us that the interaction of tradition and modernity is not automatically problematic. It is what people make of the two that counts (1997).

I eventually got through the master's degree after changing topics, and then earned a Ph.D. Anthropology is not for the impatient. It requires a commitment to taking the time to get to know a place and people in all their complexity before understanding can begin. It is about drawing connections between the events, institutions, and processes that constitute daily life.

The People and Their Landscape

Defining "North" in Canada is difficult. We could use an arbitrary latitude, the Arctic Circle, for example, or the line of continuous permafrost, or the treeline. Each case would miss people who are northerners or places that seem northern. If we take "North" to mean all areas once occupied by Inuit, that includes everything north of the treeline from Yukon to Labrador, insular Newfoundland, St Pierre and Miquelon, and the north shore of the St Lawrence River. In effect Inuit occupied all the land that was largely treeless and connected to ocean that would freeze over.

The emphasis on land is a bit misleading in depicting Inuit territory. They also lived on the ice in winter and continue to take much of the food they eat from under it. While the Inuit are the Indigenous inhabitants of this particular ecological condition and remain the majority population of it today, they are in no way restricted to living in these areas. There are important Inuit communities in Montreal, Ottawa, Winnipeg, and other places throughout the country. The lives of southern Inuit are informed equally by the values of their ancestors and Elders as they are shaped by contemporary reality. Likewise, Inuit people are not restricted to Canada; they are also Indigenous inhabitants of eastern Russia, northern Alaska, and all of Greenland. Because of the breadth of their territorial and aquatic occupation, describing a generic form of Inuit lifestyle glosses over a lot of important regional variation.

The Arctic landscape is difficult to grasp with the senses without a lot of experience within it. During the first months I spent in the North, people seemed constantly to be pointing out animals I could not see. Someone would say, "Look, 10 caribou on the hillside," and I would strain to catch a glimpse. Were they close or far? I could not tell. Eventually I realized that I had no frame of reference to judge distances. There are no trees or buildings to allow me to judge how big the animals would be in my field of vision. To make matters worse, caribou blend in with the lichen-speckled rock and juniper brush. The lesson I take from these first experiences is that landscape appears bleak if you cannot see what it holds. In popular and academic works we find repeated references to Inuit-occupied territories as representing the margin of possible human existence; cold, unforgiving, and barren. A good question to ask is, how much of this view derives from the apparent emptiness of the landscape to the foreign observer?

The Inuit, their ancestors, and their predecessors have survived well in the North. There have been three waves of technological and cultural change in the Arctic. The first, known as the Arctic Small Tool Tradition, arose in the west and moved quickly east. Sites in eastern Alaska attest that Arctic inhabitants, who were culturally and more than likely biologically distinct from contemporary Amerindians, lived there some 9,000 years ago. As the Arctic glaciers retreated about 4,000 years ago, these people applied their distinct hunting, travelling, and dwelling technologies in the new landmass and ocean areas to move across and occupy all the land from present-day Alaska to eastern Greenland. This seems to have happened very rapidly, perhaps in only a few hundred years. In Canada this original technological–cultural tradition is thought to have developed into the second phase, known as the Dorset culture.

Contemporary Inuit are descendants of people who developed what archaeologists call the Thule tradition. Thule people seem to have displaced the Dorset, perhaps through a superior technology including harpoons with floats attached, large skin-covered boats (*umiaq*), and the use of dogs for traction. These would have allowed them more easily to access and kill large marine mammals including walrus, seals, and beluga, narwhal, and bowhead whales. The size of these animals allowed for the storage of large quantities of meat and fat to cover lean periods and it appears that bowhead whale kills in particular were important to support relatively large numbers of people through several months. These technological innovations first appear in the archaeological record some 2,000 years ago on islands in Bering Strait. By 1,000 years ago, Thule culture bearers had displaced the Dorset people already occupying the Arctic. Recently an intriguing idea has been put forward, that Thule people migrated extremely rapidly from west to east in response to knowledge about a large meteoric iron deposit in Greenland.

Inuit oral tradition speaks to the existence of *Tuniit*, who are described as people who inhabited the Arctic but were not Inuit. Throughout the North the material remains of past human occupation are quite evident. Very little soil accumulates so that while simply walking around one often finds harpoon points, bits of broken cutters, soapstone bowls, and flakes from tool production. The remains of tent rings, meat caches, and semi-subterranean houses are plainly evident. The Inuktitut word for "artifacts" is *Tunirtait*, "things of the Tuniit." Some archaeologists take the Inuit mythology and oral history of the Tuniit to be evidence that groups of Dorset people persisted until relatively recently. While this may be the case, Inuit descriptions of Tuniit emphasize superhuman capacities that suggest they are not a literal retelling of contact with other peoples but perhaps a merging a historic and cosmologic events.

Tuniit are renowned for remarkable strength. They could move enormous boulders and run over deep, soft snow with ease. Some lived inside mountains in bright, crystalline-walled caves. They were capable of changing their size, of being very small or huge, and of becoming invisible. What is more, many Inuit have had encounters with Tuniit. In some cases they see them at a distance but are unable to catch up with them. In others the Tuniit come to play jokes on people in their camps or while hunting alone on the land. People have told me of getting up in the morning to find a large rock in front of the entrance to their tent. Others find things strewn about camp when there was no wind the night before. Tuniit will frustrate or tease a lone hunter by calling his name from a hiding place. While invisible they may throw rocks near a hunter, surprising him, or push him off balance. Tuniit are alternately mischievous and timid. Few people alive today have spoken with them, although I have heard stories of people who did. It seems that Tuniit are quite sensitive to human moods. They will not directly approach someone they know to be afraid or tense but will come to those who are without trepidation about them. It is interesting that where archaeology would place the existence of the Tuniit in a deep past, for Inuit Tuniit remain a presence in the world.

Similar to the archaeological depictions of Arctic prehistoric phases, there is an Inuit typology that distinguishes peoples and times in the Arctic. A number of Elders have spoken to me of three phases or styles of Arctic occupation: Tuniit, Eskimo, and Inuit. The Tuniit, as described above, were there before Inuit arrived. Today the word "Eskimo" is often taken to be derogatory and no longer used to identify Inuit. However, when used by Elders it is not pejorative, but an important marker of identity for those who were born and lived on the land before there were communities. It defines a kind of life experience that cannot now be reproduced. Their knowledge and experience was generated by a lifestyle of continuous hunting and movement on the land. In contrast to

"Eskimo," "Inuit" has come to mean "people born once communities existed" and signifies a difference in lived experience among people who nonetheless share a language and culture. Inuit, then, are politically modern, comfortable with community living, and can move from city to city anywhere in the world. For Elders the framing of time in this way distinguishes historical periods relevant to them and asserts a cultural continuity of territorial occupation in the North despite changes in the ways that people live.

The Arctic is an enormous territory that, contrary to popular conception, must have been quite rich in order to support the population growth and expansion that occurred. Indeed, Inuit today point to the wealth of the land that surrounds them as the most important element in their persistence as a people. Elders will say that, whatever happens to the rest of us, Inuit will survive because they have the knowledge to do so. From an Inuit perspective the Arctic is far from barren; rather, it is lush, comforting, and supportive. The landscape is inhabited by birds in huge numbers and large numbers of mammals—muskoxen, caribou, several species of fat-rich seals—in the sea, lakes, and rivers are fish, and in the sea are whales big and small. The land is not poor unless the people lose their knowledge of it.

The Pursuit of Animals

For Inuit, like hunting peoples everywhere, relations with animals are fundamental to the way they understand the world. Hunting provides food, which permits the continuation of society. It also forms the basis for organizing the social, spiritual, and cultural worlds. Animals figure prominently in Inuit mythology and the relations between people and animals are often represented like those of kin. Indeed, the distinctions between animals and people are ambiguous in mythology, as many stories concern animals that transform into people and vice versa.

Traditional Perspectives

In earliest time, once humans had been created, people and animals could exist by eating earth. They spoke with one another and experienced no violence. The boundaries between animals and people were flexible as transformations and marriages between them were common. With time the world became overpopulated and animals and people began to kill and consume each other.

The origins of the animals and the distinctions between them are found in transgressions of social orders. The classic myth of Nuliajuk (also known as Sedna and Napaaluk) accounts for the creation of sea mammals. There are many variations of this myth and the following version is condensed.

A woman disobeys her father by refusing to marry the man he arranged for her. She chooses one of his dogs instead and leaves with him to live on an island. Her father kills the dog, which is providing well for her, while she is pregnant. She bears the children; they are both human and dog. The father pities his daughter's life on the island and goes to bring her back in his *qajaq* (kayak). The husband has been transformed into a bird and swoops down on the *qajaq* to kill the father. In his terror, or seeing duplicity in his daughter, he throws her overboard. She clings to the edge of the *qajaq*. He cuts off her fingers one by one and each turns into an animal: seals, whales, and walruses. She sinks to the bottom of the sea where she becomes a human-fish creature controlling the animals of the sea that were created from her body.

The annual cycle of hunting is also an annual social cycle. Animal spirits associate with individuals who may travel to lands where animals and humans converse. Protector spirits (*turngait*) help people who treat them appropriately and thus help people to help others through successful hunting and sharing of game. *Turngait* can also be evil and intentionally cause misfortune. They can mislead people into thinking they are helpful. In many accounts the role of the angakkuk (**shaman**) in

Inuit society is to mediate between the invisible realms of the *turngait* and other spirits and the realm of the mundane world. Like *turngait*, shamans are seen as possibly being a positive force for people or possibly negative. In general, the intensity and complexity of human–animal relations is mirrored by the complexity of knowledge that successful hunting requires.

For people on Baffin Island the year is divided into 13 "moon months"[2] and six to eight seasons. With the input of Elders, John MacDonald of the Nunavut Research Institute published a comprehensive survey of Inuit astronomy that includes a description of the months and seasons along with their corresponding ecological and social activities (1998). Eight of the 13 months are named after ecological characteristics of food species: three for seals (*Avunniit*: March or April, *Nattian*: April or May, *Tirigluit*: May or June), four for caribou (*Nurrait*: June, *Saggaruut*: July or August, *Akullirut*: August or September, and *Amiraijaut*: September or October), and one for eggs (*Manniit*: June or July). Four moon months refer to light characteristics. *Tauvikjuaq* (December or January) means "great darkness." Two names mark the re-emergence of the sun, *Siqinnaarut* (January or February) and *Qangattaasan* (February or March), while *Ukiulirut* (October or November) simply means the beginning of winter. Only one refers to social life: *Tusartuut* ("hearing" about other people), in November or December, marks the end of a transitional season when sea ice is forming but is not thick enough to travel on. The significance of the names lies in their descriptive qualities and in the implication that social interaction is taken for granted throughout the year except during *Tusartuut*.

As parts of the year are continuously either dark or light above the Arctic Circle, clock-based time is relevant mainly to the requirements of community activities such as work, school, and commercial transactions. On the land, time markers are established by the pragmatics of travel and animal behaviours. It is easier to travel from the ice to the land when the tide is high because the transition is smoother. In Hudson Strait, tides are quite large, rivalling those of the Bay of Fundy, and getting over or between huge hummocks of broken ice at low tide can be very difficult. At low tide during full moons in winter, the heaving of the ice leaves sizable air pockets underneath. Mussels and clams can be collected by making a hole between two slabs large enough to squeeze through and climbing under the ice. In hunting it is not the amount of time that matters but the level of success. Hunters will hunt 24 or more hours continuously and sleep after they get the catch back to camp. In the warmth of late spring the snow loses its grip, making travel difficult. People covering long distances by dog team or by snowmobile will wait until 10 or 11 p.m. to leave, as it is colder then and the snow a bit more solid.

The seasonal round of hunting and gathering provides a wide variety of foods, almost all of it meat-based. Inuit distinguish between store-bought foods and *niqituinnaq*, "genuine food" that is hunted. An important component of the hunting lifestyle is expressed in cultural conceptions of health. Country food is good—wild food that has lived without human constraints. Its meat and fat provide the kind of energy people need to feel comfortable on the land. The animal blood restores the energy in human blood that is depleted when *niqituinnaq* is unavailable. Store food appears to have no blood in it and provides less energy. For Inuit, domestication of food animals was never undertaken and people are sometimes disdainful of food raised on farms. In the hunter's perspective, animals in these conditions are like pets. Dogs are the only domesticated animal in the North and were a food of absolute last resort. Despite the cultural and gustatory values attached to food from the land, there are a number of constraints on their consumption. Chief among them are the cost of

FIGURE 4.2 Butchering a Beluga whale. (© Robert Fréchette/Nunaturlik LHC)

hunting with modern equipment—gasoline can be two or three times the price that it is in southern Canada—time constraints imposed by jobs and schooling, changing weather predictability linked to global warming, and changing social patterns that make it more difficult for young people to spend time with Elders on the land. The ready availability of store-bought food, much of it high in energy but low in nutrients, is also a factor in shifting diets and activity. Elderly people today remark that modern youth are much bigger than people of their generation, something they correctly attribute to the eating of carbohydrates during growth, but have little endurance or strength for their size. Compared to store-bought junk foods, *niqituinnaq* gives you strength, just as it requires strength to capture it.

Above the Arctic Circle the return of the sun marks the beginning of spring. Below the Circle the short days begin to lengthen and it is noticeably warmer. It is a productive time for hunters, who use the breathing holes maintained by seals along the cracks and thinned areas of the sea ice to wait with harpoons and rifles. The later in spring, the more likely that seals will be found on the ice as well as in the fissures and areas of open water. When ring seal pups are born, their mothers scrape out little ice domes next to breathing holes. Pups rest under a thin layer of ice while mother searches for food. Experienced hunters can spot these small rises on the surface of the ice and wait for the mother to return or simply take the pup if it is there. Later, when days are warmer, the pups and the mother bask in the sun. Several breathing holes are established and a mother seal will call her pup from a "learning hole" to condition it to swim. At this time of the year they may be approached using canvas or skin blinds to hide the human presence or by slowly creeping up to the seal while lying on one's side and waving one hand as if it were a flipper.

This technique works particularly well for bearded seals. High-powered rifles with scopes reduce the proximity needed for a successful kill. Another technique uses the labour of the entire family hunting group by placing one person at each hole. As the seal rises it will be scared away until it is forced to rise at the hole of a waiting hunter. Seal-hunting at breathing holes can be undertaken in winter but is very demanding because of the temperatures. In spring it is easier to wait quietly behind a windbreak made of snow blocks. Early spring is also a good time for hunting ptarmigan, when they gather together in willows or brush.

In late spring, migratory birds begin to arrive as areas of open water appear along the shore of the ocean and on the lakes and rivers. The birds are looking for nesting grounds and hunters wait by good spots. Before rifles were available, people would use small bird spears and thongs weighted with stones to immobilize or kill them. As the sea ice rots, jigging along the edge for the formidable-looking *kanajuk* (sculpin) or "ugly fish" is common. The occasional northern cod is caught as well. When the ice has broken but is still floating in large pans, sleeping walrus can be caught. Before the arrival of rifles, it was difficult to kill them in the water at this time of year.

Once the birds have settled in and laid their eggs, usually after ice has broken on the ocean, parties of men, women, and children will make collecting trips to near-shore islands favoured by eider ducks in particular. On a good day a group of five or six people can find 50 or more nutritious eggs. Late spring is also prime time for small whale hunting. Beluga whales move east to west following the ice breakup through Hudson Strait into Hudson Bay. They are harpooned from kayaks or the shore, shot from larger boats. Belugas return to the same estuaries yearly to moult their skins by rubbing on the gravel bottom and to bear their young. Hunters today wait at the same well-used spots as their ancestors did. The harpoon head

detaches from the shaft as it is driven under the animal's skin. The shape of the head is such that it flips up as it enters and secures behind the skin as a button does on a coat. A cord, often made of a single strip of bearded seal skin, is attached to the harpoon head and has a float (*avataq*) made of an inflated ringed seal skin attached to the far end. The harpooned whale is easy to spot when it surfaces with the float and tires quickly because of the drag. Today harpoons are used in conjunction with rifles and the float is often an empty five-gallon gasoline container. The more northerly communities also have a significant narwhale hunt.

With the ice largely gone, bowhead whales are sought by large parties of hunters. Numerous solid harpoon hits and *avataq* are needed to kill these animals. In some places, bays with narrow entrances are used as traps. Hunters prevent the animal from leaving the bay as the tide went out. It becomes trapped in a small area and is killed by several hunters.

As summer gives way to the cooling temperatures of fall, preparations for winter are made. Before the widespread use of snowmobiles, a major concern was acquiring enough food for the dogs. While in the summer they are generally left to their own devices on small islands, they work hard in winter. Walrus is a good source of dog food. Walrus tend to congregate on the ocean side of islands and on specific points of land, but hunting them is dangerous because they are enormous and agile in the water. Several men are required to provide enough strength to hold the harpoon line once it has struck a walrus. Late summer and early fall are also good for hunting caribou. They are fat from the summer's grazing and the skins have healed from fly infestations. An adequate supply of caribou is important for meat and fat as well as for the clothing and other materials produced from the skins. In late fall, once the ice has set on lakes, fishing for Arctic char is undertaken. The most significant vegetable source in the Inuit diet is berries.

In the fall women and children collect blueberries, juniper, and cloudberries. They are so abundant in some areas that the pickers' footwear will turn purple while picking.

While the annual cycle emphasizes hunting of specific species when they are most likely to be found, many food sources are available much of the year. Fish, particularly Arctic char, can be caught year-round in lakes and the ocean, although they are taken in largest numbers at stone weirs while they make their runs to and from the sea. Likewise, caribou and seals are often hunted throughout the year.

Without dogs winter travel is very difficult. Distances covered to locate and kill game are substantial and walking often requires more energy than it can produce in game. Seals are hunted through their breathing holes and caribou may be found close to the coast in some areas and inland from the west coast of Hudson Bay. In northern Quebec the Leaf River and George River herds have recovered from a population crash in the early 1900s that was disastrous to the Inuit of the region, and now number in the hundreds of thousands. Population cycles of all the animals are familiar to the Inuit and they have strategies to concentrate on more abundant species. The timing of the last caribou crash, however, had significant impacts as it coincided with the early arrival of southern administrators and the increasing reliance of Inuit on trade goods. With the availability of some limited relief, and an increasing interest by non-Inuit in the North, the people adopted the beginnings of a community lifestyle.

Multiple preservation techniques allow for surpluses to be stored and periods of lean harvesting to be covered. Air-dried fish, thinly sliced meats, and seal entrails last for long periods of time. Beluga and seal fat are collected in containers and fermented to produce *misirak*, eaten as a dip for fish, and caribou meat and fat are buried under rocks and sod for preservation. Of course, in winter food is frozen as well. Taken together these techniques provide for the levelling out of periods of abundance and scarcity.

Contemporary Hunting

All of the above animals, with the exception of bowhead whales, are hunted regularly today. A limited catch of bowheads has been introduced with some excitement and a few challenges. Even with changing hunting equipment, knowledge of wildlife behaviour is critical to successful harvesting. The same is true of preservation and storage practices. Caches are filled and emptied. This I take to be evidence of the abundance of animals in the Arctic and testimony to the importance of self-sufficiency and *niqituinnaq* in the maintenance of Inuit culture. Nevertheless recent health and dietary surveys indicate that less nutritious store-bought foods are increasingly important in northern diets, a change that is having important repercussions on people's health. There are distressing warning signs that food availability in general is precarious for many people. There are several factors affecting food availability. Climate change is being felt in the Arctic far more immediately than in most other parts of the country, affecting the availability of food species and mobility on the landscape. Years of studies and discussion about global transport of pollutants into the Arctic and bioaccumulation in major food species cause justifiable concern about the quality of food species. As all food that is not produced through hunting must be flown to the Inuit communities, costs are astronomical. Government policies have considerable impact on store prices and recent changes in the Food Mail Program have resulted in vast increases in some basic items. It is clear that hunting is a major contributor to a healthy diet and every effort should be made to maintain the quality and quantity of the food produced this way.

In addition to the many social and environmental changes brought by sedentarization and the global transportation of pollutants, hunting today is undertaken in a broader social and political context than in the past. It is now undertaken under the gaze of people from other cultures with other preoccupations. For example, Inuit have experienced considerable economic hardship as a result of the activities of animal-rights organizations, which prompted the European Union in 1982 to ban the importation of sealskins. This has essentially eliminated the trade in sealskins and reduced economic self-sufficiency. The number of seals taken has not likely fallen very much, however, as they remain a staple food source. A small trade in fox, wolf, and polar bear skins still exists but does not cover the cost of hunting. Inuit are exempt from an international ban on whale harvesting because they conduct a subsistence hunt. Regardless, they are obliged to monitor their hunts and respect quotas drawn up by wildlife management agencies. Surprisingly, given their expert and multi-generational knowledge of animal populations, the role of Inuit hunters in these organizations has until recently been marginal. Only with the conclusion of land-claims agreements across the Canadian Arctic has Inuit participation with wildlife management boards become commonplace. One of the most significant effects of the creation of Nunavut territory in 1999 is that Inuit now have effective control over and responsibility for the management of wildlife on their land. There are still disagreements between hunters and scientists as to the status of a number of species, but in general co-operation in managing wildlife wins out over antagonism.

The settlement of land-claims agreements has played an important role in maintaining the viability of hunting and gathering as a lifestyle, or what is now termed the "subsistence economy." Despite the vastness of the North, there are increasing pressures on the land from industrial developers, tourism and hunting outfitters, newcomers, and a steadily growing Indigenous population. It has become necessary to define who can do what, where, when, and how in order to regulate land activities and avoid unintended ecological damage. Inuit have consistently defended their right to continue hunting without restrictions from outside their own cultural system. They have also developed hunter-support programs that allow people to continue these activities. In northern Quebec each municipality has a hunter-support budget to benefit hunters and the community at large. Communal freezers store meat brought in through hunter support and all can help themselves, although the elderly and incapacitated have priority. In this we see the reinvention of the Inuit ethos of sharing in a community setting being facilitated by a land-claim agreement.

In each of the four Inuit regions, the land base has been classified into several categories in which Inuit have varying rights and exemptions from the hunting, fishing, and trapping legislation that applies to others. In Nunavik, for example, the JBNQA established three basic categories of lands. Category I lands immediately surround communities and their resources are reserved exclusively for Inuit. They comprise 8,152 square kilometres. All land-use activities on Category I lands are under the jurisdiction of the landholding corporations of the communities. On Category II lands Inuit retain exclusive hunting, fishing, and trapping rights, including commercial exploitation. Category II lands cover 82,597 square kilometres and include the most productive hunting and fishing areas. Category III lands are Crown lands on which the public at large has access as they do elsewhere. Certain species are reserved for Native use on Category III lands.

In Nunavut a similar system of land categories and Inuit rights to animals exists. An additional feature of the Nunavut Agreement is that Inuit have subsurface rights on some lands. The land-claim negotiators were clearly looking for broadly based economic sustainability. Having subsurface

BOX 4.1 Whale Hunting

Bowhead whales had been hunted almost to extinction by the early twentieth century. They were prime targets for commercial whaling expeditions because of their size and the relative ease of killing them. For decades they were rarely seen and even more rarely hunted. Tight government restrictions on the remaining animals formally ended the hunt. For the Inuit, it was the loss of an important part of their culture, not to mention a significant food source.

In 1996 the hunt was back on. A large bowhead was killed close to Repulse Bay in an intensely scrutinized and somewhat disappointing hunt. The animal sank in deep water only to resurface two days later, the meat largely spoiled. Some of the *muktuk*, the thick skin and a favoured food of most Inuit, was distributed to Inuit communities as planned. The hunt was repeated in Pangnirtung two years later with new equipment and more success. The whale was landed at the old whaling station at Kekkerten and its products distributed widely throughout Nunavut.

The right to harvest at least one bowhead was negotiated into the Nunavut Land Claim Agreement, subject to federal ministerial approval. The symbolic importance of a renewed hunt in a new, Inuit-run territory is clear. It asserts Inuit political authority over sea mammals they have always used, demonstrates traditional values of sharing, and attributes prestige to those associated with hunting success.

There are long-standing tensions between Inuit hunters and fisheries and wildlife officials regarding the status of a variety of animal populations and the Inuit obligation to respect quotas and other hunting restrictions. Inuit have always felt they were the experts and the responsible hunters. It was largely non-Inuit who brought species to dangerously low levels, yet it is Inuit who must restrict their traditional activities to save them. The Nunavut Wildlife Management Board conducted a large-scale study of the eastern Arctic bowhead using the traditional methods of science and Inuit knowledge. Their research shows that an ongoing but limited hunt is sustainable. The tide seems to have turned toward an era of co-operation and mutual respect when it comes to managing these animals.

The return of bowhead whaling in Nunavut has international political ramifications. Pro- and anti-whaling nations and organizations have deeply entrenched positions about the legitimacy and ecological viability of whaling. The subsistence hunts of the Inuit and other Indigenous peoples are contested by some and are used by others to argue for the resumption of commercial hunts. Inuit are represented on many international whaling organizations to monitor these debates and to make sure that their voice is heard. Inuit hunting is now a global occupation.

rights allows for Inuit control over mines and other developments that could have significant implications for their economy. Should development prove viable, it will lessen their dependence on transfers from the federal government. This is the only Inuit territory where the Crown has ceded mineral potential to the people.

The land claims have not settled all the territorial questions or all concerns of the Inuit. Jurisdiction over oceans and navigable waters still remains in the hands of the federal government, as it does for the rest of the country, even though Inuit have a legitimate ancestral claim to seasonal (winter) occupation of the ice. There is no legal mechanism to deal with these issues. The issue of offshore islands has, however, been subject to some negotiation. When the borders of Quebec were extended north to their present locations in 1912 the question of islands close to the coast was not considered. Inuit from Quebec found themselves in the curious position of travelling from a province to a territory with completely different legal and jurisdictional requirements when they paddle five minutes to an island from which they have always hunted. Likewise, Inuit from the Belcher Islands in Hudson Bay are part of Nunavut—the capital, Iqaluit, is 1,000 kilometres away—even though they are related through family ties, culture, history, geography, and language to Quebec Inuit only 165 kilometres east. These are accidents of history that have become political issues between the Inuit and federal and provincial governments, and increasingly between Inuit regional governments. In 2007 the Nunavik Inuit Land Claims Agreement established a Nunavik Marine Region (NMR) incorporating the offshore islands into the Nunavik Inuit Settlement Area (NISA). This establishes clear occupancy rights over islands that have never been part of Quebec. Moreover, the NISA and NMR overlap with Nunavut territory, Labrador Inuit settlements and political geography, and James Bay Cree territories. A remarkable political achievement, the agreements continue the political evolution of Aboriginal governments in the provinces and territories.

Global assessments of wildlife status are also of concern to Inuit today. The global transport of pollutants has important repercussions in the North. Global weather patterns concentrate many dangerous pollutants in the North, where they are consumed by animals. PCBs and mercury, for example, are found in high concentrations in the fat and skin of some marine mammals. Inuit generally eat at the top of the food chain: animals that eat other animals. It is very difficult to determine the effects on people of relatively small doses of these chemicals, and the biophysical mechanisms that create health problems are still poorly understood. However, the potential for health risks is undeniable and quite disconcerting to Inuit. In some instances pregnant and breastfeeding women have been advised to avoid certain parts of animals. In the case of mercury, not eating seal would have a complicating effect because seal meat also contains selenium, which negates the effect of mercury. The risks of *niqituinnaq* have to be evaluated in comparison to the alternatives. Overall, people who eat country food are better nourished, have a healthier body weight, and are more active than those who do not. If people were told to stop eating *niqituinnaq*, they would eat more junk food and do less physical activity. These are the major factors in the lifestyle diseases afflicting people in industrial countries. In fact, there is already evidence that rates of diabetes and heart disease are rising among Inuit for exactly these reasons. A final effect would be on social cohesion and intergenerational communication. Social problems are already pronounced in the North. If people stopped doing what they have always done, there would be further erosion of the qualities of life that make people feel good.

At a political level, Inuit are very active in national and international environmental policy. Organizations such as Inuit Tapiriit Kanatami and the Inuit Circumpolar Conference have been effective at representing Inuit interests and in influencing environmental policy. They regularly promote the reduction of pollutants and greenhouse gas emissions that undermine their traditions and the quality of the environment for everyone. The Inuit are not a passive people. Rather, they connect local traditions to global discourses and actions in a unique and productive way.

Leadership, Individuality, and Social Solidarity

Accounts of Inuit social organization point to two distinct and quite different systems, based on the seasons. Winter life in some regions was focused around the multi-chambered snow house, *illu* (igloo), or the semi-subterranean dwelling, *qarmaq*. Several extended families would winter together, particularly when a surplus of food had been collected. At this time of the year ritual activity was frequent and intense. Spousal exchanges, shamanic divinations, competitions of strength, and so on occurred within the concentrated space of the igloo. Authority in social matters, including marriage, hunting, division of game, naming children, and the adoption of children, was concentrated in a single socially acknowledged, powerful, and knowledgeable person known as *isumataaq*. Social interaction was at its height and the people's attentions were focused indoors. Several anthropologists have described the igloo as a female realm dominated by the symbolic symmetry between domestic space and female bodies.

In contrast to winter, social organization in summer was typified by dispersal into small, autonomous family groups consisting of father and sons, or brothers and wives, and children. Older people and others who were unable to move around easily, and those who were not wanted as travel companions, tended to stay close to the winter sites, fishing and hunting seals throughout the summer. The authority in decision-making shifted from the *isumataaq* to family heads and there was much more room for individual independence. In the warm months people were mobile and life was focused outward, onto the land and sea. Relations between people and animals displaced relations among people and the female symbolic realm gave over to the male. The social distinctions between summer and winter patterns are reproduced in categorizations of summer-born and winter-born people, between the continual pursuit of the sun and the moon in mythology, and in the tensions between individual autonomy and social obligation.

This last point is quite important, as it seems from a variety of accounts that Inuit people experienced significant tensions embedded in the structures of authority and individuality. Throughout Inuit rituals we see an emphasis on sharing and giving. The first time a young hunter catches an animal of each species, he is obliged to give it to others in particular sequence. In most cases he can consume none of it himself. These gestures acknowledge the importance of Elders, midwives, and namesakes, and continuously demonstrate individual subservience to the group. Deference to familial authority, the *isumataaq*, and the shaman lead to tensions when disagreement is suppressed or ignored. There are numerous stories of people who rebelled and adopted a self-oriented, perhaps selfish, position. Sometimes they went on to become leaders through the fear they invoked, but in other cases they were ostracized or even murdered.

Denial of the self and deference to socially recognized authority continue to be important Inuit values. While these traits had an important role in maintaining group cohesion in the past, when the first non-Inuit came into the North bearing governmental authority their decisions, even dangerously poor ones, were often met with quiet acquiescence. People today talk about how they could not speak their minds to *Qallunaaq* in the past, even when asked to do so, because they had no authority to do so within their own social system. In contemporary society we see an easing of these absolute hierarchies. There is much greater latitude for Inuit to voice their opinions and, consequently, to control their own destinies.

What has happened to this way of organizing life? At one level all would seem different: people live in permanent communities, have jobs, and participate in the opportunities available today in Canada and abroad. However, it is also possible to see the reproduction of older patterns. The community has replaced the large igloo and ritual activity now includes shopping, schooling, and churchgoing. In summer, particularly in smaller communities, seasonal dispersal of family groups to hunting camps still occurs much as it always did. Hunting and consuming marine mammals, caribou, birds, and fish remain vitally important to physical and social health, as Inuit readily affirm. In this instance traditions are easily transplanted to a new context.

There are limits to the community-igloo analogy. The most obvious difference is in the pluralization of Arctic society and the roles that people can occupy. For example, the characteristic leader of the past, the *isumataaq*, is now paralleled by formally elected leadership. "Paralleled" is the key word here, as formal government neither has replaced family-based authority nor does it threaten to. Instead, it would appear that a basic challenge to the Inuit regional and territorial governments is to acknowledge the importance of that system, incorporate its cultural power into effective policy-making, and draw society into that process by linking tradition with governance.

There have been attempts to acknowledge the role of social leadership by incorporating an Elders' area into the Nunavut legislature. The area chosen was felt by some to be disrespectful of Elders because it was located behind the premier's and speaker's areas. Elders do not generally get pushed to the side. More important than seating arrangements is the role that Elders' knowledge and experience brings to the process of government. Nunavut government has adopted as policy *Inuit Qaujimajatuqangit*, "Inuit ways and knowledge." Many feel that decisions and policies should be examined from the perspective of Inuit traditions

and philosophy before being acted upon. The logic is that Inuit government should contribute to and respect traditions rather than ignore or undermine them.

Socially vested authority and formalized authority sometimes correspond, sometimes coexist, and sometimes conflict. Leadership is now specialized and rarely carries the same all-encompassing social importance it once did. Solutions to problems are increasingly sought in processes located in institutions and not in a society consisting of small groups, where all problems were once managed. A complex division of labour has developed with the cash economy. Where once one would have gone to see a leader whatever the problem, now an Inuk can seek out specialists in social matters, hunting, mechanical repairs, or medicine.

Contemporary lifestyle brings with it inescapable effects on social and familial organization. Having permanent dwellings imputes a specific kind of social structure onto its inhabitants, restricting and shaping social organization. In effect, the predominant housing style emulates that of the **nuclear family** and reifies that kinship system. This has impacts on the way Inuit social organization is conceptualized in administrative systems, and these in turn affect families. Of course, there are social problems in some families in the North, and it is through the management of tragic and complex events that we most readily see where change in Inuit society is taking place. Also, the structure of governance now in the hands of Inuit is inherited from English common law. It brings with it assumptions about the nature of society, productivity, property, and kin that in some instances counter those of Inuit customary practice. It is common to hear leaders talking about the antithesis of the idea of landownership to Inuit cultural values, for example, yet ownership is exactly what has been determined in the land-claims agreements.

An aspect of the incompatibility of Inuit and Canadian systems of social organization that I have studied closely is child adoption. The largely unacknowledged assumptions of the child welfare system, which is grounded in national legal standards rather than Inuit social or moral ones, are a continuing source of friction. In Nunavut and Nunavik roughly one child in four is adopted by customary arrangements. I define "adopted" in Inuit society as "not primarily socialized by the biological parents." Adoption is a cornerstone of Inuit social organization and essentially everyone takes part as a giver, receiver, brother, sister, and so on of adopted children. Older people in particular adopt children. Often elderly adopters talk about having young children in their lives as a requirement to staying healthy. Without them they feel unproductive, lazy, and even ill. Inuit customary adoption challenges basic assumptions about motherhood, childhood, and elderhood held in southern Canada and beyond.

These social arrangements of child-rearing run counter to fundamental truths held in the legal system and reflect back on non-Inuit ideas of property and ownership. Children *belong* to their biological parents and to give away a child imputes negligence on the part of the parents. Old people are supposed to be quiet, unproductive, and relieved that they no longer have to bear the burden of child-rearing. Rarely would we see elderly people seeking children to adopt in southern Canada. Inuit clearly do not experience adoption this way. They see giving children as a sign of respect to people they have known all their lives and care for deeply. It is, as one woman told me, "the nicest thing I could do for them." Inuit adoption is enacted within pre-existing and often multi-generational kin relationships. The quality of parenting an adopted child would receive is rarely in question and people who are seen as irresponsible are less likely to be given the opportunity to adopt. Checks and balances relying on social

knowledge and historical association are built into the system. Regardless, the role of government institutions has grown and there are clear conflicts grounded in the differences between Inuit social and bureaucratic systems. Attempts to resolve social problems involving children occur in both realms. Customary adoption practices stand out in these instances and are probed for their contribution to social problems. Rarely, however, have they been examined by the bureaucratic system for their contributions to social harmony. While there is more to write about this, it is sufficient to say that even in the context of renewed Inuit political authority, there are restrictions on the space that cultural practices can take.

The Historical Context: Communities and Coercion

Historians of English Canada have said that we stopped thinking like a colony and began acting like a nation in the wake of the collective loss and horrors of two world wars. As a nation we grew up. In World War I, Canadians began to emerge from the mentality of imperial colonials and into the mindset of independent nationals. World War II cemented a growing vision of nationhood and initiated the consolidation of national territory, including the Arctic. Our attention turned inward to our own geography and its meaning.

The changes in Canadian self-image are seen in the corresponding shifts in how the North has been represented and acted upon. In the age of exploration the impetus that drove the exploration of the North was the fabled Northwest Passage. Finding a sea route from the Atlantic to the Pacific had enormous symbolic importance and potential economic significance. Heroes of this period expanded the horizons of empire and some lived to tell the tale. Others, such as Sir John Franklin and his crew of 128, disappeared (in 1848) in the High Arctic. More than 40 expeditions tried to find them, none successfully. The only evidence of their fate came from

Dr John Rae, who travelled with Inuit in the mid-1800s as a surveyor for the Hudson's Bay Company. He heard from them of a group of white men, who could only have been Franklin's crew, hauling a large boat over the ice. He collected stories of their fate and relayed them to England, where they were largely disbelieved (Woodman 1991).

The relevance of Rae's story is in the extent to which the Inuit testimony was correct and the degree to which it was ignored. This pattern of interaction between peoples has endured for some time, although its substance has changed. This episode demonstrates that what we think we know is often determined by what we assume to be possible. Only recently has Inuit testimony regarding Franklin's fate been tested against objective criteria, primarily the discovery of artifacts and graves from the Franklin crew. In the end the Inuit testimony was found to have been highly accurate. That it was doubted for so long says something about the durability of preconceptions.

The Franklin expedition marks the beginning of the end of the imperial North and the dawn of the Canadianization of the Arctic. Early in the twentieth century a new way of talking about the North emerged, one that began to acknowledge Inuit cultural and technological mastery of the Arctic. In popular culture, notably the hugely successful film *Nanook of the North* (1922), the technological ingenuity of the Inuit was marvelled at, although it seemed to emerge from childlike explorations with simple objects. Others in this period, notably explorer and anthropologist Vilhjalmur Stefansson, argued that the North is amenable to occupation and exploitation and, more importantly, that this should be a national objective. In the period between the wars, Inuit were not considered active participants in northern development. In fact, they existed on the margins of the story, almost invisible to those who were imagining it. The leap from a passive observation of the Inuit to an active intervention in their lives would come later.

The end of World War II marked a new era. The nation had barely worked out where it stood in the world when the world crowded in on it. Americans had strategic claims to portions of the Arctic Archipelago, Danes were looking across Baffin Strait to Ellesmere Island, and Russians suddenly were capable of attacking the West by coming over Arctic Canada. Perhaps the most significant event in the ongoing relationship between the state and the Inuit occurred when the United States built radar bases across the North. In the process, Canada's Arctic peoples came to be seen by the world. In many instances what was seen were resolutely traditional-looking people, almost entirely self-reliant, living from the land. The post-war boom brought unimagined technology and comparative wealth to almost all of North America, yet the Inuit were stubbornly unchanging. Well into the 1950s many clothed themselves in skins and lived off the land, with no need of government or nation. The new sense of national confidence was threatened by the transformation of geopolitics, by the absence in Canada of knowledge about its own territory, and by the apparent indifference of Inuit to material prosperity. The earlier imaginings about the Arctic and its peoples were outdated and in need of revision. Where formerly Canada had no means of demonstrating sovereignty over its northern territory and little interaction with its Indigenous inhabitants, the post-war period was marked by the arrival of the state in the lives of the Inuit. They became, in the eyes of government, people needing administration.

Not only did Canada begin to think like a nation in the post-war period, it acted like one. The development and implementation of national social policies had a profound effect. The presence of government in the daily lives of people, seen through the development of education, health, economic, and social policies, increased dramatically. The post-war period saw Canada transformed into a wealthy, modern country. For Aboriginal peoples generally, the same period is marked by an intensification of the systematic undermining of their Indigenous social structures, traditional economies, and cultural principles. The Arctic and the Inuit posed a particular difficulty in this modernization. Transportation was erratic and distances enormous. The few non-Inuit living in the North were largely traders, priests, and the occasional RCMP officer. There was little government in the North and most people lived outside the cash economy.

Anthropology and Arctic Modernity

Anthropology has played an important role both in building the national sense of the North and in criticizing it. For a period from the 1950s to the late 1970s when Inuit were being drawn into permanent settlements, applied anthropologists addressed the question of how they were adapting to life in communities and looked at social and cultural change. Throughout the past 40–50 years the discourse of cultural contact and subsequent change in Indigenous lifeways has been invoked as an encompassing explanatory model in applied anthropology, and in psychological and psychiatric investigations of individual distress and social dysfunction. Change, as it has been expressed as a result of the encounters between Inuit and Euro-Canadians, is generally taken to be pathogenic. But change is not an accident of nature. People make decisions about what will change and how. Enforced change means that some people have authority over others.

Anthropologists took a role in analyzing the effects of change on Inuit and in making certain changes happen. Diamond Jenness, an anthropologist who travelled with Knud Rasmussen, the Danish explorer and ethnologist, in the groundbreaking Fifth Thule Expedition, later undertook a large study called *Eskimo Administration* (1964) that supported the development of a government policy of settling Inuit into new and permanent communities. It was generally taken for granted that they would ultimately be acculturated into pan-Canadian values, abandoning the subsistence economy to participate in industrial society. Throughout this period anthropologists examined the social changes resulting from community living with an eye toward easing and understanding the adjustment of Inuit to this new arrangement.

In retrospect it seems that the disappearance of traditional cultures was taken to be inevitable by government and researchers alike. Inuit today speak of this time with great sadness. They were told repeatedly that they would have to change and were better off not pursuing traditional activities. Children were encouraged to learn English and came to devalue their parents through an educational system that portrayed their lives as primitive. This period produced a disjuncture between generations that has come to be seen as a source of social distance and disintegration that people are only now coming to terms with.

The presumed inevitability and direction of change in Inuit society were forces shaping their relations with government. Early studies of Inuit social change were naive to the politics at play in describing the apparent dissolution of traditional ways in the face of new modes of social organization imposed from outside. The basic assumptions about the future of Inuit life were in effect self-fulfilling prophecies. As evidence of social dysfunction mounted, new programs and policies were created to shape and mitigate the changes. In each case Inuit were pulled further from the sources of social order and authority that had informed their lives, in many instances making things worse. Few people with authority were suggesting alternatives to the policies that disempowered Inuit.

The settlement of Inuit into communities did not happen overnight. Rudimentary towns had grown up around Hudson's Bay Company posts and missions since the turn of the twentieth century. In some cases people would gather there, usually in winter, and then return to other hunting areas in spring. In this respect social organization emulated that of the past. However, with World War II, trade goods became scarce and fur prices fell for lack of demand. Inuit who had become accustomed to semi-annual trading sessions, and the goods these provided, were often left destitute, so they were increasingly reliant on relief through the missions, the HBC, or the RCMP. From the point of view of people providing relief, the situation was chaotic. They could not plan for the future and had no idea what would happen next. Inuit were still highly mobile but when game became scarce they would arrive, needing relief, far from where they had been last encountered. It became increasingly important to control the movements of people so they could be provided for when necessary.

In the early 1950s the RCMP shot hundreds of dogs in several communities in northern Quebec and the Northwest Territories. This was explained as necessary due to rabies among the dogs and the danger this posed to people. Inuit, who are knowledgeable about rabies in wildlife populations, disagree. They view these incidents as intentional efforts to stop them from going on the land. They have also come to symbolize their powerlessness in relations with the state. Dog teams were the principal means of winter locomotion. Without them people were forced to remain in the communities. They could not hunt and became more dependent on imported goods. The significance of this period has never receded in the memories of northerners. In October 2010 a commission reported its findings on the dog killings, finding that there was no organized attempt to disrupt Inuit mobility although the actions of officers and agents of the state had exactly that effect.

The demonstration of Canadian sovereignty over the Arctic was also wrapped up in these efforts. Creating recognizable and permanent communities involved, in some instances, relocating people from one part of the North to very distant places. In 1953, people near Inukjuak, Quebec, a relatively southern Inuit community, were moved to Grise Fjord in the High Arctic under the guise of providing them access to more productive hunting grounds. The people had no experience with this landscape and the hunting was unfamiliar and certainly no more productive than where they came from. In the end, the real reason seems to have been to show the flag in a contested part of the North. Sovereignty over the outer edges of the country remains an important issue and one that is increasingly so as the sea ice thins and commercial shipping through the Northwest Passage may become possible.

Throughout this period of transition to community living, locally pertinent alternatives to a seemingly irrevocable process of settlement and modernization were never explored by those in charge. They were being put forth by Inuit, however. The rise of co-operative movements and new forms of culturally defined political representation were undertaken even before the communities of today had been formalized.

Recently, a critique of the relations of power inherent in the internal colonialism of Aboriginal peoples in Canada has pointed to the devastating effects of enforced social change. One example comes from the institutionalization of Inuit health service delivery. Epidemic tuberculosis was responsible for many deaths throughout the North in the twentieth century. Treatment involved sending people south on an annual medical survey ship for treatment in sanatoriums. The separation of families, sometimes for years and sometimes permanently as many died and a few were even lost in the "system," had an important impact on the ability of Inuit to be independent. By necessity many Inuit remained close to the trading posts, mission houses, and RCMP stations to receive relief. This pattern became regularized as their dependence on non-Inuit grew and they could not re-establish their traditional economy.

The policy of evacuating people with chronic illness for hospital treatment was eventually extended to include women in the third trimester of pregnancy. As in the case of TB, sending women to hospitals separated them from the familial and social support already in place, and isolated fathers from caring for the family and from the birth itself. It also severed cultural practices around birth that were important in establishing the child's social context. Inuit midwives had an important place in the life of children they helped deliver. Similarly,

cutting the umbilical cord created a lifelong special relationship between the child and *Sanajiik*, the one who cut the cord. Hospital births for healthy women ruptured these social ties. Sending women out of their communities was done under the guise of helping people, a justification that made it easier to intervene in cultural practice and demonstrate authority. The anthropological literature discussing these events generally supports returning control over policy to the Inuit. Regaining the power to make decisions that affect people's lives will allow for more culturally appropriate policy to be established and for the wounds of the past to be healed.

BOX 4.2 Inuit Language and Writing

Inuktitut is one of the most vigorous Indigenous languages in North America. It is widely spoken within Inuit communities and is the language of everyday life in most. Inuktitut, Inuinnaqtun, Inuttut, and Inuttitut are, respectively, the regional dialects of the majority of native speakers in Nunavut, the Inuvialuit Settlement Area, Labrador, and Nunavik. There are sub-dialects within each region as well, but all are largely mutually intelligible. Language and culture are closely linked and Inuit are keenly aware of the challenges that Inuktitut faces in a sea of anglophone North American culture. The Nunavut government has implemented a policy of three official languages in the territory: Inuit (Inuktitut and Inuinnaqtun), French, and English. A major challenge in Nunavut is encouraging the use of Inuktitut in the workplace. As the government workforce is heavily populated by non-Inuit, many of whom grew up elsewhere, and Inuit tend to be bilingual, the tendency is to favour English. In some instances Nunavut

government employees are encouraged to take Inuktitut language courses.

In Nunavik the situation is more complex, as provincial authority has grown since the signing of the JBNQA and there is a mix of Inuktitut, French, and English speakers in the workplace. In some instances Inuit have chosen to educate their children alternately in English and French in order to have a full spectrum of language skills within the family. Many young people are growing up functionally trilingual. In Kuujjuaraapik in southern Hudson Bay the community is roughly half Inuit and half Cree. Here there are some people who are comfortable in four languages, signalling a northern cosmopolitanism that is surprising to many.

Writing in Inuktitut is a relatively new invention brought by Anglican missionaries in the nineteenth century. The majority of Inuit in Nunavut and Nunavik use a syllabic script based on modified shorthand. In Labrador the roman script is used with some modifications for sounds not found in English. For example,

Continued

a capital "K" anywhere in a word indicates a combined "q" and "h" sound produced deep in the throat. In western Nunavut and the Inuvialuit settlement area a standard roman script is used for writing. When Inuit from around the world gather they also add the Cyrillic script (Russia) and Greenlandic versions of roman Kallalisut (the Greenlandic name for their language) writing to the menu. Not surprisingly, there have been calls to produce a unified Inuit writing form that would allow for simple written communication across the circumpolar North.

The cultural and political dimensions of language use in the North are complex. Variations in written and spoken language signal regional and national differences that correspond both to particular historical trajectories and to senses of identity and tradition. It is interesting to note that the arrival of social media like Facebook in the North (Internet development is slowed by the absence of land lines—expensive satellite transmission is required) has encouraged conversations about language, terminology, and dialectical variation among Inuit from many different regions. These spontaneous groups tend to use roman script when communicating, although most people participating in them have been raised using syllabics. Thus we again see how Inuit culture persists even while changing and adapting to new contexts.

Conclusion

In the past 35 years we have witnessed the resolution of Inuit land-claims agreements across the Arctic. The most significant for the country at large was the creation of Nunavut. This is the first change in Canadian political boundaries since 1949, when Newfoundland joined Confederation. Nunavut has a public government, meaning any resident may participate in it, dominated by Inuit because of their overwhelming numbers. This achievement is the culmination of more than 30 years of work by a class of politically astute Inuit that emerged in the 1960s shortly after people had been settled into communities and by Elders and others who supported them. Nunavut represents a return to Inuit regional autonomy, but its creation obviously is not a return to the past. Instead, it reflects a hybrid of Inuit and southern ways of doing things. Consequently, social and political tensions inherent to the new structure of governance place demands on Inuit that are unique in the country and serve as a model for others.

The changes that Inuit have experienced in a lifetime are profound and irrevocable. It was clear even at the beginning of the nineteenth century that many of them were going to happen. This led to almost 100 years of anthropological research that was explicitly or implicitly underpinned by the idea that, eventually, the Inuit would lose or abandon their culture to adopt that of the majority population—that they would cease to exist as a distinct cultural group. To be fair, it was not just anthropologists who assumed this process was inevitable. It was the dominant way of conceiving the future of all non-Western cultures since at least the Victorian era. Certainly, the assumption of cultural loss and assimilation was central to how government operated until relatively recently. Not only were the Inuit "disappearing," but the role of government was to facilitate their transformation. Rarely were Inuit themselves consulted or considered.

Well, we all seem to have been wrong. Since regional political autonomy has been regained and as Inuit take charge of their governments,

Inuit culture is undergoing a renaissance. Inuit culture has taken its place on a world stage. The remarkable artistic vision of Zacharias Kunuk in his film *Atanarjuat* (which Canadian novelist Margaret Atwood called "Homeric" in its scope) is a contribution to global culture. Likewise, it is not uncommon to see throat singing and drum dance performances in Paris or Osaka, or to hear Inuit popular music being played alongside American and British tunes. Not only are there more Inuit alive today than at any time in the past, but the use of the various dialects of the Inuit language is strong in most areas, particularly the eastern Arctic.

Where the use of Inuktitut has declined and been replaced by English, there are now government-funded programs and voluntary associations of people working to expand its use. Permanent housing, wage-paying jobs, television, the Internet, school buses, and airplanes have not made the Inuit any less Inuit. These are simply material things that people incorporate into their everyday lives. What is relevant to a discussion of Inuit cultural continuity and change is how their everyday lives are constrained and broadened by the flow of information and continual contact with ideas, values, rules, and laws that surround people today.

NOTES

1. Anna Mehler Paperny and Sara Minogue, "Life on the Mean Streets of Iqaluit," *Globe and Mail*, 14 August 2009. www.theglobeandmail.com/news/national/life-on-the-mean-streets-of-iqaluit/article1253119/

2. Although the terms "month" and "moon month" are commonly used, technically they are neither, but rather are named mini-seasons that follow each other in regular order. In any particular year they may come sooner or later than usual.

REFERENCES AND RECOMMENDED READINGS

Bennett, John, and Susan Diana Mary Rowley. 2004. *Uqalurait: An Oral History of Nunavut*. McGill–Queen's Native and Northern Series. Montreal and Kingston: McGill–Queen's University Press. A highly original oral history consisting mainly of direct quotes from Inuit involved in documenting life and culture in the wake of the creation of Nunavut.

Briggs, Jean. 1970. *Never in Anger: Portrait of an Eskimo Family*. Cambridge, MA: Harvard University Press. A groundbreaking and sensitive ethnography of Inuit family life, this study broke the formalist and descriptive tradition to focus on the emotional lives of a small group and includes excellent detail on children and women.

Dorais, Louis-Jacques. 1997. *Quaqtaq: Modernity and Identity in an Inuit Community*. Toronto: University of Toronto Press. Examines the process of community development and the influence of family alliances on contemporary political and social organization. A very accessible ethnography/ethnohistory of a small Nunavik community.

Grace, Sherrill E. 2001. *Canada and the Idea of North*. Montreal and Kingston: McGill–Queen's University Press. A comprehensive overview of Canada's fascination with the North. Includes consideration of poetry, performing arts, painting, and literature in attempting to grasp what the North means to us.

Jenness, Diamond. 1964. *Eskimo Administration, vol. II*. Canada: Arctic Institute of North America.

Laugrand, Frédéric, and Jarich Oosten. 2010. *Inuit Shamanism and Christianity: Transitions and Transformations in the Twentieth Century*. McGill–Queen's Native and Northern Series. Montreal and Kingston: McGill–Queen's University Press. A highly detailed review of Inuit religious thought and practice in the face of Christianity.

MacDonald, John. 1998. *The Arctic Sky*. Toronto: Royal Ontario Museum and Nunavut Research Institute.

A thematic approach to Inuit cosmogony that emphasizes the role of human–animal relations in Inuit representations of the heavens.

Mowat, Farley. 1963. *Never Cry Wolf*. Toronto: McClelland & Stewart.

Nunavut Arctic College. 1999–2001. *Interviewing Inuit Elders*, 5 vols. Iqaluit: Nunavut Arctic College. A remarkable series (vol. 1, *Introduction*; vol. 2, *Perspectives on Traditional Law*; vol. 3, *Childrearing Perspectives*; vol. 4, *Cosmology and Shamanism*; vol. 5, *Health Practices*) exploring the experiences of Elders with Inuit traditions and change in their lifetimes. Presented as extended interview transcripts, these are accessible first-person accounts.

Pitseolak, Peter, and Dorothy Eber. 1993. *People From Our Side*. Montreal and Kingston: McGill–Queen's University Press. An autobiography with accompanying photographs by Peter Pitseolak. The original manuscript was complemented with interview citations and synthesized into a genuinely Inuit view of history in the twentieth century.

Rasmussen, Knud. 1976 [1932]. *Intellectual Culture of the Copper Eskimos*, trans. W.E. Calvert. New York: AMS Press.

———. 1976 [1930]. *Intellectual Culture of the Iglulik Eskimos*, trans. W.E. Calvert. New York: AMS Press. These two volumes of the Fifth Thule Expedition Reports (1921–4) are some of the most comprehensive descriptions of Inuit life, custom, and myth in the early twentieth century. Rasmussen was part Greenlandic Inuit and spoke Inuktitut, providing an unparalleled window into the Inuit world of the time.

Stern, Pamela R., and Lisa Stevenson. 2006. *Critical Inuit Studies: An Anthology of Contemporary Arctic Ethnography*. Lincoln: University of Nebraska Press. Excellent collected volume on contemporary issues in Inuit life.

Tester, Frank James, and Peter Kulchyski. 1994. *Tammarniit (Mistakes): Inuit Relocation in the Eastern Arctic*. Vancouver: University of British Columbia Press. A finely researched and scathing reconstruction of the role of government ineptitude in the events leading up to starvation and murder in two Inuit regions.

Wenzel, George. 1991. *Animal Rights, Human Rights: Ecology, Economy and Ideology in the Canadian Arctic*. Toronto: University of Toronto Press. A veteran anthropologist documents the adverse impact of the anti-seal hunting campaigns on the Inuit, including the conscious decisions of the "environmentalists" not to exempt Inuit from their boycott.

Woodman, David C. 1991. *Unravelling the Franklin Mystery: Inuit Testimony*. Montreal and Kingston: McGill–Queen's University Press.

CHAPTER 5

The Caribou Inuit

Ernest S. Burch Jr[1]

Introduction

The people formerly called "Caribou Eskimos" lived on and near the west coast of Hudson Bay in what is now the southern portion of the Kivalliq Region, Nunavut territory. The label was coined in the early 1920s by the Danish ethnographers Knud Rasmussen and Kaj Birket-Smith, who were fascinated by the obsession the Inuit-speaking residents of the region had with caribou as a source of food and other raw materials, to the near exclusion of everything else. In this respect they contrasted markedly with other Inuit groups in the ethnographic record, most of which depended primarily on sea mammals.[2]

From the perspective of the early twenty-first century, the interesting question is less that these people were obsessed with caribou than with how they came to be that way. Also of interest is the fact that, as we now know, the members of these hunter–gatherer societies increased in numbers and expanded their territory for nearly two centuries after European contact. This placed them in direct contrast to the experience of small-scale societies in almost every other part of the world.

Field and archival research conducted during the second half of the twentieth century significantly enhanced our understanding of Caribou Inuit history, ecology, and social organization. Birket-Smith's and Rasmussen's accounts will always be essential elements in our record of Caribou Inuit life, but we now realize that those authors overlooked several important aspects of it, and they failed completely to understand the unusual historical circumstances in which they made their observations.

My own introduction to the Caribou Inuit came in 1968. I was interested in learning how people living in extreme environments were organized prior to the time of Western contact. I was looking for an Inuit group that was different enough from the Iñupiaq of northwestern Alaska, with whom I was already familiar, to provide me with an instructive contrast.[3] On more practical grounds, I had just joined the Anthropology Department at the University of Manitoba and, as a condition of getting the job, had agreed to do research among Canadian Inuit. A literature review suggested that the Caribou Inuit might solve both problems. That view was confirmed by a colleague at Manitoba, Thomas C. Correll, who had spent several years among the Caribou Inuit as a missionary-linguist before entering anthropology. Between 1968 and 1971, Correll and I spent about 14 months interviewing Elders in both northwestern Alaska and on the west coast of Hudson Bay, trying to learn what they knew about their ancestors' ways of life.

Then I turned to historical documents, both published and unpublished.

The primary unpublished documents relevant to the Caribou Inuit region were the Hudson's Bay Company (HBC) records, which spanned the entire era between the late seventeenth and early twentieth centuries. These were not made available to the general public until the mid-1970s. As I examined these amazingly informative documents, what began as a relatively straightforward exercise in sociology developed into a rather complicated project in ethnohistory. My original interest in the general structure of early twentieth-century Caribou Inuit societies expanded to include an equal, if not greater, fascination with the changes occurring in that structure over the previous 250 years. Both of those interests are reflected in the present account.

The Country

The Caribou Inuit region is located about halfway down the west side of Hudson Bay, between approximately 60° and 65° N. It extends roughly 600 kilometres from north to south and 500 kilometres inland from the coast. The landscape is an undulating plain of generally low relief that rises gradually from the shallow waters of Hudson Bay toward the west and south, where it reaches a maximum elevation of some 500 metres above sea level. A heavily glaciated portion of the Canadian Shield, the region is characterized by a variety of post-glacial landforms, such as eskers and rocky outcrops, and countless marshlands, rivers, lakes, streams, and ponds. The land is still rebounding from the release of the great continental glacier's weight, with the result that the shoreline has changed considerably over the past 300 years.

The treeline angles irregularly across the region from southeast to northwest (see Map 5.1). North of this line, the country is blanketed by barren or lichen- and moss-covered outcrops and boulders interspersed with grass and sedge meadows, and copses of dwarf trees and shrubs, which seldom exceed one metre in height. Here and there in the southern and western portions, in sheltered valleys or hollows, are islands of spruce that remained behind when the forest retreated southward during the bitter weather of the Little Ice Age, some 400 years ago. (Currently the treeline is moving north again as climate change brings warmer and longer growing seasons to the region.) Below the treeline, spruce fill the valleys and hollows, and grow progressively farther up the hillsides as one proceeds from northeast to southwest.

Plant growth even in southern Kivalliq is severely restricted by the harsh climate. Frost occurs on an average of more than 260 days per year, and the average temperature, reckoned for a 12-month period, ranges from about –5°C in the southwest to –6°C in the north.[4] Precipitation, which fluctuates considerably from year to year, is at near-desert levels most of the time, averaging between about 20 and 30 centimetres a year; 60 per cent of this usually falls as rain between early June and early October. The dominant feature of the weather, however, is the wind, which blows incessantly across the land, day and night, all year long.

The harsh climate and lack of vegetation mean that relatively few species of animals are found in the region. Historically, barren ground caribou and muskoxen were the dominant terrestrial species. Both have experienced dramatic fluctuations in numbers over the past 300 years, ranging between great abundance and near-extinction. Several varieties of fish—most notably Arctic char, lake trout, and whitefish—are found in the lakes and rivers.

The shallow coastal waters of western Hudson Bay are home to several kinds of sea mammal. The most common is the small ringed seal, but the much larger bearded seal is also present in some numbers. Walrus formerly were numerous in the central and northern sections of the coast, and belugas were abundant in some areas in early summer. Bowhead whales frequented the waters off the mouth of Chesterfield Inlet before they were nearly exterminated by American whalers in the nineteenth century. Arctic foxes, wolverines, wolves, polar bears, and several varieties of birds—particularly ptarmigan, ducks, and geese—constitute the remaining faunal resources of the area.

Origins and Early History

Precisely when and how the Caribou Inuit originated as a distinct population have long been the subject of debate. Birket-Smith maintained that they were living representatives of the earliest Inuit, and that they still occupied the original homeland of all Eskaleut-speaking peoples when he visited them in the early 1920s. Birket-Smith's conclusion followed in part from his belief that social and technological change can proceed only from less to more complex over time. He showed, through an exhaustive comparative analysis of the material culture of various historic Eskaleut (including non-Inuit) groups, that the Caribou Inuit had a less complex social structure and technology than almost all the others. Hence, they must represent the "original" Inuit. All others, therefore, had to be descendant populations. Unfortunately, while his argument was logically valid, its conclusion was wrong because its basic premise was flawed. In fact, as we now know, change is not linear, but can go from more to less complex; indeed, it actually *did* do so in the specific case of the Caribou Inuit.

A contrary view was developed by Birket-Smith's colleague on the Fifth Thule Expedition, Therkel Mathiassen. He contended that his archaeological research demonstrated that all historic Inuit were descended from rather sophisticated prehistoric immigrants who brought the Thule culture eastward from Alaska. Subsequent research has shown that Mathiassen was correct.

The Caribou Inuit are definitely the biological and cultural descendants of Thule people, but just how and when they reached the west coast of Hudson Bay is still being debated. My own view is that they migrated overland from the north Canadian coast sometime in the seventeenth century. However, regardless of when they arrived or how they got there, they were firmly ensconced in the central portion of the west Hudson Bay coast by the summer of 1719, where they were encountered by HBC traders Henry Kelsey and John Hancock.

The Founder Society

The eighteenth-century Inuit population of southern Kivalliq seems to have ranged between about 250 and 450 people, as good times alternated with bad to keep their numbers in a state of flux.[5] Their territory extended along the coast from Eskimo Point to Rankin Inlet, and probably continued inland for several tens of kilometres. A few families also wintered periodically on or near Baker Lake. The greatest concentration of people was in the vicinity of Whale Cove, in the richest sector of the southern Kivalliq coast. Observations of the location and movements of specific individuals and families, made over several decades by HBC traders, suggest that all the eighteenth-century Inuit inhabitants of the region were members of a single social system. Lacking an Inuit name for this society, I call it the "Founder Society" of Caribou Inuit.

The Founder Society way of life was an adaptation to local conditions of the Thule culture they brought with them from the west and north. Their winter houses, made of stone chinked with moss and dirt and covered with snow, were situated on the mainland coast. In spring they moved out to islands and points of land, where they lived in conical, skin-covered tents. There they hunted seals, walrus, belugas, and an occasional bowhead whale, and fished for char. They dried the meat and fish in the sun, and stored it, along with blubber, in sealskin bags. The supplies they accumulated between May and early August probably formed the bulk of their food during the following winter. In mid- to late August they walked inland to hunt caribou, acquiring skins for clothing, and meat and fat for food. In fall, they returned to their winter dwellings near the coast with the dried meat and hides. After the ocean froze, they retrieved from the islands the supplies of sea-mammal oil and meat stored there since early summer. During winter they hunted caribou or seals, as need required and conditions permitted. Overland transportation must have been by foot, since there are no references to dogs or sleds in any of the observations made of their camps by eighteenth-century explorers and traders. On water, they travelled by *kayak*, frequently lashing several together to form a raft when carrying bulk goods or large numbers of people.

The members of the Founder Society apparently were rather isolated from other Inuit. However, they were in intermittent contact with Chipewyan Indians, hundreds of whom ventured onto the tundra each summer to hunt caribou. Relations between the Chipewyan and Inuit during this period usually are depicted as invariably hostile, often violently so. HBC traders later took credit for establishing peace between the two groups. A careful examination of the archival sources, however, indicates that, while Chipewyan–Inuit relations did indeed sometimes result in bloodshed, contacts were peaceful more often than not. If anything, the HBC made things worse because members of the two groups began to compete for the traders' attention. After a smallpox epidemic decimated the Chipewyan population in the early 1780s, contacts became less frequent and overt hostility between Chipewyan and Inuit largely disappeared.

The early trade between the Caribou Inuit and the HBC was conducted from sloops sent north from Churchill during the summer. The trade was so meagre that one has to wonder why the HBC pursued it. The only furs southern Kivalliq

has in quantity are those of the Arctic fox, with some wolf and wolverine, and the market for all of them was very weak during the eighteenth and nineteenth centuries. The bulk of the trade was in caribou skins and sea-mammal products, primarily blubber, with some baleen and walrus ivory. In exchange, the Inuit received knives, hatchets, fish hooks, pots, files, beads, and tobacco. After about 1770, guns, powder, and shot were also traded. The balance of the coastal trade was much to the advantage of the Inuit, a fact realized early on by the HBC traders at Churchill, but overlooked or ignored by their superiors in London. It was finally halted in 1790, after which the Inuit had to make the long trek to Churchill if they desired goods of European manufacture.

Expansion

The end of the coastal trade, which apparently occurred during a period of increasing population—the reasons for the increase are not known—led the Caribou Inuit to expand their geographic horizons. For much of the eighteenth century, and especially after 1750, they had moved to the coast each spring to hunt seals. The HBC had kindly delivered a boatload of trade goods to their very door, receiving in return a variety of miscellaneous items having little value to the Inuit. The Inuit did not become dependent on this trade, for they headed inland as soon as caribou-hunting season arrived whether or not the trading vessel had been there.

The people whose winter houses were situated in the northern sector of Caribou Inuit territory were understandably loath to make the 700–800-kilometre round trip to Churchill to acquire trade goods after 1790. Such goods were nice to have, but they were not crucial to survival. When the coastal trade was broken off, the inhabitants of this sector began to spend more time hunting, fishing, and exploring in the Chesterfield Inlet and Baker Lake area than formerly. They probably also travelled more extensively north along the Hudson Bay coast.

About the same time that the Caribou Inuit were expanding the scope and frequency of their journeys north, the Aivilik branch of the Iglulik Inuit was expanding southward from Foxe Basin. Members of the two populations apparently came into contact for the first time around 1800. This was a major event for the Caribou Inuit because, evidently from the Aivilik, they learned the art of making a snow house, a vastly more suitable winter habitation for life on the barrens than a rock house. They may also have acquired their first dogs from the Aivilik. Conversely, the Aivilik gained their first access to iron tools and containers, which they purchased from the Caribou Inuit.

While people in the northern segment of the Founder Society were gradually reorienting their activities toward Chesterfield Inlet and Baker Lake, those in the southern segment were beginning to focus their attention on Churchill, 250–300 kilometres to the south. On 9 June 1791, 20 Caribou Inuit arrived in Churchill, bringing 50 caribou skins, 6 fox skins, and a wolf skin to trade. They were hired by the HBC to hunt seals until the ice left the coast, and subsequently to hunt beluga whales for the HBC for a week or so before returning to their own country. When they departed, the chief **factor** told them that, henceforth, all trade would be done at Churchill, and he asked them to tell that to their friends. They did so, and another group of Inuit arrived at Churchill on 22 August of that same summer. These two visits initiated a trend that was to persist, with occasional modifications, for more than 130 years.

By 1810, the members of the northern and southern segments of the Founder Society were not getting along, and by the mid-1820s they had split. HBC people at Churchill learned of this development and began to refer to them as the "Distant" and "Homeguard" Esquimaux, respectively. The former spent the winter in the interior,

near Baker Lake, and the summer along the shores of Chesterfield Inlet and Marble Island. A few made the long trip to Churchill each year, but they headed back north in time for caribou-hunting season. The Homeguards probably spent the winter along the Lower Maguse River and the spring on the islands near Eskimo Point. Several of them visited Churchill each spring, then hunted beluga for the HBC during the summer. The area around Whale Cove, the geographic centre of Founder Society and the area with the greatest supply of sea mammals, became a sparsely inhabited borderland. It was apparently during this period that the trend toward the later obsession with caribou began.

The Caribou Inuit population grew rapidly, albeit with occasional setbacks, over the next century or so. At this point reasons for this increase are purely speculative. The population reached a total of perhaps 1,100 in 1881 and some 1,500 in 1915. As the population grew in size, it also expanded in space, particularly toward the interior.

Several developments, in addition to population growth, contributed to the inland expansion. The first involved the Chipewyan, who had dominated the interior, at least in summer, until the smallpox epidemic of 1781. The lure of the fur trade led many of the survivors to move southwest, further into the forest and closer to the trading posts, and away from the Inuit. Their departure left the country open to the Inuit, although groups of Chipewyan continued to make annual summer trips into the Barren Lands in the western part of the region until at least the 1870s.

A second important development was the adoption of the snow house as a winter dwelling. As noted above, this apparently occurred between 1790 and 1810. Much warmer in the winter wind than a tent, but equally suited to a nomadic way of life, snow houses were a vast improvement over stone houses. In 1750, people had had to stay fairly close to their (stone) houses whether there was any food there or not, or else live in tents all winter

---

BOX 5.1 Caribou

. . . the importance of caribou hunting as far as the Caribou Eskimos are concerned cannot be rated high enough. To them the caribou occupies at least the same position as the seal and the walrus to their kinsmen, or as the bison of the past to the Plains Indians. The caribou is the pivot round which life turns. When it fails, the mechanism of culture comes to a stop and hunger and cold are the consequences for those tribes which, relying upon it, have created an almost incredibly one-sided culture. (Birket-Smith 1929:9)

---

long. By 1820, if food ran short, they could go anywhere they wished and be relatively comfortably housed.

A third development was a crisis, in the form of a caribou decline, along the coast. Lasting for most of the 1840s, this event led to considerable hardship, particularly among the Homeguard Esquimaux. In an effort to locate caribou, several families apparently moved west to the middle Kazan River, where they discovered an abundance of muskoxen, enough to sustain them through the crisis. Finding the country to their liking, they simply stayed there after the caribou population recovered.

As the Caribou Inuit population grew numerically and expanded geographically, it also became further divided socially. The two societies of 1850 had become five only 30 years later. I have been unable to learn what one of them was called by HBC personnel, but the others were known as the "Homeguard," "Distant," "Inland," and "Middle" Esquimaux. These societies were in operation during what I call the "Classic Period" of Caribou Inuit history.

The Classic Period

Caribou Inuit culture, as a distinctive way of life, was marked by a general emphasis on terrestrial, as opposed to marine, resources, and by an overwhelming reliance on caribou as the specific resource with which material needs were satisfied. European recognition of these characteristics in the descriptive label "Caribou Inuit" was closely paralleled in the Inuit term *nunamiut*, "inland people," which other Inuit used to designate even those groups who spent some of the year on the coast.

The economic orientation of the late nineteenth-century Caribou Inuit was markedly different from the one prevailing 150 years earlier. In the 1750s, HBC traders literally had to beg them to give up even a small portion of their precious supply of seal oil. A century later they still killed hundreds of seals and belugas each summer, but they sold virtually their entire production to the HBC and relied almost entirely on caribou, muskoxen, and fish for their sustenance. Just why this change occurred and particularly why it took such an extreme form remain mysteries.

The change from a diversified economy to a highly specialized one occurred gradually during the demographic and geographic expansion of the mid-nineteenth century and definitely was completed by 1880. That year, therefore, may be designated as the beginning of the "Classic Period." The end of the period may be designated, less arbitrarily, as 1915, the first year of the "Great Famine."

The period 1880–1915 has a number of features that commend it for special treatment. During those years the Caribou Inuit population in general was high and still growing; the extent of their territory was greater than at any other time, before or since, and, despite more than a century and a half of contact, the people remained extraordinarily uninfluenced by Western culture. Finally, this is the earliest period for which the documentary records of traders and explorers can be enriched by information obtained directly from Caribou Inuit themselves.[6]

Societies

During most of the Classic Period the Caribou Inuit were organized in five societies, the Ahiarmiut, Harvaqturmiut, Hauniqturmiut, Paatlirmiut, and Qairnirmiut (see Table 5.1). A sixth group, the Tahiuyarmiut, may have become a society before 1915, but too little is known about it to establish that as fact; it was all but wiped out by famine almost as soon as it emerged.

All five societies had developed out of the Founder Society, but they had become separate social systems—the hunter–gatherer equivalent of different countries—by 1880. Each society was a relatively (although not absolutely) discrete network of families connected to one another by marriage, descent, and partnership ties. In addition

to holding dominion over a separate territory (see Map 5.1), the members of each spoke a distinctive variant of the Caribou Inuit dialect, wore clothes that were distinctive in one or more respects, and held to a general ideology of uniqueness and a sense of superiority over other peoples.

Families

The organizational core of a Caribou Inuit society was the **extended family**. This type of organization took a variety of forms. Some examples are: a group of adult male and/or female siblings, their spouses, and children; two adult brothers, their widowed mother, spouses, and children; or an aged couple, an adult offspring (of either sex), an adult nephew or niece, and their spouses and children. There were many other variations along these same general lines.

Children were betrothed early in life, often while still infants. The arrangements were made by the parents of the prospective spouses, and the principals had no say in the matter. According to Caribou Inuit belief, the best marriages were those of first cousins, and the very best arrangement of all was a brother–sister exchange (*akigiik*) between two sets of cousins; thus, a brother and sister of one

TABLE 5.1 Caribou Inuit Societies, *c.* 1890

INUIT NAME	EST. FOUNDED	HBC NAME	POPULATION	GENERAL LOCATION
Paatlirmiut	by 1825	Homeguard Esquimaux	450	Maguse River and nearby coast
Qairnirmiut	by 1825	Distant Esquimaux	200*	Thelon River, Baker Lake, and Chesterfield Inlet
Ahiarmiut	by 1858	Inland Esquimaux	350	Middle Kazan River
Hauniqturmiut	by 1871	Middle Esquimaux	175	Wilson River and nearby coast
Harvaqturmiut	by 1890	None	200	Lower Kazan River
Estimated total population, 1890			1,375	

* The Qairnirmiut population was already being affected by European diseases in 1890.

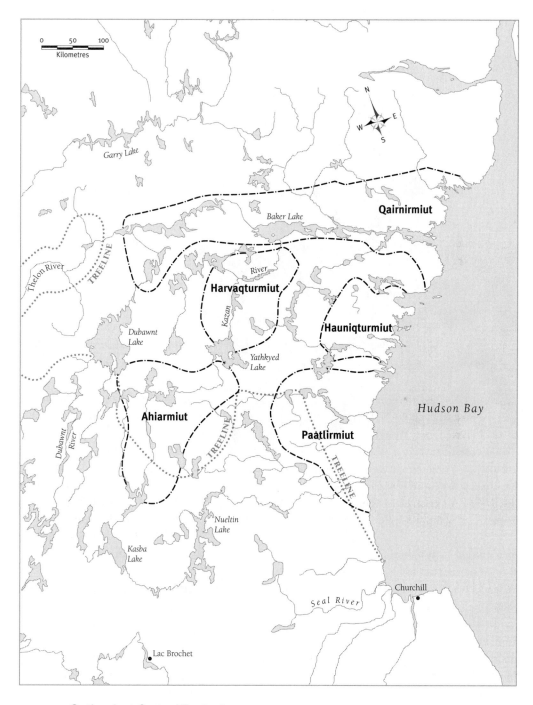

MAP 5.1 Caribou Inuit Societal Territories

FIGURE 5.1 A Paatlirmiut woman carrying her baby on her back, inside her parka, not as commonly supposed, in her hood. (By permission of the National Museum of Denmark, Department of Ethnography)

If Caribou Inuit ideology was carried to its logical conclusion, all the members of an entire society would have lived together in one place, intermarrying, having children, and generally operating as one huge family. However, tight limitations on the food supply and inevitable personality conflicts prevented them from even remotely achieving this ideal. Actual families ranged in size from simple conjugal units comprising just a married couple (or sometimes a man and two wives) and their non-adult children to relatively complex extended families of up to 35 people. Caribou Inuit had no ideological preference for either the male or the female line, and so developed neither lineages nor clans.

The members of a small family could live comfortably in a single dwelling. The larger the family, the greater its need to have two or more dwellings, since there are fairly narrow limits on the size of a snow house and more so on that of a tent. The average family seems to have involved nearly 20 people living in three tents in summer and fall, or in two snow houses in winter and spring.

Most settlements were occupied by the members of only one extended family. In times of hunger even these might split up, the constituent households spreading out over the country in the hope of finding game. In late spring or summer, though, when food supplies were greater, two or more related families often joined forces. Aggregations of more than 75 people sometimes occurred, but they were unusual and temporary,

family would marry a sister and brother of another, the two sibling pairs being cousins to begin with. When a cousin marriage occurred, people who started life as siblings, cousins, nieces, and nephews suddenly became spouses and in-laws of various kinds as well, thus building one layer of kin relationships upon another. The condition in which a small number of individuals became related to one another in several different ways simultaneously was known as *tamalrutit*, and was regarded as a highly desirable state of affairs.

generally associated with the arrival of an HBC trading vessel, a whaling ship, or an unusually large caribou kill.

A Caribou Inuit society was entirely lacking in political, economic, or other specialized institutions, such as governments, businesses, churches, or schools. Almost all functions required to sustain life were performed within the extended family. To a degree that most Canadians could scarcely comprehend, the life of a Caribou Inuk (singular of "Inuit") revolved around family—from birth until death.

Other Social Bonds

Extended family ties were supplemented in the Caribou Inuit social system by only two other types of social bond. One consisted of a series of special kin relationships created through a co-marriage; the other was a dancing partnership.

A co-marriage was established when two married couples agreed to exchange sexual partners for a night or two. This was not the casual, lustful affair implied by the common phrase "wife trading," because it really was a form of marriage. The arrangement created a number of relationships in addition to the original husband–wife ties. *All* these relationships were imbued with rights and obligations of mutual support and assistance, and these rights and obligations were binding for the rest of one's life.

A dancing partnership was established in a more elaborate way. After agreeing to become partners, two people, usually men, struck each other on the face and shoulders as hard as they could, often raising large welts. Eventually one gave up, at which point they exchanged gifts. The third and final stage was to dance together, beating drums, while the onlookers sang. By the time exhaustion finally overcame them, they had become *mumiqatigiik*, dancing partners.

Dancing partners were members of different families who normally lived in different settle-ments but visited each other from time to time. When they met after a prolonged absence, they repeated the initiation ceremony with only slight modification. At first sight they hit each other and tried to knock each other down. Later they danced and exchanged gifts. In addition to the ceremonial features, a dancing partnership was imbued with a great deal of joking and horseplay, each member trying to outdo the other in, say, an exchange of jibes or in a shoving match. *Mumiqatigiik* were very fond of each other and eagerly looked forward to their meetings.

The Political Process

Politically, each family was a hierarchical system based primarily on generation and relative age, and, to some extent, on gender differences. In general, people of a senior generation had authority over those in junior generations, older individuals had authority over younger ones, and, within a given generation or age category, males had authority over females. At the pinnacle of each of these tiny hierarchies was an *ihumataq*, or "chieftain."

An *ihumataq* was a mature adult, usually a middle-aged or older man who had lived long enough to have experienced life, acquired wisdom, and demonstrated in practice that he was qualified for the responsibilities of leadership. An *ihumataq* was also a very close relative of most of the people over whom he wielded authority. He was related to them as husband, father, older brother, older cousin, uncle, grandfather, and/or senior in-law. In short, the *ihumataq* typically was a person who wielded authority automatically by virtue of the fact that he filled a superior position in a whole series of hierarchical kin relationships. But the role always carried greater authority than would be conveyed by age, generation, and gender considerations alone, and it could be filled by any man whose extraordinary ability overrode those considerations. In a family large enough for there to be more than one candidate for the position, the actual *ihumataq* was likely to be a physically powerful individual, an excellent hunter, an understanding counsellor, an expert at human relations, and often a shaman as well. He would have more wives, more living children, better clothing, and generally more and better of everything than anyone else in the group.

An *ihumataq* led by a combination of demonstrated wisdom and ability. Where he was lacking those qualities, he might try to wield authority by brute strength, but a family headed by such a person would not stay intact for long. Individuals or conjugal family subunits could leave at any time. But where could they go? They either had to set out on their own or join another group of relatives belonging to the same type of organization as the one they left, but with different personnel. These alternatives combined to act as a check on the abuse of power by an *ihumataq*, while at the same time helping concentrate people around the most effective leaders.

An *ihumataq* had no institutionalized authority over anyone outside his own family. At the inter-family level, therefore, power and responsibility were allocated in a very haphazard manner. Families whose members could not get along very well together had to either fight or stay apart. Most of the time, they chose the latter course.

Subsistence

Caribou are remarkably useful. Their skins provide raw material for excellent cold-weather clothing, footgear, rope, tents, boat covers, sleeping bags, mattresses, insulating materials, house covers, knapsacks, blankets, and storage bags. Thread can be made from their sinew, and components of tools, weapons, and utensils can be manufactured from their antlers and bones. People who consume all the meat, viscera, stomach contents (rich in vitamin C), and fat of caribou are able to satisfy all their nutritional requirements from that species alone. If caribou are available in sufficient numbers

at appropriate times of year, and if they are fully utilized, they can provide for the *total* subsistence requirements of a human population.

Given the real benefits that an adequate harvest of caribou can bestow, it is not surprising that hunting peoples living on or near the boreal forest-tundra border all the way around the world had economies based heavily on this species (which includes Eurasian reindeer). But barren ground caribou are highly migratory animals, travelling hundreds or even thousands of kilometres each year. The only predictable feature of these movements for herds whose ranges straddle the treeline is that the majority of animals in a herd move onto the tundra for the calving season in early summer and return to the boreal forest for the winter. Hunters have three alternatives: (1) try to follow the animals over immense distances; (2) harvest caribou in great quantities when they are present and store enough meat and skins to last the rest of the year; or (3) harvest other species when caribou are not available. Within the region and time period of interest here, the Chipewyan emphasized the first strategy, while the Caribou Inuit employed a combination of the other two.

The main caribou hunt was from mid-August to late September, when the hides are in prime condition and the animals are normally fat. Hunters waited at places where caribou were likely to cross rivers or lakes, then speared the swimming animals from kayaks. While women processed the meat and hides, men continued to hunt, killing as many animals as they could. Meat, bones, and viscera not required for immediate use were wrapped in skins and cached under rocks. If the meat putrefied a bit before frost halted the process that only enhanced its taste—from the Inuit perspective. The success or failure of this late-summer hunt generally determined how comfortable life would be during the following winter.

Caribou hunting for most of the rest of the year was erratic. Whenever caribou were present they were pursued—with bow and arrow or with pit-falls dug in deep banks of snow. Occasionally they were hunted with muzzle-loading guns. But the Inuit were frequently out of ammunition, and their weapons apparently were not well maintained, so firearms provided little benefit. Sometimes thousands of caribou remained on the tundra all winter, but sometimes there were none at all. When there were not enough caribou, the people turned to muskoxen.

Muskoxen generally live in small groups of perhaps 12 to 24 animals. These groups, which travel only short distances, were widely distributed across southern Kivalliq at the beginning of the nineteenth century. They apparently were not heavily hunted by the Chipewyan. But when the Inuit moved inland in mid-century, they killed muskoxen whenever they ran out of caribou. This happened in mid- to late winter almost every year. During the Classic Period they are known (from HBC records) to have killed at least 3,000 muskoxen, and the real number must have been much higher. In the process, they all but exterminated their most important source of emergency food.

Fish also played a part in their diet, particularly in spring, when char swim out to sea, and again in August and September, when they return to the rivers and lakes. Char were caught with stone weirs, **leisters**, and hook and line. But fish were needed most in late winter, when the supply of caribou meat was often exhausted. Although the lakes of southern Kivalliq contained large populations of whitefish and other species, none of the Caribou Inuit techniques was very effective for winter fishing. Schools of fish are difficult to locate in large, deep, ice-covered lakes. Gill nets, set under the ice, are relatively productive on lakes, and particularly so on rivers. Yet almost every March found people chopping holes through the thick ice and jigging with hook and line. Sometimes they found fish, but often they did not.

The Caribou Inuit had been exposed (by the HBC) to the use of gill nets since at least 1720. They had been shown how to use them, and nets were available to them in trade. But it was not until the 1930s that they were widely adopted. Why? Birket-Smith provided the answer, which has three parts. First, they had a powerful taboo against eating fish taken dead from the water—and fish often drown in gill nets unless removed quickly. Prompt removal is very difficult in cold winter weather. Second, it was just about impossible to dry and mend nets in a snow house, where the temperature was below or near freezing most of the time. Finally, nets are heavy, bulky items to carry around, and Caribou Inuit moved quite often over the course of their yearly cycle. For all these reasons, but particularly the first, extensive use of nets was out of the question.

The Ahiarmiut and Harvaqturmiut, who remained inland year-round, lived almost exclusively on caribou, muskoxen, and fish, supplemented by ptarmigan in early spring, other birds in summer, fur-bearing animals such as foxes and wolves, and such other small game as they might encounter—right down to and including mice in extreme situations. Most members of the other three societies moved to the coast each spring. There they fished for char and hunted seals and beluga—unless caribou or other game was available.

It is worth repeating that, throughout the Classic Period, Qairnirmiut, Hauniqturmiut, and Paatlirmiut men remained active and competent sea-mammal hunters. But most of their harvest was sold to the HBC in Churchill or to whalers farther north. They regarded sea-mammal meat as suitable for dogs, but as little more than emergency food for humans. Even the blubber was hardly used. This is surprising because the meat of northern mammals is much leaner than beef, and people must have some fat in their diet. Blubber is also an efficient fuel for lamps and an excellent medium in which to store dried meat and fish for prolonged periods. However, for fatty food the Caribou Inuit relied on fish and caribou—or went without; for fuel they depended on dwarf willows and moss—or went without; and for a food preservative they relied primarily on cold temperatures. And whenever caribou, fish, or, say, geese appeared on the scene, sea mammals were all but forgotten. This utter disdain for sea-mammal blubber and oil, not the obsession with caribou as such, made the Caribou Inuit unique in the Eskaleut world.

Yearly Cycle

Caribou Inuit societies followed one of two forms of yearly cycle. One, followed by most Ahiarmiut and Harvaqturmiut, involved year-round residence in the interior of the country. The other, followed by most Qairnirmiut, Hauniqturmiut, and Paatlirmiut,

involved residence in the interior from late summer to early spring, and settlement on the coast in spring and early summer. This second pattern obviously required extensive travel between the two areas. Beyond that, the similarities among the five societies were much more numerous than the differences; the similarities receive treatment here.

In summer the Caribou Inuit lived in conical tents consisting of a frame of poles over which a cover made from several caribou skins was stretched. Cooking was done outside on a fire made of dwarf trees and shrubs. The smoke also helped to drive away some of the billions of mosquitoes that infest the country each summer. Light was provided by the sun. Although southern Kivalliq is well south of the Arctic Circle, it is still far enough north to have relatively little darkness during the late spring and early summer months.

FIGURE 5.2 Moving camp near Yathkyed Lake, early July 1922. The women and children move out first to be followed by the men and dogs. (By permission of the National Museum of Denmark, Department of Ethnography)

Children amused themselves or helped their parents, women tended to their babysitting, sewing, or butchering chores, and men roamed the country searching for game. Individuals ate whenever they were hungry (if food was available), although a cooked meal was usually prepared for the entire family each evening. When food was abundant and there were no pressing matters to attend to, the members of the tiny community often came together in the largest tent, or perhaps in two tents linked together, and danced, sang, told stories, and generally enjoyed themselves.

People usually stayed in one place as long as the hunting or fishing was good, although hunters often covered a tremendous area in their excursions around the camp. If a large kill was made at some distance from the tents, or if the hunting appeared to be better somewhere else, camp was moved.

Movement in summer was primarily on foot. People and dogs had to carry literally everything; what they could not carry, they cached under rocks. Each man carried his kayak upside down on his shoulders, his head inserted into the cockpit, while the women, children, and dogs carried almost everything else. When people reached a river or small lake, they ferried themselves and their equipment across by making repeated trips in the kayak. If two or more kayaks were available, they were rafted together. By alternately walking and camping, moving slowly but steadily across the country, an entire family, including infants and old people, could cover hundreds of kilometres in just a few weeks. Caribou Inuit were marvellous walkers.

People lived in their unheated tents until, in the fall, snowdrifts of the right depth and quality formed on the downwind side of the countless eskers and ridges. Usually the right snow conditions did not develop until November or even December. The snow houses that they could then build were of the general central Canadian Inuit type—dome-shaped structures perhaps four to five metres across at the base, made by stacking progressively smaller rows of snow blocks on top of one another in a circle until they converged at the top. To the basic house was added a long entrance tunnel, off which was built an alcove for cooking and perhaps one or two others for storage. Often the two or more houses occupied by a single extended family were linked by tunnels made of snow blocks.

Unlike all other snow-house dwellers, and, indeed, unlike most other Eskaleuts, Caribou Inuit did not normally heat or light their winter houses. A few people used seal-oil lamps, but they usually ran out of fuel by early winter. Light generally was provided by sunlight, which came directly through the translucent snow walls and through a window of clear ice placed in the roof on the south side of the building. But during the short days of early winter the Caribou Inuit spent most of their inside hours in total darkness. They did without heat altogether, except for that provided by the bodies of the house's occupants. Any cooking was done over a fire of dwarf willows built in the alcove. At most there was one cooked meal (of boiled meat or fish) a day, but during the winter months most food was consumed raw and frozen. During daylight hours people occupied themselves much as they did in the summer, but during the long hours of darkness they lay in their warm sleeping bags and chatted, told stories, sang songs, or just slept. Boredom must have been a major problem, which may account at least in part for their willingness to make long winter excursions to trade at Churchill, on the coast, or at Brochet, in the interior.

When people travelled they hauled their baggage on long (c. 750 cm), low (10 cm), narrow (42 cm) sleds, which looked more like ladders than sleds capable of hauling 500 kilograms. In the morning, people loaded the sleds and, pushing and pulling along with the dogs, moved out slowly. When travelling downwind they erected sails and let the wind do the work. When darkness began to fall, they built new snow houses and created a new settlement within an hour or two.

Religion

The Caribou Inuit believed that a spirit called Hila constituted the supreme force underlying all phenomena. This general force also had a special female form, Pinga, which dwelt somewhere in space. It was Pinga who made it possible for people to live in the world, who kept a close watch on human activities, and who intervened from time to time in people's affairs. Hila determined which acts were good and which were bad, but Pinga was the spirit who monitored people's behaviour. The soul of a person who had lived according to the rules laid down by Hila was believed to ascend at death to Pinga. That spirit received it in space and subsequently returned it to earth in the body of an animal, human, or otherwise. The souls of persons who had not lived properly, on the other hand, were condemned to eternal misery, somewhere outside the earthly domain.

Caribou Inuit did not pretend to know much about the spirit world. What knowledge they did have was acquired by their shamans, or *angakut* (plural). The primary duty of a shaman was to act as intermediary between the human and spiritual worlds. By communicating with Hila, a shaman could determine the cause of a problem and ascertain its solution. The latter invariably involved adherence to one or more taboos stipulated by the spirit. In addition, a shaman could perform magic of various kinds and make certain kinds of predictions about the future.

Caribou Inuit religion, while ostensibly quite otherworldly, had a considerable immediacy about it. One did not spend time worshipping an intangible and dimly perceived God or contemplating a satisfactory reincarnation in the next life. Rather, one tried to sustain oneself in this difficult life by conforming to an extensive set of rules governing quite specific acts. Indeed, practically every act was governed by some taboo: the technique, timing, and location of the hunt; the technique and timing of butchering; birth and death; menstruation; eating—these and more were governed by taboos so numerous that no one could remember them all.

Taboos were laid down by Hila, and obedience to them helped maintain a balance of amicable relations with that power. If people disobeyed them, on the other hand, Hila subjected them to hunger, sickness, bad weather, or other calamity. Observance of the rules was basically an individual matter, but a transgression by one person often resulted in punishment being visited upon an entire settlement. It was therefore in everyone's best interest not only to watch one's own behaviour but also to monitor that of one's neighbours.

Misfortune was usually interpreted as a sign that a taboo had been broken. In order to determine what was involved, a shaman went into a trance to contact Hila, who specified who had committed what particular offence and stipulated the procedures necessary to rectify the situation (and perhaps also to prevent its recurrence). It was through this oft-repeated sequence that the extensive body of taboos governing Caribou Inuit life gradually developed, probably over hundreds of years. Since Hila apparently would not entertain general questions, the shamans were denied the kind of comprehensive revelation that has led to the development of more complex religions in other parts of the world.

Concluding Remarks

This brief summary of the structure of Caribou Inuit societies during the Classic Period depicts a system that, even after nearly two centuries of contact with Westerners, was thoroughly non-European, not only in its basic structure but in almost every detail. The Caribou Inuit were still very much in control of their own affairs. Despite the fact that their land was one of the least hospitable areas in the world, they remained in their own country, dealt with life's problems in their own ways, and generally remained aloof from the wider world of whose existence they had long been at least vaguely aware.

Denouement

From the time of first known contact in 1631, when Luke Foxe sailed down the west coast of Hudson Bay, until 1903, when the government of Canada decided to assert its control over the region, Europeans had little interest in Caribou Inuit territory or in the people who occupied it. A few outsiders had visited the region to explore, while others had come to hunt whales or trade for furs, but all remained for just a little while, then left.

This geographic isolation began to be broken when the North-West (later, Royal Canadian) Mounted Police established a post at Cape Fullerton, on the northeastern fringe of Caribou Inuit territory, in the summer of 1903. The police established the post partly to keep an eye on American whalers, and partly to establish an official Canadian presence in a land whose ownership was not yet established in international law.

In the summer of 1912, both the Roman Catholic Church and the HBC established permanent posts on the south side of Chesterfield Inlet, right in Caribou Inuit country. Over the next two decades tiny Euro-Canadian settlements sprang up at a few widely scattered points across the region. The largest contained an RCMP post, an HBC trading post, sometimes a competing trader or two, and two missions, one Anglican, the other Roman Catholic. The missionaries often ran schools, in addition to trying to convert the Inuit to Christianity. Traders, police, and missionaries all tried to influence the Inuit in one way or another, and they competed in attempting to achieve a dominant position. During the early years, however, the Inuit remained almost as aloof as ever.

The event that did more than anything else to terminate Caribou Inuit societies was the "Great Famine" that began in 1915. For reasons that remain unclear, caribou fled the country. Unfortunately for the Inuit, the muskoxen, which had played a crucial role in their original inland expansion, had been all but exterminated.

People turned to fish, but they had only hook and line with which to catch them. Weakened by hunger, they chopped holes through the thick ice in the lakes and jigged their lures, but with little success. Eventually they slaughtered their dogs and ate them, and even ate pieces of boiled skin clothing. The famine continued for years. It was not until the fall of 1924 that caribou returned in some numbers to the Qairnirmiut sector, and not until the following summer that they reached Ahiarmiut country again. The precise figures remain debatable, but in 1915 there were probably some 1,500 Caribou Inuit. In 1925 only about 500 remained.

BOX 5.2 On Doing Anthropology

It is one of the great ironies of Arctic ethnography that Kaj Birket-Smith and Knud Rasmussen made their observations near the end of the Great Famine of 1915–25, probably the lowest point for the Caribou Inuit in 200 years. Their "definitive ethnography," which has been widely cited in the anthropological literature, was actually a description of a people on the verge of extinction.

In desperation, the Inuit turned to outsiders for help. Police, missionaries, and traders tried to assist them, but there was little they could do. The Inuit starved and died in their isolated camps as they had lived, on their own.

Eventually, the Great Famine led the Caribou Inuit to become trappers. Previously, they believed that, despite periodic fluctuations, caribou would never forsake them for long. And if they ran out of caribou meat for a while, they could always turn to muskoxen, which did not travel far, were easily killed, and whose general whereabouts were well known. By 1915, however, the muskoxen were gone, and by 1920 people realized that total reliance on caribou was fatal. But, as luck would have it, the price of a white fox pelt, which was the only fur the Barren Lands had in abundance, increased significantly after World War I. Thus, for the first time in their history, the Caribou Inuit could turn to fur trapping as a realistic way to make a living.

Somehow a few people managed to survive, but the societies to which they belonged did not. Their populations were so reduced in size that they could not maintain their independence. By 1922, what in 1915 had been five and possibly six societies had merged into a single unit consisting of five regional bands. Each of the latter was the remnant of a former society. The Tahiuyarmiut, who were in the process of splitting off from the Paatlirmiut and becoming a sixth society when the famine began, were reduced to only a few individuals.

During the period from 1915 to 1945, several additional developments contributed to the erosion of Caribou Inuit autonomy. One, noted previously, was the gradual expansion of police, missionary, and trading operations all across what was then the southern part of the Keewatin District of the Northwest Territories. Another was the migration of members of other Inuit groups to the northern fringe of the region. Some of them came from the northern Hudson Bay and Foxe Basin coasts. These were members of the Aivilik branch of the Iglulingmiut and descendants of Netsilingmiut, who previously had migrated eastward to the Hudson Bay coast, attracted there by the prospect of trade with American whalers. Both groups were drawn by the trading post at Cape Fullerton, and later by the one at Chesterfield Inlet. Somewhat later still, other Netsilingmiut from the Back River area also moved south, attracted by the timber along the Thelon River and by the opportunities for trade at Baker Lake.

While these incursions were taking place in the northeastern and northwestern sectors of the region, the people continued to suffer periodic famine farther south. None of these misfortunes was as geographically extensive or as prolonged as the disaster of 1915–25, but each regional band was struck by more than one period of extreme hunger during which many people died. The Qairnirmiut, and particularly the Hauniqturmiut, began to fragment under the pressure, and the surviving families began to disperse in an effort to find game. Epidemics took an even greater toll.

The nadir was reached in 1948, when a combination of tuberculosis, influenza, and infantile paralysis reached such an extreme state that the entire district was placed under quarantine for almost two years by the Canadian government. Seriously ill people cannot hunt, so epidemics were invariably accompanied by famine.

Concern on the part of missionaries, police, and government officials, and a storm of public outrage stimulated by the writings of Farley Mowat and Richard Harrington, led the government to take a more active interest in the early 1950s. Administrative centres were set up in the old communities of Baker Lake, Chesterfield Inlet, and Eskimo Point, and new settlements were established at Whale Cove and Rankin Inlet, the latter in conjunction with a mining operation.

In the late 1950s, the government confronted a dilemma. On the one hand, the combination of genuine concern and political pressure dictated that something be done to help the starving Inuit. On the other hand, Canadian taxpayers did not want to foot much of a bill for whatever action was taken. Regular monitoring of conditions in and the provision of adequate medical and other assistance to the tiny, widely scattered camps would have been prohibitively expensive. Consequently, officials decided to concentrate both the Caribou Inuit and the Netsilik and Aivilik immigrants in the five administrative centres.

By 1968 the centralization process was complete. Of the five settlements, only Arviat (formerly Eskimo Point) was inhabited primarily by people of Caribou Inuit extraction. Baker Lake and Whale Cove each contained, in addition to Caribou Inuit, significant numbers of Netsilik, Aivilik, and other Inuit immigrants. Rankin Inlet was largely Aivilik, and Chesterfield Inlet was primarily Netsilik.

Vastly improved medical care and other government services helped the Inuit population of the region rise dramatically during the final decades of the twentieth century. In 1996, nearly 4,900 Inuit lived in the five administrative centres, along with some 760 non-Inuit. Thirty years of living together in the same settlements and of intermarriage had blurred the ancient boundaries between Inuit groups. Elders had not forgotten their roots, but people came to be identified more by the settlement in which they lived than by the society or regional band to which their ancestors once belonged. As this transition occurred, "Caribou Inuit," which was not an Inuit concept but a useful anthropological referent until the late 1960s, rapidly lost its currency. The label remains useful with reference to the past, but not to the present.

Recent Period

On 1 April 1999, the area of interest here became the southern portion of the Kivalliq Region, Nunavut territory, instead of the southern portion of the District of Keewatin, Northwest Territories. The population is now distributed among the five previously existing administrative centres, which are now designated as "hamlets" (see Map 5.2). Locally elected councils, chaired by mayors, give the residents of each community a relatively high level of self-government. Offences against local regulations are dealt with by Inuit bylaw officers and justices, although the RCMP remains responsible for dealing with more serious issues. Formal education and health care are provided by the territorial government. Roman Catholic and Anglican missions have been supplemented by those of a number of other religious groups. Inuktitut is still the first language, but is being replaced rapidly by English.

The biggest problem facing the people of southern Kivalliq today is how to make a living without leaving their traditional homeland. Inuit can still meet many of their food needs by hunting and fishing, and they travel long distances across their territory, especially by snowmobile, to find game. However, they need a cash income to acquire equipment and fuel, not to mention clothing, and houses to keep themselves in a semi-urban setting.

Trapping can provide some cash, but not enough to live on. The country is rich in minerals, but at current price levels no one can afford to extract them and take them to market. Located far from population centres, industries of even modest size are unlikely to locate here at any time in the foreseeable future. The rivers and lakes can provide excitement for a few adventuresome canoeists and fishers as well as income for outfitters who look after them, but the landscape is too bleak and homogeneous to attract large numbers of tourists. The production of carvings and other forms of art is one possibility—and, indeed, some of the finest artists in Canada live in the region—but this can never support more than a small percentage of the population. Considerable effort is devoted

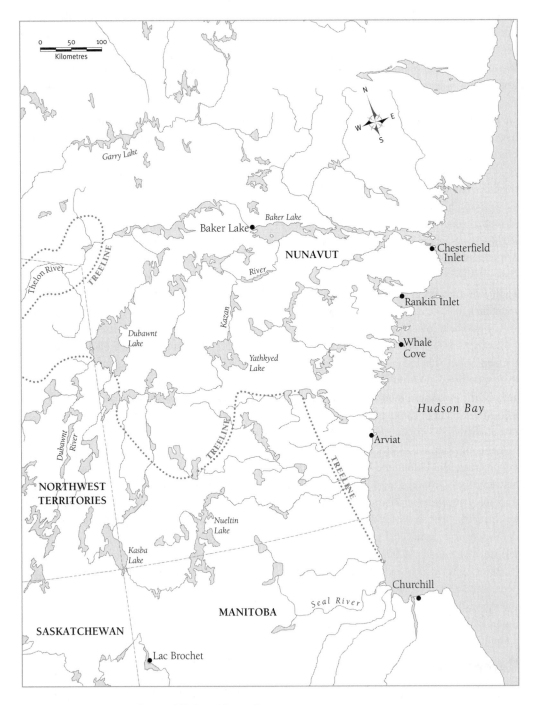

MAP 5.2 Modern Hamlets and Political Boundaries

to preparing Inuit to fill locally available jobs, but there are not enough positions to go around.

The Inuit residents of southern Kivalliq enter the twenty-first century in complex and generally difficult circumstances. On the one hand, they have regained a measure of local and regional control over their affairs, which they had nearly lost after they were concentrated in hamlets. Most live on or near lands inhabited by their ancestors, and the extended family remains a central focus of people's social networks. On the other hand, they have been forced by hard times and a rapidly changing cultural environment to abandon their traditional way of life. Because of their geographic isolation, they cannot participate as constructively as they might like in the modern Canadian way of life. As a result, apathy is widespread, and rates of sexual abuse, substance abuse, domestic violence, parental neglect, and suicide are at comparatively high levels.

The obvious alternative—leaving the North for cities in the south—does not offer much promise. Only slightly prepared by training and experience for urban life, confronted by widespread discrimination, and isolated from family and friends, the urban Inuk often has an even harder time than his rural counterpart. Most people living in northern settlements have heard about these difficulties and are reluctant to try city life themselves.

Conclusion

Having information on even the general outlines of the lifeways of a particular population of hunter–gatherers over nearly 300 years is very rare in anthropology. That it is possible in the Caribou Inuit case is due to fortuitous circumstances. Among them are the following: (1) the frequent but peculiarly casual contacts between Inuit and HBC traders during the eighteenth and nineteenth centuries; (2) splendid HBC record-keeping during that era; (3) the fact that the Caribou Inuit homeland did not offer enough attractions to Westerners to draw them there on a permanent basis until well into the twentieth century; and (4) the fact that the Inuit were content enough with life in their homeland to resist the temptation to move elsewhere.

One general lesson we can take away from the history of southern Kivalliq is that change is continuous in all human societies. This is true even of those that, like the Caribou Inuit, are organized along very simple lines. Therefore, it is incumbent on the author of every ethnographic account to state the specific period to which that account pertains. It is incorrect to treat the past as an undifferentiated whole, no matter what society is involved. Separate descriptions of Caribou Inuit societies in 1750, 1825, 1890, and 1925 would produce significantly different pictures. This is so even though the people were members of relatively simple hunter–gatherer societies throughout, and even though the people living in later periods were direct cultural and biological descendants of those in the earlier ones.

NOTES

1. Ernest "Tiger" Burch died in 2010. His scholarly and careful ethnohistoric writings are widely admired for their detail and insight. This chapter is a very lightly edited version of the one he submitted before his death. For a fuller account of his accomplishments please see: http://pubs.aina.ucalgary.ca/arctic/Arctic64-2-261.pdf

2. In the 1970s, the Native term "Inuit" began to be used instead of the foreign term "Eskimo" for the Inuit-speaking residents of the central and eastern

Canadian Arctic, with the result that "Caribou Inuit" replaced "Caribou Eskimo." In this posthumous edition of the chapter, we have used "Inuit" in all cases where this is temporally accurate.

3. From 1968 to 1974 the research on which this chapter is based was supported by the Canada Council (now the Social Sciences and Humanities Research Council of Canada). Since 1974, I have continued it on my own as time and resources permitted.

4. At the beginning of the twenty-first century, the climate is probably warmer than these late twentieth-century temperature figures indicate. In the eighteenth and nineteenth centuries, the climate was noticeably colder.

5. The sources on which this historical summary is based include a number of published documents, and the following unpublished records: (a) HBC Archives: Churchill post journals, sloop and ship logs, correspondence, accounts of trade, and miscellaneous other records, from 1717 to the early twentieth century; (b) National Archives of Canada: Record Group 18, Records of the RCMP; Record Group 85, and Records of the Northern Administration Branch; (c) original field journals and other records compiled by J. Burr Tyrrell in 1893 and 1894, housed at the National Archives of Canada, Record Group 45, Reports of the Geological Survey of Canada, and in Manuscript Collection No. 26, in the Thomas Fisher Rare Book Library, John P. Robarts Research Library Complex, University of Toronto.

6. This reconstruction of the "classic period" is based primarily on information acquired from Inuit Elders interviewed by T.C. Correll or me from 1968 to 1970, on HBC records of the period, and on Birket-Smith (1929, I), Boas (1901, 1907), Rasmussen (1930), Turquetil (1907, 1926), J.B. Tyrrell (1897), and J.W. Tyrrell (1898).

REFERENCES AND RECOMMENDED READINGS

Birket-Smith, Kaj. 1929. *The Caribou Eskimos: Material and Social Life and Their Cultural Position.* Copenhagen: Report of the Fifth Thule Expedition 1921–4, vol. 5, parts I and II. Part I of this substantial work, together with Rasmussen's 1930 volume, constitutes the basic ethnography of the Caribou Inuit. It focuses primarily on economic and technological matters. Part II, a reconstruction of Inuit history and prehistory, is an extraordinary example of reasoning that was outmoded even at the time it was published, using atemporal distributional data to draw temporal conclusions.

Boas, Franz. 1901. "The Eskimo of Baffin Land and Hudson Bay," *Bulletin of the American Museum of Natural History,* 15, part I.

———. 1907. "Second Report on the Eskimo of Baffin Land and Hudson Bay," *Bulletin of the American Museum of Natural History*, 15, part II.

Burch, Ernest S., Jr. 1976. "Caribou Eskimo Origins: An Old Problem Reconsidered," *Arctic Anthropology* 15, 1: 1–35. A comprehensive review of the literature dealing with Caribou Inuit origins. The historical sequence outlined in the present chapter begins where this article ends.

———. 1977. "Muskox and Man in the Central Canadian Subarctic, 1689–1974," *Arctic* 30, 3: 135–54. This article describes how and why the Caribou Inuit nearly exterminated muskoxen from their country. It was published at a time when most scholars believed that only Westerners were capable of destroying one of their major resources.

Csonka, Yvon. 1995. *Les Ahiarmiut. À l'écart des Inuit Caribous.* Neuchâtel, Switzerland: Editions Victor Attinger. This elegantly written study of the Ahiarmiut concerns a Caribou Inuit group that the Fifth Thule Expedition entirely missed. It contains a thorough literature review, information on social change and Chipewyan–Inuit relations, and many useful maps and photographs.

Fossett, Renée. 2001. *In Order to Live Untroubled: Inuit of the Central Arctic, 1550 to 1940.* Winnipeg: University of Manitoba Press. A general historical summary of most of the Inuit populations of the central and eastern Canadian Arctic. The sections dealing with the Caribou Inuit region are particularly well informed.

Rasmussen, Knud. 1930. *Observations on the Intellectual Culture of the Caribou Eskimos.* Copenhagen: Report of the Fifth Thule Expedition 1921–4, vol. 7, no. 2. This monograph is a companion to Birket-Smith's. The two stand together as the major ethnographic account of Caribou Inuit culture. Rasmussen, like Birket-Smith, was a poor historian, but he had as much insight into Inuit thought processes as anyone who ever wrote on the subject.

Smith, James G.E., and Ernest S. Burch Jr. 1979. "Chipewyan and Inuit in the Central Canadian Subarctic, 1613–1977," *Arctic Anthropology* 16, 2: 76–101. The Chipewyan and Caribou Inuit were invariably described in the pre-1979 literature as having been in a state of perpetual armed conflict. This article shows that Chipewyan–Caribou Inuit relations were more complex than previously thought, and were often peaceful.

Turquetil, Arsène. 1907. "Première tentative d'apostolat chez les Esquimaux," *Missions de la Congregation des Missionnaires Oblats de Marie Immaculée* 45: 330, 353, 484–503.

———. 1926. "Notes sur les Esquimaux de Baie Hudson," *Anthropos Ephemeris Internationalis. Ethnologica et Linguistica* 21: 419–34.

Tyrrell, J. Burr. 1897. *Report on the Doobaunt, Kazan and Ferguson Rivers, and the North-west coast of Hudson Bay, and on two Overland Routes from Hudson Bay to Lake Winnipeg.* Ottawa: Geological Survey of Canada. (Ninth Annual Report, part F.)

Tyrrell, James Williams. 1898. *Across the Sub-Arctics of Canada, a Journey of 3,200 Miles by Canoe and Snowshoe through the Barren Lands.* London: T.F. Unwin.

Vallee, Frank G. 1967. *Kabloona and Eskimo in the Central Keewatin.* Ottawa: Canadian Research Centre for Anthropology, St Paul University. The most comprehensive account of the Caribou Inuit in the late 1950s, it is arguably one of the best monographs on any Inuit group from that era. Its focus is on the northern part of Caribou Inuit territory.

VanStone, James W., and Wendell H. Oswalt. 1959. *The Caribou Eskimos of Eskimo Point.* Ottawa: Department of Northern Affairs and National Resources, Northern Co-ordination and Research Centre (NRCRC–59–2). This short monograph describes Caribou Inuit life in or near Eskimo Point (now Arviat) in the middle and late 1950s. It is a useful summary of the southern sector of the Caribou Inuit region at the time.

PART III

The Eastern Subarctic

CHAPTER 6

The Eastern Subarctic: A Regional Overview

Jennifer S.H. Brown and C. Roderick Wilson

The Eastern Subarctic is sometimes referred to as the Northern Algonquian culture area because the entire region is occupied by a branch of the widespread Algonquian-speaking peoples. The surviving languages form two series of closely related dialects that are grouped into two languages, Cree and Ojibway. That is, both languages have spread over such vast distances that considerable variation has arisen, yet with enough continued interaction between regions that the differences between adjacent dialects is relatively minor. Confusingly, both Cree and Ojibway are simultaneously also spoken of in English as being two "tribes" (see Chapter 1). Our usual terminology does not reflect this understanding very well: old-fashioned terms, such as "Naskapi," implied the status of being a separate language, rather than being a dialect of Cree. Its modern replacement, Innu, has the same implication. Another older term, "Tête-de-Boule Cree," had the advantage of clearly indicating linguistic affinity, as its contemporary replacement, "Atikamekw," does not. The latter term, however, has the still greater advantage, like Innu, of being what the people call themselves! It must also be noted that in recent years the term "Anishnabe" has largely replaced "Ojibway."

In any case, Cree and Ojibway seem to have developed independently from Proto-Algonquian, possibly separating about 3,000 years ago. The relationship between the dialects of these languages is quite complex, in part because in historic times (and earlier?) whole groups of people have shifted from one dialect to another.

The inhabitants of any region must come to terms with their environment. The Eastern Subarctic is characterized by long winters, short summers, and a continental climate. The generally cold climate is also related to the jet streams, which, passing from west to east, tend to draw arctic high-pressure air masses to the southeast. In spring and summer, intensified sunlight decreases the dominance of arctic air, so seasonal contrasts are strong. Minimum–maximum daily mean temperatures in the Severn River drainage in northern Ontario, for example, range from between –29°C and –19°C in January to between 11°C and 21°C in July. But even hot summer days may soon be followed by frost, and variations from the average can be considerable in either direction.

Precipitation in much of the area is relatively light. Total annual precipitation in northern Ontario averages only about 60 centimetres, most of it coming in summer thunderstorms. However, the climate east of James Bay is much affected by Hudson Bay. Air currents in fall and early winter pick up moisture from Hudson Bay to dump it along the eastern shores and inland. From midwinter to early summer, the Bay remains ice-covered, depressing temperatures and delaying the coming of spring in lands to the east. As a consequence, this area experiences very heavy snowfall and cold temperatures.

The presence of such extreme climatic conditions in these latitudes was difficult for Europeans to accept. When in 1749 the Hudson's Bay Company faced a parliamentary inquiry into its conduct, critics complained that it had not established agriculture and colonies around Hudson Bay and asserted that company representatives must be lying about the climate; after all, Fort York was on the same latitude as Stockholm, Sweden, and Bergen, Norway; and the Severn River was on a level with Edinburgh, Copenhagen, and Moscow. The critics' ignorance was pardonable, however. Fuller understandings of the effects of large-scale and even global weather patterns on the region have only recently been developed. Current research, in fact, is drawing on Hudson's Bay Company journals from the eighteenth and nineteenth centuries to trace the regional weather patterns.

Northern Algonquians have therefore long been adapting, with a success that startled their early, ill-equipped European visitors, not only to cold, but to unpredictable and extreme climatic conditions. A late spring, for instance, would mean late breakup of lakes and rivers for travel and late arrival of migrating geese and other birds important as food. Less moisture than usual meant, among other things, less snow cover, meaning in turn less shelter and lower survival rates for some basic food sources such as ptarmigan, hare, and other ground-dwelling animals. Drying of streams is a serious impediment when the movements of people to different seasonally used food resources (between winter hunting camps and summer fishing spots, for example) depend on canoe transport. Excess precipitation would bring floods, mud-filled portages, and swollen rapids dangerous to small vessels.

The landforms, rocks, and soils of the Algonquian Subarctic support many forms of life, but they, too, pose challenges and constraints. The Canadian Shield is the single topographic feature that has most influenced the shape of Northern Algonquian life. Even a casual traveller sees how this rough rock base, polished clean in places by glaciers and overlain in other places by glacial clays, sand, and gravel, provides the contours for countless lakes, streams, and swamps—ideal habitat for beaver, muskrat, and other animal species long important for food and furs. The French who reached present-day Ontario in the seventeenth century found that the Hurons valued the trade furs and leather they received from the Algonkin, Nipissing, Odawa, Ojibway, and others who made their home in the Shield region. And these Algonquian groups in turn valued their trade with the Hurons, prizing in particular Huron cornmeal.

The Shield country in central Ontario and Quebec is transitional between temperate and Subarctic. The observant traveller notices, going north, that the mixed deciduous trees of the south yield increasingly to evergreens—white and red pines mingled with spruce—then to a predominance of black spruce. Continuing northward the landscape changes again. The rocks of the Canadian Shield mostly disappear. The Hudson Bay Lowland—a spruce-dominated forest on poorly drained, clayey soil—covers an area west and south of James Bay. The growing season is short and intense throughout the Algonquian Subarctic. People intensify their activities, taking advantage of the open waters, the fisheries and waterfowl, and such plants as blueberries, which can be harvested only for a few short weeks.

The landscape presents limits of various kinds to its occupants, and anthropologists and other Western scientists are only now beginning to appreciate the extent to which Aboriginal peoples interacted with the environment. Europeans, for example, have always described the forests they found in America as "virgin," "primeval," "wilderness," and so on. In contrast, the forests not only were occupied, but their productivity was actively managed and maintained. We have long been aware that one could manage game directly by varying the intensity of hunting; it is now clear that Native peoples also managed game levels indirectly by manipulating the environment, primarily through the selective use of fire.

Small, carefully located and timed fires were extensively used to hasten new growth in the spring, which would attract desired animals and birds, foster desired plants such as blueberries and raspberries, create a more varied habitat that would support larger numbers of animals, and open up areas for travel and hunting. Some species that benefited from controlled burning were moose, deer, beaver, muskrat, bear, and ducks. Other species, notably caribou, require the mosses and lichens of mature, "climax" forests. Where caribou was the preferred basic resource, as it was in the northerly parts of the region, the use of fire was lessened. The choice was not simply a matter of food preferences but ultimately one of social organization, since the strategies for hunting solitary and herd animals vary substantially. In either case, the forest was not something simply provided by nature.

Changing patterns of human activity have also been major determinants of Northern Algonquian life. Because the following chapters are strongly historical in orientation, the historic context for the region will be limited to two generalizations. First, despite the fact that large numbers of its contemporary inhabitants pursue lifeways that are seen as strongly "traditional," this region had an extremely long period of contact with Europeans. Almost certainly its southeastern reaches along the St Lawrence River were visited by Bretons before 1500, and by 1670 the Hudson's Bay Company had initiated trade in the more northerly Hudson drainage. First European contact for the Cree in the

northwestern corner of the Eastern Subarctic was only a few years prior to the first direct contacts for their closest neighbours in the Western Subarctic, the Chipewyan. As a whole, contact in the east of the region was substantially earlier—in some cases more than 350 years earlier.

Partly because of the length of the cultural contact, people's lives over the years have changed substantially. Again, this is most true of the south and of the coastal regions, but it also places the Eastern Subarctic as a region in contrast to the Western Subarctic. This region saw very early missionizing of its people, early exposure to new diseases, and generally a greater involvement in the fur trade than similar zones further west. As an extreme example, by the end of the era of competitive fur exploitation (1763–1821) between the Hudson's Bay Company and its Montreal rival, the North West Company, in some areas the dominant resource bases, caribou and moose, had been virtually exterminated. A consequence of this longer and more intense period of cultural contact in the Eastern Subarctic than in the West is that we are less sure of what the eastern Aboriginal life patterns and beliefs were. On the other hand, in the east there is substantial historic (European) documentation of events dating from the early seventeenth century, for which there is no parallel in the Western Subarctic.

There follow three final points of general relevance. First, there is always the problem of sources—which voices have spoken to us and why. Native voices are rarely heard from the documentary record, and, when they are, they are often reported at second or third hand.

A second matter is that of homogeneity versus local variability. A superficial observer sees a great sameness: Algonquian hunters inhabiting a vast, cold, mainly spruce-covered region. In fact, local variations—the shape of a lake, the slope of the land, pockets of soil—produce a considerable range of micro-environments. Where local food

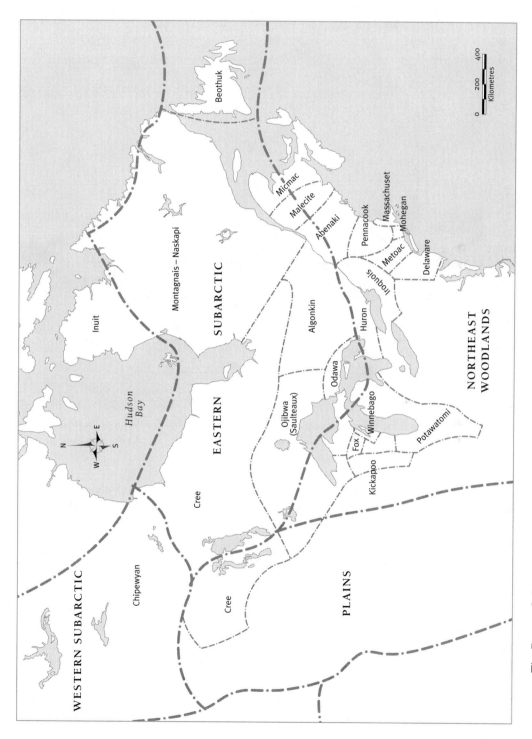

Beothuk

Micmac

Malecite

Abenaki

Pennacook

Massachuset

Mohegan

Metoac

Delaware

Iroquois

Montagnais – Naskapi

SUBARCTIC

Inuit

Algonkin

Huron

EASTERN

Hudson
Bay

Odawa

N
E
W
S

Winnebago

Ojibwa
(Saulteaux)

Fox

Potawatomi

NORTHEAST
WOODLANDS

Cree

Kickapoo

WESTERN SUBARCTIC

Chipewyan

Cree

PLAINS

0   200   400
Kilometres

MAP 6.1 The Eastern Subarctic

FIGURE 6.1 Hudson's Bay Company post at Moose Factory on James Bay, 1934. (Courtesy of the Hudson's Bay Company Archives, Archives of Manitoba. HBCA 1987/363-M-100/22 HBC post at Moose Factory.)

resources, particularly game, are not evenly distributed, people have reacted in even more complex fashion. Furthermore, their lives have never been solely subsistence-oriented. They evolved distinctive social traditions, world views, and cultural and religious patterns that had their own dynamics of variability and conformity.

Superficial generalization is accordingly to be avoided. The challenge is to get beyond the simple traditional stereotype of hunters in wigwams, or the more modern one of isolated northern villages, to begin to know the Northern Algonquians as complex, diverse human beings whose lives have their own historic richness and vitality. We close with a series of contemporary facts that

have implications worth pondering. Cree children who first learn to read in Cree, reading stories produced in their home community, later learn to read English or French better than their older siblings did. Some families strategize by ensuring that some children learn the old bush skills and sending others to university. The Grand Council of the Crees and similar regional Aboriginal governing bodies are rooted in traditional ways of doing things; they also are contemporary political innovations of the first order. A final word: however momentous contemporary innovations in Aboriginal life may seem, they always seem also to be rooted in and flow from established ways of doing things.

CHAPTER 7

Hunting and the Quest for Power: Relationships between James Bay Crees, the Land, and Developers

Harvey A. Feit

Introduction

Hunting and "quests for power" mean different things to different people. The "quest for power" is a metaphor the James Bay Crees might use for the life of a hunter; it is also a metaphor other Canadians might use for the goals of both northern developers and government bureaucracies. In this chapter I consider these different ideas of hunting, power, and development, and I show how the way each group uses them is related to their relationships to the environment and to other peoples.

The way I approach these questions is to look first at how James Bay Cree people typically talk and think about themselves and about others in their world, and at what kind of relationships they develop. Some people, such as the Crees, approach relationships as the foundations of life. Family relations make it possible to grow into adulthood, social relations make it possible to become a full individual by learning how to be a person from interactions with others, and careful environmental relations make it possible for present and future generations to survive in the world. Many others approach relationships solely as things which individuals create for their own purposes. For them relationships can be ignored because they think that individuals are separable from their relations to kin, society, and the world. In the

second half of this chapter I focus on how the governments of Canada and Quebec have tried to use or deny relationships in order to control the James Bay Crees, and how the Crees have sought to exercise their autonomy by enhancing recognition of relationships. This part traces the court challenges, the environmental campaigns, and the negotiations and agreements that the Crees have used to continue to coexist with developers on the Cree's homeland. In doing this I show how environment and politics are intertwined in relationships and conflicts over who governs the James Bay region and how it is to be developed.

The James Bay Cree region lies to the east and southeast of James Bay and southeast of Hudson Bay. Crees have lived there since the glaciers left about 9,000 years ago. They now number some 14,000 people and live in nine settlements from which they hunt approximately 375,000 square kilometres of land. (In this chapter the word "Crees" refers specifically to the James Bay Crees.)

I first visited the region in 1968 when I began my doctoral research on hunters of the Cree community of Waswanipi. My interest in hunting arose from a concern for the relationships between Western societies and their environments. I had read often in the human ecology literature that Indigenous peoples had a different relationship with nature, but I found the accounts in that literature often vague and romantic. I thought an "on-the-ground" study of Cree–environment relationships could help revise the popular images of Indigenous peoples as ecological saints or wanton over-exploiters and could develop a practical understanding of the real accomplishments and limitations of one group's approach to environmental relationships. I think I was partially able to accomplish this goal, but with Cree tutelage and encouragement I also learned things I had not foreseen. These are probably best described as lessons in the sacredness of the everyday, the practicality of wisdom, and the importance of relationships and **reciprocity**.

When the Crees began their opposition to the James Bay hydroelectric scheme in 1972, they asked if I would present some of my research to the courts and then use it in the negotiations. It was an unexpected happenstance that my research proved to be of some use to the Crees, and one for which I was thankful. I served as an advisor to Cree organizations during the negotiation and implementation of the James Bay and Northern Quebec Agreement, regularly from 1973 through 1978 and occasionally thereafter.

Contemporary Cree Hunting Culture

Hunting in a Personal and Social Environment

We can develop an understanding of how the Crees think about hunting and themselves and their world by considering the different meanings conveyed by their word for hunting. Their concept of hunting is very different from the everyday understandings of most North Americans. However odd the Cree conception may appear at first, it not only has logic when understood in the context of Cree life and environment, but also has important affinities with the discoveries of eco-

logical scientists. These analogies may help us to better understand Cree thought, although they will not make the Crees out to be secular scientists or transform scientists into effective but responsible hunters.

Animal Gifts

Ndoho, the Cree term that is roughly translated as "hunting, fishing, and trapping on the land," is related to a series of words about hunting. At least five basic meanings are associated with this root term for hunting: to see or to look at something; to go to get or to fetch something; to need something; to want something; and to grow or continue to grow.

That hunting should be thought of as a process of looking is apparent. Hunting is typically a process of seeing signs of the presence of animals—tracks, spoor, feeding or living areas—and of then seeking to encounter the animals to kill them. But the proposition that hunting is "looking" also emphasizes uncertainty. The Cree view is that most animals are shy, retiring, and not easily visible, and hunting therefore involves an expectation as well as an activity.[1] The hunter goes through a process of finding indications of possible encounters with animals; if the animal appears and the hunt is successful, they fulfill their anticipation. We will see below how this anticipation plays a role in Cree understandings.

That a successful hunt should also be conceptualized as getting or fetching animals is also apparent, but part of what the Crees mean by this is different from what non-Crees might assume. To get an animal in the view of many Crees does not mean to encounter it by chance, but to receive it. The animal is given to the hunter. A successful hunt is not simply the result of the intention and work of the hunter; it is also the outcome of the intention and actions of animals. In the process of hunting, a hunter enters into a reciprocal relationship: animals are given to hunters to meet their needs and wants, and in return hunters incur obligations to animals. This understanding of hunting involves a complex social and moral relationship of reciprocity in which the outcome of the hunt is a result of the mutual efforts of the hunter and an active environment. This is a subtle and accurate perspective, somewhat like the ecological insights that have become prominent recently both in science and popular culture.

It may seem odd or self-serving that animal kills should be conceptualized by hunters as gifts, and it is important therefore to note that Crees do not radically separate the concepts of "human" and "animal." In their everyday experience on the land they continually observe examples of the intelligence, personalities, and willpower of animals. They say that animals are "like persons"; animals act, they are capable of independent choices, and they are causally responsible for things they do.

For the Cree hunter these are everyday observations. Evidence of intelligence is cited from several sources. One type is that each animal has its own way of living and thinking. Each responds to environmental circumstances in ways that humans can recognize as appropriate. Each has its own preparations for winter: beavers build complex lodges; bears build dens; ducks and geese migrate. Each also relates to, and communicates with, members of its species. For example, beavers establish three-generational colonies built around a monogamous couple. Geese mate for life and have complex patterns of flock leadership. And inter-species communication is indicated by the intelligent response of animals to the efforts of hunters. Some beaver will place mud on top of a trap and then eat the poplar branches left as lure and a gift by the hunter. Each animal has special mental characteristics: beavers are stubborn and persistent, bears are intelligent, wolves are fearless,

grouse are stupid. Further, animals have emotions and may be "scared" or "mad" when they avoid hunters.

That animals give themselves is indicated in part by their typical reactions to hunters. When a bear den is found in winter, a hunter will address the bear and tell it to come out. And bears do awake, come out of their dens sluggishly, and get killed. That such a powerful, intelligent, and potentially dangerous animal can be so docile is significant for Crees. The behaviour of moose is also telling. Moose bed down facing into the wind, so that air does not penetrate under their hair. When a hunter approaches from downwind, he comes upon it from behind. A moose typically takes flight only after scenting or seeing a source of danger. It therefore rises up when it hears a hunter approach and turns in the direction of the noise to locate and scent the source. In this gesture, taking 10 to 15 seconds, the moose gives itself to the hunter by turning and looking at the hunter.

The extensive knowledge Cree hunters have of animals becomes, therefore, a basis for their understanding that animals are given. The concept of an animal gift indicates that killing an animal is not solely the result of the knowledge, will, and action of humans, however necessary these are, but that the most important reasons for the gift lie in the relationships of the givers and receivers. Because animals are capable of intelligent thought and social action they are not considered as being like children, as is common among other Canadians. For Crees animals are autonomous persons who live free lives on the land, and who act as responsible and caring adults. It is not only possible for them to understand humans and their needs, but for them to give themselves for humans. Doing so helps humans and it creates the conditions for animals and humans to coexist. Saying that the animals are gifts therefore emphasizes that the hunter must responsibly adapt his hunt to what he learns from and knows about the animals he hunts. To see how this works we must examine the Cree world.

The Hunters' World

Because animals are gifts, it is appropriate to ask Cree hunters, "Who gives the animal?" Their answers lead us to important features of Cree logic and cosmology. Recurrent answers are that animals do not only give themselves, but they are given by the "wind persons" and by God or Jesus.

Just as animals are like persons, so are phenomena that we do not consider to be living. Active phenomena such as winds and water, as well as God and various spirit beings, are all considered to be like persons or to be associated with person beings. Because all sources of action are like persons, the explanations of the causes of events and happenings are not in terms of impersonal forces, but in terms of the actions of social persons. Explanations refer to a "who" that is active, rather than to a "what" (Hallowell 1955). The world is volitional, and the perceived regularities of the world are not those of natural law but, rather, are like the habitual behaviour of persons. It is therefore possible to know what will happen before it occurs, because it is habitual. But there is also a fundamental unpredictability in the world: habits make action likely, not certain. This capriciousness is also a result of the diversity of social persons, because many phenomena must act in concert for events to occur. The world of personal action is therefore a world neither of mechanistic determination nor of random chance: it is a world of intelligent order, but a very complex order, one not always knowable by humans.

This way of thinking and talking captures the complex relationships among phenomena that are experienced in the environment and the world. In different cultures people understand environments using analogies from their own experiences. Scientists, for example, use mechanical metaphors when they talk of the environment as having energy flows, or having nutrient or material cycles, and they employ market metaphors when they talk of investing in the environment or the decline in biological capital, and organic metaphors when they talk of biodiversity and an ecosphere.

The Crees, for their part, know the environment as a society of persons, and this view emphasizes the relationships humans have to non-human phenomena and the detailed interactions they have with them every day. Their view does not try to know an environment from outside but as a society of which Crees are part. It does not imagine environments without humans, nor does it envision the possibility of protecting environments by trying to remove humans. Environments are social networks of relationships that must be understood and respected by living in them.

For example, the relationship of the wind persons to human activities and animal lives is constantly confirmed by everyday experience. The wind persons bring cold or warmth and snow or rain, and with the coming and going of predominant winds the seasons change. They are responsible for the variable weather conditions to which animals and hunters respond. The bear hibernates and is docile only in winter when the cold north wind is predominant. The geese and ducks arrive with the increasing frequency of the warm south wind and leave with its departure. In a myriad of ways, the animals and hunters, and the success of the hunt, depend in part on the conditions brought by the winds.

When a hunter is asked by young people who have been to school why they say that animals are given by the winds, the answer often is that they must live on the land to see for themselves. These relationships can be discovered by anyone who spends enough time on the land. The wind persons also link God to the world. They are part of the world "up there," but they affect the earth down here. They thus link the spirits and God who are up there to the humans and animals who live on earth.

"God" and Jesus are the ultimate explanation for all that happens on earth, but He also gives all the personal beings of the world intelligence and will in order to follow His Way, or abandon it.[2] Persons are responsible for their actions. God therefore plays a key part in the gift of animals to hunters, but only a part. He is the leader of all things, and He is assisted by the wind persons and a hierarchy of leaders extending to most spirits, animals, and humans. The idea of leadership is persuasive in the Waswanipi world, alongside egalitarianism and reciprocity, and the hierarchy of leaders is spoken of as one of power. Hunting therefore depends not only on the hunter and the animals, but on an integrated chain of leaders and helpers acting together to give and to receive animals.

In this chain, human beings fit somewhere in the middle, closely linked to those above and below. Humans are mutually dependent on animals, who are generally less powerful than humans, and on spirit beings, who are generally more powerful. But the linkages are close and the positions flexible. As Cree myths indicate, some less powerful spirit beings were formerly humans who have been transformed into spirits. Animals used to be "like us," and in the "long ago" time they could talk with one another and with humans.

The Power of Hunting

The power of God and humans is manifest in the relationship between thought and happenings in the world. What God thinks or knows happens; His thought is one with happenings and thus He is all-powerful. Spirit beings participate in this power to a lesser degree; only some of what they know and think will happen. Their thought and happenings frequently coincide. God and spirit beings may give their powerful knowledge to humans in dreams, in waking thoughts, and by signs in the world, but they never tell all that humans would like to know. People can often be said to "discover" their understandings rather than create them; thus thought or insight "come to us" as a gift from God and spirits, in everyday thoughts, or in dreams. Thinking and prayer may be one. The knowledge that spirits and also animals give anticipates what is happening with some effective, but always unknown, degree of certainty.

Humans not only differ from animals by the degree of power they receive but also from each other. Powerful and effective knowledge increases with age and with the care and attention individuals give to interpreting and cultivating their communications with God, spirit beings, and animals. These differences in power and wisdom are reflected in the patterns of leadership within human communities.

The meaning of power in the Cree perspective, therefore, differs in important ways from that common in North American societies. People in the latter typically think of power as the ability to use relationships to control others and/or the world. For the Cree it is more complex. Human knowledge is always incomplete, and there is often a gap between what humans think and do and what actually happens. In hunting, for example, a hunter will frequently dream of an animal that will be given before he or she begins to look for it. When they then go out hunting they may find signs that confirm this expectation. When the things they think about actually come to be—when they are given the animal—that is an indicator of power. The power is an emerging coincidence between the anticipation (social thought and action) and the configuration of the world (other persons and events), a congruence that this anticipation helps to actualize. Thoughts, actions, events, and persons are all social processes. The social person who thinks and the personal environment in which he or she acts are not radically separable. Power is not an individual possession, it is a gift, and in this view a person cannot usually bring thought to actuality by individually manipulating the world to conform to personal desires. At each phase of happenings, humans, spirit beings, and other beings must interpret and respond to the communications and actions of other beings around them. "Power" is a social process, a relationship in thoughts and actions among many beings, whereby potentiality becomes actuality.

Hunting is an occasion of power in this sense, and the expression of this is that animals are gifts, with many givers. Power in this Cree sense may have analogies to a concept of truth, i.e., thoughts that come to be. We might say that in this view the power that is worth seeking is truth unfolding in social relationships, rather than power as a seeking of control of one person over another.

This complex understanding of hunting links intimately with basic Cree attitudes toward human life itself. The symbols conveying Cree concepts of hunting also order the Cree understanding of the life and death of animals and of the hunters themselves. The life and ultimate death of both the hunted and the hunters are as enigmatic for the Crees as they are for everyone else. That humans must kill animals to feed themselves and their families in order for humans and animals as social collectivities to have healthy lives, and that humans themselves all die, are fundamentally mysterious features of life (Tanner 1979). Cree symbols of hunting elaborate this and bring the wonder of life and death into the world of everyday meanings.

The hunt is conceptualized as an ever-changing cycle at many levels. Successful hunters will bring game back to their families and others in camp. Having received gifts, hunters are obligated to respect the givers by reciprocating with gifts of their own. These gifts go partly to other Crees, as most large kills are shared with kin, neighbours, or with the wider Cree community. By giving meat to others they are said to find more animal gifts in return. Many hunters also reciprocate to the

spirits who have participated in the hunt, often by placing a small portion of meat into the stove at the first meal of each day. The smoke of the gift goes up the stovepipe as a sign of appreciation and respect to the spirits "up there." This return offering is part of an ongoing relationship of reciprocity: it not only expresses respect and repays an obligation, it continues the exchange as a statement of anticipation that the hunter will again receive what is wanted when in need. Many Cree rituals follow a similar structure.

In hunting, when bad luck occurs with a particular animal, hunters turn their attention to other species or they hunt in another area until the animals are ready to be caught again. This allows animal numbers to grow. But if animals want to be caught and are not hunted, that is also bad luck, because they become overpopulated and more easily succumb to diseases or predation, as well as having fewer young survive. Thus, proper hunting is responded to with increases in the health and numbers of the animals. However, if a hunter kills animals that are not given, if they over-hunt, then the spirits and the animals of that species will be "mad" and the hunter will have no luck. Thus, in hunting, the life and death of animals forms a delicate reciprocal process.

The alteration in hunting luck brings us to the last of those meanings of the word "hunting." Hunters say that when they decrease their hunting they do it so that the animals may cease being mad and may grow again. Hunting involves a reciprocal obligation for hunters to contribute to the conditions in which animals can grow and survive on the earth. The fulfillment of this responsibility provides the main criterion by which hunters evaluate one another. In everyday conversation people speak extensively about the reputations and actions of hunters. What is emphasized is hunting competence (Preston 2002). A hunter who masters a difficult skill and through his or her ties with spirits receives hard-to-get gifts exhibits his or her competence and participates in power. Men and women who are respected for exceptional competence are contrasted with those who take chances, who fool around with animals by not killing them cleanly, and who seek self-aggrandizement by making large kills or wasting animals. Hunters who consistently have good luck but not excessive harvests also demonstrate competence because they maintain that delicate balance with the world in which animals die and are reborn in health and in continuing growth.

This image of the competent hunter serves also as a goal of the good life, or *meeyou pimaat-tahsee-win* (see Awashish 2006). The aims of both hunting and of life are, in part, to maintain a continuing sensitivity to and a balanced participation with the world, in which humans and animals reciprocally contribute to the well-being and survival of the other. The aim of life is the perpetuation of a healthy, meaningful, and bountiful world. This aim includes those now alive and those yet to be born. The social universe thus extends beyond the human world, beyond the temporal frame of an individual human life.

Hunting is not just a central activity of the Crees, nor is it simply a body of knowledge or a spiritual activity. Hunting is an ongoing experience of truth as power in the course of human lives and in the social world in which they are lived.

Hunting Practices: Subsistence Economy, Kin and Society, and Environmental Conservation

Contemporary understandings of hunting and gathering peoples can be dated from the mid-1960s when it was "discovered" that the hunting and gathering peoples of Africa and Australia efficiently, abundantly, and reliably produced their subsistence. This came as a revelation to both popular and professional ideas about hunting life. The hunting way of life was often thought to be precisely the opposite—inefficient, impoverished,

and completely unpredictable. Studies of the Crees tended to confirm the application of the new view to Subarctic hunters as well, although with some qualifications.

Efficiency, Abundance, and Reliability

It was found that hunters do not encounter game haphazardly but by careful planning, knowledge, and organization. Hunting is organized so that each species of game is used at times likely to produce an efficient, abundant, and reliable supply of food. Thus Crees know how to kill moose in almost any season, but they tend to concentrate their hunting at specific periods. One period is during the fall mating season, or rut, when moose call to attract partners. Hunters often look along shores for signs indicating the places where moose have visited to drink; they then wait or return at appropriate times to call moose to the location. After the rut, moose are not hunted extensively until deep snow has accumulated. As the snow deepens, the widely dispersed populations progressively concentrate and are often found on hills where the wind has blown away some of the snow accumulation. When the snow in these concentration areas exceeds one metre in depth, moose tend to restrict their movements to a series of trails. Under these conditions Crees know where to look for moose, and moose move outside the trails only reluctantly. If moose do take flight, hunters on snowshoes can exhaust them by pursuit until they stand their ground, face the hunter, and give themselves to the hunters.

A third period of intensive moose hunting occurs in late winter when snow may form a crust. Moose can walk, breaking through the crust with each step, but if they run they tear their legs against the jagged edges of the crust. Again, they will often stand their ground and face the hunter.

Cree moose-hunting practices therefore depend on extensive knowledge of the animals' habits in relation to weather, habitat, and the actions of hunters. Hunting is concentrated in periods when moose most clearly give themselves to hunters and when hunters can best fulfill the obligation to kill them with a minimum of suffering.

The proficiency and knowledge of Cree hunters make their hunting quite reliable. Bush food is also abundant, providing hunters' families with 150 per cent of the calories they require and eight times the daily protein requirement. Up to half the food some hunters harvest is circulated in gift exchanges to kin and friends back in the settlement, and some is kept for later village consumption, so everyone in the community can receive some "bush food."

Social Relations, Hunting Reciprocity, and Conserving Animals

The Cree have a distinct system of rights and responsibilities concerning land, resources, community, and social relations—a legal system of land and resource tenure, and of self-governance. This system enables hunters to fulfill their responsibilities to animals and spirits and to contribute to the conditions necessary for their mutual survival and well-being.

Cree society is organized around principles of community, responsible autonomy, and reciprocity. The central resources of land and wildlife are not owned. The land and the animals are God's creations, and, to the extent that humans use or control them, they do so as part of a broad social community united by reciprocal obligations. These gifts and obligations are not solely individual; they involve the wider human community as well, so that all people have a right of access to land and resources to sustain themselves. This right extends to all Crees, and to others, but along with the rights go responsibilities to contribute to the continued well-being of the land, animals, and other people. The exercise and fulfillment of such responsibility implies a willingness to exercise self-control and participate in a community of responsibility.

The Crees are efficient enough at hunting that they could deplete the game. Restraint is both an individual and a community responsibility and is assisted through a stewardship system. All hunting land is divided into territories (*Eeyou Indoh-hoh Istchee*) under the governance and stewardship of custodians (*Indoh-hoh Ouje-Maaoo*). The approximately 300 territories vary in size from about 300 to several thousand square kilometres, each supervised by a custodian (see Map 7.1). They are part of larger blocks, each associated with a community. While rights to land and resources are distributed to the whole community, as a continuing society extending over generations, the stewards exercise authority over the territories in the name of their family, the community, and the common interest and are thus obligated to protect and share the resources.

In general, all community members have the right to hunt on any land on a short-term basis, while travelling through, while camping for brief periods, or while using small game or fish resources. However, extended and intensive use of the larger game resources is under the supervision of the stewards.

Stewards usually have grown up in a territory on which they hunt repeatedly over many years before they inherit their role. They have built up extensive ties with the spirits of the land and acquired a vast knowledge of it. Most are constantly aware of the changing conditions and trends in the game populations. They discuss these trends with other stewards and Elder hunters, comparing patterns in different territories and relating them to changes in weather, vegetation, and hunting activity. Some of the trends observed by the stewards are the same ones used by wildlife biologists to monitor game populations, although few biologists have such long-term and detailed knowledge of a particular area. The trends are also important because they are communications from animals and spirits. Thus, if too many animals were

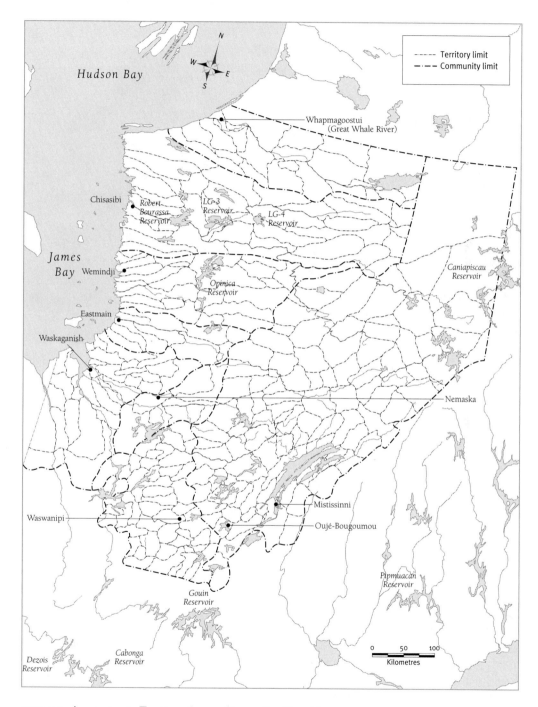

MAP 7.1 Approximate Territory Areas of James Bay Cree Hunters

FIGURE 7.1 The late Joseph Ottereyes from Waswanipi hunting geese while travelling to get wood for his fall bush camp. (Courtesy H. Feit)

killed in the past, the animals would be mad and have fewer young or make signs of their presence harder to find. This would indicate that the animals wish to give fewer of themselves, and, out of reciprocal respect, the hunters would take less.

Stewards use their knowledge to direct the intensive hunting of the animals on their territories. Each steward has the right to decide if the territory will be used intensively in any season, how many and which people can use it, how much they can hunt of each key species, and where and when they can hunt. However, stewards do not exercise these powers in an authoritarian manner. Stewards usually act by suggestion and by non-personal public commentaries on the situation, and their knowledge, their spiritual ties to the land, and the sacred sanctions for their statements give them considerable influence.

The system is part of the network of social reciprocities. At the individual level, the system of allowing hunters to join groups generally assures each a place to hunt every year. For the community as a whole, the system permits the distribution of hunters to respond to changes in the conditions of the game populations. The right to steward land and animals is inherited as a gift from previous generations, and the present stewards view their own actions as implying the same respect and responsibility to future generations. A territory is an inheritance and a legacy to be cared for.

In practice, the system of hunting-territory stewardships works to maintain an ongoing balance between harvests and game of those species that can be conserved. Several studies supply quantitative evidence that the Cree system works for the moose, beaver, fish, and geese populations, by keeping harvests below sustainable yields of the game populations. The best indicator of success is the relative stability of big-game populations over the two decades during which estimates were made before the influx of sport hunters and forestry into the region accelerated. These data indicate that the ecological balance sought by the Cree can, in general, be achieved. Furthermore, the Cree have been highly responsive to changing environmental and historical circumstances in pursuing a balanced hunt.

The Cree have also responded to important demographic, technological, and economic changes. They have generally maintained viable game populations through a period in which their own numbers have risen by as much as fivefold since the early twentieth century. To increase their food production they have intensified and diversified their use of some game populations but have also limited their bush food production to sustainable levels. They now purchase a significant proportion of their food when on the land.

The more intensive harvesting has occurred with the aid of important additions to their technological repertoire, including improved rifles and shotguns, new traps, and mechanized means of transportation. But the use of this technology still depends on Cree knowledge, cultural values, and social practices. The technology, therefore, has not led to over-hunting. The Crees have also maintained the balance despite periods of cash shortages. In such times they have done without some trade goods rather than exhaust animal resources. And they have continued to treat cash and trade goods as socially modified forms of property, often using them for co-operative ends by distributing and consuming them through sharing practices.

The Crees have thus maintained their hunting and the animals in their region despite important changes in their environment and in historical circumstances. However, rare periods of breakdown in the balance of hunters and animals have also occurred. The most serious of these happened in the 1920s and 1930s, when beaver were severely depleted. Non-Native trappers, encouraged by temporarily high fur prices, entered the region from the south, trapped out a place, and moved on. Some Crees say that they themselves trapped out the beaver in their areas because they did not see the possibility of maintaining animal populations if non-Native trappers continued to deplete their lands. But they continued to conserve moose and other game that were not hunted by the intruders. This example emphasizes the limits of the means at the disposal of the Crees for maintaining viable long-term balanced relations with animals. The culture and social organization of the Crees are effective aids for their self-governance, but they did not regulate or control the impact of what outsiders do on their lands. Further, where outsiders did not act responsibly and with respect, and when they did not acknowledge and act on their relationships to the Crees and the land, their activities threatened the animals and the Crees themselves.

The Crees recovered from the impact of these intrusions when non-Native trappers were banned from the area, but a crisis developed again in the 1970s when the government of Quebec started to build a massive hydroelectric project on their hunting lands. To understand the events of this second crisis, we have to turn from an examination of Cree culture and hunting to an account of the relationships of Crees to governments and developers.

The Crees Struggle to Maintain Autonomy in the Face of Government Intervention

Crises in the Fur Trade and the Incorporation of the Crees into Canada and Quebec

Fur traders have been present in the James Bay region since the mid-seventeenth century, and missionaries have visited trading posts since the mid-nineteenth century; but the arrival of the government and corporate resource developers characterizes the twentieth and twenty-first centuries. In the early 1930s the Quebec government's first intervention in the region occurred when it responded to requests from Crees and fur traders to help solve the beaver crisis created by non-Native trappers. In doing so the government recognized Cree hunting territories and their leaders. Quebec first made the killing of beaver by non-Indians illegal and then in the mid-1930s outlawed all killing of beaver. When hunting resumed, after 10 to 20 years depending on the region, the response had worked: beaver were numerous, and they wanted to give themselves again. The Crees and the government had worked together to re-establish beaver populations and agreed on the timing for beaver hunting to be reinstituted.

For the Crees, the government was recognizing their system by working with the custodians to conserve beaver and organize the new hunt. By recognizing the system of hunting-territory custodians, governments were also giving Crees an additional source of authority that they could use to limit the hunting activities of people from outside their communities, including non-Natives, who often were less responsive to their social and spiritual authority. But, an important and not yet fully apparent conflict developed between the Crees and the governments. The governments used the Cree system of hunting territories and custodians, but they thought that now Cree hunting was regulated and supervised by government regulations and authority, and that these determined the Crees' rights to hunt. The Crees thought the government had clearly recognized their system of tenure, custodianship, and self-governance, and initiated a form of relationship and co-governance.

An element of the government response to the crisis of the 1930s was to establish a band government structure for each community and to start issuing rations and, later, social assistance. In fact,

however, a chief and council system had been adopted in most communities before this time. Nevertheless, these responses also represented a turning point in Cree society. They bound the Crees within the fabric of Canadian political society, law, and economy for the first time, and in circumstances that did not make clear how government views threatened their autonomy. The Crees were still exercising extensive control and autonomy in their hunting society and on their lands, but they were now doing so, in part, within the Canadian polity.

Government Assistance Turns to an Assertion of Dominance

Government presence in the region accelerated rapidly throughout the 1950s and 1960s as governments sought to develop and "open the North." This involved making the region more accessible to southern Canadians and corporations. It also involved extending government administration and authority. These changes were not intended to aid the Crees but to promote the interests of southern Canadians and corporations. Programs specifically affecting the Crees were not developed in consultation with them, and were aimed at their assimilation rather than at supporting their self-governance or recognizing relationships of co-governance.

The expansion of the rail and road networks into the southern portions of Cree territory occurred in the 1950s and 1960s, and several mines, mining towns, commercial logging operations, and pulp mills were established. Their impacts on the Crees were neither foreseen nor considered. Hunters said animals became much less calm and less willing to be caught over large areas affected by noise generated by logging, railways, road traffic, and airplanes. Logging disrupted and destroyed large areas of forest animal habitats. Crees reported frequent finds of dead fish and aquatic animals and changes in the taste of animals over large areas. The extensive

Cree use of the environment and their knowledge of it made clear to them the extent of the impacts these developments were having, but no mechanism was established by governments or companies to give them a voice in the projects. That the government did not consider the Cree system of land use and management as a system of land tenure, rights, and governance, and that it did not consider that government and developers had relationships and mutual obligations with the Crees, was becoming clear.

The opening of the region to development projects not only affected the land, it affected the choices open to the Crees. When fur prices declined in the 1950s and 1960s, hunters began to meet the cash shortage by taking summer employment. They chose jobs primarily in work that was compatible with continued hunting, used their bush skills, allowed them to work in Cree groups, and was not organized by industrial time or authority structures. Although they continued to hunt, the number who did not pursue hunting as their main occupation rose significantly. Other changes also influenced this process: the formation of reserves, the construction of permanent settlements, and the establishment of schools.

Taking these jobs provoked a new crisis. Agents of government saw this as the first step in an irreversible process of abandoning hunting for wage labour. This fit the popular image of hunting as an unreliable, unproductive, and insecure means of living, one that any person would willingly give up for a steady job and a better life. Combining hunting and employment as a way of life was not considered a viable option by governments. Crees developed it as their option, and they knew the combination was better than just depending on jobs. During their summer jobs in the 1960s they were aware of often being given the hardest work, of being paid lower wages than non-Natives, and of being the first fired. The non-Native sawmills, exploration companies, fisheries, and hunting outfitters for whom they worked were constantly failing or moving. In their experience hunting and work could be compatible, and hunting was more reliable than many kinds of employment.

Although some schooling had been provided earlier, during the 1960s a significant portion of Cree youths began to attend schools. The government tried to force parents to send their children, sometimes threatening to cut off social assistance if they did not. Most parents wanted their children to have some schooling, and an increase in the number of children also affected their willingness to send some to school. The trauma of residential schooling away from Cree homes, in programs not significantly adapted to Cree culture, separated parents from their children in more than a physical sense. The longer children stayed in school the harder it was for parents and children to understand each other. As people saw what was happening, up to one-third of a community's children were kept out of school each year to live in their family and to learn hunting skills and the hunting way of life. Thus, the Crees kept some control over the type of education their children got.

The result was not to limit the continuation of the hunting economy but to diversify the range of skills and interests of the young adults. The effect of schooling paralleled that of the crisis in fur markets, creating a need for a more diversified economy in which both hunting and employment would be viable activities. However, schooling also created new resources for continuing efforts to define their own future. One effect was to bring a generation of Crees with high school, and some with higher education, back to the communities and into active roles in social and political life.

Cree Opposition to Quebec's Quest for Power

When the government of Quebec announced its plans for hydroelectric development in the James Bay region in 1971, it followed its practice

FIGURE 7.2 The late Emily Saganash from Waswanipi preparing a beaver as her granddaughter watches. She will remove the pelt for commercial sale and cook the animal for sustenance. (Courtesy H. Feit)

of neither involving the Crees in the decision nor examining its impact on them, nor recognizing any relationships or obligations to them.

Several young Crees called a meeting of leaders from each village to discuss the project. At the time, the Crees comprised eight separate communities and bands having limited regional integration or political structure. At the meeting, all were opposed to the project because of the severe damage it would cause to the land, the animals, and the Crees. In their view, the project was to serve non-Natives and they would not benefit substantially. They discussed ways to oppose the project and attempted to get discussions going with the Quebec government and its Crown corporations. They wanted to avoid complete opposition to the project, to see if they could re-establish respectful relationships and co-governance with

governments, and to get modifications to reduce the project's impact. However, the government refused to do anything but inform the Crees as the plans developed. The Crees were left with no choice but to oppose the project (Feit 1985).

Joined by the Inuit of northern Quebec, as Inuit also lived on some of the rivers to be diverted by the project, in 1972 they initiated a legal injunction in Canadian courts. Basically, they had to prove that they had a prima facie claim to rights in the territory, that the project would damage their exercise of these rights, and that these damages would be irreversible and irremediable. They asked the court to stop construction until further hearings on their rights could be completed.

The court hearings provided a detailed description of the project planned for the La Grande region. The La Grande complex involved diverting three major rivers into the La Grande River to increase its flow by 80 per cent. The construction of roads and power transmission lines would require cutting three or four corridors 960 kilometres long through the forest. And all this was only the first of three phases.

In the Crees' view, many of the damages were like those they had previously identified from earlier developments, although now over a much larger area. In addition, the particular effects of flooding were of special concern because about 50 per cent of the region's wetlands would be under water, destroying important beaver, waterfowl, and game habitat. The number of animals would be significantly reduced, and the variability of water levels in the reservoirs would restrict the ability of many animals, particularly beaver, to re-inhabit the areas. In short, they argued that animals would be adversely affected, and that hunters would suffer a serious and permanent loss of subsistence resources and a major threat to the continuity of their culture and society. Dozens of Cree hunters went to Montreal to testify, explaining to Judge Albert Malouf, government representatives, and the public how they lived on the land and why they had to have a say in what was done there. Their tone was not confrontational but truthful and firm.

Their lawyers then argued that the Crees had been exercising rights to the land since time immemorial, including the rights to hunt, fish, and trap, which constituted an Indian title over the land. At that time, the case was one of the most important on the concept of Aboriginal rights and Indian title.

The government lawyers argued that the project would affect only a small percentage of the land directly, that it would improve its productivity in many respects, and that in any case the damages were temporary or remediable. They claimed that the Crees no longer lived primarily off the land: they lived in settlements, had houses, used manufactured clothes and equipment, and now ate purchased foods predominantly. They argued that Cree culture had been substantially transformed and replaced by Canadian culture. They said the Crees were dependent on government financial assistance and support for their settlements. They argued that the use of wildlife, especially beaver, was completely institutionalized by the government as a result of establishing beaver reserves. They claimed that most Crees now had jobs. Finally, they argued that the Crees had no Aboriginal title to the land, or at most had a right to some monetary compensation and small reserves such as were provided in other treaties made elsewhere in Canada.

In November 1973, Judge Malouf ruled that the Cree and Inuit people did appear to have Aboriginal title to the land; that they had been occupying and using the land to a full extent; that hunting was still of great importance, constituted a way of life, and provided a portion of their diet and incomes; that they had a unique concept of the land; that they wished to continue their way of life; that any interference with their use comprom-

ised their very existence as a people; and that the project was already causing much interference. He ruled that the province was trespassing. The ruling was a stronger affirmation of Cree rights than many people had thought possible at that time and forced the government to negotiate with the Crees.

To people in the villages the ruling was a great victory, but it was also a straightforward recognition of the truth about their way of life and the dangers inherent in development conducted without their involvement and consent. It was also interpreted as a statement of good sense, reaffirming that relations between Crees and non-Natives could be guided by the principles of respect and reciprocity that should inform relationships among all beings in the Cree world. Reciprocity implied mutual respect for the needs and autonomy of others, ongoing obligations and relationships to others, and the possibility of sharing the land and its governance responsibly (Scott 1989).

Crees' Autonomy and the Aboriginal Rights Agreement

Negotiating Recognition of Aboriginal Rights

The Crees approached negotiations cautiously, despite the effort they had put into trying to get discussions started. They were in a difficult position as they were already experiencing the impacts of massive construction work on the project, which had been permitted to continue while Justice Malouf's ruling was appealed.

Early in the negotiations the Crees formed their own political association, the Grand Council of the Crees of Eeyou Istchee (GCC). The full Cree name for the Grand Council means roughly "the people from inland and the people from the coast helping each other," and Eeyou Istchee means "Cree land."

Negotiations continued for nearly two years through 1974 and 1975, and there was a sense that neither the government nor the Cree could agree on more.[3] The negotiations included several changes to project plans. The location of a main dam was changed. Funds were provided for remedial work to be undertaken as future impacts were experienced, and the negotiators agreed that any future changes would require new approvals.[4] These limited compromises meant very substantial impacts on the land and wildlife of the region.

The government recognized the right of all Crees to hunt, fish, and trap all kinds of animals at all times, over all the lands traditionally harvested by them, on the understanding that their harvesting rights would be subject to conservation of wildlife. Conservation was an objective Crees were pursuing themselves, and they negotiated agreements on the meaning and means of implementation of conservation that recognized their practices and needs. In addition, it was agreed that Cree harvesting would take precedence over sport hunting and fishing by non-Indigenous hunters, but not that they had priority over other uses of natural resources (see below). Approximately 17 per cent of the land area, called Category I and II lands, was set aside for exclusive Cree use. From the government point of view the Cree recognition of the principle of conservation and of non-Indigenous access to some game made the wildlife provisions acceptable. From the Crees' point of view the government recognition of their rights and of their priority of access to wildlife over sport hunters made the provisions acceptable.

Differences also arose over whether the governments or the Crees would have jurisdiction to implement these provisions. The terms agreed to would have to be interpreted and applied each year, as game populations shifted and hunting activities varied. The Crees argued that the fact that game existed in the region today demonstrated the effectiveness of their governance, and they claimed a right to manage the wildlife and to continue to co-govern the region. The representatives of Quebec and Canada argued that par-liamentary legislation gave the responsibility to manage wildlife to the governments.

This conflict was addressed in two procedures. It was agreed that all parties would recognize the Cree system of hunting territories and that there would be a minimum of government regulation. Second, the provincial and federal governments would exercise legal authority and enforcement powers over all the region except lands immediately adjacent to Cree communities, but only after receiving the advice of a joint committee composed equally of Crees, Inuit, and government appointees. This would be a part of their new and ongoing relationships. On lands adjacent to communities, the Cree governments would act with the advice of the joint committee.

Both the Crees and the governments agreed that development had to be controlled. The Crees did not oppose all development, envisioning sharing the land with non-Natives, but they wanted the right to decide on whether specific projects should be permitted, and if so, under what terms and conditions. And they wanted to be sure that they benefited from projects that went ahead by mutual agreement. The governments argued that they had the right to final decisions authorizing future developments, and they wanted to avoid situations in which the Cree could again tie up projects in courts. The governments hoped the other recognitions in the agreement would lead to Cree acceptance of government authority over the development in the region and prevent future confrontations. The conflict over this issue was not resolvable, and what was established was more co-management than co-governance, although this changed somewhat over time for the better.

The insistence of the governments that the region be open for development limited the land base over which the Crees could negotiate control. The province took the position that land under Cree control should be limited to areas immediately around the settlements and to the adjacent hunting locations. The greatest amount of land the province would transfer to Cree control, Category I lands, was only 5,500 square kilometres of the approximately 375,000-square-kilometre region.

The Crees sought to reduce their dependence on governmental authority and administration during the negotiations and to take more control of their own affairs in the settlements through increased self-government. They therefore sought regional autonomy and recognition of self-governance through the formation of distinctive, ethnically defined governments and boards for education, health, and other social services. Crees got agreement to special legislation for a Cree-Naskapi Act, extending the powers of their band councils as new community governments and replacing the provisions of the Indian Act and the powers of the Department of Indian Affairs.

The Agreement in Principle, reached after eight months of negotiation, was discussed in each Cree community, where the provisions were outlined in detail. People did not consider the draft agreement to be fair or just but thought it would recognize relationships of governments and Crees, and increase their chances of maintaining their way of life, culture, and economy, given the ongoing dam construction that was already affecting them. The final agreement followed a year later. The outcome was summarized by Chief Billy Diamond of the GCC, announcing to the press that all Cree communities had accepted the Agreement in Principle:

> The Cree People were very reluctant to sign an Agreement in Principle. . . . We feel, as Cree People, that by coming to an Agreement in Principle, that it is the best way to see that our rights and that our land are protected as much as possible from white man's intrusion and white man's use ["white man" is a general term James Bay Cree use for non-Indigenous people]. We . . . believe this agreement

> supports and strengthens the hunting, fishing and trapping rights in/over all of the territory, and restricts non-Native activity in that area. . . . I hope you can all understand our feelings, that it has been a tough fight, and our people are still very much opposed to the project, but they realize that they must share the resources. That is why we have come to a decision to sign an Agreement in Principle with the Quebec Government. (Diamond 1974:8–9)

Implementation: Enhancing Cree Autonomy Despite Government Betrayal

Accounts of the results of the James Bay and Northern Quebec Agreement (JBNQA) have been presented from several different perspectives. Here I want to emphasize six general but diverse aspects: (1) the agreement considerably aided Cree hunting; (2) it strengthened the Cree collectively and politically; (3) the socio-economic aspects of the agreement have failed; (4) government respect and support for the agreement have been mixed but mostly absent; (5) the Cree lands have been opened to rapid resource developments in which Crees do not have an effective voice; and (6) the Crees are more autonomous than before the agreement, but real threats to Cree autonomy remain.

The protection and recognition of Cree hunting rights and the provision of income security payments for hunters enhanced the perceived viability of hunting as a way of life, and participation in hunting intensified. In 1975, about 700 families or single adults were hunting as a way of life. The number of intensive hunters increased immediately following the agreement to approximately 900 and then to about 1,200, where it has stayed for over two decades. The time spent in hunting camps has also increased, and the average number of days intensive hunters stayed in the bush

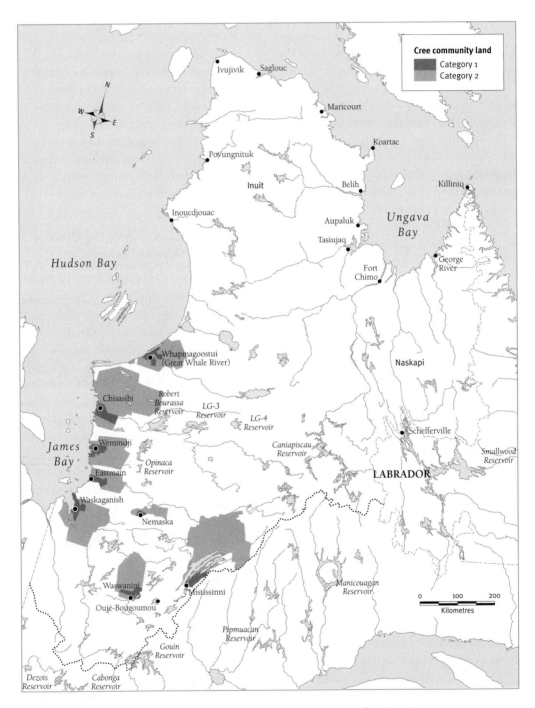

MAP 7.2 Division of Cree Lands under the James Bay and Northern Quebec Agreement

hunting during a year increased by 20 to 25 per cent after the income security program was begun. Most of these families live six months or more in bush camps.

The increased number of intensive hunters and the increased time they spend in bush camps present complex challenges to the stewards of hunting territories, who wanted to assure these changes do not result in over-hunting of game. In the initial year after the JBNQA, harvests of the most intensively used wildlife—geese, beaver, and moose—increased significantly. Stewards responded quickly, speaking widely of the problems in the villages, and reorganizing their hunting groups accordingly. By the second and third years, harvests had returned to earlier levels. This adjustment of harvests to the significant and rapid increase in the numbers of hunters and the length of time people spent on the land was a dramatic test and confirmation of Cree conservation practices.

In terms of changes in social relations, several commentators anticipated that the increased cash available to both hunters and to the growing number of employed Crees might result in widespread increases in the independence of individual nuclear families and in reduction of extended social relations and reciprocity. These changes are emerging although they have been slow to develop. The families who hunt intensively continue to do the work necessary to make additional harvests of foods that they give to kin, friends, and those who do not hunt so intensively. In general, customary stewardship therefore continues to express social responsibility and mutual aid despite considerably more intensive use of lands. The gifts of bush foods and other goods are a sign both of the continuing value of those foods and of the value of the social bonds that motivate the distribution and are confirmed by it. The fact that such exchanges are less of a material necessity today highlights their social value.

A rapid increase in Cree population has meant that while the number of intensive hunters has not declined during the nearly four decades since the JBNQA, the total population continues to grow at a rate that the land cannot support, so that the 1,200 intensive hunters and their families are now roughly one-sixth of the adult resident population. The majority of other Crees hunt on a part-time basis. Extensive linkages exist between families living most of the year in the settlements—who hunt on weekends, in the evenings, on school breaks, and holidays, and between jobs—and those kin and friends who live half of the year in bush camps and for whom hunting is their primary activity. Those in the settlements often provide equipment and cash for those in the bush, while the latter provide access to hunting camps and lands, advice and knowledge of hunting conditions, and regular gifts of food to the former. Hunting is critical to the identities and relations of the majority of Crees, and it binds together the diverse sectors of the communities. Whereas cash and market conditions can lead to an attenuation of social relations, hunting reciprocity and kin-based sharing continue to re-create wider social relationships, which are accompanied by a desire to enhance collective local autonomy in the face of forces that might otherwise radically weaken Cree society.

Social linkages are also expressed in the growth of more formal community-based decision-making institutions. Crees took over formal control of the many organizations that provided services in their communities more or less as they had existed, but as Crees received on-the-job training, Cree control has grown and policies and programs have become increasingly innovative (Salisbury 1986).

In the villages, school and health committees composed of local Crees, especially women, play decisive decision-making roles. This has empowered local people and provided them with enhanced skills and experience. These processes have not been easy, and numerous mistakes have been made. Nevertheless, the overall process has showed how effective self-government can be established.

This process has had important consequences for community economies. The Cree takeover and expansion of administrative services and programs have increased employment opportunities in the communities. The 30 or so Crees who were fully employed as administrators before the agreement have increased to over 800 administrators and supporting employees.

It is clear, however, that the number of administrative positions is insufficient to employ fully all those Crees in the rapidly growing population who do not hunt as their primary activity. The Crees have therefore begun to emphasize the creation of Cree economic enterprises in the communities. The structures being developed sometimes combine elements of modern business practices with structures adapted from Cree hunting society. However, these enterprises are not sufficient to employ the growing numbers of Cree youth, and there are still many obstacles to full Cree participation in the regional resource-based economy. One limitation is the small land base of the Crees and their inability to access natural resources for their development, as almost all resources continue to be allocated to large corporations.

The socio-economic development provisions of the agreement have not greatly benefited the Crees. Nor has the hydroelectric project contributed systematically to community-level economic development within the villages. The economic benefits of the project have been directed to southern urban centres. Indeed, nearly all socio-economic provisions of the agreement have suffered negligence, and often explicit subversion, on the part of governments.

When the first major parliamentary review of the implementation of the agreement was conducted in 1981, five years after the signing, it was clear that the federal government had not budgeted any special funds to meet its new obligations under the agreement, nor had it established any agency with responsibility for overseeing its role in the implementation processes. As a result of this review several initiatives were undertaken, including setting up the Cree-Naskapi Commission. The commission, an independent organization that reports every two years to Parliament on the implementation of the Act putting the JBNQA into law, reported a decade after the JBNQA:

> It is difficult to believe that a federal department responsible for negotiating and implementing self-government arrangements with Indian nations, and charged with improving their conditions, could persistently misinterpret a negotiated arrangement of this nature. The Department's attempt to circumvent clear obligations . . . is unjust, and must not be allowed to continue. Such actions cannot be dismissed as merely an honest difference of opinion. (Cree-Naskapi Commission 1986:27–8)

Similar attitudes and actions prevail with respect to the development of natural resources. The governments of Quebec and Canada have repeatedly tried to avoid their obligations to the Crees, and to the wider public, to regulate developments, instead facilitating large-scale projects that primarily meet the interests of corporations and investors. They have opened the territory to rapid resource developments, and repeatedly ignored, subverted, or minimized legally mandated obligations they undertook for Crees to be involved in decisions.

BOX 7.1 A Cree's View of the JBNQA

Philip Awashish, a youthful negotiator of the JBNQA and now a Cree Elder wrote that the implementation of the JBNQA has

> marginalized Eeyouch [Crees] and has led to their exclusion in the overall governance of the territory and exclusion in economic and resource development and benefits. . . . [The] consultative and advisory bodies have not had any significant impact on the making of policies and enactment of legislation by Canada and Quebec for the proper management of wildlife and acceptable environmental protection. . . . [Provisions for] economic and social development . . . [are] another dismal failure as Quebec continues to pursue and implement policies that exclude *Eeyouch* from direct participation and full benefits from economic development. . . . *Eeyou* communities are suffering from the soul-destroying effects of inadequate . . . housing, unsafe or lack of water supply and rampant unemployment. (Awashish 2002:156–9)

He also says that

> governments presently continue to exercise outright domination and control over lands and resources of *Eeyou Istchee* [Cree lands] with the exclusion of *Eeyouch* in the exercise of power.

> Broken promises, lies and deceit perpetuated by greed in pursuit of profit and the exercise of power through exclusive domination and control are serious flaws of the heart and spirit. These flaws of the heart and spirit cannot be rectified by laws, treaties and constitutions of nations and governments. For the truth is that the essential element in any righting of wrongs eludes law and morality because justice lies in the will of the powers that be. Therefore, the powers that be must find within themselves the will, the wisdom, the courage, and good faith and sense of justice to end the politics of exclusion and denial of rights and recognize and affirm the inherent right of *Eeyou* governance . . . (2002:162)

A New Kind of Campaign, and a New Agreement

Creating a Transnational Campaign against Development

In 1989 Hydro-Québec announced that it would build the second phase of its hydroelectric projects for James Bay, the Great Whale River (GWR) project north of the La Grande (McCutcheon 1991). Its view was that with the JBNQA some rights of the Crees had been recognized, but the agreement also recognized the right of the government to develop the hydroelectric resources of the region, with or without Cree participation or agreement.

The Crees decided to oppose the project and embarked on a campaign that lasted five years and created innovative ways of seeking recognition for Indigenous rights. At the heart of their campaign was a sophisticated linking of Indigenous rights to the environmental movement and to decisions in transnational markets. Opposition to the project was led by Whapmagoostui, the community at the mouth of Great Whale River, but was supported broadly. Nevertheless, it was not an easy decision to stand against further development in the region. The failure of the socio-economic development provisions of the JBNQA meant that there was a widely felt need for jobs and contracts that properly regulated natural resource developments could bring, and there were now some Crees with businesses and jobs who voiced support for the development. The discussion was wide-ranging, and in the end there was strong support not just to oppose the project but to stop it.

The Cree people and leadership were in a better position to try to do this than they had been in the early 1970s, but there are few examples of small communities stopping multi-billion-dollar development projects. The Crees had a strong organization, experienced leadership, and a broad base of community support for the campaign. They also had some funds as a result of the JBNQA. The provisions of both the JBNQA and general environmental legislation that had been passed since 1970 required that environmental and social impacts of large-scale developments be assessed before construction could begin. The governments tried to bypass key requirements, but the Crees challenged them in court to assure the full application of the law and prevent construction from proceeding, as it had in the 1970s, while the Crees were opposed.

This time, however, the Cree strategy was not to fight mainly in the courts but to carry their campaign to the public, politicians, and public utilities—the decision-makers in the United States where the energy would be sold—and to the international investors whose capital Hydro-Québec needed. The Crees reasoned that if US contracts for the bulk purchase of this electricity could be blocked, or if it could be demonstrated that project timetables and work could be disrupted and therefore costs would be increased, it would make the investment of billions of dollars in Hydro-Québec bonds look riskier to the managers of capital from world markets in New York and Europe, thereby making it harder for Hydro-Québec to finance the project.

The Crees set out a multi-scale campaign without a fixed plan, developing it as the situation progressed, approaching it as they did hunting (Craik 2004). Leaders spoke to environmental groups in the United States and built campaign alliances with national and international organizations who opposed the project on environmental and social grounds. They commissioned videos, slide shows, and Web presentations, sought newspaper and magazine articles, and gave talks at massive environmental rallies such as Earth Day in New York City. All were aimed at convincing environmentalists and the public at large that hydroelectricity from northern Quebec was not "clean" power simply because it did not burn fossil fuels or was generated outside the United States. They pointed out that the project involved damming and diverting rivers which in the United States would be protected by environmental legislation. They also noted it would disrupt habitats and wildlife, including migratory waterfowl protected by US and international treaties. They also said it would endanger the "way of life" of Cree hunters.

Not only leaders were involved. Hunters and their families, especially those from communities threatened by the project or who had experienced the effects of development on the La Grande River, travelled to the United States to speak directly with people in towns and cities in the northeastern states where the electricity would be consumed. They travelled through Vermont, Massachusetts, and New York, stopping each night to meet environmentalists, church groups, and social activists. They built understanding, support, and long-term relationships, and some of the people they met made return journeys to James Bay. Some of those they met say that working with the Crees and seeing the connections between communities so far apart, yet struggling with similar issues of how to keep control of their lands and their lives, has changed how they live and work in their own communities (McRae 2004).

The Cree campaign argued so successfully that Americans must care about what was being done to provide them with power that a significant number of new members joined the major US environmental group that partnered the campaign. The Crees commissioned pollsters to survey public opinion and show that there was growing public opposition in the United States to buying power from Hydro-Québec. They made sure that US politicians up for re-election saw these results and they urged candidates privately and publicly to stand against the contracts.

But public and political support was not enough. The Crees also sought to show that the contracts did not make good economic sense, and that there were alternatives. They were convinced that, without these economic arguments, the political pressure would be ignored or undermined by power utilities and US companies wanting cheap electricity. The Crees commissioned US experts to evaluate critically the Hydro-Québec and US utility company figures on how quickly energy demand would grow and what prices could be charged for it. They studied how demand could be met if more electricity were not available from Hydro-Québec. These technical studies showed that it would be cheaper to apply energy conservation measures in the United States than to buy GWR power, and that conservation could fully meet the expected demand. They also showed that energy conservation would create jobs in the United States. These studies helped to convince some senior officials in US electric utility companies that new contracts with Hydro-Québec were not economically desirable.

The multi-year campaign had many twists and turns, but the Crees renewed their commitment to it each year and pursued an extraordinarily diverse

set of means to their goal of preventing the new dams. They lost some fights opposing contracts and won others, such as when the New York state power authority cancelled a large contract with Hydro-Québec. Several months later, early in 1995, the premier of Quebec, Jacques Parizeau, announced that the Great Whale Project would be delayed indefinitely.

It was an extraordinary victory, and it had ramifications for everyone involved. It was now clear that groups like the Crees could not be simply ignored even in the context of transnational economies and markets. Hydro-Québec opened offices in New York and in Europe, realizing it needed an ongoing presence in the political and economic centres where its power was sold or where it sought to raise capital. This was partly in response to realizing that the victory of the Crees and their international environmental allies had damaged the corporation's image. They also sought to be in a better position to oppose similar campaigns in future. The Cree campaign changed things for social, environmental, and Indigenous rights activists, and in corporate boardrooms.

Shortly after the decision cancelling the GWR project, the referendum campaign on whether Quebec should separate from Canada went into high gear, and the Crees were drawn into it. They argued that they were not objects that could be incorporated into an independent Quebec against their will, that they were a nation with Indigenous rights. They also argued that their lands would not necessarily become part of an independent Quebec, should Quebecers separate from Canada (GCC 1998). The Cree used some of the techniques they had learned in the GWR campaign during the referendum debates. They commissioned a public opinion poll that showed the percentage of Quebecers supporting separation was significantly lower if a separate Quebec would not include the northern Cree and Inuit lands. Some Cree leaders were told that this survey was one of the factors that influenced the federal government to argue more publicly against separation. When the referendum to separate was defeated by the narrowest of margins, the Cree leadership thought that its campaign had played an essential role in that outcome.

Trying to Build a New Relationship, Again

Following this intense half-decade of political action, Crees and Quebec slowly sought to rebuild relationships. For the Crees it became increasingly urgent during the later 1990s that the overexploitation of forests and wildlife by industry and sport hunters be dealt with. Commercial cutting of forests and sport hunting were both increasing, despite Crees attempts over many years to raise concerns and despite provisions of the JBNQA.

Under the JBNQA, forestry development was to be reviewed through Cree input to Quebec government forestry management plans. In practice, Cree input has not been sought at critical stages of the planning, and those discussions that were held had not resulted in any significant modification to forestry practices or plans. Quebec turned over forestry management and the monitoring of compliance to forestry companies themselves. This made it impossible for Crees to get agreements as companies claimed it was a government responsibility, and vice versa. Consistent with Quebec's denials that forestry clear-cutting has a significant impact on the Crees, it permitted forestry companies to cut without regard to the Cree hunting-territory system. The scale of this exploitation threatens some Cree hunting territories as effective hunting and conservation units. Over 40 per cent of several hunting territories have been cut, and the cut on one area is already 80 per cent of the commercially forested land (Feit and Beaulieu 2001). The rapid development of logging and significant increases in non-Cree hunting directly threaten Crees' use of lands and the fabric of Cree society. Nevertheless, Cree hunters are convinced that if they have a say in how the forests are cut and at what pace, timber harvesting could be compatible with forest and wildlife regeneration and conservation.

Crees also want greater economic participation in forestry activities. Few Crees work for the major companies, and those who do are mostly in unskilled jobs. The Cree set up logging and sawmill operations to meet some of their social development needs, but they were allocated limited forest resources and were kept to a very small scale by Quebec.

In the late 1990s it was clear to Quebec and Hydro-Québec that the JBNQA had not led to a "social peace" with the Crees as they had thought it would in 1975. Hydro-Québec began talking to Cree communities about building a hydroelectric diversion to the south of the La Grande River complex, which would divert the water from the Rupert River through dams on the La Grande. These discussions, and some preparatory work, extended over several years. In 2001 the Quebec government proposed new negotiations about Cree and Quebec relationships. It was clear that they preferred to try to establish new agreements rather than initiate a large project without Cree involvement. Only weeks later an agreement in principle was completed and called "Agreement Concerning a New Relationship (Paix des Braves)."

When the agreement in principle was made public, it surprised many Crees and their supporters in the environmental community, because the Cree negotiators had agreed not to oppose the river diversion to the limits of their means. Quebec agreed not to build the third hydro project it had envisaged, which would have involved not only the Rupert but several other rivers as well, and flooded up to 20 times the area that the Rupert

BOX 7.2 Testimony of Alan Saganash Sr, in 1999

I am the Ndoho Ouchimau ["hunting boss" or custodian]. . . . I am 80 years old this year. All my life has been spent on the land. . . .

Our land is uncut now but a Hydro road passes close to it. . . .

Poachers use that road now. . . . Many people come there now. There is garbage left everywhere. . . . The lake is over-fished. . . . Our camps in that area have been vandalized and things are stolen.

Our land is very rich elsewhere. There are all kinds of animals and fish . . . but I know [a forestry company] plans to build a road into it. They want to put a camp. . . .

The road will change all that [it] will damage the habitat and open it up. . . .

I am afraid once the road comes there will be many mines opened. . . .

I want all of this considered in a full environmental assessment but they won't do it. I know the government well. I have seen how they work throughout my life. They refuse to consider all the development together. I have no chance to get all these issues looked at. I worry all the time about what will happen when the road comes.

The road is not to come to the heart of my land. I don't want it. The government is not trustworthy. . . . We are pushed out of our land again and again. We are told to move our hunting grounds. I have seen this happen many times in Waswanipi.

The companies and the government don't listen to us. They take what is ours and push us aside. This must stop.

—From an affidavit of 22 July 1999 by Allan Saganash Sr. of Waswanipi submitted in the court case the Crees initiated against forestry companies and the governments.[5]

diversion would flood. This agreement was probably facilitated by a shortfall of water supply to the La Grande River dams, and the lower costs of this way of utilizing the Rupert water.

The agreement involved important concessions by both sides. Forestry practices in the region were to be modified, under the supervision of a joint government–Cree committee, so that logging would be planned in relation to Cree hunting territories, and limits were established for how much land could be logged on a territory before there was adequate regeneration.

In addition, the Cree would be guaranteed substantial funds needed for socio-economic development. This was of vital concern, as JBNQA provisions for socio-economic programs had been largely ignored by governments. This time the Cree wanted to undertake to do it themselves and Quebec guaranteed annual block funding. Funding would come throughout the 50-year term of the agreement through payments from royalties and incomes collected by government from development of natural resources in the region, with a minimum amount guaranteed and increased payments if resource exploitation exceeded certain levels. The Crees also agreed to withdraw their several lawsuits that were pending over forestry, other development activities, and unfulfilled JBNQA undertakings. The Quebec government agreed that its relationship with the Crees would henceforth be on a nation-to-nation basis, a principle that had previously been refused.

The Cree negotiators believed the agreement met needs that previously they had been unable to address. In their view, the main challenge they faced was to balance protecting the land with creating the social and economic conditions for healthy, viable communities for those whose primary activity was not hunting. This would require jobs and new Cree businesses. The agreement would help Crees to achieve these goals in their own way.

In the Cree communities people faced a difficult decision. On one hand, Crees have participated in commercial trade and market relations for 350 years. They have repeatedly been able to create a balance between their ties and obligations to the land and their production of commodities and wage labour for commercial trade. Yet, the failure of social and economic development programs in recent decades was clearly taking a high toll on community health and the ability of village-based Crees to have productive and meaningful lives. The whole history of marginalizing Indigenous people in Canada on reserve lands, with limited ownership of or say in the use of the natural resources on their traditional lands, has condemned them to communities riddled with severe economic, health, and social limitations. This agreement promised new resources and means for Crees themselves to meet these challenges. But it did not improve Cree rights to natural resources or give them a stronger say in developments, with the possible exception of forestry. On the other hand, the substantial funding received by Crees could be used to have certain kinds of influence over those developments

in which Crees chose to invest or participate. And recent court rulings, which affirm the requirement that developers consult Indigenous peoples have particular force in the James Bay region where Crees have successfully fought large-scale development projects.

Many Crees did not support permitting more dams, nor were they sure the right balance had been struck between socio-economic development and protecting the land. There were also concerns that by accepting money tied to new developments, they could weaken public support from other Canadians in future relations with governments, including over projects they might oppose. There was some agreement that the Crees should seek to have good working relationships with governments, but also that they should be careful not to endanger their effective autonomy. In addition, the speed with which the draft agreement had been reached, without prior consultation, was a concern to some Crees.

Grand Chief Ted Moses, who negotiated the agreement for the Crees, said in 2002:

> I told [Quebec] Premier Landry that we were not opposed to development. We want to be included in a way which will be respectful of our nationhood and our right to maintain our own way of life. . . .
>
> We want to determine the pace of our own development. We want to choose for ourselves what is best for our communities and our people. . . .
>
> We know, however, that we cannot make our choices without appreciating the interests and concerns of Québec society. We have far too many common interests to be able to do that, and we live, after all, on the same land. . . .

We Crees still attach great reverence to the land. We continue to hunt, fish, and trap, and none of this will really change. . . .

[The agreement] is a Québec-Cree production.[6]

In early 2002, 55 per cent of Cree voters turned out for the referendum, and 70 per cent voted in favour of the agreement. Their votes expressed diverse thinking: outright support, a desire to build a new relationship with governments and Canadians based more on mutual respect and reciprocity, a desire to have the means to take responsibility for their own socio-economic development, and a desire for the Crees to stay united. Crees took a risk that this time an agreement could work.

In 2008, the Crees and the government of Canada negotiated and signed an agreement in which Canada provided a substantial lump sum to the Crees for socio-economic development, and Canada was released from its obligations in that area in the JBNQA, obligations that it had not met as was noted above. The agreement also provided for accountability and governance measures for Cree governments. The agreement lasts for 20 years, at which time it may be renegotiated or the JBNQA provisions come back into effect.

Having signed these agreements, the Crees face formidable challenges of which many of them are well aware. The new financial resources and access to development opportunities are vitally needed, but turning cash and investment opportunities into local or regional development that benefits Crees has not proved any easier for Crees than for other First Nations or small but hard-to-access communities anywhere in Canada. It is clear that standard development planning does not work. Very few Crees presently work for regional companies and innovative measures will be needed. One challenge is how to make regional corporate employers responsive to the scale of Cree employment needs

while taking account of the other Quebecers who also live and work in the region.

Another problem is how to create long-term jobs and viable enterprises beyond those already established in administration and community services. In separate agreements Hydro-Québec has made detailed commitments to Crees to make the economic opportunities its projects offer more effectively available to Crees. These commitments offer some hope, but there is limited employment at dams after the boom in construction jobs. Similarly for mining projects, the number of jobs simply does not meet Crees' needs.

Because the new agreements do not give Crees more say in resource development decisions in general, the developments are likely to proceed solely in response to market conditions, which tend to favour quick returns on investments and limited attention to long-term socio-economic needs in communities and regions. Most corporations and investors are highly mobile, and jobs are quickly cut or moved elsewhere in response to changing market conditions. As a result many new developments will repeat the histories of previous corporate resource developments: short-term boom followed by bust. Crees know this from their experiences dating back to the 1960s when the first mines and sawmills came to the region, few surviving for more than a decade, and from hydro development construction. Crees may use their development funds and influence to try to modify development decisions, but without control of the resources themselves, and without effective functioning of the 1975 agreement processes that were intended to regulate development on social and economic grounds, their means are limited. Thus the new agreements do not provide solutions for these problems, but they do provide the Crees with some additional means to try to find some improvements and more effective answers.

The long-term success or failure of the new agreements will depend not only on what the

Crees do, but also on how the governments approach their undertakings, and on whether relations to corporations change. The governments can pursue nation-to-nation relationships with the Crees in a way that give Crees an effective voice in future decisions about development. Alternatively, the governments may continue to ignore the Crees in decision-making in the hope that the communities will need jobs so badly, or be so dependent on the cash provided by the agreements from new developments, that they could not say "no" to development again.

The agreements were probably intended by Quebec and Canada to demonstrate to the investment community that the governments can "manage" the conflicts with the Crees, making some concessions but assuring investors that resource development could go ahead smoothly in the future on terms the investors want. If the governments and corporations also implement the agreements by effectively involving Crees in decisions about developments and how they proceed—decisions that take account of long-term Cree needs for jobs and land—they may avoid conflicts that can undermine the investment climate.

But if corporations and the governments still seek simply to maximize the speed and size of resource developments, and marginalize Crees' long-term goals while offering cash compensation and temporary jobs, then they will likely face new and unpredictable conflicts with Crees.

Most Crees want to be effectively involved in resource development decisions so that their long-term needs for socio-economic development and their responsibility to the land and future generations can be fulfilled. If relationships to the future and the land are not part of what governments intend when they speak of new nation-to-nation relationships with Crees, if they think of Crees only as market partners, then Crees may again initiate new campaigns against developments.

Conclusions: Continuing Autonomy, Seeking New Relationships

Over the last four decades, the autonomy of Cree communities has clearly been enhanced by sustaining their society and hunting economy; by Crees' greater control of regional government, services, and financial resources; and by their ability to take political, economic, and legal initiatives. The ability to sustain their autonomy, and to enhance that autonomy in the face of repeated government attempts to erode and manage Cree governance and visions, is also clear.

The Crees continue to face major threats. The regulation of resource development was addressed in the JBNQA in 1975 and it has been addressed with new commitments in the forestry provisions of the 2002 agreement, but it needs to be implemented and made effective. Resource developments present both important opportunities to Crees and major threats to the land and long-term Cree livelihoods. The land of the region has been rapidly and intensely occupied by corporations and non-Cree Canadians. Crees have recently negotiated recognition of their nation-to-nation relationship to other Canadians, and a significant share of the economic benefits that developments produce, with the aim that they will address Crees' socio-economic needs. The challenges they face are how to break or moderate the historical pattern of limited employment in highly mechanized resource extraction projects, and the boom and bust development that unregulated market developments create. The new nation-to-nation relationship implies that they will have a say in how developments occur, so that they can better serve regional socio-economic needs, but the new agreements do not specifically address these challenges, and much depends on how governments and corporations respond to the challenge of co-governing with Crees.

The Crees have repeatedly sought and hoped for new relationships with other Canadians and Quebecers, based on mutual respect; on responsible and long-term sharing of land, resources, and wealth; and on enhancing their co-governance. Governments and corporations have repeatedly responded with agreements that recognize some Cree engagement and autonomy, but the implementation and the effects of those recognitions have also worked to limit Crees and to subordinate them. That Crees have shaped these agreements and challenged their effects demonstrates that they have retained considerable autonomy. In the most recent agreements Crees have again reaffirmed their commitment to renewing relationships with Canadians, governments, and developers: relationships of co-existence and co-governance that have continued through both agreements and conflicts for over half a century.

ACKNOWLEDGEMENTS

This chapter draws on the work of many Cree people and scholars from whom I have drawn insights, including Philip Awashish, Mario Blaser, Monique Caron, Matthew Coon Come, Brian Craik, Paul Dixon, Sam C. Gull, Jasmin Habib, Peter Hutchins, Deborah McGregor, Monica Mulrennan, Brian Noble, Alan Penn, and Colin Scott. I also want to acknowledge financial support from the Social Sciences and Humanities Research Council of Canada and the Arts Research Board of McMaster University.

NOTES

1. The term "hunter" includes both men and women hunters and their spouses. Women typically fish and hunt small game, but some engage in all types of hunting. Some also say that they have dreams of where game may be caught and assist their husbands with this knowledge. How animals are butchered, prepared, distributed, and consumed can also affect the hunt. So post-harvest tasks that are typically, but not exclusively, done by women are an integral part of the hunting process.

2. In Cree the word for "God" does not specify gender. But Cree, who are mostly Christians, generally use the masculine pronoun when speaking English. I follow their usage when paraphrasing their statements.

3. The negotiations were conducted jointly with the Inuit of Quebec, but this discussion only addresses aspects relevant to the Cree.

4. As it turned out, later changes were agreed to on several occasions, including an agreement to relocate the dam that had been moved and to build it on its original site. The move was requested by Hydro-Québec because it found construction at the new site to be technically impossible. The developers also claimed that it was nearly impossible to protect the village on Fort George Island from erosion by the greater flow in the river, and they funded the construction of a new site on the shore of the river at Chisasibi, which the Cree agreed to. The old site has not eroded substantially or become uninhabitable.

5. *Mario Lord et al. v. The Attorney General of Quebec et al. and Domtar Inc. et al.,* Superior Court, District of Montreal, No. 500–05–043203–981.

6. Grand Chief Dr Ted Moses, Grand Council of the Crees (Eeyou Istchee), notes for a statement "La société québécoise et les Autochtones," 26 March 2002.

REFERENCES AND RECOMMENDED READINGS

Awashish, Philip. 2002. "Some Reflections on Eeyou Governance and the James Bay and Northern Quebec Agreement 1," In *Reflections on the James Bay and Northern Quebec Agreement*, edited by Alain C. Gagnon and Guy Rocher. Montreal: Québec Amérique. A valuable and critical assessment by a Cree negotiator and leader of the JBNQA and the history of Cree–government relations.

———. 2006. "Eeyou Law and Eeyou Governance," In Cree-Naskapi Commission, *2006 Report of the Cree–Naskapi Commission*. Ottawa: Cree–Naskapi Commission.

Blaser, Mario, Harvey Feit, and Glenn McCrae, eds. 2004. *In the Way of Development: Indigenous Peoples, Life Projects and Globalization*. London and Ottawa: Zed Books and IDRC.

Craik, Brian. 2004. "The Importance of Working Together: Exclusions, Conflicts and Participation in James Bay Quebec," in Blaser et al. (2004).

Cree–Naskapi Commission. 1986. *1986 Report of the Cree–Naskapi Commission*. Ottawa: Cree–Naskapi Commission.

Diamond, Billy. 1974. Press Statement. "A Time of Great Decision Has Come for the Cree People."

———. 1977. *Highlights Leading to the James Bay and Northern Quebec Agreement*. Val d'Or, QC: Grand Council of the Crees.

———. 1990. "Villages of the Damned: The James Bay Agreement Leaves a Trail of Broken Promises," *Arctic Circle* (Nov.–Dec.): 24–34. A valuable account of the JBNQA by the foremost Cree leader of the period, and a critique of its implementation.

Feit, Harvey A. 1985. James Bay Cree Responses to Hydro-electric Development, In *Indigenous Peoples and the Nation-State: Fourth World Politics in Canada, Australia and Norway*, edited by Noel Dyck. Social and Economic Papers no. 14. St John's: ISER books, Memorial University of Newfoundland.

———. 1989. "James Bay Cree Self-Governance and Land Management." In *We Are Here: Politics of Aboriginal Land Tenure*, edited by Edwin N. Wilmsen. Berkeley: University of California Press. A review and assessment of relations between the Cree and Quebec governments in the decade following the JBNQA.

——— and Beaulieu, R. 2001." Voices from a Disappearing Forest: Government, Corporate and Cree Participatory Forest Management Practices," in Scott (2001).

Francis, Daniel, and Toby Morantz. 1983. *Partners in Fur: A History of the Fur Trade in Eastern James Bay, 1600–1870*. Montreal and Kingston: McGill–Queen's University Press. The first comprehensive history of the James Bay Cree in the period up to the twentieth century.

Grand Council of the Crees (GCC). 1998. *Never Without Consent: James Bay Crees' Stand Against Forcible Inclusion into an Independent Quebec*. Toronto: ECW Press.

Hallowell, A. Irving. 1955. *Culture and Experience*. Philadelphia: University of Pennsylvania Press.

McCutcheon, Sean. 1991. *Electric Rivers: The Story of the James Bay Project*. Montreal: Black Rose Books. An account of the James Bay hydroelectric project and its initial environmental and social impacts by an independent science writer.

McRae, Glenn. 2004. "Grassroots Transnationalism and Life Projects of Vermonters in the Great Whale Campaign," in Blaser et al. (2004).

Niezen, Ronald. 2009. *Defending the Land: Sovereignty and Forest Life in James Bay Cree Society*, 2nd ed. Boston: Allyn and Bacon. A very readable account of the changes and continuities in Cree society and culture from the 1970s to the 1990s.

Preston, Richard J. 2002. *Cree Narrative: Expressing the Personal Meanings of Events*, 2nd ed. Montreal and Kingston: McGill–Queen's University Press. An extensive exploration of core Cree symbolic meanings and knowledge as revealed through the analysis of myths, songs, stories, and conjuring performances.

Richardson, Boyce. 1991. *Strangers Devour the Land.* White River Junction, VT: Chelsea Green Publishing. A richly personalized account, by a skilled journalist, of Cree hunting and the 1972–3 court case against the hydroelectric project.

Salisbury, Richard F. 1986. *A Homeland for the Cree: Regional Development in James Bay, 1971–1981.* Montreal and Kingston: McGill–Queen's University Press. A major review and synthesis of the organizational and economic changes in Cree society in the initial years following the signing of the JBNQA.

Scott, Colin H. 1989. "Ideology of Reciprocity between the James Bay Cree and the Whiteman State." In *Outwitting the State,* edited by Peter Skalnik. New Brunswick, NJ: Transaction Books.

———, ed. 2001. *Aboriginal Autonomy and Development in Northern Quebec and Labrador.* Vancouver: University of British Columbia Press. The most up-to-date collection of papers reviewing the relations of Cree and neighbouring Indigenous societies with the nation-state and world markets in changing times.

Tanner, Adrian. 1979. *Bringing Home Animals: Religious Ideology and Mode of Production of the Mistassini Cree Hunters.* Social and Economic Studies No. 23. St John's: Memorial University of Newfoundland, ISER Books. A detailed ethnography of Cree hunting, emphasizing the ritualization of productive activities and the symbolic organization of the social life of hunters.

CHAPTER 8

The Atikamekw: Reflections on Their Changing World

Sylvie Poirier

Introduction

The Atikamekw live in the boreal forest and rich watershed of the upper Saint-Maurice River (Tapiskwan Sipi) of north-central Quebec (see Map 8.1). In traditional times, these waterways facilitated numerous contacts and exchanges with neighbouring groups. These include the Innu of Lac Saint-Jean to the east, the James Bay Cree to the north (mostly Waswanipi and Mistassini), and the Anicinabe (or Algonkins) to the west. All these groups are Northern Algonquians, and they share strong linguistic, social, cultural, and territorial affiliations. Their alliance and exchange networks may, however, have extended far beyond these groups, including some Ojibwa bands. In contrast to their neighbours, who are well known in the literature through the writings and records left by missionaries and traders as well as through anthropological studies, there are very few such records of or studies on the Atikamekw. Today, they number about 6,000 people, living in the three communities of Wemotaci, Manawan, and Opitciwan.

In this chapter, I present some facets of my understanding, as an anthropologist, of the Atikamekw world. In the face of many challenges that confront them, the Atikamekw are involved in a dynamic redefinition of their culture and its institutions. Their intimate and complex relationship with the forestland forms a focal point for much of their struggle. They have experienced decades of colonial denigration and dispossession in an unequal struggle. Nevertheless, they persist and practise what some would call the art of resistance, a process I am profoundly moved by. I am particularly interested in the methods they creatively employ to preserve and pass on their ways and their knowledge, methods that involve reinterpreting their culture and devising new initiatives and strategies in the hope of taking their rightful place in today's world.

A discussion of the Atikamekw people necessarily involves a consideration of the forest and their intimate relationships with it, a forest that for the last 100 years has been coveted and transformed by loggers and the builders of dams, with little consideration for the "original people," *Nehirowisiw*. As a result, the contemporary reality of the Atikamekw cannot be grasped without an understanding of their prolonged contact with the *Emitcikocicak*, "the whites" or Euro-Canadians. That reality provides the context for the persistence and transformation of their language,[1] their knowledge, and their practices as semi-nomadic hunters and gatherers, and of their specific way of engaging with the land (*aski*) and with the forest (*notcimik*), as a social space containing networks of living places. What I wish to describe here are

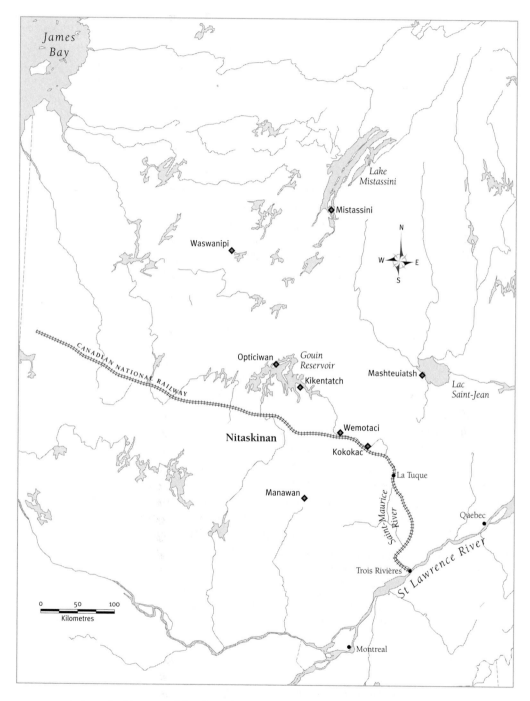

MAP 8.1 Atikamekw Territory (Nitaskinan) and Contemporary Communities

some of the ways in which the Atikamekw are rethinking their new realities in relation with the dominant society and some of the strategies they are developing to accommodate to these new realities.

Doing Fieldwork

Before I began doing research with the Atikamekw in the early nineties, I underwent an enriching initiatory journey in the Australian Western Desert with the Kukatja and neighbouring groups. My research and long-standing relationship with these Australian Aborigines (since 1980) had introduced me to many of the realities of contemporary hunters and gatherers and of Fourth World peoples (colonized Indigenous peoples within modern nation-states). The experience and knowledge I gained as an individual and as an ethnographer with my Kukatja friends, and the comparative basis it has given me, were invaluable when I decided to pursue my anthropological research itinerary with the Atikamekw. Although the path from the Australian Western Desert to the Canadian boreal forest is a long one, the social worlds of the Kukatja and the Atikamekw nonetheless share much in common. For example, they both come from a hunting and gathering tradition that entails a nomadic or semi-nomadic (in the case of the Atikamekw) way of life. Flexible and dynamic social and territorial networks inform their respective social orders and identities, each in their own ways. Both value an intimate and reciprocal relationship with the land and with non-human agencies, including animals, plants, spirits, and places. Both come from an oral tradition, where their knowledge and their history are best expressed and passed down through the idiom of stories.

As for their respective colonial history, and current experiences as Indigenous peoples in modern liberal nation-states, there are both similarities and differences (Poirier 2010). For both, the gradual yet irreversible process of settling in confined communities started in the 1950s, with all the accompanying bewilderment and sense of loss felt at the time and during the following decades. For both, that process also gave rise to economic dependence on the state. However, then as now, both groups have continued to have access, at least to some degree, to their ancestral territories, giving them a sense of continuity as well as a medium through which they can express and hand down their knowledge, values, and memories. For both, in spite of two decades of a residential school regime, the local languages are still very much alive.

By the beginning of the twentieth century the Atikamekw had converted to Christianity and by the 1950s Catholic beliefs and practices had become an intrinsic dimension of their identity and culture.

The Kukatja, in contrast, strongly resisted missionary attempts to convert them. Very few identify themselves as Christians and their cosmology and ritual life still follow their Ancestral Law (commonly known as the "Dreaming"). To some extent, the same is true of their attitude toward political structures imposed from the outside. While the Atikamekw seem to have readily adopted the band council system, as stipulated under the Indian Act, the Kukatja still refuse to adopt a political structure (the Aboriginal community councils implemented by the Australian government in the 1970s) that runs counter to their own decision-making processes. Since the late 1970s, following a major change in Canadian policies concerning Indigenous people, the Atikamekw Nation has been negotiating with the federal and provincial governments toward a comprehensive land-claim agreement. A similar possibility was presented to the Kukatja and neighbouring groups only in 1993 with the implementation of the Native Title Act by the Australian government.

I first encountered the Atikamekw in the early 1990s. In 1992, while a post-doctoral fellow at the

University of Montreal, I took a small contract with the Atikamekw and Montagnais Council.[2] At the time, there was a dispute between some Atikamekw families who had built permanent camps on their ancestral lands and a local town council over municipal taxes for resort leases. The town council wanted these Atikamekw families to pay annual taxes just like the few Euro-Canadian families who had resort leases and cottages along the river. From the perspective of the Quebec government and the town council, these Atikamekw were outside the law unless they agreed to pay taxes. According to the government, the only area where the Atikamekw are allowed to build permanent camps on public Crown lands is within the beaver reserve, an area reserved exclusively for Atikamekw trapping and hunting (see below). As for the Atikamekw, they argued that on the basis of the families' historical and customary affilia-

tion with that particular territory, they should be treated differently from the vacationers. In addition to these permanent camps, a number of temporary campsites in the same area were being used by members of related families. The mere presence of "Indians" was a great irritation, not only to the authorities but also to the cottage owners and sport hunters.

My task was to demonstrate the historical presence of these Atikamekw families in the area since at least the middle of the nineteenth century. Alongside a number of written (and official) records, the oral testimony and memory of Elders, both men and women, were central to the research. I met with Elders at their house in La Tuque (the neighbouring Euro-Canadian town), in Wemotaci, or at their camps. With the help of an Atikamekw research assistant who introduced me to them and acted as interpreter, I drew up genealogical charts

FIGURE 8.1 Once a year the Atikamekw Elders of the three communities gather for a few days to discuss and exchange views on social and political issues. (Courtesy of the Conseil de la Nation Atikamekw)

and recorded the oral life histories of these families. The genealogies covered at least six generations (from the great-grandparents of today's Elders to their own grandchildren) and were most helpful in showing the matrimonial alliances between the families.

It turned out that all the families still frequenting the disputed area were related to the band formerly connected to Kokokac. The Hudson's Bay Company had operated a trading post at Kokokac from 1863 to 1911. In 1894, following an official request by the Atikamekw chiefs, an area of 1.5 square kilometers was surveyed and Kokokac officially became reserved land. However, in 1931, Kokokac was flooded following construction of the Rapide-Blanc dam, at a time when Indigenous land rights were not recognized and there was no possibility of land claims; no compensation was received. The families affected by the flooding, who had used Kokokac as a summer gathering site and whose ancestral affiliations and hunting territories lay in the vicinity, nonetheless continued to occupy the area, as do their descendants to this day. According to official records, the Kokokac band no longer exists; its members had been transferred to the Wemotaci band. After our report was completed (Poirier 1992), the town council (following a recommendation by the Quebec Ministry of Municipal Affairs) agreed to the Atikamekw demands. No taxes on their permanent camps have since been requested. However, the Atikamekw refusal to pay taxes was motivated more by politics than economics (the tax bill was rather low). For the Atikamekw Nation, it was a small yet significant victory within their broader political agenda of achieving recognition of their land rights and a form of political autonomy.

During the research I was introduced not only to the struggle of the Atikamekw for their land rights but also to their recent history and their life as contemporary hunters and gatherers. Since then, I have returned many times to the

Atikamekw lands, visiting their communities and conducting research on customary practices, local knowledge, and oral traditions in their changing contemporary expressions. Over the years, my work and relationship with them have evolved into an exchange: whatever I produce in terms of anthropological knowledge may be used by their leaders as anthropological proof of their enduring and ever-changing relationship with the land and the forest. I view my role and my responsibility as an anthropologist as a mediator and translator between worlds (a **cultural broker**). I hope that my role may eventually contribute to the empowerment of Indigenous peoples. Escobar (1997:510) has aptly identified such a position as "a new ethics of anthropological knowledge as political practice." As an anthropologist, I think that we have to embrace this role if we are to continue to have a dialogue with Indigenous peoples. As ethnographers, we have to continue to explore and take seriously the manifold forms and expressions of cultural differences if we are to meet our responsibilities as "translators between worlds."

Atikamekw Colonial History

Due to a lack of written reports, very little is known of Atikamekw early contact history. A first and brief mention of the "Attikamègues," a name given to them by the Algonkins, is found in the *Jesuit Relations* of 1636, written by Father Le Jeune (Gélinas 2000:32). It was reported that a few of these hunters who lived in the northern basin of the Saint-Maurice River had travelled to the trading post of Trois-Rivières, founded in 1634, to trade their furs. There is no doubt that like their Cree, Innu, and Algonkin neighbours, the Atikamekw had been engaged in the fur trade for some time. In the absence of trading posts in their own territory, however, they travelled to those of the Lac Saint-Jean and James Bay areas and, after 1634, to the one established at Trois-Rivières. During the last quarter of the seventeenth century,

Atikamekw families suffered significant losses due to smallpox epidemics and to raids by the Iroquois, who ventured into their territory in search of furs. According to oral tradition, some families decided to travel further north into Cree territory for a few decades before coming back to their own lands. Between 1775 and 1821, a few short-lived trading posts were established in Atikamekw territory, mostly by the North West Company. In 1821, the HBC established a trading post at Wemotaci (not far from the present-day community), and two others, at Kikentatch and Kokokac, were established in the following decades. Atikamekw families already used these places as summer gathering camps. Well into the 1960s, the Atikamekw continued to be involved in trapping; to a great extent it guaranteed their autonomy and pride as hunters. Today, while hunting, fishing, trapping, and gathering remain intrinsic dimensions of their experience and of their relationship with the forest, no one earns a living as a trapper.

With traders generally came missionaries. In 1651, Father Jacques Buteux, a Jesuit, was the first to venture into Atikamekw territory. During his three months of perilous travels, he met with three Atikamekw "assemblées." On a subsequent visit, a few years later, he was killed in an Iroquois raid. During the eighteenth century there seem not to have been any missionaries in Atikamekw territory, which does not, however, mean that they were not influenced by Christian cosmology and rituals. From 1837 onward, priests from Trois-Rivières visited Kikentatch and Wemotaci annually in July, when Atikamekw families were gathered there. While their contact with travelling missionaries—people who would only stay a few days during the summer at Atikamekw gathering places—had been sporadic until the end of the nineteenth century, the Atikamekw were sensitive and to some extent receptive to their messages. By the beginning of the twentieth century the Oblates maintained a permanent presence in

the newly established Atikamekw "reserves," even though the Atikamekw themselves would only gather there during the summer. The influence and "power" of the missionaries increased over the following decades. There, as elsewhere, they strongly forbade and denigrated hunting and shamanic rituals that they identified with the devil. They also forbade polygamy. According to Atikamekw oral tradition, in the 1890s the last man living in a polygamous relationship engaged in open confrontations with the priest. Catholicism became an intrinsic dimension of Atikamekw culture; they appropriated Catholic cosmology, ceremonies, and praying practices. Some people continued, however, to perform traditional hunting rituals and ceremonies such as the first-steps ceremony (*orowitowasowin*), the sweat lodge (*marotsowin*), and drum (*tewehikan*) beating, all of which they practised on a sporadic basis while out on their territories and unbeknownst to the missionaries. In today's context, Elders who have grown up in a solely Atikamekw Catholic tradition sometimes look with suspicion on the revitalization of some of these ritual practices in the communities; the movement of revitalization started in the 1980s and has since gained momentum (Jérôme 2010).

In the 1850s, when the first timber concessions were granted to a logging company, the Atikamekw were confronted with what was to become a major activity on their land. Logging has grown significantly since then, and with the introduction of heavy equipment in the 1970s the forest industry has transformed the Atikamekw forestscape on a larger and different scale than any of the area's forest fires had ever done. Significantly, the Atikamekw word for Euro-Canadian people (particularly the Québécois) is *Emitcikocicak*, "the ones who use wood."

Their involvement with the forestry industry has evolved over the decades. Until the 1970s, a fair number of Atikamekw men worked seasonally as lumberjacks. Today, faced with the increasing presence of forestry activities, the Atikamekw have developed a bold strategy. They want to participate in the decision-making processes concerning the forest (with the hope to better protect it); they also want to share the economic benefits. To achieve these ends, the three communities have started joint ventures with forestry companies operating in the area. Opitciwan has even been operating a small sawmill for several years now. In spite of these initiatives, it is still too early to speak of an Indigenous forestry industry since the Quebec government and forestry companies continue to control the industry. However, one can sense mixed feelings and growing concerns among the Atikamekw regarding forestry activities, and the extent and the nature of their own participation in such activities (Wyatt 2004).

In 1881, concerned by the growing presence of Euro-Canadian people and interests on their land, the council of chiefs, *Kice Okimaw*, of the then four Atikamekw bands of Wemotaci, Manawan, Kokokac, and Kikentatch, petitioned the federal government to set aside lands for them. Four communities ("reserves") were surveyed shortly thereafter. The Kikentatch and Kokokac sites have since been flooded by the construction of the La Loutre hydroelectric dam in 1918 (which created the vast Gouin reservoir) and the Rapide-Blanc dam in 1930. The families who frequented Kikentatch asked to be relocated at Opitciwan; those from Kokokac, as we have seen, officially merged with the Wemotaci band while maintaining their activities and presence in the Kokokac area.

It must be stressed, however, that the Atikamekw did not settle in communities right away. Until the 1950s, and for some families well into the 1960s, the communities were simply places where they established their summer camps for a few weeks. There, the children would attend summer school while their parents fulfilled their commitments as Catholics. By the end of the summer they would start travelling back to their territories,

their places of belonging, their "homes." As a general rule, it was only in the 1970s that Atikamekw families really began living on a permanent basis on the reserves, and even then many of the adult men went back to their territories during the winter months, often accompanied by their wives. However, that practice declined significantly in the following decades.

The first decades of the twentieth century brought about other changes, including construction of a railroad through Atikamekw territory. While the railroad meant an increase of Euro-Canadian workers and visitors, it also made it easier for Atikamekw to travel to trading and supply posts. In spite of an increased infringement of *Emitcikocicak* activities on their land, the Atikamekw adapted fairly well to the changes while maintaining their autonomy and self-determination as semi-nomadic hunters. Up until the 1970s, many of the men worked seasonally as lumberjacks or guides for the (mostly) American sport hunters and fishers who came to the private clubs. These activities gave them some income but did not significantly infringe on their lives as hunters and trappers. They maintained their camp lives and trapping activities, as well as their responsibilities toward their ancestral territories. The flexibility that characterizes the world of hunters—an openness to change that allows them to reassess constantly the resources and potentialities of the land and of their social environment and to act accordingly—served them well.

Government Policies of Assimilation

The Canadian policies of assimilation of Indigenous people that were implemented more systematically from the 1950s to the 1970s marked a turning point in the world of the Atikamekw. The impacts of those policies, wherein Natives were pressured to move into permanent settlements (reserves) to "take advantage" of educational and health services, for instance, are still felt. One of these policies, the off-reserve residential schools, created a breach in the local processes of handing down knowledge, skills, and practices to younger generations. Several men and women, now in their fifties and sixties, shared with me their memories of childhood, when they were taken from the security and warmth of camp life to faraway and foreign places. One of them recalled the sadness and loneliness he felt around Christmastime when his parents would send him a two-dollar bill that smelled of the reassuring scents of the forest and of camp life, of the wood stove and the fir ground cover. He kept it secretly and affectionately under his pillow. Another recalled the awkwardness he felt when he returned to live with his parents during the summer holidays. He would try to assist his father in making wooden snowshoe frames, unable to understand the technical Atikamekw terms of his father. As children and later on as adults, men and women of that generation have lived through many hardships and painful experiences. Paradoxically, the residential school generation is the one that has initiated, with the support and the knowledge of the Elders, the reaffirmation and the revitalization of the Atikamekw ways, language, and traditional ritual practices. For the last 30 years, they have been pushing for Indigenous rights, land claims, and political change. It is the members of that generation who established, in the 1990s, a bilingual program in Atikamekw elementary schools.

In the early 1950s, at a time when the beaver population was declining dramatically to the point of jeopardizing the fur market, the Quebec government implemented beaver reserves over large areas of central and northern Quebec. The reserves were intended as a resource management strategy; the government believed the beaver population could recover if areas of land were delimited and secured where only Aboriginal people could hunt and trap. The Abitibi beaver reserve covered just over half the territories used by Atikamekw families, thus reducing significantly the territories where the Atikamekw were legally allowed to hunt and trap. At the time, the government also imposed a five-year ban on beaver trapping and even brought some beavers from elsewhere to allow the resource to regenerate.

According to the Atikamekw, the decline was the result of over-trapping by Euro-Canadians who did not have the necessary knowledge to ensure the reproduction of the species. As early as the 1930s, the Atikamekw, accompanied by Father Joseph-Étienne Guinard, a missionary, had brought their concerns about the abuses of Euro-Canadian trappers to the attention of Quebec Premier Louis-Alexandre Taschereau. Most Atikamekw, however, also explained this disappearance as a result of the beaver's decision. The following comment made in 1997 by an Elder of Manawan, who was a young man at the time, is revealing:

The Elders had told us. One day, the beaver will come back. He has dived into the water, but one day he will surface again. He stays underground, but we don't know where. And when they know that their number has increased, they will surface again. When they know that they are sufficiently numerous to give themselves as food. All the animals do that, even the moose. They disappear for a while, unwilling to give themselves as food, and then they come back.

In the late 1940s and 1950s, in the absence of the beaver and until he decided to "surface" again, the Atikamekw trapped other species, such as marten, muskrat, mink, fox, lynx, and otter. While the focus of trapping has varied, throughout the same time period the moose has remained central to hunting activities.

Within the beaver reserve, trapping lots were granted to the heads of family groups, more or less respecting traditional territorial affiliations. The beaver reserve represented the first tangible gesture by the Quebec government to set limits on Atikamekw hunting (and living) territories. As a result, the Atikamekw were directly confronted, perhaps for the first time, with Western ways of mapping and drawing boundaries. Again, they adjusted to this new reality, evolving a synthesis between these new regulations and their own customary practices of sharing and handing down territories, including resource management practices and ethics. Those families whose ancestral territories lay outside the beaver reserve continued, whenever possible, to use them as before.

This brief overview of Atikamekw colonial history is meant to outline the main events and policies that have shaped recent Atikamekw experiences and the forms that their resistance has taken. These events and policies have played a sig-nificant role in the transformation of their world. Their social order, their cultural consciousness and identity, and the ways in which they relate with the forest have all been affected.

Contemporary Social and Political Structures

The Atikamekw Nation, as a modern social and political entity, took shape gradually throughout the twentieth century as the semi-nomadic bands and families of this vast territory consolidated their alliances and united their forces in the face of the intruders. Over the last three decades and in their struggle for self-determination, the Atikamekw have created institutional structures and representative bodies that allow them to relate to and negotiate with the state and the dominant society in ways that they feel they can be heard. These structures and bodies give them an opportunity to

---

BOX 8.1 Reserved Lands

The reserved lands of the Atikamekw communities of Wemotaci, Manawan, and Opitciwan occupy 32, 7.83, and 9.35 square kilometers. These reduced spaces contrast sharply with the amount of territory that not so long ago they occupied as semi-nomadic hunters. Such spatial reduction has meant a rethinking of interpersonal and inter-group relationships and a transformation in gender and generational relationships. At the political level, as stipulated under the Indian Act, every three years each community elects a band council, that is, a chief and councillors. Until recently, the council was solely a male domain. This contrasts with traditionally egalitarian gender relationships and contradicts somehow the fact that *kokum*, the grandmother, to this day stands as a most respected, knowledge-able, and even authoritative figure. In the last 10 years, however, women have been increasingly present in local and "national" political bodies and agendas, putting forward their concerns on community matters and on social healing, re-establishing a more egalitarian balance in the decision-making processes. Following the implementation of federal policies of self-determination toward First Nations, Atikamekw communities have gained increased autonomy in dealing with their own affairs, particularly in health and social services, justice, and education. This leaves political and legal recognition of their rights and title on ancestral territories as their most important struggle.

reaffirm their difference and the vitality of their dynamic tradition. From the 1970s onward, following on the Canadian government's policies of self-determination for Indigenous people, the Atikamekw founded institutions that have enabled them to assert themselves as a distinct social, cultural, historical, and political entity. Among these are: Atikamekw Sipi, the Council of the Atikamekw Nation; Nehirowisiw Wasikahikan, the Atikamekw language institute; Nehirowisiw Kitci Atisokan, the Atikamekw historical society; and Mamo Atoskewin, the Atikamekw trapper's association (now defunct). Through these institutions, the Atikamekw are able to represent their interests vis-à-vis the dominant society.

Among themselves, however, at both the individual and the collective levels, Atikamekw affiliation is community based, as in Wemotaci Iriniwok (the people of Wemotaci), Manawan Iriniwok (the people of Manawan), and Opitciwan Iriniwok (the people of Opitciwan). Within each one of these community-based identities are a number of family groups, which some people today refer to as "clans." Each family group strongly identifies with its ancestral territory. The guardianships and responsibilities toward these territories are still being passed down according to Atikamekw customary practices, even for the territories that cannot be used anymore because of clear-cutting or other *Emitcikocicak* activities or regulations. An Elder expressed this in the following manner:

> We have to maintain our territories, always and irrespective of what happens. We have to do all what is in our power to maintain (our relationships to) those territories. . . . My territory that was my grandfather's and father's before me, even if today it is clear-cut, it will always be my territory. . . . One day the animals will come back. They always come back.

For the Atikamekw, as for other First Nations, there is a direct correlation between the loss of territories, the loss of self-determination, and their confinement in reserves and a significant increase in a variety of social problems. These include, in the last decades, a high rate of suicide among young people.

Even in the confines of the new communities, however, the Atikamekw have evolved a different sense of belonging, interacting, and moving about that still reflects some aspects of their semi-nomadic traditional ways and values. They have redefined their hunting and nomadic traditions to meet the requirements of today's world. Ancestral territories are now visited only on a sporadic basis. This does not, however, mean that their ties and sense of responsibility toward the land have diminished; territorial affiliations sometimes may be neglected, but they are never denied. The Atikamekw social order still values and recognizes each person's identification with the family territory inherited from their fathers and grandfathers. People still visit their territories, even if it is only on weekends, on holidays, or during cultural weeks.[3] These visits are facilitated by motorized transport (outboard motor, four-wheel drive vehicle, and snowmobile). Over the years, many Atikamekw hunters have been fined or arrested and their hunting equipment has been confiscated for hunting outside the beaver reserve, such as within the limits of an outfitting camp that has been given exclusive rights to the area by the government. Far from being discouraged, more and more Atikamekw are now "occupying" their family territories. They are making their presence known by establishing both temporary and permanent camps, in spite of the tensions this may create with the sport hunters and fishers they encounter. These signs of their presence and activities in the forest represent for them the most tangible evidence of their rights and responsibilities toward their ancestral territories. The traditional identification of land with family groups still lies at the core of Atikamekw identity, social networks, and interpersonal relationships, and is an intrinsic part of their sense of responsibility toward the land. Even the territories that cannot be used anymore, for example, because of clear-cutting, are still identified with their traditional owners.

Atikamekw Land: Identity and Knowledge

In societies like that of the Atikamekw, which value oral traditions, storytelling plays a paramount role in the process of individual socialization. It is also a means of sharing knowledge and skills. Through the telling of stories, including myths, life histories, personal experiences, and anecdotes, children learn the values and moral codes of the group. For the ethnographer, stories represent a privileged medium through which one can access a culture and the way a group of people understands its own history. The following sections are inspired mostly by stories told by elderly women and men of the three communities, as they recalled their lives in the first half of the twentieth century and well into the 1960s.[4]

These narratives refer to a time when the Atikamekw were still living independently on the land and the signs of *Emitcikocicak* presence were few. Through stories, these Elders share their experiences, knowledge, practices, and interactions, not so much on the land and in the forest but with the land and within the forest, and with the trees, animals, and plants. As hunters, they acquired the art of deciphering the various sounds, signs, and traces left by all living beings that share the land with them; it is a fundamental dimension of their intimate and knowledgeable relationship with their dwelt-in world. From their point of view, the decrease in recent decades in the various signs and traces left by the Atikamekw (the campsites, for example) and the increase in the signs and traces now left by the Euro-Canadians represent

the most tangible indication of their dispossession. Interestingly, in their narratives, they never referred to themselves as Atikamekw. They used instead the word *Nehirowisiw*, that is, "the first human inhabitant," which also means the one who has an intimate and knowledgeable relationship with the land and the forest. It is precisely such a relationship that has made it possible for them to live autonomously on their territories. *Notcimik*, the Atikamekw word for "forest," can be translated by "where I come from."

Ancestral Territories

The Atikamekw language distinguishes between an inclusive "us" that encompasses the one who speaks (and other related persons) and the listener, and an exclusive "us" that includes only the one who speaks (and other related persons) but excludes the listener. This distinction is evident in the different ways they designate their ancestral territory. In the context of land claims and negotiations with states and Euro-Canadians, Atikamekw refer to their ancestral territory by using the word *nitaskinan*: the listeners are here excluded from territorial affiliation. When, on the other hand, they speak between themselves of their ancestral territory, they use the word *kitaskino*: the speakers and the listeners share then the territorial affiliation.

The territory of a multi-family group can be defined as a more or less bounded area delimited by permanent landmarks (rivers, lakes, or mountains). Overlapping between different territories was (and is) frequent. These rather large multi-family territories may in turn be divided into extended family hunting territories, which are sometimes called *nehirowisiw aski*, "the land within which one can be autonomous." From the Atikamekw point of view, territorial boundaries are permeable and flexible, something that can be reassessed according to needs, events, or the accessibility of resources. These areas of land, as areas of responsibility, are inherited, usually along the father's line, but again some flexibility is needed. For example, some people have inherited rights over their mother's father's territory, while others have inherited areas of land from their adoptive father, or their father-in-law. The Atikamekw rules of sharing, delimiting, and passing down territories—rules that are grounded and recognized solely through oral tradition—are flexible and dynamic, constantly adapting to circumstances, perhaps more so in today's context. But now as before, what is most important for the Atikamekw is that no territories be left alone without a traditional "guardian" to look after them. The main guardian, the head of a family territory, who must be an accomplished hunter, is called *kanikaniwitc*, "the one who walks in front" or "the one who leads the way," referring to portaging, or *okimaw*, the "chief" of a family territory. His main responsibilities are to ensure that the territory is well looked after, that local resource management practices are respected, and that every hunter within the extended family has his hunting and trapping area. If someone from outside the extended family wishes to use an area within the territory for a season, permission must be requested orally of the *kanikaniwitc*.

What is handed down is not so much a bounded area of land as a series of named places along travelling routes, as well as campsites and traplines. All these are imbued with memories, stories, and traces from the ancestors (*kimocomnok*), those who lived there before, taking care of the land and leaving their mark on it. An Elder from Manawan expressed it in the following manner, "When you give your territory to your son and your grandson . . . you give your *onehirowisiwin* (a way or a place for being autonomous). You don't give the territory itself but everything that lives and grows on the territory . . . so people can in turn live from it. My grandfather did not 'give' his territory to anyone, he simply said, 'This is where you will find whatever you need to feed yourselves and to live.'" The importance of the territory in providing food is crucial. A way of life and a path to self-sufficiency, and thus to autonomy and pride, are also passed down with the territory. From the point of view of the Elders, the responsibility and commitment to one's territory make an individual a *Nehirowisiw*.

Delimiting and Sharing Traplines

Extended family territories, within the larger multi-family domains, must in turn be distinguished from the traplines. Within each extended family territory are a number of traplines (*atoske meskano*) that are shared among the hunters of an extended family and reassessed every year according to Atikamekw resource management strategies and ethics. It is the responsibility of the main guardian to ensure that the hunting and trapping areas are shared among hunters. Each year, in August or early September, before the trapping season, hunters visit their territories—and the hunting and trapping areas they know best—to evaluate the state of the land and its resources, paying particular attention to the beaver population. Circling around their territory (*waskackan*), they identify the lakes and streams where there are families of beavers. At each place, they evaluate the number of beavers and know how many can be taken and how many should be left to ensure reproduction. Along the way—and Atikamekw insist that traplines are always circular—in order to mark the identified places but also to delimit trapping areas for the coming season, hunters make notches on the trees (*wasikahikan*). They may even make as many notches as the corresponding number of beavers they plan to trap there. These notches—signs—represent a highly efficient system of communicating to other hunters that this place, and this colony of beavers, is already set aside for the coming season. In no way, according to Atikamekw customary rules, should these trapping spots be infringed upon. Once the trapping season is over, these seasonal boundaries are lifted and will be reassessed the following year.

An Elder from Wemotaci described the marking of territory:

> I have seen my father. He made a notch on a tree, and planted a branch in it, meaning that this is as far as he would go. The other hunter does the same thing; he comes to the limits of his trapping area and does a notch next to my father's. Like that, they both know their respective limits where their trapping territories meet, so they would not encroach on each other's territory. *It is not the territory itself that they were measuring, it is the streams and the lakes where they trapped that they were indicating* [my emphasis].

It is worth noting that it was (and is) common for a group of hunters to share the same trapping and hunting area for a season. The group of hunters (*mamo atoskewin*) may be composed of a father and his adult sons (or grandsons, nephews, or sons-in-law), a man and his brothers-in-law, or a hunter and some friends he has invited for the season. This brings us to a widespread practice embedded in the Atikamekw social order and in resource management strategies: the practice (or institution) of inviting other hunters to share one's territory for a season. This principle (*wicakemowin*) serves mainly as a resource management strategy. It means that whenever one's territory, or trapping area, has to be left for a season to replenish itself, the hunter can seek an invitation to share another territory. Or, whenever a hunter considers that he has surplus resources on his territory, he can invite family members or friends to share the trapping season (and resources, and income from the sale of furs) with him.

Learning the Languages of the Forest

In handing over the responsibility for an extended family territory or a hunting area within it, a number of factors are taken into account, among them the degree of knowledge one has of the territory. One knows a country when one has walked over it; when one can name and recognize the myriad places and the trails connecting them; when one knows the paths and travelling routes according to the seasons, over the land (*icawin* or *motewin*), along the water ways (*itohiin*), and across the snow in winter; when one has the skills to evaluate the state of the land and its various resources. This knowledge must be balanced with an equivalent degree of respect toward the land and its non-human inhabitants. In the past, a boy of 10 would start following his grandfather during the trapping and hunting season. After five years of learning from his grandfather, he would go hunting with his father for a few seasons. Not only did he have to acquire hunting skills, but he had to be able to make the necessary materials out of local resources (bark canoe, snowshoes, sledge, axe handles, etc.). This meant, for example, that to make a frame for snowshoes, he had to be able to recognize the right birch tree, one that would bend easily and not split during the process. In his early twenties, once he had acquired the skills and values to be self-sufficient, he would be given responsibility for an area within the family territory. Throughout the learning process, each time he killed a type of game for the first time, the event was underlined by a *makocan*, a ceremonial meal. An Elder from Opitciwan told the story of his own experience:

> I was a boy, and I was helping my mother to lift the fishing net. My father and my brother had gone to trap muskrat. I saw the loon. I took the gun, it was a short one, and shot it. This was the first time that I killed a loon. With my mother, we took it and brought it to the camp. My grandfather was there; he was blind. He told us to prepare it right away. My mother plucked it, cleaned it, and cooked it. Then, when everybody had come back,

we made the *makocan*. We all sat in a circle. I sat next to my grandfather, and we ate and shared the loon. During the meal, I was asked to sit in the middle of the circle; they gave me the fat and they told me to rub my hair with it. This is what they did.

In the meantime, young girls were initiated by their grandmothers, mothers, or aunts into the skills and knowledge needed by women. While the men were out on their traplines or travelling to and from the trading posts, often for weeks at a time, the women stayed at the winter camp and had to ensure the well-being of the household. Among others things, women's skills included setting snares for hares and other small game; fishing; preparing the game men brought back from hunting; cooking, smoking, or drying the meat or fish; gathering medicinal plants; tanning the hides (mostly moose and beaver hides); and making and decorating birchbark containers and leather clothing (such as moccasins and gloves), etc. These skills and practices are not simply things of the past. Although they are no longer part of everyday life, many women from all generations still have these skills.

It would be wrong to believe that this knowledge, these practices, and these values are things of the past, or that they have been eroded or become obsolete as a result of the major changes in the Atikamekw way of life and the growing constraints on using their territories. While some of the knowledge and skills that used to sustain a nomadic and self-sufficient way of life have indeed disappeared, most of them are still very much alive. They remain part of contemporary Atikamekw reality, in spite of the fact that the knowledge is acquired and practised differently by the younger generations and may have different meanings for them. In today's context, it is usually in their thirties that men and women will start to show an interest in learning about and practising traditional activities on the land, seeking then guidance from the Elders.

The Seasonal Cycle

The Atikamekw recognize six seasons, rather than four, and whenever the opportunity arises, they are proud to point out this difference to non-Indigenous people. Each season corresponds to a state of the land, to the availability of particular resources, and thus to specific hunting, trapping, fishing, and gathering skills and practices. *Sikon* (March and April) starts the seasonal cycle. It is the period when the lakes start to break up; travelling on the land during this season is problematic. It is the time for collecting and making maple syrup, a traditional activity. In traditional times, it is during *sikon* that the Atikamekw started the journey to their summer gathering place. *Miroskamin*—"new earth, new shoot"—corresponds to May and June. In addition to fishing and trapping and hunting animals, it is also a time for hunting geese and other migratory birds. *Nipin* (July and August), a word derived from "water," is the summer season. Fishing is the main activity, with no trapping and very little hunting being done, aside from duck hunting and some snaring. It is the time to gather bark (mostly from birch, to make baskets and canoes in traditional times), medicinal plants, and blueberries. The latter are abundant in the area. They are cooked, made into a paste, mixed with bear fat, and stored for the winter. Traditionally, it was the time when families, who were spread over a wide territory the rest of the year, would gather together to socialize and meet with friends and family members. *Takwakin* (September and October) is the season of "chilly times." The family groups would start their journey back "home" to their respective hunting grounds. They had gathered the necessary material (food, hunting equipment, clothing, etc.) and would take a few weeks to get to their winter camps. They would establish temporary

FIGURE 8.2 An Elder stretching a beaver skin to dry it. The skin will be used for making various items of clothing. These skills, though less widespread than in earlier generations, are still part of Atikamekw reality. (Photo, 1965, by Camil Guy. Courtesy of the Conseil de la Nation Atikamekw)

camps along the way, travelling on rivers and lakes, portaging, etc. *Takwakin* is also the best time for moose hunting; the bulk of the meat would be smoked and kept for later and harder times. *Pitci pipon* (November and December) is the "false winter." By this time, families usually had arrived at their winter camps; hunting, fishing, and trapping are the main activities during this season. *Pipon*, "winter" or "coldest times" (January and February), is the best time for trapping. Some fishing is done by cutting holes in the ice. *Takwakin, pitci pipon*, and *pipon* are the best seasons for trapping, when an animal's fur is thickest. The best seasons for fishing are *miroskamin, nipin*, and *takwakin*. Today, Atikamekw still strongly identify with the six-season cycle and its associated activities.

Named Places and Campsites

The Atikamekw have an intimate relationship with the forest as a social space and a series of living places. Their deep knowledge of it is eloquently expressed in a rich profusion of place names for locales that, not so long ago, were home to those who are Elders today. Nomads are not content to name only the most obvious features of the landscape; instead, they name the smallest meaningful unit. Place names are inspired by a permanent or peculiar feature of the landscape, by whatever can be gathered or hunted there, or by a particular event or action that occurred there. The comments of two Elders of Opitciwan in regard to a small portion of their ancestral territory help us to understand this reality:

There is a place, it is a shortcut; it is all covered with a lot of moss. There is only moss at that place, so we call it Mickekonikimici. At another place, the water level is higher, so we call it Eskowipew or Eskowpekw. There is a trail that we call Miro Mitiso Meskano, which means "the trail where one eats well." Another place, it is a long portage and over the years as people walked over and over, the roots have been coming out, so we call it Ka Otapihocomokw, "the trail of roots." Another place where they come up to with the canoe for a portage; there are a lot of cypresses at that place, so we call it Ka Oskikecimokw.

There is a place where a female Elder once prepared some strips out of moose hides for snowshoes, so we call it Ackimin. There is another place where the passage to go from one lake to another is very narrow; we call it Ka Arokopetciwokw. A place where the edge of the forest is scattered, we call it Ka Meskwaskokamak. Another one, it is the highest point in the area where one can see all around; it is as if there were waves, as if one could hear the humming of the waves, we call it Ka Mokwaskak. Another place is called Ka Atikamekwskak—this is where there is cisco [a fish]. There is a mountain we name Ka Nicokotewci Matana because it is as if the mountain had two peaks.

From the Atikamekw point of view, these place names represent signs of their intimate and enduring relationship with the land and the forest. Other signs of Atikamekw presence and dwelling within *notcimik* are also highly valued. Such traces include sites of old and more recent temporary camps, places where imprints left on the ground by tents are visible. Another sign is the *tecpita-kan*, a wooden structure used to store hunting and trapping materials (traps, snowshoes, canoes, sledges, etc.) in the bush at the end of the hunting season. Atikamekw stopped building and using these caches about 30 years ago because of Euro-Canadian break-ins and vandalism. The decrease in these signs of Atikamekw activity, as expression and proof of their connection to the land, makes the Elders, both women and men, quite nostalgic. Part of their nostalgia is also due to their observation that Euro-Canadians perceive and act upon the forest in ways that lack the basic values of respect and reciprocity that formerly orchestrated the relationship between the human and non-human inhabitants of the land.

A Sentient Forest

At the beginning of the chapter, I mentioned that an anthropologist acts as a translator between worlds. This role becomes especially challenging when we come to radical cultural differences, particularly when they relate to questions of **ontology** and **epistemology**. An example of this radical difference is seen in how the Atikamekw view, experience, and relate to the forest and its non-human constituents. An answer to this question can be found by exploring and taking seriously local ontological (ways of being) and epistemological (ways of knowing) principles and comparing them with those dominant in the West. Western thought, and by extension its scientific models, establishes a clear distinction, if not an absolute dichotomy, between the world of "natural" objects and the world of "cultural" (human) subjects. This mode of thought is based on an anthropocentric view of the world, giving humans priority over the rest of nature. As members of a community that embraces that view, we see it as normal, as the "logical" way to look at the world. However, such a dualistic mode of thought is far from universal. One has only to look at the world of hunter–gatherers, as well as the world view of many other non-Western societies around the world, to realize that the Western scientific outlook is but one way of defining reality.

What anthropological studies seem to emphasize, insofar as the world view of hunters is concerned, is the centrality of relatedness (Bird-David 1999; Ingold 1996; Viveiros de Castro 1998), that is, the relational nature of being, knowing, and becoming. Relationships dynamically unfold in time and space through the interactions between interconnected constituents, whether these are human or non-human. Hunters engage in intimate and reciprocal relationships with the animals they hunt insofar as they share the same land, trees, and waters, breathe the same air, and walk over the same ground. Furthermore, the non-human constituents of the world are considered sentient entities that act consciously upon their world. Animals, for example, are endowed with intentionality. They have purposes, identities, and points of view so that they experience the world from their own perspectives and act accordingly. Let us see now how these considerations find echoes in the world of the Atikamekw.

In a hunting tradition, like that of the Atikamekw, knowledge and practices, ethics and aesthetics, and values and emotions are all closely intertwined. The Elders also make it clear that sharing and reciprocity are at the core of their understanding of their relations with the animals. As hunters, the Atikamekw value and engage in an intimate and reciprocal relationship with the non-human constituents of their world and with whom they cohabit—animals, trees, plants, mountains, including also the spirits of deceased relatives. Atikamekw ethics, their resource management strategies and practices, and even their aesthetic sense can only be understood by taking into account this particular dialogue with the forest and its inhabitants. The land, as a sentient landscape, "speaks" to the hunter. Asked about the beauty of the mountain, as part of a landscape, an Elder answered that "the mountain is delicious," referring to all the different food that the mountain offers to humans. The animals *are* food, but the Atikamekw hunter is always reminded that the animals "give themselves" and by that conscious gesture they earn the hunter's respect. It is in that sense that their relationship is said to be reciprocal. If humans do not act properly, the animals may decide to go away and not give themselves anymore. The trees and plants, as food for animals and humans, are just as valued and respected. An Elder spoke of the trees as the sole "guardians" and "chiefs" of the *Nehirowisiw*.

These examples suggest that, for the Atikamekw, the animals, plants, trees, and waters are resources. But they are also sentient entities who share the forest with humans. This view contrasts with the Western one in which only humans are said to be conscious agents who have a mandate to act as sole masters over an objectified world of "nature." The Atikamekw concept thus entails a different code of ethics and a different mode of resource management based on a holistic system of knowledge. The Atikamekw system of knowledge is holistic in the sense that it is not specialized and compartmentalized. Trees, bears, and people are not put into separate "boxes." When walking in the forest or visiting a hunting territory, a knowledgeable person should be able to read, both qualitatively and quantitatively, the state of the land as a whole. The availability of so-called resources as well as the state of their interrelations and interactions, and thus of their becoming, should be apparent. Such a qualitative and quantitative process of assessment implies listening to, reading, and interpreting the different languages within the forest, and responding to them appropriately.

In the Atikamekw language, this holistic process of assessment and reconnaissance over the extent of one's territory is referred to as *tipahiskan*. *Tipahiskan* implies a whole range of knowledge and practices, from visiting a territory and evaluating its resources to passing on knowledge and telling stories. It can be translated as "land and resource management," though the term has a different meaning from what Westerners, or scientific models, usually understand by it. The main difference between the Western concept of resource management and that of the Atikamekw is that the former aims to modify the land and exploit resources through technical manipulation of the natural world in order to suit the needs and purposes of humans. From an Atikamekw perspective, considering the principles of relatedness and reciprocity, management and ethics mean adapting one's behaviour or future purposes and actions on the basis of the information received from the forest, including the needs and well-being of non-human others. If the needs and purposes of the latter are not taken into account, the well-being of humans will be affected. From the perspective of Euro-Canadian "users," whether logging companies or sport hunters, the forest is viewed as a commodity and as "raw nature"; it is neither a "home" nor a "sharing partner." Furthermore, *tipahiskan* implies the whole person, as a centre of relationships, and his or her engagement within *notcimik*, not merely a disembodied, technical knowledge over an objectified world of "nature." Even the concept of "sustainable development" is inadequate to express all that is implied in the concept of *tipahiskan* because it usually is construed in a dualistic manner and so limits what is taken into account in assessing resource needs. In the rhetoric of sustainable development, resources remain merely resources; they are not non-human agents who interact with humans and share the forest. *Tipahiskan*—the Atikamekw mode of resource and land management—currently must take into account the Euro-Canadian presence, activities, and boundaries, demonstrating once more their tremendous

ability and willingness to transform their ways in order to adapt to the new conditions of their changing world.

Conclusion

In this chapter, I have portrayed some aspects of the changing world of the Atikamekw. We have reviewed their colonial history, their participation in the fur trade, and their gradual passage from a nomadic way of life to settled communities subsequent to the narrowing of their hunting and living territories. Elders' stories have offered some understanding of the lives, values, and seasonal practices of the Atikamekw prior to the 1960s, at a time when they still felt they could live autonomously, following in the footsteps of their ancestors. We have also tried to understand how Atikamekw hunters view and experience their relationship with the forest, as a world of interacting and interconnected sentient entities. With the same determination and flexibility as their ancestors, but also with much disillusion, frustration, and suffering, today's Atikamekw have accommodated to their new realities and adjusted their practices. In their ongoing attempts to accommodate *Emitcikocicak* activities and interests on their land, they have made many compromises, while others they have resisted.

After decades of colonial marginalization, dispossession and humiliation, Atikamekw women and men are involved in a number of initiatives in an effort to build a meaningful future and to regain their dignity and pride. I have already referred to the creation of political, cultural, and linguistic bodies and institutions at the level of the Atikamekw Nation. In order to promote the Atikamekw language and ways, a primary school bilingual program has been implemented in the three communities. Smaller-scale programs aim to initiate young people to life in the forest and to hunting skills. Alongside these initiatives, a growing number of Atikamekw are involved in the revitalization of traditional ritual practices such as the first-steps ceremony, the sweat lodge, and drum beating, all practices that were strongly denigrated and forbidden by the Roman Catholic Church. To these practices we could add also the reactivation of networks of ritual exchange with neighbouring First Nations such as the Ojibwa. While some Atikamekw express opposition to these practices, they are gaining momentum and contributing to the process of social healing. The revitalization

and reinterpretation of these ritual practices are not only culturally interesting, but are also politically empowering as significant gestures in the struggle toward self-determination. All these initiatives, along with their territorial claims, are political statements insofar as they are contemporary expressions of their identity and of their unique relationship with the land.

As a rule, the Atikamekw are conscious that their relationship with the land is the only

---

BOX 8.2 Ancestral Territories

In the 1970s, public access to Crown lands was democratized by the Quebec government and private hunting and fishing clubs were suppressed. Since then, Atikamekw ancestral territories, apart from the reserves, have been subject to an administrative system that places them in one of four categories: controlled harvesting zones, outfitting camps (with either exclusive or non-exclusive rights), resort leases, or logging leases. This means that, on the ground, the Atikamekw must deal with two systems for "mapping" the land and for setting boundaries: theirs and that of the *Emitcikocic*. While the Euro-Canadians' boundaries and regulations contrast with Atikamekw ways of sharing, delimiting, and passing down family and hunting territories, a synthesis—or compromise—between the two has evolved. However, all the decisions about policies, leases, and boundaries have taken place with almost no consultation with the Atikamekw, let alone their active participation. This seems to deny not only their history but their very existence. On the other hand, the Atikamekw Nation has been negotiating with the federal and the provincial governments since the mid-

1970s toward a comprehensive land-claim agreement over the extent of their ancestral territories, but with no tangible results to this day. The Atikamekw refuse to comply with the federal policy of extinguishing Indigenous rights and title. Like other First Nations, they seek a form of modern treaty based on a mutual recognition and affirmation of rights and interconnections between them, the state, and the dominant society; they seek to shape a relationship based on equality and sharing (Asch 1997).

The following statement by César Néwashish, a most respected Elder who died in 1994 at the age of 91, is emblematic of Atikamekw territorial claims:

> Witamowikok aka wiskat e ki otci pakitina-mokw kitaskino, nama wiskat ki otci atawanano, nama wiskat ki otci mecko-tonenano, name kaie wiskat ki otci pitoc irakonenano kitaskino. (Tell them we have never given up our territory, tell them we have never sold or traded it, tell them that we have never reached any other sort of agreement concerning our territory.)

guarantee of the vitality of their language, and thus of the Atikamekw ways. Indeed, it is a leitmotif in the various claims, strategies, and struggles to regain their self-determination. The initiatives and strategies being developed today by the Atikamekw aim to maintain and reconfigure their relationship to their territories while accommodating the dictates of modernity and development. They are waiting, patiently but not passively, for the political recognition of their land rights. In so doing they hope to gain their rightful place as equal "partners" within the decision-making processes that govern their territories and preside over the destinies of *notcimik*.

ACKNOWLEDGEMENT

The research on which this chapter is based was supported by the Social Sciences and Humanities Research Council of Canada.

NOTES

1. The Atikamekw language is an r-dialect of Cree, using "r" where other dialects might use a "th" or an "l." Sometimes they are simply included among the Cree. The phoneme "kw" is pronounced "ak". From the end of the eighteenth century until the 1950s, they were known as the Tête-de-Boule Cree.

2. The Atikamekw and Montagnais Council was founded in 1975 as a political and representative body. It was dissolved in 1994, each of the First Nations preferring to negotiate separately (see Charest 1992).

3. Twenty-five years ago, the Atikamekw instituted cultural weeks—two weeks in spring and autumn when schools and offices are closed so people can set up camps on their territories during the hunting seasons for migrating birds.

4. These narratives were collected between 1995 and 2000 by myself, two Atikamekw research assistants, Jean-Marc Niquay and Gilles Ottawa, and two MA anthropology students, Kathia Lavoie and Marie-Josée Roussy.

REFERENCES AND RECOMMENDED READINGS

Asch, Michael. 1997. "Affirming Aboriginal Title: A New Basis for Comprehensive Claims Negotiations." In *Aboriginal and Treaty Rights in Canada: Essays on Law, Equality, and Respect for Difference*, edited by Asch. Vancouver: University of British Columbia Press.

Béland, Jean-Pierre. 1978. "Atikamekw Morphology and Lexicon," Ph.D. thesis, University of California, Berkeley. This is the only thorough description and analysis of the Atikamekw language, with some analysis of contemporary dialects and comparisons with neighbouring Cree and Innu.

Bird-David, Nurit. 1999. "Animism Revisited," *Current Anthropology* 40, supplement: S67–S91.

Charest, Paul. 1992. "La prise en charge donne-t-elle du pouvoir? L'exemple des Atikamekw et des Montagnais," *Anthropologie et sociétés* 16, 3: 55–76.

Clermont, Norman. 1977. *Ma femme, ma hache et mon couteau croche: Deux siècles d'histoire à Weymontachie*. Quebec: Ministère des Affaires Culturelles. A comprehensive analysis of Wemotaci from the end of the eighteenth century to the 1950s, this study offers historical data and information on social organization, material culture, and hunting practices.

———. 1977. "Les Kokotchés à Weymontachie," *Recherches amérindiennes au Québec* 8, 2: 139–46. Ethnographic data on Atikamekw oral tradition, myths, and cosmology. The Kokotchés are strong and malevolent beings who look like humans but are cannibals and masters of the wind.

Cooper, John M. 1926. "The Obidjiwan Band of the Têtes de Boule," *Anthropos* 21, 3/4: 616–17. A historical, social, and territorial overview of Opitciwan hunting groups. Cooper conducted extensive fieldwork and underlines the linguistic, social, and cultural affiliations among northern Algonquians.

———. 1928. "Field Notes on Northern Algonkian Magic," *XXIII International Congress of Americanists*: 513–18. Based mostly on ethnographic data from Opitciwan, a short and unique early description of Atikamekw hunting rituals, including notes about the shaking tent.

———. 1945. "Tête-de-Boule Cree," *International Journal of American Linguistics* 11, 1: 36–44. The evidence of the Atikamekw language being a Cree dialect is presented here. Mention is made of sub-dialectic differences between Atikamekw bands.

Davidson, D.S . 1928. "Decorative Art of the Têtes de Boule of Quebec," Museum of the American Indian, *Indian Notes and Monograph* 10, 9: 115–43. A thorough analysis of Atikamekw material culture and art designs, with a focus on birchbark containers, cradleboards, and moccasins. The author makes some comparisons with Cree and Innu.

———. 1928. "Notes on Tête de Boule Ethnology," *American Anthropologist* 30, 1: 18–46. One of the first anthropologists, with Cooper, to conduct fieldwork among the Atikamekw, Davidson provides invaluable data on their social and territorial organization in the early twentieth century.

———. 1928. "Some Tête de Boule Tales," *Journal of American Folklore* 41: 262–74. An early account of Atikamekw oral tradition, with a number of stories about the Iroquois raids. One tale about an old woman who finally succeeded in cheating and killing them is widespread among Algonquians.

Escobar, Arturo. "Anthropology and Development," *International Journal of Social Sciences* 154: 497–515.

Gélinas, Claude. 2000. *La gestion de l'étranger: Les Atikamekw et la présence eurocanadienne en Haute-Mauricie, 1760–1870*. Quebec: Septentrion. The first comprehensive ethnohistoric study of the Atikamekw. Gélinas analyzes the organization of hunting groups, material culture (including the trade of imported goods), relations with Euro-Canadians, and their changing character over 100 years.

———. 2003. *Entre l'assommoir et le godendart. Les Atikamekw et la conquête du Moyen-Nord québécois, 1870–1940*. Quebec: Septentrion.

Guinard, J-É. 1945. "Mémoires: Journal des missions," manuscript in Seminaire de Trois-Rivières, Québec. Father Guinard was an Oblate missionary in the upper Saint-Maurice from 1899 to 1940. His narration contains information on daily social realities in the communities. It is most instructive regarding Catholic and French-Canadian attitudes toward "Indians" in the early twentieth century.

Ingold, Tim. 1996. "Hunting and Gathering as Ways of Perceiving the Environment." In *Redefining Nature: Ecology, Culture and Domestication*, edited by R. Ellen and K. Fukui. Oxford: Berg.

Jérôme, Laurent. 2010. "Jeunesse, musique et rituels chez les Atikamekw (Haute-Mauricie, Québec): ethnographie d'un processus d'affirmation identitaire et culturelle en milieu autochtone". Unpublished Ph.D. diss., Université Laval. An in-depth analysis of the movement of ritual revitalization among the Atikamekw with an emphasis on intergenerational relationships and knowledge transmission.

Labrecque, Marie-France. 1984. "Des femmes de Weymontachie," *Recherches amérindiennes au Québec* 14, 3: 3–16. This work is based on the life stories of Atikamekw women from four generations. The author shows some of the changes in their lives and their main concerns.

———. 1984. "Développement du capitalisme dans la région de Weymontachie (Haute-Mauricie): Incidences sur la condition des femmes Attikamèques," *Recherches amérindiennes au*

Québec 14, 3: 75–87. A Marxist analysis of the fur trade, colonial history, and the development of capitalism in Atikamekw territory and how such external influences have affected the sexual division of labour and the social roles of women.

McNulty, Gérard E., and Louis Gilbert. 1981. "Attikamek (Tête de Boule)." In *Handbook of North American Indians.* Vol. 6, *The Subarctic,* edited by June Helm and William C. Sturtevant. Washington: Smithsonian Institution. A useful summary of Atikamekw history, population movement during the fur-trade period, and material culture, with bibliographic sources.

Poirier, Sylvie. 1992. "L'occupation et l'utilisation du territoire dans la région du Lac Flamand, McTavis et Windigo," report filed with Conseil Atikamekw et Montagnais, Québec. An analysis of the occupation of the Kokokac area and the merging of the Kokokac and Wemotaci bands, including maps showing family hunting territories and detailed genealogical charts.

———. 2000. "Contemporanéités autochtones, territoires et (post)colonialisme: Réflexions sur des exemples Canadiens et Australiens," *Anthropologie et Sociétés* 24, 1: 137–53. A critical approach to colonial doctrines, such as *terra nullius,* and their current effects through a comparative analysis of the Atikamekw and Kukatja (Australian Western Desert): their dealings with "modernity," their land-claims processes, and their cultural consciousness and resistance.

———. 2001. "Territories, Identity, and Modernity among the Atikamekw (Haut St-Maurice, Quebec)." In *Aboriginal Autonomy and Development in Northern Quebec and Labrador* edited by C.H. Scott.. Vancouver: University of British Columbia Press. The Atikamekw as contemporary hunters and gatherers: the consolidation of their nation, their perceptions of the land, and their resistance to Euro-Canadian activities and interest on their land.

———. 2010. "Change, Resistance, Accommodation and Engagement in Indigenous Contexts: A Comparative (Canada-Australia) perspective," *Anthropological Forum* 20, 1: 41–60.

Viveiros de Castro, Eduardo. 1998. "Cosmological Deixis and Amerindian Perspectivism," *Journal of the Royal Anthropological Institute* 4, 3: 469–88.

Wyatt, Stephen. 2004. "Co-existence of Atikamekw and Industrial Forestry Paradigms: Occupation and Management of Forestlands in the St-Maurice River Basin, Quebec." Unpublished Ph.D. diss., Université Laval. Based on the example of Wemotaci, it offers a comprehensive and critical analysis of "Indigenous forestry."

PART IV

The Western Subarctic

CHAPTER 9

The Western Subarctic: A Regional Overview

C. Roderick Wilson

Although the region strikes most southerners as definitely inhospitable, people have lived in the Western Subarctic longer than in any other part of Canada. As discussed in Chapter 2, bone tools discovered in the Old Crow region of Yukon have been widely accepted as indicating human presence some 25,000 years ago. Some archaeologists think that other artifacts found in the region are much older. Whatever dates are ultimately demonstrated, Amerindian people have clearly lived in the region from "time immemorial."

The physical environment of the region can be characterized as the zone of discontinuous permafrost in western Canada. The southern half is boreal forest (spruce, fir, and pine, with some poplar and white birch) and the rest is primarily a transitional zone of boreal vegetation intermixed with patches of lichen-dominated tundra. (As a cultural region the Western Subarctic in places extends north of the treeline into the tundra because some Subarctic societies made extensive use of tundra resources.) In absolute terms the region receives little precipitation (annual average about 40 cm), yet it has two of the largest river systems on the continent and innumerable lakes. The ground is snow covered six months of the year, and few places have more than 50 frost-free days. Temperature extremes typically range from lows of -50°C to summer highs of over 20°C.

Large game animals, particularly caribou, constituted the primary resource base for Aboriginal peoples. Moose, goats, sheep, and even bison were locally important. Small animals (especially the snowshoe hare), fish, migratory waterfowl, and grouse were of secondary importance.

The entire Western Subarctic culture area is inhabited by people speaking a series of closely related Athapaskan[1] languages. Linguists believe that these languages were undifferentiated as recently as 2,500 years ago and that from their "ancestral" homeland they expanded further west in Alaska and eastward into the Northwest Territories and then southward. Some, notably the Apacheans, became physically separated from the others and ended up thousands of miles to the south, but for Northern Athapaskans, because of limited linguistic variation, communication is still possible across considerable distances. This implies frequent communication between people from different localities from ancient time into the present. Correlatively, the ethnographic evidence is that few Northern Athapaskan groups had significant relationships with non-Athapaskans. The exceptions are the Denesuline (formerly Chipewyan, with Cree), the Gwich'in (formerly Kutchin) and Hare (sometimes called K'ahso Got'ine, with Inuit), and the Kaska (with Northwest Coast groups).

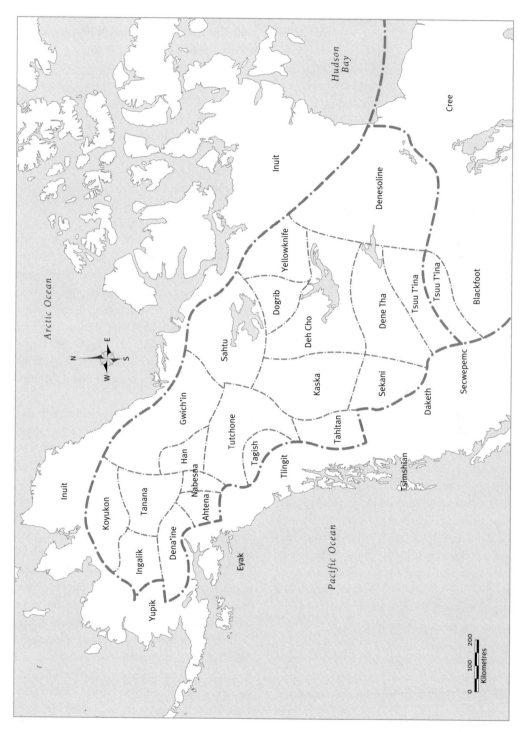

MAP 9.1 The Western Subarctic

In this context it seems significant that the kinship systems of people in this region could be extended in such a way that usually one could find a "relative" even in bands quite far distant, and hence a legitimate basis for establishing a relationship. In general these people developed social strategies characterized by great flexibility and informal institutional arrangements. For example, leadership among groups in the east of the region was largely situational: People were listened to or followed not because they had the power to make people obey but because they had demonstrated an ability to lead in that particular activity. An outstanding hunter might attract a considerable following; nevertheless, he had no permanent power. The overall picture thus was of individuals, family groups, and even larger groupings making short-term decisions about where and how they would live. These decisions were based on a large number of factors: the local supply of game, reports from elsewhere, degree of satisfaction with fellow band members, which relatives lived where, and so on. In the western part of the region, the existence of clans correlated with a more complex and formal social life; nevertheless, that life also was characterized by remarkable social flexibility.

Another key to Aboriginal Athapaskan society is its egalitarianism (autonomy and self-reliance are closely associated). This was true even among the most westerly people of the region who, like their maritime neighbours, had "chiefs." As McClellan and Denniston (1981:384–5) point out, these positions were conditional, and stratified rank was not possible for them until the fur-trade period. The staples necessary for life were, in general, equally accessible, and the skills necessary to transform them into finished products were shared widely in the community. Although some people were more competent than others, and more respected, there was no basis from which an exclusive control over goods, and hence people, could develop. Even in the realm of spiritual power, the ultimate basis for

any success and an aspect of life in which people varied conspicuously, the possibility of becoming a shaman was in principle open to all.

The initial contact of Canadian Athapaskans with Europeans was consistent with the general trend of the frontier moving from east to west. Direct trading contacts were made by the easternmost group, the Chipewyan, in 1714, while none of the westernmost tier of Canadian Athapaskans had direct contacts prior to 1850. There was not, however, a single frontier: Athapaskans in southern Alaska had trading contacts from 1741.

Helm (1975) makes the following points concerning the early contact process: European goods and diseases usually preceded direct contact with traders; the first-contacted tribes obtained guns and expanded their fur-collecting operations at the expense of their western neighbours; trading posts were welcomed by those living in the "new" territories; traders tended to act as peacemakers in this newly competitive context. The latter three points particularly contrast with Russian–Native relationships in Alaska.

The fur trade had numerous consequences, and it constituted a social revolution. The introduction of new goods, especially guns and traps, is salient. New social roles, such as trading chiefs, and changing social relationships are also striking. Perhaps most startling are features that are now identified as traditional, such as dogsleds, which were introduced during this period. Somewhat simplified, the guns, traps, and sleds enabled people to engage in old and new bush activities more efficiently, and the trading chiefs allowed traders to deal with the people more efficiently. However, the new elements made their own demands: a dog team in a year would eat thousands of pounds of fish, thereby increasing the "need" to obtain new goods such as fish nets and to harvest bush resources at a higher level. Further, an innovation frequently had a cumulative impact. The effect of the gun, an early trade item, in contributing to higher harvest levels becomes most evident

FIGURE 9.1 Chipewayan hunter with caribou he has shot, northern Manitoba. (Courtesy Hudson's Bay Company Archives, Archives of Manitoba, HBCA 1987/363-T-200/28)

after 1900. Nevertheless, these early changes were limited in scope, and continuity with the past was evident. The ensuing way of life was remarkably stable for many groups for almost a century and a half. Even the general acceptance of Christianity resulting from the activities of Oblate and Anglican missionaries was as notable for people's continued adherence to old beliefs as to new.

The impact of introduced diseases is not clear. Aboriginal population levels of the time are not well known, nor are the consequences of the various outbreaks. Are they isolated events, as a narrow reading of the sources would indicate, or do they represent merely the documented cases of widespread epidemics? What is evident is that a number of new diseases (smallpox, scarlet fever, influenza, measles, venereal diseases, and tuberculosis—in rough chronological order) became common, and that there were at times very high mortality rates, both because the new diseases were in themselves devastating and because in their wake small groups might well starve to death. Nevertheless, the recuperative powers of the population were such that the region as a whole appears not to have experienced significant demographic change until recently. With the advent of modern medicine some 60 years ago, the Yukon and Northwest Territories have experienced the highest rates of population increase in Canada.

For most of the area, the fact that Native societies had become incorporated into Canada did not become a social reality until the early 1950s. There were two major exceptions. Much of Dunne-za (Beaver) traditional territory, the Peace River country of northern British Columbia and Alberta, is arable. Farmers began displacing Natives in this area around 1890. Even more dramatic was the Klondike gold rush. Dawson alone had grown to 25,000 by 1898, while the Han "tribe," occupying adjacent portions of Alaska and the Yukon, numbered only about 1,000. The gold rush, and the government and commercial presence it created, resulted in an early marginalization of Native people in the Yukon to a degree that the people of the Northwest Territories generally have still not experienced.

A few generalizations about contemporary life are in order. First, for much of the region, most adults over about age 60 have personal memory of what life was like before significant government–industrial presence. For some the "traditional life" is a still present reality. Second, even for severely impacted groups, truly significant features of traditional life remain important.

Third, the treaties continue to be living documents. As Wishart notes, there is active debate over how Treaty Nos. 8 and 11 should currently be interpreted, but both sides agree that they help define the constitutional debate on what it means to be Native in those regions. A unique element of this debate is Judge Morrow's 1973 investigation of the circumstances under which Treaty No. 11 had been signed in 1921—unique because at the time there were signatories to the treaty still alive and able to testify in court that the treaty had been everywhere presented as a gesture of friendship and goodwill and not, as a literal reading of the English-language written text would indicate, as a means of extinguishing Aboriginal title.

A fourth point is that Athapaskans have attempted both to maintain themselves as distinctive peoples and to accommodate the powerful forces for change thrust upon them. In the late twentieth century the primary mechanism in the Northwest Territories for doing this, the Dene National Assembly, was profoundly rooted in traditional values. Events, however, have overtaken it, so that currently regional organizations and the Territorial Assembly are the primary arenas in which Aboriginal people attempt to regain effective control over their lives. As Wishart documents for the NWT (and as Goulet shows for Alberta and Parlee et al. for northern Alaska, Yukon, and NWT), political and economic control are intimately connected, and currently are being negotiated in various venues, including both formal treaty processes and commercial deal-making.

The end result will not be something closely resembling Nunavut. The Inuit case is unique for Canadian Natives; they are numerically dominant in their region and therefore a politically open system is very workable. The Dene, like most Natives in Canada, must find mechanisms other than a territorially based legislature for political accommodation. Presumably that means some form of limited, shared, or joint arrangement with Euro-Canadians. Their recent history demonstrates a willingness to seek workable solutions. A wide range of options has been actively explored by the various Native groups in recent years. Two questions that remain, however, are whether or not Euro-Canadians will be as open to accommodation and what kinds of futures will be locally possible in the wake of "developments" like tar sands and diamond mines.

NOTE

1. The term "Athapaskan" has recently come into disfavour in some circles because it is not Indigenous. At this time, however, it cannot be avoided as it is thoroughly embedded in the literature, and professional linguists are not considering any change. Simply substituting some variant of "Deneh" for "Athapaskan," as has been suggested, will not work since the terms "NaDene" and "Dene" are already part of the taxonomic tree.

REFERENCES

Helm, June, et al. 1975. "The Contact History of the Subarctic Athapaskans: An Overview." In *Proceedings: Northern Athapaskan Conference,* vol. 1, edited by A. McFayden Clarke. Ottawa: Canadian Ethnology Service Paper No. 27.

McClellan, C., and G. Denniston. 1981. "Environment and Culture in the Cordillera." In *Handbook of North American Indians.* Vol. 6, *Subarctic.* edited by June Helm and William C. Sturtevant. Washington: Smithsonian Institution.

CHAPTER 10

The Dene Tha' of Chateh: Continuities and Transformations

Jean-Guy A. Goulet

Introduction

Young Dene in high school or university are taught about Canada, a Canada with a life expectancy of over 80 years for women and over 75 years for men. The Canada they know, however, is strikingly different. Their average life expectancy is 20 to 30 years less, largely due to a high rate of tragic juvenile and adult deaths related to alcohol abuse. Many Dene Tha' end their days in conditions that were unknown only one generation ago. They strive to live meaningful lives in the midst of grieving their lost ones. They do so in the light of their Aboriginal knowledge and convictions. They also do so in the midst of Euro-Canadian institutions established over the last century: the church, the store, the residential school, and later the government-operated day school, the RCMP detachment, and the nursing station. To this day they continue to bridge cultural divides and persistently seek to transform the legal and administrative relationships that bind them to government and non-government institutions.

I first visited Chateh in northwest Alberta in the summer of 1979 to ask the Dene Tha' if they would teach me their language and way of life. I explained that I intended to spend six months of each year with them as part of an extended research project. My goal was to find out if the Dene Tha' had repudiated their own institutions and values as they were exposed to Euro-Canadian institutions in the fields of politics, economy, religion, education, and health. During six years of close association with them, I found that a century of interaction with Euro-Canadians has not eradicated or rendered obsolete Dene ways of knowing and living. The Dene Tha' saw Western institutions as a complement to, rather than a substitute for, their Aboriginal ways.

The presentation of contemporary Dene Tha' lives proceeds in four steps. First, I offer a brief historical sketch of events to explain how the Dene Tha' of Chateh came to live in their present location. Second, I explore their understanding of the world, including their relationship to individuals who are reincarnated and their recourse to healing powers received from animals. Third, I examine Dene Tha' domestic life. I focus on their views of education and learning as well as on the challenge posed over the past 50 years by violent behaviour associated with the consumption of alcohol. Last, I discuss contemporary social, economic, and political issues that are shaping the future. Dene Tha' are preparing to invest millions of dollars to exploit vast oil and gas fields in their traditional homeland.

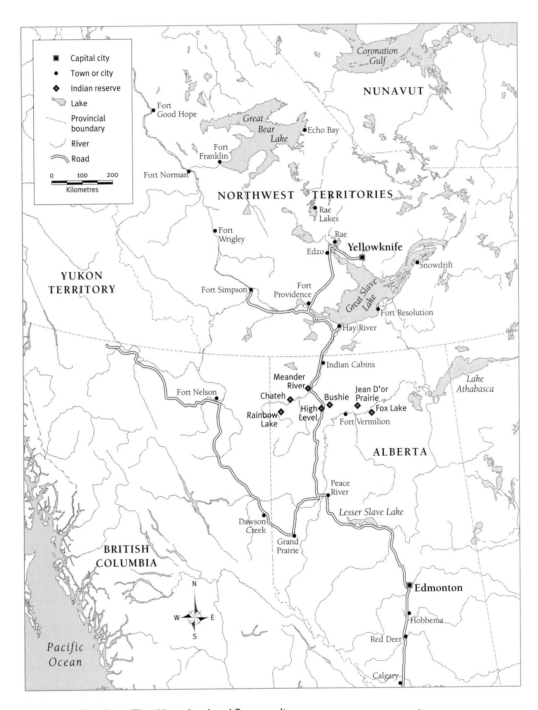

MAP 10.1 The Dene Tha: Homeland and Surroundings (Map courtesy of Robin Poitras)

The Slaveys of Alberta Become the Dene Tha' of Chateh

In the anthropological literature the people of Chateh are referred to as Slavey, Hay River Indians, Albertan Beaver Indians, the Dene Tha' branch of the Beaver Indians, and the Hay Lakes Alberta Dene. Chateh, also known as Assumption, is listed by the Department of Indian and Northern Affairs as the Hay Lakes Reserve (the name given to the band in 1953 by the federal government), with a population of 951 in 2006.

Three Names, Three Historical Phases of Dene Tha' Life

Hay Lakes, Assumption, and Chateh are names that reflect distinct phases in the history of the Dene Tha'. Following battles lost to the Cree in the nineteenth century, the Dene Tha' moved northward from the Lesser Slave region. Contemporary Dene Tha' know the place along the Hay River where they last battled with the Cree. They remember that a Dene Tha' woman survived by hiding on the riverbank. Elder Louison Ahkimnatchie comments, "Today, if you want to camp there, you have to make an offering of tobacco. If you don't, you will hear crying and screaming of people who were killed in the battle. Dene Tha' have tried to stay there without making an offering and they had to leave before morning—they couldn't stand the terrible noises" (Dene Tha' First Nation 1997:40).

In 1900 the Dene Tha' signed Treaty No. 8. Unknowingly, they became subject to the Indian Act. A band membership list was drawn, specifying who could live on the land set aside for them. They received **patronyms**. Adult male members were called upon to elect a chief and a council to act as counterparts to federal officials whose primary mandate was to open Aboriginal territories to peaceful settlement and exploitation.

In 1900, when the Dene Tha' signed Treaty No. 8, they continued to move freely around their territory in search of game and fur irrespective of provincial and territorial boundaries. The politicians working in Edmonton, established as Alberta's capital in 1905, were keen to develop their interests in northern Alberta. The construction of rail transportation made possible the transfer of resources and crops from the north to the south. Lobbying led to the appointment to the federal cabinet of an Edmontonian, Frank Oliver, as Minister of Interior and Superintendent General of Indian Affairs. In 1906, to respect the intent of Treaty No. 8, "the Indian Act was amended to ensure that games laws in the prairie provinces and in the NWT would not apply to aboriginal people without the consent of the Superintendent General of Indian Affairs" (Bouchard 2006:13). In other words, provincial game laws may apply to Indians without their consent, but with the consent of the government whose **fiduciary** duty it is to look after the interests of its wards.

The Dene Tha' understanding of the treaty was as a means of establishing a kinship-like alliance between themselves and the government. The treaty-signing ceremony had been concluded with a gift of money from the federal government to each band member. This money, Elder Jean-Marie Tally told me, was "not to sell anything but to make us brothers and sisters [and therefore inclined to assist each other]. That is what my father, who saw them give money to the people, used to say. It [the treaty] will not be a lie for God as long as night follows night, and as long as the sun lasts, and as long as the water flows." Every year since, in midsummer, Dene Tha' line up to receive from an RCMP officer the five-dollar bill promised annually to each band member. In Dene Dhah, the language of the Dene, treaty day is appropriately called "the day they give money to people."

Following the signing of Treaty No. 8, Dene Tha' had little exposure to Euro-Canadians, since they spent most of the year making a living on the land. Contact was limited to occasional visits to the Hudson's Bay Company trading post in Fort

Vermilion. There they sold furs and purchased supplies of flour, lard, tea, sugar, ammunition, and the like for the next round of trapping. Until about 1950, government policy throughout the Subarctic, in the absence of economic development, was to preserve unchanged the "traditional" fur-trading way of life as much as possible. In this way Indigenous populations contributed to the **market economy** while providing for all their needs at a minimal cost to the Canadian government.

The Dene Tha' then lived and hunted over a wide expanse extending into northeastern British Columbia and the Northwest Territories. Until the mid-1940s, Hay Lakes, some 13 kilometres north of the present-day site of Chateh, was an important gathering place. In spring and fall Dene Tha' found in Hay Lakes plentiful wildlife (fish, moose, deer, beaver, muskrat, ducks, and geese) and abundant pasture for their horses. When winter set in, extended families dispersed to their traplines.

During that period, anthropologists living with the Dene could not see them as victims or as dispossessed of their land or their means of living. Richard Slobodin (1975:285), who worked among the Gwich'in, asked how anthropologists could "depict as mere victims the men, women, and children who had hauled us through the broken ice, disentangled dogs, given us dry clothing, and poured hot caribou soup down our throats." In those days Dene could well feel superior to the occasional white man who ventured into their midst and who depended on them for food, shelter, and orientation.

Anthropologists were then motivated by the desire to record distinctive ways of life threatened by Euro-Canadian colonization. In the course of these investigations, the Dene Tha' of Chateh, along with many other Aboriginal populations north of them, became known as the Slavey. This name, a translation of the Cree term *awahka'n*, "captive, slave," was already widely used by traders,

explorers, and missionaries to refer to Indians in northern Alberta and the NWT. People so designated eventually adopted the term to refer to themselves when communicating in English. A new system of social identity began to coexist with the Aboriginal one, according to which people identified themselves in reference to geographic sites, as "people of the swift current" or "the brushwood people." When anthropologists adopted "Slavey" as the English term to refer to all these populations, they collapsed into one general category various groups dispersed over a wide area.

After the Fur Traders, the Missionaries

After the fur traders, the missionaries were the most significant outsiders to enter Dene Tha' lives. Roman Catholic missionaries first sought to convert them and later operated a residential school. In 1917 Father Joseph Habay, an Oblate missionary, built a log chapel on the shore of Hay Lakes, where he carried out his missionary work (the site was named after him in 1953). He was followed by Father François Arbet, OMI, who built another chapel there in 1927–8. Elders recall how he travelled by dog team to visit families on their traplines. They remember how he ate with them and slept in their house, lying, like them, on the floor. Hospitality was mixed with puzzlement. "Before we go to mission," that is, the residential school, said a devout Catholic woman, "Father Arbet used to come to visit us in the bush. We get pictures of Mary and Jesus, but we do not know what they are. We laugh and say, 'This woman looks like this woman.' We learn to do the sign of the cross when we pray, and we laugh a lot then. It's funny to us. But when we got in mission, then we learned a lot."

In 1938 and again in 1948, Dene Tha' requested a residential school and a hospital. In a letter dated 17 July 1948, the band chief wrote to the Minister of Mines in Ottawa as follows:

We Hay Lakes Indians take the liberty of submitting to you some communications and asking you a few questions. We are Indians, poor, igno-rant, and we start to realize our situation among white people. We are trappers, part in Alberta and part in British Columbia. But trapping is getting so poor that some of us might have to find work amongst white people but only 6 of us have been at school at Fort Vermillion [sic] and can speak English.

The chief underlined the need for a local hos-pital, given the band's hardships and the 17 deaths the previous year, "3 of old age, 1 childbirth, 1 pneu-monia, the other 12 were TB." The chief then added that the band wanted a boarding school, "because it is impossible for us to send our children to a day school" and it was "very difficult, not to say impos-sible to carry with dogs enough supplies 80 miles away, for big families like we have."

Following this petition, construction of a boarding school soon began, not at Hay Lakes but at a site 13 kilometres inland. The missionaries deemed this site, named Assumption, less liable to flooding and more appropriate for a residential school and a farm to support its staff and pupils. In February 1951 the new school received 74 chil-dren (28 boys and 46 girls). The following month 16 other children joined them. From 1951 to 1969 the number of students ranged from 72 to 125 (the peak year being 1960). Over these years more families built their log cabins closer to the mis-sion site and residential school. A cemetery was created nearby, and so the people of Hay Lakes became the people of Assumption. The relation-ship between church, local people, and cemetery continues to this day. Only for a funeral does the church fill with people, before they follow the cof-fin to their burial ground.

Closing the Residential School, Opening up to Global Developments

In 1965 major discoveries of oil and natural gas west of Assumption led to construction of a road between High Level and what was to become the town of Rainbow Lake. The disparity in liv-ing standards between the Dene Tha', who had lived in the area for centuries, and the Euro-Canadians moving into High Level and Rainbow Lake by the hundreds soon became obvious to all. Differences in employment opportunities, housing, types of vehicles, and the like clearly indicated that the Dene Tha' were disadvan-taged. Band members marched on the steps of the Alberta legislature, asking for jobs and better living conditions. In response, the federal gov-ernment built simple two- and three-bedroom frame houses in Assumption. These were most often built next to log cabins erected a genera-tion earlier. As they moved into their new homes, families also kept log cabins in the bush. Here men in their fifties and older, along with sons or other relatives, spent extended periods trapping and hunting in winter and spring, a pattern that still continues.

In 1966, 120 Dene Tha' were living in Habay and 575 in Assumption. As more people were living permanently around the local store and boarding school, the federal government estab-lished a day school there in 1969. That same year, the missionaries closed the boarding school and the band named the settlement Chateh, in hon-our of the chief who had signed Treaty No. 8. This change of names came at a time of world-wide Aboriginal political mobilization. Other Northern Athapaskans (Slaveys, Chipewyans, Hare, Dogribs, Mountain Indians, Bearlake Indians, and Kutchin) living in the NWT adopted the name "Dene" to designate themselves in English. In the same breath they referred to the

Western Subarctic as Denendeh, "the land of the Dene," to stand beside Nunavut, "our land," the land of their Inuit neighbours. This was the context in which the Slaveys of Assumption became the Dene Tha' of Chateh.

One could argue that Chateh could have been included in Denendeh. The Dene Tha' share many features of social organization, culture, and language with the Slavey of the NWT. The hunting and trapping activities of Dene Tha' extended into the Territories. Slaveys from Assumption have many family ties with NWT Dene. Moreover, in the mid-1960s Dene Tha' prophets had played an important role in a revitalization movement among Dogribs and other groups in the NWT. In the following years members of these groups travelled regularly to Chateh to consult with local Elders. Why, then, were the Dene Tha' not included in the wider project of Dene self-determination? The reason is political. In Canada Aboriginal peoples must claim their Aboriginal rights without challenging provincial and territorial boundaries. This was the condition under which the federal government would negotiate. The claim to nationhood and self-determination can be made only on a political stage defined by Euro-Canadians. If the Dene Tha' were to claim Aboriginal rights, they would have to do so in Alberta.

The assertion of Aboriginal nationhood and the adoption of Aboriginal names to identify oneself in the world publicly emphasized the existence in Canada of two categories of people, with a broad semantic contrast between them. One category comprises people with Aboriginal rights to land and to self-government, the original inhabitants of Chateh, Denendeh, and Nunavut. The other category is made up of non-Aboriginals, whose privileged economic opportunities in the land of the Dene are due to Canada's control of those territories. As shall be discussed in the last section, these political developments constitute the back-ground to the current agreements between the Dene Tha', government, and business to generate employment and exploit resources in the Dene Tha' homeland.

Being at Home in the World

What has been stated so far about the Dene Tha' is based on an examination of the historical record and observable reality in northern Alberta. Much of social reality, however, consists not of events and material objects but of people's interpretation or understanding of them. A crucial part of the anthropological endeavour consists precisely in grasping these understandings. For this, anthropologists depend on their hosts to help them learn about what is really going on.

In my experience, an important way to learn from the Dene Tha' about how things really were in their lives consisted of asking them to translate into Dene Dhah a statement initially made in English, and then to have them translate this statement back into English. For instance, in English, Dene Tha' would sometimes refer to someone's "superstition." When translating this into Dene Dhah, people always said *dene wonlin edadihi*, which they translated back to English as "a person who knows an animal." Similarly, when speaking in English about individuals dying and being born again, a few Dene Tha' spoke of "reincarnation." Most, however, would use phrases such as "he or she was done to us again" or "he or she was done again." When translated to Dene Dhah, it became apparent that these phrases were close to the Dene expression denoting such a person: *Dene andat'sindla*, "a person made again by others." In these cases, as in countless others, Dene meanings are attached to English vocabulary. These Dene meanings are to a large extent shared by old and young alike and taken for granted by contemporary Dene Tha'. To grasp these meanings is to truly enter the Dene Tha' world.

Living in Our Land and in the Other Land

Dene Tha' differentiate between *ndahdigeh*, "our land," and *ech'uhdigeh*, "the other land." Dene Tha' do not draw this distinction in the way Euro-Canadians conceive of binary opposites such as the natural and the supernatural or the field of science and the field of mysticism, magic, and religion. The other land, also referred to as *yake*, "heaven," is experienced first-hand in dreams when the soul journeys away from the body. It is in the other land that one meets relatives who have passed away, as well as Christian figures such as Mary and Jesus. In conversation, Dene Tha' Elders easily followed an account of a trip to a nearby town with a story of a journey to the other land. To the nearby town in our land they had travelled by car. To the other land they had travelled with their souls. Elders often bring songs back from their journey to heaven and sing them in "our land" during healing ceremonies. Similarly, young people would describe bouts of acute illness and near-death experiences as a period of time when their soul or spirit had begun to travel on the trail leading to heaven. In such circumstances, individuals called on Elders and their animal helpers to help recover their souls and, hence, their health.

In the Dene Tha' world, events in the other land and in our land are intimately associated. For instance, atmospheric events in this land are an expression of someone's condition in the other land or in this land. When a violent storm swept over Chateh the day after a young man was shot to death, people said the storm was his feelings. When low clouds drizzled over Chateh for three days, a Dene Tha' healer explained that it was his power (animal helper) feeling let down because his patients had not brought appropriate gifts as promised. When exceptionally bright red northern lights were seen in the sky, Dene Tha' said it was because

their leading prophet had lost much blood in the course of an operation. Thus, a continuous flow of interpretations accompanies changes in weather patterns, weaving threads of meaning between social and atmospheric events.

In this land the Dene Tha' share a deep sense of dependence on animals, to whom signs of respect are faithfully given lest animals stop giving themselves to hunters who seek them as game. A child learns this respect from his parents as they dispose properly of the bones of animals or the feathers of fowl. People also avoid talking negatively about animals since they know how one talks about them and will not present themselves in the bush to those who speak negatively about them. Children learn that the little feathers at the end of a duck's wings are not to be burned. "If you burn that little feather, real pointed ones, if you burn them, you don't shoot ducks as you would like to; you miss them. You don't throw them to the dogs. You throw them in the bush or in the water." And so the child is sent to drop the feathers in the creek behind the house. The guts are removed from a dead moose and its eyes pierced before its head and brain are put high in a tree. "This is so he will not see where we go. If he knew, he would be mad at us and we would not shoot moose next time around," says a hunter. Eagles are never killed, for they tell hunters where the moose are and in some cases fly very low to look at people and communicate with them. A woman commented, "We are afraid of the eagle; we do not kill it. If we kill it in the fall, then it comes and kills one of the family the same year. It all goes back to the time when animals were like human beings, and they could talk and everything." This woman refers to a distant time when animals and human beings spoke the same language, married, and cohabited. Although this is no longer the case, animals and human beings continue to entertain intimate relationships, particularly in the realm of healing.

FIGURE 10.1 Drumming and singing from the other land. (Courtesy J.-G. Goulet)

Seeking a Power to Heal, Going for a Song

Until very recently, virtually all Dene Tha' children, before the onset of adolescence, went on a vision quest and experienced an encounter with an animal who gave them a song and a power to heal. Dene talk little, if at all, of these things, lest they lose their power or have it turn against them. When asked what it means to know an animal and have an animal helper, a woman answered:

> I don't really know. Like my older brother, he never talks to us about it, but my mom told us once that one day [he] went in the bush with little provisions, and was supposed to come back the same day, but stayed two days and two nights. On his way he met wolves who had come to meet him, and he had been with them all that time. I guess they became his helpers.

But that is all I know. We do not talk about these things.

This, as we shall see, is also the reason invoked by Dene Tha' not to include on maps of their homeland the sites where they collect *yu*, "powerful medicine."

In the early and mid-1980s, most Dene Tha' were known to have an animal helper even if they had spent years in residential school. As one former student commented, "You need an animal helper to survive in this community." Although some children still go for a song, many parents despair that their children will ever get a vision. Pointing to her young son and nephew, who were listening to our conversation, a young woman told me, "They are always on the road. You get that kind of thing [a vision] in the bush, not on the road." Voicing her opinion in this manner, the woman was reminding the children that they should get on with it and go

for a song. In another Dene Tha' family, teenagers admitted that although their grandfather had often told them "to go and look for medicine, to learn what they had to do and receive a song to sing on people," they had been too scared to go. These adolescents were growing up without a power but in the company of grandparents, parents, and siblings who had animal helpers.

Dene Tha' say that, "Long ago there were no doctors, and people who had visions were like doctors [who] would cure others." To cure others, Dene Tha' would draw on *ech'int'e*, the power to heal received from an animal helper. To this day, every Dene Tha' knows someone who has had a vision and has received a power; everyone knows a relative or a friend whose health has recovered through the assistance of someone with a power to heal. When in need, every Dene Tha' calls on someone who knows an animal. Dene Tha' also use *yu*, substances that have medicinal properties, such as animal parts, herbs, roots, bark, and leaves. For instance, beaver testes are often seen hanging up to dry in homes. The gum-like material inside relieves toothaches, or the whole can be boiled and the potion drunk for a chest cold. It is also used as an efficient bait for lynx. Rat root is used for stomach ache and head colds. Poplar bark is used for headaches. And so on, with a wide variety of parts of animals and plants.

In a sense *yu* is in the public domain. It is part of the knowledge of every family and is in principle accessible to anyone who cares to go into the bush with the proper attitude and knowledge. This knowledge is nevertheless special. To benefit from the medicinal power of these entities, one does not simply take it. One places tobacco where an uprooted plant stood or by a tree from which a part is taken. "If you pluck a 'rat eye' or stinkweed, you don't just take it. You have to put a gift there to replace what you took." Without this acknowledgement, the plant's power is withheld. So profound is this attitude to *yu* and the places

where it may be gathered that these places were not included on any of the Dene Tha' maps drawn for their traditional land-use study. As Dene Tha' stated, "Not everyone should know about them [medicine, or powers]" and "Any person cannot just pick ground medicine. It is dangerous if one does not know how to use it."

Some Dene Tha' men and women are reputed to gather and keep *yu* properly. They dispense it as medicine in exchange for appropriate payment in tobacco, other goods, and sometimes cash. Dene Tha' also apply the term *yu* to Western medication—the pills, syrups, and ointments bought in drugstores or administered by doctors and nurses. A medical professional is referred to as *yu dené*, "medicine person." In Dene Dhah, *yu koan*, "medicine house," refers to the local health clinic or to hospitals in urban centres where they are often taken for medical treatment. They never refer to a fellow Dene as *yu dené* or to a dwelling of theirs as *yu koan*.

Reincarnation, or "Being Made Again"

I have mentioned cases of reincarnation and journeys of the soul that led to near-death experiences. The following account contains all the Dene Tha' themes associated with death: grief over the death of a loved one; the apparition of the dead relative in the narrator's dreams; fear that the visitation would cause harm; and reassurance by the deceased relative that it would not.

> You remember my little niece [Lucy, deceased in her early twenties], she died; she had an accident. About two months after she died I was just crying and then I dreamed about her. Just like a person in person. I could hear that foot, foot, you know [with her hands on the kitchen table she makes the movement and noise of footsteps]. She was carrying a paper like

this [she rolls the TV guide in her hands to show me]. When I was dreaming, looking at her, first thing I see her, I say, "She is gone; how come she is back?" First time she says, "Where's Peter [the narrator's son]?" He was sleeping in the next room. "I want to see Peter and Rose [his wife]," she said. I was surprised, scared. She could ask for something if she couldn't go to heaven. She said, "No, I will not do nothing; I just want to see again."

The narrator went on to explain that when Rose woke up the next morning, she was screaming and shaking, terrified by a dream in which she had seen Lucy coming back. Was Lucy coming back to take someone's soul away and cause another death in the family? A month later Rose found out that she was pregnant. Rose then knew that Lucy had come back to her to be made again and raised once more as a child in our land.

Identification of someone as a reincarnated person may be a gradual process. Prior to Beverly becoming pregnant with her third child, her father had dreams of his late hunting partner. Her father, who suspected that his partner might be made again to his pregnant daughter, nevertheless kept his dreams to himself. The child reached the stage when she was grasping things and taking them to her mouth, when one day she began to cry inconsolably. Many objects were offered to the child, who turned them down and kept on crying. Beverly's father then said, "Try giving her an onion." Beverly did so. To everyone's surprise, the child eagerly took the onion, bit into it, ate, and smiled. Beverly's father then explained that following his dreams he had expected other signs that would confirm his suspicion that his close friend was reincarnated. His suggestion that the child be given an onion reflected the fact that his late hunting partner loved onions. The child eagerly eating the onion confirmed that the baby

was his hunting partner growing among them as a young girl.

Among Dene Tha', the individual going into a woman to be born again is a known relative. When the child is born in a sex opposite to its previous sex, the latter determines what kinship terms of address are used. A boy may be addressed as my daughter, my sister, or my aunt. Conversely, a girl may be called my son, my brother, or my uncle. In turn, these kinship terms of address trigger a wide range of accounts of the child's previous life that progressively enter the child's sense of his or her own identity. The grandmother who constantly greets her grandson with the exclamation, "Ha ha, the child who is made again," sets the stage for others to engage in recollections of events lived by the child in an earlier life. Through such interaction adults teach a child knowledge that is defined as recollection of a past life. Within this process of socialization, one's sense of identity is mediated by others who know who one is because they saw the spirit come back to be made again.

Household and Daily Life

Dene Tha' homes in Chateh are distributed over the land in a clear pattern. Bilingual and bicultural Dene Tha', that is, those most closely associated with Euro-Canadian institutions, dwell in the central townsite. This area also includes the day school, the band-owned general store, the police station, the nursing station, and the residences of the non-Dene professionals (school principal, teachers, nurses, police officers, store manager, band-office personnel, and missionaries) living on the reserve. Many Dene Tha' women who reside in the central townsite find employment with these professionals as receptionists, clerks, teaching aides, secretaries, or cleaners. Families who associate less closely with Euro-Canadians and their institutions tend to live further away from the townsite in houses built along the road to Habay or along the Gun River, running through what is called the First, Second, and Third Prairie. Over the past 20 years, population increase has led to the creation of a trailer park near the airstrip for younger couples and their children.

Households on "the prairies" most often consist of a three-generation family living under one roof and addressing one another by kinship terms. English is seldom heard in Dene Tha' homes, except for the omnipresent voice of the television. Most adults under 40 are fluent in English, but raise their children in their Native tongue, although some parents now speak English at home. All children eventually attend the local public school where they are instructed in English, but to this day they play in the schoolyard speaking Dene Dhah. In Dene Dhah, people refer to individuals according to their relationship to the first-born child. When this child receives a name, for instance Dih, the parents and siblings become known as Dihta, "the father of Dih"; Dihmo, "the mother of Dih"; Dihdéédzé, "the sister of Dih"; Dihchidle, "the younger brother of Dih"; and so on. The status achieved in parenthood is immediately reflected in the change of kinship terms of reference.

Learning by Observation or by Instruction

In all societies children learn from their elders the knowledge, attitudes, and skills that allow one to live with confidence as a competent individual. The manner in which learning occurs varies, however, according to kinds of social organization. Among the Dene, as among hunters and gatherers generally, learning proceeds through observation and imitation with what appears to outsiders to be a minimum of intervention and instruction. From the Dene point of view, to explain is to take away someone's opportunity to learn for herself or himself. To the Dene, knowledge derived from others is suspect. True knowledge comes through direct experience.

When I began fieldwork among the Dene Tha', I took up a Dene Tha' woman's offer to teach me how to cook bannock. She came to my house, and while we talked in the kitchen about community matters she proceeded to mix flour, water, and lard and to bake the resulting dough without offering a single word by way of instruction. One hour later, while we shared the freshly baked bannock, I asked if she was going to give me the recipe or the instructions necessary to replicate her baking. She immediately told me, "I just taught you; you've seen me do it!" Obviously, I had not watched as a Dene Tha' would have watched. A 40-year-old Dene Tha' father asked me once how many sports I could engage in. I mentioned swimming, whitewater canoeing, scuba diving, skiing, and skating. With tears in his eyes he said that we non–Dene Tha' could learn so much because we had instructors to teach us all manners of activities, whereas the Dene Tha' must take the much longer and more arduous route of personal observation and imitation.

Given this attitude to learning and dispensation of knowledge, it should come as no surprise that schooling organized according to Euro-Canadian principles of education is problematic for Dene Tha'. Thirty years ago, anthropologist Catharine McClellan wrote that in regard to schooling Indian children, "The increasing emphasis on verbal instruction in advanced grades, regardless of subject matter, helps to cause the withdrawal of older native children about which White teachers so often comment" (McClellan 1972:xvi). The same observation was made recently after the psychoeducational assessment of Dene Tha' children. That report stated:

> Assessments revealed, first and foremost, that the students at DTCS [Dene Tha' Community School] are capable and show personal strengths in many areas. The *DTCS students are not "stupid," "dumb,"*

or lacking in ability. Virtually all students showed strengths in their ability to work with their hands and to learn by doing and seeing. However, *they displayed weaknesses in their ability to learn through language. This pattern of strong visual and poor verbal learning skills was pervasive. This pattern of abilities will have a significantly negative effect on students' abilities to function effectively within the classroom,* particularly when students with these types of abilities are taught via conventional teaching methods (i.e., verbally based teaching methods). (DTCSTI 1996; my emphasis)

The report clearly states that in the current schooling system Dene Tha' children are deficient and disadvantaged. There is no suggestion that one could design an educational system that would build more on Dene values and ways of learning.

Being Autonomous and Responsible

The Dene Tha' emphasis on experiential learning through observation and imitation is closely associated with their value of autonomy. People's ability to realize their goals on their own, including the acquisition of personal knowledge, is highly respected. This respect for autonomy is experienced throughout life. It is experienced by the year-old child who moves toward a broken window, pulls himself up onto a chair, moves his hand through the gaping hole, feels the cold outdoor air, and safely withdraws his hand without touching the windowpane's jagged edges. All along, the child's parents and grandparents quietly observe as they carry on with their own activities, while I, not believing my eyes, silently cringe at the thought

FIGURE 10.2 Self-directed learning on the prairie. (Courtesy J.-G. Goulet)

of an impending injury. At the other end of life, the consideration for one's right to accomplish one's goals on one's own is experienced by elderly people who, in their seventies, climb aboard pickup trucks unaided. It may take them several minutes to pull themselves partially up, slip down, and pull themselves up again, sweating and breathing heavily in the process. As they do so, able-bodied adults casually carry on with their conversation in the vehicle, while I wonder if it would not be more respectful, and easier for everyone, to give the old person a helping hand.

The differences between my view and that of the Dene Tha' reflect our very different upbringings. According to the Dene Tha', to interfere with the child's exploration of his environment would violate his right and ability to pursue and achieve his goals. According to my point of view, to stop the child from approaching the broken window is to protect him from possible injury. I must, however, acknowledge that over the years the accidents and the injuries that I expected in the course of the Dene Tha' children's free-ranging explorations did not occur. This fact, I believe, accounts for the relaxed attitude of Dene Tha' adults, who supervise their children with a minimum of interference in their activities. Children proceed with confidence in their exploration, secure in the knowledge that no one will interfere. Similarly, to help an elderly individual get into a vehicle would be insulting, for it would suggest that he or she cannot climb on board the vehicle on his or her own. What outsiders see as non-interference in other people's lives, Dene see as preserving the other's ability to truly live life to the fullest extent.

To affirm that "the behavioural mode by which the autonomy rights of others is observed can best be summed up as non-interference" (Helm 1994 [1961]:176) is to view them as not acting as we would act. To engage in this kind of description is to miss the point that in behaving as they do, the Dene promote *their* values and view of life. They

consistently maximize the number of occasions in which one can learn by oneself and for oneself what it is to live an autonomous life competently. This is why they do not step in to stop a small child from approaching a broken windowpane, to take a chainsaw and a new pair of gloves from a boy who imitates his father, or to snatch liquor away from young children who are drinking it. The following statements reflect the Dene attitude toward their children and fellow Dene: "At home I pretty much let them do what they want to do." "It's up to this certain person to make up their mind; no one is going to make their mind." Since it is the Dene world that we anthropologists strive to grasp, the onus is on us to write, as much as possible, in a manner that conveys their view. We should, therefore, write about the Dene ethical principle of personal responsibility for one's own life, where in the past we spoke of non-interference.

Dene Tha' children make decisions that non-Dene parents or professionals would never consider letting them make. For example, when a six-year-old girl was bitten by a dog, I expressed my concern about rabies to the parents and suggested the need for a medical examination and, possibly, vaccination. I offered to take them to the nursing station in my vehicle. The parents listened and sat in silence. They then told me that their daughter did not want to go see the doctor. The girl looked at me with a smile. She knew that it was up to her to make up her mind and that everyone would respect her decision. A week later the wound had properly healed, and the girl could be seen merrily playing with her siblings and cousins.

Dene Tha' similarly respected another girl's decision when a doctor and a nurse came into a home, explaining that they had flown to Chateh specifically to vaccinate a few children also at risk of contracting tuberculosis. They asked where they might find an eight-year-old girl whose name they had but whom they did not know. It happened that the girl they were looking for was in the house. The five adults present remained silent as six children quietly moved around. The nurse asked if the girl they were looking for was in the house, but no one answered. Growing impatient, the doctor explained that he was on a tight schedule and must soon leave. He reiterated that without the proper vaccination the girl could become very sick. He obviously expected the adults to co-operate and to answer his questions. From the Dene Tha' point of view, however, it was the girl's responsibility to identify herself to the doctor. The girl knew that no one would point her out to the doctor. In the end the doctor and nurse left without finding the girl. The parents of the girl looked at me with a smile, happy that I had not stepped in to undermine the child's ability to make up her own mind.

Note that in all of this the Dene responsibility for one's own life is accompanied by a well-developed sense of one's position relative to others. Everywhere the older and more capable individual has a responsibility to exhibit competent and respectful behaviour for younger individuals to observe and learn well. Kinsmen and friends keep an eye on one another to offer protection, important information, or food, when needed, without being asked. Parents are also careful to store firearms and ammunition away from the reach of children. Stories are repeated again and again to illustrate the kind of behaviour that leads to well-being and the kind that leads to undesired consequences or disaster. And so one learns that true knowledge is personal knowledge, that generosity brings general esteem, and that consideration for the well-being of others and for the community is the foundation of a life well lived.

Dene Tha' social life is therefore informed by a pattern of subtle verbal and non-verbal interaction oriented toward the well-being of others while respecting each person's own autonomy. This pattern was observed again and again by Peruvian-born anthropologist Kim Harvey-Trigoso in her recent investigation of Dene Tha' childhood socialization and the transmission of traditional knowledge. She notes that, "The more children engaged in traditional subsistence activities with their caretakers, the more they exhibited a positive attitude towards the community based on co-operation and reciprocity" (Harvey-Trigoso 1999:18). In her study, the greatest exposure to activities related to hunting, gathering, and trapping are designated as High Traditional Subsistence Activities (High TSA), as opposed to Low TSA, whereby children have little exposure to these activities.

In their drawings, High TSA children drew more scenes of life in the bush, of local and distant hunting grounds, and of service institutions within the community. Important differences between High and Low TSA children were also noted in terms of group process and behaviour when drawing. High TSA groups consulted each other more, engaged in mutual planning, and stimulated each other with humour to co-operate with each other while avoiding conflict. The High and Low TSA groups both spoke about the dark side of life in Chateh. This included fatal car accidents due to drunk driving, people being shot at, people drowning in the river, and so on. Harvey-Trigoso's observation was that the High TSA groups ended their fantasies with positive outcomes. The boy who had fallen in a river would be saved. The one who had been shot at would survive. The one who ventured into the bush would be visited by an animal. This positive outlook on life was absent in the fantasies of Low TSA children, whose "mutual criticism of what was drawn inhibited interaction, co-operation, and enthusiasm" (ibid.:17).

Yesterday and Tomorrow: The Power of "Fire Water"

The dark side of life alluded to above is a recent development in the lives of the Dene and of Aboriginal peoples worldwide. Everywhere, the intrusion of Western institutions and officialdom, often supported by military might, into Aboriginal economy, politics, and religion brings about massive social disruption. Aboriginal peoples cease to enjoy unimpeded access to their ancestral land and the resources that supported their way of life. The social fabric of old is torn along generational and gender lines as young and old, men and women, are drawn differently into a new social order. Adults participate as they may as cheap labour in the new frontier economy. Tensions and frustrations increase. Men, especially, take to drinking, vent their anger toward family members, destroy property, and sometimes take their own lives or those of other community members.

It is against this global background of colonization and its aftermath that we can best understand the alternation among the Dene Tha' between two contrasting states of affairs: the attentive and joyful climate of sober life, on one hand, and the uninhibited outbursts and violence associated with drinking, on the other. These opposing states I came to see as phases in a continuous, complex process of social interaction. The ideal and practice of respecting each other's autonomy, which is so characteristic of Dene social life, give way, with alcohol, to violent intrusions into the lives of others. Following violent incidents, the most often-heard comment is that the person acted when his or her mind was gone. Hence the person is not accountable for these violent actions.

To read generalizations about Dene Tha' patterns of behaviour is not the same as coming face to face with individuals whose behaviour fully fits the pattern. This was the case when two strongly built Dene Tha' men in their early thirties came to visit me and have tea early one February afternoon. It was our first meeting, as I was in the initial weeks of my first fieldwork. Full of laughter, they introduced themselves as very best friends and sat next to each other, shoulder to shoulder, on the living-room sofa. I could not help but notice one man's bluish, bruised face, the nose covered with a wide bandage. He spontaneously explained his injuries, first telling me that his friend sitting next to him had hurt him. Both men then laughed and elbowed each other. They insisted that they could not get angry over this incident because the broken nose had been unintended.

The circumstances were as follows. While at a drinking party, the drunken victim's friend, who had a large piece of lumber in hand, had waited behind a door to smash it in the face of a drunken foe, who was soon expected. It was not the foe but the friend, however, who entered the room. As they told me about this turn of events, both men broke into laughter. The broken nose and bruised face were really nothing at all, they said. The victim reiterated that his friend did not know who he was when he delivered the blow. Laughing again, both men repeated how much they enjoyed each other's company. Later, when they walked away, I doubted that it was possible not to feel anger toward someone who had inflicted such injury, friend or not.

Through numerous accounts of this kind I learned that the Dene Tha' operate within a complex system of management of self and of social relationships. When a Dene Tha' woman reported that the neighbours' drunken son had slashed the four tires of her pickup, I spontaneously asked, "What have you done?" She immediately replied, "I'm keeping my niece away from him. We might have to move for a while to Edmonton" (approximately 800 kilometres south of Chateh). In typical Dene fashion, under the cover of drunkenness, a teenager has retaliated against a woman who thwarted his ambitions. Her response is also typically Dene, to withdraw temporarily from the scene with her niece, rather than confront the teenager or to lay charges with the police. Conflict thus is avoided and people's autonomy is respected to the fullest extent.

Contemporary Issues in a Competitive World

As noted earlier, the year 1965 represents a major turning point in the lives of the Dene Tha'. The discovery of a vast gas field in Rainbow Lake, a few kilometres southwest of Habay, led to the construction of a major highway linking it to High Level and other economic centres. In the years to follow, government and industry promoted the construction of a major pipeline to connect gas fields in the Beaufort Sea to Zama Lake, in the Dene Tha' homeland. It was already the hub of a distribution system extending from northwest Alberta to Canadian and American markets far to the south.

Dene Tha' were then eager to see this project go ahead. They hoped to play a significant part in its implementation. In the mid-1970s they trained with heavy equipment in the dense forest around Chateh in anticipation of the contracts they would get to open roads and to dig trenches in which to lay the proposed pipeline between Zama Lake and the NWT. When I arrived in Chateh in 1979, huge mounds of trees and earth piled at one end of the reserve were testimony to the determination with which the Dene Tha' had prepared for the economic development to come. That dream failed to materialize, but it is revitalized today.

A Squandered Opportunity?

To speak of revitalization is to posit a relationship between the past and the present interest in building a pipeline from the Beaufort Sea to Zama Lake. Twenty-five years ago, provincial, territorial, and federal governments, allied with powerful business interests, were deciding to open the entire length of the Mackenzie Valley corridor. This would have involved construction of gas and oil pipelines, building a highway and possibly a railway to the Arctic coast, and the massive influx of non-local labour. New towns, more housing, hydroelectric

transmission lines, and telecommunication facilities would follow.

In 1973 this socio-economic revolution was in the making without the participation of the Aboriginal communities it would affect most. The response of Aboriginal peoples to the federal government's intentions was to present a caveat to the Supreme Court of the Northwest Territories, asking it to prevent economic developments that did not consider their Aboriginal rights and interests in the land. In June of the same year, following extensive hearings in Dene communities, Judge Morrow ruled in favour of the Dene and upheld their claim to over 1 million square kilometres of land. In March 1974, the federal government appointed Justice Thomas Berger to conduct an inquiry into the social, ecological, and economic impact of the proposed pipeline project. In his report, released in May 1977, Justice Berger recommended a 10-year moratorium on the development of the project to allow for a satisfactory conclusion to necessary comprehensive negotiations between the federal government and the Aboriginal inhabitants of the land.

Extensive and intensive negotiations followed, and in April 1990 an agreement in principle between the Metis, the Dene, and the federal government was in place. Three months later, however, the agreement was rejected when put to a vote of the Dene Assembly. With the collapse of this comprehensive claim, regional groups soon indicated that they were prepared to sign regional agreements. This was the case first for the Dinjii Zhuh (Gwich'in), who signed a regional agreement with the federal government in September 1991, soon to be followed by the Sahtu (Bearlakers) and the Dogribs. In August 1993 these three groups declared that they no longer recognized themselves as members of the Dene Nation.

Today, provincial, territorial, and federal governments are once more allied with powerful business interests, promoting the construction of a

Mackenzie Valley pipeline. They do so, more and more, in partnership with regional and local Dene First Nations.

There is, however, one outstanding Dene regional group, the Deh Cho First Nation, that has not settled its claims with the federal government. Their lands constitute 40 per cent of the area along the southern part of the Mackenzie Valley that the pipeline must go through before reaching Alberta. Without participation of the Deh Cho, construction of the pipeline cannot proceed. Their participation hinges on the successful completion of what is known as the Deh Cho Process, negotiations with the federal government entered into by the Deh Cho First Nation to protect their lands and resources and implement their oral understanding of Treaty Nos. 8 and 11. The Dene Tha' see the successful outcome of the Deh Cho Process as vital to their interests. It is not surprising, therefore, that at the National Treaty Conference held in Yellowknife in October 1998, Chief James Ahnassay of the Dene Tha' First Nation seconded a motion tabled by Chief Rita Cli, Liidli Kue First Nation. This motion asked for the support of the First Nations at the National Treaty Conference and of the First Nation members of the Assembly of First Nations for the Deh Cho First Nation's stated agenda.

Treaty Rights and Aboriginal Rights

The Dene Tha' have supported the Deh Cho Process for two main reasons. First, without its successful completion a major economic project they may benefit from cannot proceed. Second, one day they may also, like the Deh Cho First Nation, formally claim their Aboriginal and treaty rights. A recent statement by Chief James Ahnassay reminds people that the Dene Tha' "are still striving to assert ownership of the traditional lands as it was supposed to have been included in the Treaty negotiations back in June 23, 1900." He adds, "The true spirit and intent of the Treaty as understood

and told by the Elders has yet to be implemented by Canada to this day. The Elders maintain that none of our traditional lands have ever been given up and will never be given up" (Dene Tha' First Nation 1997:4).

In these matters of treaty rights, the views of the Dene Tha' and of the federal government and the provincial government of Alberta are diametrically opposed. These governments maintain that a simple reading of the English-language text of Treaty No. 8 makes it clear that any rights the Dene Tha' may have had to lands outside their reserves were extinguished absolutely. The political implications of this understanding are stark. Building on its view of property rights, the provincial government grants leases of this "Crown" land (i.e., traditional Dene Tha' territory) to corporations for resource extraction. Forestry and oil and gas companies exercising these rights pay royalties to the provincial and federal governments, but none to the Dene Tha'. What are the Dene Tha' to do when Euro-Canadians claim property rights and exercise these rights over their homeland? How are they to maintain any control over their homeland? To do so they must speak in a language that can be heard by the powerful. That language is the language of property rights.

For Aboriginal people to claim rights in the language of property, however, is to attempt to speak a language that is alien to them. We have seen that the vocabulary of superstition, reincarnation, power, and medicine stands for very different realities in the words and worlds of the Dene Tha' and of Euro-Canadians. The differences in meaning are just as significant in regard to such words as "land," "animals," "ownership," and "right." Consider this. An Aboriginal leader surveys his community's land to map out what belongs to them and what belongs to others. When he tells his mother what he is up to, she tells him it is "a crazy thing to do, for no one can own the land—neither white men nor Indians." She tells him that Aboriginal land claims ought to mean that government and Aboriginal people get "together to try to figure out how to keep the land and animals safe for their children and grandchildren" (Nasaday 2002:247). Is this not the standard against which to measure the value of any Aboriginal people's attempt to co-operate with government and industry, both to create employment and also to preserve its traditional ways for future generations?

In 1995, in an attempt to bridge the gap between themselves and governments regarding their interests in their homeland, the Dene Tha' commissioned a Traditional Land Use and Occupancy Study. It had positive outcomes, particularly growth in community pride, in awareness of the importance of traditional sites and traditional knowledge, and in understanding government and industry perspectives on economic development. Nevertheless, the results have fallen short of expectations. Outsiders' recognition of their traditional lands as Dene Tha' territory has not increased. Neither has communication between the community and forestry companies improved.

Presently, however, the Dene Tha' appear to pursue immediate economic benefits. Corporations and governments remind them that hoped-for benefits will be jeopardized if they enter a land claim with the federal government, asking for recognition of Aboriginal rights to the land, or if they initiate a legal case that could take years to come to a conclusion. The time to invest in gas and oil extraction and distribution is now. This view is in sharp contrast with the attitude expressed recently by a Deh Cho Elder: "We haven't had a pipeline for thousands of years. I don't see why we should be worried about waiting a little longer" (Anderson 2002).

Dene political leaders are caught between immediate worries and a concern for the long-term well-being of their people. They fear missing out on an imminent economic boom. That is why, in April 1998, the Dene Tha' signed with the fed-eral government an Enhanced Co-Management Agreement to build capacity at the band level to prepare for full control of local oil and gas resources. Following this agenda, in September 2002 the Dene Tha' accepted $1.96 million in assistance from the federal government to enable the band to acquire a 50 per cent interest in two oil and gas drilling rigs to be used for a minimum of 760 drilling days over the next four years in northern Alberta and northeastern BC. As they implement this project that will create 32 new jobs, Chief Stephen Didzena highlights the dilemma facing the Dene Tha': "We are determined to work with industry and government to maximize economic benefits from resource development, while ensuring the protection of our Treaty rights and the enhancement of our traditional ways." Significantly, in all existing agreements with governments leading to economic development in the Dene Tha' homeland the federal government has yet to meet fully its obligations toward the people. This, as we will see shortly, constituted the basis for a Dene Tha' claim against the Crown.

While negotiating with the Deh Cho First Nations, three levels of governments (federal, provincial, and territorial) and business corporations established the framework for the Mackenzie Gas Project (MGP). First, the Aboriginal Pipeline Group (APG) was created in 2000 following meetings of leading Aboriginal politicians and businessmen in Fort Liard and in Fort Simpson. These leaders represented APG's three founding Aboriginal groups: from north to south the Inuvialiut, the Gwich'in, and the Sahtu. In June 2001, APG "negotiated a Memorandum of Understanding with the Mackenzie Delta Producers—Imperial Oil, ConocoPhillips, Shell and Exxon Mobil" whereby it would eventually gain one-third ownership of the MGP (Reid 2004). Second, in June 2003, the Mackenzie Valley Producers Group, of which APG is a partner, filed with the Minister of Resources a Preliminary

BOX 10.1 Standards of Consultation

The standards of consultation imposed on the Crown acting in its fiduciary capacity (when it acts in its role as trustee for Aboriginal peoples) are more onerous than those that arise out of statutory obligations and procedural fairness requirements. Some of the key findings of Monique Ross (1997), a research associate at the Canadian Institute of Resource Law, include:

- The constitutional obligation, and the ability to discharge that obligation, rest squarely with the Crown. As a result, government must be involved in the consultation process and cannot simply delegate that duty to a third party without supervising it. The courts scrutinize how government, not industry, has consulted.
- Aboriginal and treaty rights are collective rights. Therefore, consultation must involve not only individuals directly affected in their exercise of those rights, but also community representatives.
- Government must initiate the consultation process and obtain sufficient information (including information on the practices and

views of the affected First Nation) upon which to base a conclusion regarding the impact of proposed developments and land-use decisions on Aboriginal and treaty rights.

- Government must provide to potentially affected Aboriginal people full information on the proposed action or decision and its expected impacts, so that they have an opportunity to express their concerns and interests.
- Consultation is expected at a minimum to be "meaningful" and the Crown must be prepared to "substantially address the concerns of the Aboriginal peoples whose lands [or rights] are at issue." Depending on the nature of the proposed infringement of the right, this may translate into a duty to obtain full consent, notably in the context of title lands.
- Case law suggests that any decision affecting the balance between Aboriginal and treaty rights and non-Aboriginal interests in natural resources (such as setting harvesting limits and allocating resources between various users) requires prior consultation with Aboriginal people.

Information Package (PIP), a 205-page document describing the scope of the project and a timetable for its implementation.

The filing of the PIP triggered the creation of the Northern Gas Project Secretariat, which was established in December of the same year. Third, on 18 August 2004, the Minister of the Environment appointed a Joint Review Panel (JRP), "a seven-member, independent body that will evaluate the potential impacts of the MPG on the environment

and lives of the people in the project area" (AANDC 2005) Finally, also in August, along with the Inuvialuit Game Association and the Mackenzie Environmental Impact JRP, the Minister of the Environment issued the JRP's Terms of Reference, a 77-page document outlining the MGP and the scope of the assessments to follow. The stage to launch the MGP was set, the actors were identified, the principles to guide the expert assessment of the pipeline on sensitive environments and remote communities were established, and a public consultation process was about to be launched.

Noteworthy is the fact that the Mackenzie Valley Producers Group includes four corporations (Imperial Oil, ConocoPhillips, Shell Canada, Exxon Mobil) and "the Aboriginal Pipeline Group (APG), which was formed by representatives of various aboriginal groups to represent the ownership interest of the aboriginal people of the Northwest Territories in the Mackenzie Valley Pipeline" (Imperial Oil et al. 2003:8). Its motto is "Maximizing economic benefits through ownership in a Northern pipeline." On the Mackenzie Gas Pipeline web page the APG offers a summary translation of the MGP in four Aboriginal languages: North Slavey, South Slavey, Gwich'in, and Invuialuktun.[1]

Also noteworthy is that the APG, like the federal government, ruled out the participation of the Dene Tha' in the MGP. The Dene Tha' argued that they ought to be included, because the Mackenzie Valley Pipeline would be constructed through 65 kilometres of Dene Tha' territory in northwestern Alberta, down to Zama Lake to a connector to the Alberta gas distribution system. The National Energy Board maintained that the Dene Tha' could not have a voice on a major development that was to take place in the NWT (National Energy Board 2005:73). The Dene Tha' insisted that they still had claims to territory that is part of the NWT, a territory on which they have continued to trap and hunt since the signing of Treaty No. 8. "Canada's position was that it would consider Dene Tha' 'activities' in the NWT, but not rights" (Phelan 2006:20).

In July 2004 the Dene Tha' received from the government copies of draft Environmental Impact Terms of Reference and the draft of the Joint Review Process Agreement. The Dene Tha' were given 24 hours to file a response to these complex documents. This led the Dene Tha' to appeal to the Federal Court, which they did on 18 May 2005.

Following a lengthy trial, on 10 November 2006, Judge Michael L. Phelan of the Federal Court of Appeal found the federal government in breach of duty to consult the Dene Tha' in respect of the MGP. While he noted that all parties recognized the Crown's "duty to consult," he ruled that four federal ministers had "breached their duty to consult" and reminded them that "The duty to consult cannot be fulfilled by giving the Dene Tha' 24 hours to respond to a process created over a period of months (indeed years) which involved input from virtually every affected group except the Dene Tha'." Judge Phelan also ruled that "The location of the Dene Tha's affected territory (south of 60) also is irrelevant to justification for exclusion because the scope of the JRP includes the Connecting Facilities [in Alberta] as part of its consideration of the whole MGP" (Federal Court 2006:28).

Judge Phelan also noted that in three recent cases the Supreme Court had described the duty to consult as a duty more general than the fiduciary one, a duty "arising out of the honour of the Crown" (Federal Court 2006:29). In the light of these legal precedents, Judge Phelan recognized that a remedy was called for. He noted, however, that "The difficulty posed by this case is that to some extent 'the ship has left the dock.' How does one consult with respect to a process which is already operating?" (Federal Court 2006:46).

Twenty days following the judgment of the Federal Court of appeal, Jim Prentice, Minister for Indian Affairs and Northern Development (MIAND), appointed Tim Christian as Chief Consultation Officer for the Dene Tha' First Nation and charged him with the task of "negotiating a Settlement Agreement with the DTFN, as part of Canada's commitment to fulfilling its obligations to consult" (AANDC 2007a). Seven months later, on 23 July 2007, an agreement was signed. According to a press release of the MIAND, Chief Ahnassay is reported to have said, "The potential impact on our communities of big energy sector projects has been a concern for us in the past, and remains a concern with the MGP. This Settlement Agreement is a signal that, going forward, governments and industry will work with us to ensure our Treaty and Aboriginal Rights, and our rights as first peoples of this great land, are respected." (AANDC 2007b).

An important question remains: Will the intensification of oil and gas exploration enhance Dene Tha' traditional ways? The new jobs will be held by men who are part-time hunters and trappers. The land continues to provide Dene Tha' families with substantial amounts of food (fish, rabbit, duck, moose, etc.) and medicine or *yu*. These life forms are more than material resources; they are vital links to their history and identity. This heritage and land base, however, are rapidly changing. Trappers describe their traplines as being close to or toward "Mobile Road," "Esso Road," or "Husky Road," using the different oil companies as reference points. The impact of this development is further reflected in the fact that when people "stay for a week or longer in the bush they take drinking water" (since natural water is polluted due to industrial development).

The Dream of Full Employment

The economic opportunities pursued in recent years may exacerbate rather than improve social problems. It is well known that drinking is tied to the flow of cash in the community. Dene Tha' men, for instance, observe that "firefighting money is for firewater." They do not, however, spend all their firefighting money on drink. Typically, they buy gifts for their parents and spouse (a piece of furniture, a major appliance, or a television, for instance), give some money to siblings and cousins, and keep some for drinking in High Level. The same pattern is likely to repeat itself in the years to come in the context of higher male employment.

As we have seen, the Dene Tha' continue to privilege observation over instruction and individual autonomy over subordination. In this respect, there is great continuity from generation to generation. The consequences of living by these values, however, are quite different today than they were in the past because the physical and social environments have changed so drastically. To live by these Dene values in the context of a hunting and gathering economy, in which extended families or small bands were dispersed over a large territory for most of the year, is one thing. To live by these same values on a reserve where almost 800 people, the majority under 16 years old, dwell in constant proximity, is another. Earlier generations of Dene Tha' dealt with their children in the context of a dwelling they had built in the bush, in which their children would fall asleep at night as the fire went out, and everything was dark, indoors and out. Nowadays children may keep their parents awake night after night in a single-family dwelling serviced with electricity, permitting light and television after dark. Children play and watch television in the presence of parents who will not turn off the lights or pick up the children and put them to bed, because that simply is not done. To do so would infringe on their autonomy.

In the past, men and women had clear and complementary productive domestic roles. Through observation, girls would learn from their mothers and sons from their fathers. Dene then experienced themselves as largely autonomous and self-governing. They sought gifts and songs from animal helpers and developed strong minds with which to know how to conduct themselves competently. This is no longer the case, with most men and women unemployed and, to a significant degree, dependent on unemployment and welfare cheques. The tragedy is that for contemporary adults on the reserve, there is a lack of constructive challenges to meet and overcome.

The dream of full employment was vividly expressed by a young girl. Her father had been drinking with his brothers and friends for four consecutive days. One man in the group was paying for all the liquor, since he had received three cheques of $340 each. Once the men were drunk, the girl and her mother hid one of the cheques. When the man asked for his last cheque, the girl told him he would not get it back until he was sober. She added, "I am tired of you drinking. I will buy the band store, you will be the meat cutter, and your brother will be the meat grinder for hamburger, and your mom, she is old, her, she will work on the food side, and Mom will work on clothes, and my sister will be at the Post Office, and Dad will be the manager. I will buy the nursing station, and I will buy the school too, and Dad's brother will be the principal. And I will buy the coffee shop and I will run it." In reality, except for the positions of school principal and store manager, held by non-Dene hired by the band, all the positions mentioned by the girl were already held by Dene Tha'. In this light, current Dene Tha' initiatives to foster a type of economic development that will provide employment opportunities to a greater number of individuals may well represent the lesser of two evils. But such a choice must only be embraced with a view to mitigating as best as possible the potential negative consequences.

A significant step was taken in that direction on 28 May 2008, with the opening of the Hay-Zama Lakes Wildland Park. The 486-square-kilometre park covering Dene Tha' hunting and fishing grounds is home to approximately 600 wood bison and seasonal habitat for large numbers of migratory ducks and geese. Protecting the area from industrial development means that the 23 wells currently producing oil and the 10 ones producing gas in the park will cease to operate by 2017. No new drilling will be allowed. The park, twinned with the Dalai Lake National Nature Reserve in China, may well attract eco-tourists from near and far, providing the Dene Tha' with an opportunity to diversify their economy and to continue hunting and fishing in a cleaner environment (AANDC 2008).

Conclusion

For centuries, the Dene Tha' have lived in their homeland according to a rich Indigenous tradition. This accomplishment is reflected in the comment of an Elder who proudly told his son, "If our stories and ways were wrong, we would not be here today." The son, however, faces circumstances that his ancestors did not. Treaty No. 8 was signed by people thinking they would be able to pursue their traditional way of life with a minimum of external control. Their descendants are now accepting millions of dollars in loans from the federal government to invest in the exploitation of gas and oil fields in their homeland to fuel the economy of the Canadian and American heartland.

Such a development would have been unimaginable 20 years ago. Its occurrence demonstrates the degree to which the Dene Tha' have come to shape their lives in the context of Western institutions designed to promote Euro–North American values and standards of life. Up to this point, the various non-Dene institutions have not eradicated or rendered obsolete Dene ways of living in this land and in the other land. The cumulative impact of sustained interaction with non-Dene is nonetheless undermining the relatively homogeneous view of the world and the practices characteristic of Dene life. This is true of the school, the police station, the nursing station, and the church. It is even true of the band office, which now functions more and more as the local gateway to industrial economic development on the Dene Tha' homeland.

There is little evidence that Euro-Canadians can truly be receptive to an agenda other than their own. For some time to come outside professionals who are unaware of much of Dene Tha' reality will continue to staff the school, court, hospital, nursing station, and church. These professionals will continue to dispense Eurocentric forms of education, justice, medication, religious service, and employment.

Given current political and economic developments, it is also likely that the differences between families who pursue different economic strategies will increase. In and out of school one will be able to distinguish between children who still know the land and children who do not. The former will continue to have a positive outlook on life; the latter will see only disaster looming before them. The source of this contrasting outlook on life will continue to stem from the children's participation, or lack of participation, in traditional subsistence activities.

In the meantime, the environmental crisis will continue to impact the Dene Tha'. People already see damage to the land undermining their ability to move around their homeland. Water in some streams and lakes is polluted by industrial activity. Vast tracts of forest are harvested by international corporations. The harm to their homeland will persist for decades, if not centuries, to come. Throughout the Subarctic, cleaning up the environment in the wake of ecologically insensitive mining, drilling, and harvesting of trees is a huge task that government and industry have yet to undertake seriously. Slow progress on this front means that it will take more than a generation before Dene Tha' can hunt and trap in the bush for extended periods and drink again with confidence the water that is now polluted and undrinkable.

Finally, the Dene Tha' will continue watching the Deh Cho Process and learn from their northerly neighbours how best to launch their own claims to Aboriginal self-government and Aboriginal stewardship over the land. If they take that route, governments and their legal advisors are likely to argue that the willing participation of the Dene Tha' in current agreements governing exploitation of resources indicates their recognition that what exists within the global economy are not Aboriginal rights but economic opportunities open to all regardless of race or creed. Once again, Dene Tha' leaders will have to face the deep disjunction between Euro-Canadian and their own understandings of their history and their relationship to the land and its inhabitants. Sadly enough, in the present circumstances I see little likelihood that Euro-Canadians and Dene Tha' will be able collectively and jointly to create a just and balanced political and economic environment. Such an environment would truly enhance the quality of life for all the inhabitants of Chateh and beyond. Such an environment would then respect the invisible web of interpretations drawn by the Dene Tha' to constitute a distinctively meaningful Aboriginal world that, to this day, is much richer and more complex than ever imagined by outsiders. Such an environment would foster a world in which parents could still proudly say to their children, "If our stories were not true, we would not be here today."

ACKNOWLEDGEMENTS

I want to express my gratitude to Monique Ross of the Canadian Institute for Resource Law and to Kim Harvey-Trigoso for making available to me, on short notice, valuable material they had recently published or written concerning the Dene Tha'. Thanks also to Christine Hanssens, who, based on her first-hand experience with the Dene Tha', has provided valuable insights and comments on the organization and content of this chapter. Except for references to events and developments that have taken place since 1987, the ethnographic material (including the map of the Dene Tha' homeland) pertaining to the Dene Tha' contained in this chapter is adapted from Jean-Guy A. Goulet, *Ways of Knowing: Experience, Knowledge, and Power among the Dene Tha* (Lincoln: University of Nebraska Press, 1997).

NOTE

1. See www.mackenziegasproject.com.

REFERENCES AND RECOMMENDED READINGS

Aboriginal Affairs and Northern Development Canada (AANDC). 2005. "Mackenzie Gas Project Environmental Assessment and Regulatory Review". Accessed 31 July 2013 at: www.aadnc-aandc.gc.ca/eng/1100100023680/1100100023682

———. 2007a. "Backgrounder—Dene Tha' Settlement Agreement." Accessed 31 July 2013 at: www.aadnc-aandc.gc.ca/aiarch/mr/nr/m-a2007/2-2894-bk-eng.asp

———. 2007b. "Government of Canada and Dene Tha' First Nation Reach Settlement Agreement." Accessed 7 February 2013 at: www.aadnc-aandc.gc.ca/aiarch/mr/nr/m-a2007/2-2894-eng.asp.

———. 2008. "Indian Oil and Gas Canada. Annual Report 2007–2008." Accessed 7 February 2013 at: www.pgic-iogc.gc.ca/eng/1100110010500/1100110010520#chp4_1.

Anderson, M. 2002. "Not All Aboriginal Groups Support New Developments," *Edmonton Journal*, *National Post* supplement, 17 September, EJ14. A journalistic account, supported by a wealth of colour photographs, of current economic developments and contemporary actors in the NWT.

Bailey, Sue. 2006. "Ottawa Offers Land Deal to Only First Nation Offside with Pipeline Project," Associated Press. 31 May. Accessed 28 January 2008 at: ca.news.yahoo.com.

Bouchard, Randy. 2006. *Dene Tha' Presence in Northwestern Alberta and the North West Territories*. Manuscript report prepared for Robert Freedman, Cook Roberts Lawyers, counsel, Dene Tha' First Nation.

Brant, C. 1990. "Native Ethics and Rules of Behaviour," *Canadian Journal of Psychiatry* 35, 6: 534–9. A Mohawk psychiatrist discusses the ethics of non-interference and individual responsibility among Natives.

Dene Tha' First Nation. 1997. *Dene Tha' Traditional Land-use and Occupancy Study*. Calgary: Arctic Institute of North America. Verbatim statements on issues affecting individuals following their transition from the bush economy to contemporary development and welfare. Many photographs.

Dene Tha' Community School Testing Information (DTCSTI). 1996. Unpublished manuscript, 3 April.

Federal Court. 2006. *Dene Tha' First Nation v. Canada (Minister of Environment)*, Docket T-867-05. 10 November. Available at: http://decisions.fct-cf.gc.ca/en/2006/2006fc1354/2006fc1354.pdf. Accessed 23 June 2009.

Fumoleau, René. 1994. *Aussi Longtemps que le Fleuve Coulera. La Nation Dènèe et le Canada*. Quebec: Septentrion.

Goulet, Jean-Guy. 1998. *Ways of Knowing: Experience, Knowledge, and Power among the Dene Tha*. Lincoln: University of Nebraska Press. A study that illustrates with anecdotal accounts how it is possible to understand another culture.

Harvey-Trigoso, Kim. 1999. "Ecological Knowledge of the Dene Tha': Traditional Subsistence Activities and Childhood Socialization," MA thesis, University of Calgary. A study of childhood socialization among contemporary Dene Tha' that reveals the unique perspective of children on their world.

Helm, June. 1994 [1961]. *Prophecy and Power among the Dogrib Indians*. Lincoln: University of Nebraska Press. Traces origins of a revitalization movement among NWT Dene to activity of Dene Tha' prophets.

Horvath, S., L. McKinnon, M. Dickerson, and M. Ross. 1997. *The Impact of the Traditional Land-use and Occupancy Study on the Dene Tha' First Nation*. Sustainable Forest Management Network, Project Report 2001–18. Edmonton: University of Alberta.

Documents the impact of traditional land-use study on the Dene Tha' and on industry and government.

McClellan, C. 1972. *The Girl Who Married the Bear.* Publications in Ethnology No. 2. Ottawa: National Museum of Man.

Mills, Antonia, and Richard Slobodin, eds. 1994. *Amerindian Rebirth: Reincarnation Belief among North American Indians and Inuit.* Toronto: University of Toronto Press. Excellent collection of reincarnation studies among contemporary Native peoples.

Moore, Patrick, and Angela Wheelock, eds. 1990. *Wolverine Myths and Visions: Dene Traditions from Northern Alberta.* Edmonton: University of Alberta Press. Dene Tha' stories from when animals and humans talked and intermarried.

Nasaday, P. 2002. "'Property' and Aboriginal Land Claims in the Canadian Subarctic: Some Theoretical Considerations," *American Anthropologist* 104: 247–61.

National Energy Board. 2005. Annual Report to Parliament. Accessed 7 February 2013 at: www.neb-one.gc.ca/clf-nsi/archives/rpblctn/rprt/nnlrprt/2005/nnlrprt2005-eng.pdf.

Phelan, J. 2006. Dene Tha' First Nation (Applicant) and Minister of Environment, Minister of Fisheries and Oceans, Minister of Indian and Northern Affairs Canada, Minister of Transport, Imperial Oil Resources Ventures Limited, on behalf of the Proponents of the Mackenzie Gas Project, National Energy Board, and Robert Hornal, Gina Dolphus, Barry Greenland, Percy Hardisty, Rowland Harrison, Tyson Pertschy, and Peter Usher, all in their capacity as panel members of a Joint Review Panel established pursuant to the Canadian Environmental Assessment Act to conduct an environmental review of the Mackenzie Gas Project (Respondents). Citation: 2006 FC 1354.

Reid, Bob. 2004. "The APG: An Exceptional Deal." A presentation to the Senate Standing Committee on Energy. 8 Mar. Accessed 7 February 2013 at: www.mvapg.com/media/docs/an-exceptional-deal.pdf.

Ross, Monique M. 1997. "The Dene Tha' Consultation Pilot Project: An 'Appropriate Consultation Process" with First Nations?,' *Newsletter of the Canadian Institute for Resource Law* 76 (Fall): 1–7. A legal analysis of current agreements between the provincial government and the Dene Tha' from the perspective of the federal government's legal obligations toward Aboriginal peoples.

Slobodin, Richard. 1975. "Canadian Subarctic Athapaskans in the Literature to 1965," *Canadian Review of Sociology and Anthropology* 12: 276–89.

Smith, D.M. 1993. "Albert's Power: A Fiction Narrative," *Anthropology and Humanism* 18, 2: 67–73. An insightful narrative based on the Dene understanding of animals as a source of power that humans can draw upon.

CHAPTER 11

The Mackenzie Valley Dene: The Continuing Relevance of Asch's Ethnohistory to Development

Robert Wishart

In previous editions of this book, serially updated versions of "The Slavey Indians: The Relevance of Ethnohistory to Development" by Michael Asch have been central to the section on the Western Subarctic. This piece has become a classic and many, including myself, assign it as such in university courses and recommend it those who ask about the economic and political history of the Mackenzie Valley Dene. Asch's original piece focused primarily on the Slavey of Pehdzeh Ki (Wrigley), with whom he did fieldwork in the late 1960s and early 1970s. Pehdzeh Ki is in what has become known as the Deh Cho region. However, Asch argued that the piece was indicative of the history of the Mackenzie Valley Dene as a whole. Despite my fieldwork being with the Gwich'in in the Mackenzie Delta, Asch's work was of primary importance in the way that I came to understand the history I was being told by the Gwich'in and uncovering in the archives. Simply put, the history of anthropology's involvement with the Dene and the development debates of the late twentieth century are entangled with the anthropological understanding of current Dene life to such an extent that it warrants attention.

Therefore, the goal of this piece is to demonstrate why the historical evidence that Asch and others brought to light in such forums as the Berger Inquiry[1] is still relevant to ongoing debates and political manoeuvres surrounding petroleum development in the Mackenzie Valley and, indeed, in wider contexts as well. The contemporary situation will thus be examined in relation to the economic history of these people through the Aboriginal period, the early contact period, the height of the fur trade, and the collapse of the fur trade. As Asch argued, the primary goal should be to relate these histories to contemporary social, political, and economic structure and to evaluate the impact of proposed petroleum development. Maintaining the relevance of this ethnohistory allows for an argument that, should Dene jurisdiction and their well-informed choices about development not be upheld and respectfully heard, then the negative impacts of the collapse of past economic developments could be repeated and magnified.

Pipeline Development in the Mackenzie Valley Today

The meteoric overall rise in the price of petroleum in the last decade has put tremendous pressures on Aboriginal groups in the Mackenzie Valley to participate in the development of the Mackenzie Delta and Beaufort Sea natural gas reserves. These reserves are estimated to contain trillions of cubic metres of available hydrocarbons. While the spike in prices has heightened the effect, the contemporary pressure really reflects a series of events that began in the mid-1990s with more gradual increases in prices. Moreover, the pressure also has precedence in the spike in petroleum prices in the 1970s. While the actual exploration and development of gas wells in these northern regions has continued since the 1980s, the rate of development generally follows the increase and decrease of energy price speculation. The increased efforts to bring gas to market with the most recent boom in prices highlighted what has always been the problem with energy development in this region: how best to deliver the product to southern markets and consumers.

The answer to this problem has not changed. Then as now, from the standpoint of energy producers, it is necessary to construct a pipeline that will feed directly into the existing natural gas pipeline grid that begins in northern Alberta. Therefore, since the early 1970s, the Dene of the Mackenzie Valley have been under significant pressure to allow or to participate in the development of a Mackenzie Valley pipeline that would efficiently deliver petroleum products to market. The current proposed pipeline would be 1,200 kilometres long and follow the Mackenzie River south to Fort Simpson and then take a direct route to the northernmost part of the existing network. It is estimated that it could bring as much as 18.5 billion cubic metres of natural gas to market annually.

The intense pressure placed on the Dene to allow this gas to reach its market is multiplied by two other factors. First, there is competition between four potential pipeline routes proposed by several petroleum companies for delivering natural gas to southern markets. Of these, two routes are being taken most seriously. One is along the Mackenzie Valley, estimated to cost about $8 billion (not including gas gathering systems and other necessary development projects that raise the price to more than $16 billion); the other is along the Alaska Highway and would cost $6.5 billion to build, but it could possibly be constructed faster

because it parallels an existing highway. Both routes are "stand-alone," meaning that one or the other will be built, but not both. This competition has placed considerable pressure on the First Nations of both of these regions to approve proposals (Crump 2001:2). More recently, the potential for a US$26 billion natural gas pipeline from Alaska's North Slope to the Canadian network has raised the question of a competing pipeline to link across the Beaufort Sea and deliver Mackenzie Delta gas to market.

The second factor is the steady decline in demand and price for the Dene's renewable resource products, especially for fur. Despite these declines, continuing to practise traditional hunting, fishing, and trapping is described by Elders and younger generations as being of prime importance. There are many reasons for this concern with maintaining tradition; however, relevant here is the economic importance of wild foods to the local diet and the importance of cash brought in from the fur trade for purchasing goods. In many of these communities, bought foods are expensive due to the high cost of shipping goods to remote areas, and the availability of fresh foods is severely limited. Therefore, people who live in these areas continue to rely on wild foods[2] and on the money received in exchange for furs to purchase expensive goods—many of which are used for hunting and fishing. Despite this continued reliance on hunting, fishing, and trapping, people are again realizing that trapping cannot provide sufficient cash income to meet the local demand for imported goods and services (e.g., Barrera 2001). One of the ramifications of declining outside demand for renewable products is the pressure on First Nations governments to create jobs in the wage-labour sector. Many (e.g., Antoine 2001), but certainly not all, see the extraction and delivery of non-renewable resources such as oil, gas, and diamonds as an answer to the problem of the severe fluctuations and overall historical decline in the relative price of furs.

In 2000, in response to these pressures, 30 members of Aboriginal groups from the Mackenzie Valley and Delta formed the Aboriginal Pipeline Group (APG), whose mandate was to maximize the economic benefits of petroleum development in the region and work with petroleum companies to get the Mackenzie Valley Pipeline built. The leaders of the Deh Cho First Nation, part of the Dene people, hesitated to sign on to the APG because of concerns over a lack of consultation with Elders, but signed in the end with the understanding that it did not commit them to building a pipeline, but rather that it was an agreement to investigate the maximization of Aboriginal ownership and benefits and the drafting of a business plan. Friction between the leaders of the Deh Cho and other signatories then appeared when the premier of the Northwest Territories, Stephen Kakfwi, and some of the other members of the APG declared that they had a mandate to negotiate the building of a pipeline. The Deh Cho members did not feel that this was what they had signed on to. They then refused to sign any of the other Memorandums of Understanding presented by the APG. Neither did they sign a Memorandum of Understanding on 15 October 2001 with the other members of the APG and Imperial Oil, ExxonMobil, Shell Oil, and ConocoPhillips (known as the Mackenzie Valley Producers), agreeing that the Aboriginal members (under the umbrella of the Mackenzie Gas Project) would have one-third ownership of the proposed pipeline. The Mackenzie Gas Project began the regulatory application process in January 2002. This process, along with the "definition phase," was long in the making. Hearings before the National Energy Board (NEB) began in 2006; in 2010 the NEB approved both the construction project and the transmission of gas through the pipeline, despite the fact that the Deh Cho have an unsettled land claim with the federal and territorial governments. The Deh Cho First Nation does not want to sign any pipeline agreements until they have

the same assurances as the other First Nations who have settled comprehensive land claims. The Deh Cho have been negotiating with the federal government for several years for a self-government agreement. They believe that they do not need to "claim" land which is already theirs and that their treaty rights should not be extinguished in what they consider to be "land sales" (Nadli 2001:14). In exchange for the extinguishment of certain treaty rights, the claims of the Inuvialuit, Gwich'in, and Sahtu Dene and Metis include private blocks of land, which means that corporations must seek Aboriginal approval for any development affecting these lands. The Deh Cho First Nation is seeking an interim resource development agreement with the federal government which would give them similar powers until a final agreement can be made. The federal government has been hesitant to negotiate such a deal outside of a comprehensive regional land claim.

The question is, how did a situation arise where different groups within the Dene Nation came to hold these different positions regarding today's proposed pipeline development and to have different political relationships with Canada? Answering these questions requires knowledge of the economic and social history of the region and the political events that unfolded after the Berger Inquiry.

The Berger Inquiry and the Dene

Following the discovery of ample reserves of hydrocarbons in the Mackenzie Valley and Delta in the late 1960s, a consortium of multinational petroleum corporations decided in the early 1970s to construct a pipeline to transport Alaskan and Canadian Arctic gas to markets in southern Canada and the United States. Named the Canadian Arctic Gas Pipeline Ltd. (CAGPL), the consortium proposed to construct a line along the Arctic coast and up the Mackenzie River Valley to northern Alberta.

The region through which the pipeline was to pass included the homeland of two Aboriginal nations: the Dene and the Inuvialuit. The Canadian government commissioned the Mackenzie Valley Pipeline Inquiry to ascertain the potential social and economic impact of this pipeline. Under Justice Thomas Berger this inquiry spent more than two years listening to testimony from experts and community members. It was anticipated that the project would be given rapid clearance to proceed; after all, it would provide economic development to a region that was understood to be economically deprived. In fact, this economic rationale became the main argument of the consortium. According to them, Aboriginal culture was dead or dying, the bush economy had collapsed along with the fur trade, and the people would welcome wage labour while construction proceeded.

It is this assumption about the collapse of traditional economies and cultures that is closely tied to the history of anthropology in the region. Some anthropological theories on culture change were certainly informing this particular understanding, for was it not the case that all traditional cultures were being rapidly swamped in the wake of capitalist expansion? Then there were those such as Michael Asch who were in the field and discovering that the theories were overly simplistic, if not wrong, and that the eulogy for Aboriginal culture being delivered by development interests reflected wishes rather than facts.

When the Berger Inquiry began, the academic debate about culture change became front and centre in the conversation about the effects of economic development. Michael Asch was one of the experts called to give evidence. His own explanation for his involvement is crucial and indicative of the potential impacts of social theory and the action anthropology of the time:

I became involved in the Berger Inquiry because I had done research among the

Slavey regional grouping of the Dene in 1969–70. I had collected much information of the contemporary economy of the Slavey at Wrigley (Pehdzeh Ki in Slavey) and Fort Simpson during my fieldwork and on their economic history.

The Berger Inquiry dealt with the social and economic consequences of a major construction project on contemporary Native people. Crucial to this kind of evaluation is the status of the Aboriginal society: is it "dead" or "dying" or does it remain "viable"? At the heart of this matter lies our perception of hunting–gathering society. Dominant in academic thought today is an evolutionary view that sees such societies as of intellectual interest primarily because of the data they provide on the "past" of human history. Hunter–gatherers are in this view our "contemporary ancestors." Part of the intellectual baggage pertaining to this idea is the belief that such societies today are mere vestiges of their former statuses and, like vestigial organs, are about to self-destruct. Evidence for this conclusion appears to abound in transparently obvious symbols of precipitous assimilation. . . . After all, the Dene now wear Western clothing, speak English, go to school, ride on snowmobiles and in cars, listen to country music, and complain about lack of disposable income. One could easily presume that fundamentally these are just poor people who happen to be Dene and not members of an autonomous culture.

The proponents of the pipeline firmly supported this view. On the basis of studies into the contemporary economy of the Dene and Inuit and by reference to some of the ethnographic literature, expert witnesses (including economists and sociologists)

who appeared on behalf of the applicants argued that the traditional way of life was "dead" or "dying." As a consequence, they argued that in the near future the Dene would slip from high unemployment to endemic poverty. Seen in this context the pipeline was a good thing, for it would provide jobs enabling the Dene to make a "smooth" transition from a traditional existence to a middle-class way of life.

Because of my work at Wrigley, I was asked by the Indian Brotherhood of the Northwest Territories (now renamed the Dene Nation) to provide evidence for the Berger Inquiry. However, it was not supposed to be about evaluating this way of thinking. Rather, it was to focus on ethnographic and historical evidence on land use and the fur trade. Indeed, my evidence was titled "Past and Present Land Use of the Slavey Indians." Yet, although the title never changed, the content did, for I found myself confronting an idea for which evidence was lacking.

Upon reading the data provided by the applicants' witnesses, I became convinced that something was fundamentally wrong with their work, for it did not jibe with my own recollections of the time I spent at Wrigley. These people were being miscast as impoverished, marginalized Canadians, for, to paraphrase what Dr. Peter Usher stated about the Inuit, if these are poor people, they are the only ones who go to bed with stomachs filled with good meat provided from their own larders. It was a view that was further confirmed by the Dene themselves, for they argued almost unanimously in opposition to the immediate construction of the pipeline. Their reason? It would interfere with their traditional land-based activities. In short,

the Dene were presenting the view that their traditional way of life (as currently practised) could remain viable in the modern world. If one agreed that their way of life was dead or dying, the point of view presented by the Dene could make no sense, and, indeed, the applicants characterized their assertions as "romantic" and "politically motivated." If, on the other hand, their assessment of their economy was taken to be valid, then their orientation could be understood as based on a realistic appraisal of the situation.

My testimony focused on determining which perspective was more appropriate and, although facts concerning these matters were used, did not present a story concerned with land use or economic history. In this respect, it represented my first attempt to grapple with how members of our society frame facts about Aboriginal peoples, for although one might argue that the assertions made by the applicants were merely "politically motivated" they appropriated a way of looking at Aboriginal peoples that dominates contemporary Western thought (including theorizing in anthropology). My work indicated that there was little factual basis for the assumptions made about the Dene as contemporary hunter-gatherers and sought to piece together an analysis that made better sense of the facts of cultural contact. (Asch with Wishart 2004:178–80)

As indicated by Asch's own words, he had to work against the grain of the anthropological theory of culture change that was dominant in his day. He was thus effectively able to deconstruct the assumptions that informed the view being put forward by the development and governmental interests, because these were much the same as the anthropological ones. At the same time, his testimony allowed for an alternative ethnohistory to be given in evidence at the Berger Inquiry.

When Berger tabled his recommendations in April 1977, they came as a shock to the development interests. He recommended a 10-year moratorium on petroleum development so that the Inuvialuit and Dene could have time to negotiate their claims with the territorial and federal governments. Furthermore, he recommended, for environmental and economic reasons, that an alternative stand-alone pipeline through the northern Yukon should never be built. In short, Berger was convinced by the Dene, the Inuvialuit, and their experts that the arguments put forward by the development interests were not based in fact. Furthermore, he was persuaded that the development position had more to do with an understanding of de-populated frontiers than it did of an area that was occupied and home to two nations. He cautioned:

> It is not always easy to remember, as one flies over the unbroken boreal forest, the tundra, or the sea ice, that the Canadian North has been inhabited for many thousands of years. The populations that have used this great area were never large by European standards, but their skills as travellers and hunters made it possible for them to occupy virtually all the land. (Berger 1977:5–6)

In the case of the Dene, they disagreed that their contemporary way of life was vestigial or dying. They did not want the pipeline built, because it would interfere with their way of life; they recognized it as a threat to their economy and way of life, not as a solution to their problems. They did not want a pipeline built until they had assurances that their way of life would protected and their already existing economy would be sup-

ported and developed, as guaranteed in Treaty No. 11. Berger summarizes:

> It is an illusion to believe that the pipeline will solve the economic problems of the North. Its whole purpose is to deliver northern gas to homes and industries in the south. Indeed, rather than solving the North's economic problems, it may accentuate them.
>
> The native people, both young and old, see clearly the short-term character of pipeline construction. They see the need to build an economic future for themselves on a surer foundation. The real economic problems of the North will be solved only when we accept the view that the native people themselves expressed so often to the inquiry: that is, the strengthening of the native economy. We must look at forms of economic development that really do accord with native values and preferences. If the kinds of things that native people now want are taken seriously, we must cease to regard large-scale industrial development as a panacea for the economic ills of the North. (1977:xxi)

From the Dene viewpoint, negotiations were needed on a nation-to-nation basis to create a regime suitable for their way of life and give them control over their own affairs. Moreover, they should be consistent with the spirit and principles of the 1975 Declaration of Dene Nationhood (Dene Declaration) and precede any large-scale development on their lands.

As Asch argued, it is not surprising that the development interests used the argument that the Aboriginal way of life was dead or dying; it reflected a larger narrative of the history of Canadian policy in the North and corresponded to the evolutionist theory of the time.

BOX 11.1 Justice Thomas Berger, 1977

This process of cultural transformation has proceeded so far that in the North today many white people—and some native people, too—believe that native culture is dying. Yet the preponderance of evidence presented to this inquiry indicates beyond any doubt that the culture of the native people is still a vital force in their lives. It informs their view of themselves, of the world about them and of the dominant white society.

Euro-Canadian society has refused to take native culture seriously. European institutions, values and use of the land were seen as the basis of culture. Native institutions, values and language were rejected, ignored or misunderstood and—given the native people's use of the land—the Europeans had no difficulty in supposing that native people possessed no real culture at all. Education was perceived as the most effective instrument of cultural change; so, educational systems were introduced that were intended to provide the native people with a useful and meaningful cultural inheritance, since their own ancestors had left them none.

The assumptions implicit in all of this are several. Native religion had to be replaced; native customs had to be rejected; native uses of the land could not, once the fur trade had been superseded by the search for minerals, oil and gas, be regarded as socially important or economically significant.

—Thomas Berger, *Northern Frontier, Northern Homeland: The Report of the Mackenzie Valley Pipeline Inquiry* (1977:5, 85)

Both of these tended to understand culture contact between Europeans and First Nations in northern Canada as immediately damaging to the Aboriginal people and their way of life. Furthermore, this argument was often couched in the terms of necessary progressive steps toward a modern way of life (Asch 1979a, 1979b, 1982). There were alternative views on the effects of culture contact in the work of other scholars who did fieldwork with Dene (e.g., Slobodin 1962), but these tended to be ignored in favour of the culture-collapse model (Wishart and Asch 2009), which aligned with the consortium's interest in building a pipeline as quickly as possible. Asch therefore set out to evaluate the development position using historical evidence. The resulting argument was extensive, covering three periods of economic history: the Aboriginal period, the fur-trade period, and the 1950s to the 1970s. He believed that independent factual evidence demonstrating that the contemporary way of life was not dying would help in understanding why the Dene did not want the pipeline built immediately and why they argued that, prior to its construction, a regime protecting their traditional way of life and controlled by themselves should be in place. This evidence is summarized and augmented by my own research in the next section. However, each sub-section maintains the scope and focus of Asch's argument—one that has become crucial to the academic understanding of culture contact in this region, and that also illustrates how I have come to understand positions and arguments recently presented by Dene.

The Evidence

The Aboriginal Period

The pre-contact period is by far the longest. Human habitation began in this area at least 12,000 years ago (Dickason 2002:17), with some archaeologists arguing that it may be at least twice that old. Whatever the date, these First Nations understand that for as long as they have been who they are, they have lived in this area. What we know about the Aboriginal period can be gleaned from sources related to late pre-contact life.

Life in the region was characterized by the dominance of groups of approximately 20 to 30 related persons, often referred to as bands. In order to maintain themselves economically, these groups relied on harvesting the many kinds of bush resources found throughout the region by hunting, fishing, and gathering wild plants for food, clothing, and shelter. Big game, such as moose, caribou, bears (black and grizzly), mountain sheep,

and woodland buffalo, were hunted, along with small game such as snowshoe hare, migratory waterfowl, beaver, and muskrat, which could be hunted or trapped using a variety of techniques and technologies. Fish, such as whitefish, inconnu (another whitefish), herring, grayling, arctic char, salmon, and northern pike were extremely important in most areas. Plant life, such as several species of berries, wood from spruce and birch, and some seasonal broad-leaved plants provided food as well as fuel, building materials, and medicine.

The primary techniques used in collecting animal resources were snaring with **babiche** or sinew, and larger-scale entrapment. Moose, caribou, and other big-game animals were also hunted with bow and arrow, club, or spear when they were crossing water or open country. Caribou were hunted in the mountains often by using surrounds, pens to contain the animals. Two long fences would be built flaring out from the mouth of the surround; the caribou would then be driven

FIGURE 11.1 Slavey shaman (right), his son (left), and Dogrib boy (centre), Fort Rae, NWT, 1913. (© Canadian Museum of Civilization, photographer J.A. Mason, 1913, 26079)

into this funnel. Once the caribou were in the surround, their exit was blocked and they could be
speared or shot with arrows. Evidence of these
surrounds can still be found. Fish were taken
using nets made of woven willow **bast**, sinew,
or babiche. Fish traps of various sorts were constructed, including weirs.

Given these technologies, large-game capture
and successful fishing often required co-operative
labour. Co-operation was also important for
women's production tasks that often produced a
more reliable supply of foodstuffs such as berries
and small game like hares, grouse, and ptarmigan
that could be snared. Moreover, safety from large
predators like wolves and bears and even unruly
behaviour of large herbivores[3] can be found in co-
operative harvesting relationships.

Within bands, bush resources were distributed
on the basis of reciprocity or mutual sharing. It
was the whole local group, and not each family
or individual, that defined the self-sufficient unit.
All would share in the success or failure of finding
food. This reciprocal formula is further complicated
and extended by sharing between groups as well as
inter-regional trade, so these bands should not be
thought of as isolates. In fact, many bands would
often come together in summer or winter around
lakes or on rivers to share in the massive fish runs.
In some areas, bands would also come together in
the mountains in winter to hunt caribou and preserve meat.

As Asch argued, the primary problem with
sustaining this economic system was the redistribution across local groups, some of which
may have a surplus and some of which may not
have the minimum resources for survival. There
were two possible solutions to this problem. The
resources could move, or the people could be
brought to the resources. In most cases, the evidence indicates that the latter solution was most
often used. The kinship networks linked all the
local groups and allowed for the reciprocal rights
and obligations that gave the use of resources to
all within the region.

The Fur-Trade Period

Direct involvement in the fur trade started in different locations at different times in Dene country.
However, in all cases European goods flowed into
the area along Aboriginal trade lines prior to direct
European contact. Russian goods came from the
west; British, American, and French goods from
the east and south. Alexander Mackenzie travelled through the heart of this area in 1789–93,
down the river that now bears his name, and was
arguably the first European in the area; he noted
on several occasions that the Aboriginal people
were already familiar with trade goods and were
trading with their neighbours. However, direct
trade between Aboriginal people and Europeans
in the Mackenzie Valley as a whole did not begin
until late in the eighteenth century, and in more
northern areas not until quite a bit later. During
the early years of the fur trade, availability of goods
was severely restricted due to poor transportation, and Aboriginal people maintained their reliance on bush products. Important items of trade
tended to be decorative or luxury goods; items
most requested were beads, blankets, metal pots,
sugar, flour, and tea. Dene would often refuse to
trade if the particular goods they wanted were not
available. For instance, a scarcity in the right kind
of trade beads caused a crisis for traders at a couple
of posts in these early times.

During this time there was some competition between the North West Company and the
Hudson's Bay Company, but not on the scale of
other areas in Canada. The North West Company
enjoyed a near monopoly at first, as the HBC had
only just begun to explore this area economically;
the HBC had a monopoly beginning in 1821 upon
the amalgamation of the two companies. It was not
until the HBC lost its monopoly in the late 1860s
that competition became a factor in the destabil-

izing of the fur-trade economy. Most of the early trade from the Aboriginal side was in bush resources such as meat and fish that were meant to sustain and provision the traders; fur was of secondary importance. While opening these new trade routes was of primary importance to the HBC, and initial shortfalls in furs were expected as the company could not provision the forts themselves, the continuation of this situation did not sit well with the company, which was running a deficit in the Mackenzie District of approximately 1,500 made beaver[4] by 1830 (HBC Archives B.200/d/27/3d). HBC governor George Simpson was particularly frustrated with this situation in his district, a region he was sent to make profitable. He argued that trade in luxuries like beads should be done away with and the Dene should be forced to trade in dry goods and metal works in exchange for furs alone, a situation which he thought would create dependency and thus larger profits, as had been done elsewhere (HBC Archives D.4/92). However, this situation did not change until the introduction of steamships on the major rivers of the Subarctic in the late nineteenth century, which provided access to provisions from the south, so now the traders could focus on the more profitable trade in furs (Tough 1996:44). Asch asserts:

> The economy of the Native people changed little during this period from its Aboriginal strategy. It was still "total" in that the people of the region, including Natives and Bay personnel, depended for their survival almost exclusively on local resources. This was achieved by Bay personnel through the exchange of trade goods for food and by the Natives through the continued use of a wide range of bush resources and the organization of the people into self-sufficient local groups. For the Native people, production, despite the new utensils and implements, was still

primarily a collective activity: distribution of goods within and between local groups was still based on the principle of sharing. The only significant changes in Native economic life during this time were the adoption of certain trade-good items that made life a little easier and a shift in seasonal round to include both occasional trips to the trading posts for supplies at various times in the year and, especially later in the period, the occasional use of the trading posts rather than the major lakes as places for encampment during the summer. (Asch with Wishart 2004:183)

The Hudson's Bay Company lost its monopoly with the sale of its territories in 1870 and, with new competition from independent or free traders, they lost the ability to secure furs at prices far below market value. With profits decreasing, the HBC was pressured to deliver more trade goods at a lower cost. They did this by introducing steamships in the 1880s, and when the rail link was built between Calgary and Edmonton in 1891 they were able to cut the cost of shipping goods and furs dramatically. The result was that the HBC shifted their focus away from direct trading into the shipping of trade goods and furs and into retail sales. It was a focus on these two activities that maintained the company's profitability until recently.

The new transportation system had multiple effects on the fur trade. First, it allowed traders to supply their own sustenance needs; therefore they did not need to trade for provisions. Second, it meant that the Dene now needed to rely on fur alone to obtain trade goods. Third, it meant that the HBC and the independent traders could subsidize provisions so that the Dene could focus more of their labour on trapping for fur rather than hunting for meat.

With these changes also came a change in the types of goods the Dene could now receive

FIGURE 11.2 Slavey Indian camp at Fort Simpson, NWT, 1934. (© Canadian Museum of Civilization, 80042)

some individualization of trapping activities, but Asch argued that these effects were not total:

As a result of these externally initiated developments in the fur trade, the Native economy in some areas had shifted by 1900 (and throughout the region by World War One) away from its virtual independence of trade goods to a situation where both trade goods and local subsistence resources were significant. Yet the internal organization of the economy did not change greatly. The primary economic unit remained the local group, which in most cases still wintered at fish lakes. Labour was still organized on the basis of age and sex; women and children were responsible for collecting small game, the men, for hunting, fishing, and now trapping. . . . Aboriginal hunting techniques were still employed in hunting most game, including big-game animals, and co-operation therefore remained a significant component of production. . . . (Asch with Wishart 2004:184)

in trade. Repeating rifles and steel traps were incorporated into the Dene way of life, as were prefabricated clothing and other luxury items. In addition, the quantity of traditionally exchanged goods increased considerably. By the end of the nineteenth century, the fur trade had been revolutionized, and it would be tempting to argue that the Aboriginal way of life must also have been changed beyond recognition in its adaptation to this social force, but this argument was short-sighted. Certainly there were changes in mobility, some shifts in residence, stays at the trading posts were incorporated into the seasonal round, and

While there was a change in the amount of trade between the Dene and the traders, the distribution of the goods within the regional economy maintained the features of mutual sharing that could be found in the Aboriginal period.

Recent Decades

By "recent decades," Asch meant those decades between about 1950 and the Berger Inquiry of

1977. To a contemporary reader these may seem to be distant history, but they are a highly significant period to the Dene, and the Elders I worked with in the early 2000s would also inform the present with these "not so long ago" times. I leave the heading unchanged to remind us of the importance of this historical information to the inquiry and the lessons it still has for the present.

Recent economic history was marked by the collapse of the fur trade following World War II, the advent of government interventions, and the coming of new industries to the North.

The high price of furs during the early part of the twentieth century led to an ever-increasing reliance on trade goods among the area's Aboriginal peoples. Despite this reliance, they continued to make their living from the bush. However, these increasing prices for fur led to an influx of European trappers and settlers and to new competition for land bases. Now the stability and success of the economy depended largely both on external economic conditions, such as a high market price for furs in relation to trade-good prices, and on the local availability of a productive surplus in one resource, furs. The focus on furs led to chronic problems, and after the influx of Europeans into the North during the 1920s, a period when many returning soldiers of World War I headed north and took up trapping, it almost led to economic collapse due to intense competition. On the other hand, the relationship between the price for furs and trade goods remained fairly constant through the two world wars and even the Great Depression. Yet, ultimately, it was this price factor and not fur production itself that led to the collapse of the fur-trade economy when, beginning after World War II and lasting at least through the Korean War, there was a long depression in the value of furs and an astronomical rise in the prices of trade goods. So it was not a collapse in the Dene side of the economy that led to the problems with the fur trade but rather world economic forces that put a premium on goods.

By the middle of the twentieth century, it became apparent that the fur trade would not recover its economic importance. The boom was over. The federal government, rather than bringing in price supports and other factors to support the economy as it had done in some sectors such as family farming, assumed that the collapse of the fur industry meant the loss of a way of life.

As a consequence, they encouraged and coerced Dene to move into towns where children would attend school and then take jobs rather than become hunters and trappers. However, this program was not successful. There were few jobs and the government erred in concluding that, because most Dene now lived in towns rather than in their bush communities, Dene had lost their way of life. However, to live in towns with little income to support these capitalist structures, many communities became reliant on welfare and transfer payments. It is an issue that continues to be a central concern, as direct government payments have replaced labour as the main method for obtaining trade goods. For example, one Elder I worked with used her house as an example:

> My elders told me, "Don't take that house, stay in one that you build yourself. If you take that house then you have to take their water, take their fuel, pay with their money, pretty soon eat their food. If you stay in your house then you have to go get your own water, go out and cut wood, get everything yourself, you know meat, fish and berries. This means your kids got to do that too and they will be OK."

However, many Dene did not have a choice and, as a consequence, a pattern has been established in the relationship between Native people and external agents—both governmental and business—during the past few decades. The pattern is best described as a massive intrusion of southern Canadian institutions, values, and powerful personnel into the ongoing social and economic processes of Dene society. The implementation of family allowances and pensions gave the government a tool for requiring, as a prerequisite, that children attend schools in towns; as a consequence, the families must settle in these places rather than be out in the bush.

These new circumstances had partially fractured the Dene economy. Officials distributing monies tied to social assistance made it clear that they favoured nuclear families and disfavoured the local group. The trade economy therefore became dependent upon a shift in social structure. This was not the case with the bush economy.

Production, distribution, and reciprocity in the bush sphere did not change very much. Men were still going out into the bush to secure large-game resources, to fish, and to trap; however, settlement in towns meant they were now travelling large distances to do so. Women were still securing small game and plant materials; however, with settlement and the need to be near the children in school, the resources around towns for these types of bush products were soon depleted. This depletion shifted more emphasis to the men's contribution to the bush economy.

The trade-good sphere was put under different pressures. With the collapse in fur prices, families had to supplement the goods they would have received from trading furs with cash that at first came primarily from government sources and then increasingly also from wage labour. Cash was treated according to values of both the Aboriginal economy and the Euro-Canadian one. Cash became the private property of the person who received it, as were the luxuries bought with it. It may have often been lent out to relatives and others (at no interest) but was not regulated as strictly by the rules of reciprocity. However, once converted into traditional trade goods, these goods circulated along the lines dictated by the bush

economy and formed a significant part of the reciprocity system of distribution.

Asch summarizes what he found to be recent conditions:

In sum, the collapse of the fur trade and the concomitant rise of governmental intervention in the economic and social life of the people did not produce a qualitative shift in the focus of the Native economy away from its reliance on both local subsistence and the use of trade goods, although in recent years the latter has become increasingly important. The past 40 years have been a period of marked change in the internal organization of the economy: production and circulation in the spheres of bush subsistence and cash-trade-good subsistence became virtually independent of each other, creating what is known as a **dual economy**. . . .

The contemporary Native economy has not solved the problem of dependency on external agencies. Indeed, the problem has deepened: direct government payments have replaced productive labour as the main resource for obtaining trade goods—payments that are seen by most people, Native and non-Native, as handouts to the poverty stricken. In short, post-contact economic history is dominated by a single theme: the acceptance by Native peoples of immediate well-being in exchange for long-term economic dependence. (Asch with Wishart 2004:187)

Dene Opposition to the Pipeline

At the time of the Berger Inquiry, the Dene were nearly unanimous in their opposition to the pipeline despite the offer of increased wage labour that this development would bring. As Asch demonstrated with his ethnohistoric evidence, this should have been predictable; however the assumption was that the only way to escape the problems of modern life in these northern regions was to strengthen the wage-labour economic sphere. This is precisely what the Dene did not want, and from the lessons of their own history, they knew this would not accomplish what it was meant to solve; it would further the process of accepting today's comfort in exchange for tomorrow's economic dependence and social problems.

With the coming of wage labour many traditional Aboriginal institutions and values were put under tremendous strain, which contributes to social problems such as alcoholism, poor housing, high welfare rates, poor health, and increased crime. One theme that Berger described in detail was how the intrusion of southern values and institutions without control by the Dene and Inuvialuit had always been accompanied by massive social disruptions and problems. In short, the contemporary period has produced social and political dislocations derived mainly from the imposition of strong external influences on the Dene and from their need, in attempting to maintain their way of life, to accept short-term solutions that have long-term negative impacts. These social repercussions are not due to the adaptation to culture contact but rather result from direct government policy and actions (Asch 1993:20).

As the Dene argued, and as Asch reported, these problems can be solved only by strengthening the Dene way of life, not by imposing another form of dependence on worldwide economic trends and further government intervention. Asch concluded that the Dene recognized that they had lost control with the intrusions of various policies and that they were attempting to regain control and reassert the importance of the aspects of their lives that were assumed to be dead or abandoned. Regaining control could be recognized in the various territorial political organizations like the Indian Brotherhood of the Northwest Territories, which later became the Dene Nation. Again, pursuing political power resulted in the Dene Nation claim and political statements such as the Dene Declaration.

As Asch argued:

> It is ironic but significant to note that among the strongest supporters of the land claim are the young and well-educated, the very individuals the industry-sponsored studies suggest are most alienated from the traditional way of life and most willing to embrace the Western one. An overwhelming majority of young people do not want to abandon their traditional lifestyle, and they see the land claim settlement as a way to protect themselves in future from what has happened to their society in the past.[5] The most important point is that they are not sitting around waiting for us to solve their problems; they have arrived at a proposed direction for a solution themselves. The question is whether we will allow them to take that path and make it work. Where local people have some control over the internal organization of economic institutions, those institutions can be run to maintain traditional values such as mutual sharing even in the cash sector of the economy. (Asch with Wishart 2004:191)

Berger heard these oppositional arguments and was convinced by the evidence presented to him. His recommendations reflected his "far-reaching vision" that the Dene economy could exist in modern times with the right kind of support that would entrench their rights to the land, their rights to determine their own future in relationship to the lessons from their history, and to "ensure their place, but not their assimilation, in Canadian life" (1977:xxiii).

BOX 11.2 Excerpts from the Dene Declaration

Statements Of Rights

We the Dene of the N.W.T. insist on the right to be regarded by ourselves and the world as a Nation. Our struggle is for the recognition of the Dene Nation by the Government and the people of Canada and the peoples and governments of the world.

The New World like other parts of the world has suffered the experience of colonialism and imperialism. Other peoples who have occupied the land—often with force—and foreign governments have imposed themselves on our people. Ancient civilizations and the ways of life have been destroyed.

Colonialism and imperialism are now dead or dying. Recent years have witnessed the birth of new nations or rebirth of old nations out of the ashes of colonialism.

The African and Asian peoples—the peoples of the Third World—have fought for and won the right to self-determination, the right to recognition as distinct peoples and the recognition of themselves as nations.

But in the New World the Native peoples have not fared so well. Even in countries in South America where the Native peoples are the vast majority of the population there is not one country which has an Amerindian government for the Amerindian peoples.

Nowhere in the New World have the Native peoples won the right of self-determination and the right to recognition by the world as a distinct peoples as a Nations.

While the Native people of Canada are a minority in their homeland, the Native people of the N.W.T., the Dene and the Inuit, are a majority of the population of the N.W.T.

What we the Dene are struggling for is the recognition of the Dene Nation by the governments and peoples of the world. And while there are realities we are forced to submit to, such as the existence of a country called Canada, we insist on the right to self-determination as a distinct people and the recognition of the Dene Nation.

Our plea to the world is to help us in our struggle to find a place in the world community where we can exercise our right to self-determination as a distinct people and as a Nation.

What we seek then is independence and self-determination within the country of Canada. This is what we mean when we call for a just land settlement for the Dene Nation.

—Second Joint General Assembly of the Indian Brotherhood of the Northwest Territories and the NWT Metis Association in Fort Simpson, 19 July 1975. The Dene Declaration can be viewed in its entirety at www.denenation.com/dene_declaration.html.

However Berger's report failed to gain political support and only his 10-year moratorium was given any real consideration. In the end, the fall-ing price of hydrocarbons allowed the government simply to stop discussion of the pipeline development issue for a few years. When prices began to increase again in the early 1980s, coupled with a looming recession, the government was able to give permission to smaller petroleum development projects "for national good." No mention was made of the moratorium.

The Rise of Comprehensive Claims and Present-Day Effects

As they realized that the government was simply going to approve development projects without Dene support or without taking their concerns into consideration—other than citing them as secondary issues—the Dene found themselves under differing levels of pressure to enter into regional negotiations. In the Far North, the Inuvialuit signed a comprehensive claim in 1984 which gave them some control over development on Inuvialuit private lands. This claim meant that their Dene neighbours to the south were at a serious disadvantage in negotiations over projects that would have a direct effect on their lives. The Gwich'in and the Sahtu Dene and Metis therefore negotiated comprehensive claims in 1992 and 1993 respectively. In the south in the early 1990s, the Dogrib were witnessing the fastest diamond development project in history, so like their northern national members they were being forced to the comprehensive claims table in the real fear of losing all control over development on their lands. The Dene had a tough choice to make: either settle and have some say in development, or not participate in a comprehensive claims process while development would proceed without their consent. It is a difficult choice and one that can only be understood in relation to the history of development and Canada's intervention in these areas. According to the work of Asch and the recommendations of Berger, it is a choice that the Dene should never have had to make because they had already formed a political relationship with Canada that should have taken precedence. It is this relationship that the Deh Cho Dene have continued to uphold.

As far as the Deh Cho Dene are concerned, there was already a special relationship with the rest of Canada that guarantees protection of Dene interests: Treaty Nos. 8 (1899) and 11 (1921). Dene assert that these treaties recognized that they would maintain peaceful relations with Euro-Canadians in exchange for the acknowledgement of their own land and cultural rights "as long as the sun shines and the river flows," a solemn promise that they have upheld. In general, the Dene sought recognition of the rights they maintain through the treaties as they were negotiated, and they simply wanted Canada to fulfill its own treaty promises.

The comprehensive claims process has traded the acknowledged general rights of the treaties for specific rights to have a part in determining what happens over certain pieces of land within the settlement areas. At a local level, comprehensive claims have partially worked to give control over development to the claimants, and corporations have had to adjust their wage-labour policies to provide time for bush-sector activities for their workers. These are recognized as positive effects. However, another effect of this process has been the division of the Dene into those with a clear working relationship with corporations seeking to extract resources and those who continue to uphold the idea of nationhood and jurisdiction over all the Dene lands but have been losing their say about development. As the Deh Cho have argued, the essential concern is having a fundamentally different conversation with Canada than negotiating a regional claim that would extinguish their pre-existing rights. As a result, the APG has argued that it will proceed with its plans to get the pipeline built, even without Deh Cho support for about 40 per cent of the route, but it will hold 34 per cent (the Deh Cho share) of its profits for the Deh Cho in trust until they settle a claim. As before, the Deh Cho are left with a very stark choice.

Conclusion

In Asch's conclusion he summarized why he believed that the Dene were right when they told Berger they did not want a pipeline until a land deal had been reached. From what we know of the economic history of the region, the proponents of the pipeline were offering a "remarkably" similar deal to that of the fur traders: "immediate material well-being in return for long-term economic dependency." But in the fur trade there was a difference; the Dene received material well-being but did not have to seriously alter their traditional activities and organization. The deal proposed by the pipeline consortium assumed that the traditional elements were irrelevant because they were doomed. They offered instead temporary economic well-being in exchange for greater dependence on the cash sector and assimilation into the Euro-Canadian way of life. This assimilation means a total reorganization of the labour force into the one sphere, wage employment:

> Whether wage employment is secure anywhere in Canada, given our economic system, is an open question. Of concern here, however, is that the petroleum industry will not be secure in the North over a long period. That is, just as the fur trade's viability depended on the availability of furs and a high world market price for them, so the viability of petroleum development will depend on the availability of oil and a high world market price for it. But what happens when the resource gives out, or we in the south find a cheaper source of fuel? What happens if the world market price of petroleum products declines to a point where it is uneconomic to exploit and transmit northern oil and gas to southern markets? The petroleum corporations, just like the fur traders before them, will pull out. They must leave if the proposition becomes uneconomic and, of course, that day inevitably will come.
>
> What will happen to Native northerners? The history of the fur trade provides the answer: there will be a general collapse in the cash-trade goods sector of the economy. (Asch with Wishart 2004:191)

During my own research with the Gwich'in, they expressed a similar concern. This concern is captured in the following quote from one Elder who was reflecting on his life of working various jobs and of being a hunter: "In my life, four times someone said, this job will help you, help your people. Four times in my life that job goes away. Good thing there is still caribou, still fish about. My grandson is now going through training. They tell him it is all he will ever need." From the Elder's perspective, he can still shift his labour to the bush sector as needed. But this is not in accordance with the deal put forward by the development proponents, who would prefer a total refocusing of the economy to suit their own interests for an indefinite time, even though this refocusing will rob the people of their ability to sustain themselves in their own lands. In the time of the Berger Inquiry, the Dene saw through the details of this deal and rejected it in favour of upholding what they regarded as their right, as affirmed by treaty, to effectively control development to suit their own interests. Berger believed that the only way to make development responsive to Dene interests was to proceed with settling the land issue prior to any permit being issued to build the pipeline.

At this time, there is still one land settlement in the Mackenzie Valley outstanding, and should development of the pipeline proceed without the expressed consent of all the Deh Cho, the decision about their future will have been made without their approval; the consequences are potentially dire. At the same time, just to the south, other First Nations in Alberta and British Columbia are also witnessing the effects of petroleum development without their control. They are also now being approached with pipeline deals and are under pressure to accept these deals. Once again there are Nations who are referring to the treaties they signed or the fact that they never signed a treaty and wondering what became of the guarantee to protect their way of life as long as the sun shines and the river flows.

NOTES

1. "The Berger Inquiry" is shorthand for the Mackenzie Valley Pipeline Inquiry, the results of which were tabled by the commissioner, Mr Justice Thomas R. Berger, in 1977. In the Mackenzie Valley it is referred to as the Berger Inquiry or more simply as Berger.

2. Analyses of the continuing importance of "country food" in this area clearly show that these foods are still consumed on a daily basis (e.g., Usher 1976, Wein and Sabrey 1988). My own more recent experience in the community of Fort McPherson (a Gwich'in community) concurs with these analyses.

3. There are times of the year (particularly when the cows have small calves in the spring and when the bulls are rutting in the autumn) when the bison and moose pose greater threat to safety in the bush than do predators.

4. "Made beaver" was a term used early in the trade to designate the value of trade goods. Thus one made beaver was the value of one blanket, one brass kettle, or eight knives.

5. In the present day this trend can be seen as continuing. A perusal of Deh Cho–based social networking Web pages demonstrates a strong desire for the negotiation to continue along the lines of the original land claim. My thanks to Julie Sinclair for bringing this to my attention.

REFERENCES AND RECOMMENDED READINGS

Antoine, Jim (Minister of Aboriginal Affairs, Minister of Justice, Government of the NWT). 2001. "The Emerging Aboriginal Business Community in the Northwest Territories," Speaking notes for AFN-NEXUS Conference, 17 July, Halifax.

Asch, Michael I. 1979a. "The Ecological Evolutionary Approach and the Concept of Mode of Production." In *Challenging Anthropology*, edited by D. Turner and G.A Smith. Toronto: McGraw-Hill Ryerson.

———. 1979b. "The Economics of Dene Self-Determination." In *Challenging Anthropology*, edited by D. Turner and G.A Smith. Toronto: McGraw-Hill Ryerson.

———. 1982. "Dene Self-Determination and the Study of Hunter-Gatherers in the Modern World." In *Politics and History in Band Societies*, edited by E.B. Leacock and R.B. Lee. Cambridge: Cambridge University Press.

———. 1988. *Kinship and the Drum Dance in a Northern Dene Community*. Edmonton: Boreal Institute for Northern Studies. Discusses the social life of Wrigley in the late 1960s. Its focus is on the connections between the drum dance, kinship, and economics in the lives of these Dene people. It is particularly valuable for its approach, which does not isolate the drum dance from political and social organization but instead incorporates these elements into a holistic picture of kinship structure.

———. 1993. *Home and Native Land: Aboriginal Rights and the Canadian Constitution*. Vancouver: University of British Columbia Press.

Asch, Michael, with Robert Wishart. 2004. "The Slavey Indians: The Relevance of Ethnohistory to

Development." In *Native Peoples: The Canadian Experience*, edited by R.B. Morrison and C.R. Wilson. Oxford: Oxford University Press.

Barrera, Jorge. 2001. "We Can No Longer Make a Living," *Inuvik Drum*, 18 October.

Berger, Mr Justice Thomas R. 1977. *Northern Frontier, Northern Homeland: The Report of the Mackenzie Valley Pipeline Inquiry*, 2 vols. Ottawa: Department of Supply and Services. Reproduced with the permission of the Minister of Public Works and Government Services Canada, 2013 A detailed account of the Dene and Inuit economy in the Mackenzie Valley. Berger describes the potential impact of the massive pipeline proposed by industry and makes recommendations on how to maintain a viable hunting–trapping way of life within a contemporary northern economy.

Brody, Hugh. 1981. *Maps and Dreams: Indians and the British Columbia Frontier*. Vancouver: Douglas & McIntyre. This volume presents a concise portrait of how the Dene in northeastern BC are working to maintain a traditional way of life based on hunting and trapping in the face of those who would transform their lands to extract resources. Written in a style accessible to the non-specialist, this work still maintains a high standard of scholarship and thus succeeds at explaining in a humanistic manner the central battle all northern Native groups now face.

Crump, John. 2001. "Return of the Pipeline," *Northern Perspectives* 27, 1: 1–3.

Dickason, Olive. 2002. *Canada's First Nations: A History of Founding Peoples From Earliest Times,* 3rd ed. Toronto: Oxford University Press.

Gemini North Limited. 1974. *Social and Economic Impact of Proposed Arctic Gas Pipeline in Northern Canada*. Study prepared for Canadian Arctic Gas Pipeline Limited.

Helm, June. 1961. *The Lynx Point People: The Dynamics of a Northern Athapaskan Band*. National Museum of Canada Bulletin 176. Ottawa: National Museums of Canada. A summary of Slavey life in the 1950s, with discussion of social and cultural changes. Of particular interest is her discussion of Slavey culture and values and their attempts to incorporate a commercial fishing operation into their way of life.

——— ed. 1981. *Handbook of North American Indians*. Vol. 6, *Subarctic*. Washington: Smithsonian Institution. Authoritative reference source on the ethnology, ethnohistory, and archaeology of the Mackenzie Valley Dene, including the Slavey.

Honigmann, John. 1946. *Ethnology and Acculturation of the Fort Nelson Slavey*. Yale University Publications in Anthropology 33. New Haven: Yale University Press. This is a general account of traditional culture and society and of the effects of contact with Western societies as analyzed from the perspective of the acculturation model. Honigmann emphasizes that in his view Slavey subsistence patterns result in a minimum of social and political complexity and in a high regard for individual autonomy.

Hudson's Bay Company HBC Archives. B. 200/d/27/3d. "Fort Simpson Accounts, 1824–1834," Winnipeg: HBC Archives.

———. A D. 4/92. "Governor George Simpson Correspondence Outward, 1828," Winnipeg: HBC Archives.

Mitander, Victor. 2001. "A Look Back at the Mackenzie Valley Pipeline Inquiry and the Alaska Highway Pipeline Inquiry: What Has Changed Since Berger and Lysyk Made their Recommendations," *First Nation Rights and Interests and Northern Pipeline Development*. Materials prepared for a conference held in Calgary, 18–19 June. Vancouver: Pacific Business and Law Institute.

Nadli, Michael. 2001. "Grand Chief Michael Nadli— The Deh Cho View," *Northern Perspectives* 27, 1: 14–15.

Ridington, Robin. 1990. *Little Bit Know Something: Stories in a Language of Anthropology*. Vancouver: Douglas and McIntyre. This book speaks to the theme of anthropological transformations resulting from work with the Dene. In this case it is about stories and what it means to know something rather than directly about economy.

Slobodin, Richard. 1962. *Band Organization of the Peel River Kutchin*. Ottawa: National Museum of Canada, Bulletin 179.

Tough, Frank. 1996. *As Their Natural Resources Fail: Native Peoples and the Economic History of Northern Manitoba, 1870–1930*. Vancouver: University of British Columbia Press.

Usher, Peter J. 1972. *Fur Trade Posts of the Northwest Territories: 1870–1970*. Northern Science Research Group—14. Ottawa: Department of Indian Affairs and Northern Development.

———. 1976. "Evaluating Country Food in the Northern Native Economy," *Arctic* 29, 2: 105–20.

Watkins, Melville, ed. 1977. *Dene Nation: The Colony Within*. Toronto: University of Toronto Press. The book is composed primarily of edited versions of the testimony presented by witnesses called by the Indian Brotherhood of the Northwest Territories at the Mackenzie Valley Pipeline Inquiry. It encapsulates the "case" presented by the Dene at those hearings. Some contributors were Dene, describing such matters as their educational and other experiences. Others were expert witnesses called by the Dene, such as Scott Rushforth, who evaluated country food and Asch, who provided a much reduced version of the material in this chapter.

Wien, Eleanor E., and Henderson Sabrey. 1988. "Use of Country Foods by Native Canadians in the Taiga," *Arctic Medical Research* 47, supplement 1: 134–8.

Wishart, Robert, and Michael Asch. 2009. "Writing against the Grain of Materialist Orthodoxy: Richard Slobodin and the Teetł'it Gwich'in." In *A Kindly Scrutiny of Human Nature: Essays in Honour of Richard Slobodin*, edited by Richard J. Preston. Waterloo, ON: Wilfrid Laurier University Press.

CHAPTER 12

Offerings of Stewardship: Celebrating Life and Livelihood of Gwich'in Women in the Northwest Territories

Brenda Parlee, Alestine Andre, and Ingrid Kritsch

Introduction

*W*omen the Gatherer (Dahlberg 1982) was intended to balance the portrayal of hunter–gatherer societies in *Man the Hunter* (Lee and DeVore 1968). Her investigation of the gendered dimensions of subsistence was a catalyst for the development of this chapter and our discussion of Gwich'in women in the Northwest Territories.

The Gwich'in people make up one of the largest Athapaskan groups in northern Canada. Extending through present-day Alaska, the Yukon, and NWT, the 11 Gwich'in populations are locally adapted. Walking through mountain berry patches or boating down the Peel or Mackenzie River to a family fish camp, even the uninformed visitor can see and feel the power of the land which has shaped and been shaped by the generations of people who made lives here. Early explorers, missionaries, traders, and anthropologists tell us much about life here at the beginning of the twentieth century and before. Recent Indigenous oral histories offer Gwich'in perspectives on this way of life. Other kinds of interdisciplinary and collaborative research with organizations like the Gwich'in Renewable Resources Board and Gwich'in Social and Cultural Institute add depth about contemporary issues of social, economic, cultural, and ecological change including those related to con-taminants and changing diet and health, self-governance, economic development, and the effects of resource development and climate change on the land, water and wildlife of the region.

My (Brenda's) earliest memories of the Gwich'in region are of the mountains above the Peel River where I spent many hours with the women of Fort McPherson looking for what they call *nakal*, also known as yellow berries, cloudberries, bake apple, or *Rubus chamaemorus*. I was privileged to be with a group of women known as expert berry pickers. Although I was/am a slow and clumsy harvester by comparison, I seemed an acceptable and useful member of the group due in part to my four-wheel drive extended-cab pickup that could ferry my elder friends up the Dempster Highway to this "shangri-la of berry patches."

Subsequent memories are bittersweet. On 11 September 2001, as planes flew into the twin towers in New York City, Ingrid and I were in Fort McPherson. We sat with an Elder watching the events unfold on her big-screen TV as the first winter snow fell outside. While Rosie worked solemnly on her beaded slippers and sent her grandchildren on their way to school, I found myself paralyzed by the collision of worlds occurring in her tiny living room. Rosie, born in a tent in the Richardson Mountains 85 years previously, would have seen many crises—the tuberculosis and influenza outbreaks of the late 1920s and early 1940s, the beginning and end of World War II, changes in lifestyle and diet when the caribou did not come in the 1950s, and the loss of her children to residential schools in the 1960s. Despite her physical frailty, Rosie was a very strong woman, with knowledge, experience, and perspective on both local and world events that I could only imagine. Rosie has since passed away, but is still highly regarded for her beading and sewing skills as well as her knowledge and experience.

When I returned to Winnipeg that fall and began my doctoral studies, I was surprised to discover that there was very little in the historic or contemporary literature about the kind of women I had gotten to know. I was caught off guard by the obvious gender bias in many historical texts about the Gwich'in and other northern Indigenous peoples. As aptly framed by Miller and Chuchryk, "Ethno-historical descriptions of tribal life in the past placed the focus on men and men's roles—man-the-warrior, man-the-chief, man-the-hunter, and man-the-provider. The roles of women have either been ignored altogether or placed in a position of subservience and/or secondary importance" (1996:6).

This bias in the ethnography of Indigenous societies has been answered by a revisionist trend in anthropology, archaeology, and other disciplines and a growth in the breadth of scholarship related to Indigenous women in general. A recent review reveals emerging research on the impact of colonization on women and their roles in society, ceremonial and spiritual roles, traditional socio-political roles, and social issues including sexual abuse and addictions (Strong 2005). In Canada, Indigenous women are an important focal point in research related to Canadian history, Aboriginal rights, land tenure, health, education, food security, biodiversity conservation, traditional clothing, and resource management. On the whole, however, our knowledge of Indigenous women and their

contributions to the shaping of their communities still remains limited. "Women are virtually invisible, their voices stilled by the infrequency with which their work is noted and by the implication, when it is noted, that it was less important to the group's survival and to the cultural complex" (Peers 1996:39). Accounts of subsistence, for example, have virtually ignored the role that women played within the family—as providers, caregivers, and healers.

It is no surprise as one looks to the North, that the archetype of "man the hunter" is deeply ingrained in the archaeological and anthropological record. Although the tendency is toward male knowledge and practice, a discussion on "hunting" does not necessarily exclude women. Many who have thoroughly explored and deconstructed this practice in the North and elsewhere have revealed complex systems of knowledge and practices attributed to both men and women.

A common northern reference to women's role in hunting is Bodenhorn's paper, "I'm Not the Great Hunter, My Wife Is," quoting a successful Inupiat hunter referring to his wife's abilities to attract animals as well as to butcher, share meat, and sew clothing, all of which are described by Inupiat as hunting skills (1990). While women's role in hunting is noted to be significant in some cultures, it is only one dimension of a more complex system of knowledge and practices unique to women. Theory on "woman the gatherer," which emerged in response to the classic 1966 symposium and subsequent volume entitled "Man the Hunter" (Lee and DeVore 1968), attempted to explore these alternatives to hunting.

The "man the hunter" model stresses that primitive males hunted for meat and provided food and protection for their mates and children, who stayed near the home base. The competing hypothesis suggests that major food of early human beings consisted of plants, obtained by women with the use of tools and shared with their offspring. The contrast focuses on how female behavior is conceptualized: as mobile and active or as sedentary and passive. Responses to both theories, however, depend on which anthropological evidence is used, how it is interpreted, what animal models are used, and which behaviors form the starting point. (Zihlman 1989)

Using the classic "woman the gatherer" model as the starting point for investigating the knowledge and practices of Indigenous women, this chapter discusses the role of Gwich'in women in historical and contemporary contexts; specifically we expand the largely economic notion of Indigenous women as simply gatherers to the multifaceted notion of stewardship.

Stewardship is an important concept in many Indigenous cultures. In the resource management literature it refers to acts of protecting, nurturing, or managing the environment sustainably. In the context of Indigenous peoples, it often refers to a broad set of social, cultural, and spiritual roles and responsibilities to each other and to the environment. Unlike notions of ownership and property, Aboriginal stewardship is based on the assumption that valued resources are not commodities to be bought and sold but rather are collective and sacred entities, the values of which cannot be measured by the physical alone but must be considered in the context of spiritual values and beliefs. Land, water, and wildlife are thus not merely resources in the conventional economic sense but are sentient and anthropomorphic beings inextricably linked to a people's past, present, and future. It is this interconnectedness to the land which underlies ideas of stewardship for Indigenous peoples around the globe. Recognizing these cosmological roots for the idea of stewardship and the challenges around the use of the term "resources," we offer steward-

ship as a means of discussing the knowledge and practices of Gwich'in women in relation to environment, health, and culture.

Getting There: A Reflection on Methods and Collaboration

I have travelled many times between Fort McPherson and Inuvik on the Dempster Highway. It is always a time of reflection since I am rarely able to keep the CBC radio signal going for more than an hour of the two and a half–hour trek. It is always a surprise to see whom you meet along the way and who emerges from their mud-spattered four-by-fours (or bicycles—amazing!) when you arrive at the ferry landings at Tsiigehtchic or on the Inuvik side of the Mackenzie River. After my borrowed Chevy truck spit out its transmission on the Peel River ferry, I once made the journey back to Inuvik as the co-pilot in the fruit-and-vegetable truck. I have travelled the road with chiefs and leaders, Elders, and "taxi" drivers, and made good friends along the way. Ingrid, Alestine, and I have from time to time found ourselves together on the road or at the ferry landing in Tsiigehtchic, a likely location given that Tsiigehtchic is both Alestine's home and a home of the Gwich'in Social and Cultural Institute. The river view is one of the most spectacular in the region. The Mackenzie is very wide here, and wider still after the Arctic Red River joins it.

In keeping with this river imagery, this chapter is a confluence of different streams of experience, discipline, and outlook on the places and people of the region. As an academic who has worked with the Teetł'it Gwich'in for only a short time (since 2001), my position in this collaboration is distinctly an outsider's whose approach to cultural research is informed by academic training in development and in environmental resource management. My perspectives are tempered by those of both Ingrid and Alestine whose collective experiences—Ingrid as a northern scholar and anthropologist and

Alestine as a Gwich'in ethnobotanist and northern scholar—provide more grounded and insider views. In addition to our own views, we bring forward the voices of our collaborators—the women who tell the stories of their lives. Thus this chapter really has many authors with many perspectives.

First we explore the role that Gwich'in women traditionally played in their communities—in domains stereotypically dominated by men as well as in fields uniquely attributable to women. We challenge and expand on these notions as the chapter develops. The ecological knowledge of Gwich'in women is the first challenge; specifically the paper speaks to the knowledge and practices associated with harvesting berries and plants for medicinal and nutritional value. The role of Gwich'in women in health and health care is specifically considered through the disciplinary lens of ethnobotany and the experiences and perspectives of Gwich'in scholar Alestine Andre who shares narrative on her work with Gwich'in Elder Ruth Welsh. Finally, the paper focuses on the important role Gwich'in women play as stewards of culture. Historically, the work associated with the development of clothing, tools, and household items was fundamental to the livelihood and well-being of their communities. Today, these practices are equally important expressions of Gwich'in cultural identity and self-determination. We discuss how Gwich'in women are celebrating their cultural heritage through work of the Gwich'in Social and Cultural Institute.

The Land of the Gwich'in Settlement Region

For many Canadians, their first and only visions of the Gwich'in region are found on calendar photos posted on their mom and dad's kitchen wall. Next to June's Bay of Fundy in Nova Scotia and January's Moraine Lake in Banff, you find images of the Roman Catholic Church perched on the banks of the Arctic Red River at Tsiigehtchic, the

autumnal mountain landscape of the Richardson Mountains, and the weaving channels of the Mackenzie Delta at Aklavik. These images are all the more powerful if you place them within the local geography of the Gwich'in Settlement Area. In a space of 300 kilometres of highway, travellers wind their way through the alpine habitats of Dall sheep and barren ground caribou on the northern edge of the boreal forest, across the Peel River, and finally to the banks of the majestic Mackenzie River. The communities of Fort McPherson, Tsiigehtchic, Aklavik, and Inuvik are equally as diverse and complex as the environment around them.

The Gwich'in (formerly Kutchin or Loucheux) are part of the Athapaskan language family. They are the most northerly of Canada's Athapaskans, occupying most if not all of the southern slopes of Alaska's Brooks Range, the river valleys and floodplains of the northern Yukon, and east to the Anderson River in the NWT. Oral tradition indicates that the Gwich'in have occupied this area since time immemorial or, according to conventional belief, for over 10,000 years. Today the Gwich'in of the NWT occupy an area defined in their 1992 Gwich'in Comprehensive Land Claim Agreement as the Gwich'in Settlement Region (see Map 12.1) which includes traditional lands in both the NWT and the Yukon.

Each of the 11 contemporary bands constitutes a dialect and identifies itself by a major river or a prominent feature within their traditional lands. The two groups we focus on are the Gwichya Gwich'in, "those who dwell in the flats" and now live primarily in Tsiigehtchic, and the Teetł'it Gwich'in, "those who dwell in the headwaters of the Peel River" and today largely make Fort McPherson home.

Gwich'in ethnography starts with Osgood's classic work (1936). He, in particular, is credited with extensive ethnographic contributions on the Gwich'in, including the Alaskan groups. Gwich'in

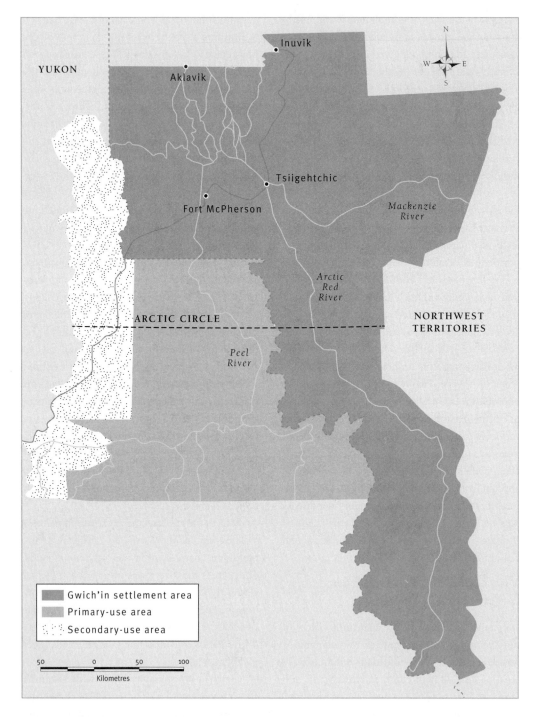

MAP 12.1 Gwich'in Settlement Region

history is also being constructed and reconstructed through more recent oral history research (Heine et al. 2001) and the analysis of historical documents such as Hudson's Bay Company journals.

Gwich'in population in the Mackenzie basin is estimated to have been in the tens of thousands prior to European contact. First contact along the Mackenzie occurred in 1789 when Alexander Mackenzie arrived en route to the Beaufort Sea. Post-contact diseases are thought to have resulted in significant mortality, particularly among northern and eastern populations. Disease in this time period resulted in the disappearance of the Dihaii Kutchin, who lived in the Chandalar River and Koyukuk River area. Later, the Daghoo (Dagudh) Gwich'in also disappeared as a separate band following epidemics (Osgood 1936; Slobodin 1981).

The main sources of food of the Teetł'it Gwich'in have notably been caribou, moose, and the array of freshwater fish found in rivers and lakes of the region. Although such foods have always been the core of the diet, there is growing recognition among cultural ecologists and health-promotion academics and practitioners that the consumption of berries and plants is under-reported and poorly understood in its importance to northern nutrition and health (Turner and Cocksedge 2001). Consequently, early ethnography focused heavily on male-dominated subsistence activities, especially caribou and moose hunting. Assertions regarding the importance of these subsistence activities were based not only on estimates of the quantities of a resource harvested and consumed but also on perceptions of the relative complexity of these harvesting activities compared to other forms of subsistence. As Slobodin noted:

> The socio-cultural importance of larger
> mammals is evidenced in elaboration
> of hunting ritual, in many refinements
> and variations in stalking and taking the
> game, in the customs for sharing out the

kill—practices that were relatively rigid for a culture marked by pragmatic flexibility—as in the prestige attached to successful hunting of these animals. (1981:517)

To be fair, other resources important to subsistence were peripherally noted. Slobodin referred to the contributions of flora to their diet. "Almost every type of edible fauna, from the wide variety of these available and many types of flora, were utilized by the Kutchin" (1981:515). Leechman (1954) was among the few ethnographers who documented the ethnobotanical knowledge of the Gwich'in—he concluded that at least 22 plants were employed medicinally by the Crow Flats Kutchin (now known as the Van Tat Gwich'in). Documentation of traditional clothing including various forms of hide clothing design and decoration and skin and hair adornment were also made from early times (Slobodin 1981; Osgood 1936). The use of mineral pigments such as red ochre and dried seeds as beads for clothing decoration and for skin colouring was also noted. In addition, early explorers, traders, scientists, and missionaries collected samples of clothing and tools which were, for the better part of the nineteenth and twentieth centuries, deposited in museums worldwide (Kritsch and Kreps 1997).

Details about the roles and responsibilities of women in providing these valued nutritional and cultural resources are, however, conspicuously absent. Only generalized interpretations can be found. According to Jenness, the contribution of Gwich'in women to the overall livelihood of the community was more than significant; however, their status in the overall decision-making was limited; they "received no gentle treatment; they performed nearly all the hard work in camp, transported all the family possessions, ate only after the men had eaten and had no voice in family or tribal affairs" (1972:403). The characterization of Gwich'in women as traditionally having low status, was contested, however, by others, including Osgood

(1936) as well as by contemporary oral history work, much of which has been carried out under the auspices of the Gwich'in Social and Cultural Institute[1] (GSCI) and its partners (Heine et al. 2001; Thompson and Kritsch 2005).

The Diverse Roles and Practices of Gwich'in Women

Sitting over a cup of tea with Elizabeth Colin, Dorothy Alexie, or Mary Teya, one learns a great deal about the role that Gwich'in women played in their communities prior to settlement in the community now known as Fort McPherson. This included many pursuits and domains stereotypically dominated by men including leadership, hunting, trapping, and fishing, as well as other practices uniquely attributed to women.

More than Hunting

Knowledge of when and where to travel was particularly important, given the mixed reliance on caribou in fall and winter and fish in summer months. Women were often influential in deciding where families would move. In addition to knowledge about where the caribou were most abundant, such decisions included consideration of what terrain was best for travel and what sites were most valuable for setting camp (e.g., shelter and the availability of fuel wood and water). These decisions were also determined by social networks. Given the importance of working together to survive, decisions of when and where to go required consideration of who was nearby and could be called upon in times of need.

Gwich'in Elder Tony Andre remembers that sometimes his mother, the eldest in the family, decided when they would move camp (Heine et al 2001:66). When it came to work at the camp, Gwich'in women and older children worked alongside the men. Elder Ruth Welsh recollects her own upbringing at Husky River. "We lived at Husky River year round. (We) hunted and trapped in the winter time, muskrat trapping in the spring,

fishing in the summer. Every year all families did that and we all survived. It was hard work" (Andre 2006:130). Teaching and learning were part of the hard work as older children of both genders watched and helped their parents, setting traps for fine fur or muskrats, or setting nets for fish at good eddies along the river or at points on lakeshores.

At traditional camps, women were trained to carry out the various tasks required around the house and camp as well as when travelling on the land. Such work would include washing dishes and clothes, making snowshoes and caribou-skin sleds or canvas wrapper sleds, tanning hides, making caribou-skin babiche, sewing, fishing, snaring rabbits, and some hunting. Both young women and men would learn camp skills, as Ruth Welsh explains, "Even the boys had to learn how to mend their clothes or make a new pair of mitts or duffels because everyone was out in a different place on the land, hunting or trapping" (Andre 2006:34). The periodic absence of men at seasonal camps required that women do "a man's job." They had to know the best locations to get firewood and how to chainsaw the dry standing trees, and haul and chop firewood. Around camp the women still worked at various household chores, helping with cutting moose or caribou meat as well as tanning hides. In this way young people, both girls and boys, were taught how to work and survive on the land.

While men were the primary hunters and often possessed medicine related to hunting, women possessed their own medicine power and learned from an early age that their conduct could impact the outcome of a hunt. Carefully controlling their behaviour as proscribed by rules set out during puberty training was critical to a balanced management of power—and the success of a hunt. "The women accepted the responsibility to exercise this control and to behave in the appropriate manner; this was one of their indirect contributions to the hunters' work" (Heine et al. 2001:98). If women failed to do their part, the hunt might not be successful.

Puberty was an important transition in women developing their power. Specific teachings were associated with this transition time (Zhatie et al. 1993). Only women had access to this knowledge. The following statement from Gwich'in Elder Therese Remy Sawyer highlights how this knowledge was shared between women. "They taught me how to respect all those things that were associated with the way you lived in those years. But these things were brought to me by other women in the later years. By that time you became a woman, so now these women were telling me, I should be respecting the women" (Heine et al. 2001:98).

While the men were away hunting, women were in charge of the camp and camp life. As Therese Remy Sawyer notes:

> The men were there to hunt, to trap, but I was always in charge of camp. It didn't matter how late we got there, I made sure the first thing I did—even before you had hot tea—I went and unhitched the dogs and made a bed for them with branches, while my grandfather went out to get wood or, if there was wood, he made fire while I was tying down the dogs, feeding them.

BOX 12.1 *Dene Kede:* **Passage to Womanhood**

The Rites of Passage of our Dene Women Ancestors

Dene women were given special counselling and training during their "transition time" (puberty) to prepare them for womanhood.

Spiritual Development
During the transition time, young women were made ready to receive medicine power.

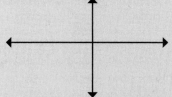

Relationship to Others
During adolescence, young women were counselled on how to behave respectfully toward others.

Self-Development
During the transition time, challenges helped develop courage, stamina, and self-reliance.

Relationship with the Land
During the transition time, young women learned to survive on the land, learning all the skills required to be a contributing member of the community and respectful of the land.

(Adapted from Northwest Territories Department of Education, Culture, and Employment 1993:15)

TABLE 12.1 Phases of Tanning Caribou Hides

PREPARING AND STORING THE HIDE

Caribou harvest	Caribou are typically hunted in fall and winter months. Historically, people lived in camps in the mountains near places where caribou were known to migrate and overwinter.
Fleshing the hide	After the meat was brought back to camp, the remaining flesh was removed from the hide using a flesher made from the leg bone of a caribou or moose. In some cases the hide was first pegged to the ground with small sticks placed through holes made at the corners of the hide. Fleshing could take 1 or 2 days, depending on the hide's size.
Removing the hair	The hair was removed from the outer side of the hide using a long knife and a downward scraping movement. Care was taken not to damage the hide, which reflected poorly on the tanner.
Storing the hide	The hide would be rolled or folded to be frozen through the winter. Care was taken to keep it away from dogs and to ensure that it did not thaw, lest it rot. Alternatively, the hide was hung, resulting in it both drying and bleaching in the winter sun.

TANNING THE HIDE	**SPRING AND SUMMER WORK**
Preparing "brains"	During the winter, brains of caribou, bear, or lynx had to be found for the tanning process; women would pack the brains away in a container away from people and animals for 2–3 months until they were sufficiently fermented for use.
Soaking the skin	Once thawed, the hides had to be soaked in the river or lake for about 1 week.
Gathering wood for smoking the hide	Before tanning could begin, the women gathered *dahshaa*, the inner part of a tree (usually poplar) that had turned brown and rotten.
Singeing the hair side	Before wringing out the water, the hair side had to be singed to take off any remaining bits of hair. A pan was heated and placed upside down on the ground and the hide drawn across it. When this was completed, the hide was black where it had been singed. Care had to be taken not to scorch the hide.
Thinning the neck	The exterior neck area was thinned with a long knife (it being the thickest part of the hide).
Wringing out the water	The hide was wrung out and then rinsed in clear water in a wash tub. This was repeated several times, using fresh water for each rinse.
Twisting the wet hide	To prepare the hide for twisting, small loops were cut out along its outer edge. A solid stick was placed into the ground, and about 3 of the loops were slipped over it at the same time. Three loops on the opposite side of the hide were slipped over a loose pole about 1 m long. This pole was rotated, twisting the hide. After being twisted, it was rinsed and twisted again. This continued until only clean water came out when the hide was twisted.
Soaking the hide in brain water	To soften the hide further, it was then soaked in a mixture of water and fermented brain. After soaking, it was again twisted, then soaked and twisted again.

TABLE 12.1 *(Continued)*

TANNING THE HIDE	SPRING AND SUMMER WORK
Preparation of a pole and tripod/stretcher	Two tripods support a horizontal pole about 1.5 m off the ground, from which the hide hung while being scraped. The pole could be raised or lowered, depending on the part of the hide being scraped. To tighten or stretch the hide to make it easier to scrape, women would kneel or sit on the bottom of the hide. A stretcher could also be created by lashing 4 poles together to make a frame to be leaned against a tree or building. Small holes would be made every 15–30 cm around the edge of the hide and thongs used to stretch it within the frame. This was done while the hide was wet; care had to be taken not to stretch the hide too tightly, since it would shrink while drying.
Preparing the hide for smoking	The hide would be smoked to soften it to make it into moccasins, pants and coats. Before smoking, the twisting holes would be sewn up and edges trimmed off. The hide was hung on a stick 1 m off the ground with a canvas sometimes attached to the bottom to act as a funnel for the smoke.
Smoking the hide	The smoking fire was made of rotten wood and had to be well tended so it would not go out or break into open flame and scorch the hide. The smoking fire would be kept going for 8–10 hours. Once the inside of the hide was smoked, it was taken off and scraped to soften.

Adapted from Heine et al. (2001)

You always carried dry fish or something like that out for them when you are traveling ... you never sat doing nothing, your day was full. The best time was when they came back with moose or a caribou. The first thing they brought back was a pack sack and there was blood in it and you knew you could eat the best meal ever. You know you were so happy for all the good things that you could cook and eat and that you'd have fresh meat. (Heine et al. 2001:142)

The preparation of hides was a particularly important responsibility and involved a great deal of work, particularly in spring, summer, and fall.

Sitting with women at their kitchen tables or in band-office board rooms, we hear these stories of traditional life on the land; they are poignant and touching, particularly knowing the hardships that women and families endured. But it is not a sad process. For many of the Elders telling these stories,

there is a great deal of laughter and joy and feelings of well-being that come with the memories of being connected to the land, connected to family and to a way of life that has endured for many generations. At some points in these interviews, this way of life seems a world away. Yet, in the midst of the background noise of the television and children running in and out the front door, the Elders are able to reconstruct what life was like in the past. Tapping into this other world of experience, we have learned a great deal about the environment, health, and culture.

Stewards of the Environment[2]

In 2001, a group of Teetł'it Gwich'in women gathered together at the Fort McPherson Complex to talk about the possibility of a research project on berries and berry picking. There was initially much laughter in the group. How could their knowledge of berry picking be worthy of scientific study? It was something they did for fun with their aunties, sisters, and daughters, for the pleasure of making

Louisiana surprise (whitefish and cranberries) or jelly for morning bannock. The science behind berry picking would become obvious over the next two years, however, as we worked together to map and document where, when, and with whom they found and harvested the plants of the region.

Although many berries and other plants are valued, the focus of our study was on three species: blueberry (*Vaccinium uliginosum*, elsewhere known as northern bilberry), cloudberry (*Rubus chamaemorus*), and cranberry (*Vaccinium vitis-idaea*) (known by many names: in Labrador as partridge berry and more widely in North America as lingonberry). Successful harvest of these berries required knowledge of the phenology (life cycle within differential ecosystems) of the plants themselves and also of broader ecological elements and processes.

Like many other resources of the Subarctic ecosystem, the abundance and distribution of berries is highly variable. Mary Ruth Wilson described this variability in terms of change: "Sometimes there are a lot of changes. One year, there would be a lot of blueberries and no cloudberries; then the next year there would be a lot of cloudberries and no blueberries. It's always been like this but we have never seen a year when there were no berries of any kind" (Parlee 2005, 20 February 2003).

Women in Fort McPherson noted that there are a variety of ecological factors influencing abundance and distribution of good berry patches: continual erosion of the Peel River along cutbanks, spring flooding, forest fires, and the succession of invasive willow into good picking areas were some of the disturbances described during interviews. As Bertha Francis said, "The weather is the main thing that affects the berries" (Parlee 2005, 20 February 2003). Different weather conditions from year to year significantly affect harvest yield across the region. Rebecca Francis exclaimed, "This year it was too much, ohh!!! (laughs) There were lots of berries around; especially cranberries. I heard there was a lot down in the Delta. Up in the hills and mountains too. I heard it was lots! All over the place, there were berries!" (Parlee 2005, 15 October 2003). Dorothy Alexie confirmed this: "There was lots!! Yeah! Everywhere you went there were berries" (Parlee 2005, 16 October 2003).

Rebecca Francis noted that berry picking in 1998 and 1999 were also very good (Parlee 2005, 15 October 2003). In 2002, however, a late frost and a very hot, dry summer resulted in virtually no berries across the region due to extreme weather events. This was described by May Andre:

> I hardly got any cranberries this past fall [2002]; nobody did in this area anyway. Out this way, I checked (toward Tsiigehtchic) and there was hardly any where it used to be. I think it was the weather conditions. First, it was too hot— in June. Then in July, it snowed! And I think that was the cause of no berries— extreme weather change. . . . I notice a lot of these changes—extreme weather condition changes. Like this last summer—it was extremely hot. It wasn't good for the health of the people. Lots of elders couldn't stand it. It was pretty dangerous. It switched from one extreme of heat to cold rain. . . then for about five days it snowed. I was at Eight Miles and it was very, very cold. And that is crazy weather!" (Parlee 2005, 17 April 2003)

Given the ecosystem dynamics associated with cranberry, blueberry, and cloudberry, women have had to develop complex and sophisticated strategies for harvesting. Many people we interviewed said that they pick berries where their grandmothers or mothers used to pick; some people have been picking blueberries and cranberries in the same patches for more than three generations. Alice Vittrekwa commented, "My grandmother used to pick berries a way up the Peel. She always used this place because of her grandmother. The trail to that place is worn into the ground. These places, you really have to walk a long ways to get there, but it is worth it" (Parlee 2005, 20 February 2003).

Many of these places, passed on from mother to daughter through the generations, are associated with fish camps and/or other resources that are also important to women and their families. Fort McPherson Elder Mary Kendi describes her mother's berry patch where she finds a variety of berries as well as medicinal plants:

I know my [mother's] berry patch; and it's a really good one. There is a good berry patch that I know where there are really a lot of cranberries, blueberries, blackberries and all kinds of berries around there. When you go for berries you pick berries; you have to go for a picnic; you have something to eat and then you start picking again. You pick until 6 pm in the evening. Then you can start your journey back home. On the way back from berry picking, that is when you pick sticky gum; it's very good medicine for colds or anything like that. (Parlee 2005, 25 February 2003)

Not all women pick in areas where there are so many different kinds of berries. Many said they go where they can find the most berries, or where it is "easy to pick." Rachael Stewart noted that in many cases, the patches where women find the most berries are species-specific, having only blueberries, cloudberries, or cranberries.

There is one place just down the road [that we found blueberries] that were that big! They came with us to get to that place. We checked it out. It was just blue! We picked just a little ways back and we heard trucks coming. The boys were playing on the road. The trucks passed and slowed down. They asked them, "What are you doing?" They told them, our

Grandmothers are picking berries. (Parlee 2005, 11 March 2003)

As described here by May Andre, some women pick their berries in different places every year and will often find good berry patches by accident. "Well, I go anywhere. You know me, I will go anywhere with my dog. Yeah! I check all over. Some places are good, and in some places, I waste my time. Where I think it is good, it's not good. . . . It's just like it changes every year. Every area is not the same all the time. I notice that" (Parlee 2005, 7 April 2003).

Whether it is their grandmother's berry patch or a recently discovered area, most women make use of different micro-climates within their favourite berry patches. Women will pick in open or sheltered areas depending on the time of the season. Cloudberries, for example, that grow in open and well-sunned areas tend to ripen and spoil the fastest and so are picked first; berries that are more sheltered and are in cooler areas tend to ripen slower and last longer.

Margaret Vittrekwa put it this way:

I usually pick on the hills because it's cooler and berries last longer there. Around the lakes on the top of the hills—anywhere it's flat around Red and Black Mountain. Along the shore of the river and up past the bushes towards the mountain is good for blueberries and cloudberries. You can sit there all day and pick—there are no end of berries there. (Parlee 2005, 11 July 2003)

The perspective of Bertha Francis was that:

[Blueberries] grow better in the shade like under the willows. It has not been good berries for a very long time (few years). I told my daughter to check the berries last year—I told her to check under the willows. That is where there are lots. When the trees fall down, it's good. There is lots of shade. I sometimes think I should tell the boys to cut them down but then I think it might affect the berries so I just leave it—I end up crawling under the willows looking for the berries. (Parlee 2005, 3 July 2003)

As May Andre notes, the use of these micro-climates is particularly important during extreme weather conditions:

The [cloudberries] that I got, the ones I found, they were sheltered by the spruce trees and willows so they were in good shape. They were delicious, juicy, and plump. But the others that I found in the open in a different area, those ones were cooked [over-ripened from the heat] and it was not worth [picking them]. Even the blueberries in that area; there were very little blueberries. [I was thinking that] I went a long ways for nothing but [there was one place]—when I got to where that area was eh, I found 'em lots of blueberries. It was just full of it. It was really damp in that area. But it was getting late so I left it. I was thinking that I was going to come back to it, to pick them. Because to me, it looked like two good days of picking for myself. I would have gotten really lots and lots. And then the next day it started raining. I think it rained for a couple of weeks . . . you remember? And then I went back. After that awful weather started, all the berries were gone. They dropped eh, in the rain. Rain and snow, I think, made them drop early, much too early, plus that extreme heat too that we had. So that's [what I found] berries in certain places that were shaded. That is where I found blueberries and cloudberries. (Parlee 2005, 7 April 2003)

Berry harvesting, like other harvesting activities of northern peoples, is not simply a circumstantial effort; when and where women harvest is based on a significant body of ecological knowledge.

Stewards of Health and Healing[3]

Gwich'in women also play an important role in their communities in health and health care and as traditional medicine practitioners. Their knowledge and practices include many aspects of preventative health care, including nutrition, midwifery, child care, and elder care. They also possess important knowledge and practices for treating illness. The Gwich'in have suffered significantly from illnesses and diseases related to colonization and settlement. Elder Julienne Andre describes the impact of influenza on the community in the early part of the twentieth century:

That night after mass they all went down to dance. A chant was sung. We really had lots of fun. Everybody danced; some rested and then took the place of the dancer. That's when the flu came. Everybody was sick and lots of people died. Ones that were well worked with the sick. My mother and I were very sick too. There was no medicine and we heard every day that someone died. (Heine et al. 2001:262)

Plants have both nutritional and medicinal purposes. Women collecting plants would often leave something of value behind as a token of their gratitude; this is still done today. Tobacco, for instance, might be sprinkled at a place where juniper berries were collected. It is said that not to leave something might rob the plants of their special power.

The work began with the recognition that there are many and diverse plants and resources available in the Gwich'in region that are valuable for healing and which may present as a viable alternative to western health care and medicine in the North.

TABLE 12.2 Plants and Medicine Plants Identified at the Traditional Camps

PLANT TYPES	PLANTS IDENTIFIED	MEDICINE PLANTS
Tree and shrubs	27	18
Flowering plants	50	18
Grasses and grass-like plants	9	0
Ferns and fern-like plants	1	1
Mosses and lichens	5	0
Fungi	5	1
Aquatic plants	4	2

Adapted from Andre (2006:98)

Andre and Fehr (2001) documented more than 30 species of flora used by the Gwich'in for food, medicine, shelter, and tools. Gwich'in researcher Alestine Andre carried out ethnobotanical research with Gwich'in Elder and plant specialist Ruth Welsh to learn more about their medicinal use of plants. Andre used two methods to learn about and document traditional plant knowledge: traditional "hands-on" or experiential learning and conventional research. Her family's summer fish camp on the Mackenzie River became one of the research sites. "During this time my grandmother, my parents, my aunt and uncle harvested and prepared plants as we needed them for medicine and other purposes or we consumed plants as food with our regular meat and fish diet" (Andre 2006:18).

Andre's master's thesis, entitled *Nan t'aih nakwits'in ahtsìh* (*"The Land Gives Us Strength"*), expresses the importance of resources available from the land that Gwich'in people used for medicine to maintain good health and well-being. Equally important was the need to document Ruth Welsh's extensive traditional medicine plant knowledge for future generations of Gwich'in. Ruth's plant and cultural knowledge and stories were passed down to her by her mother:

What we call "traditional medicine" has been used for thousands of years. All native people in this land have used these medicines. These medicines have been gathered by these people and prepared for use by their elders or parents who in turn were taught by their elders before them. Children and young men and women in each family were taught how to identify, gather and use the plants that they could use for minor illnesses. These days we call this first aid. (Ruth Welsh in Andre 2006:13)

Andre and her Gwich'in teacher documented 40 plants with medicinal properties and identify how they are to be harvested, prepared, shared, stored, and used. They are used to treat and heal skin and eye conditions, internal, respiratory, nasal, and urinary problems, common colds and influenza, as well as broken limbs, insect bites, stings, and burns, and to maintain good health. Prominent medicine plants used by the Gwich'in in the NWT include birch (*Betula papyrifera*), poplar (*Populas balsamifera*), juniper (*Juniperus communis*), black and white spruce (*Picea mariana* and *P. glauca*), tamarack (*Larix laricina*), willow (*Salix* spp.), plantain (*Plantago major*), wintergreen (*Pyrola grandiflora*), wormwood (*Artemisia tilesii*), yarrow (*Achillea millefolium*), and horsetail (*Equisetum arvense*) (Andre 2006:ii). Some of these are included in Table 12.3.

TABLE 12.3 Medicinal and Other Uses of Some Plants in the Gwich'in Region

GWICHYA GWICH'IN (G) TEETŁ'IT GWICH'IN (T)	ENGLISH AND SPECIES NAMES	PURPOSES
Lidii Maskeg/Maskig (G) Lidii Masgit (T)	Labrador Tea *Ledum palustre*	Labrador tea (muskeg tea) is very commonly used medicinally as a preventative and as a treatment for various illnesses. It is a good source of vitamin C. Many Elders recommend drinking a cup of Labrador tea daily to maintain good health. Concentrated tea is used for internal health problems. All parts of the plant can be used in making tea.
Natł'at (GT)	Cranberry (Lingonberry) *Vaccinium vitis-idaea*	Cranberries are highly valued for food and medicinal purposes. Historically they were one of the few vital sources of vitamin C in the Gwich'in diet and were easily stored by drying, mixing with caribou or moose grease, or freezing for winter use. The berries could also be made into teas. Elders note their value in treating cold and flu symptoms as well as kidney and urinary tract infections. Today cranberries are eaten raw and in various kinds of sweet and savoury baking and cooking. Cranberries and the liver and eggs of Burbot or Loche (*Lota lota*) are also ingredients in a nutritious dish sometimes called "Louisiana Surprise." The name probably comes from the similarities of Burbot with Catfish, a delicacy in the southern United States.
Ts'eevii/Ts'iivii (G) Ts'iivii (T) Dzèh kwan' (G) Dzih drinh' (T)	Spruce (white and black) *Picea glauca* *Picea mariana* Spruce Gum	Spruce gum has multiple uses. It can be administered internally (in a tea) or topically as a salve. The darker or older sap, commonly called spruce gum, is chewed as a treat and preventative health measure. The clear or new sap is known to reduce the risk of infections when applied to skin irritations or wounds. The inner layer of spruce bark is also used to treat cuts and skin wounds. Spruce cones from young trees are considered particularly good for healing. Boiling the cones (or spruce gum) for half an hour to an hour makes a good digestive tea or to prevent or treat colds and other illnesses.
K'oh (G/T) K'aii (G/T)	Red Willow (Green Alder) *Alnus crispa* Green Willow (Balsam Willow) *Salix pyrifolia*	Young red willow can be used to treat rashes or burns. Boiling the leaves and small branches provides a sticky film which can be skimmed off and administered to the affected area. Eczema can be treated by bathing in the tincture. Young buds are chewed to treat a cold. Roots can be pulped and eaten as a treatment for stomach ailments. The alder is preferred by some Elders as fuel wood for drying/smoking fish because of the flavour. The boiled bark is used as a dye for decorating goods made from hides. Green willow has many practical uses, such as constructing drums, snowshoes, pelt stretchers, fish traps, and nets. It was used by some in the construction of smokehouses and as flooring in tents and cabins. Bark from young green willow can be used like a poultice to treat skin irritations and cuts.

TABLE 12.3 *(Continued)*

GWICHYA GWICH'IN (G) TEETŁ'IT GWICH'IN (T)	ENGLISH AND SPECIES NAMES	PURPOSES
Aat'oo	Paper Birch (White Birch) *Betula papyrifera* Dwarf Birch *Betula glandulosa*	Sap from the paper birch, collected in spring, is a valued sweet and nutritious treat. The stems, twigs, and leaves of both the paper and dwarf birch are boiled to make a tea to treat ulcers and heartburn. One cup would be drunk at breakfast and at night. Tea made from the inner bark is also used to treat stomach ailments. Boiled roots also have medicinal uses. Due to its flexibility and strength, paper birch is the preferred material for making snowshoes as well as other tools such as sleds, paddles, shovels, knife and axe handles, and fish net needles.
Nichih t'àn	Prickly Wild Rose *Rosa acicularis*	Petals are picked in early summer and boiled and strained. A drop of the liquid can be used to clean out any eye infection. Rosehip berries can be boiled and made into a tea.
Ts'iiteenjùh (G) Tsiiheenjoh (T)	Tamarack *Larix laricina*	The tamarack is considered to be a very good source of medicine. According to many Elders, an offering must be left when collecting any part of a tamarack. The tincture made from boiling branches can be used for stomach ailments and colds and as a preventative. The inner bark can be prepared as a poultice for wounds. The tamarack is also valued as fuel and for making tools.
At'an tsoo	Alpine Arnica *Arnica alpina*	The yellow flower can be made into an ointment for treating muscle aches and related illness by mixing the petals and stamen with warm oils.
Duu'iinahshèe (G) Doo'iinahshìh (T) Ts'eedichi (T)	Northern Ground Cone *Boschniakia rossica*	The northern groundcone, commonly called "the pipe" in some Gwich'in communities, has useful medicinal properties when applied topically or eaten. The inner part of the cone, sometimes described as potatoes, can be chewed or ground into a powder, mixed with oils or grease, and applied to relieve skin irritations. The cones and roots can also be boiled and the tea drunk medicinally. As the name "pipe" implies, the ground cone, once dried, was used as tobacco, with dried willows or dried roots.
Dineech'ùh (G/T)	Crowberry *Empetrum nigrum*	The crowberry is referred to locally as blackberry. It is valued for food and is eaten directly or included in jams and baking. *It'suh*, a Gwich'in dessert similar to pemmican, is made from crowberries, cranberries, and pounded dry fish. Teas made from the berries and roots are used to treat stomach aches and colds.

(Adapted from Andre 2006; Parlee 2005; Andre and Fehr 2001; Heine et al. 2001)

Today, as in the past, the land also provides for the health and well-being of the people when they live on it, even for short stays. As noted by Ruth Welsh, "medicine" has a broader meaning in Gwich'in than in English: "When we work with (medicine plants), it's not only plants and the medicines that we make from plants [that are important], a lot of times you have to change what you're drinking and what you're eating. Change your diet . . . your lifestyle really has to change in order to get the full benefits and to stay well after that" (Andre 2006:106).

Knowledge and skills for harvesting plants and preparing traditional medicines were not considered to be the exclusive responsibility of women. Ruth Welsh (Andre 2006:13) explains, "All members of the family groups used to be familiar with the use and application of certain medicine plants for basic ailments . . . everyone knew the use and application of spruce gum and they could prepare a tea for the treatment of colds or as a body application for healing internal and external conditions." The use of plants for medicine or food continues to be important today. As they are needed, medicine plants are gathered and prepared to treat many different ailments.

Stewards of Culture

Many aspects of women's knowledge have been passed down through the generations. Finding ways of preserving it for current and future generations is increasingly important to women and their families. Knowledge about traditional clothing is one such subject.

While there is still a strong tradition of Gwich'in women sewing slippers, mitts, mukluks, and hats using caribou, moose, beaver, rabbit, and other hides—often home-tanned—a key area of knowledge lost until recently is that of making traditional caribou-skin summer clothing decorated with porcupine quillwork, silverberry seeds, and leather fringes. The following description

explores women's knowledge related to this type of clothing gathered primarily during the Gwich'in Traditional Caribou Skin Clothing Project carried out by the GSCI in partnership with the Prince of Wales Northern Heritage Centre (PWNHC) in Yellowknife and the Canadian Museum of Civilization in Gatineau between 2000 and 2003.

My (Ingrid's) interest in Gwich'in crafts and clothing started in 1983 when I carried out archaeological fieldwork in the Van Tat Gwitchin (Old Crow) area for a research program based at the University of Toronto. At both the beginning and the end of the field season, the archaeological crew stayed in Old Crow for a few days, visiting with people and exploring the area around the community. It was during this time that I first saw the stunning beaded baby belts that the Gwich'in are renowned for and still use to carry babies, as well as elaborately beaded "high top" beaded slippers (also called Crow boots). The fine artistry and skill of the women who sewed these items impressed me and made me curious to know more about other kinds of traditional Gwich'in clothing and crafts. Upon my return to Toronto, I discovered with delight a book by Judy Thompson (1972) describing nineteenth-century Gwich'in traditional clothing in the collections of the Canadian Museum of Civilization and other museums in North America and Europe. I was amazed at the craftsmanship of these garments and that the style of clothing in these collections—largely tunics and pants with attached feet—had changed little during the century they were described and/or collected. About 10 years later, in 1994, I was able to rekindle my interest in this clothing through a partnership between GSCI and the PWNHC. The goal of the project was to identify the location and extent of Gwich'in and other Athapaskan and Metis material collections from the Northwest Territories in museums and archives around the world (Kritsch and Kreps 1997). This research grew out of possible requests to governments to repatriate these items, following the signing of the Gwich'in and Sahtu Comprehensive Land Claim Agreements respectively in 1992 and 1993, and with an eye to possible requests from other Athapaskan groups in the Mackenzie Valley as their claims are settled.

Working with staff at the PWNHC we identified 160 heritage institutions worldwide with possible collections, and determined that Gwich'in material was housed in at least 30 heritage institutions across North America and Europe. Items in collections included clothing, hunting and fishing equipment, containers, objects related to transportation, and models and reproductions (Kritsch and Kreps 1997). Of these institutions, those housing the finest collections of Gwich'in materials in North America were the Canadian Museum of Civilization and the Smithsonian Institution (Kritsch and Wright-Fraser 2002: 205–6).

Following discussions with the GSCI Board of Directors, who represent all four Gwich'in communities and the Gwich'in Tribal Council, we decided that attempting to repatriate cultural items from museums to the NWT would be very time consuming with no guarantee of success. The board recognized that the items held in these museums were likely acquired ethically, and therefore museums were under no obligation to send them back to their place of origin. Instead, board members felt there would be much greater cultural, educational, and possibly even economic benefits if they were to initiate a series of "knowledge repatriation" projects, using Gwich'in cultural materials in museums as a way to relearn skills and knowledge no longer practised. Given the beauty of Gwich'in traditional caribou-skin clothing and the special relationship the Gwich'in have with caribou and the land, this seemed an ideal place to start (Kritsch 2001: 108–9).

Ethnohistoric records and museum collections show that this type of clothing was worn in the late eighteenth century and into the nineteenth century. With increased contact with Euro-Canadians, styles changed, and by the end of the nineteenth century this style of traditional caribou-hide clothing was no longer worn. Within a few generations, women no longer learned and passed on the skills required to make this clothing and their knowledge was largely lost, with only glimpses of it in the oral history. Fortunately, because the clothing was so elegant and portable, they were particularly sought after as souvenirs by traders, missionaries, and others travelling in the NWT. Consequently, there are more than 25 examples of this type of clothing (including 18 multi-piece outfits), preserved in North American and European museums today (Thompson and Kritsch 2005:1–3).

From 2000 to 2003, the GSCI in partnership with the PWNHC and the Canadian Museum of Civilization (CMC) embarked on a project to repatriate the knowledge and skills to make traditional caribou-skin summer clothing by replicating a nineteenth-century example from the collection of the CMC. Such traditional clothing had not been made in Gwich'in communities for over a century, and no examples of this clothing remained either in these communities or elsewhere in the NWT. The project was carried out over two and a half years with the goal of producing five examples of the multi-piece outfit for display in each of the four Gwich'in communities of Aklavik, Inuvik, Fort McPherson, and Tsiigehtchic, and also at the PWNHC. These multi-piece summer outfits were replicated by 42 seamstresses who ranged in age from 20 to 88 years old. Replicating each outfit entailed several hundred hours of sewing in the seamstresses' homes and in a series of two- to seven-day workshops. The workshops reintroduced old skills and materials no longer used, such as decorating with porcupine quills and silverberry seeds (*Elaeagnus commutata*). They also gave the seamstresses an opportunity to work together cooperatively to solve sewing puzzles, and reach consensus about decorative expression. Many other people in the two museums and Gwich'in communities also contributed their time, materials, knowledge, and expertise to the project.

Each replicated outfit is made from eight caribou skins and sewn with sinew. Silverberry seeds, porcupine quills, beads, wool, embroidery floss, and fringes were used to decorate each garment, with the wool and floss being substitutes for wrapping the fringes with quills. The overall look of each community's outfit is slightly different, as the seamstresses from each community decided to use different colours and combinations of quills, beads, wool, and floss.

The five outfits were completed and presented to the public by five proud Gwich'in male models in a ceremony held at the PWNHC on 28 March 2003, to an overwhelming reception by a packed and enthusiastic audience. The project had a tremendous impact on everyone involved, including seamstresses such as Maureen Clark:

> I became interested [in this project] after I realized that I would be helping to replicate a 100-year-old garment. It brought chills right through my body, just knowing that I [would] re-create history from 100 years ago, [that] I'm going to learn the old skills, the old ways. I'm honoured to be here. I've never touched quills in my life. I've seen my grandmother's quills, but I've never seen anybody working with them. I've heard about it, I knew we had it in our history. . . . I'm so grateful I've been chosen to work on this garment. (Thompson and Kritsch 2005:42).

The project also generated a book (Thompson and Kritsch 2005), an exhibit at PWNHC (2006–7), and permanent exhibits in the four Gwich'in communities. One outfit is currently stored in the collection of the PWNHC. The garments are a fine testament to Gwich'in women's skills, knowledge, and artistic expression.

What did we learn from this project about the skills and knowledge needed to produce such garments? We learned that the acquisition of raw materials requires much planning and good timing, and that great skill was involved in the construction of garments. When examining the prototype CMC outfit and replicating the knife sheath for the Tsiigehtchic outfit, seamstress Agnes Mitchell noted,

> The stitching is so fine. I'm so impressed. It makes me wonder—no lighting, needles, nothing. You have to use a magnifying glass [to see the stitches]. I thought I saw sewing machine stitches but we examined it. Even this sheath, it took me almost one week. It looks simple but it's intricate. My stitches are showing. Not on that one. Their sinew must have been fine and tough and hard to see stitches. . . . It's amazing. I've been sewing all morning and remembering my mother. I want to thank her. She's here with me now. I'm glad to see young people working with quills. It won't die. (December 2001)

As Agnes indicates, making clothing was a very labour-intensive activity—just one of many tasks that the women were responsible for to ensure the well-being of their families. It also became clear that making clothing required the efforts of the whole family—from men hunting the caribou in the right season and skinning it properly, to women (and young girls) tanning, sewing, and decorating. Below are some of our other findings.

Highly functional and elegant design: Individual components of an outfit were designed to fit and cover the body (thus providing protection from weather, rough terrain and especially from stinging, biting insects—the scourge of a northern summer), while enabling arms and legs to move freely.

Caribou and moose hides: The timing of the caribou hunt, quality of the hide, and the way the caribou was skinned and tanned were important. According to Gwich'in oral history, the preferred hides for summer clothing were from caribou killed in late August or early September. The hide at this time lacks holes caused by the larvae of warble flies that burrow out through the skins in spring. Also the fur on the hide is relatively thin, making de-hairing easier. Caribou hide, once tanned, is lightweight, flexible, and breathable. (Thompson and Kritsch 2005:14–17)

FIGURE 12.1 Gwich'in models and project coordinators at the unveiling ceremony of the nineteenth-century Gwich'in Traditional Caribou Skin Clothing Project at the Prince of Wales Northern Heritage Centre, Yellowknife, 28 March 2003. (Back L–R): Adolphus Lennie, Brandon Albert, Ryan Vittrekwa, Ryan Moore, Chas Saddington. (Front L–R): Judy Thompson, Karen Wright-Fraser, Ingrid Kritsch, Joanne Bird. (Photo Tom Andrews , PWNHC)

The summer clothing reproduced was only one example of clothing made traditionally from caribou. Billy Cardinal describes how, in earlier days, the Gwich'in wore two sets of clothes in winter. "The heavier and warmer one was worn outside, when the family travelled on the trail. This coat was too warm for inside, so a lighter one was worn inside . . . because the outside coat was made from caribou skins with the hair left on, it could not be put into a warm place. The hair would have fallen out, and so the outer clothing was left outside" (Heine et al. 2001:146). Smoked skins were most commonly used for clothing as they would last longer in warm or wet weather, but unsmoked skins were used to make clothing for special occasions, such as the reproduced outfit.

For example, the way in which the sleeves were cut wide at the armhole and set deeply into the side seams enable easy movement of the arms, particularly in a forward motion. Similarly, the high sides and pointed bottom edge of the tunic allowed for unencumbered walking, while also providing the wearer with added protection from cool breezes and an extra layer to sit on. Wrist and neck openings on the tunic were small, to inhibit drafts and insects. The all-in-one fitted lower garment also offered excellent protection against insects and the elements. Soft and flexible, it was ideal for summer travel in birchbark canoes. When the sole wore out, it could be replaced without sacrificing the body of the garment. (Thompson and Kritsch, 2005:14–15)

Caribou and moose hides have long had many valued purposes in the community. For example, hides were cut up and used to make babiche of varying strengths for ropes, twines, or string for making snowshoes, dog harnesses, and snares—with a fine caribou twine used to snare rabbits and five to six strands of moose-hide babiche for moose. Almost all parts of these hides were used with even moose leg skins being made into long bag-like toboggans and caribou leg skins into hunting bags and dog pack bags.

Women's role in the success of a hunt: According to Elder Joan Nazon of Tsiigehtchic, at puberty young girls lived separately from their families for up to a year, during which time they learned from the family's older women their roles and responsibilities. It was at this time, according to Elders Therese Remy Sawyer and Noel Andre that the girls learned how important it was to show respect for men's hunting equipment and hunting clothes, as their conduct could affect the outcome of the hunt. Women controlled their power by following certain rules. Some of the rules included not stepping over men's equipment or clothing but moving them aside before going further, and not stepping over the blood, feet, or hair of moose or caribou (Joan Nazon, 28 July 1992; Therese Remy Sawyer, 31 July 1992; Noel Andre, 14 July 1992).

Porcupine quills: According to Annie Norbert of Tsiigehtchic, quills were best harvested in the coldest winter months of January and February. Annie remembers her mother procuring them at that time because of their pliability. Later in the year, they become more brittle. About handling the quills, Annie recounts, "Mom used to take little piece of moose skin like that and poke all the quills on it and it gets stuck to that end and won't come out no more. And she cut it with scissor and throws it away. That way it's not [a] danger. But it's better to get rid of the end quick. Try and keep it away from the kids" (January 2001). Various materials were traditionally used to dye the quills including berries, lichens, roots, bark, and flowers. Annie recalls her mother using blackberries and cranberries to dye her quills, giving them "nice colour." Sarah Simon of Fort McPherson recalls women using red willow, boiling it to make a red dye, and berries. "They used plants from the land to dye the quills. They had it [the quill] in their

mouth and from there they sewed with it. They bit it and wet it in their mouth and made it flat and then they sewed with it" (January 2001).

The original outfit from the CMC was elaborately decorated with thousands of porcupine quills—an estimated 3,000 on the tunic alone. Including the quills on the footed trousers, hood, mitts, and knife case, there may be 4,000 or more in total. There are approximately 30,000 quills on an adult porcupine, and while not all of the quills would be suitable, one porcupine would likely be enough to decorate at least one set of clothing. After plucking the quills, which some people liken to plucking a duck, the quills need to be washed several times to remove their natural oils, dried, dyed, and sorted according to size, and then the barbed tip is removed (Thompson and Kritsch 2005:37). The time needed to do this work, plus sewing the quills on the garments, is impressive. The seamstresses at the initial workshop said that it took approximately an hour to sew an inch of quills (Kritsch and Wright-Fraser 2002:208). It is not surprising therefore that we saw quillwork that appeared to have been reused on a number of garments in the museums we visited. Because the quilled decorative motifs are largely separate from the body of the garment, this work could have been carried out by a number of hands separately and then attached when the garment was ready to be assembled.

Silverberry seeds: There were almost 400 seeds from the silverberry (*Elaeagnus commutata*) bush used on the fringes and tags on the CMC outfit. The small brown, fluted seeds are found inside spongy, silvery-green coloured balls of fruit. The fruit grows in clusters and ripens in the early fall. The shrub is quite distinctive in the spring, as the blossoms emit what has been described as a "haunting fragrance." Elder Hyacinthe Andre of Tsiigehtchic recalls them growing in the mountains up the Arctic Red River (Kritsch and Wright-Fraser 2002:208). Alestine Andre has seen them growing near her fish camp at Tree River on the Mackenzie River and just above the high water level of the Mackenzie from Tree River to Tsiigehtchic. According to botanists, the bush grows extensively across the Canadian Subarctic and beyond along river gravel bars and dry slopes (Schofield 1989). Elder Sarah Simon recalled that these berries are called "grizzly berries" in Gwich'in, because they are a food source for grizzly bears (Kritsch and Wright-Fraser 2002:208). The fruit is ready for harvesting in September, and considerable effort is needed to extract the seeds and drill holes through them so they can be threaded on the fringes and tags. As Karen Wright-Fraser explains, "The silverberry seeds were cleaned by hand. We took the flesh off the berries, and then washed them to take the sticky stuff off the seed. Then we boiled the seeds for a bit [to make them soft] and . . . stuck a darning needle through each bead and strung a large thickness of sinew through—but that didn't work too well, so we used an electric drill press and drilled a hole through the center" (Thompson and Kritsch 2005:38). Before the advent of electric drills, drilling holes in the seeds must have required considerable time and effort.

Conclusion

All ethnographies are situated in a particular socio-cultural and political context, bringing forward differing perspectives on particular peoples, relationships, and events. This project offers an alternative perspective on the history and contemporary worlds of Gwich'in drawn from community-based research with women from the Gwich'in Settlement Area.

Indigenous women are now being represented in many aspects of anthropological study. The contribution of women to traditional subsistence is an area of research which was overlooked for the better part of the twentieth century. Feminist critiques of "man the hunter" archetypes revealed new perspectives on the roles and contributions of women. The development of Indigenous feminism in the last decade has been particularly important in developing our understanding of women in the social sciences. As noted by the Status of Women group in Ottawa reporting on Aboriginal women's policy research, the literature still has some major gaps. In particular, they argue that the literature addresses only a limited range of issues and pays little attention toward **non-status** and Metis women and to Aboriginal women with disabilities. The literature is distinctly negative in orientation. "With surprisingly few exceptions, work dealing with Aboriginal women has tended to be highly problem-focused, and it has pathologized these women's agency and realities" (Stout and Kipling 1998:6).

Representation of women in academia is only part of a larger battle waged by Aboriginal women in their communities and in Canadian society. Women play a fundamental role in their own communities, not only in the ways stereotypically defined in the academic literature, but as mothers, grandmothers, aunts, social support workers, nurses, teachers, researchers, and leaders. As this work has explored, women also hold important roles as stewards of the environment, of health, and of culture.

NOTES

1. GSCI was established as the cultural and heritage arm of the Gwich'in Tribal Council in 1992 and began operation in 1993 with the mandate to document, preserve, and promote Gwich'in culture, language, traditional knowledge, and values (www. gwichin.ca). This was in response to concerns about the long-term viability of Gwich'in culture and language. In the past 20 years, GSCI has fulfilled

its mandate through a comprehensive program of research, education, and language promotion. More than 80 research projects, many of them multi-year, have been initiated. Research has included the study of place names and traditional land use, ethnobotany, ethnoarchaeology, Elder's biographies, genealogy, a Gwich'in dictionary, the replication of nineteenth-century caribou-skin clothing, and the identification of territorial and national historic sites in the Gwich'in Settlement Region.

2. This section is primarily based on Parlee (2005).

3. This section is primarily based on the research of Gwich'in scholar Alestine Andre.

REFERENCES AND RECOMMENDED READINGS

Andre, Alestine. 2006. "Nan t'aih nakwits'in ahtsih (The Land Gives Us Strength): The Medicine Plants Used by Gwich'in People of Canada's Western Arctic to Maintain Good Health and Well Being." Unpublished MA thesis. Victoria, BC: University of Victoria.

———— and Alan Fehr. 2001. *Gwich'in Ethnobotany: Plants Used by the Gwich'in for Food, Medicine, Shelter and Tools*. Tsiigehtchic, NT and Inuvik, NT: Gwich'in Social and Cultural Institute and Aurora Research Institute.

Balikci, Asen. 1963. *Vunta Kutchin Social Change: A Study of the People of the Old Crow, Yukon Territory*. Ottawa: Northern Co-ordination and Research Centre, Dept. of Northern Affairs and National Resources. Still a classic ethnography.

Bodenhorn, Barbara. 1990. "I'm Not the Great Hunter, My Wife Is: Inupiat and Anthropological Models of Gender," *Études/Inuit/Studies*, 14, 1–2: 55–74.

Dahlberg, Frances, ed. 1982. *Women the Gatherer*. New Haven, CT: Yale University Press.

Heine, Michael, Alestine Andre, Ingrid Kritsch, Alma Cardinal, and the Elders of Tsiigehtchic. 2001. *Gwichya Gwich'in Googwandak: The History and Stories of the Gwichya Gwich'in*. Tsiigehtchic, NT: Gwich'in Social and Cultural Institute. A deep look at the history and experiences of the Gwichya Gwich'in from the Elder's perspectives, from creation stories to current events.

Jenness, Diamond. 1972. *The Indians of Canada*. Bulletin No. 65. Ottawa: National Museums of Canada.

Johnson, Leslie Main, and Eugene S. Hunn, eds. 2010. *Landscape Ecology: Concepts of Biotic and Physical Space*. Toronto: Berghahn Books. A global view of how environments and resource management systems are cultural constructed. While gender is not a specific theme, it provides an understanding of why the traditional ecological knowledge and practices of Gwich'in women matter.

Kritsch, Ingrid. 2001. "The Gwich'in Traditional Clothing Project." In *Fascinating Challenges: Studying Material Culture with Dorothy Burnham*, edited by Judy Thompson, Judy Hall *and Leslie Tepper, in collaboration with Dorothy K. Burnham*, : 107–11. Mercury Series. Canadian Ethnology Service Paper 136. Hull: Canadian Museum of Civilization.

———— and Bart Kreps. 1997. *A Guide To Northern Athapaskan and Metis Collections Residing in Museums and Archives Outside of the Northwest Territories*. Tsiigehtchic: Gwich'in Social and Cultural Institute.

———— and Karen Wright-Fraser. 2002. "The Gwich'in Traditional Caribou Skin Clothing Project: Repatriating Traditional Knowledge and Skills," *Arctic* 55, 2: 205–11.

Lee, Richard B., and Irven DeVore, eds. 1968. *Man the Hunter*. Chicago: Aldine.

Leechman, Douglas. 1954. *The Vanta Kutchin.* National Museum of Canada Bulletin No. 130. Ottawa: National Museums of Canada.

Miller, Christine, and Patricia Chuchryk, eds. 1996. *Women of the First Nations: Power, Wisdom, and Strength.* Winnipeg: The University of Manitoba Press.

Nelson, Richard K. 1973. *Hunters of the Northern Forest: Designs for Survival among the Alaskan Kutchin.* Chicago: University of Chicago Press. Still a classic ethnography.

Northwest Territories Department of Education, Culture and Employment. (1993) *Dene Kede: Education, a Dene Perspective: Grade 7, Module One, Passage to Womanhood.* Yellowknife: Northwest Territories Department of Education, Culture, and Employment.

Osgood, Cornelius, 1936. *Contributions to the Ethnography of the Kutchin.* Yale University Publications in Anthropology, no. 14. New Haven, CT: Yale University Press. This is the classic pioneering ethnography of these people.

Parlee, Brenda. 2005. "Dealing with Ecological Variability and Change: Perspectives from the Denesoline and Gwich'in of Northern Canada." Unpublished Ph.D. thesis. Winnipeg: University of Manitoba.

Peers, Laura. 1996. "Subsistence, Secondary Literature, and Gender Bias: The Saulteaux," in Miller and Chuchryk (1996).

Schofield, Janice J. 1989. *Discovering Wild Plants: Alaska, Western Canada, the Northwest.* Anchorage and Seattle: Alaska Northwest Books.

Slobodin, Richard. 1962. *Band Organization of the Peel River Kutchin.* Ottawa: Dept. of Northern Affairs and National Resources.

———— 1981. "Kutchin." In *Handbook of North American Indians* Vol. 6, *Subarctic,* edited by June Helm and William C. Sturtevant., Washington: Smithsonian Institution.

Stout, Madeleine Dion and Gregory D. Kipling. 1998. *Aboriginal Women in Canada: Strategic Research Directions for Policy Development.* Ottawa: Status of Women Canada.

Strong, Pauline Turner. 2005. "Recent Ethnographic Research on North American Indigenous Peoples," *Annual Review of Anthropology* 34: 253–68.

Suzack, Cheryl, Shari M. Huhndorf, Jeanne Perrault, and Jean Barman. 2010. *Indigenous Women and Feminism: Politics, Activism, Culture.* Vancouver: UBC Press. The focus of this diverse collection is understanding the social positioning of Indigenous women in relation to the unique social, economic, and political experiences in Canada and globally.

Thompson, Judy. 1972. *Preliminary Study of Traditional Kutchin Clothing in Museums.* Mercury Series. Canadian Ethnology Service Paper 1. Ottawa: Ethnology Division, National Museum of Man.

———— and Ingrid Kritsch. 2005. *Yeenoo Dài' K'ètr'ijilkai' Ganagwaandaii: Long Ago Sewing We Will Remember: The Story of the Gwich'in Traditional Caribou Skin Clothing Project.* Ottawa: Canadian Museum of Civilization.

Turner, N.J., and W. Cocksedge. 2001. "Aboriginal use of Non-timber Forest Products in Northwestern North America: Applications and Issues," *Journal of Sustainable Forestry* 13, 3–4: 31–57.

Zihlman, A. 1989. "Woman the Gatherer: the Role of Women in Early Hominid Evolution," in Sandra Morgan, ed., *Gender and Anthropology: Critical Reviews for Teaching and Research,* Washington, DC: American Anthropological Association.

PART V

The Eastern Woodlands

CHAPTER 13

Farmers and Hunters of the Eastern Woodlands: A Regional Overview

Mary Druke Becker and Thomas S. Abler

Environment

The region south of the boreal forest in eastern Canada and the adjacent United States was (and to some extent still is) homeland to a dense population of speakers of languages in two great North American language families—the Algonquians and the Iroquoians. Each of these two language families consisted of a large number of distinct languages. The languages within each family are clearly related to each other, and likely have evolved though time from two "proto-languages" which existed in the distant past. Collectively, they are grouped together by anthropologists in the Eastern Woodlands culture area (both language families are also found in other North American culture areas). The Eastern Woodland peoples exploited a land whose climate supported a mixed deciduous–coniferous forest. Lakes and rivers abound in the region, and the territory of a First Nation was often defined in terms of a particular river drainage. The St Lawrence River, linking the Great Lakes to the Atlantic Ocean, was an important feature in both the social and the physical landscape of the region.

Staples in the economy for most of the region in historic times were cultivated crops, maize (or corn), beans, and squash. Early European visitors to the region did not discover a wild "forest primeval," but rather extensive areas where the forest had been cut back for use as corn fields or meadows, regaining their fertility after the soils had become exhausted through years of use as agricultural lands. What has been appreciated only recently is the degree to which many other vegetable products were not simply gathered; the plants in one way or another were tended. Edible fruits, nuts, roots, and in places, wild rice, were harvested. The forests which surrounded the cleared land of the settlements and towns were home to a number of animals desired primarily for their meat and hides, but also for other purposes. These included deer, bear, moose, rabbit, beaver, otter, muskrat, fox, wolf, racoon, skunk, bobcat, and numerous fowl. These were hunted with bows and arrows or spears, or caught in traps, round-ups, or dead-falls. Aquatic resources, including salt- and freshwater fish, sea mammals, crustaceans, eels, and turtles, were also of major importance to most peoples in the region. Tools used for fishing were bone fish hooks, nets, harpoons, spears, and basketry traps and weirs. Animal skins and bones, wood and bark, clay, shell, stone, and other such items provided the raw materials from which people created the necessities of life: clothing; shelter; tools for building, hunting, fishing, gardening, and other domestic tasks; and objects that served ritual or recreational purposes.

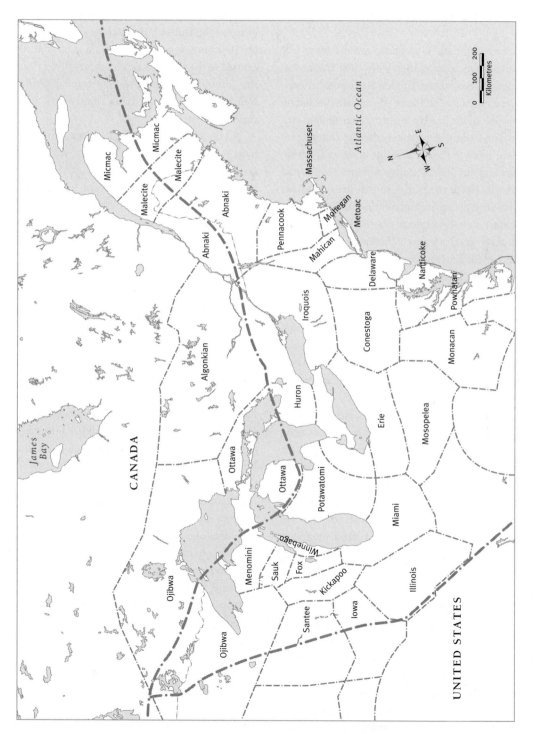

MAP 13.1 The Eastern Woodlands

Social Organization

Some Algonquian-speaking groups were less focused on farming than were their Iroquoian-speaking neighbours. This led to alliances between some Iroquoians and some Algonquians (including peoples of the Eastern Subarctic culture area) centred on trade, with corn and other agricultural produce going to the Algonquians in return for meat, fish, and furs. However, all groups in the region had broadly based economies, so that the Iroquoians also engaged in fishing, hunting, and gathering, while many Algonquians practised **horticulture**. In the warmer portions of the Eastern Woodlands, i.e., present-day New England and the mid-Atlantic states, where farming was more reliable, the contrast was less marked.

Farming anchored populations to villages or towns, but inter-village contact was extensive and common. A complex system of trails linked villages to one another and to hunting areas. Travel was frequent between villages to attend ceremonial, political, or recreational events such as planting or harvest ceremonies, councils, or lacrosse games. In the north, birchbark canoes facilitated travel over waterways, but since water travel in southern Ontario and the adjacent United States was limited to clumsy elm bark or dugout wooden canoes, foot travel over the well-worn trails was more important.

Social organization varied among Algonquians. Mi'kmaq had a band organization similar to that found in the Subarctic in that it was based on principles of friendship and **cognatic** (bilateral kin-group) relations. Nevertheless, these maritime people are considered to belong in the Eastern Woodland culture area because of the diverse, intensive nature of their subsistence activities and because of their internal political organization and their external political alliances. In the upper Great Lakes, Algonquian communities were organized into totemic descent groups, usually patrilineal (the word "totem" has come into English from the language of the Ojibwa). The Mahican and Munsee (or Delaware, a portion of whom migrated to Canada in the late eighteenth century) lived near the Iroquoian-speaking Mohawk and like the Mohawk were organized into three matrilineal clans or **phratries**.

All the Iroquoians in the northeast appear to have recognized matrilineal kinship, with children belonging to their mother's group. Thus they belonged to their mother's nation, and within that nation they also belonged to the exogamous clan and lineage of their mother. The number of clans within each Iroquoian nation varied, from 3 to 10.

A division of labour based upon gender was important. Men were primarily responsible for hunting, fishing, warfare, councils, construction of houses and village fortifications, manufacturing implements for hunting and fishing, and, among those who farmed, clearing the fields. Women were responsible for gathering wild foods, and for planting, cultivating, and harvesting. Gathering firewood was a vital female occupation, and they also fished, cleaned and processed fish and game, cooked, cared for children, and made clothing and household utensils.

Political organization among inland Algonquians took the form of local chieftainships. In some cases, as among the Passamaquoddy and the Maliseet, these chieftainships were patrilineally inherited. Among the maritime people, leadership was band-based, usually with one leader per band. Some Algonquian local groups united to form national or confederate councils, as in the case of the Wabenaki Confederacy, composed of the Maliseet, Mi'kmaq, Passamaquoddy, Penobscot, and Eastern and Western Abenaki. Iroquoians had local chieftainships, which in the case of the Six Nations (Mohawk, Oneida, Onondaga, Cayuga, Seneca, and Tuscarora) were based on both heredity and merit. The Confederacy of the Iroquois

FIGURE 13.1 (After Edward Chalfield) Nicholas Vincent Isawanhonhi, Principal Christian Chief and Captain of the Huron Indians established at La Jeune Lorette near Quebec, holding a wampum belt, 1825. (Courtesy of the National Archives of Canada, c38948)

(the Hodenosaunee) is famous, but confederacies were also found among other Iroquoians, such as the Huron.

History

The earliest French, Dutch, and English explorers of North America found a thriving population in the Eastern Woodlands. Dire effects, however, soon followed contact. Smallpox and other contagious illnesses for which First Nations peoples had no immunity led to enormous and frightful population losses. Warfare centring on the fur trade further depleted numbers. We do not know how many entire groups, let alone families and individuals, were completely lost during the very early historic period.

Other changes were also forthcoming. For many Iroquoians and Algonquians the fur trade resulted in specialization in trapping and trading and less reliance on traditional subsistence practices. For some Algonquians farming became more feasible because they no longer had to break into small groups to search for food in times of scarcity and because, although horticulture was still less reliable than hunting in a relatively northern climate, there was now the security of an "outside" source of supplies in the event of crop failure.

Through time a number of Woodlands people accepted Christianity. Many were induced by missionaries in the seventeenth and eighteenth centuries to move to mission settlements. These settlements were in effect the first Indian reserves in Canada. A number of communities in eastern Canada were formed this way. Others did not accept the new religion, and today Christianity is found side by side with Indigenous traditional religion in many Indian communities.

The disruptions caused by historic events following the European invasion of North America led to great shifts in locale for many Eastern Woodlands groups. Some moved far from their sixteenth-century homeland, to points as distant as British Columbia, Oklahoma, or Mexico. Others migrated to Canada from homelands in what is now the United States. Others became extinct as social entities, although surviving members of such groups frequently were received as refugees and incorporated into populations which have survived and have become an integral part of the Canadian multicultural mosaic. The following chapters provide more detail concerning their culture and history.

CHAPTER 14

Iroquois and Iroquoians in Canada and North America

Thomas S. Abler

Introduction

"Canada" has entered the vocabularies of the world as the name for northern North America as a result of an encounter in the sixteenth century between Iroquoians and French on the St Lawrence River. On 2 October 1535, Jacques Cartier and his crew sailed up the St Lawrence River and reached the island now known as Montreal. There they found Hochelaga, a town of 2,000 or more people. The lands surrounding the town had been cleared, and there the inhabitants grew crops (much of which we expect would have been harvested before this October meeting) unknown in Europe just five decades earlier—maize (or corn), beans, squash and pumpkins, and tobacco. The town itself made an impressive appearance, for it was surrounded by a triple wall or palisade constructed of straight tree trunks approximately five metres long. These were planted in the earth and the outer and inner palisades inclined to the middle, so all three walls intersected at the apex. On the interior near the top of the walls were platforms from which to defend the town. Cartier's account suggests that 50 multi-family houses were found within the walls. They were rectangular, approximately 7 metres wide and 40 metres long. A hall ran the length of the house and would have had five hearths or fire pits placed along the passageway, each shared by two families. Cartier noted that the people lived primarily on the products of their fields and on fish and commented about the quantity of maize stored in the rafters of the houses and the dried fish stored in barrels. These substantial houses were made of timber frames covered with slabs of bark. Later observers of similar dwellings, which have come to be called longhouses, noted that each was about as high as it was wide, had an arched roof with smoke-holes to allow the smoke from each fireplace to escape, and was entered through doors at each end of the house.

The Hochelagans spoke a language in the Iroquoian language family[1] and the residents of Stadacona, on the site of present-day Quebec City, spoke another one. Cartier's interactions with these peoples led him to use the name "Canada" to refer to the lands bordering the great river he had ascended. "Canada" is a word recorded in the vocabularies he collected from these peoples, and means "town."

European troubles prevented the French from returning to the St Lawrence during the second half of the sixteenth century, and these Iroquoians had disappeared when Europeans next ventured up the St Lawrence. Various hypotheses have suggested European diseases or conflict stimulated by competition over the fur trade may have led to their demise. All that is known for certain is that when Samuel de Champlain sailed up the St Lawrence in the first decade of the seventeenth century, Hochelaga and Stadacona and all other St Lawrence Iroquoian settlements were gone, and none of the Iroquoian peoples encountered subsequently spoke a language identical to those recorded by Cartier.

However, we now know that a vast portion of eastern North America was occupied by speakers of languages classed in the northern branch of the Iroquoian family. In what is now Ontario, between Lake Simcoe and Georgian Bay, Champlain found the Huron, a confederacy of five nations—the Attignawantan (Bear Nation), Attigneenongnahac (Cord Nation), Arendaronon (Rock Nation), Tahontaenrat (Deer Nation), and Ataronchronon (Swamp Nation). "Huron" is the French name for these people; they called themselves "Wendat." Immediately to the west were the Petun or Tionontate (also known as the Tobacco Nation). The Neutral Nation was a populous group occupying southwestern Ontario. Champlain called them "Neutral" because on his initial encounter with them, they remained at peace with both the Huron and the Iroquois, despite the fact that these two peoples were then engaged in bitter conflict. Residing between the Neutral and the Iroquois Confederacy were the Wenro. The region south of Lake Erie was the homeland of the Erie, sometimes referred to as the Cat Nation, although Raccoon Nation would be more accurate. The Iroquois Confederacy was found south of Lake Ontario, in New York's Finger Lakes region and the Mohawk Valley. From west to east the members of the Confederacy were the Seneca, Cayuga, Onondaga, Oneida, and Mohawk. Other Northern Iroquoian speakers lived to the south—the Susquehannock on the Susquehanna River and even farther south, the Tuscarora, Nottoway, and Meherrin. Also in the south were the Cherokee, a populous group speaking a language classified as a separate branch of the Iroquoian language family.

This large grouping of Iroquoian-speaking peoples frequently had political and trading relationships with Algonquian neighbours. The Huron enjoyed trading relationships with the Ojibwa, Nipissing, Ottawa, Algonquin, and Montagnais (Innu). The Iroquois had a complex (varying from political alliances to open warfare) relationship with their Mahican and Delaware neighbours as well as with the Algonquian-speaking populations of New England. Looking westward, the Iroquoians interacted with many Algonquian-speaking nations in the upper Great Lakes and in the Ohio country. The so-called Neutral in fact are recorded as sending major military expeditions against the "Fire Nation" (the Algonquian-speaking Mascouten) inhabiting lands west of Lake Huron.

Of Northern Iroquoian languages, only the six languages of the Iroquois Confederacy have survived the twentieth century. Of these, Tuscarora is quite distinct from the other five, while Mohawk and Oneida are most closely related. Today Mohawk has by far the largest number of speakers of a Northern Iroquoian language and is divided into distinct dialects.

Because of severe population losses from European diseases and dislocations caused by warfare intensified by the fur trade and the colonial presence in eastern North America, many of these Iroquoian nations ceased to exist as independent political entities within a century of first contact. One exception is the Huron, although they were driven from their historic homeland in Ontario. A small portion of the Huron migrated to a settlement outside Quebec City where they continue to reside. *La Nation Huronne-Wendat*, also known as the Wendake First Nation, has a registered membership of 3,027 of whom 1,326 live on reserve. Some Huron and their Petun neighbours came to be known as Wyandot and settled in various locales in the upper Great Lakes. The Wyandotte of Oklahoma relocated to that state in the nineteenth century when it was known as Indian

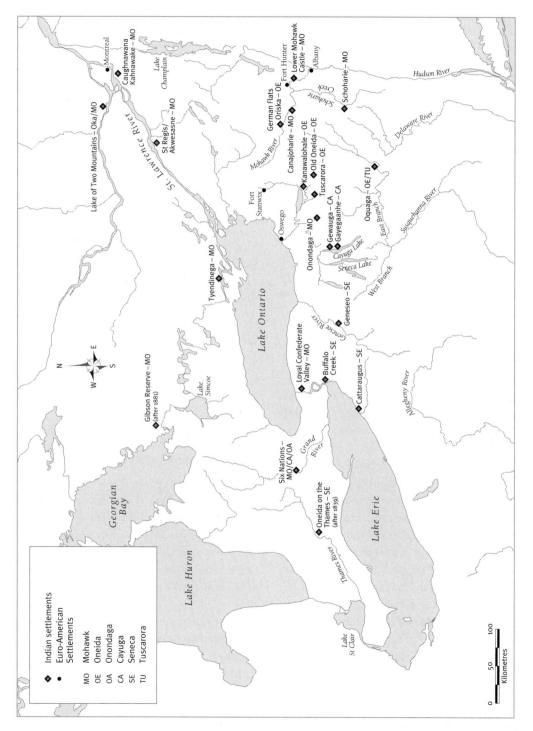

Legend

Indian settlements ◆
Euro-American ● Settlements

MO   Mohawk
OE   Oneida
OA   Onondaga
CA   Cayuga
SE   Seneca
TU   Tuscarora

Caughnawana Kahnawake – MO
Montreal
Lake Champlain
Lower Mohawk Castle – MO
Fort Hunter
Albany
Hudson River
Oriska – OE
Schoharie – MO
Schoharie Creek
Delaware River
German Flats
St Regis/ Akwesasne – MO
Lake of Two Mountains – Oka/MO
St. Lawrence River
Mohawk River
Canajoharie – MO
Kanawalohale – OE
Old Oneida – OE
Tuscarora – OE
Oquaga – OE/TU
Susquehanna River
Fort Stanwix
Oswego
Onondaga – MO
Gewauga – CA
Gayegaanhe – CA
Cayuga Lake
Seneca Lake
East Branch
West Branch
Tyendinega – MO
Lake Ontario
Geneseo – SE
Genesee River
Loyal Confederate Valley – MO
Buffalo Creek – SE
Cattaraugus – SE
Allegheny River
Gibson Reserve – MO (after 1881)
Lake Simcoe
Six Nations – MO/CA/OA
Grand River
Oneida on the Thames – SE (after 1839)
Thames River
Georgian Bay
Lake Huron
Lake St Clair
Lake Erie

N
E
W
S

0   50   100
Kilometres

MAP 14.1 Iroquois Settlements, c. 1784

Territory. Pioneering Canadian anthropologist Marius Barbeau worked among them early in the twentieth century. They are recognized by the US federal government as Indians but another group of Wyandottes in Kansas are not.

It is the descendants of the Haudenosaunee or Iroquois who have survived in the greatest numbers. Table 14.1 lists the population of various Iroquois communities in Canada and the United States.

Sources on Northern Iroquoian Cultures

There is rich documentation for some Northern Iroquoian cultures dating back to their first contacts with Europeans. For others, who disappeared or were dispersed early in the historic era, we have little or no documentation. Disease and warfare eliminated many Northern Iroquoian nations prior to details of language and culture being recorded. Thus it is only on recorded testimony from the seventeenth century that it can be asserted that the Erie spoke an Iroquoian language. No word lists or documentation of their language exists. Only for the Huron and Iroquois do we have extensive documentation of their language and culture.

Several major sources document Huron culture from the first half of the seventeenth century. These are readily available, in both French and English translations. The earliest are the writings of Samuel de Champlain and the Recollet friar Gabriel Sagard. Jesuits later began a mission among the Hurons, and the *Jesuit Relations* are a rich record of this mission and the people with whom they dealt. Of greatest importance are the writings of Jean de Brébeuf, especially those in the *Relation of 1636*.

The cultures of the Iroquois Confederacy, particularly the Mohawks, were initially described by the Dutch who settled the Hudson River valley and established a trading post at Fort Orange, now Albany, New York. By the second half of the seven-

TABLE 14.1 Contemporary Iroquois Reserves and Reservations

RESERVE OR RESERVATION	ENROLLED POPULATION
ONTARIO	
Akwesasne (St Regis)	9,500
Tyendinaga	7,046
Six Nations	20,876
Wahta Mohawk (Gibson)	659
Oneida of the Thames	4,776
QUEBEC	
Kahnawake (Caughnawaga)	8,888
Kanesatake (Oka)	1,943
NEW YORK	
Seneca Nation (Allegany and Cattaraugus)	6,241
Tonawanda Band of the Senecas	1,050
Oneida	1,100
Onondaga	1,600
Tuscarora	1,200
Akwesasne (St Regis)	5,638
WISCONSIN	
Oneida	11,000
OKLAHOMA	
Seneca–Cayuga	2,460

SOURCE: *Lex and Abler (2004:744)*

These figures reflect the enrolled or registered membership of the above communities in or about 1990 for the United States and 2000 for Canada. Many enrolled members live off reserve or off reservation. The reserves and reservations also are home to many non-enrolled individuals, Indian and non-Indian, who have married into or otherwise have a right to reside on the reserve or reservation.

teenth century, Jesuits were residing in Iroquois country and describing what they heard and saw. In 1724, the French missionary scholar Joseph François Lafitau published his four-volume study, *Moeurs des sauvages amériquains*, which devoted the bulk of its text to a comparison of Mohawk customs to those which Lafitau knew from his study of classics and ancient history. In that same decade, the New York colonial official Cadwallader Colden published *The History of the Five Indian Nations depending on the Province of New-York in America* (1727), arguing how the Iroquois were vital to the English colonies in America because of their political and economic importance.

The Iroquois contributed to the birth of anthropology as an academic discipline. In the 1840s a lawyer named Lewis H. Morgan obtained the aid of Ely S. Parker, a young bilingual Seneca. They collaborated in an investigation of traditional Seneca culture. The resulting publication in 1851 of *The League of the Ho-dé-no-sau-nee or Iroquois* has been hailed as the first scientific description of a Native American society. It set the standard for the ethnographic monograph for the next century. Since Morgan, a large number of professional anthropologists, some of Iroquois ancestry, have investigated various contemporary Iroquois communities.

Iroquoians, Anthropology, and Ethnohistory

Thus for the Iroquoians we have a particularly rich record, with almost 500 years of historical documentation of Iroquoian peoples and languages and more than 150 years of anthropological documentation of the culture of the nations of the Iroquois Confederacy.[2] It was this rich record which initially attracted me to explore Iroquois culture and history. As a teenager I read Morgan's *League* and devoured Francis Parkman's histories of the French experience in the Great Lakes. I then discovered our local public library had the 73-volume edition of *The Jesuit Relations and Allied Documents*, and I could read the sources Parkman had used in his depictions of the wars between the Huron and the Iroquois Confederacy. As an undergraduate I was attracted to both history and anthropology. Much of the history that attracted me, however,

was that of exotic regions and peoples undergoing a colonial or frontier experience. Eventually I chose anthropology as a major. I had discovered that a number of anthropologists were engaged in ethnohistory, looking at historical documents for information on the past of the peoples they had studied, examining issues of stability and change in these cultures. For a senior independent study project I produced an ethnohistoric investigation of Northern Iroquoian settlement patterns, using the writings of the Jesuits, Champlain, Sagard, and others.

As a master's student I encountered William Fenton, a major figure in Iroquoian scholarship, at an academic meeting, and this led to writing a Ph.D. thesis on political change among nineteenth-century Allegany and Cattaraugus Seneca and researching the project on the Allegany Reservation. Various historical issues in Iroquois culture have occupied most of my research time since. The rich historical documentation of Iroquoian cultures has enabled me to pursue my dual interest in culture and history. Both historians and anthropologists pursue ethnohistoric studies, but anthropologists frequently ask different sorts of questions of documents than do their siblings in history.

The Iroquoian Story of Creation

Among the aspects of culture documented by this long historical record are variant forms of the creation story shared by these Iroquoian peoples. The Recollect brother Gabriel Sagard alluded to the story in his 1624 publication, but it was first recorded in full among the Huron by Jean de Brébeuf in 1636. Since this first publication of the Huron version of the myth, some 40 other versions have appeared in print and new variants continue to be recorded.

The basic story describes this world as covered by a primeval sea inhabited by water creatures and water fowl. This world is covered by a sky dome and people lived atop this dome. There they received light and sustenance from a great tree that grew from the apex of the sky dome. For various reasons, depending on who is telling the story, the tree is uprooted and a woman is pushed through the resulting hole in the dome. As she falls toward the waters below, water fowl catch her on their backs and the creatures decide that the turtle is strong enough to hold the woman on her back. Various creatures dive to fetch earth from the bottom of the sea; one is successful, and the land grows to become the continent of North America, on the back of the turtle.

Sky Woman gives birth to a daughter. After the daughter reaches adulthood, she too becomes pregnant. As she nears term, the daughter is distressed to hear the twin sons in her womb arguing. One wishes to be born the normal way; the other suggests it would be shorter to exit through their mother's side and announces his intention of doing so. Recognizing that she will die in childbirth, the daughter instructs Sky Woman how she should be buried. The first-born twin is born normally; his brother bursts through his mother's side, killing her. When found by their grandmother, the younger twin blames his elder brother, who is then cast by their grandmother into the bush. The daughter is buried and from her breasts grow corn, from her fingers beans, from her feet squash, and from her head tobacco.

The elder twin survives, and upon maturity he and his brother begin to create the world. The elder twin, known as Sapling or Good Mind, creates humans and all that is good for them. The younger twin, known as Flint or Evil Mind, makes things that will plague humans and make life difficult. Neither is able to destroy his brother's creations, but each modifies that of the other to reduce its impact, for good or ill, on humans. In this process, Flint is aided by their grandmother, Sky Woman.

The brothers engage in a cosmic, earth-shattering battle. Using an antler as his weapon, Sapling destroys Flint (antler tines are commonly used in shaping chipped-stone tools). Flint is cast into a pit, and Sapling, the Creator, ascends into the sky world.

Northern Iroquoian Cultural Adaptation

Subsistence

With the possible exception of the people visited by Cartier, all Northern Iroquoians made extensive use of the four domesticated crops mentioned in the creation story. Maize, beans, and squash were known as "the three sisters" or "the life supporters." Tilling these crops was a female task, with a group of female kin working under the direction of an elder matron. Maize was planted in hills, frequently with beans and squash. As the corn stalks grew, the beans twined about them for support while the broad-leaved squash grew about the base of the hill, shading out weeds competing for nutrients.

Tobacco, while not a food plant, was (and is) viewed as essential for communication with the Creator and other deities. Burning tobacco is a ritual activity. Cultivating tobacco seems to have been the responsibility of males, who also may have been responsible for the numerous clay effigy pipes found on late prehistoric Iroquoian sites.

The fields where these crops were cultivated surrounded a rather dense settlement. Houses were the multi-family longhouses described by Cartier. Built of a framework of posts and poles covered with elm bark, the roof was arched, and early European observers compared its shape to an arbour or a bower. The house length depended upon the number of families residing there. Spaced seven metres apart down the four-metre-wide central passageway of the house were a series of hearths, each shared by a pair of families. In the roof above each fireplace was a smoke hole, the only outside source of light for the interior of the longhouse. Doors were at the ends of the longhouse; ends might be rounded or square. The core residents of the house consisted of a group of women related to each other through uterine links—a woman and possibly her sisters plus any daughters of the senior woman or women and so on, with their husbands and unmarried children of these women. In the seventeenth and early eighteenth centuries houses were typically 30 metres long with three or four hearths. Most Iroquoians lived in rather large villages, with up to 50 longhouses or 400 families, but there were also small hamlets. In times of conflict the larger villages were often enclosed with a palisade, such as Cartier encountered at Hochelaga.

Men built houses and cleared the fields surrounding the village. Women planted, cultivated, and harvested the fields. Women also gathered firewood, for cooking and for maintaining a comfortable temperature inside the longhouses over the winter. Because fields lost their fertility and firewood within easy transport to the village grew scarce, villages relocated to new sites after 10 to 25 years.

While food from the fields was sufficient to sustain the village, the woods beyond were important. Wild foods, such as strawberries and maple sugar, flavoured Iroquoian cuisine. Men brought in meat through hunting, but equally important were the hides and other raw materials obtained in the hunt. Prior to the fur trade, deer hides were essential for clothing. Deer skin remained vital for the production of moccasins throughout the seventeenth and eighteenth centuries, but trapping furs for European markets allowed Iroquoians to replace leather garments with cotton and wool ones. Thus the male economic role matched that of their sisters and wives in importance.

Clans and Lineages

Northern Iroquoians organized themselves around exogamous matrilineal clans. In turn, each clan was composed of one or more matrilineages. The clans bore names, and one could identify oneself, for example, as a member of the Wolf or Bear clan. One felt a sense of kinship with other clan members, even if they were of a different nation. For example, a Mohawk of the Turtle clan would view an Onondaga of the Turtle clan as a fellow clan member and hence a relative. However, one might not know exactly how one was related to other members of one's clan. The smaller unit, the lineage, recognized their common kinship because they all knew their relationship to the lineage founder and/or the lineage matron, the eldest competent and knowledgeable woman in the lineage. Usually all members of a lineage would live in the same community; almost always all female members of the lineage did so, perhaps residing in a single longhouse. Those females would own the longhouse or longhouses occupied by the lineage and had the right to farm particular fields. The image of the clan eponym might be painted or inscribed above the doors of the lineage longhouse. Strangers visiting a village would seek out a longhouse associated with their clan. Within a nation, a small clan might consist of a single lineage, whereas large clans would consist of multiple lineages.

Jesuit missionaries to the Huron and Iroquois occasionally alluded to men having more than one wife, but in fact both peoples were monogamous. What the Jesuits suggested was **polygyny** was simply divorce (relatively common among Iroquoians, as it often is in matrilineal societies) and remarriage. However, despite relatively relaxed attitudes toward non-marital sexual activity, a leading cause of suicide among both Hurons and Iroquois was the infidelity of a spouse or the breakup of a marriage.

Upon marriage a man typically moved to this wife's longhouse. If all apartments in the house were occupied, the house could be simply extended. There is some suggestion that a male who held a political position within his lineage and clan might continue to live within a longhouse of his matrilineage.

Among the Iroquoians, our knowledge of lineage and clan organization is most extensive for the Iroquois, where clan and lineage affiliation are still important for at least some. Clan structure was not static. A small clan could become extinct. A large clan might split, although all in a community might not recognize that split.

It seems likely that other Northern Iroquoians were divided into similar matrilineal clans. Eight clans have been reported for the Tuscarora, including Great Turtle, Sand Turtle, Wolf, Bear, Beaver, Deer, Snipe, and Eel. Some Tuscarora have suggested that, as was the case with Turtle, there were two Wolf clans (Grey Wolf and Yellow Wolf) and two Bear clans. The Wyandot descendants of the Huron and Petun were divided into eight clans: Turtle, Wolf, Bear, Beaver, Deer, Hawk, Porcupine, and Snake. There are, however, reports of several Turtle clans, named according to size or species,

numbering from three to five. Seventeenth-century reports of Huron social structure also suggest eight clans, and many ethnohistorians have suggested these were the eight Wyandot clans listed above. Others have suggested that the inclusion of Porcupine and Snake clans as Huron clans is mistaken and that the final two Huron clans are Sturgeon (or Loon) and Fox. Refugee Hurons who settled at Lorette near Quebec City belonged to Turtle, Wolf, Bear, Deer, and possibly Beaver clans. When two or more clans are somehow linked for social purposes, anthropologists refer to these larger groupings as phratries. If clans divide into two units or sides, anthropologists speak of these units as **moieties**. The Wyandot grouped their clans into three or four phratries while among the western Iroquois the clans were divided into two moieties.

Individual names were associated with each clan and lineage, and when an infant was born into a lineage, the matron would select one of the lineage's currently unused "baby names" for the child. Again, when the child came of age, a name would be selected from the adult names available. Thus everyone bore a name long used in the past

TABLE 14.2 Clans of the Nations of the Haudenosaunee or Iroquois Confederacy

SENECA	CAYUGA	ONONDAGA	ONEIDA	MOHAWK
Wolf	Wolf	Wolf	Wolf	Wolf
Turtle	Heron	Turtle	Turtle	Turtle
Bear	Snipe	Snipe	◊	◊
Beaver	◊	Beaver	Bear	Bear
◊	Deer	Ball		
Deer	Turtle	◊		
Snipe	Bear	Hawk		
Heron	Ball	Deer		
Hawk	Beaver	Bear		
	Eel	Eel		

Note: The above lists of clans are divided into moieties. Among the Seneca Nation, the moiety containing the Wolf Clan is known as the Animal Clans, while the moiety containing the Snipe Clan is known as the Bird Clans. The Onondaga in New York state term the moiety with the Wolf Clan the Longhouse Moiety, while the moiety with the Hawk Clan is the Mudhouse Moiety.

within the matrilineage and destined to be used for future generations. Among the Iroquois these names were publicly announced during the Green Corn festival or the Midwinter Ceremony. Some names were associated with political office (see the story of the Peacemaker outlined on page 261), so a lineage matron had the power to select which of her lineage had the right to assume that political office by assuming that name.

Matrilineages and lineage matrons also played an important role in the warfare complex. If a lineage matron was grieved by a death in her lineage, she could call for a captive or a scalp to replace the deceased individual. She did not ask her own sons (or those of her sisters) to engage in this dangerous task, however. Instead she approached the children of her brothers (or sons fathered by males in her lineage) to take on this task. This aspect of Iroquoian behaviour has been described by historian Daniel Richter (borrowing a phrase coined by anthropologist Marian W. Smith) as "a pattern known as the 'mourning-war'" (Richter 1983:529). Thus every male in Iroquoian society owed this service to the matrilineal kinsmen of his father. But it is also of interest that women played a primary role in initiating military action, yet when they did so they did not send their own sons to war, but rather called on the sons of their brothers.

Religion

Much of Iroquoian ritual activity was concerned with human health. Health was strongly associated with one's mental condition. A troubled mind could lead to physical sickness. It was true that some illnesses had natural causes (and the Iroquoians had a rich pharmacopoeia of herbal remedies), but illness could be brought on by an unfilled desire of one's soul or by witchcraft. In the former case, the desire might be revealed in a dream or it might be guessed by one's fellow villagers in a dream-guessing rite. The unfulfilled desire might be met either literally or symbol-

ically. Psychological anthropologist Anthony Wallace (1958) argued that Iroquoians anticipated Freud's emphasis on the importance of dreams. Frequently the soul desired the performance of one of the rites of a medicine society or another sacred action such as playing a game of lacrosse. Members of one Huron curing society handled coals from the fire and red-hot stones as part of their rituals. Witnesses described another Huron curing ritual involving masked dancers, hunchbacked and carrying staves, recalling the Society of Faces, which continues to perform rituals for individual and communal health in a number of Iroquois communities.

The Society of Faces is one of several medicine societies found in contemporary Iroquois communities which function to cure illness. A second masked society is the Husk Faces or Bushy Heads, who wear masks made of woven corn husk. The most powerful of medicines is held by the Little Water Society, which must periodically hold nightlong rituals to renew the medicine. Only the initiated may attend such a ceremony. The Pygmy Society or Dark Dance, the Eagle Society, the Bear Society, the Otter Society, and the Buffalo Society are each charged with the treatment of specific illnesses.

Both the Huron and the Iroquois were also convinced that witchcraft, either conscious or unconscious, could bring on illness or misfortune. If a community concluded that one of its members was indeed a witch, an executioner was appointed and the witch was killed. It is likely that Mohawks killed Jesuit missionary Isaac Jogues in 1646 because they believed the epidemic and famine which had struck their villages were results of his witchcraft.

Death

Both mourning and recovering from bereavement were themes important in the Iroquoian world view. The Huron and Iroquois felt that a

---

BOX 14.1 The Huron Feast of the Dead

The Huron practised an important and impressive rite of solidarity associated with death that was not found among their Iroquois neighbours. The Huron referred to the ceremony as *yandatsa*, meaning "the kettle," but it is known in the ethnohistoric literature as the Feast of the Dead. It was held every 15 years or so to bury in an ossuary a major village's dead; smaller nearby and allied villages (sometimes from a considerable distance) would also take part.

Three days after death, a body was placed on a platform encased in a bark coffin high above the ground in a village cemetery. (Those who had died a violent death, including those who had drowned or frozen to death, were not treated in this fashion; their remains were disposed of separately.) At the time of the Feast of the Dead, the kin of the deceased removed the bodies from the platform tombs and cleaned the bones if decomposition was well along. A large pit was dug and lined with beaver pelts. At the climax of the rituals the bones and the undecomposed bodies of the recently deceased were deposited in the pit, and men with poles stirred them to mingle them together. Fur robes were placed over the remains of the thousand or so individuals deposited in the ossuary, and the pit was filled and topped with a low mound.

---

death should lead the principal relatives to mourn intensely for 10 days. Among contemporary conservative Iroquois, this is followed by the Ten-Day Feast in which the property of the deceased is distributed. A less intense period of mourning follows, for a calendar year for the Huron and until the next major calendrical ceremony among conservative Iroquois. The Huron ultimately moved almost all the dead to a single large burial pit or **ossuary** in a ceremony known as the Feast of the Dead.

Since the pioneering studies of Lewis H. Morgan, anthropologists have consulted with ceremonial specialists among the various Iroquois communities and have provided detailed descriptions of the structure of Iroquois ceremonialism. Especially noteworthy are the researches conducted by Frank Speck and Annemarie Shimony on the Six Nations territory near Brantford, Ontario. It is important to remember that these ceremonial events have all been influenced by the teachings of the Seneca prophet Handsome Lake, who preached for the first 15 years of the nineteenth century, and that each Iroquois community exhibits its own local variation.

The Green Corn Ceremony and the Midwinter Ceremony are most important; each lasts several days while other ceremonies currently last but a single day. Midwinter is held five days after the first new moon to appear after the Pleiades appear directly overhead at sunset (early January). It is a time for announcing the names of the newborn and the newly adult, a time for the practice of the four sacred rituals of the Iroquois (the Great Feather Dance, the Individual Thanksgiving [Adowa], the Skin Dance, and the Bowl Game), and a time for the public performances of the rites of the Medicine Societies, sponsored or requested by individuals who have been cured. On the first day of the Green Corn Ceremony, women carry ears of new corn in the Women's Dance, following the performance of the Great Feather Dance. On the third day of Green Corn, the Women's Society

TABLE 14.3 Calendrical Ceremonies of the Iroquois

CEREMONY	DATE
Bush	Within 10 days of Midwinter
Maple	Late March/early April
Sun	April
Thunder	April or in time of drought
Seed Planting	April/early May
Strawberry	June
Green Bean	Early August
Corn Testing	Late August/early September
Green Corn	Late August/early September
Harvest	Late October/early November
Midwinter	The new moon of midwinter—January or February

rite honours the "three sisters" or "life supporters," maize, beans, and squash. Both Green Corn and Midwinter conclude with the moieties playing against each other in the Bowl Game.

The Origins and Structure of the League of the Haudenosaunee

Both the Huron and the Iroquois were confederacies, as probably were other Iroquoians such as the Neutral. Despite the enormous demographic, economic, social, and political impact of the European invasion of North America, the structure of the Haudenosaunee or Iroquois Confederacy Council has survived into the twenty-first century. It should be emphasized that the Confederacy is a living tradition, being modified through time by its participants, yet documented through this time in various manifestations, with greater or lesser

detail and with greater or lesser accuracy, by both anthropologists and Indigenous participants in the tradition.

Prior to the establishment of the Great Peace, the five nations of the Iroquois Confederacy were continually at war with one another. Blood feuds dominated relations between nations and clans. At this time a son was born to a Huron virgin living on the shores of the Bay of Quinté on the north shore of Lake Ontario. Upon reaching maturity, he vowed to preach a message of peace to the warring five nations to the south. He went first to the country of the Mohawks where he encountered Hiawatha,[3] a fierce warrior who had just butchered a victim for a cannibal feast. The Peacemaker climbed the roof of Hiawatha's house and looked in through the smoke hole. As Hiawatha was placing the kettle on the fire, he mistook the reflection of a man's face (it was the face of the Peacemaker staring from above) for his own. Thinking this could not be the face of one who had performed the violent acts which he had just perpetrated, Hiawatha vowed to reform. As he emerged from his longhouse, he encountered the Peacemaker, and the two agreed to carry the message of peace to all the five nations. In some versions of this story the Peacemaker stammers and so Hiawatha becomes his speaker.

Travelling from nation to nation, they convince almost all of the utility of the Great Peace. Only the Onondaga refused to join. They were led by a formidable chief named Thadodaho. He was an infamous sorcerer, misshapen with seven crooks in his body and with snakes in his hair. The Peacemaker and Hiawatha eventually convinced Thadodaho and his Onondagas to join the Great Peace by making that nation central to the affairs of the Confederacy. Thadodaho was recognized as first among the chiefs on the Confederacy Council, although in fact all are equals. The Onondaga were recognized as the fire keepers of the Confederacy. It was in the large village of Onondaga that the

FIGURE 14.1 Wampum belts and strings were exchanged in diplomatic activity by the Iroquois and their neighbours as pledges of honesty and sincerity on the part of the speakers at council and treaty sessions. Such speakers often arrived at council with a belt draped about their shoulders. Here in an 1870 photograph a Mohawk from Kanasetake carries a belt in this fashion while holding a second belt in his left hand. (Courtesy of McCord Museum of Canadian History, McGill University, Montreal, I-48873)

or woven into belts. A speaker holding a string or belt of wampum in his hand is demonstrating the truth of his words. In diplomatic negotiations, passing strings or belts of wampum from one side to the other cements and documents the pledges being made. Hence as wampum keepers, the Onondaga received the strings and belts given to the Iroquois in diplomatic negotiations and so held the archive of the treaties and alliances made by the Haudenosaunee.

Wampum strings and belts retain political significance among contemporary Haudenosaunee. In communities with traditional hereditary chiefs, the matron of the lineage holding the position or title possesses a wampum string or strings associated with that chieftainship. Some belts are purported to date from the founding of the Iroquois Confederacy and other mark important treaties negotiated with colonial powers and other First Nations. Over time important belts came by various routes into the hands of museums. Many of these have been repatriated in recent decades. Among the most important is the Two Row wampum, a white belt with two horizontal rows of purple beads. The two bands of purple have been interpreted to represent a large ship and a canoe travelling parallel but separate routes. Thus the cultures of the European invaders and the First Nations should remain distinct, each never to interfere with the other. The origins of the belt are debated, but many believe that it marks the earliest treaty negotiated between the Haudenosaunee and a European power.

It was at Onondaga that the Peacemaker and Hiawatha convened a council to establish the Great Peace. Fifty chiefs attended. Hiawatha combed the snakes from Thadodaho's hair. The Peacemaker dug a pit into which he cast the weapons of war. Over this he planted a pine tree, the Tree of Peace. Its white roots of peace grow in the four cardinal directions. The Haudenosaunee and their allies sit in the shade of this great Tree of Peace.

council fire for the Haudenosaunee burned. Moreover, an Onondaga chief on the Confederacy Council was given the privilege and responsibility of being wampum keeper for the Confederacy.

Wampum is a cylindrical shell bead with a sacred quality. It comes in two colours; white wampum is made from the shell of the whelk, and purple wampum from the shell of the quahog clam. These shell beads were threaded on strings

The 50 chiefs who attended this council were not evenly distributed among the nations. Mohawk and Oneida each had 9, Onondaga 14, Cayuga 10; and Seneca only 8. The names of these chiefs continue to this day, for when a chief dies, he is replaced by a member of his matrilineage who then assumes the name or title associated with the position (recall that one always takes a name from one's matrilineage). The names of all 50 chiefs are also recited in a roll call which lists them by nation and presents the nations from east to west. Within each nation there is a specific ordering of the titles; thus one can refer to a title, such as *Skanaawadi* ("Across the Swamp"), as the fourteenth or final title on the Onondaga list or the thirty-second title overall. The matron of the matrilineage plays a major role in deciding who among her brothers, sons, and nephews (sister's sons) or other matrilineal kin will assume the position. She also holds the wampum string which is associated with that particular title. She also watches the behaviour of the incumbent in office, for she has the power to remove him if warranted.

Not all Iroquois clans have positions on the Confederacy Council. The three Mohawk and three Oneida clans each have three seats on council (although the second Mohawk title, a Turtle Clan position, was that of Hiawatha and traditionally is not filled). For the remaining three nations, some clans enjoy multiple seats while others have none. In Morgan's listing of Seneca members of the Confederacy Council, neither the Beaver, the Deer, nor the Heron clans are represented, while two titles are affiliated with the Turtle Clan and the Snipe Clan has three positions. If a matrilineage had no suitable candidate for its position on the council, the title could be "borrowed" by another matrilineage, perhaps even of a different clan. For example, the first Seneca title is associated with the Turtle Clan, but from 1795 to 1815 it was held by a member of the Wolf Clan. This has led to differing clan affiliations for many of the titles on the roll call of chiefs as these roll calls have been recorded at different places and times.

When death leaves a position vacant on the Confederacy Council, there is an elaborate ritual to install the new candidate into office after he has been selected by the lineage matron in consultation with the female and male members of the lineage. This ritual is known as the Condolence Council, and it reflects a moiety division that formally governs council behaviour. The nations of the Haudenosaunee sit as a pair of moieties. On one side of the fire sit the Mohawk, Onondaga, and Seneca. This side is sometimes referred to as the "elder brothers" or the "three brothers." On the opposite side of the fire sit the "younger brothers" or "four brothers": the Oneida and Cayuga plus any client nations brought into the shade of the Tree of Peace. The minds of the moiety that lost a member are troubled. It is the duty of the other side, the moiety with a clear mind, to remove this grief, to recite the wonderful story of the founding of the Great Peace, to recite the roll call of the founders, and finally to call forth the candidate to fill the vacant position. Thus a Cayuga or Oneida chief conducts the rite and installs a chief to fill a Mohawk, Onondaga, or Seneca vacancy. Similarly, a speaker from the Mohawk, Onondaga, or Seneca recites the rites and rituals to install a successor to a deceased Cayuga or Oneida chief. The necessity for this ceremony to install a man into office has led to some contemporary Haudenosaunee to refer to those installed as "Condoled Chiefs."

Iroquois political thought and speech is particularly rich in metaphor. Metaphorically, the Condoled Chiefs wear the antlers of office. Those who sit on the Confederacy Council are peace chiefs and as such cannot go to war without first removing their antlers of office. If a lineage matron is dissatisfied with a chief's performance, she has the right, after appropriate warning, to "dehorn" the chief, removing his antlers of office.

The moiety division governs the discussion of matters in council, although the Onondaga sit as moderators rather than with the other nations of the elder brothers. When a matter comes to council it is considered first by the elder brothers' side, initially by the Seneca and then by the Mohawk. If these chiefs are in agreement, the matter is passed across the fire to the Oneida who consider it, and, if they agree, pass it on to the Cayuga. If all four nations are of one mind, the issue is passed to the Onondaga and if they agree, then it is the acknowledged policy of the Haudenosaunee. Because of this requirement for unanimity, the differential representation of nations and clans was of no significance since a single dissident could block any decision.

The Impact of the Fur Trade on the Iroquoians

The story of the Peacemaker tells of the intense conflict that existed among the Iroquois. Archaeological evidence also suggests intense early warfare among Iroquoians. While land was abundant for agricultural purposes, it seems likely that groups came into conflict over deer-hunting territories. These conflicts were exacerbated by the European invasion of the Americas and the involvement of Indigenous people in the fur trade. The French used the St Lawrence to establish trading links into the interior and soon established strong ties with the Algonquians of the St Lawrence and Ottawa valleys and the Huron farther inland. Initial French contacts with the Iroquois were violent. Samuel de Champlain was with an Innu and Algonquin expedition in 1609 that encountered a Mohawk war party at the southern end of Lake Champlain. Probably these Mohawks had never before encountered firearms, and Champlain reported shooting three chiefs who appeared at the front of their men clad in wooden armour. Champlain assisted in a second expedition which defeated Mohawks in 1610, and in 1615 he accompanied an army of Huron and Algonquin who unsuccessfully attacked a village in the heart of Iroquoia.

These hostile encounters with the French led the Mohawks to seek trading links with the Dutch. The Mohawk drove the Algonquian-speaking Mahican from the lower Mohawk Valley and established direct trading links with the Dutch at Fort Orange. Trade goods had reached far into the interior long before any Europeans set foot there. Brass kettles and iron and steel tools became vital as old technologies were abandoned. Cloth replaced leather for clothing. Glass beads supplemented quillwork and moose hair in decorating clothing. Even starting fires came to depend on flint and steel. Finally, throughout the seventeenth century obtaining firearms became increasingly vital for waging war. In 1640 a Mohawk warrior would have desired a gun; by 1680 it was necessary that his primary weapon be a musket.

Beaver pelts were the major commodity desired by Europeans. As they exhausted the beaver supply in their own country, the Iroquois turned increasingly to warfare to maintain a supply of peltry. The Mohawk in particular fought as pirates, intercepting fleets of Huron and Algonquian canoes taking furs to the French posts on the St Lawrence. At the western end of the Iroquois longhouse, Seneca policy was to expand their territory. By 1638 Seneca attacks had driven the Wenro from their homes and the survivors sought refuge in Huron villages.

As the fur trade intensified inter-ethnic conflict, a far deadlier infestation struck. Europeans brought with them previously unknown diseases. Smallpox, measles, and mumps killed large numbers; half the population of a village might be lost in a single epidemic. By the winter of 1648–49, the population of Huronia was less than half what it had been when Champlain first visited less than 30 years earlier. The Huron were also divided, some favouring the new religion preached by the Jesuits and some seeing the Jesuits as witches who had brought disease and destruction.

In March of 1649 a large Mohawk and Seneca army, perhaps 1,000 men, attacked two Huron towns bearing the mission names of Saint-Ignace and Saint-Louis. A Huron counterattack drove the attackers from Saint-Louis, but they were still surrounded. In a desperate and bloody battle the Hurons were defeated. The Mohawk and Seneca returned with their captives and booty to their homeland.

The demoralized Huron abandoned all their villages that summer and, without crops, many starved the next winter. Surviving Hurons sought refuge. Some settled outside Quebec City, others among the Petun and Neutral, and large numbers among the Iroquois. Iroquois culture as now known may well reflect ideas brought by the many Hurons who settled among them.

The dispersal of the Huron led the Iroquois to turn on the Petun. In December 1649, an Iroquois army destroyed the principal Petun town of Etharita, which had housed more than 500 families. Two Neutral villages were destroyed in the next two years and southwestern Ontario lay open to Seneca and other Iroquois beaver hunting. The major town of the Erie Nation fell to an attacking army, principally Onondaga, in 1654.

This warfare strained the resources of the Confederacy, so a peace was negotiated with the French prior to commencing hostilities against the Erie. This brought Jesuits, who had long worked among the Hurons, into Iroquoia. This first mission at Onondaga lasted only five years, and the remainder of seventeenth century was marked by alternating episodes of peace and war between the French and the Nations of the Haudenosaunee (it was not unusual for one or more of the Nations in the Confederacy to be at war with French Canada while the remainder were at peace). The French invaded and destroyed Iroquois towns—those of the Mohawk were burned in 1666 and 1693;

Seneca towns were destroyed in 1687 (the Seneca retaliated by destroying Lachine outside Montreal in 1689), and in 1696 a French invasion led to the destruction of both the Oneida town and that of the Onondaga.

Possibly more devastating than these invasions was the work of Jesuit missionaries. Not content to allow their converts to continue close to the English and Dutch Protestant influences from Albany (New Netherland had become New York upon surrender to the British in 1664), the Jesuits encouraged their converts to move to the St Lawrence Valley. These were largely Mohawks, and by the end of the seventeenth century there were as many Mohawks living outside Montreal as in their Mohawk Valley homeland.

The Haudenosaunee occupied a highly strategic position between French Canada and the English colonies on the Atlantic seaboard. Both European powers curried their favour. In 1701 the entire Confederacy negotiated separate treaties with both the French and the English, effectively making the Confederacy neutral. Generally this path was followed until the British conquest of French Canada. The Mohawks living on the doorstep of Albany were drawn at times to fight as ethnic soldiers in British expeditions. The Seneca, particularly the western branch, were at times seen fighting alongside the French, particularly after the French established a trading post in their country at the mouth of the Niagara River. The Catholic Mohawks who had moved to the St Lawrence frequently fought alongside the French, raiding into New England. Captives taken during these raids were adopted and sometimes successfully incorporated into the culture and society of Kahnawake and other Mohawk settlements.

The Four Kings of Canada

In an effort to impress the Haudenosaunee with the power of the British Crown and to impress the bureaucracy in London with the importance of

Indian affairs on the colonial frontier, New York sent three Mohawk chiefs and one Mahican (or River Indian) to London in 1710. Hailed as "the four Kings of Canada," they were a sensation in London. At the request of Queen Anne, their portraits were painted by John Verelst and these and other images of the four chiefs were published. A goal of the delegation was to obtain a commitment for Anglican mission activity among the Iroquois to counter the French Jesuit influence. Queen Anne supported this and supplied to "Her Majesty's Chapel among the Mohawks" a set of communion silver. The Royal Chapel was established, but when the Mohawks were forced to leave their homes in the Mohawk Valley after the American Revolution, the silver was divided between the two new Mohawk settlements established in Canada—on the Grand River and at Deseronto.

The Tuscarora

In recognition of the nature of their Confederacy, British colonial officials usually referred to the Haudenosaunee as the Five Nations. Numerous groups of refugees were encouraged by the Haudenosaunee Council to settle in Iroquoia to offset the periodic population losses caused by epidemics. Most were simply assimilated into the five founding nations of the Confederacy. In the 1720s, however, the Tuscarora from the Carolinas arrived to sit in the shade of the Tree of Peace, fleeing conflict with English settlers. They were given lands within Oneida territory. Like their hosts, the Tuscarora spoke a Northern Iroquoian language. Unlike other refugees, the Tuscarora maintained their ethnic distinctiveness and so the "Six Nations" became a name commonly used for the Haudenosaunee. They were never granted seats on the Confederacy Council, but their political agenda was expected to be voiced by chiefs from the younger brothers' side of the council fire.

Sir William Johnson and Mary Brant

William Johnson was a young Irishman in 1736 when he was sent by his uncle, British admiral Peter Warren, to look after lands which Warren had purchased in the Mohawk Valley. Johnson quickly began to amass his own fortune through participation in the fur trade, initially trading to the southwest at the village of Oquaga on the Susquehanna River. Part of his success was the intensity of his bonding with his Mohawk neighbours. He learned their language and the formal metaphors of their public speaking. He was comfortable wearing their clothing. He slept in their houses. He sang and danced with them. He then began to acquire their lands. In 1739 he bought over 800 acres on the north side of the river, opposite Fort Hunter (Tiononderoge). There, a decade later, he built a country estate worthy of a man of his wealth, Fort Johnson.

The final episode in the struggle between the French and British empires in North America burst upon the scene and Johnson was in a strategic position to benefit from the conflict. Because of his influence with the Mohawks, and through them, the Confederacy, he was appointed by the commander-in-chief for North America, General Edward Braddock, to represent the Crown in dealings with the Six Nations. London confirmed this, giving Johnson a royal commission in 1756 as Colonel and Superintendent of "the Six united Nations of Indians, & their Confederates, in the Northern Parts of North America."

In 1755 Johnson provided the one bright spot for the British in that year's disastrous campaigns. As a major general in the forces of colonial New York, he was instructed to capture Crown Point. While he did not capture his objective, in the Battle of Lake George his 3,000 provincials and 300 Iroquois decisively defeated a force of French regulars commanded by Jean-Armand Dieskau.

Dieskau was wounded and captured. The elderly Mohawk chief Hendrick (Theyanoguin) perished in the battle, bayoneted by a French regular. For his victory, Johnson was knighted, made a baronet, and awarded £5,000 by Parliament.

Sir William had been living with Catherine Weissenberg, an escaped indentured servant who bore him three children. Weissenberg contracted tuberculosis and died in April 1759. By the fall, a young Mohawk woman, Mary (Molly) Brant, pregnant with her first child by Sir William, moved into Fort Johnson. There, and at their later residence, Johnson Hall in Johnstown, New York, Brant helped Sir William entertain dignitaries from both sides of the frontier while she bore him a total of eight children. She used her extensive influence with her own people, and she and Sir William fostered the education and development of Mary Brant's younger brother, known to the non-Indian world as Joseph Brant and to the Mohawk as Thayendanegea. Young Joseph was with Sir William when the British captured the French fort at the mouth of the Niagara River in July 1759.

Molly Brant was firmly in charge of Sir William's household. Johnson moved from Fort Johnson to Johnson Hall in 1762. The decision to move was probably related to estate management, but Johnson Hall was closer to Brant's home village of Canajoharie than was Fort Johnson. Inland from the Mohawk River, Johnson Hall was the centre of a vast estate. Johnson brought in a large retinue of highland Scots to work his lands as tenants. At the time of the move, Johnson and Brant already had two children and another arrived soon after. Johnson Hall was the social centre of the Mohawk Valley, and as chatelaine of Johnson Hall, Brant managed the bevy of visitors whose origins ranged from deep in the western forests to across the ocean.

Johnson did much to perpetuate the view that the Iroquois possessed an "empire" in North America. Several factors contributed to this view.

The Iroquois had achieved real military victories, and the Iroquois Nations acting individually or collectively had, in the words of one Iroquois chief, "won beaver hunting lands by the sword." Some of their opponents in these wars were destroyed or dispersed, while others became tributary to the Confederacy. However, they were not vassals; rather, they sat in the shade of the Tree of Peace as allies of the Haudenosaunee or even as junior members of the league. Given Johnson's influence with the Iroquois, and given the importance to the Iroquois of a political and economic alliance with Britain, it was in the interest of both parties to exaggerate the degree of Iroquois control over distant nations.

The capture of Quebec City and Fort Niagara in 1759 and Montreal in 1760 left Britain the sole political and economic power in northern North America. In addition to competing with each other in the fur trade, both the British and the French had dispensed large quantities of goods to the Indigenous nations on their borders to maintain alliances or at least neutrality in their colonial conflicts. With the vanquishing of French military and political might, the British commander in North America, Jeffery Amherst, saw no useful purpose in spending government funds to convey goods to the Native peoples on the frontier. The river of gifts that had cemented the Indian–British alliance ceased to flow and other elements increased the friction between Native peoples and the red-coated soldiers who had replaced the French military in posts along the frontier. The western Senecas were circulating wampum belts calling for war as early as 1761.

There was a general uprising along the entire frontier in 1763, and many forts and posts were destroyed and their garrisons killed or captured. The name of the Ottawa chief Pontiac is associated with this war, but there were a number of leaders, including the western Seneca chief Guyasuta, who urged attacks on the British. The influence of Johnson kept the eastern Seneca and the other four Iroquois Nations out of the fray, but the western Seneca were active, destroying three British forts south of Lake Erie and intercepting a British column and driving it into the Niagara gorge at Devil's Hole. With no source of arms and ammunition, the uprising was doomed to failure and the Indians, including the western Seneca, eventually sued for peace. The price that Johnson demanded and received for Seneca participation in the war was surrender of a strip of land along the Niagara River, including Grand Island.

In some ways, however, the Indians had achieved a victory. The government in London determined that diplomacy and trade was cheaper than military action to deal with the First Nations and that transactions with these Nations must be conducted in an orderly fashion. The result was the Royal Proclamation of 1763, which ever since has influenced the relationship between First Nations and the Crown. A boundary was drawn separating Indian lands from those available for non-Indian settlement (recognizing Aboriginal title to those lands) and, perhaps more importantly, the Royal Proclamation declared only the Crown had the right to purchase lands from their Indian owners.

Sir William Johnson gathered some 3,400 Indians at Fort Stanwix (now Rome, NY) in 1768. There he negotiated a treaty to formalize the boundary between the areas open for non-Indian settlement and that remaining under Indian title. Lands ceded in this treaty included lands south of the Ohio River to the mouth of the Cherokee River. The treaty was signed on 4 November 1768 by only five chiefs, one for each of the five founding nations of the Haudenosaunee. Both Johnson and the Iroquois claimed that the Iroquois had held title to those lands through right of conquest. People who lived and hunted there, especially the Shawnee, disagreed.

Sir William Johnson died in the midst of a conference held at Johnson Hall in 1774. His son-in-law, Guy Johnson, took the reins of the Indian Department. Next year conflict broke out as some of the American colonies rebelled against Britain. Initially the Six Nations were largely neutral, but when Joseph Brant (Thayendanegea) returned from Britain in 1777,[4] he and his sister Mary worked hard with the loyal British Indian Department officials to bring the Six Nations onside as allies to the Loyalists and the Crown. They were largely successful (some Oneida under the influence of New England missionary Samuel Kirkland fought with the rebels) and the Mohawks, Senecas, and Cayugas achieved several notable victories. However, the Mohawks were forced to flee their homes in the Mohawk Valley, and many Cayuga and Seneca towns were burned by an invading American army in 1779. Britain wearied of the conflict, and made peace with the Americans, signing the Treaty of Paris in 1783. The government in London ignored the loyal allies of His Majesty and no mention of them was made in the peace settlement. The boundary between the new United States and the British in North America was drawn through Lakes Ontario, Erie, Huron, and Superior. Hence the British surrendered all interest in the traditional homeland of the Haudenosaunee. Recognizing the injustice of this, Governor Frederick Haldimand negotiated for tracts of lands in Canada to be made available to those allies of the Crown who did not wish to live under the "yankee" government. Thus the Fort Hunter Mohawks under chief John Deserontyon settled on lands set aside on the Bay of Quinté. Most of the Seneca chose to remain in western New York, and Joseph Brant was persuaded to seek lands for his followers near those of the Seneca, but on the Canadian side of the Niagara frontier. On 25 October 1784 Governor Frederick Haldimand of Canada granted to "the Mohawk Nation, and such other of the Six Nation of Indians as wish to settle in that Quarter ... allotting to them for that Purpose Six Miles deep from each Side of the [Grand] River beginning at Lake Erie, & extending in the Proportion to the Head of the said River, which them & their Posterity are to enjoy for ever" (Johnston 1964:50–1). Of the 1,843 who originally settled the Grand River tract, 464 were Mohawks, 381 Cayuga, 245 Onondaga, 129 Tuscarora, 162 Oneida, 78 Seneca, 231 Delaware, 11 Nanticoke, 74 Tutelo, and 68 assorted others. The communion silver presented to them by Queen Anne was hidden during the American Revolution and divided between the two Mohawk communities in Ontario.

Shortly after the American Revolution, Handsome Lake, who held the first Seneca title (the forty-third title on the Roll Call of Chiefs) of the chiefs of the Confederacy Council, experienced a vision which led him to preach a doctrine of religious and social reform. Anthony F.C. Wallace termed this a "revitalization movement," and indeed Handsome Lake was able to convince many of the errors of their ways and to bring a new vitality to Iroquois culture. His followers were told to abandon vices introduced by the Europeans, especially alcohol. The sale of lands was viewed as evil, to be punished in the afterlife. The yearly ceremonial cycle was to be renewed and the practice of the Four Sacred Rituals emphasized. However, he was also critical of some aspects of traditional Iroquois culture. He felt the nuclear family should be strengthened relative to the matrilineage. He saw a need to discourage divorce and encourage marital stability. He travelled and preached this message from the experience of his first vision in 1799 until his death in the Onondaga community near Syracuse, NY, in 1815.

At this time the Iroquois were largely housed in single-family dwellings (or a house containing a minimally extended family). However, each community retained a large structure, called a council house or a longhouse, used for religious and political meetings. Handsome Lake's teachings became associated with the ceremonies performed in the longhouse, and the terms "Longhouse Religion" and "Longhouse People" have come to be applied to those who follow his teachings. One recent survey noted that the Six Nations territory on the Grand River has four longhouses and that other Canadian communities with longhouses include Oneida on the Thames, Kahnawake, Akwesasne, and Kanesatake. In New York, longhouses are found at Allegany, Cattaraugus, and Tonawanda (all Seneca territories) and at Onondaga, where Handsome Lake is buried.

Two additional Iroquois reserves were established in Canada in the nineteenth century. Despite the role the Oneida played as allies in the American Revolution, their lands were stripped from them through aggressive negotiations by New York state. A large portion moved west to settle at Green Bay on Lake Michigan, but others purchased lands to be held in common in Ontario in 1839. This community is known as Oneida on the Thames, near London, Ontario. The festering land dispute, which still continues, between the Mohawks of Kanesatake and the Roman Catholic Sulpicians at Oka, Quebec, led the Canadian government to attempt to settle some of the Mohawks on the Gibson Reserve (Wahta) established on Georgian Bay in Ontario in 1881.

For many years the Six Nations Reserve was governed by the hereditary chiefs of the Iroquois Confederacy Council. Although divided by religion (many chiefs were Christian, while a minority were Longhouse adherents), the Council provided effective local government for Grand River. However, a group known as "Dehorners," because they wished to remove the metaphorical antlers of office worn by the hereditary chiefs, agitated for an elected council. On 7 October 1924 the federal agent to the Six Nations Reserve announced that the Confederacy Council would be replaced by an elected council, and since then the issue of the proper form of government (hereditary chiefs or elected council) has divided the community.

Only some Kanesatake Mohawks moved to Georgian Bay, and the dispute over ownership of lands at Oka led to the dramatic and tragic Oka crisis of 1990. The town of Oka planned to expand a golf course into lands which were claimed by the people of Kanesatake and which had been used as a cemetery. The Mohawk blockade to stop the construction resulted in an armed assault by the Sûreté du Québec and the death of one police officer. The Canadian Forces were called in, and the Kanesatake militants and others who had joined in the protest found themselves surrounded by the Canadian army. Mohawks at Kahnawake in support of those at Kanesatake blockaded the Mercier Bridge out of Montreal. On 26 September 1990, after a siege of 78 days, those remaining people at Kanesatake attempted to walk out, catching the military by surprise. Thirty-four were arrested, and the immediate crisis was ended; the golf course has not been built, but the underlying disputes and claims over land issues remain.

Many Iroquois communities are divided by the issue of gambling. Some argue that the Iroquois are a sovereign people, and that Canadian or provincial laws do not apply on their reserves. Hence gaming operations can be mounted without reference to federal or provincial laws. Others, while they may agree on the issue of sovereignty with those who favour gambling, oppose casinos on moral or social grounds. There have been violent clashes at Akwesasne over this issue, leading to arson and even killings. Smuggling is a second issue at Akwesasne, on the border between Ontario and New York, which has led to internal violence. A dispute about the placement of armed members of the Canadian Border Service on the reserve flared as this chapter was being written, and it seems likely that further disputes will arise.

More recently matters of land and sovereignty have brought Haudenosaunee to the attention of the press. There have been clashes in Ontario as residents from the Six Nations on the Grand River occupied a real-estate developer's site in Caledonia, Ontario. As in the Oka crisis, portions of the neighbouring communities responded to this assertion of rights with threats and violence. The Caledonia dispute is part of a larger land claim resulting from the clouded nature of land transfers involving most of the lands in the Haldimand tract in the nineteenth century.

The media focus on militants and conflict masks the considerable number of success stories found in Iroquoia. One might point to two examples, a century apart. The poetry and performing skills of Pauline Johnson from Six Nations became well known across Canada in the two decades preceding the outbreak of World War I. Another Mohawk woman from the same community, Roberta Jamieson, served as ombudsman for the province of Ontario from 1989 to 1999. She went on to become the first female chief of the Six Nations Reserve under the elective system and later became CEO of the National Aboriginal Achievement Foundation.

Despite internal conflict, contemporary Iroquois share an immense pride in the role their ancestors played in the history of North America and a conviction of the independent place they should enjoy in the current socio-political scene in North America. As part of the ritual of condolence (as translated by pioneering Canadian anthropologist Horatio Hale [1883] 1963:125) used to install chiefs on the Confederacy Council, a speaker laments: "Oh, my grandsires! Even now that has become old what you established,—the Great League [sic]. You have it as a pillow under your heads in the ground where you are lying." But the speaker also notes "that far away in the future the Great League would endure." Despite predictions of government officials, journalists, and some anthropologists, the Haudenosaunee have endured, and the sounds of the water drum and the turtle shell rattle will continue to be heard in Iroquois communities in Canada and the United States.

NOTES

1. Most authors now distinguish between "Iroquoian," referring to members of the family of languages spoken in parts of eastern North America, and "Iroquois," which was the Confederacy of five (later six) nations. These latter people refer to themselves as *Haudenosaunee* (but found with variant spellings such as *Hotinoshonni*). Although in the past some archaeologists, anthropologists, and historians wrote of the St Lawrence Iroquois and the Ontario Iroquois, contemporary usage has replaced these and similar designations with ethnonyms such as St Lawrence Iroquoians and Ontario Iroquoians.

2. Despite this, the Iroquois have formed part of the demonology of the Euro-American and Euro-Canadian history of North America. For Americans, there is the fact that most Iroquois sided with the British and Loyalists during the American Revolution and inflicted telling blows on supporters of the Continental Congress. One might expect their loyalty as allies to the Crown would lead the Six Nations to be praised in conventional Canadian history, but instead they are demonized because of their attacks on early French colonial settlements and on the Huron towns that had substantially converted to Christianity, in the middle of the seventeenth century. These attacks involved the execution (in the Christian Jesuit view, the martyrdom) of several Jesuit priests, notably Jean de Brébeuf.

3. "Hiawatha" is the conventional spelling of this name. Mohawk chief Seth Newhouse spelled it *Ayonhwathah*. There are numerous other spellings. The American poet Henry Wadsworth Longfellow wrote the story of an Ojibwa culture hero in verse but purloined the name of the co-founder of the Iroquois Confederacy for the Algonquian-speaking hero of his poem.

4. Thayendanegea had been pursuing land issues while in London. He went in the company of Sir William Johnson's sons-in-law, Guy Johnson and Daniel Claus, who were attempting to shore up their positions in the British colonial establishment. Joseph Brant created a sensation while in London, and his portrait was painted by the prominent painter of British aristocracy, George Romney. The portrait is now owned by the National Gallery of Canada in Ottawa.

REFERENCES AND RECOMMENDED READINGS

Fenton, William N. 1998. *The Great Law and the Longhouse: A Political History of the Iroquois Confederacy.* Norman: University of Oklahoma Press. Fenton over seven decades published seminal works on Iroquois culture, as expressed in those communities where he conducted fieldwork (Allegany and Tonawanda reservations in New York and Six Nations of the Grand River in Ontario). Some Haudenosaunee, removed from times and places where he conducted his research, now express hostility toward him and his work. This is unfortunate, for Fenton had only respect and admiration for Iroquois culture. However, Fenton, unlike Morgan and Shimony, never produced a volume synthesizing his knowledge of Iroquois culture. Despite this, no serious scholar interested in Iroquois can ignore his rich, incredibly knowledgeable contributions. For more than half a century Fenton pursued an interest in the Condolence Council, which installed chiefs in the League Council, and this book links his detailed observations of actual Condolence Councils he recorded among the Six Nations on the Grand River with historic usage of the Condolence ritual over two centuries of treaty negotiations and forest diplomacy.

Hale, Horatio, ed. (1883) 1963. *The Iroquois Book of Rites.* Reprinted with an Introduction by William N. Fenton. Toronto: University of Toronto Press.

Johnston, Charles M., ed. 1964. *The Valley of the Six Nations: A Collection of Documents on the Indian Lands of the Grand River*. Toronto: The Champlain Society.

Lafitau, Joseph François. (1724) 1974–1977. *Customs of the American Indians Compared with the Customs of Primitive Times*. Edited and translated by William N. Fenton and Elizabeth L. Moore. Toronto: The Champlain Society [originally published as *Moeurs des sauvages ameriquains, comparées aux moeurs des premiers temps*]. Lafitau was a missionary to the Mohawks on the St Lawrence and here provides a strong collection of data on their culture (particularly the social structure) in the early eighteenth century.

Lex, Barbara W., and Thomas S. Abler. 2004. "Iroquois." In *Encyclopedia of Medical Anthropology*, vol. 2, edited by M. and C. Ember. New York: Human Relations Area Files and Kluwer/Plenum, 743–54. With kind permission from Springer Science+Business Media B.V.

Morgan, Lewis H. 1851. *The League of the Ho-dé-no-sau-nee or Iroquois*. Rochester: Sage. The prime source on Iroquois culture. Morgan was not a historian so the history must be taken with caution. Information was gathered with the assistance of Ely S. Parker, from Parker's home community, the Tonawanda Seneca, in the 1840s.

Richter, Daniel K. 1983. "War and Culture: The Iroquois Experience," *William and Mary Quarterly* (3rd series) 40, 4: 528–59.

Shimony, Annemarie A. 1994. *Conservativism among the Iroquois at the Six Nations Reserve*. Syracuse: Syracuse University Press. Other than Morgan, the most essential work on conservative Iroquois culture. As with Morgan, it has a local and temporal focus—the Six Nations of the Grand River in the 1950s.

Speck, Frank G. 1949. *Midwinter Rites at the Cayuga Long House*. Philadelphia: University of Pennsylvania Press.

Tooker, Elisabeth. 1970. "Northern Iroquoian Sociopolitical Organization," *American Anthropologist* 72, 1: 90–7. For this topic, this is required reading.

———. 1978. "The League of the Iroquois: Its History, Politics, and Ritual." In *Handbook of North American Indians*, vol. 15, edited by Bruce Trigger. Washington: Smithsonian. One must read this alongside Morgan and Shimony.

Wallace, Anthony F.C. 1958. "Dreams and Wishes of the Soul: A Type of Psychoanalytic Theory among the Seventeenth Century Iroquois," *American Anthropologist* 60, 1: 234–48.

———. 1970. *Death and Rebirth of the Seneca*. New York: Knopf.

Wallace, Paul A.W. 1946. *White Roots of Peace*. Philadelphia: University of Pennsylvania Press. The elder Wallace (father of Anthony F.C. Wallace) provides a readable retelling of the story of the founding of the Iroquois League.

Weaver, Sally M. 1978. "Six Nations of the Grand River, Ontario." In *Handbook of North American Indians*. Vol. 15, edited by Bruce Trigger. Washington: Smithsonian. The classic synthesis on this important community.

———. 1994a. "The Iroquois: The Consolidation of the Grand River Reserve in the Mid-Nineteenth Century, 1847–1875." In *Aboriginal Ontario: Historical Perspectives on the First Nations*, edited by Edward Rogers and Donald Smith. Toronto: Government of Ontario.

———. 1994b. "The Iroquois: The Grand River Reserve in the Late Nineteenth and Early Twentieth Centuries, 1875–1945." In *Aboriginal Ontario: Historical Perspectives on the First Nations*, edited by Edward Rogers and Donald Smith. Toronto: Government of Ontario. In her two chapters in *Aboriginal Ontario*, Weaver presents a nuanced and sensitive portrait of the changing face of the diverse community descended from those who followed Joseph Brant to the Grand River after the American Revolution.

CHAPTER 15

The Mi'kmaq: *Ta'n Mi'kmaqik Telo'ltipni'k Mi'kma'ki*—"How the People Lived in Mi'kma'ki"

Roger Lewis and Trudy Sable

In the last quarter-century there has been an increased awareness within the academic community of the need to reconceptualize its thinking to be more consistent with and inclusive of Mi'kmaw[1] perceptions of their history. More importantly, many Mi'kmaq are becoming aware of the discrepancies between whom they perceive themselves to be and what is written about them. This chapter addresses those concerns and combines the perspectives of two individuals of different heritage—one a Mi'kmaw from Nova Scotia, Roger Lewis; the other an American–Canadian of English–German descent, Trudy Sable.

While past academic discourses have provided an essential foundation for our understanding of Mi'kmaq and their culture history, they have rarely included voices and perspectives of the people about whom they are written. As well, what has been written regarding the Mi'kmaq, traditionally an oral culture, has been articulated in languages and through media that are both foreign and oblique to their way of thinking. Some writing is also based on archaeological interpretations of remnants of their material culture, plotted carefully into different time periods, attesting to whom they were as a people. Our view is that history is not just about written words and material objects but also about contexts and relationships, and movements and rhythms, as well as patterns of thinking communicated through time.

Ta'n Mi'kmaqik Telo'ltipni'k Mi'kma'ki—"How the People Lived in Mi'kma'ki" (see Lewis 2006) provides both an explicit and an alternative view of Mi'kmaw culture history, and demonstrates the value of understanding the history of the Mi'kmaq from the perspective of those who have lived and experienced it. This concept serves to address three needs: inclusivity, the need to include Mi'kmaw perceptions in academic thinking; cultural identity, the need to broaden public understanding of the Mi'kmaq as a distinct people; and cross-cultural validation, the need to encompass both Mi'kmaq and Western scientific perspectives and for both perspectives to emphasize and validate the continuity of Mi'kmaq culture, including its language, values, and settlement patterns. The difference in approaches naturally leads to conflict in determining who has authority to interpret Mi'kmaw history, how it is presented and written, and on what sources that interpretation should be based.

Through this approach, we hope to articulate the deep and complex attachment Mi'kmaq have to land and place, and how "Mi'kma'ki" is embodied within them, something that has not been well articulated to date. We will discuss how the Mi'kmaw language and expressive culture (e.g., legends, songs, dances, and pictoral art/symbols) embody this deep relationship with the land, as well as change and adapt to new conditions.

Therefore, to better understand a Mi'kmaw view of culture history, there must be a greater appreciation of language and expressive culture as ways of knowing that link the conceptual to subtle and sensory detail.

Moreover, the devastation wrought from foreign diseases, wars, and other disruptions that decimated and continue to plague the Mi'kmaw population, has persistently flavoured writings attentive to a history of cultural loss versus a history of continuity and resilience (which is not to say that the two perspectives cannot be combined). The position taken here is that the archaeological delineation of distinct cultural periods such as Paleo-Indian and Archaic may lead to confusion and conflict between members of the academy and Mi'kmaq who have their own conception of cultural history.[2] Local archaeologists and academics from the Atlantic region largely support the more inclusive recognition expressed in *Ta'n Mi'kmaqik Telo'ltipni'k Mi'kma'ki* that acknowledges continuity of ancestry despite cultural disruptions or changes in material culture.

The word *weji-sqalia'tiek* perhaps helps us come the closest we can to understanding the sense of rootedness Mi'kmaq feel for their ancestral lands. According to linguist Bernie Francis, from the Membertou First Nation in Cape Breton:

> The Mi'kmaw verb infinitive, *weji-sqalia'tiek* a concept deeply engrained within the Mi'kmaw language, a language that grew from within the ancient landscape of Mi'kma'ki. *Weji-sqalia'tiek* expresses the Mi'kmaw understanding of the origin of its people as rooted in the landscape of Eastern North America. The "we exclusive" form, *weji-sqalia'tiek*, means "we sprouted from" much like a plant sprouts from the earth. The Mi'kmaq sprouted or emerged from this landscape and nowhere else; their cultural memory resides here. (Sable and Francis 2012:2)

Another word, *ko'kmanaq*, is also important and means "our relations," "our relatives," or "our people." According to Francis, because it conveys the notion of relatedness and kinship, it also carries an implicit set of values and obligations. The extended and bilaterally related family was, and continues to be, the most important unit for the Mi'kmaq. These extended families were the basis of close-knit communities of related households. The extension of family members is based on reciprocal relationships, whether formal or informal, allows a young Mi'kmaq flexibility in residence, to live with uncles or aunts or other relatives to learn particular skills.

Personal and reciprocal relationships extend to animals and other objects considered inanimate in Western world view, such as rocks, mountains, winds, and certain plants, as will be seen below in the discussion on legends. This implies that one's relationship to the world requires a kind of respectful vigilance of the various forms of power, which in turn requires proper conduct, depending on the relationship one has with them.

This way of thinking preceded the arrival of the Europeans and survived because this world view has been communicated from one generation to another through the legends, songs, dances, and oral histories in the language of the Mi'kmaq. In recent years Mi'kmaq have asserted control and authority over their culture and the telling of their story in response to the disconnection they have come to feel within their ancestral lands.

As noted, to better understand a Mi'kmaw view of cultural history we emphasize that language and expressive culture are ways of knowing that link the conceptual to subtle and sensory detail. Together, Lewis's archaeological, environmental, and historical research and Sable's cultural/historical research on language with linguist Bernie Francis, and on legends, songs, and dances attempt to show the threads of that continuity, despite immense disruptions that occurred following European contact. Therefore, we will util-ize Mi'kmaw language and other expressive forms as a prerequisite for discussion of the culture, and show how these expressive forms embody a deep relationship to the land, while also changing and adapting to new conditions. Through this approach we hope to articulate the deep and complex attachment Mi'kmaq have to land and place, and how Mi'kma'ki is embodied within them.

Ta'n Mi'kmaqik Telo'ltipni'k Mi'kma'ki

Mi'kma'ki is the traditional homeland of more than 27,500 Mi'kmaq. Their territory is divided into in eight *sagamowits* (districts) throughout present-day Nova Scotia, Prince Edward Island, eastern and western New Brunswick, the Gaspé Peninsula, and parts of Newfoundland.

Mi'kma'ki has a long tenure of human habita-tion as well as critical land and resource use, which is divided into four cultural periods that Lewis

(2006) recently redefined from a Mi'kmaw per-spective after consultation with Elders and other advisors.

Lewis felt the need to redefine these time per-iods from a Mi'kmaw perspective as a result of the personal disconnect he experienced as a Mi'kmaw person throughout his studies and career as an archaeologist. Currently, as the ethnologist at the Nova Scotia Museum, he and his colleagues strug-gle to present accurately inclusive representations of Mi'kmaw history that do not negate Mi'kmaw ways of knowing, but rather recognize them.

Since efforts of Canadian Aboriginal peoples to redefine their own archaeological time per-iods from their own perspectives have been denounced as ill-conceived and dangerous "aborig-inalism" (McGhee 2008), it is important to point out that, in this case, renaming culture periods from a Mi'kmaw perspective does not change the archaeological taxonomy through which history

TABLE 15.1 Comparative Chronologies in Mi'kma'ki

PERIOD	RADIOCARBON YEARS[1]	CALENDAR YEARS
Sa'qewe'k L'nu'k "Ancient People" Paleo-Indians	11,500–8500 BP	13,500–10,000 BP
Mu Awsami Kejikawe'k L'nu'k "Not-so-recent People" Archaic period	8500–3000 BP	10,000–2500 BP
Kejikawe'k L'nu'k "Recent People" Woodland period and early contact era[2]	3000–300 BP	2500–400 BP
Kiskukewe'k L'nuk "Today's People" Early European contact and colonial era	1000 BP–present	900 BP–present

1. *The relationship between radiocarbon and calendar years is not constant.*

2. *Overlapping dates in last two periods reflect earliest infrequent European contact. No evidence of material culture exchange until c. 1500.*

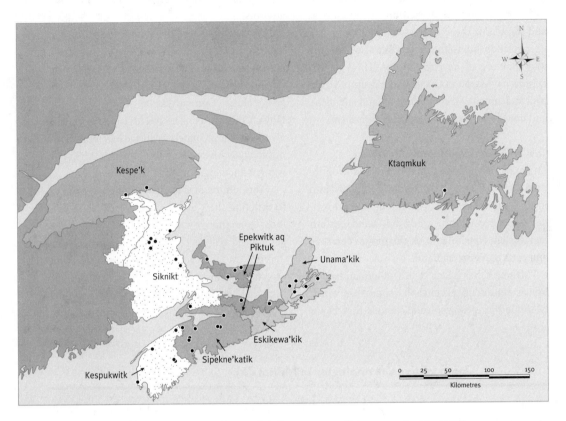

MAP 15.1 Mi'kmaw Cultural Landscape Areas and Communities (Map compiled by William Jones from concept developed by Roger Lewis with additional content input from Trudy Sable, William Jones, and Bernie Francis. Sourced by exp. Services Inc. Base map layers © 2012 ESRI. In Sable and Francis [2012:23])

Kespukwitk: "water's end"
Sipekne'katik: "ground nut place"
Eskikewa'kik: meaning uncertain, but possibly "skin dresser place"
Unama'kik: a variation of Mi'kma'ki meaning "Mi'kmaw territory," but often
   mistakenly translated as "land of fog"
Ktaqmkuk: "across the waves"
Epekwitk aq Piktuk: "laying in the waves" or "the explosive place"
Siknikt: "drainage area"
Kespe'k: possibly "the last land"

is measured and understood. Rather, it expands it, and reflects a more holistic perspective of relatedness and descent as expressed in words such as *weji-sqalia'tiek* and *ko'kmanaq*.

Several subsistence models have been developed for traditional Mi'kmaw economy. Generally they flow from a review and interpretation of seventeenth-century literature, and reinforce the idea of Mi'kmaw reciprocal relationships with their environment. That interpretation has recently been expanded by archaeological research providing further insight into Mi'kmaw economy and allowing us to show its continuity to the present.

Understanding *Ta'n Mi'kmaqik Telo'ltipni'k Mi'kma'ki* means that Mi'kmaq must have been keen and knowledgeable about the surrounding physiographic features with which they had to relate in order to sustain themselves. These include climate (regional and local), physical landscape (topography, soils, bedrock, and water), and ecological landscape (species associations, seasonality, and the availability of sustaining resources). However, these factors are inseparable from cultural use and people's interaction with their environment.

Generally, populations of Mi'kmaq tended to be located near critical land- and resource-use areas, characterized by outstanding biodiversity and availability of resources, which extended about 50 kilometres around an area of habitation. These areas were flexible and dynamic, with their use determined by generational changes in resource availability (populations/ecological cycles) as well as the seasonal availability of resources.

Aquatic and terrestrial resources, associated with myriad lakes, rivers, and mixed forests are basic to Mi'kmaw existence in Mi'kma'ki. These critical land- and resource-use areas occur along principal rivers and favour both habitation and resource exploitation. Although some academics have emphasized that Mi'kmaq ranged widely

through their territories and resource extraction was not limited to the major rivers, Lewis's research supports the consensus view that Mi'kmaq resource use nevertheless has long been focused on the principal river systems.

Lewis's examination of the strategies which facilitate land and resource use has determined that they can be modified to exploit resources in a variety of habitats. For example, four types of fish **weirs** can be found on rivers throughout southwestern Nova Scotia. Overlapping seasonal availability of aquatic resources allows for a successional harvesting of one river using different types of weirs. Fence-stake weirs at the mouths of rivers trapped larger fish such as sturgeon, bass, and shad entering the river to spawn or feed. Their use was dictated by the rise and fall of tides. Smaller V-shaped, upstream-oriented stone weirs were placed in rivers just below the heads of tides to harvest mackerel, gaspereaux (alewives), bass, and male eels. Large rectangular stone weirs with adjoining ovate traps on a river just above the head of tide were designed to harvest spawning salmon when they would still have high caloric values. Larger, V-shaped, downstream-oriented stone weirs located at the outflows of interior lakes caught the out-migrating female black eels during a four- or five-week window of opportunity in the fall dictated by fluctuating water levels and temperature. Higher water levels allowed fish to bypass the weir, while water temperatures below 5°C would render out-migrating eels torpid. The brief period available required intensive, specialized, and rapid harvesting. Generally, however, stone fish weirs were common in the smaller tidal rivers of southwestern Nova Scotia, while netting and spearing fish was more prevalent in the much larger tidal rivers of central and northern Nova Scotia.

Those same archaeological investigations reflected a coastal–inland pattern of land use on the mainland portion of Mi'kma'ki, with a reversed inland–coastal pattern of use and occupancy occurring for Unamaki (Cape Breton Island). This pattern of land and resource extends from the last period of glaciation, approximately 10,500 years ago.

While most resource use and habitation occurred along principal rivers, family networks extended at the same time further inland within the critical land- and resource-use area. The myriad rivers served as principal transportation routes for social, economic, and political interactions. For example, in Nova Scotia there are 44 principal rivers that were the focus of settlement and resource activity.

Lewis's archaeological research in Nova Scotia demonstrates that contemporary Mi'kmaw communities are not significantly displaced from traditional land and critical resource areas. This is significant given the disruptions of traditional lifeways resulting from diseases, wars, Indian settlement policies, encroachments on reserve lands during the mid- to late 1800s, the placement of generations of Mi'kmaw children in residential schools, and the centralization efforts of the 1940s. Even today, Mi'kmaq are drawn to these same rivers for subsistence activities, as established under treaty rights, though not necessarily for settlement.

Weji-sqalia'tiek

Continuity and sense of place are not just about temporal and spatial patterns of physical land use and occupancy, two terms used in contemporary land-claims hearings in which Mi'kmaq have to prove their ancestral presence in Mi'kma'ki. Sable's research into Mi'kmaw culture began in 1989 with her desire to study the dances of the Mi'kmaq, along with songs and chants, as non-verbal, unwritten forms of communication through time. She began with the early missionary documents, digging through archival research, anthropological and archaeological studies, and meeting with scholars of the culture. It soon became evident that spending time in Mi'kmaw communities, sitting

around kitchen tables sipping tea, socializing in smoky bingo halls, dancing at powwows, doing sweats, and walking and travelling through the landscape with Mi'kmaw friends was more important. Sable soon realized that much of Mi'kmaw culture was danced and sung into being, and that history was largely about contexts and patterns of relationships, and, as mentioned in the introduction, about rhythms.

Leaving the history books and looking at other means of preserving knowledge quickly led to a deep appreciation that Mi'kmaw language, dances, stories, and songs are storehouses of information. As with many oral cultures, these expressive forms act as "libraries" of valuable knowledge hidden within the memories of Elders and others, and evoked by features of the landscape as it is recalled and as it still exists.

For instance, in Sable's 1991 research into traditional land-use practices of the Mi'kmaq and Maliseet for the Canadian Parks Service (CPS, now Heritage Canada), several Mi'kmaq suggested that place names be integrated into any interpretation of the land. Place names in Mi'kmaq not only tell of features of the landscape and important resources, they also act as mnemonic devices and are associated with stories that guide peoples' conduct. It became apparent that while CPS was looking for in situ, visible evidence of land use within park boundaries, the Mi'kmaq and Maliseet placed more emphasis on the oral traditions associated with various regions, most likely corresponding to the critical resource areas outlined by Lewis. We suggest that this oral tradition is valid evidence of Mi'kmaw prehistoric presence in the area, although in land-claims hearings the courts still require physical evidence of use and occupancy.

Ironically, Mi'kmaw language, dances, stories, and songs offer probably our best access to understanding the biophysical environment of Atlantic Canada as it existed in pre-contact and early contact periods. At the same time, the "scientific"

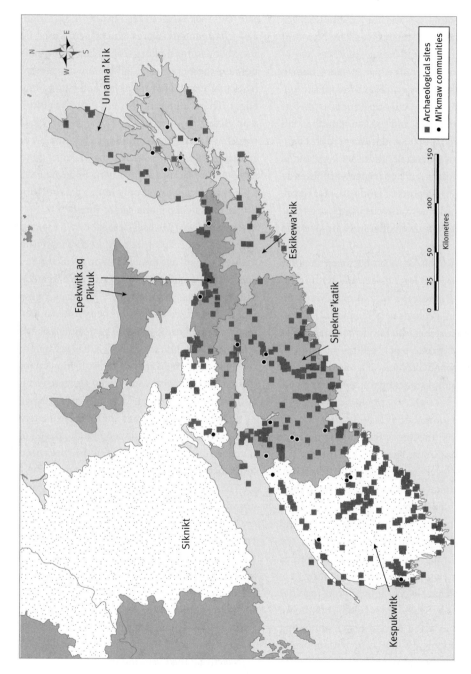

MAP 15.2 Mi'kmaw Cultural Landscape Areas, Communities, and Archaeological Sites (Map compiled by William Jones from concept developed by Roger Lewis with additional content input from Trudy Sable, William Jones, and Bernie Francis. Sourced by exp. Services Inc. Base map layers © 2012 ESRI. In Sable and Francis [2012:23])

information is embedded in a larger narrative about how Mi'kmaq reflected, perceived, and acted in the world, a world they did not experience as separate from themselves. Their sense of identity, collectively and individually, was part of a network of relationships which included human and non-human beings, visible and invisible forces, and features of the landscape such as mountains, rock formations, and the Grandmother and Grandfather rocks that are documented throughout the province. Generally these are large and of no particular shape, and associated with legends. They acted as guideposts or landmarks for travellers, were regarded as conscious beings or as having power, and were given offerings in respect and supplication.

Since 1993, Sable has been documenting how creation myths and legends abound with information about landscape formations. Based on archaeological, geological, glaciological, historical, and oral histories, she has demonstrated that legends acted as oral maps, telling travellers of the geography and resources of an area and most likely delineating distribution routes and territorial markers.

There are a number of legends that refer to sites throughout the Minas Basin (eastern Bay of Fundy) in Nova Scotia. They speak of the exploits of Kluskap, a legendary *ginap* (powerful person, trickster) who moved throughout the area, chasing moose, turning them and his dogs into islands, killing beavers and opening up their dams, and generally creating, destroying, and shaping the landscape. Throughout the area are numerous place names related to these tales. Putting geological and archaeological information together with the legends, Sable argues (1996, 2005, 2006) that the names acted as oral maps, reminding people who and where they were within a landscape that is both social and physical.

Geologically, legends associated with the Minas Basin mention places on an ancient rock forma-

tion stretching from Briar Island on the south side across the Minas Basin to Cape D'Or on the north side. This rock is rich in high-quality lithic materials—chalcedonies, agates, and jaspers—used by the Mi'kmaq for making stone blades and tools because their cryptocrystalline structures were particularly suitable for flaking and getting fine edges. These minerals also are quite beautiful, with chalcedony's swirls of colour, or jasper's deep, waxy reddish colour. Archaeologically, a number of sites in this area were used by the Mi'kmaq up to late prehistoric times for quarrying lithic material. Chalcedonies are found only in this part of Nova Scotia; native copper also can be found.

Archaeologist Michael Deal excavated a quarry site dated to the *Kejikawe'k L'nuk* (Middle to Late Ceramic period) around 1540 BP in the Scots Bay area of the Blomidon Peninsula, an area noted by Elsie Clews Parsons in the legend "Gluscap's Moose Hunt." Deal's research into this quarry site, supplemented by archaeological and geological research into the whole Minas Basin area, has led him to conclude that two distinct lithic distribution routes existed throughout this area (1989). Other research also points to large networks of material exchange in the southern Maritimes from approximately 700–1200 CE. These continued into the period of European contact. Many sites, however, have been lost to extensive erosion along the shore.

The mapping skills of the Mi'kmaq are also well documented. The seventeenth-century missionary Father Chrestien Le Clercq and M. Dièreville, a French traveller to Nova Scotia in 1699, made similar observations, also noting the use of wampum, sticks, and simple drawings to convey extensive information.

> . . . they have much ingenuity in drawing upon bark a kind of map which marks exactly all the rivers and streams of a country of which they wish to make a representation. They mark all the places

thereon exactly and so well that they make use of them successfully, and an Indian who possesses one makes long voyages without going astray. (Le Clercq [1691] [1910] 1968:136)

In fact, it was this use of rudimentary marks and drawings as mnemonic devices that led Le Clercq to develop his system of hieroglyphics with which he taught the Mi'kmaq lessons in Christianity in the Gaspé area.

The intimate relation of the Mi'kmaq to their physical world can also be seen in the extension of kinship terms to animals, stars, and other beings, as found in many legends. Numerous legends tell of animals and people being transformed, or transforming themselves, into stones, trees, mountains, and islands. In "The Two Weasels," two sisters, by choosing their favourite stars while lying awake one night, inadvertently cause the stars to transform into humans and become their husbands.

The whole way of life in Mi'kmaw culture was literally woven and encapsulated into the fabric of their clothing, painted on their canoes, wigwams, and other material items. Not only was everything children wore directly taken from nature, but motifs and animal figures painted and incised into the clothing were sources of power and attributes of their relation with the rest of the world. In her work on Mi'kmaw material culture, Ruth Holmes Whitehead of the Nova Scotia Museum discusses how porcupine quillwork, skillfully collected, dyed, and woven, adorned girls' hair and clothing. *Matachias* (ornaments made of shells, quills, beads, etc.), dew claws (vestigial digits found on some animals), and tinkler cones (small conical ornaments sewn onto clothing) of native copper all sang and danced with them as they moved through the world (1980). In other words, communication with their world was both very personal and universal at the same time, with the tiniest details expressing that relationship.

Communication of knowledge occurred throughout life. Learning from direct experience and through example and imitation, animal movements and the natural rhythms of the world included, was a constant for children. Early on they participated in the daily activities of their parents and family. Their classroom was, and in some cases still is, the world around them.

These experiences were further reinforced and expressed through stories, songs, and dances that provided children with metaphors for how to be in the world. Babies were carried on mother's backs as they went about their daily activities. When a child cried, the mother would dance and sing until the crying ceased. As they grew out of their cradle-boards, they would join in the activities according to their capacity. Nicholas Denys, a seventeenth-century French merchant who traded among and wrote extensively about the Mi'kmaq, observed, "Daughters help carry when moving camp depending on their strength. They were thereby accustomed at a young age to work, as well as to do everything they had to do, even to masticating the gum of Fir trees for sealing the seams of canoes" (Denys [1908] 1968:424). Similarly, young boys would hunt small animals and mimic the actions of men.

Mi'kmaw Elder Isabelle Knockwood writing about her life growing up in the mid-twentieth century, describes her memories of her childhood:

My mother passed on some of her traditional knowledge to me. Like other Mi'kmaw mothers, she took care to teach us things which would keep us safe.

When we were taken into the bush as tiny children we began learning about the environment from the cradle-board strapped to our mother's back or from sleeping and waking up in a hammock between two trees. As our mother walked along, we saw the changing landscapes.

Day after day, from sunrise to sunset, in all kinds of weather, the sky, the trees, the ground, and the waters are what we saw. Upon wakening in the morning, our first sight was usually the branches and leaves silhouetted against the ever-changing sky and the last thing before the dream world took over, we saw the moon and stars and the Milky Way of the night world. (1992:18–19)

Dance, whether formal or informal, suffused Mi'kmaw culture in prehistoric, proto-historic, and early contact periods. As with the legends, Sable has demonstrated that many of these dances were storehouses of multiple layers of information and meaning encapsulated in the bodily movements and choreography. Though dances could be spontaneous, many mirrored the turning of the seasons and constellations of the sky or the movement and life cycles of animals and plants, including medicinal plants.

Important values were also communicated and reaffirmed through dance and songs, such as the play between individuality and communality, gift-giving and reciprocity, honouring the lineage of oneself and others, and so forth. Abbé Pierre-Antoine-Simon Maillard, a seventeenth-century French missionary, described a very lengthy dance during an all-night feast that included orations regaling the host, long recitations of personal ancestries, silences, smoking the pipe, and alternating male and female dances (1758:12–15).

Joey Gould of the Apaqtnkek (Afton) First Nation community described dance competitions of a celebration dance, Ko'jua, during the annual St Anne's Day celebrations in the 1950s. St Anne, the grandmother of Jesus, became the patron saint of the Mi'kmaq following their conversion to Catholicism, and she continues to be regarded as their own grandmother. Each August, Mi'kmaq congregate at Chapel Island, Merrigomish, Restigouche, and other sites for a large celebration that include carrying St Anne's statue in a procession across the island.

On Sunday evenings, there would be a Ko'jua competition to see who would "take the Ko'jua home." Dancers would get up on the stage and start competing to see who was the best dancer, and who could take the Ko'jua home to their reserve. Joey said: "As soon as I heard people hollering at the dancers, "It's going to Eskasoni, It's going to Membertou, It's going to Nyanza—nobody would mention Wycocomaugh—then that would give me a feeling to get up there . . . I'm going to beat them all. As soon as I started dancing my style, I could hear my people from my reserve and even from Eskasoni where I have relatives, they would start calling, "it's going to Wycocomaugh. It's going to Wycocomaugh." You'd dance the Ko'jua until you just tired out and can't dance anymore. I think that's the way you'd compete. You started and go out on stage until you can't dance anymore. (Joey Gould, personal interview with Trudy Sable, Feb. 1990)

Dance competitions between powerful *ginap* occur in the legends. Individual strength and the survival of communities, often consisting of extended kin networks, worked hand in hand. As well, there is still a dance ring on Chapel Island where the Grand Council would meet. The *Neskewet* was a formal dance done during these meetings, remembered by Elders into the twenty-first century. For example, Dr Margaret "Granny" Johnson (1915–2010) of Eskasoni as a young girl living on Chapel Island mischievously peeked under the edge of the *wi'kuom* (wigwam) to watch the council gatherings.

Like stories, dance contexts changed over time as new cultural influences were adopted. The Roman Catholic Church played a primary role in discouraging dance, particularly shamanic ones as priests assumed the role of spiritual power brokers. However, like stories, certain cultural themes and values endured. *Pestie'wa'taqtimk*, the "Naming Ceremony," was done on designated days throughout the Christmas season. This was a Christian ceremony, likely introduced by missionaries, which celebrated the names of saints. People would go from house to house giving gifts to those who had the name of that day's saint. After offering a gift to the person whose name was being celebrated, the visiting group would enter the house and dance the Ko'jua. This dance was an offering in exchange for food provided by the host. Similarly, at powwows on Mi'kmaq reserves, the dancers are said to be giving energy to the drummers and vice versa. At the end of every powwow is a gift-giving ceremony in thanks to all who helped host it.

Sable has also demonstrated how Mi'kmaw chants mirror the rhythms and sounds of the natural world in much the same way that the dances do. There is a snake song, a wind song, a pine needle song, an eagle song, a toad song, and many others. However, chants and songs held a power far beyond mere mimicry. They were a means of communicating with the natural world. Frank Speck documented Penobscot men canoeing across Penobscot Bay, "The singer tempered his voice to follow the pitching of the canoe as it mounted wave after wave. He said that the boat rode the waves much more easily while the old man was singing" (Speck [1940]1985:167).

The Mi'kmaw language itself reflects a view of an interdependent world in constant motion. The nineteenth-century Baptist missionary Silas Rand wrote the following description of the Mi'kmaw language:

> The language of the Indians is very remarkable. One would think it must be exceedingly barren, limited in inflection, and crude; but just the reverse is the fact—it is copious, flexible and expressive. Its declension of nouns and conjugation of verbs are as regular as the Greek, and twenty times as copious. The full conjugation of one Micmac verb will fill quite a large volume; in its construction and idiom it differs widely from the English. . . . The verb is emphatically the word in Micmac. Whole sentences, and long ones too, occur constantly, formed wholly of verbs. All adjectives of the animate gender are real verbs, and are conjugated through mood and tense, person and number. . . . Even the numerals are verbs, and any noun can assume the form and nature of a verb without difficulty. ([1894] 1971:xxxiv, xxxvii)

One of the most distinguishing factors about the Mi'kmaw language, as noted by Rand, is that it is verb-based. The verb is the focus of the language, with prefixes and suffixes added to determine gender, tense, plurality, animacy, and inanimacy. This focus on the verb, and the many suffixes that can be added to it, allow for extraordinary adaptability, breadth, and creativity of expression.

Mi'kmaw language reflects a universe in a continuous state of flux, ever-changing and non-static. For instance, Mi'kmaw linguist Bernie Francis explains that all the colours are intransitive verbs that can be conjugated. The translation of *maqtew'k* ("black") means "in the process of being black," implying that there is no fixed state of blackness, but rather a stage in a process that could change. The fluid nature of reality can be seen through the many words for "creator," each one describing some particular quality or process. None of these words are nouns that connote one central being as a source of creation; they are transitive verbs conveying different *processes* of creation. They can be conjugated 400 different ways, and can move and change constantly. This implies the relative nature of any particular form, and its interdependent relationship with all other forms.

In the 1970s Francis and linguist Doug Smith developed a Mi'kmaw orthography, revising earlier writing systems developed by missionaries. The work of these early missionaries is valuable documentation of linguistic change and continuity over time, and was combined with the analysis of contemporary speakers in developing the new orthography. The Smith–Francis orthography is widely accepted, although coexisting with other orthographies.

Francis, during a taped session at a Native Council of Nova Scotia award ceremony for his and Smith's work, described how he as a Mi'kmaw speaker experienced the difference between the Mi'kmaw and English languages:

> We find it (Mi'kmaq) seems to cut up reality differently, as every language cuts up reality in a certain way. Mi'kmaq does it as well, and very different from English in that it seems to cut it up less in my mind. And it seems to reflect reality in a way that the English language, I find, fails to do. That is, it just seems to demonstrate in its verb-like way that the world is in constant motion, constant flux. That is one major difference I find. The second thing is that even the so-called nouns in Mi'kmaq, I realize now, that you don't have to dig too far to realize that these are what I call now recycled verbs and they

just sort of changed an ending on them and made them into nouns. Words like *ikan* and *aqan* are suffixes that usually come at the end of words, which gives them that noun-like quality. But I have no difficulty showing that these are old verbs. . . . I tend to picture it in the sense that the English language seems to take a photograph of the world—a still photograph—whereas Mi'kmaq is more like a videocamera. (Sable, Smith, and Francis, video interview, 30 Sept. 1994)

In the same interview, Smith also mentioned that "in the Mi'kmaw language, there is an inherent dynamism or movement that Mi'kmaw speakers themselves are always aware of."

Mi'kmaw is said to be **holophrastic**, compressing multiple meanings into a single word. An image that might take many sentences in English to write can be expressed in one word or one movement. There may be implicit meanings not conveyed in the literal translation of the Mi'kmaw word.[3] Eleanor Johnson described how frightening it was to be told that she had to write a 1,000-word essay for a university class. "I come from a one-word language where one of my words is a whole sentence in your language. Can you imagine how it felt to write trying to think out 1,000 words?" (Johnson 1995).

This means that the profundity of Mi'kmaq is often lost when translated into English. Furthermore, the conventional assumptions of objective and subjective experience are inherent in English, and so translation distorts the dynamic and interdependent world view offered by the Mi'kmaw language (although, again, these are features that plague most translations).

Francis has also described how the reality of these linguistic differences between Mi'kmaw and English is seen daily in the courts as Mi'kmaq on trial miss the simple meaning of a preposition, a legal concept, or even the notion of the word "guilty." Similar disconnects happen in land-claims proceedings as Mi'kmaq are asked to identify exactly where they used and occupied a place.

As these examples show, the Mi'kmaq do not view their environment as an inanimate, unconscious object, but rather as a network of relationships which they mirror and communicate with through various forms of cultural expression. The world is a network of relationships that requires attention, proper protocol, and knowledge of the various powers that be. At the same time, what Westerners would view as "practical information" was embedded inseparably within these expressive forms.

The Period of "Aggressive Civilization"

Maillard's description of the long feast orations recounting the accomplishments of the dancer's ancestors reinforces the importance of lineage and personal and collective identity. Yet, we also have to reconcile the sense of lineage and identity with a young woman's dream of a small island floating toward Mi'kma'ki with what she perceived to be bears climbing the masts. This dream was later interpreted as foreseeing the coming of Europeans to Mi'kma'ki, and the devastating repercussions of colonization on the Mi'kmaq over the next 400 years.

Faced with shifting demographics from reserve-based communities to an ever-growing urban population, Mi'kmaq currently struggle with their sense of connectedness to a physical place while still hoping and fighting for cultural continuity for future generations. These contemporary struggles arise out of what has been termed the period of "aggressive civilization" (Davin 1879), particularly with the formation of reserves, the creation of the Indian Act and associated policy, and especially

the "cultural bombs" dropped on the Mi'kmaq—dispossession of lands and resources, disease and starvation, the Indian Act, residential schools, and centralization (Christmas 2009).

The "contact" period is an obvious turning point in any history, but for the Mi'kmaq its beginnings were almost ephemeral. For centuries, starting with the arrival of Vikings at L'anse aux Meadows in Newfoundland around 1000 CE, there were numerous fishing, exploratory, and merchant enterprises visiting the area, some even setting up seasonal fish- and whale-processing sites. Maps of the Atlantic region from the fifteenth to the seventeenth century are dotted with Portuguese, Basque, French, and English names, as cartographers sought to document the landscape reported by itinerant sailors.

In 1534, the first documented contact between the Mi'kmaq and Europeans occurred when Jacque Cartier, who first claimed "Canada" for France, entered the Bay of Chaleur. The Mi'kmaq who went out to meet the ships in canoes seemed familiar with the rules of trade, and knew some trade language or pidgin.

More significant change began with colonization. Pierre du Gua, Sieur du Monts under Royal Charter of Henry IV of France, arrived in 1604, establishing Acadia as a colony. Acadia encompassed the entire eastern seaboard from present-day New Jersey to Cape Breton. Initially landing on St Croix Island (on the border between Maine and New Brunswick), and then after a disastrous winter moving to Port Royal, Nova Scotia in 1605, du Monts sought to establish a fur-trade monopoly. As with many mercantile expeditions of the time, spiritual conversion went hand in hand with colonial expansion. A religious fervour following the Wars of Religion (1562–98) had seized the ruling classes, and empires competed for both material wealth and the souls of Indigenous peoples. Merchants, seeking monopolies on the lucrative fur trade, were required to carry out a holy mission as well, as did du Monts and his companion and later successor, Seigneur de Poutrincourt.

While the great Saqmaw Membertou, from Kespukwitk district, and his band established friendly relations with the new colonists, du Monts succumbed to rivalries with other merchants, and the subsequent loss of sponsorship forced him to abandon the colony. When, in 1610, Poutrincourt returned to re-establish the colony, he discovered Membertou and his band had safeguarded it. As historian John Reid points out, without the Mi'kmaq the fledgling colony would not have survived (1987). In fact, the Mi'kmaq could easily have allowed the French to perish, letting scurvy and starvation take their toll.

However, disease had already begun to alter Mi'kmaq society, though historians disagree about the pre-contact population (estimates range from 11,900 to 35,000) as well as when its decimation began. The Jesuit Pierre Biard wrote that Membertou, thought to be over 100 years at the time of contact, remembered the Mi'kmaq population being as "thick as the hairs upon his head" in his youth. Membertou and Mesomoet, the chief of the La Have Mi'kmaq, are believed to have died of dysentery, while 60 others at La Have are thought to have died from the parasite-borne respiratory diseases pleurisy and severe tonsillitis (Wickens 2002:32).

Decimation of Mi'kmaq populations through diseases such as typhoid, dysentery, and smallpox has been estimated at between 70 to 90 per cent, a loss of life now unimaginable and unacceptable. Today, diabetes and cancer are the major killers of Mi'kmaq.

Poutrincourt and his colonial colleagues spread more than disease. Accompanied by two Jesuit missionaries, Edmond Massé and Pierre Biard, a condition imposed on Poutrincourt by his sponsor Mme de Guercheville, Membertou and his band were baptized in 1610. Membertou was given the Christian name Henri, after King Henri IV of France.

In 1613, Poutrincourt returned to Port Royal only to find it in ruins after an attack by the British admiral Samuel Argall. While he abandoned Port Royal shortly thereafter and returned to France with most of the colonists, some remained, moving to Cape Sable. Intermarriage became common. Throughout the century, other newcomers followed, expanding their settlements from Port Royal to the border with New Brunswick. These early Acadians posed no threat to the Mi'kmaq. The reciprocal exchange of cultural practices included music and dance traditions, clothing styles, and marriage vows. The majority population in both communities was Catholic. Many Mi'kmaq today bear the names of these early French Acadian colonists, such as Meuse, Labrador, Doucette, and Louis.

A series of wars between France and England starting in the 1650s had a profound impact upon both Mi'kmaq and Acadians. Parts of Mi'kma'ki/Acadie were negotiated back and forth with the signing of each of the nine treaties, culminating in the Treaty of Paris in 1763, ceding all French-claimed territories to the English. Mi'kmaq featured strongly in these wars, often being entreated by both French and English with gifts, including guns, medals, blankets, great coats, and a variety of "gewgaws" to assist in their efforts.

Throughout these wars missionaries played an influential role as intermediaries between the French and Mi'kmaq, as well as between the Acadians and English. Abbé Maillard, who spoke Mi'kmaw, established missions throughout Nova Scotia, including the beloved St Anne's mission on Chapel Island in 1754. He also documented numerous events, including gift-giving and exchange ceremonies between the Mi'kmaq and French, as well as between the Mi'kmaq and British. Abbé Jean-Louis Le Loutre, who came to Acadie in 1737 to assist Maillard, featured strongly throughout those tenuous war years as well.

Historians writing about this era generally leave the impression that following the defeat of the French at Louisbourg in 1758, Aboriginal relations had little further significance for the non-Native settlement history of the Atlantic region. Contrary to that assumption, several peace and friendship treaties were signed between the British and Mi'kmaq throughout those decades, most notably the Treaty of 1752 (the Treaty of Peace and Friendship), which set the stage for Mi'kmaq rights and title in the Atlantic provinces today. Often lost within these histories is recognition that Mi'kmaw leadership had the foresight to see the changing political climate in the colony and to lay a foundation for protecting future rights.[4]

However, as we shall see, these rights were not readily recognized. The arrival of Loyalists in 1783, following the British loss of the War of Independence to the Americans, had a tremendous impact on the region, doubling the population. This resulted in settlements expanding into lands rich in timber and marine and agricultural resources, and to the creation of New Brunswick as a distinct colony in 1784. The early 1800s, particularly after the Napoleonic wars ended in 1815, saw the Mi'kmaw population being relegated to remote and unproductive lands, as settlers—English, Irish, Scots, Welsh, and others—along with deserters from the British military, began to settle what they perceived as unsettled tracts of richly timbered lands.

This displacement and encroachment upon traditional Mi'kmaq lands was well underway as the "golden age" of ship building began. Timber mills soon began sprouting up along principal waterways and ancient travel routes of the Mi'kmaq and Maliseet, including the Saint John and the Miramichi Rivers in New Brunswick.

By 1807, Nova Scotia had been divided into 12 districts, with an Indian agent assigned to each to oversee Indian Affairs and report conditions back to the colonial government's Indian Commissioner. New Brunswick was far less organized, with little control exerted over the settlement and outright squatting on Mi'kmaq lands.

The "plight" of the Mi'kmaq became a concern of the newly established Indian agents, as the consequences of colonization became evident. Diseases and poverty racked communities, along with another introduced scourge, alcoholism. One agent, Moses Perley, saw the assimilation and civilization of the Mi'kmaq as a means to counter these conditions. With the consent of Lieutenant-Governor William Colebrooke, he toured New Brunswick reserves in 1841 to conduct a census and to investigate settler encroachment. In his extensive report, he recommended the development of permanent settlements for the Mi'kmaq, assistance in developing agriculture, and education in integrated schools. Although he recognized the need for gradual acculturation and for Mi'kmaq to continue their traditional hunting and fishing, he regarded these activities as merely recreational, ones that could readily be replaced by agriculture (Bock 1966:18).

Furthermore, Mi'kmaq had to petition the government for lands, as squatters made liberal use of what they claimed were unoccupied lands. In 1841, three chiefs—Joseph Malie, François Labauve, and Pierre Basquet, from the Miramichi area of New Brunswick—travelled to England to see their "Noble Mother the Queen" Victoria. They went to protest unjust land settlements and to challenge the appointment of Thomas Burnaby as chief by the colonial government. The queen did not receive them, but charged the colonial secretary, Lord Stanley, to present each chief with a medal, to send them back home quickly, and finally, to ask New Brunswick authorities to take care of their Indians (Bock 1966:18). Similarly, colonial documents show that in 1847, Louis Luxey, then chief of the Queens County Mi'kmaq, petitioned the governor to be allowed to fish the rivers and lakes at Fairy Lake (now Kejimkujik) Reserve as they always had, but never received a response. Coincidentally, this land was considered prime land for the Queen's timber (Crown land).

Confederation in 1867 had a profound effect upon Mi'kmaq. The Dominion of Canada established under the British North America Act resulted in the federal government having exclusive responsibility for Native people. The Indian Act of 1868 led to the appointment of Indian agents, the creation of reserves, and chiefs being appointed by the government. The early to mid-1880s saw colonial Indian agents governing and dictating the local affairs of Mi'kmaq. During this time there was also new and sustained interest in the acquisition of and encroachment upon what little was left of traditional Mi'kmaq hunting and land-use areas. Along with encroachment came game laws and regulations. In the 1920s, travel writer Clarissa Archibald Dennis documented Chief Louis Luxey of Yarmouth County, a descendant of the previously mentioned Chief Louis Luxey, telling how the enactment of provincial game laws limited their moose harvest to one animal annually. He remembered how only 60 to 70 years earlier, there were many encampments of 100 people or more able to hunt moose, bear, and other animals and follow their ancestral ways. Families now had hardly enough to feed their families (Dennis 1923).

Chief Luxey also recalled how his people used to be healthy, collecting their own medicines, and living to be 100. Now, due to encroachment on their lands, they could not collect their own medicines. Worse yet, the Elders viewed the medicine of the new doctors as poison, a view many Elders still hold today.

The building of railway lines, one of the primary conditions for Nova Scotia and New Brunswick joining Confederation in 1867, also had a profound impact on traditional Mi'kmaw lifeways and economy. These railways became the new steel "rivers" connecting townships and markets otherwise isolated. Sam Gloade, a decorated World War I Mi'kmaw hero, talked about his father and grandfather hunting their last caribou prior to that war. Gloade cited the negative impact on caribou migration of the railroad's construction between Middleton to Bridgewater, Nova Scotia, because it crossed the migration route (Raddall 1944).

Railways also allowed access to the interior, where big game and fish could be taken by "gentlemen sportsmen." Mi'kmaq, with their knowledge of the forests and waterways and the movement of game, became valued guides to these hunters and fishers. Although it was a relatively lucrative means of subsistence for Mi'kmaq, the cost to animal populations was often high. For instance, in Yarmouth County, Nova Scotia, Lord Dunraven left hundreds of slaughtered caribou to rot in what is still known as Dunraven Bog. There was also a kind of romanticism in having a Mi'kmaw guide; Gloade was brought as a guide to the mountains of Montana even though he knew nothing of the landscape or animals there.

As circumstances shifted, Mi'kmaq adapted to their changing world. Margaret Johnson is an outstanding example of how Mi'kmaq survived through the nineteenth and twentieth centuries, prior to the establishment of social assistance. Her mother, a red-headed, freckled Irish woman who was adopted by Mi'kmaq after being abandoned as a baby, grew up speaking only Mi'kmaw. She married a Mi'kmaw named Michael Paul and lived in Barrahead, now Chapel Island First Nation, raising her family. They farmed, fished, made baskets and axe handles, and traipsed the roads of the Atlantic provinces selling their wares door to door. They were Catholics and their children went to the community school, as well as joining in the many activities of their community, including dances and an "old-fashion" ball game. Johnson was herself an accomplished step dancer, winning a dancing contest in Halifax in 1975. She bore 14 children in two marriages, eventually moving to Eskasoni where she died in 2010 at the age of 95. She became known as "Dr Granny" after receiving an honor-

FIGURE 15.1 Judge Christopher Paul and his family. Mr Paul died at Shubenacadie in 1905 and his wife, Margaret (Babaire), in 1902. (Ethnology Collection, Nova Scotia Museum)

ary doctorate from St Francis Xavier University in 1994, acknowledging her contribution to Mi'kmaw culture. But despite her example, it must be noted that the general life span of Mi'kmaq today is far shorter, with many dying in middle age due to cancer, diabetes, heart disease, and other ailments.

Residential School

Assimilation was the governmental policy and practice of the day and continues to the present. Nowhere was this practice more painfully enacted than in the educational policies that created residential schools. Dr "Granny" Johnson, like many Mi'kmaq in the twentieth century, saw a number of her children "survive" residential school, while others did not.

The federal government developed an Indian residential school policy as a result of the Bagot Commission of 1842. In 1846, a report was published based on the ideas of Egerton Ryerson,

"father" of public education in Ontario from 1844 to 1876. The Gradual Civilization Act soon followed in 1857. Ryerson's ideas formed the basis for future directions in policy for Indian education:

> There is a need to raise the Indians to the level of the whites . . . and take control of land out of Indians hands. The Indian must remain under the control of the Federal Crown rather than provincial authority, that effort to Christianize the Indians and settle them in communities be continued, . . .that schools, preferably manual labour ones, be established under the guidance of missionaries. . . . Their education must consist not merely training of the mind, but of a weaning from the habits and feelings of their ancestors, and the acquirements of the language, art and customs of civilized life. (www.shannonthunderbird.com/residential_schools.htm)

Such statements, unacceptable today, represent a "we are civilized—they are not" attitude of not only early colonial governments but of those that followed. In 1879, Nicholas Flood Davin, a lawyer, journalist, and Member of Parliament, produced the *Report on Industrial Schools for Indians and Half-Breeds*, also known as the Davin Report. He advised John A. Macdonald's federal government to institute a residential school policy. These schools were administered by various churches, which lobbied the government for control of the schools as a means of religious conversion and increased influence. For example, the residential school in Shubenacadie, Nova Scotia, was administered by Oblates of Mary Immaculate (OMI) and the Sisters of Charity and served all Atlantic Canada. From 5 February 1930 until 26 June 1966, more than 1,000 Mi'kmaw children attended it.

FIGURE 15.2 Mi'kmaq family c. 1890, no provenance. (Ethnology Collection, Nova Scotia Museum)

Parents unable to feed their children due to poverty, illness, or loss of a spouse assumed that their children would be cared for spiritually and physically if sent to residential schools. They believed it would be a temporary solution, not realizing their children were going to be incarcerated for years with no option to leave. Not only was the negative impact on Mi'kmaw families astounding, this institution weakened the social structure of Mi'kmaw communities in numerous ways.

The regimented structure of the school forbade any expression of Mi'kmaw culture and identity, including speaking their language. Both pedagogy and curriculum were based on Victorian European concepts and values, which were contrary to Mi'kmaw teaching styles of observation of Elders and the natural surroundings. Children were separated from their siblings, often maltreated and punished with little provocation, and sexually abused, with many suffering ill health and quietly dying of unknown reasons. In fact, high rates of ill health and death of up to 24 per cent of students were openly acknowledged, and another 18 per cent suffered ill health after leaving school. Recommendations by the medical examiner of the Department of the Interior to improve conditions were not instituted, primarily due to economic concerns, particularly under the rule of Superintendent of Indian Education Duncan

Campbell Scott (Neu and Therrien 2003:104–206). Graves near residential schools are just now being discovered and the reasons for death determined.

This entire residential school process was a failed social experiment to assimilate Mi'kmaq, which unfortunately disrupted the roles and responsibilities of Mi'kmaw Elders, parents, and youth and left three generations of Mi'kmaq unable to speak their language. The cultural values and norms of the Mi'kmaq were no longer passed from Elder to parent and to child. Such values and norms are critical for the continued identity of a distinct people, which, of course, was exactly the point. Today many of those who experienced the residential schools are scarred both emotionally and physically and consider themselves to be survivors. In 2008, a settlement was reached to recompense Indigenous peoples in Canada for their suffering, and a healing process has begun under the federal government's Truth and Reconciliation Commission.

Centralization

Surprisingly little is written about centralization, though it is considered by Mi'kmaq as one the most destructive policies ever enforced by the Canadian government. Prior to centralization, Mi'kmaq lived on scattered reserves. In Nova Scotia prior to 1942, there were 2,100 Mi'kmaq living in approximately 20 locations. One such reserve was Franklin Manor in Cumberland County, where the population fluctuated between 82 and 102. They were employed in nearby lumber mills and on farms, as well as in making and selling baskets and axe handles, and farming their own land. Some spoke only Mi'kmaw, and one, Sam Knockwood, walked the land blind. They also made some of the finest hockey sticks in the country.

The idea of centralization was put forth as early as 1918 by H.J. Bury, a senior federal official in Nova Scotia, who saw that the creation of a few large reserves would simplify administration. The policy was finally implemented as a cost-saving device in 1942 as the expense of wartime efforts escalated. Vacated reserves would be sold off.

Dire warnings were issued against the wisdom of the move, citing lack of resources, such as timber for proposed lumber mills and for housing, wildlife to hunt for food, arable land for farming, and employment opportunities since these reserves were in remote locations. Ben Christmas, chief of Membertou Reserve, along with other Mi'kmaw leaders, accurately foresaw the future of their people if centralization was enacted. They all predicted increased lawlessness, social problems, and unemployment due to the lack of resources to support an increase in population and the remoteness of the locations.

Indian agents and missionaries threatened people into moving by saying they would not receive any services or support if they remained on their home reserves. Many Mi'kmaq, upon returning from World War II, were told they could receive the normal grants for veterans under the Veterans' Land Act only if they moved to Eskasoni, Shubenacadie, or Big Cove, the three reserves designated for centralization. Building funds on the other reserves had been curtailed.

Some people moved in the winter with just tents; some refused outright. Those who moved found the quality of houses poor. Some were only shells, the wood was often green and shrank when

---

BOX 15.1 Early Days in Eskasoni after Centralization

Me and husband first lived in States. It was in 1942 when we came back from Portland. We were originally from Whycocomagh. When we came back, nobody was in Whycocomagh, only one family. We were told older people needed help. A teacher named Alex MacDonald called John and told him he would get a job as a truck driver. He got paid thirty-five cents an hour. My in-laws wanted to move to Eskasoni, so we followed them. We were told we would get new houses, but the houses were only tar paper shacks.

My husband drove people here to Eskasoni. We would get a food order, called one or two rations. One ration was eight dollars, and two was twelve dollars. Then we would take it to the community store, the old band office. We got our stuff at the community store. The agent got a lot of money that we were supposed to get. But he sent it back or kept it. It was a hard life. They treated Indians very badly.

Our house was very cold. They could have helped our people but they didn't. The agents got cows that were supposed to [have been for] our people. But they didn't [get the cows], they kept them. If you got water for your house, you had to pay yourself. I went to ask for help, but this woman told me, "I heard that story before," so she didn't help me. Even the doctor was mean, and would throw people out. The older people could not communicate because they didn't understand any English. Older people were really poor, because they could not ask for help. The houses were only shells with a wood burning stove. The people that first came in Castle Bay lived in tents until they got a tar paper shack. It is hard to believe we lived in those conditions.

—Annie Claire Googoo as interviewed by Florence Dennis

www.cbu.ca/mrc/oral-histories#annieclaire-googoo

it dried, leaving gaps in the structure, and there was no insulation. Promised land for livestock and farming could be miles away from the homes, and visions of lumber mills employing people soon wilted as timber reserves diminished and the mills went silent.

Centralized reserves simply did not have the land base to support the increased local population. By the end of 1948, the failure of the scheme began to be noticed, though Indian Affairs continued to promote it as a positive and original social experiment creating model communities. As such it was called the first social experiment of its kind in Canada (Neu and Therrien 2003).

Before the government realized its efforts were a failure, half the Mi'kmaw population had moved to Eskasoni and Shubenacadie. By end of 1948, 100 houses had been built at Eskasoni and 80 at Shubenacadie, but these numbers were short of what was needed. Welfare costs had risen, unemployment was high, little or no schooling existed, and traditional governance was compromised by an increasing number of federally supported institutions now dealing with the social problems that arose.

From Centralization to Institutionalization

As a result of the failure of centralization, a new and more insidious social experiment in the form of social welfare institutions arose, causing what Frances Widdowson and Albert Howard (2008) cynically describe as the "Aboriginal Industry." What we are terming the institutionalization of reserves has created an even greater dependence on the government and has further undermined traditional family networks, forms of governance, and values. Following centralization, employment of Mi'kmaq on reserves increasingly came from federal institutions such as Health Canada, Family and Child Services, Social Assistance, the Department of Education, the RCMP, Service Canada, Economic

Development, Resource Management, and so on. The governance of reserves was defined by the Indian Act, and the reserve government became the largest employer of Mi'kmaq. This was even more disempowering and hindered hopeful aspirations for true self-governance.

An unexpected rallying cry for Aboriginal peoples throughout Canada in 1969 came following the articulation of Prime Minister Pierre Trudeau's vision of a just society in the form of the White Paper on Indian Policy. Trudeau's proposals would wipe out the special status of Aboriginal peoples. These proposals and the Aboriginal responses they generated are dealt with elsewhere (see Chapter 26). The point here is that in Mi'kma'ki, Mi'kmaw organizations came to realize the implications of gaining a larger voice within the larger framework of Aboriginal politics.

To respond to the structural infiltration of federal institutions on reserves to deal with "social" problems, the Union of Nova Scotia Indians (UNSI) drafted and presented to the government of Canada the *Nova Scotia Micmac Aboriginal Rights Position Paper*: "The Pre-contact History Factor." This paper essentially expressed this concept of *Ta'n Mi'kmaqik Telo'ltipni Mi'kma'ki*—"How Mi'kmaq Lived in Mi'kmakik," a concept that had been largely overlooked in the context of Mi'kmaw rights and title. Central to that paper was the UNSI resolution that the Canadian government must recognize and compensate the Mi'kmaq for Aboriginal title as the only avenue through which Mi'kmaq of Nova Scotia could achieve economic and social justice.

The federal government initially rejected this outright, but it sowed the seed for future legal and political challenges such as the Donald Marshall case, by reinforcing traditional use of resources and the occupation of traditional use resource areas. Marshall, a Mi'kmaw, was charged with three offences under the federal fishery legislation for selling eels, fishing without a licence, and fishing in a closed season with illegal nets. As the result of the *Marshall* cases (1999, 2000), the courts recognized and re-established Mi'kmaw rights to moderate livelihood through fishing but with an ironic qualifier—that the onus was on the Mi'kmaq to prove regular use and occupancy of their ancestral lands in future negotiation processes. Oral histories, so far, are not recognized as valid proof of those rights.

A Tripartite Process resulted from these court challenges, establishing a federal, provincial, and Mi'kmaw negotiation process to resolve outstanding rights and title issues. Prior to that, in 1998, Canada, Nova Scotia, and the Assembly of Chiefs had also agreed to pursue a "made-in-Nova Scotia process" to deal with outstanding treaty, title, and Aboriginal rights questions in Nova Scotia. Though the "made-in-Nova Scotia process" appears to be merely a regional treaty negotiations process, there are broader implications for Mi'kmaq throughout Mi'kma'ki and for Aboriginal groups everywhere.

These discussions could affect Mi'kmaw rights to fish, rights to be involved in forestry, rights to land and resources, and to real self-determination and governance with the goal of improving the lives of all Mi'kmaq. For example, the Assembly of Nova Scotia Chiefs has assumed the role coordinating land-claims negotiation strategies in Nova Scotia.

The Native Women's Association was yet another organization which arose in the 1970s to challenge Clause 12(1)b in the Indian Act, which took away the legal status of Aboriginal women and their children if they married non-status men. This was not true for Aboriginal men. The act virtually exiled these women, denying them the right to reside on reserves. In 1985, those challenges resulted in amendments to the Indian Act

---

BOX 15.2 Made-in-Nova Scotia Process

The Made-in-Nova Scotia Process is the forum for the Mi'kmaq, Nova Scotia and Canada to resolve issues related to Mi'kmaq treaty rights, Aboriginal rights, including Aboriginal title, and Mi'kmaq governance. The participants are the Mi'kmaq of Nova Scotia as represented by the Assembly of Nova Scotia Mi'kmaq Chiefs, the provincial government and the federal government.

The Process began with the signing of the Umbrella Agreement in June 2002, in which the Parties confirmed their intention to begin a negotiation process to address these issues. On February 23, 2007, the Parties signed the Mi'kmaq-Nova Scotia-Canada Framework Agreement, which outlines procedures that will guide the negotiations and the topics to be covered.

The Framework Agreement states that the objectives of the Process are "to create stable and respectful relationships and to reconcile the respective interests of the Parties through a Mi'kmaq of Nova Scotia Accord that sets out the manner in which the Mi'kmaq of Nova Scotia will exercise constitutionally protected rights respecting land, resources and governance, to the extent the issues are dealt with in the Accord".

—Mi'kmaq Rights Initiative http://mikmaqrights.com/page.asp?ID=16

through Bill C-31. Ostensibly, these women were given their status back and could return to their home communities with full status and benefits.

Bill C-31 redefined who is and who is not "Indian." Since Bill C-31, all such people are registered and defined under Section 6 of the Indian Act. A child with two status "Indian" parents falls under the regulations of Section 6(1). A child with only one "Indian" parent is registered under Section 6(2). Those registered under Section 6(2) must marry a status Indian to pass status on to their children (their children will lose their status if they marry a non-status Indian or person not of Aboriginal descent).

A May 2009 *Toronto Star* article by immigration reporter Nicholas Keung, entitled "Status Indians Face Threat of Extinction," pointed out that in some communities no children will be born with status after 2012, as a consequence of literally no person with Aboriginal status marrying another such person. Keung argues that the amendments to the Indian Act continue to be designed to assimilate and extinguish the rights of Canada's Aboriginal peoples.

The view that for many Aboriginal peoples Bill C-31 is a form of legislated extinction was affirmed in the *MacIver v. Canada* case in the Supreme Court of British Columbia in 2009, which deemed the existing requirements under Section 6 to be discriminatory and instructed the government to make changes.

Emerging from these court cases and the subsequent negotiation processes, a new nation-to-nation approach was taken by the Mi'kmaq as a sovereign government. But, in order to become truly a self-governing nation, Mi'kmaq have recognized the need to develop and implement an effective self-government strategy to counter institutional dependency. On Treaty Day, October 2008, the Mi'kmaq signed a proclamation of nationhood in Province House in Halifax. In March 2009, they met to determine what form nationhood would take. Instead of 13 separate bands, for instance,

resources would be pooled and Mi'kmaq would negotiate nation-to-nation on equal footing with the federal and provincial governments.

The greatest issues facing Mi'kmaq involve dealing with the effects of the Indian Act, such as beneficiary and governance questions, for example, determining who is actually entitled to be Mi'kmaq and what form a Mi'kmaw government would take. Off-reserve and non-registered Mi'kmaq are currently represented by such organizations as the Native Councils of Nova Scotia and Prince Edward Island and the New Brunswick Aboriginal Peoples Council. However, tensions persist around unresolved questions of governance and beneficiaries impacting off-reserve registered Indians, non-status Indians, and an ever-growing number of people who self-identify as Metis.

Conclusion

The influence of the Mi'kmaq is today being experienced and integrated into all aspects of society in Mi'kma'ki. No longer on the margins, they are now becoming the centre, including in the negotiation and consultation processes. The government has realized that because of unique treaty rights, any discussions that may adversely impact Mi'kmaw rights and title issues have to be dealt with on a nation-to-nation basis. Despite past policies and failed social experiments, the concept of *Ta'n Mi'kmaqik Telo'ltipni Mi'kma'ki* is communicated from one generation to another, with a growing population of educated Mi'kmaq, and in publications such as this.

Mi'kmaq are strong today, but, like the colours in their language, they are in the process of becoming who they have always been, once again. This has major importance for the growing number of Mi'kmaw youth, the largest population of youth in Atlantic Canada. Better educated, more sophisticated youth are also aware, taking pride in and reclaiming their traditional lifeways that were displaced but never fundamentally lost.

In this chapter, we have looked at different elements of cultural continuity that are often overlooked—the silent and intangible factors, as well as fundamental treaty rights that have never been relinquished or extinguished. There is growing awareness in the academies and the political arenas, which are becoming more inclusive of Mi'kmaw and other cultural perspectives. More importantly, the depth of the Mi'kmaw connectedness and the inseparability of their cultural psyche, their language, and their values, with the landscape of Mi'kma'ki has never been extinguished, though much healing is still to come.

NOTES

1. "Mi'kmaw" is the singular as well as the adjectival form of "Mi'kmaq."

2. On the other hand, any good teacher emphasizes that the appearance of a new trait such as pottery in the archaeological record, while marking a significant event that is worth noting, does not necessarily mean that other aspects of life changed dramatically, or even at all. Continuity of culture through time is, in fact, normative [the editors].

3. This is true of all languages [the editors].

4. The treaties signed with the English established and defined the right of Mi'kmaq to hunt and fish and to live upon the land unmolested. The Treaty of Peace and Friendship was put to the test in the famed Donald Marshall decision, establishing the right of Mr Marshall to hunt and fish for subsistence purposes. The 1999 *Marshall* case was a landmark victory for the Mi'kmaq, validating their treaty rights. Each year on 1 October, hundreds of Mi'kmaq travel to Halifax where they celebrate the upholding of this treaty at Province House.

REFERENCES AND RECOMMENDED READINGS

Bock, Phillip K. 1966. *The Micmac Indians of the Restigouche: History and Contemporary Description.* Ottawa: National Museum of Canada, Bulletin 213, Anthropological Series no. 77.

Christmas, Dan. 2009. "Presentation to the Antigonish Chamber of Congress." Keating Millennium Centre, Antigonish, Nova Scotia, 11 Feb.

Davin, N.F. 1879. *Report on Industrial Schools for Indians and Half-breeds.* Ottawa: Canada, Ministry of the Interior.

Deal, Michael. 1989. "The Distribution and Prehistoric Exploitation of Scots Bay Chalcedonies." Paper prepared for the twenty-second annual meeting of the Canadian Archaeological Association. Fredericton, NB. 10–13 May.

Dennis, Clarissa Archibald. 1923. "Journals of Clarissa Archibald Dennis, Notebooks 1&2. " Halifax: Public Archives of Nova Scotia, MG1, vol. 2867.

Denys, Nicholas. (1672, 1908) 1968. *Descriptions & Natural History of the Coasts of North America (Acadia).* New York: Greenwood Press. [Originally published as *Champlain Society Publication II*].

Gould, Joey. 1990. Videotaped interview on Mi'kmaw dance. Afton Reserve, 19 Dec.

Keung, Nicholas. 2009. "Status Indians Face Threat of Extinction," *Toronto Star*, 10 May, A1.

Knockwood, Isabelle. 1992. *Out of the Depths.* Lockeport, NS: Roseway Publishing. A first-hand account of her experience in the Shubenacadie Residential School.

Johnson, Eleanor. 1995. Lecture at Gorsebrook Research Institute, St Mary's University, Halifax.

Le Clercq, Father Chrestien. (1910) 1968. *New Relation of Gaspesia With the Customs and Religion of the Gaspesian Indians.* Edited and translated by William F. Ganong. Toronto: The Champlain Society; New York: Greenwood Press.

Lewis, Roger. 2006. "Mi'kmakik Teloltipnik L'nuk," *Mi'kmaq–Maliseet News*, Jul./Aug.

McGhee, Robert. 2008. "Aboriginalism and the Problems of Indigenous Archaeology," *American Antiquity* 73, 4: 579–97.

Maillard, Abbé Pierre-Antoine-Simon. 1758. "An Account of the Customs and Manners of the Micmakis and Maricheets, Savage Nations, Now Dependent on the Government of Cape Breton." London: S. Hooper and A. Morley. From an unpublished French manuscript.

Neu, Dean, and Richard Therrien. 2003. *Accounting for Genocide: Canada's Bureaucratic Assault on Aboriginal People*. Blackpoint, NS, and Winnipeg, MB: Fernwood Publishing/Zed Books. A good overview of the Canadian policies and processes for dealing with Aboriginal peoples.

Raddall, Thomas H. 1944. "Notes of Personal Interview with Sam Gloade, Micmac Indian." Halifax: Nova Scotia Museum of Natural History.

Rand, Rev. Silas. (1894) 1971. *Legends of the Micmacs*. New York and London: Longmans, Green, and Co.; and New York: Johnson Reprint Corporation. Legends written down by the nineteenth-century Baptist minister Silas Rand, who lived and worked among the Mi'kmaq.

Reid, John G. 1987. *Six Crucial Decades: Times of Change in the History of the Maritimes*. Halifax: Nimbus Publishing.

Sable, Trudy. 1994. Videotaped discussion on Mi'kmaw Language with Doug Smith and Bernie Francis. 30 Sept.

———. 1996. *Another Look in the Mirror: Research into Developing an Alternative Science Curriculum for Mi'kmaw Children*. MA thesis, Saint Mary's University, Halifax.

———. 2005. "Legends as Maps." Presentation to Confederacy of Mainland Mi'kmaq. Debert, NS. Oct.

———. 2006. "Preserving the Whole: Principles of Sustainability in Mi'kmaq Forms of Communication." In *Indigenous Worldviews: Scholarly Challenges to Anti-"Indian" Hegemony*, edited by Wahinkpe Topa. Austin: University of Texas Press.

——— and Bernie Francis. 2012. *The Language of this Land: Mi'kma'ki*. Sydney, NS: Cape Breton University Press.

Speck, Frank. (1940) 1985. *A Northern Algonquian Sourcebook: Papers by Frank Speck*. Edited by Edward S. Rogers. London: Garland Publishing.

Whitehead, Ruth Holmes. 1980. *Elitekey: Micmac Material Culture from 1600 AD to the Present*. Halifax: Nova Scotia Museum.

Wickens, William C. 2002. *Mi'kmaq Treaties on Trial: History, Land, and Donald Marshall Junior*. Toronto: University of Toronto Press. History of treaties since the 1700s and discussion of high profile treaty negotiations.

Widdowson, Frances, and Albert Howard. 2008. *Disrobing the Aboriginal Industry: The Deception Behind Indigenous Cultural Preservation*. Montreal and Kingston: McGill–Queen's University Press.

PART VI

The Plains

CHAPTER 16

Myths and Realities: An Overview of the Plains

C. Roderick Wilson

No Aboriginal people anywhere have so captured the popular imagination as have the "historic" Plains Indians. Frozen in mid-nineteenth century by strips of Hollywood celluloid, or for our grandparents by dime novels and Wild West shows, the Plains Indian has for millions become "The Indian." So much is this the case that Indians from culture areas thousands of miles distant at times feel compelled to don Plains-style feather headdresses and assorted other finery—so that others will recognize them as Indians.

Non-Indian devotees of Plains culture are found around the world. Black celebrants at Mardi Gras in New Orleans and throughout the Caribbean annually celebrate, by means of elaborate costume, song, and dance, an essentially mythic kinship with Plains Indians. European Boy Scouts devour both highly romanticized popular works and technical treatises on Plains (and Woodland) Indians, with some scrupulously following every possible detail in creating their own medicine bundles and actually becoming, in their own minds, members of their chosen tribe. Some North American hobbyists spend thousands of dollars and hours in perfecting historically accurate costumes and dances, and in performing them. A number of Canada's national myths have to do with events by which Plains Indians were incorporated into the Canadian state: the North-West

Mounted Police protecting Canadian Indians from unscrupulous American whisky traders; the Canadian Pacific Railway, the ribbon of steel that tied Canada together, being made possible by the pacification of the warriors of the Plains; the stark contrast in levels of violence on the Canadian and US frontiers. In myriad ways, both conscious and unconscious, the dominant Indian image, in Canada and the world, is that of the Plains Indian of about 1850.

What relationship, if any, exists between the popular image and the reality?

There are several ways to answer the question. One is to emphasize that the stereotype has virtually no relationship to the reality of the time that Indians have occupied the region. In the 12,000 or more years of its existence, the economic basis of Plains society changed substantially. The earliest known Plains dwellers appear to have relied mainly on spears to dispatch the large animals they hunted. Three major technological innovations transformed Plains hunting prior to the advent of European contact: the spear thrower, the bow and arrow, and the buffalo pound. Each brought new efficiencies to the hunt and in turn affected the life of the people. The real Plains Indians thus are part of a millennia-old pattern of dynamic change and development, of adjusting to major shifts in climate and environment, to altering frequencies of

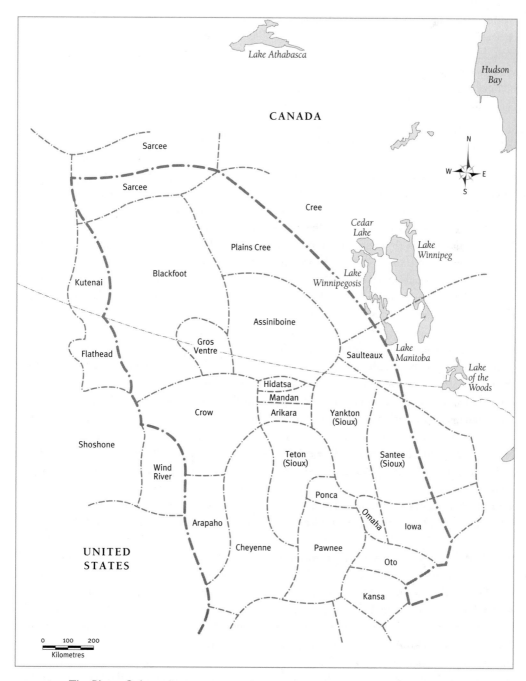

MAP 16.1 The Plains Culture Area

game population (including the extinction of major species such as the mammoth, the mastodon, and ancient species of buffalo), and to new hunting tools that demanded new skills and new forms of social co-operation. The stereotype, in contrast, has no roots and does not speak to change. In fact, it denies change.

To further emphasize this point, it can be noted that the list of "tribes" on the Canadian Plains during the "classic" period is substantially different from what it was earlier. (1) Stoney (Assiniboine) people broke off from the Yankton Sioux and thereafter associated largely with the Cree. They lived in Minnesota 300 years ago at the edge of the parklands and Plains, hunting both deer and buffalo, and engaging in some horticulture. (2) Blackfoot, like the Cree and Saulteaux, speak an Algonquian language. They seem to have lived on the Plains for a very substantial period of time. (3) Although recent evidence indicates that Cree have lived in the parkland regions of the West for some time, the Plains Cree came into existence and moved onto the Plains through involvement in the fur trade. (4) Saulteaux, who once referred to themselves as Bungi and today often prefer Anishnabe, could as well be called the Plains Ojibway. They also may have moved onto the Plains in early historic times. (5) Tsuu T'ina (Sarsi) are Dene immigrants from the North who became buffalo hunters associated with the Blackfoot in recent times. Thus, of five tribes inhabiting the Canadian Plains in 1850, only one probably was not a newcomer. If one considers the Metis a tribe, the case is even stronger. Conversely, three tribes (and possibly a fourth, the Hidatsa) that in late prehistoric times lived in the Canadian part of the Plains, the Ktunaxa (Kutenai), Shoshone, and Atsina (Gros Ventre), had been displaced by 1850. Again, the stereotype gives no sense of the dynamic changes in the region. To put it more strongly, the 1850 Plains region was flooded with people (and peoples) compared to anything that had ever gone before.

Another indicator of the discrepancy between the stereotype and the tradition of Plains culture is the extent to which life changed as a result of the horse and gun. Each in turn increased the efficiency of the hunt. People not only could get more food and hides quickly, they could also carry bigger tepees and more goods, men could keep more women productively working and so were more likely to be polygynous, infant mortality dropped, and women at least were likely to live longer. Perhaps most significantly, high status now depended on having horses, creating a new impetus for raiding—and with the gun the level of violence increased dramatically. In addition, life on the Plains was no longer entirely Indigenous: the Europeans were also there. Although Plains life in 1850 was still grounded in the past, in many regards it was conspicuously different from anything that had gone before.

The stereotype, however, was not wholly invented. There were buffalo-hunting nomads who sought visions, counted coup, and ate pemmican. Dempsey writes graphically of Blackfoot in this period, and much of what he describes could also be said of other Plains tribes. Although Dempsey's portrait corresponds quite substantially with elements of the stereotype, major differences include: (1) as a generalization dealing with typical patterns, it allows for the fact that people's real behaviour is quite variable; (2) it recognizes that real Blackfoot had a past and that in many ways their present is markedly different from their life a century ago; and (3) in recognizing that today's changed Blackfoot are rooted in the life and values of the past, it implies that they have a future as a culture. The implicit denial of an authentically Indian future is perhaps the most damning feature of the stereotype.

This discussion originated in a consideration of the popular stereotype of the Plains Indian. Part of our argument about the pervasiveness of this image is that it has affected also the perceptions of

FIGURE 16.1 Assiniboine warrior. (Courtesy Saskatchewan Archives Board, R-A4945-1)

gists as well, and any other academics who have discussed these people. The personal example she provides is straightforward: her research of the facts dispelled the presuppositions with which she started. Some connections are not so easily traced, however. One of our unfinished tasks is to rethink not only our national and regional history, but also the disciplines themselves.

Our fundamental conclusion is the observation that the Plains stereotype has been, and continues to be, a factor in the Indian–government relationship in Canada. Although there are earlier treaties, the formal treaty-making process that created the modern reserve system is fundamentally a phenomenon of the Plains. That is where the numbered treaties started, and most treaty Indians still live in the Prairie provinces. The necessity of settling the Canadian Plains, of protecting them from a neighbour whose vision of manifest destiny conflicted with our own, and of tying the nascent nation together prompted the treaties. The treaties and reserves were also a product of the US Plains, a deliberate attempt to avoid the bloodshed and expense associated with the US frontier; such events as that of the Little Bighorn, where the Seventh Cavalry was routed by concentrated Indian forces, loomed large. It is no accident that Canadian reserves, generally, are both smaller and more scattered than are reservations in the United States.

The treaties called for reserves. The government not only established reserves for the treaty

government officials and academics. Carter's chapter contains a thorough and depressing analysis of the extent to which the stereotype was one of the factors that effectively prevented Plains Cree and other Plains Indians from becoming productive farmers in the late 1800s. Unfortunately, what she documents for these groups could easily be extended in both time and place.

Carter also mentions, almost in passing, that the Plains stereotype has affected the view of historians. She could have mentioned anthropolo-

Indians but for thousands of non-treaty Indians who did not live on the Plains and with whom the government saw no necessity of signing treaties. But the reserve system, as legislated by the Indian Act, embodies an assumption that Indians are not competent to govern their own affairs, that land and money must be held by the government in trust for them. The Plains stereotype, it must be remembered, is in part a fusion of two conflicting stereotypes, both held by Europeans for centuries—the Indian as the uncivilized and barbaric savage and the Indian as the noble savage, the untutored child of nature. Noble he may be, but in the eyes of the law, a child. Most Canadians would be shocked to realize the domination that Indian agents legally exercised on reserves until recently, as well as the reluctance that is still frequently encountered among professional "carers-for-Indians" to allow their "noble charges" the simple dignity of running their own lives. The fact of the non-adult legal status of the Indian is central to most of the public controversies concerning Natives in recent years. Even the current attempt to revise substantially the Indian Act (as noted more extensively in Chapter 26), even though it incorporates numerous changes designed to "give Indians greater self-determination," is fundamentally flawed by a process that brings in Natives for consultation after the process is designed. Look again at the last sentence. To speak of "giving" anyone self-determination is at heart paternalistic.

Perversely, the benefits of the reserve system have in turn spawned their own stereotypes. In the spring of 2009, for instance, the University of Saskatchewan declined a half-million-dollar endowment because it was to be given on condition that the scholarships so created would be available only to non-Aboriginal students. The donors apparently were convinced that Aboriginal students "had it made," and they desired to help students who had to struggle to acquire an education!

The Plains stereotype does not alone explain the history and current conditions of Canadian Indians, but it certainly served, and continues to serve, to reinforce unfortunate tendencies toward paternalism.

CHAPTER 17

The Blackfoot Nation

Hugh A. Dempsey and L. James Dempsey

Introduction

Hugh Dempsey's interest in Blackfoot Indians is due to his personal and professional relationships. As a reporter covering the Indian Association of Alberta's 1949 meetings in Edmonton, he met the daughter of its president, James Gladstone, and soon married her. This family connection led to constant exposure to Blackfoot history and contemporary life. Employment with the Glenbow Museum, an institution focused on Canadian Indians, combined with an interest in writing, led to a desire to present Native insights into historic events.

Dempsey chose biography as his medium, believing that the personal aspects of a life provide human interest that cannot be gained in formal history, while the political and social events of the period become the study's background. Tragedy and triumph become more significant when related to real lives.

Dempsey considers himself basically a historian, but one familiar with related fields such as anthropology, political science, and geography. He also made extensive use of Native oral history before the technique was widely accepted by academic historians.

To illustrate the sometimes unique perspective of oral history, Dempsey notes that Prime Minister John A. Macdonald saw Crowfoot as a friend of the government for his actions in the North-West Rebellion of 1885. Crowfoot, however, was acting only in the best interests of his people. If his actions helped the government, it was a coincidence.

Another example comes from the negotiation of Treaty No. 6 in 1876. The official transcript has Big Bear professing his fear of being hanged, which was understood to mean that he intended to do evil. What Big Bear actually said was that he did not want a rope around his neck. He was equating himself to a wild horse that, once roped, forever lost its freedom.

Ethnohistorian James Dempsey, a member of the Blood Tribe, also includes Native oral history in his multidisciplinary studies of Plains Indian warfare, Blackfoot warrior art, and western Canadian Native veterans. For instance, he has proposed that a cultural desire to gain war honours (raising their status in their community), a historic connection through the numbered treaties to the idea of protecting the Crown, and a desire to escape the stifling life on reserves appears to have motivated many Natives to enlist in Canada's armed forces.

The Ethnographic Blackfoot

Beginnings

Napi (Old Man) was travelling about, south of here, making the people. He came from the south, travelling north, making animals and birds as he passed along. He made the mountains, prairies, timber, and brush first. So he went along travelling northward, making things as he went, putting rivers here and there, and falls on them, putting red paint here and there in the ground, fixing up the world as we see it today. . . . The first people were poor and naked, and did not know how to get a living. Napi told the people that the animals should be their food, and gave them to the people, saying, "These are your herds. . . ." Also, Napi said to the people: "Now, if you are overcome, you may go and sleep, and get power. Something will come to you in your dream that will help you. Whatever these animals tell you to do, you must obey them, as they appear to you in your sleep. Be guided by them . . ." He started off again, travelling north, until he came to where he began to slide down a hill. The marks where he slid down are to be seen yet, and the place is known to all people as the "Old Man's Sliding Ground." This is as far as the Blackfeet followed Napi. He said, "Here I will mark you off a piece of ground. There is your land, and it is full of all kinds of animals and many things grow in this land. Let no other people come into it. This is for you . . ." Of late years we have let our friends, the white people, come in, and you know the result. We, his children, have failed to obey his laws. (Grinnell 1962:137–44)

Regardless of the evidence provided by anthropologists, the Blackfoot believe that they were created and have always lived in an area bounded on the west by the Rocky Mountains, the east by the Cypress Hills, the north by the Battle River, and the south by the Missouri River. Their Plains culture lifestyle, combined with their world view

and language, which has few if any references to another lifestyle, support this belief. This is not to ignore the evidence that the Blackfoot at one time migrated from the east; however, it has no relevance to how the Blackfoot perceive themselves. Around 1750 Blackfoot territory was as far north as the North Saskatchewan River, but pressure from the Cree and the buffalo herds beginning to congregate further south resulted in the northern range shrinking to the Battle River.

The Blackfoot Nation consists of three tribes—the Blackfoot proper, or Siksika (today called the Siksika First Nation); the Blood tribe, or Kainai (today known as the Kainaiwa First Nation); and the Peigans, or Pikuni, who are further divided into two groups: the North Piegan, or Aputohsi-Pikuni (Piikani First Nation), and the South Piegan, or Amiskapi-Pikuni (Blackfeet Indians of Montana). The population size and historical distinctiveness of the North and South Peigans have led to them being seen, at times, as separate tribes. Collectively all the tribes were referred to in Blackfoot as *Saukitapix*, or "Prairie People," or as *Nitsitapix*, "Real People." The Blackfoot Confederacy comprised these three tribes along with the Sarcee and the Gros Ventres. The latter, however, left the Confederacy in 1861 due to a dispute over stolen horses and became enemies.

Literally speaking, "Siksika" means "black foot" while "Kainai" translates to "many chiefs" and "Pikuni" means "scabby robes." A number of myths explain how these tribal names came to be. The most popular is that at one time they were an unnamed group beset by enemies on all sides. They agreed to divide into three groups—one to guard the northeast, another to protect the southeast, and a third the southwest. After some time someone from the northern tribe decided to visit the others. On his way he passed over a large area burned by prairie fire. When he reached the southeast camp, his moccasins were black with ashes. Entering the village, he asked a man who was the

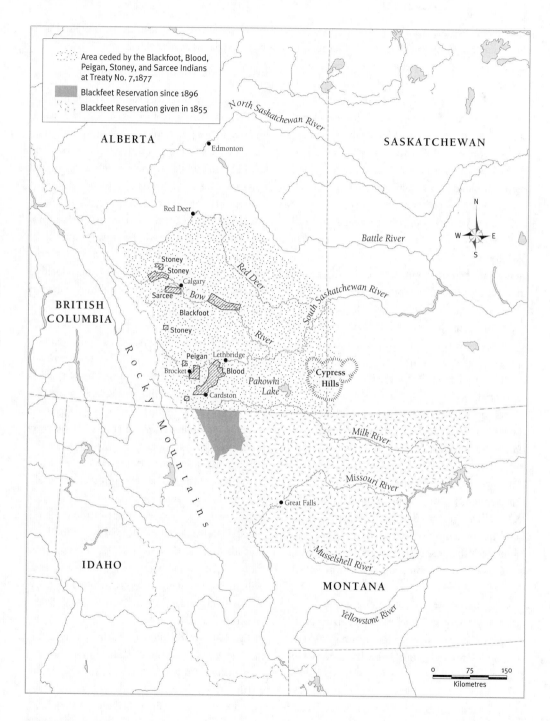

MAP 17.1 Blackfoot Reserves

chief. "I am," he said. Another person stopped and said, "I am the chief," and soon the northerner was surrounded by several people, all claiming to be chiefs.

"I shall call your tribe 'A-kainah,' Many Chiefs," he said, "for everyone here seems to be a chief." Meanwhile, the Crees gave this tribe the name of Red People, for the ochre they spread on their clothes, and this was later translated as Blood People, or Bloods. Continuing the story, the Bloods looked at the visitor's moccasins and said, "Very well, you have given our tribe a name, so we will reciprocate; your people shall be called 'Siksika,' Blackfoot."

The man then went to the southwestern tribe where their territory was rich in buffalo. The people had become lazy and the women had tanned their hides so badly that men walked about with pieces of dried flesh and hair on their robes. "I shall call you 'Apikuni,' or badly dressed robes," he told them. Over time the word changed to "Peigan."

Because the Peigan nation is divided between the United States and Canada, a number of contradictions have arisen regarding spelling tribal names. For example, Canadians generally and those on the Peigan Reserve in southern Alberta use the term "Peigan," while in the United States it is spelled "Piegan." But most controversial has been the correctness of "Blackfoot" or "Blackfeet." Some insist that one term is correct and the other wrong, but no evidence supports either opinion. The word "sik-sik-a" is taken from two roots: "Sik-si" from "siksinum" or "black," and "ka" from either "okat" (foot) or "okats" (feet). When the chiefs signed a US treaty in 1755, the document identified the "Blackfoot Nation" but was signed by four "Blackfeet"; similarly, in the Canadian treaty the term "Blackfoot Tribe" was used but an adhesion to the document was signed by "Blackfeet." Today, most Canadians, anthropologists, and Natives in Canada use the term "Blackfoot," while many in the United States use "Blackfeet." Therefore both terms appear to be acceptable.

Environment and Economy

The weather in Blackfoot country was marked by hot dry summers and long cold winters, with warm chinook winds providing some respite during winter. Spring was often cool and wet, interrupted by late blizzards, while autumns were warm, dry, and pleasant; the term "Indian summer" was most appropriate for the region. Spring and summer saw violent thunderstorms, to which was attributed religious significance. The first thunderstorm of spring heralded a ritual of the medicine-pipe owners, while the thunder itself was considered to be a powerful deity. Death by lightning was not uncommon.

Blackfoot territory was primarily short-grass plains interspersed by east-west running coulees and streams. A number of these watercourses dried up completely during the summer. Lakes often were so alkaline that the water was virtually undrinkable. Most of the river areas and lakeshores were devoid of timber. When groves of trees were found, they became favourite wintering areas. The large mammals in Blackfoot country were the buffalo, grizzly bear, black bear, antelope, deer, elk, mountain sheep, and mountain goat. Of these, the buffalo was the primary source of food; people called its flesh *nitapiksisako*, "real meat," implying that all other meat was inferior. Besides being used for food, the buffalo was used for many articles of utilitarian and religious objects, such as lodge covers, tools, clothing, drinking vessels, storage containers, expungers, and shields.

Buffalo were killed in various ways. One method was the "surround." When hunters located a small herd they crept forward, sometimes disguising themselves as wolves or buffalo calves, and when close enough picked off animals on the fringe of the herd. If they were lucky, the herd merely milled in a circle instead of running away, and the hunters might kill several animals before the rest took flight.

For thousands of years, the dominant hunting method used by the Blackfoot was the buffalo jump, using cliffs near streams. Those not killed by the fall were quickly dispatched. With the introduction of horses and guns, this method gradually fell into disuse and was abandoned during the mid-nineteenth century. The acquisition of the horse in the early 1700s created the "chase" which was perhaps the most thrilling way to kill buffalo. Specially trained horses were guided by knee pressure and often would press so close to the quarry that the hunter's leg would touch the buffalo. So valued were these buffalo runners that they had no other duties to perform.

Lesser mammals were used as food only when buffalo was unavailable. These included porcupine, rabbit, and squirrel. Ducks, geese, partridge, and swans were sometimes eaten, and eggs were collected for food. Children often had the responsibility for obtaining smaller animals and birds which were hunted on foot; young boys killed rabbits and partridges while girls waded among the reeds to kill water birds. Blackfoot rejected all fish as food; they considered them part of an evil Underwater World.

A wide variety of berries and edible roots were gathered by women: most prominent were the saskatoon or **service berry**, chokecherry, bull berry, high- and low-bush cranberry, gooseberry, pin cherry, raspberry, strawberry, wild turnip, wild onion, bitter root, and camas root. Picking berries and digging roots were entirely women's responsibility, although a teenaged boy usually accompanied them to protect them in case of attack by a bear or other animal. Some of the berries were stewed or sun-dried for winter use. Other plants had practical or medicinal uses: bearberry and the inner bark of the red willow were smoked, as was wild tobacco. Because of its bitter taste, the latter was mixed with herbs and, in later years, with commercial tobacco.

Under ideal conditions an abundance of food could be found by the Blackfoot; they could also starve during periods of drought or blizzards. If they went into their winter quarters and the buffalo remained far out on the Plains, if prairie fires drove the herds away, or if blizzards prevented hunters from leaving camp, hunger and privation would result. As nomadic hunters and gatherers they could not store large quantities of food and thus depended on a regular supply of fresh meat. In autumn some meat was cut into long thin strips and sun-dried, but this provided emergency rations for relatively short periods of time. Other dried meat was pulverized and mixed with crushed, dried sarvice berries and hot fat, producing pemmican. This, too, provided a limited but important source of food in winter.

Mythology

To explain phenomena around them, the Blackfoot created myths and legends, some based on spiritual experiences. Myths explained the origins of medicine bundles and painted tepee designs; they recounted the exploits of great warriors; they told of the origin of the Blackfoot and of man himself.

The most common type of legend was related to a trickster-creator called Napi or Old Man. It was Napi who enlisted the aid of a number of water animals to dive into the water and find what was at the bottom and bring it back. Muskrat was successful and returned with some earth in his paw. From this small beginning Napi created the world. In addition, he was responsible for making the first man and woman, creating life and death, and making all the flora and fauna in Blackfoot country. Yet Napi was not a god who was revered; rather, he was a supernatural personification of man, with all his wisdom and foolishness, bravery and cowardice, honesty and greed. Some tales caused listeners to double over in laughter as Napi was outwitted by an opponent or did something foolish.

There are many tales about Napi, such as those explaining why the bobcat has a flat face, why the skunk has a striped back, and how the Rocky Mountains came to be. These stories were told partly for entertainment, but also to explain the world to young people, to allay their fears of strange phenomena, and to teach the customs and mores of the tribe. Through these stories children learned about how their world worked and about the importance of making wise decisions.

The Blackfoot were known for their extensive legends about the stars. Most stars were said to have their origins on earth as Indians who had used their supernatural powers to join the Sky People. Even Blackfoot tepees pay homage to the stars; on the upper ears or flaps of most lodges are white circles depicting Ursa Major and the Pleiades. In fact, a Blackfoot painted tepee is rich in mythology; its main design is often the result of a vision. Another element of the design may relate to the Morning Star or to the butterfly, the spirit of sleep.

Stories about great warriors almost inevitably are rooted in supernatural feats. The Blackfoot believed that if a man performed some brave or important deed, he succeeded only because of the spiritual help he received. Crowfoot, a chief of the Canadian Blackfoot, was said to have received his power from the owl's head he wore in his hair; Red Old Man, a great warrior, had a mouse as his spiritual helper. When faced with a crisis these men often had visions or were led from danger by

FIGURE 17.1 Blackfoot warriors. (© Canadian Museum of Civilization, 73462)

an animal or bird. A famous story deals with the warrior Low Horn, killed by the Cree in the 1840s. According to tales, bullets could not kill him, and he died only when an elk antler was driven into his ear. The Cree then burned his body, but an ember exploded from the fire and turned into a grizzly bear that attacked the Cree. As they fled, a thundercloud overhead sent down lightning bolts to kill even more Cree. The Blackfoot believe that Low Horn was later reincarnated in a young boy who ultimately became a medicine man among the Bloods and died in 1899.

Spirituality, World View, and Religion

Religion pervaded almost every aspect of life. A woman beginning her quill working would pray; an old man waking in the morning would sing a prayer of thanks; a person before eating placed a small morsel of food in the ground for the spirits.

The Blackfoot believed that their entire universe was inhabited by spirits. Some were beneficial and others harmful, although generally the spirit world was not seen as falling into distinct categories. Rather it was specific attributes of the event, person, or season which would determine how people interpreted actions of the spirit world. One of the most important deities was Sun, who was head of a holy family including his wife, Moon, and their boy, Morning Star. The thunder spirit also was a powerful deity, while even a lowly mouse had its supernatural role. A strangely twisted tree or an unusual rock formation was considered to be the manifestation of spiritual power and, as a result, passersby left offerings for good fortune.

Often the most important spirits were those directly related to an individual's experiences. A teenaged boy, for example, might go on a vision quest, looking for a spiritual helper. He would go to a secluded place—if he was particularly daring, to an area of great danger, such as a high precipice or a burial ground. Constructing a simple shelter, he lay down with a pipe beside him and fasted and

prayed for four days. During that time he hoped that he would slip into a trance and that a spiritual helper would come. Sometimes it would be an animal in the form of a man, while at other times a creature itself might speak.

A famous leader, Red Crow, was hunting gophers with bow and arrow while still a boy. As he lay near a gopher hole he fell asleep and in his dream the gopher spirit came to him and promised to help him if he would go away and leave him in peace. "When you go against an enemy," advised the spirit, "take a blade of grass and stick it in your hair. Then you'll never get hit" (Dempsey 1980:10). Red Crow followed this advice and although he was in 33 battles, he was never wounded.

As a result of their visions, young men wore amulets or ornaments in their hair or around their necks. As noted earlier, Crowfoot kept an owl's head in his hair, while others could be seen wearing the skins of animals or other objects that represented their spirit helpers. Usually, each had specific songs and rituals performed by the owners. The objects themselves were unique to the individual; when he died, they were buried with him.

Some men had visions of benefit to the whole tribe. As a rule, such people already were recognized as holy men and as a result of their dreams, they created sacred pieces called "medicine bundles." This is a generic term for objects wrapped together and used for ritualistic purposes. Some medicine bundles contained war shirts decorated with scalps or weasel skins; others had animal skins, fossilized ammonites (known as "buffalo stones"), or other parts of costumes. Perhaps most common was the medicine pipe, a long, bowl-less pipe stem decorated with eagle feathers. Used in a dance, it brought good luck to the tribe or helped someone who was sick. Medicine-pipe men—the owners of the pipes—led a distinctive lifestyle; they wore their hair in a certain way, painted their faces, carried the pipe on its own travois, and had many taboos. They possessed the spiritual power to keep harmful spirits away from the tribe and to help those in need. Although they did not constitute a society, they would gather together periodically to open their pipe bundles, perform dances and rituals, and renew their vows. Every spring after the first thunderstorm, each medicine-pipe bundle was opened in response to the call the owner received from the thunder spirit.

Besides these revered medicine pipes, lesser pipes were individually owned. Most common was the black-covered medicine pipe, which was small enough to take to war and often was presented to a fledgling warrior by an older relative.

Medicine pipes and other medicine bundles originated in visions but, unlike personal amulets, could be transferred or sold. If a man wished to become a bundle owner, he went to someone who had such a bundle, offered to smoke with him, and announced that he wanted it. The owner could not refuse, so a price was arranged and a formal transfer ceremony took place.

The most ancient Blackfoot medicine bundle was the beaver bundle that, according to legends, was given to a hunter who camped by St Mary's Lake in what is now northern Montana. He was killing too many birds and animals, so one day when his wife went for water a Beaver Man came out of the lake and captured her. Later she led a procession from the lake to her husband's lodge; this group consisted of the Beaver Man, Sun, and Moon. The hunter was told that if he would stop killing game unnecessarily, his wife would be returned to him and he would be given a medicine bundle. Then, one by one, animal and bird skins were taken from the walls of his lodge and he was taught the songs and ceremonies for each. These were wrapped together with sweetgrass and face paint to make the beaver bundle.

Most medicine bundles contained a few standard items, such as braided sweetgrass used for incense and ochre to paint the user's face. The rest of the objects were worn or held during ceremon-

ies, usually with each accompanied by its special song. The whole bundle was contained within a large rawhide case that hung on a tripod behind the owner's lodge by day and was placed above his bed at night. Incense was burned and prayers and songs were performed each morning and night.

Medicine bundles also were used by the various secret societies. Most common were the warrior societies, discussed earlier. Each member of a warrior society had his own bundle, which was simply a packet of paints and the costume he needed for his society's dances and ceremonies. A society had one or two leaders, each with a distinctive headdress and face paint. For example, a head man in the Raven Carriers society wore a coyote skin and had an eagle feather in his hair; while he danced, he carried a long red stick trimmed with cloth and feathers.

The Blackfoot were unique in that they had one society exclusively for women. It was called the *Motoki*, popularly translated as "Old Women's Society," but, more accurately, it should be called the "Sorority." Like the Longtime Medicine Pipe, some of the society's rituals came to the Blackfoot from the Mandans in 1832, but they have been given a mythical origin relating to the actions of a white crow among a buffalo herd. The primary function of the Motoki was to acknowledge the importance of the buffalo to the Blackfoot people. In their rituals the women took the roles of buffalo killed by hunters and paid homage to the power of the buffalo spirit. The primary intention was to appease the spirits so that the tribe would have good fortune in future hunts. Among the costumes worn by the women were headdresses made of scalps from old buffalo bulls, worn by leaders of the society.

The Sun Dance

As can be seen, spirituality among the Blackfoot ranged from personal visions and a constant concern with the supernatural to more structured societies collectively performing rituals. The most complex ceremony, the Sun Dance, involved an entire tribe. This ceremony lasted for several days and had social and political overtones besides its purely religious function.

The term "Sun Dance" is a misnomer, implying a simple dance to the Sun spirit rather than a series of religious ceremonies. The Blackfoot term for the Sun Dance, *Okan*, refers to the centre pole of the Sun Dance lodge—the most sacred object of the ritual.

The basic purpose of the Sun Dance was to allow everyone to reaffirm faith in the Sun spirit. Its nucleus consisted of constructing a lodge, presided over by a holy woman, where various dances and rituals were performed. The assembling of the entire tribe also became the occasion for secret societies to perform their dances or to exchange their memberships, for medicine-pipe bundles to be opened, for war exploits to be recounted, and for the self-sacrifice ritual to be performed. None of these latter ceremonies was a direct part of the Sun Dance but, because they were performed at the same time, they were inextricably linked to it.

The decision to hold a Sun Dance was made by a pure woman—i.e., a virgin or faithful wife—who had a male relative in danger of losing his life. A husband might be ill or a son may not have returned from a raid. The woman made a public vow that if the person's life was spared, she would sponsor a Sun Dance. Then, if her prayer was answered, she became a holy woman and began preparations for the summer ceremony.

The sponsoring of a Sun Dance was expensive, so the extended family and other relatives of the holy woman began to assemble blankets, horses, and other gifts to be given away. Others sought out a woman who had previously sponsored the ritual and made arrangements for her to transfer her medicine bundle, called the *natoas* bundle, to the new sponsor.

The Sun Dance was held in July, as soon as the sarvice berries were ripe, for they were needed for sacramental purposes. A site was chosen by a warrior society in consultation with the chiefs—a location offering good protection against enemies, providing good grazing, and being close to the buffalo.

During the first several days while bands assembled, social activities such as gambling, horse racing, and re-establishing family ties dominated. The Motoki then held their ceremonies in the centre of the camp circle, building a lodge of travois and tepee covers that served as their home during the four-day ritual. On the last day, the women had a public dance and gave away gifts to visitors and friends.

By this time the grass near camp had been grazed over by the hundreds of horses, so a new campsite was chosen four or five miles away. There warrior societies, such as the All Brave Dogs, Pigeons, Horns, or Prairie Chickens, held their dances. At last the holy woman moved her lodge inside the camp circle, decorating its base with green boughs to signify that she was beginning her fast.

The main sacrament of the Sun Dance was the buffalo tongue. While fasting, the holy woman was instructed by the former bundle owner on how to cut tongues into thin strips and smoke-dry them over the fire. During the four days that the holy woman remained in her lodge, she could not touch water, even to wash, lest it rain. Instead, she wiped her face with a muskrat skin and prepared for the building of the main lodge. On the first day of her fast a huge sweat lodge was built just outside the northern edge of camp. This lodge was made of 50 willow sticks and was painted half black, for night, and half red, for day. Then 50 stones were heated in readiness for the sweat. This lodge symbolized the actions of Scar Face, a legendary Blackfoot who had visited the Sun spirit and had his scar removed in such a sweat lodge.

When the stones were ready, the holy woman and her teacher went to the lodge and sat beside it while their husbands went inside. While water was being placed on the stones and the men sweated in the steam, the holy woman painted a buffalo skull with symbols of the Sun, Moon, Morning Star, and Sun Dogs; later it was placed at the base of the Sun Dance pole. Women never enter a sweat lodge, so when the men came out the party returned to the holy woman's lodge to finish the fast.

These ceremonies were repeated for the next three days and each morning the participants moved to a new campsite. Finally, at the end of the fourth day, they arrived at the site of the main Sun Dance camp.

The following morning a warrior society left camp in search of a forked tree that would serve as the holy centre pole. When they found one they returned to camp as though they were scouts who had discovered an enemy camp. Then others in the society crept up to the tree. When it was cut down, they attacked it as a fallen enemy. The tree was taken back in triumph to the camp, there to be laid on the ground in readiness for building the lodge. Others in the camp built the frame of the lodge, which was similar in shape to a circus tent. At last the holy woman ended her fast and went to the unfinished lodge where she prayed over the centre pole before it was raised into position.

Among some tribes that practised a Sun Dance, building the lodge involved little ceremony. For the Blackfoot, however, raising the pole was the highlight of the entire ritual. Guns were fired in the air, men gave war whoops, and everyone yelled joyously as the forked pole was fitted in place and rails from the outer walls were fastened to it. The happy mood continued as scores of people, young and old, collected green branches to place around the lodge as an outer wall. This part of the ceremony symbolized the beginning of new life, just as their faith in the Sun spirit was being renewed. Taboos were relaxed as young men lifted unmarried girls and sweethearts onto their horses as they went to collect greenery. By sunset the lodge had been completed and was ready to be sanctified. With the lodge completed, the work of the holy woman was finished and her fast was over. She provided a huge feast for the camp, and her family gave gifts to everyone who had helped. One particular symbol of opulence was the pathway between the holy woman's lodge and the Sun Dance lodge; when the woman travelled that route, it was carpeted with blankets and robes provided by her family. The farther the carpet of goods extended, the greater the prestige. After the ceremony, the blankets were given away. The Sun Dance lodge was a holy place, so activities taking place there brought good luck for the participants.

That night, four warriors would build a small bower within the Sun Dance lodge and remain their all night, singing their holy songs. In the morning, men known as weather dancers lined up in two rows facing each other and, with faces elevated toward the sun, performed their ceremonial dance. Various warrior societies also performed public dances. A warrior might proclaim one of his war deeds and re-enact the entire episode in pantomime; if he lied or exaggerated, people believed that he would not live to see another summer.

Young men who had made vows to submit to the self-sacrifice ceremony had skewers thrust through slits cut in their breasts and backs. The skewers in front were fastened to lines attached to the centre pole, while those at the back were used to suspend a shield or buffalo skull. As he danced the young warrior thrust himself backward in order to tear the skewers free from his chest and then to wrest the obstruction from his back. This ritual is sometimes referred to as "making a brave," implying that one did it to become a warrior. This is not true; the ordeal was suffered by a young man who had made a vow to the Sun for the good health or protection of someone in his family. It was an act of gratitude to the Sun spirit for an answered prayer.

The Sun Dance was in sharp contrast to more individualistic aspects of Blackfoot religion. The use of personal amulets and medicine bundles was a much older practice. Only with the acquisition of the horse and the availability of leisure time could the Blackfoot develop such a complex series of rituals as the Sun Dance.

Social Organization

The movement of the buffalo and the seasonal availability of resources dictated that the Blackfoot follow an annual cycle. In winter they gathered in small bands along wooded river bottoms, often near the foothills where they were within easy reach of the buffalo. There they stayed for weeks at a time, particularly when hunting was good. In such winter camps, tepees were strung out for miles among the protective cottonwoods of a river valley. Each band might have a separate camp, but they remained within a mile or two of another camp for mutual protection.

In spring people moved out into the prairies, sometimes in small family groups or bands, depending on the buffalo movements. Some would go deep into the foothills to cut new tepee or travois poles, while others went to trading posts or killed enough buffalo to make new lodge covers. By early summer they congregated in large camps, comprising whole tribes, so that the Sun Dance and other rituals could be held. When gathered in such large numbers they seldom remained in one spot for more than a week, as their horses soon grazed off all the nearby grass. After the ceremonies the people moved off in small groups again, picking berries, drying meat, and making pemmican to sell to the trading posts. In early autumn they completed their fall trade and chose winter campsites. Often these were close to buffalo jumps, which provided a source of food as long as buffalo stayed in the area.

During all this, of course, there were small family groups seeking other bands to visit and young warriors raiding enemy horse herds, but the general practice was to follow the buffalo.

The smallest political unit was the band, usually having an extended family as its nucleus. Bands with particularly good leaders or that were constantly successful in the hunt attracted people from other bands until they became too large to be economically viable. For example, a band of Bloods called the Followers of the Buffalo kept growing in size because of wise leadership and every few years a group would break away, forming such new bands as Many Fat Horses, All Tall People, and Knife Owners. On the other hand, a band that experienced repeated misfortune or a significant disaster often simply disappeared. The Bear People lost their leading men in battle in 1872 and the band ceased to exist as the survivors joined other bands.

Blackfoot bands received their names because of some distinctive feature or attribute of their members, or because of some incident. For example, when blizzards caused starvation among a band isolated in the foothills, its members were forced to subsist on fish. They became known as the Fish Eaters. Another band was named Gopher Eaters through a similar experience. Other names, like All Black Faces or All Short People, were purely descriptive. The names could change, if an old one became outdated or a new incident occurred. After settling on their reserve, the Followers of the Buffalo were renamed Camps in a Bunch while the Shooting Up band was renamed the Interfering band. The latter happened when a river changed course, leaving the band without water; joking friends said its members had interfered with the stream by taking all the water for tea.

A band was a self-contained unit small enough to find food yet large enough to protect itself. Nineteenth-century bands are estimated to have contained 20 to 30 families. Each band had a leader recognized as the political chief; another man was war chief. During normal times the political chief controlled the movements of the band, but should there be danger from enemy attack or other causes, the war chief immediately assumed control. The political chief took the role of chief magistrate, presiding at council meetings, giving instructions to the camp "police," and settling disputes within the band. His police were members of one of the warrior societies.

When a boy reached his early teens he joined one of these societies made up of comrades his own age. Then, about every five years, his society took over the membership of the group that was older than themselves and transferred their membership to a new cohort of younger males. Those who were between, say, 20 and 25 years of age, or between 25 and 30, were most often chosen to act as camp police. They patrolled at night, acted as guardians during buffalo hunts, and protected the band while on the trail. They also carried out edicts of punishment decided by the chief. For example, a thief might be banished from the camp, or a man who went out alone to hunt buffalo and frightened the herds away might have his horse seized and riding gear destroyed.

When bands joined together to hunt or camp in winter, one leader was recognized as head chief; he presided at all council meetings. There was no single head chief of a tribe, but if an entire tribe was together, one man was chosen as the presiding authority over the camp. Yet if they should suddenly be faced with danger, the head chief would be replaced by a war chief, just as was done in smaller bands. For example, Red Crow was considered to be a great chief of the Bloods in the mid-nineteenth century, but if the camp was threatened by an enemy, White Calf became war chief and had complete control over the warrior societies.

Council meetings were usually attended by the head chief, the war chief, and the heads of leading families. Decisions were made by consensus and the head chief seldom tried to give direct orders to councillors. He knew they were too independent to be intimidated and they could always withdraw from the camp if they disagreed with him. Instead, the head chief tried to win adherents through oratory; when he felt that he had enough support, he would announce his own intentions. If there was a dispute as to whether the camp should move north or south, the chief might present his arguments, gain support, and then say that he was going south. He did not order or dictate the others to follow, but he knew that they probably would go with him.

Family Life

When a child was born, he or she was named by his or her mother. If a girl, her name was sometimes based on the first thing the woman saw when the child was delivered: Sky Woman, Spider, or Kit Fox Woman. This might become the girl's official name, but more often a senior male member of the family, an uncle or grandfather, would select a name based on his own war experiences. Blackfoot women often had warlike names: Killed At Night, Double Gun Woman, Attacked Towards Camp, or Stabbed Twice. Others had names associated with the namer's spiritual helper: Elk Woman, Big Rabbit, Fisher Woman, or Yellow Squirrel.

Boys were given their first official name when a few days old. Most often an older member of the family would announce his right to choose the name, and, when he was ready, would perform a ceremony and go into a sweat lodge to sanctify his choice. The name chosen was based on the man's war or religious experiences but was recognized as a child's name, such as Shot Close, Little Child, or Berries. This name was used until the boy was old enough to earn an adult name on the warpath or in hunting.

Boys and girls played together until about five years old, at which time their formal education began. Girls learned to carry out simple chores, such as collecting firewood and water or looking after younger children. The boys were taken in hand by an uncle or older brother and taught to use a bow and arrow, guard and round up horses, follow game trails, and become good riders. The first time a boy killed food for the lodge, such as a rabbit or partridge, the father announced the achievement throughout the camp and sponsored a feast for his comrades.

There were no special puberty rites among the Blackfoot. When a girl began her menstrual periods, she was taken away to a separate shelter. They believed that a woman at this time would bring bad luck if she stayed in the lodge with hunters. Her scent would be carried by the hunters and frighten game away.

When boys reached the age of 12 or 13, their comrades or older brothers often gave them derisive nicknames, like Lately Gone or Little Shine, to encourage them to go to war to earn adult names. On their first expeditions boys went as servants, making fires, cooking, repairing moccasins, and looking after the camp. They did not take part in the actual raid and received no share of the plunder, but if they acquitted themselves well they might receive an adult name and be invited to go again. At this age, the name chosen would be one belonging to the family. Names were considered material possessions; when a person died, his name was the exclusive property of the extended family until it was taken by someone else. If a man had gained a particularly outstanding war record or had died under heroic circumstances, the name might be reserved until someone in the family performed a notable deed of valour. For example, a warrior named Crowfoot was killed while on a peace expedition to the Shoshone in 1828; because of the circumstances, his name was revered within the family. Not until the 1840s did a younger relative perform a deed of sufficient daring for him to take this name.

When a young man reached marriageable age he began a courtship, often meeting a girl on her way to get water or gather wood, or near her tepee at night. Clandestine meetings were discouraged

by the girl's parents, as virginity was held in high esteem and had religious significance. A young man, particularly if he was handsome, might spend hours combing his hair or painting his face in a place where he was sure to be seen by the girl of his choice.

Marriage was arranged in a number of ways, depending on the wealth and social status of the participants. Most frequently, negotiations were held between the father of the girl and his prospective son-in-law or between the two fathers. Once an agreement was reached there was an exchange of gifts, with the groom and his family making a payment of about double the amount received. In some instances where the families were poor, the boy might agree to work for his father-in-law for a year, herding horses, hunting, and performing other duties. Usually, however, the bride moved to her husband's camp, her family providing her with a new tepee and furnishings. These were her property and in the event of separation, she kept the lodge and all household utensils. The acquisition of horses provided many benefits for the Blackfoot but it also caused an increase in male deaths due to war and to hunting accidents, resulting in a surplus of women. Polygamy thus became common, the number of wives limited only by a man's wealth. Men commonly had 2 or 3 wives, while a chief at the treaty of 1877 was said to have had 10. Normally the first wife was the senior member of the female household and was referred to as the "sits beside him" wife. She directed the duties of the lodge and accompanied her husband to feasts and ceremonies. It was not unusual for a man to marry sisters, with the belief that they could live together in harmony, while an older brother might marry the widows of a younger brother should that man die.

If a woman proved to be lazy or unfaithful, a man could divorce her simply by sending her back to her parents and demanding return of the gifts. A woman also could leave her husband, but only on the grounds of extreme cruelty or neglect. Most often if a bride returned home she was promptly sent back to her husband so that the family would not suffer the humiliation of being accused of having raised an incompetent daughter.

In daily life there was a clear division of labour between men and women. Wives were responsible for pitching and striking tepees, packing, cooking, manufacturing and decorating most clothing, caring for infants, training girls, and generally maintaining the lodge. Men provided food, protected the camp, manufactured some objects related to religion and war, looked after horses, and carried out raids on enemy camps. Men painted exterior designs on lodges, although women were responsible for decorating liners, backrests, and parfleche bags. Women did virtually all the beadworking and quillworking; men painted religious symbols on shields, robes, and rattles, and carved or produced weapons.

When a man was dying he was dressed in his best clothes and his personal possessions were placed around him. After he died the camp was abandoned, as the Blackfoot believed that his spirit would haunt the area before leaving for the sand hills. His lodge was sometimes sewn up and used as a death lodge; otherwise the body was placed in a tree or on a hill and covered with rocks for burial. It was not buried underground, for the spirit had to be free to come and go. A man's horse might be

---

BOX 17.1 Blackfoot Graphic Art

The Blackfoot word for all types of picture-writing—rock art, robes, and tepee covers—is *sinaksin*, which literally means "to make marks." This term was later applied to writing, causing an interpreter to tell artist Karl Bodmer in 1833 that the Blackfoot greatly admired his drawings and that they thought he "could write very correctly."

Pictographs had two principal intents: to aid in the recollection of information, or to convey information. The function in the first case was mnemonic, in the second, notificational. Mnemonic pictography was used chiefly for keeping records, such as tribal chronicles or "winter counts." In these winter counts, each year is represented by one or more pictographs depicting memorable events occurring in that year. Forms of religious symbolic art may be found on tepees, as well as shields and their covers. Tepees featured animal and other spirit-helper figures that had come to their owners in dreams.

An important use of pictographs was to record and extol the war exploits of individuals and groups. This is referred to as biographic art in that it often consists of images or scenes relating to battles, horse raids, hunting scenes, and an individual's acts of bravery. By placing these figures on an object which was frequently on view, a successful warrior was able to proclaim his achievements to friend or foe. With no written language, Blackfoot communicated through images. Thus picture-writing effectively recorded the war exploits of individual tribal members. Such biographic art was also a means of expressing thoughts or transmitting facts by marks representing the subject in either a realistic or an abstract form.

During the latter part of the eighteenth century and through the twentieth century, Blackfoot biographical art depended more upon the proclivity of the artist than on any general trends of accepted styles. Images ranged from simple to complex, crude to

killed to provide transportation when he finally left for the spirit world.

When a man died, women mourners cut off their hair, gashed their legs, sometimes cut off a joint of a finger, and wailed ritualistically in sorrow. Male mourners cut their hair and left camp, either on a raid or to visit another band. During mourning, men wore old clothing and lived simply, and women carried out their mournful wailing at frequent intervals for up to a year.

Blackfoot clothing was similar to that of other northern tribes. In fact, persons were known to walk into an enemy camp and not realize where they were until they heard a strange language being spoken. In 1810, fur trader Alexander Henry the Younger, when describing Blackfoot men, said:

> Their dress consists of a leather shirt, trimmed with human hair and quillwork, and leggings of the same; shoes are of buffalo skin dressed in the hair, and caps, a strip of buffalo or wolf skin about nine inches broad, tied around the head. Their necklace is a string of grizzly bear claws. A buffalo robe is thrown over all occasionally. Their ornaments are few—feathers, quillwork, and human hair, with red, white, and blue earth, constitute the whole apparatus. (Coues 1897, vol. 2:525)

skilful, and traditional to contemporary. Some artists who painted robes or tepees in the second half of the twentieth century followed the styles of a century earlier while others ignored traditional conventions and tried to make figures lifelike and three-dimensional.

A man who earned war honours had a number of ways to proclaim them. One of the most public and enduring demonstrations of his bravery was to embellish a buffalo robe with a series of symbols representing his experiences. These experiences were painted along the length of the robe, so when worn with the head pointing to the left, the length of the animal was wrapped around his body, displaying the war designs horizontally. Only in later years, when robes were painted for sale, were the figures placed randomly on the hide so that they could be viewed simply as paintings or art.

Buffalo robes were the most versatile of all skins and pelts available to the Blackfoot. They were large, durable, and provided excellent protection against the elements. If a robe was to be worn, the inner surface was often decorated, sometimes with porcupine quills or beads, but more often with paint. Painted robes fell into three broad categories of decoration. Most common was the purely decorative design, usually consisting of geometric patterns and often painted by women. Second were religious and symbolic designs, such as winter counts and ritual records. Finally there were the distinctive designs and symbols used to portray war records on biographic robes. The latter two styles were painted only by men. As a general rule, a biographic robe was worn by the man whose exploits were portrayed. Other men wore robes that were simply painted with no designs, or were richly ornamented with a combination of quillwork and painted geometrical designs. A painted robe had twice the value of an unpainted one (although this may be more related to the pliability and softness of a painted robe than to its artistic merit). Traders knew that the best robes were those the Blackfoot reserved for themselves, and painted ones had first received a full tanning treatment.

In 1833, when Prince Maximilian saw the Blackfoot on the Upper Missouri, he described women's clothing as consisting of a dress

> ... coming down to their feet, bound round the waist with a girdle, and is often ornamented with many rows of elk's teeth, bright buttons, and glass beads. The dress wraps over the breast, and has short, wide sleeves, ornamented with a good deal of fringe.... The lower arm is bare. The hem of the dress is likewise trimmed with fringes and scalloped. The women ornament their best dresses, both on the hem and sleeves, with dyed porcupine quills and thin leather strips, with broad diversified stripes of sky-blue and white glass beads. (1906:249)

Of course, for everyday wear, both men and women had plain, unadorned clothing. The women, in particular, required such costumes when butchering or skinning buffalo. Children's clothing was virtually a miniaturization of adult costumes, though very young boys and girls went entirely naked in summer. However, the Blackfoot were extremely modest and even in the warmest weather a man would retain a breechcloth while a woman would simply unfasten the sides of her dress below the arms to create a cooling effect.

The average tepee used 12 to 14 buffalo skins and required as many as 23 poles of lodgepole pine. Tepees were erected upon a basic foundation of four poles tied together at the top, the others being laid against them. Tepees always faced east, both as a protection against the prevailing winds and for religious reasons, in order to face the rising sun. The ears of the lodge, which regulated the draft, were controlled by two poles fitted through eyelets cut into their upper corners.

Some wealthy men had lodges made of 30 buffalo skins. These were unique structures, used only by warriors who had performed great feats of a dual nature, e.g., killing two enemies with a single shot. The lodges were made in two sections, each forming one horse travois load. Such a lodge had two entrances and two fireplaces, one of the latter being reserved for religious purposes. A tepee of this size was an obvious sign of opulence. Prior to the acquisition of the horse, lodges were much smaller, as they had to be dragged about on a dog travois. The travois was made by tying two poles together near the end; this was placed at the pack animal's neck, with the poles dragging behind on either side. A net or rack between the poles behind the animal provided the means for carrying several hundred pounds of goods. The only other method of transporting goods was in packs carried by dogs, horses, women, and sometimes men. The Blackfoot did not use canoes.

Although life was at times difficult for the nomadic Blackfoot, they enjoyed themselves whenever opportunity arose. Winter nights were spent telling stories—Napi tales to the children and war experiences and culture tales to adults. Some would be invited for an All Smoke Ritual, lasting from sunset to sunrise, each participant singing his or her own religious and personal songs in turn, taking breaks from time to time to smoke or eat. Some gathered to gamble, playing a hand game[1] for hours as they sang gambling songs. Young men rode around camp after sunset, singing songs beside the lodges of the wealthy in hope that they would be fed.

There were plenty of games for children—hide and seek, archery contests, races, throwing mud balls, or sliding down hills on sleds made of ribs. A popular game for young boys was to pretend that they were a war party. Two scouts would be sent ahead to see if they could find meat drying on a rack in camp. Then, on a signal, the boys raced forward and helped themselves. Often, the scouts were seen by their mothers; instead of getting dried meat, the boys received a severe clubbing from the owner of the lodge.

Besides sledding in winter, boys played a spin top game, whipping rocks on ice to make them spin and to knock their opponents out of a circle. Each pretended his rock was a warrior and the opponent an enemy; if he knocked the rock away, it became his prize. Another winter game was a contest to see who could throw a long stick, called a snow snake, the farthest. Properly hurled, the snake could slide for hundreds of metres along the crust of the snow.

Horse racing was popular with young and old. Some men trained horses used only for racing. Large amounts of goods and possessions might be bet on races. In some instances, the Blackfoot made a temporary peace with other tribes just to hold horse races.

A pastime of the women, besides shinny[2] and gambling, was to have working bees, which gave the opportunity to visit and tell stories. Sometimes they got together to make a new tepee for a friend or a prospective bride, while in other instances several quill workers would bring their work to a lodge where they could visit and drink tea while working. In times of peace when buffalo were plentiful, life became pleasant. During these periods people took time out from their labours to play, gamble, sing, and visit.

Warfare

The Blackfoot were in an almost constant state of warfare during the historic period. On one hand, they coveted the rich horse herds of the Crow, Shoshone, and Nez Perce to the south and southwest. To the north and east Cree and Assiniboine preyed on Blackfoot herds and also envied the heavy concentration of buffalo in Blackfoot hunting grounds. If war parties were not out raiding tribes to the south, they were being attacked from the north. To the southeast on rare occasions they even came into contact with the Sioux.

The closest translation of the term "warfare" in Blackfoot is "gambling" or to "take a gamble." This illustrates that warfare for the Blackfoot did not include taking over an enemy's territory or attempting to eliminate the enemy. Generally, Blackfoot went to war for booty or revenge. In the former case, a small war party might set out on foot, in expectation of capturing horses and returning in triumph. Killing an enemy was not their primary objective and scalping was not among the most heroic deeds. Rather, a warrior was praised for audacity and fearlessness in battle. Sleeps On Top was remembered because he rode into conflict armed only with a club and when he saw two mounted enemies he deliberately knocked one off the left side and the other off the right, just to show his bravery. Young warriors entering an enemy camp at night took the horses tethered to their owners' lodges, not just because they were the best animals but to display their skill as raiders. Most Blackfoot went on raiding parties between ages 13 and 20. After then most were content to hunt and to breed horses, but others continued to go to war until they were old men. For them, wealth in horses was less important than the glory and excitement of war.

Revenge parties were entirely different. Usually a revenge party was formed after an enemy war party successfully attacked a Blackfoot camp and killed people. Then grieving relatives called on fellow tribe members to form what could become a huge war party, sometimes consisting of 200–300 men. If the killing had been done by Cree, the war party made no attempt to seek out the actual perpetrators; they were satisfied to kill any Cree in revenge. Often, non-Natives did not understand that this practice also applied to them. If, for example, a whisky trader killed a Blackfoot, then his relatives might kill the first non-Native they found.

Less frequently, tribes were raided for trespassing on Blackfoot hunting grounds. Kutenais, Pend d'Oreilles, and Flatheads, who lived across the mountains, travelled to the prairies once or twice a year to hunt buffalo and usually sent scouts ahead to avoid conflict. If the Blackfoot learned of their presence, either a temporary peace treaty was made or the mountain tribe was forced to retreat. The frequent hunting parties of Cree and Metis (or Half-breeds, as the Blackfoot called them) were deeply resented because of their incursions. The Metis were particularly disliked because their huge, organized hunts resulted in the wholesale destruction of buffalo herds. As very little Blackfoot inter-marriage with non-Natives occurred during the nomadic period, the Metis always were associated with the enemy Cree.

Blackfoot History

Pre-Contact Period

Some controversy exists about the earliest hunting grounds of the Blackfoot. Considerable credence has been given to an account given by a Cree to explorer David Thompson in the winter of 1787–8. The Cree man, who had been adopted by the Peigans, claimed that the Blackfoot had lived in the woodlands near the Eagle Hills, in present-day Saskatchewan, and had moved from there onto the Plains. Other information suggests that in the 1600s the Shoshone and perhaps the Crow were in possession of southern Alberta and that the foot-hills area was occupied by Kutenais. A smallpox epidemic in the early 1700s is said to have severely depleted the Kutenais and left the region vacant for Blackfoot to occupy.

There can be little doubt that Blackfoot were absent from southern Alberta and northern Montana in the 1600s, but this does not necessar-ily mean that they were a Woodland people. At that time frequent fires kept the prairies free from trees right to the banks of the North Saskatchewan River. It is therefore probable that Blackfoot occu-pied the region from the Bow River to the North Saskatchewan for countless generations before moving south. As a people without horses they could move only short distances at a time and did not require a vast hunting area. Furthermore, their culture is almost completely devoid of Woodland traits, even though these characteristics have per-sisted among the Plains Cree, who are known to have a Woodlands origin.

The Eagle Hills may well have been included in the Blackfoot hunting grounds, for this area was simply an extension of the Plains. The depletion of the southern tribes by smallpox coincided with the Blackfoot acquisition of horses and guns, and a southern movement became practical; even at that date the foothills were one of the richest hunt-ing regions and offered the added advantages of mild winters and chinook winds.

Fur-Trade Period

Blackfoot did not meet a white man until the mid-1700s, but through inter-tribal trade, they already knew about him and his technology. When the first traders arrived on Hudson Bay in the late 1600s, they bartered metal objects, beads, and other goods to local Indians. These passed from tribe to tribe until they reached the Plains. Such utensils as knives, axes, and pots were bought by Blackfoot from Indian middlemen, usually Cree. Initially, one of the most important objects they obtained was the gun, for it was unknown to their enemies to the south. With it they were able to make the Shoshone and others flee in terror.

During this same period, between 1700 and 1725, the Blackfoot also obtained horses. These were descendants of those brought by the Spanish when they invaded Mexico in the 1500s. Over the years the animals had been acquired by southern tribes and were traded and/or raided northward. David Thompson was told how the Shoshone first attacked the Blackfoot using horse that "they rode, swift as the Deer, on which they dashed at the Peeagans, and with their stone Pukamoggan [clubs] knocked them on the head" (Glover 1962:241–2). But the Blackfoot soon acquired horses as well, and by the time the first white man, Anthony Henday, visited them in 1754 they were skilled riders.

By the late 1700s, the first trading posts of the British had been built within reach of the Blackfoot; by the 1790s, posts such as Fort Edmonton and Rocky Mountain House were located at the edge of their hunting grounds. Because their territory lacked good water routes and had few beaver or fur-bearing animals, traders had no reason to build forts south of the North Saskatchewan. As a result, the tribes were able to acquire European trade goods but were free of non-Native influences and were not obliged to alter their hunting and subsistence patterns as did some of their northern neighbours.

During this time the Sarcees, an offshoot of the Woodland Beaver tribe, became allies of the Blackfoot, as did the warlike Gros Ventres from the south. The Blackfoot had good relations with British, although the Gros Ventres proved to be intractable and ultimately destroyed a trading post before withdrawing to the southern part of their hunting grounds, in what is now eastern Montana.

In 1806 the Blackfoot had their first experience with white men travelling the Missouri River. The Lewis and Clark expedition was returning from the Pacific when they became involved in an altercation with the Piegans and killed a man. For the next quarter-century anyone coming up the river was considered to be an enemy. Not only were the Blackfoot incensed about the killing, they soon discovered that American fur-gathering methods were unacceptable. Whereas British companies established forts and encouraged Indians to hunt and trap, Americans operated independently, with trappers and mountain men invading Indian hunting grounds and doing the trapping themselves. The Blackfoot saw these men as thieves and treated them accordingly.

In 1831 hostilities virtually ceased when the American Fur Company finally made peace with the Blackfoot tribes and built Fort Piegan on the upper waters of the Missouri. From that time on the Blackfoot became keen traders who pitted American against British to get the best prices for their robes, furs, and dried meat.

The population of the Blackfoot tribes varied considerably during the nineteenth century, being affected primarily by smallpox epidemics in 1837 and 1869, and measles and scarlet fever epidemics in 1819 and 1864. In 1823 the populations were estimated to be 4,200 Blackfoot, 2,800 Blood, and 4,200 Peigan, but in 1841, just after the smallpox epidemic, they were reduced to 2,100 Blackfoot, 1,750 Blood, and 2,500 Peigan. The tribes made a rapid recovery, and in 1869, just before the next epidemic, there were 2,712 Blackfoot, 2,544 Blood, and 3,960 Peigan. After further losses in 1869–70, the tribes maintained a relatively stable population until they settled on their various reserves.

Treaties and the Reservation Period

In 1855 the Blackfoot made their first treaty with non-Natives. The American government was considering building a railroad across the northern Plains and clear title to Indian lands was required. In the treaty the Blackfoot surrendered the major part of the Montana Plains in exchange for exclusive hunting grounds, annuity payments, and other benefits. Two additional treaties, although never ratified, were made in 1865 and 1869, and the vast reservation was cut down in size by executive orders of 1873 and 1874 and by agreements in 1888 and 1896. These pacts were made almost exclusively with the South Piegan tribe, as the Bloods, North Peigans, and Blackfoot considered themselves to be "British" Indians.

Within a few years of the 1855 treaty, non-Natives began trickling into Montana Territory. First there were free traders, missionaries, and government officials. Then the discovery of gold along the mountains brought a flood of prospectors, merchants, and ranchers. The opening of steamboat navigation on the Missouri River provided easy access as far upriver as Fort Benton.

This influx resulted in clashes between Indians and settlers, reaching such proportions by 1866 that Montanans were referring to a "Blackfoot war." The events culminated with an attack in January 1870 by the US cavalry, under command of Major Eugene Baker, upon a peaceful camp of Piegans. The soldiers, looking for Mountain Chief's camp where they expected to find a number of men wanted for murder, mistakenly attacked Heavy Runner's camp, killing 173 persons; the majority were women and children. This event became known as the Baker Massacre.

The attack drove a number of bands to the Canadian side, but there Indians were exposed to the unlimited sale of whisky by American traders at such posts as Fort Whoop-Up, Standoff, and Slideout. Catholic missionary Constantine Scollen observed, "The fiery water flowed as freely ... as the streams running from the Rocky Mountains, and hundreds of poor Indians fell victims to the white man's craving for money, some poisoned, some frozen to death whilst in a state of intoxication, and many shot down by American bullets" (Morris 1880:248). The traders operated with impunity on the Canadian side because the territory had been recently transferred from British to Canadian jurisdiction and no means of maintaining law and order existed. Finally, in 1874, the North-West Mounted Police were sent west to stop the illegal traffic. The police established friendly relations with the Blackfoot, and in 1877 the Canadian government successfully negotiated Treaty No. 7, the Blackfoot Treaty, with the tribes that had chosen to live in Canadian territory. In the treaty Indians gave up all rights to their hunting grounds in exchange for reserves (in the United States these lands are called "reservations"), annuity payments, and other benefits. Besides the Blood, Blackfoot, Peigan, and Sarcee Indians, their mortal enemies, the Stoneys, also signed the treaty.

BOX 17.2 Chief Crowfoot

In 1877, when the Blackfoot Nation agreed to sign a treaty with the Canadian government, the final acceptance speech was made by Crowfoot, chief of the Siksika Nation. He stated:

> While I speak, be kind and patient. I have to speak to my people, who are numerous, and who rely on me to follow that course which in the future will tend to their good. The plains are large and wide. We are children of the plains, it is our home, and the buffalo has been our food always. I hope you will look upon the Blackfeet, Bloods and Sarcees as your children now, and that you will be indulgent and charitable to them. They all expect me to speak now for them, and I trust the Great Spirit will put into their breasts to be a good people—into the minds of the men, women and children, and their future generations. The advice given me and my people has proved to be very good. If the Police had not come to the country, where would we be all now? Bad men and whiskey were killing us so fast that very few, indeed, of us would have been left to-day. The Police have protected us as the feathers of the bird protect it from the frosts of winter. I wish them all good, and trust that all our hearts will increase in goodness from this time forward. I am satisfied. I will sign the treaty. (Morris 1880:272)

By 1880 the buffalo herds had been virtually exterminated in Blackfoot territory as the result of extensive slaughter by white hide hunters and the increasing incursions of Cree and Metis from the north. The buffalo had been the staff of life for the Blackfoot. With its destruction they had no recourse but to go to the reserves. In Montana, the South Piegans went to the Blackfeet Indian Reservation, while in southern Alberta the Bloods settled on their reserve—the largest in Canada—south of Fort Macleod, the Peigans near Pincher Creek, and the Blackfoot east of Calgary.

Although each tribe developed along separate lines after that date, particularly where two countries and two administrations were involved, there were many similarities in their history. All were obliged to turn to farming and ranching as a means of livelihood; log houses replaced tepees; Catholic, Methodist, or Anglican missionaries built boarding schools and took children away from their homes; and the ration house became the centre of reserve life. Both governments expected Indians to become self-supporting through farming within a few years, and when this did not happen the authorities turned to a welfare system to keep them fed and quiet. Few, if any, long-range programs were introduced, and for many Indians it was as though time were standing still. Many believed that governments were simply feeding them until they all

FIGURE 17.2 Anglican Mission, Blackfoot Reserve, c. 1900. Although teachers were dedicated, students faced massive cultural conflicts as well as the threat of tuberculosis because of the confined facilities. (Courtesy of the Glenbow Archives, NC 5–61)

died from such common diseases as tuberculosis, venereal disease, and scrofula.

The introduction of ranching in the 1890s improved the lot of many Indians, for they found parallels between hunting buffalo and raising cattle. However, when the agricultural industry became mechanized, capital was required, which the Indians did not have, and the problems of severe winters left many destitute and unable to cope with the demands of the dominant society. For Indians the reserves became a haven from the avariciousness, discrimination, and hostility they experienced in neighbouring towns. In Canada, efforts were made between 1907 and 1921 to force Indians to surrender large parts of their reserves. The Peigans gave up almost a third of their reserve in 1909 and the Blackfoot ended up losing about half their reserve in 1912. Only the Bloods resisted all attempts to give up parts of their reserve. In Montana the Blackfeet were allotted individual lands in 1907, and unclaimed areas were sold. In 1918 Indians were given permission to sell their allotments, and as a result the reservation became a checkerboard of Indian- and white-owned lands.

Recent Trends

From the point of view of the governments, little progress was made on the reserves until after World War II. Prior to that time, children were sent to residential schools and came out either to farm or to go on welfare. The Sun Dance continued to be the main ceremony, and warrior societies still met to hold dances and rituals. During the first half of the twentieth century the reserves became a mixture of the old and new. Elders still wore braids and spoke only Blackfoot, while young men dressed in contemporary clothes, participated in rodeos, and tried to find work on or near the reserve. Government policies discouraged anyone from getting an education beyond the age of 16. Some exceptional ones did become nurses and teachers, but most merely subsisted within the protection of their reserves. The mortality rate was high, particularly among infants, and the average life span was less than half the national norm. Although conditions were depressed and depressing, people still enjoyed family life, visiting, dancing, and participating in Indian events.

After World War II the governments of both countries began to provide more funds for better schools, improved health services, economic development, and the encouragement of self-reliance. In the 1960s the first graduates of integrated schools began to assume more significant roles. Most employees on the reserves were Native, including band managers, welfare officers, public works staff, police, and teachers. With better education some chose to leave reserves to work in nearby cities, although they usually returned after a few years. Attempts were made to introduce new industries to the reserves, but with only moderate success. Such businesses as a pencil factory, a mobile-home plant, a post-peeling plant, a commercial potato industry, a moccasin factory, retail stores, and other firms have been opened. Some existed for only a few months but others carried on successfully, employing dozens of people from the reserves.

Although opportunities for education and employment improved, many serious problems remained. The extension of liquor privileges to the Blackfoot occurred during the late 1960s after a court case made it illegal to restrict alcohol from Indians. This caused a traumatic social upheaval, which, while eventually levelling off, remains a serious problem. To this has been added a drug problem, which also has been calamitous, particularly among the young. Welfare and a lack of employment on the reserves continue as major difficulties. Coupled with a rising youth population, these issues cause concern for the future. Yet many Blackfoot would prefer to put up with a welfare system and lack of employment than to leave their extended families and go to the alien world of the cities. While there has been a migration to nearby cities such as Calgary, Lethbridge, and Great Falls, it is nowhere near the mass exodus that has taken place on other western reserves.

At the same time, the Blackfoot have assumed more responsibility for their own affairs and have taken over many jobs formerly performed by outsiders. One finds areas such as education, financial services, justice, construction, and administration being performed by band members. Members of tribal councils serve on many boards and committees, both on and off the reserve. Still others have reputations as artists, musicians, rodeo performers, and in other fields.

By the 1970s television began to make rapid inroads into Blackfoot life and culture. English replaced Blackfoot as the primary language in many households and oral traditions were becoming lost. The Sun Dance was almost abandoned on most reserves, while Indian Days flourished. **Pan-Indianism** began to replace tribalism as dances, songs, and even ceremonies were borrowed from other regions. However, a consciousness of their unique history and culture also resulted in the formation of museums, cultural centres, dancing clubs, and other activities designed to help preserve cultural elements. Even the Sun Dance has regained strength as conscious efforts were made to interest young people in Blackfoot religion and culture.

The 1980s and beyond have seen dramatic changes in Blackfoot life. This came about due to a combination of government changes to the Indian Act, which had legally dictated Indian lifestyle, and the self-determination of the reserves themselves to re-establish control over their future. As part of a political and cultural awareness, the Blackfoot Tribe has officially changed its name to the Siksika Nation, while the Peigans are called both the Peigan Nation and the Piikani Nation, and the Bloods the Kainaiowa Nation. The term for the Blackfeet Indians of Montana has remained unchanged, but a new cultural institution does use the term "Piegan" in its title. The Sarcee tribe is now called the Tsuu T'ina Nation.

Although the economies of all reserves are still basically rural, attempts have been made to provide basic retail services to tribal members rather than relying on nearby towns. The Siksika tribal office is located in a shopping mall. Among the many reserve-run businesses are service stations, a chartered bank, and a post office. The Blood Reserve has an administration building with a mall and has six Native-run service stations. The Peigan Reserve has a store, service station, and craft shop, while the Indians in Montana are still served by merchants in Browning—a white town located on the reservation.

Similarly, efforts are being made to provide more educational facilities on reserves. Many students are still being educated in nearby integrated schools, but all reserves now have their own schools, to the high-school level. The Blood Reserve, in particular, has placed considerable emphasis on Indian-run schools where language and culture courses are in the curriculum. In addition, the Bloods operate Red Crow College, affiliated with Lethbridge Junior College, while courses are offered on the Siksika reserve by Mount Royal University of Calgary. Many Indians from the region are attending colleges and universities, their numbers limited only by the amount the government is willing to invest in education.

All reserves are now close to being self-governing. No Indian department or other federal officials reside on reserves and the bulk of employees, administrators, accountants, outside workers, etc. are Native. Decisions of tribal councils still must be approved by the government, but usually this is a formality. The reserves, in varying degrees, are also assuming responsibility for education, social welfare, and the administration of justice.

Self-government is moving ahead rapidly—perhaps too rapidly, as people are given powers and authority that may clash with traditional practices. For example, nepotism was an integral part of Blackfoot family life, but may be detrimental to tribal administration in the future.

Problems do exist. On the one hand, the effects of higher education are being felt with more Blackfoot being members of most professions and trades. At the same time, the loss of language and culture has become so widespread that attempts are being made to stem the tide. Language courses are offered on all reserves and efforts are being made to interest young people in cultural programs. These have had only limited success as the pervasive influence of television has virtually eliminated the Blackfoot language from many homes.

In the economic and social spheres, the situation on most reserves has not greatly improved in recent years. Alcohol and drug offences continue to be a major social problem while unemployment remains in the 75–80 per cent range. Yet, some progress has been made through rehabilitation programs, and gradually intoxication is becoming less socially acceptable. Many social dances and meetings are now completely alcohol-free at the insistence of the sponsors.

Conclusion

It should be apparent from this chapter that the Blackfoot have been a proud and independent people. As long as there were buffalo to hunt they needed no outside help, but once their primary means of subsistence was gone they had to settle on reserves. After almost one and a half centuries of sedentary life, they have retained many parts of their culture, but other elements have virtually disappeared.

There can be no question that the future will continue to bring the loss of cultural practices. If, however, they are sometimes replaced with newer practices such as those offered by Pan-Indianism, a Native, if not traditional Blackfoot, identity will remain. The changes will bring pain and hardship, yet the Blackfoot are an adaptable people. In spite of setbacks, their progress is as impressive as it is inevitable.

NOTES

1. The hand game is a team game, usually with four to a side, that involves players guessing which hand or hands hold one or more markers.

2. "Shinny" is a term applied to a number of team games involving sticks and a ball or puck. Thus, in Canada, street or pond hockey is sometime called shinny.

REFERENCES AND RECOMMENDED READINGS

Coues, Elliott, ed. 1897. *New Light on the Early History of the Greater Northwest: The Manuscript Journals of Alexander Henry and of David Thompson, 1799–1814*, 2 vols. New York: Francis Harper.

Dempsey, H.A. 1972. *Crowfoot, Chief of the Blackfeet*. Norman: University of Oklahoma Press.

———. 1978. *Charcoal's World*. Saskatoon: Western Producer Prairie Books.

———. 1980. *Red Crow, Warrior Chief*. Saskatoon: Western Producer Prairie Books. Hugh Dempsey is best known for his biographies. Although deal-

ing with individuals, they are placed in a historic and cultural context and so relate to wider, even contemporary issues. Red Crow, for instance, is portrayed as a political realist who adjusts to the reserve system but at no point loses his Indianness.

———. 1994. *The Amazing Death of Calf Shirt and Other Blackfoot Stories*. Calgary: Fifth House.

Dempsey, L.J. 1999. *Warriors of the King: Prairie Indians in World War I*. Regina: Canadian Plains Research Centre, University of Regina. A study of some 400 prairie Indians who enlisted in World War I, only a generation after the treaties. Although living in poverty under an oppressive reserve regime, they enlisted at rates comparable to other Canadians and acquitted themselves with honour.

———. 2007. *Blackfoot War Art: Pictographs of the Reservation Period, 1880–2000*. Norman: University of Oklahoma Press. A uniquely Native perspective on the importance of warrior art in Blackfoot history and culture,, based on extensive interviews as well as museum and archival resources..

Ewers, J.C. 1958. *The Blackfeet: Raiders on the Northwestern Plains*. Norman: University of Oklahoma Press. This is the most important book on the Blackfoot in the pre-reserve period. Also of interest to students of change is Ewers's *The Horse in Blackfoot Indian Culture*, published in 1955 by the Smithsonian Institution, Washington, DC.

Glover, Richard, ed. 1962. *David Thompson's Narrative, 1784–1812*. Toronto: Champlain Society.

Grinnell, G.B. 1913. *Blackfeet Indian Stories*. New York: Charles Scribner's Sons.

———. (1892) 1962. *Blackfoot Lodge Tales*. Lincoln: University of Nebraska Press. These are classics on traditional Blackfoot culture.

Hungry Wolf, Beverly. 1980. *Ways of My Grandmothers*. New York: W. Morrow. This contemporary Blackfoot writer is not to be confused with Adolf Hungry Wolf, a prolific German-born Californian writer often assumed to be Indian.

Maximilian, A.P. 1906. Travels in the Interior of North America, In *Early Western Travels*, vols. 22–4, edited by R.G. Thwaites. Cleveland: A.H. Clark.

Morris, Alexander. 1880. *The Treaties of Canada with the Indians of Manitoba, the North-West Territories, and Kee-Wa-Tin*. Toronto: Willing and Williamson.

Mountain Horse, Mike. 1979. *My People the Bloods*. Calgary: Glenbow Museum. Written during the 1930s, this is a fascinating Native viewpoint of history and culture by one of the first graduates of the local mission school system.

Wissler, Clark. 1910. "Material Culture of the Blackfoot Indians," *Anthropological Papers of the American Museum of Natural History* 5, 1: 1–175.

———. 1912. "Social Life of the Blackfoot Indians," *Anthropological Papers of the American Museum of Natural History* 7, 1: 1–64.

———. 1913. "Societies and Dance Associations of the Blackfoot Indians," *Anthropological Papers of the American Museum of Natural History* 11, 4: 359–460.

———. 1918. "The Sun Dance of the Blackfoot Indians," *Anthropological Papers of the American Museum of Natural History* 16, 3: 223–70. Intended for the specialist, these are the most comprehensive works on the Blackfoot.

CHAPTER 18

The Plains Metis

Heather Devine

Introduction: The Making of an Ethnohistorian[1]

It was never my intention to become a scholar: certainly not an ethnohistorian. Like most researchers, ethnohistorians are motivated to investigate topics out of a personal interest to discover the "truth" about something. In my case, my interest in the Metis was personal, in that I am Metis—a discovery I made in early adulthood after a childhood spent living in a town with a large Native population.

When I was eight, our family moved to northern Alberta. I did not then understand the roots of Aboriginal poverty. Nor did I understand what made one person Indian and another Metis, and on what criteria these identities were assigned by the Canadian government. I certainly did not understand why treaty Indians had benefits and rights, and why non-status Indians and Metis, who seemed culturally identical, had no rights or protection.

Two decades after moving away from home, I decided to figure out for myself exactly how a person came to be Indian or Metis. More specifically, I decided to focus on this question for my doctoral thesis in Canadian Native history. My dissertation, "Les Desjarlais: Aboriginal Ethnogenesis in a Canadien Family," explored the development of Aboriginal ethnic identities in general and

Metis ethnicity in particular. Those themes were examined by tracing the origins, development, and dispersion of the various mixed-race descendants of one Canadien family. Generations of Desjarlais men left Quebec in the eighteenth and nineteenth centuries to engage in the fur trade in the Great Lakes, Rupert's Land, and the Missouri basin, where they intermarried with Natives.

Although the thousands of Desjarlais descendants share common roots, they are ethnically and culturally diverse. Many identify as Metis. Others are legally and culturally Indians, residing on reserve communities in Canada and the United States. Still others are fully integrated into mainstream society, with little or no awareness of their Aboriginal heritage. How did this variation evolve?

My research set out to identify political, social, and economic factors governing the development of individual and collective ethnic identities by various branches of the family. More specifically, I asked:

1. What cultural values, motives, skills, and behaviours did family members exhibit which influenced their political, social, and economic contacts with Aboriginals, and what beliefs, needs, and practices influenced the manner in which Aboriginal groups dealt with outsiders, specifically Canadien *engagés* and freemen?

2. What were the social, cultural, economic, and political factors which influenced Desjarlais descendants to identify (or be designated) as Indian, as Metis, or as Euro-Canadian in the eighteenth and nineteenth centuries?

3. Which Euro-Canadian and Aboriginal cultural repertoires did family members draw upon to respond to these external pressures, and why?

4. How do the adaptive responses of the family reflect the larger experience of Aboriginal ethnic development?

My goal was to explain how Aboriginal identity formation in Canada evolved from a flexible process based on kinship to a rigid, ascribed phenomenon dictated by government. I chose to investigate this issue through the "lens" of kinship, because my personal and professional experiences suggested that kinship was, and is, the organizing principle governing most social, economic, and political activity in Aboriginal communities.

What Is Ethnohistory?

Until the 1960s, "ethnohistory meant, for anthropologists and historians alike, the use of documentary sources to talk about the past" (Krech 1991:347). During this period, oral historical accounts from present-day informants were discounted as credible sources of information about the past.

Ethnohistory, both theoretically and methodologically, is primarily a phenomenon of the last 50 years. The sources of information used by ethnohistorians are as diverse and eclectic as their theories. Historical sources are not only manuscripts, books, and oral interviews. Ethnohistorians use "maps, music, paintings, photographs, folklore, oral tradition, ecology, site exploration, archaeological artifacts (especially trade goods), museum collections, enduring customs, language, and place names, as well as a richer variety of written sources" (Axtell 1979:4).

Is ethnohistory a discipline or a method? In many ways, it is an attitude toward knowledge.

As an ethnohistorian, I utilize all primary and secondary sources of information, and do not "privilege" any source because of its form. Each type of source—an interview with an Elder, an archaeological artifact, a baptismal certificate, or a census record—yields a certain kind of information which can be combined with other sources to provide more complex understandings.

My own research has relied heavily on tracing Metis individuals and groups through genealogical reconstruction. The primary data comes from censuses, parish documents, business records, land-claim affidavits, oral accounts, and historical narratives. These are then compiled into a computerized database and interpreted through a socio-historical lens provided by a multiplicity of primary and secondary ethnographic and historical sources. The resulting narrative is a combination of quantifiable and anecdotal data from primary sources interpreted within a socio-cultural context.

Who Are the Metis?

The answer to this question depends largely on whom you ask, and when. A "metis" was once simply a person of mixed European and Aboriginal ancestry. More recently, the term "Metis" has been used to refer to unique and identifiable contemporary populations of mixed ancestry who can trace their origins to the fur and robe trade as practised in the West and Northwest between the sixteenth and nineteenth centuries. In the words of the Metis National Council:

> Written with a small "m," metis is a racial term for anyone of mixed Indian and European ancestry. Written with a capital "M," Metis is a socio-cultural or political term for those originally of mixed ancestry who evolved into a distinct indigenous people during a certain historical period in a certain region of Canada. (Peterson and Brown 1985:6)

Although this definition is also problematic (as discussed later), it distinguishes between the different historical experiences of metis/Metis peoples.

In recent years, however, we have come to understand that ethnicity defined only through biological and cultural traits is incomplete and therefore inaccurate. Ethnicity at the grassroots level is determined by three criteria operating simultaneously: biological ancestry ("race"), a person's own perception of their ethnicity, and what other individuals and collectivities (such as government bodies) see that person's ethnicity to be.

Two Cultures Meet

Some wag once wrote that the first metis was born nine months after the first European arrived in North America. Whatever the truth of this, we can be sure there were no babies without some prior negotiation. When Aboriginal peoples and Europeans first met, each dealt with these strangers based on their own cultural "toolkit" of values, attitudes, behaviours, and skills.

Most Aboriginal peoples had, and still have, very specific cultural values and practices regarding land and harvesting its resources. They did not have a concept of owning parcels of land; what they had was a notion of a group's territory, based on the systematic, seasonal use of resources in an area. Their territorial boundaries were flexible, in keeping with the vagaries of climate and soil (for agriculture), and the availability of animals, birds, fish, and plants for harvesting. When others crossed the "border" of a territory—a river, a range of hills, a stand of timber—they could expect any number of responses from the locals. One response was simply to kill intruders. A second was to permit the group temporary access to cross the territory, or for limited harvesting.

In these cases, negotiations were essential. Aboriginal groups did not trade with strangers or enemies; they traded with kin. So they would establish kin relations through ceremonies, with gift exchange as a temporal and spiritual means of establishing and securing reciprocity. These agreements were not permanent—conditions change—but it was expected that they would be renewed from time to time with further ceremony. These agreements were seen to be broken if either party did not live up to them.

The language of these negotiations reflected their familial nature. At the conclusion of the ceremonies the participants were considered to be kin, with the privileges and responsibilities that kin (in this particular agreement) could expect. A common result was the prolonged residence of a member of the visiting group with the host group—to learn the language, to learn their cultural practices, and to familiarize themselves with the territory.

What anthropologists call "fictive" kin relations often became real when members of two groups married. Children served to strengthen bonds between the groups, and increase the levels of reciprocity.

These methods for dealing with outsiders—a combination of ceremony, negotiation, and sharing—were also applied to relationships with the Europeans who arrived in the sixteenth century and chose to stay in the New World. And did children come from these early relationships? Yes, but were they Metis?

Trade Practices and *Metissage*

Initially most European traders in what is now Canada established coastal posts—factories—and insisted that Natives come there to trade. This was the practice of the Hudson's Bay Company, the "Company of Adventurers" as it was called, that received its Royal Charter in 1670 from Prince Rupert of England to exploit the lands of the Hudson Bay watershed. The day-to-day operation of the company evolved from the strategy originally devised by Pierre Radisson and Médard Chouart, Sieur des Grosseilliers, two Canadien freebooters who had switched loyalties to the British.

They contended that the speediest access to the best fur country lay via ship to Hudson Bay, rather than through the maze of waterways from the St Lawrence, then held by the French.

The company established forts at the mouths of the major rivers flowing into Hudson Bay. They relied on Cree and Assiniboine middlemen ("trading Indians") to travel overland to acquire pelts in the interior (from "trapping Indians"), and return to trade these skins for goods at the posts. The furs would be shipped from York Factory to London.

The clerks manning these posts did no trading themselves with the trapping Indians. Nor did they seek provisions for themselves. Instead, they relied on bands of Swampy Cree (called "Homeguard Indians") to provide fish, fowl, and game for food, and to manufacture leather clothing, snowshoes, and other necessities.

In the early years, HBC policy regarding relations with Aboriginals was that no informal fraternization was permitted. This was impossible to enforce. The posts were male-only establishments, and the closest English settlements were thousands of miles away, in New England. The need for food and clothing, not to mention companionship, soon undermined the edicts from London.

Over time, a population of metis children grew up in the bands circling Hudson Bay. But, because they could not be taken back to England, and were not officially permitted to live within the posts, they were raised within the Cree culture. They, and their descendants, became Cree.

The Fur Trade of New France to 1760

The French had a different relationship with Indigenous people from the outset. Like other European countries, France wanted to find a shorter trade route to Asia. Although most countries travelled the western overseas route to North America after 1492 in their search for Asia, France was restricted from travelling to North America

for approximately 30 years. Part of the delay was due to a series of papal edicts, reserving the New World to Portugal and Spain and forbidding other European Roman Catholic nations from staking claims. The French managed to circumvent this by claiming that their overseas activities were intended to propagate the Christian faith. Although Spain and Portugal protested, France succeeded in persuading the Pope that its overseas projects were religious. King Francis I also proposed that effective occupation of a country, and not simply discovery, should constitute the right of possession. This allowed France to introduce settlement schemes and to establish commercial and military relationships with Natives under the guise of religious conversion.

In order for the French to be successful in religious conversion, settlement, and trade, they had to establish good relations with the Natives. For the earliest French traders and colonists in Acadia and New France, fraternization with Natives was both a survival and a financial necessity.

The French quickly discovered that northeastern America was unsuitable for agriculture and would not support large numbers of settlers. Its northerly latitude resulted in long, cold winters and boreal forests yielding little but timber and furs. Agriculture was thus confined to riverine lowlands. In Acadia the French settlers successfully adapted European diking practices to reclaim salt marsh lands and support abundant crops and farm animals.

The Mi'kmaq and Maliseet of Acadia and the Wendat of the St Lawrence were generous with these early arrivals, teaching them how to survive the harsh winters, use local plants to prevent disease, build fishing weirs and canoes, manufacture snowshoes and hide clothing, and navigate in the bush. They also provided a variety of animal furs and an abundance of "country produce"—meat, fish, birds, musk, and quills. In return the French (like their British and Dutch counterparts) provided trade goods—metal fishhooks, knives, traps, kettles, and files; red ochre, glass beads, and silver ornaments; and woollen blankets. Perhaps the most important European commodities were guns and ammunition, providing short-term military advantage against their Aboriginal enemies until they, in turn, were also armed.

Furs were valuable in Europe, and obtained at a nominal cost from Natives who harvested them in their own hunting territories. The subsistence agriculture practised in the St Lawrence Valley and Acadia did not displace Aboriginal peoples, as did farming in the British colonies. Because the French chose to concentrate on the fur trade—a mutually rewarding activity where both parties benefited—interpersonal relations between them and their trading allies tended to be more stable than those experienced by English settlers.

The French eventually expanded their influence into the heart of North America using a three-pronged strategy involving the simultaneous establishment of Roman Catholic missions, French military and civil structures, and fur-trading establishments—all operating out of military fortifications established at the junctions of major waterways.

The *En Derouine* Trade and Metissage[2]

French success in penetrating North America was possible because they established strong familial ties with Aboriginals, a result of traders, military personnel, and clergy living for extended periods in isolated hinterland posts.

These trading houses were bases of operations for *negotiants* (independent traders) and their *engagés* (servants under contract), who traded with Indians directly, without intermediaries. In order to ease the provisioning requirements of the trading houses over the winter, *engagés* were commonly sent into the bush to winter with a Native family. This practice of living and trading with hunting bands was known as living *en derouine*.

The process of "wintering" served several purposes, all of which enhanced trade. First, inexperienced *engagés* could learn Native languages, familiarize themselves with the territory, and master hunting, trapping, and woodcraft skills. Cree was the lingua franca of the Canadian fur trade, along with French, which was the birth language of the Canadien *engagés* hired from parishes along the St Lawrence. Although most Canadien employees were adept at paddling and portaging, they generally required training in specialized skills such as canoe construction and repair. Whatever the *engagé* could not make himself, he could acquire from Indian friends and relations.

Wintering enabled *engagés* to develop personal relationships with Natives essential for personal survival and trading success. As noted, trade was inextricably linked to kinship. Kin ties meant responsibility as well as benefits. *Engagés* would be expected to look after the Aboriginal families in times of need by securing extra trade goods and provisions from the post. They were expected to defend their relatives against attacks by other Natives, and to avenge wrongs committed against their kin. They were encouraged to participate in raids, to acquire horses or slaves, or to push into new hunting territories. The children resulting from marriages *à la façon du pays* ("according to the custom of the country") further attached the wintering trader to the band, cementing the loyalty of Indian relatives—and their hunts—to specific trading establishments.

The *engagés* who wintered in the interior generally were descended from or affiliated with Canadien families with connections in the French regime. Wintering was an accepted part of doing business, as was the *metissage* that resulted.

Early in the regime, the *en derouine* trade was viewed as a lucrative and effective instrument of diplomacy. Authorities were confident that French culture and religion would prevail. Therefore they did not anticipate possible negative consequences of closer economic and social relations with Amerindians.

Racial mixing was encouraged by civil and religious authorities as a means of creating "one people," a non-violent approach to conquest and occupation. The baptism of Amerindian brides prior to marriage by priests contributed to achieving the Christianizing goals justifying France's presence in America. A policy of *metissage* also addressed the need to provide a sanctioned outlet for sexual activity in a society with few European women. Mixed unions also helped to stabilize and expand the population of the colony, necessary to its long-term survival.

However, the authorities underestimated the appeal of Aboriginal culture. Young men living with Natives often contracted unions *à la façon du pays*. These "country" relationships were attractive because they provided access to women's companionship and labour without the permanence of formal marriage. Responsibility for children was usually assumed by the mother and her family, though the father could acknowledge and support his metis children if so inclined.

Under the French regime, *metissage* did not result in a distinct Metis "people." Although the isolated posts of the Great Lakes region developed a unique metis culture based on cultural mixing, the children from these unions were socialized as French. The presence of clergy and military personnel ensured the regulation of marital unions and the baptism of metis children, who were then considered Christian and French. The metis children born and raised in Indian camps, however, remained Indian, though their names might allude to their mixed background, and their roles in their communities might evolve into those of traders, diplomats, or other intermediaries.

The same can be said of Acadians. Although *metissage* took place from the beginning (and today's Acadian population has much Amerindian ancestry), Acadians were considered not Metis, but rather a French colonial culture. Again, the presence of even limited colonial authority prevented the emergence of a distinct Metis culture.

The florescence of a uniquely Metis culture would not take place until French traders reached the *pays d'en haut*—the upper country to the west beyond the Great Lakes.

The French Presence in Western Canada

Although we are unable to determine precisely when the first biracial people appeared in what is now western Canada, we know that several small companies formed in New France in the early eighteenth century to carry out trade beyond the Great Lakes. Ostensibly established to extend France's military influence into the heart of the continent, their founders also sought to explore the lands south and west of Hudson Bay, where they knew that the HBC had yet to establish a permanent presence. To receive the blessing of the authorities, their activities were couched in language that reflected nationalistic goals. As records of their *congés* (trading passes) reveal, a goal of these expeditions was to find a passage to *la mer d'Ouest*—the Western Sea—gateway to the lucrative China trade.

With the assistance of the Assiniboine and Cree, the French familiarized themselves with the region to the west of Kaministiquia, a post first established at the western edge of Lake Superior by Daniel Greysolon Sieur du Lhut (Duluth) in 1678, and later rebuilt by Robertel de la Noue in 1717. Under the command of Pierre Gaultier de Varennes, Sieur de la Vérendrye, the next 25 years would see a series of posts built at the junctions of key river systems west of the Great Lakes. In 1727 La Vérendrye was appointed assistant commandant of Les Postes du Nord; by 1729 he was appointed commander of the Western Posts until his retirement in 1744. The following posts were built under his orders: Fort St Pierre on the Rainy River, 1731;

Fort St Charles on Lake of the Woods, 1732; Fort Maurepas on the Winnipeg River, 1733; Fort Rouge on the Red River, 1738; Fort La Reine at Portage La Prairie, 1738; Fort Dauphin on Lake Manitoba, 1741; Fort Bourbon on Cedar Lake, 1741; Fort a la Corne on the Saskatchewan, 1741; and Fort Paskoyac on the Saskatchewan, 1741 (Shaw 1973).

The French inched their way west to the Rocky Mountain foothills by 1752, intercepting Aboriginal trading parties that might otherwise reach Hudson Bay, where the English sat, waiting for furs. Using the farthest western post (always called *la fort des prairies*) as a jumping-off point, the French continued to extend their commercial influence by canoe, by dog sled, on horseback, and on foot.

Many of these posts were temporary, with a life of one or two trading seasons. Others may have closed at the onset of the Seven Years' War, which suspended the push westward until after 1763. A handful of these western posts may have operated during the conflict, possibly with trade goods shipped by canoe from posts in Illinois and Missouri.

The Northern Metis

An aged Metis patriarch named François Beaulieu (1771–1872), resident on the shores of Great Slave Lake, was descended from these French regime traders. He informed Father Emile-Fortuné Petitot that he was the son of a Frenchman named François Beaulieu, an employee of la Compagnie des Sioux. When Peter Pond arrived in 1780 to establish a trading post, its construction was assisted by local Metis. A succession of traders and explorers— Alexander Mackenzie, Sir John Franklin, Sir John Rae—benefited from the services of Beaulieu and other Metis who served time and again as canoe-men, guides and interpreters, and provisioners.

Note that I referred to these people as "Metis" rather than "metis." Established as early as 1771, this is one of the earliest permanent Metis populations west of the Great Lakes (Petitot 1891).

Naming the Other—Aboriginal Terms for Metis

We know when Metis people began to be seen as separate and distinct people: when there is record of these nascent collectivities being ascribed a separate identity—a name—by others. These Aboriginal names served to describe not only the physical characteristics of these new people but also the unique cultural values that set them apart. Naming is an important diagnostic characteristic for defining ethnic separateness, as is the development of a distinctive language.

Perhaps the earliest distinctive name for mixed-race people refers to a physical characteristic. *Les Bois-Brulé*—"the scorched-wood people" was a term referring to Metis skin colour, tan as opposed to brown.

Aboriginal terms for Metis often referred to their unique occupational status. The Nehiyawak (Cree) referred to them as *otipaymisiwak*—"their own boss," or "the people who own themselves" in reference to their tendency to work independently rather than as employees of fur-trade companies. The Dakota (Sioux) referred to Plains Metis as *Slota* ("Grease People"), possibly in reference to pemmican production, a major nineteenth-century economic activity which brought them into conflict with Dakota over bison hunting territories. Of the Northern Metis of Great Slave Lake, Father Petitot noted that their Dene nickname was *Banlay*, roughly "he to whom the land belongs," in reference to their dominant position in local trade, transport, and provisioning (1891:78).

The Anglo-Canadian Fur Trade (1763–1821)

The 1763 Treaty of Paris ended warfare between the French and British in North America. France ceded Canada, and claims to all North American territory east of the Mississippi River, to England, opening rich territories to British exploitation. Almost immediately, itinerant traders or "pedlars"—many of them American Scots who had moved northward to Montreal—made their way to the eastern slopes of the Rockies. One of them, James Finlay, first wintered in the *pays d'en haut* in 1766. His son Jacco Finlay, born about 1768 to an Ojibwa woman, entered the service of the North West Company in 1798 and soon was a fixture on the eastern slopes.

Between 1806 and 1821, prior to the coalition of the Hudson's Bay and North West Companies, it is argued that mixed-race people in what is now western Canada were "small-m" metis,—biologically biracial, but culturally part of either ancestral community. The first generation of metis children who emerged from unions *à la façon du pays* were generally raised as Aboriginals. They inherited the privileges, responsibilities, and loyalties associated with membership in Aboriginal families. But if not, they might be physically removed from the fur country and returned to their father's ancestral home for upbringing and education. Or, if they remained in the country and their father remained employed by a major trading company, they would likely be socialized within the company's corporate culture.

However, not all *engagés* chose to remain employed by fur-trade companies. Although all servants signed contracts binding them to their company, many chose to leave once their contracts expired. They possessed the wilderness skills and social connections to live independently in their own extended family groups—separate from the trading establishments and the Indian bands. Known as "freemen" or *gens libres*, they assumed independent roles as brokers, trappers, and provisioners. Their children—raised "betwixt and between" the trading post and the Indian lodge—were to establish a cultural identity that achieved its florescence in western Canada—the Metis.

What is Michif?

Language is culturally important for any group. And Michif, the language of the Metis, is truly unique. Today it is endangered, numbering approximately 1,000 speakers in western Canada and the northern United States, though three times this number once spoke it. This mixed language (and it is a language, having formal linguistic structures) is made up primarily of French noun phrases and Cree verb phrases. Unlike most hybrid languages which have a very simplified grammar, these noun and verb phrases retain very complex patterns of agreement from both parent languages. This strongly suggests that it was created by people fully functional in both languages.

Metis Community Life

As time passed, these loosely knit groups of freemen formed semi-permanent communities used as a base for seasonal rounds of hunting, trapping, and trading. Most posts had a contingent of Metis families living nearby, and the annual reports of post journals kept enumerations of them, along with estimates of the numbers of other Aboriginal groups.

Family life in the early years reflected the demands of the northern fur trade. Hunting large animals such as bison or moose was primarily a man's occupation, as was trapline maintenance; the movement of goods and people by dogsled, horse, and canoe (known as "tripping"); trade negotiations; and paramilitary activities. Patriarchs of the first generations of Metis also had Euro-Canadian family responsibilities, and extended trips back to Montreal or Britain were common.

The prolonged absences of males were reflected in flexible and highly extended family structures intended to ensure the continued well-being of family members and economic arrangements. In this "pre-industrial" subarctic fur trade, business and family life were one and the same—

one's relatives were one's employees or employers. Female cousins, where permissible under religious codes, became marriage partners. Widows married their dead husband's relatives or business associates, and on and on.

In the *pays d'en haut*, Euro-Canadian fur traders, particularly freemen, amalgamated their **endogamous** marital practices with marriage *à la façon du pays*. Much has been written about the practice of "turning off"—the process whereby a departing trader arranged for the care and support of his country wife and children by providing financial support—often in the form of another husband—prior to leaving the country permanently. Less talked about is the practice of designating "protectors" for women and children when a fur-trade father was away—either on furlough in Lower Canada or on extended trading trips. The vagaries of life in the fur trade necessitated such flexible arrangements, as the Indians certainly knew and the traders grew to appreciate. The "Ile-a-la-Crosse Post Journal" of 1825–6, kept by HBC trader George Keith, contains a list entitled "Families Whose Protectors are Retired or Dead" (HBCA 1825–26). In it he notes the original "protector" (i.e., the original father and husband of the family), his country of origin, the composition of the family, where they lived, the immediate protector (i.e., the new father and husband), and any remarks. That this information was enumerated in the journal suggests that it had become standard practice. Not noted is whether these "protector" arrangements were temporary or permanent.

The genealogical records, particularly of the earliest generations of Canadien freemen, suggest that these arrangements were extremely flexible. Freemen sometimes had two wives simultaneously. Some freemen ended one country union in order to take another woman to wife, only to resume relations with the original woman later. A hunter might break off relations with a woman, who would then form a union with his close hunting companion. A man might leave, returning years later to reclaim his country family.

Women with these largely absent partners socialized their children in an Aboriginal environment where an intricate web of family obligations provided the moral and behavioural foundations for daily activity. The Cree term describing this web of familial obligations—*wahkootowin*—was operative in most Aboriginal families in the fur country where Aboriginal values were preferred "on the ground" (Macdougall 2006:431–62).

The result of combining Euro-Canadian and Aboriginal families was a complex network of kinship which grew more intricate with each generation. Related to one another by descent through both mother's and father's family lines, these ties were further strengthened by multiple unions which produced siblings, half-siblings, step-parents, and temporary "protectors."

Understandably, these marriage practices caused consternation for the priests who arrived, bringing us to the next key factor in the formation of distinctive Metis community—the nature of spiritual practices and beliefs in the *pays d'en haut* prior to widespread Euro-Canadian settlement.

Spiritual practices in the more isolated regions of western Canada reflected the social environment of its inhabitants—a boreal/parkland hunter–gatherer culture dominated by Aboriginal beliefs and customs. Biracial children raised here did not necessarily see themselves as culturally separate from their Aboriginal cousins. With few distinctive European cultural markers to differentiate them, their cultural separateness was based largely on the strength of the Euro-Canadian cultural influences established by their fathers and grandfathers. If the father was absent, and there were no dominant cultural influence present from another Euro-Canadian person or institution, the child became Indian culturally. The continued intermarriage of metis children into local bands further attenuated these already weak links. However, the continued residence of Euro-Canadian patriarchs of these metis groups generally ensured that children got a nominal exposure to Christian beliefs and practices, whether "sprinkling" newborns in the absence of priests, the saying of prayers or other religious observances, or the repeated requests for priests by elderly Canadiens eager to have their country marriages regularized, their children baptized, or their bodies buried in hallowed ground.

Culturally, these Metis communities were a mixture of Aboriginal and European customs and values. From their European ancestors they developed a passion for fiddle music, jigging and dancing, European foodstuffs (Scots bannock in particular, as well as tea), card playing and games of chance, and embroidery and handicraft. From their Aboriginal ancestors they inherited attachment to the land and its wildlife, and respect for personal freedom. From both cultures they inherited a love of family and community.

Metis Politics to 1821

The fur-trade world was split between a corporate hierarchy dominated by European commercial values and practices and a backcountry culture comprising extended families of Indigenous hunters and gatherers, whose practices and values were shaped by kin obligations, survival imperatives, and Aboriginal spiritual beliefs. Metis success depended on their employing a repertoire of skills and behaviours acquired from both parent cultures, enabling them to straddle both environments without alienating either—a cultural "high-wire" act that few people mastered completely.

For freemen to maintain their independence, enhance their status, and ensure their families' well-being, it was necessary to establish dominance over the local fur trade. Freemen bands functioned best when they could maintain familial relations with adjacent Indian bands and with personnel at trading companies simultaneously, a task best accomplished when family members contracted marriages à la façon du pays, secured employment in trading posts, and wintered with Indian bands. Having family in both environments facilitated the flow of goods, enabling freemen to profit from their role as fur brokers between their Indian kin and Euro-Canadian traders, while ensuring a steady supply of trade goods through relatives employed in the posts.

Should kin relations not enable freemen to achieve their goals, strategies would be adjusted. In choosing alternatives, they selected from both cultural repertoires. Some family members might seek power among local bands as shamans, hunters, or warriors, forcibly moving into hunting territories through the threat of physical violence, sorcery, or hunting skill. Others would apply pressure to the companies by threatening to work for opposing firms, by withdrawing their service as engagés, interpreters, and hunters, or by pressuring other engagés to desert. They would use their mobility to avoid trade sanctions, and manipulate their kin connections to foment discontent.

These techniques, however, only worked where freemen's services were deemed essential, or where freemen could gain access to alternative markets or employment. Unfortunately, Metis ability to manipulate working conditions in their favour began to disappear once the major companies united into a single corporate monopoly—the HBC.

This temporary decline in Metis fortunes was largely due to HBC policies implemented after 1821, intended to "systematize and regularize" its business practices and to consolidate its monopoly. To achieve this, they needed to control activities of individuals both inside and outside the firm. A key element was developing policies targeted at "freemen," "half-breeds," and "Indians," intended to undermine their power and autonomy by restricting access to goods and services. Freemen who did not pay their debts, who flouted the new trapping regulations, or who deserted the company were denied access to guns, ammunition, and other essential goods at all HBC posts.

The time from 1821 to 1830 was one of economic and social transition for the freemen. Despite the initial hardships brought about by the HBC monopoly, the freemen's unique skills remained indispensable. The continued trade in pemmican and buffalo robes, essential to HBC survival, soon brought a degree of economic prosperity to those freemen who stayed in Rupert's Land. As time and distance slowly eroded kin relations with their families in Lower Canada and their tribal kin in Rupert's Land, stronger kinship bonds were established with other freemen families. In one or two generations, thriving new communities whose cultural, political, and economic ethos embodied the nexus of European and Aboriginal values, attitudes, and behaviours became well established.

By the 1860s the Metis dominated the day-to-day operation of the fur and robe trade. They trapped, processed, and traded animal pelts and bison robes. They caught and dried fish and manufactured pemmican for distribution to distant posts. They piloted York boats, operated dog trains and cart brigades, and moved people and goods. They provided the services to incoming scientists, travellers, clergy, politicians, and military personnel that only a broker people could. They were guides, interpreters, provisioners, and protectors. To their First Nations kin, they acted as go-betweens with traders, government officials, and military personnel, assuming the roles of chiefs and headmen on request when it came time to negotiate treaties and reserves with incoming government officials.

The Metis Buffalo Hunt

No field of endeavour epitomizes the culture and ethos of the Plains Metis as did the communal buffalo hunt. The migration of Metis to the northern Plains after the creation of the HBC trade monopoly, and their success in carving for themselves a distinct economic niche, enabled them to survive as a distinct Aboriginal people, despite the presence of other Natives competing for the diminishing bison herds.

Historian John E. Foster spent his career documenting the emergence and florescence of the Plains Metis. Below is his description of their bison hunt:

> Late in spring, most Metis left their river lots, some with small plots planted with root vegetables and barley, harnessed oxen or horses to their two-wheeled Red River carts, and set out south to the rendezvous point near Pembina, on the border with United States territory. Only the elderly, the sick, and the crippled remained at home. Many households, having a very skilled buffalo hunter or more than one hunter, hired *engages*, no doubt from among kinsmen, to drive additional carts and to participate in the processing.
>
> At Pembina, a general assembly of the hunters met to select officers and promulgate basic rules. Images of the militia in New France and Lower Canada are suggested both in the selection of officers and in the promulgation of hunt rules. The first order of business was to choose 10 *capitaines* who in turn would each choose 10 *soldats*. The foremost of the *capitaines* was the hunt leader, variously styled as the "War Chief" and *le President*. In addition, 10 guides were selected from among the hunters past their physical prime. No doubt the selection of the 10 captains and the 10 guides reflected the socio-political concerns of the Metis in terms of the major extended families in the community, but no documentary evidence has been found, as yet, to confirm such a pattern.

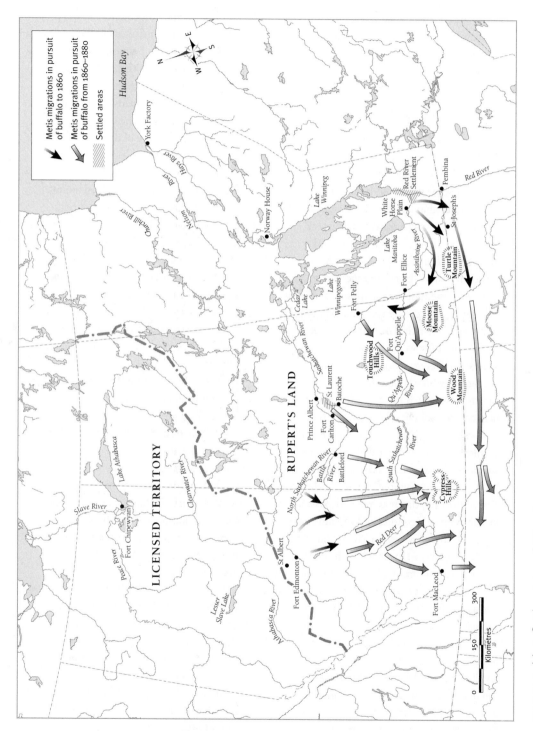

MAP 18.1 Metis Settlements and Migrations

Social and political authority among the Metis was a function of an individual's achievements—his reputation—and it was characterized by limited powers, in terms of both duration and extent, authorized by the community. On the buffalo hunt each guide and each captain commanded for a day. In a cycle of 10 days all of the guides and captains would have command of the hunt. At dawn, the raising of the hunt flag above a guide's cart signaled his command for that day. With camp struck, carts packed, and livestock harnessed or herded, the hunt, in two or more lines of carts abreast, set out on a course determined by the guide-of-the-day. The captain-of-the-day positioned his soldiers ahead, abreast, and to the rear of the line of march. The soldiers sought buffalo, but they were also on guard against the Dakota (sometimes known as the Sioux), who claimed the resources of the lands on which the Metis frequently hunted. Two soldiers always rode together: by riding away from each other at a gallop or toward each other they could signal the hunt as to whether buffalo or Dakota had been sighted. Whatever the quarry, the hunt flag was lowered, passing authority from the guide and captain-of-the-day to the hunt leader. At any hint of danger the carts were circled with shafts inward to corral the stock. If buffalo were sighted the hunters assembled in line abreast under the command of the hunt leader.

Slowly the line of hunters advanced. Severe sanctions in the rules of the hunt awaited any brash hunter who broke the line to rush the herd. At the quarter-mile mark the command *allez* launched the hunters forward into a crescendo of gunfire, stampeding buffalo, galloping horses, and exulting or cursing hunters. Clouds of dust, permeated with the smell of sweat and blood, would part momentarily to reveal possibly a downed rider lying lifeless or perhaps seeking assistance from those nearby. Others, surprisingly unaware of the chaos and confusion about them, closed with their prey. At the command *allez*, the individual hunter, astride his prized mount, had galloped forward. His horse then chose a target and closed with it. When nearly abreast of the buffalo the hunter in a single fluid motion lowered the barrel of his gun, fired his ball, and dropped a personal article, usually an article of clothing, to mark his kill. Instinctively his horse sidestepped the tumbling carcass and sought out another target while the hunter on his mount's back reloaded. Pouring a "guesstimated" amount of gun powder from his powder horn into the barrel of his gun, the hunter then spat a lead ball, from those he carried in his mouth, into the barrel. The charge was rammed home with an abrupt smack of the butt on the saddle pommel or the hunter's thigh. Holding the gun upright until his mount closed with another quarry the hunter, again in a single fluid motion, lowered the barrel of his gun and fired.

In a matter of minutes the hunt for the day was over. The dust and noise receded to reveal hunters busy butchering their kill. From two to five buffalo would be killed by each hunter, depending on ability and particular circumstances. Later, when repeating rifles were introduced in the closing years of the 1860s, kills of over 25 buffalo for one hunter would be recorded. Beginning with his last kill the hunter began butchering the carcasses in preparation for the women to dry the meat and manufacture pemmican. Cut into strips the meat was hung on racks to dry in the sun and over fires. When dried meat was pounded to flake into a coarse powder and an equal amount of melted fat was added, together with berries and other edibles in season, the resulting product was pemmican. Cooled and sewn into 90-pound buffalo-hide bags, pemmican could be transported and stored with ease. The Company's provisioning posts on the North Saskatchewan and the Red and Assiniboine rivers purchased pemmican and dried meat for their own needs, with the surplus being delivered to Norway House to provision the York boat brigades and for transshipment to northern posts to supplement the diet of fish.

Metis hunters and Plains Indians preferred the meat of the heifer or young cow. With the horse this target could be selected with much regularity. This practice contributed substantially to the demise of the buffalo.

The hunt remained a dangerous undertaking. In addition to the accidents associated with it there was the hostility of the Dakota. In most instances, violent confrontations were relatively short-lived and involved small numbers. In July 1851, however, the hunt from White Horse Plain, a Metis settlement a few miles to the west of Red River, came under sustained attack. They withstood the onslaught with only one dead and a few wounded while inflicting casualties that forced the Dakota to break off the action. On this occasion the Metis had

corralled their stock behind the encircled carts while the women and children took positions behind them. The men charged forward the distance of a gunshot to scrape gun pits in the prairie sod. From these vantage points they kept the attacking Yankton Dakota from destroying their stock and thus, at the very least, leaving them stranded on the prairie. The Canadien priest who accompanied the hunt stood astride a cart, crucifix in one hand, tomahawk in the other, exhorting his flock to persevere. The Metis victory at Grand Coteau confirmed in their own minds their paramountcy on the prairie west of Red River.

The return of the summer hunt to Red River saw "recognized hunters" rather than individual hunters negotiate the sale of their pemmican and dried meat, at prices that remained low and varied little over the years. The recognized hunters appear to have been in many instances the heads of extended families with whom the Company sought influence. A smaller autumn hunt left the settlement late in October or early November to provision the Metis for the winter months. It was sufficient to sustain the leisurely round of visits among kinsmen, punctuated by celebrations associated with numerous weddings. During these months not a few Metis found themselves, over the years, increasingly attracted to the illicit trade in furs.

The summer hunt returned to Red River Settlement usually in time to harvest what insects, drought, or floods had allowed to survive on their small plots of cultivated land. To sustain their stock over winter each settler looked to the mile of land behind his river lot for hay. For some

BOX 18.1 Rules of the Hunt

1. No buffalo to be run on the Sabbath-day.
2. No party to fork off, lag behind or go before without permission.
3. No person or party to run buffalo before the general order.
4. Every Captain with his men, in turn, to patrol the camp, and keep guard.
5. For the first trespass against these laws, the offender to have his saddle and bridle cut up.
6. For the second offence, the coat to be taken off the offender's back, and be cut up.
7. For the third offence, the offender to be flogged.
8. Any person convicted of theft, even to the value of a sinew, to be brought to the middle of the camp, and the crier to call out his or her name three times, adding the word "thief," at each time.

—Ross (1972)

families this hay was insufficient. Each year they joined others waiting for the local Council of Assiniboia to declare the opening date for haying on the prairie lands beyond the hay privilege. Having spotted a likely area prior to the beginning of haying, the hunter and his family rushed to the area on the appointed date, claiming all the hay that he could encircle in a single day's cutting. The introduction of mechanical reapers in the late 1850s gave some farmers in Red River a notable advantage over Metis hunters. (2004:305–7)

The Decline of the Bison Economy: Treaties, Scrip, and Unrest

The disappearance of the Plains bison economy in the latter half of the nineteenth century has been viewed, understandably, as a causal factor linked to the weakened political and cultural autonomy of the Metis. However, it is incorrect to assume that Metis people and their culture disappeared along with the buffalo. The boreal forest Metis continued much as they had, hunting and trapping when not freighting goods and people. In the Parkland and Plains regions, Metis adapted as best they could. The transition to a changed economic and social environment was neither smooth nor completely successful for all—but it did not signal Metis extinction. Rather, it became yet another period of adaptation and change.

The profitability of the always volatile buffalo robe trade could not survive the continued decline of the herds. By the 1840s observers noted that the herds were smaller and migrating west and south. The disappearance of the large herds was accompanied by increased violence, as tribal groups and Metis fought for the remaining animals. Directors of the fur companies, along with clergy, military, and government officials, recognized that the fur and robe economy was ending. It was time for the socio-cultural transition that was both necessary and inevitable.

The first step was the HBC transferring Rupert's Land to the new Canadian Confederation, established in 1867. The Canadian government was low on funds and vulnerable politically and militarily, despite their purchase of this huge territory that could be exploited economically. Because they feared that Americans would move to annex their vulnerable new region, the government acted quickly to secure the area.

By the spring of 1868 Anglo-Protestant colonists from Ontario had already established themselves at Red River, followed in the fall by a survey crew assigned to map a trail between Lake of the Woods and Upper Fort Garry (now Winnipeg). The survey party was made up largely of annexationists who promoted their vision of an Anglo-Protestant settlement in the local newspapers. By July 1869 the federally appointed governor of the territory, William McDougall, ordered the survey team to begin mapping the Red River Settlement itself in preparation for Canadian takeover of the region, at which time he would travel to the settlement to assume his position.

The local Metis had been watching these developments with increasing alarm, but nothing substantial had been done to challenge the newcomers. Louis Riel, a young Metis who had returned to the Red River parish of St Vital after study in Montreal, took the initiative and in October 1869 led a group of Metis who physically stopped the surveyors. Riel and his followers, supported by the Roman Catholic Church, established a National Committee to prevent McDougall's entry into the settlement without prior negotiation by the Canadian government with local residents. On 2 November, after McDougall entered Manitoba from the American border village of Pembina, he was ordered back across the border by an armed Metis patrol. On the same day, Riel and 400 armed Metis took possession of Upper Fort Garry without resistance.

Shortly thereafter a provisional government comprising both English- and French-speaking Metis was established to replace the Council of Assiniboia (a community council created by the HBC) and to negotiate terms of amalgamation

FIGURE 18.1 Louis Riel and his associates. Back row, left to right: Le Roe, Pierre DeLorme, Thomas Hunn, Xavier Page, Andre Beauchemin, Baptiste Tereaux; Middle row: Pierre Poitras, John Bruce, Louis Riel, W.R. O'Donoghue, Francois Dauphinais, Thomas Spence; Front row: Bob O'Lone, Paul Prue. (Courtesy of the Glenbow Archives, 1039-1)

with Canada. The provisional government asked for representation in Parliament, a bilingual provincial government and judiciary, protection of Metis lands, and treaties for Indians. While the Metis representatives negotiated with government representatives, Anglo-Protestant annexationists escaped from Fort Garry and succeeded in persuading a group of men to attempt to recapture Fort Garry, a gambit that failed. The annexationist leader, John Christian Schultz, escaped, but his men were jailed. Because of the destabilizing influence of the annexationists, the provisional government sought to make an example of the rebels, and sentenced the head of the Protestant militia, Major Charles Boulton, to death. One of his fellow prisoners, a young Orangeman named Thomas Scott, responded to the verdict by insulting his Metis captors to such an extent that he was subsequently executed by firing squad.

The unreasonable and unnecessary execution of Thomas Scott was a serious error in judgment by Riel. The news travelled swiftly to Ontario and Quebec, arousing sectarian tensions. By March 1870, when negotiations began between Red River representatives and the Canadian government, strong opposition to the Metis delegates and their absent leader Louis Riel had been fomented in Ontario. Despite opposition, the Red River visitors succeeded in extracting guarantees from the Canadian government that would be enshrined in the Manitoba Act of 1870. These concessions included provincial status for the territory, now called Manitoba, as well as a substantial amount of land (1.4 million acres) for local Metis. Although the negotiators also managed to achieve a bilingual judiciary and provincial government, they were unable to get amnesty for crimes committed during the transfer of Rupert's Land to Canada.

As a result, Riel was forced to flee to the United States to avoid militias eager to avenge Thomas Scott. During the years that followed, the concessions negotiated in the Manitoba Act were undermined by the slowness of the federal government in implementing scrip and by the influx of settlers who soon overwhelmed the Metis and First Nations inhabitants. By 1875, when scrip distribution was finally implemented, many Metis had already left the province.

What Is Scrip?

Scrip was a special certificate or warrant issued by the Department of the Interior which entitled the bearer to receive homestead lands, at a later date, upon presentation of the document to the proper authorities. Scrip allowed the Department to issue a land grant without specifying the actual parcel involved. For individual claimants, it had the advantage of allowing them to choose any western lands which were open for settlement without having to restrict their selection to specific reserves, as was the case with some immigrant groups from eastern Europe.

The scrip notes issued by the Department resembled government bonds and were printed by the Canadian Bank Note Company in denominations of $20, $80, $160, and $240; and in 80, 160 and 240 acres. When lands in western Canada were first made available to homesteaders under the Dominion Lands Act of 1872, the federal government arbitrarily valued farm land at $1.00 per acre. Therefore, money scrip in the value of $160 or $240 entitled the bearer to the equivalent number of acres in land.

Money and land scrip could only be redeemed at face value in the purchase of homestead lands through a Dominion lands office. Despite this restriction, a considerable black market in scrip existed in western Canada, where these documents were sold and traded at less than their face value to pay debts and to purchase goods other than land. Although its official policy was to the contrary, the federal government to some extent encouraged such practices. This was particularly true of money scrip, which was not registered in the name of the Metis claimant, but was simply made out "to the Bearer." Without some form of registration, money scrip could be used by anyone—both Metis and non-Metis alike—in their acquisition of western lands, and consequently, it was actively sought by land speculators. (Murray 1993:12–14)

There has been considerable debate over whether the Manitoba Metis were forced out of Red River by the hostility of incoming settlers and the slow distribution of scrip, or whether they left to pursue economic opportunities elsewhere. As with most cultural and economic change, the most successful transition to the new order was made by those who had the skills to adapt and the resources to sustain themselves until the transition was complete. The introduction of Manitoba scrip, intended to recognize and extinguish Metis Aboriginal claims to land, was shortly followed by the negotiation and signing of treaties with the Aboriginal groups. The first of these numbered treaties were intended to purchase territory from Native groups as a precursor to populating the land with agricultural settlers.

The person responsible for supervising scrip distribution and negotiating the first treaties was Alexander Morris, who had been appointed chief justice and later Lieutenant-Governor of Manitoba and the newly created North-West Territories. Unlike most of his government colleagues, Morris took pains to learn about these First Nations and

Metis groups, noting in particular variations in lifestyle exhibited by the Metis.

Experiencing a series of increasingly difficult treaty negotiations, Morris learned that meeting the needs of different Aboriginal populations—particularly the Metis—would be more complicated than first envisioned. Based on his travels throughout the west and his consultations with local informants, he observed:

The Half-Breeds in the territories are of three classes—1st, those who, as at St. Laurent, near Prince Albert, the Qu'Appelle Lakes and Edmonton, have their farms and homes; 2nd, those who are entirely identified with the Indians, living with them, and speaking their language; 3rd, those who do not farm, but live after the habits of the Indians, by the pursuit of the buffalo and the chase. (1880:294)

Morris recognized that the diverse lifestyles of the Metis had to be reflected in any agreement to extinguish their claims:

As to the first class, the question is an easy one. They will, of course, be recognized as possessors of the soil, and confirmed by the government in their holdings, and will continue to make their living by farming and trading.

The second class have been recognized as Indians, and have passed into the bands among whom they reside.

The position of the third class is more difficult. The loss of the means of livelihood by the destruction of the buffalo presses upon them, as upon our Indian tribes; and with regard to them I reported in 1876, and I have seen no reason to change my view, as follows:

There is another class of the population in the North-West whose position
I desire to bring under the notice of the
privy Council. I refer to the wandering
Half-breeds of the plains, who are chiefly
of French descent and live the life of the
Indians. There are a few who are identified with the Indians, but there is a large
class of Metis who live by the hunt of the
buffalo, and have no settled homes. I think
that a census of the numbers of these
should be procured, and while I would
not be disposed to recommend their being
brought under the treaties, I would suggest that land should be assigned to them,
and that on their settling down, if after an
examination into their circumstances, it
should be found necessary and expedient,
some assistance should be given them to
enable them to enter upon agricultural
operations. (1880:294–5)

The delays in awarding scrip, compounded
with the disappearance of the buffalo and economic reverses in the Red River Settlement, contributed to an exodus of mostly French-speaking
Metis from Manitoba westward to Saskatchewan
and Athabasca and southward into North Dakota
and Montana. Some established residence where
missions had been established or where they had
previously fished or wintered. Others pursued the
dwindling herds of bison on the Plains, or migrated
northward into the boreal forest to hunt and trap
in places where their ancestors worked as *engagés*.
There they reunited with both Indian and metis
cousins.

Because no enumeration of Metis communities
had been undertaken west of Manitoba, a number
of metis chose to "take treaty" under Treaty Nos. 4, 5,
and 6. Most were individuals whom Morris described
as the "second category of Half-Breed"—who were
part of Indian bands, spoke Indian languages, and

lived Indian lives. However, a small but significant
portion of the Metis signatories to treaty were those
whom Morris described under "Category Three"—
nomadic hunters—*hivernants*—who were culturally Metis but chose to follow the buffalo and had
no fixed abode, living apart from Indian bands in
their own mobile brigades. Although most were
indigenous to Saskatchewan or northern Alberta,
others had migrated from Manitoba or elsewhere,
or had been born since 1870, the "cut-off" point for
eligibility for Manitoba scrip. The delays in negotiating scrip resulted in large mixed-race populations
taking treaty; they may or may not have considered
themselves culturally "Indian," but required the
benefits of treaty for survival.

Despite the Canadian government having
promised scrip to Manitoba Metis to extinguish
their claims, no such provision was made in the
NWT. Instead of negotiating with these Metis,
the government chose not to make any provision
for scrip. Instead, they permitted mixed-bloods to
take treaty as Indians, if they chose. Because no
separate agreement was negotiated with Metis,
several groups who hunted and trapped for their
livelihood and/or had extensive Indian kin connections, chose to enter Treaty Nos. 4, 5, and 6.

The North-West Rebellion of 1885

By 1885, the rapid pace of change and its severe
impact on Aboriginal economies created political
repercussions. Settlers were discontented because
the promised transcontinental railroad was still
being planned, obstructed by lack of funds and
government infighting. The Cree, Assiniboine,
Blackfoot, and Ojibwa who had signed treaties
were equally disillusioned. Their land base was
under constant threat from interlopers, and the
animals upon which their survival had depended
were gone. The promised annuities and provisions,
intended to assist them into a settled economy,
were insufficient; starvation and disease reigned
in the western reserves.

The Metis were also suffering the aftershocks of settlement. Despite scrip being awarded to the Manitoba Metis, its implementation was flawed, resulting in the dispossession and exodus of Manitoba Metis who were unable or unwilling to redeem their certificates for land. Many joined relatives in the NWT, where people of mixed race were living either under treaty as "Indians" or as squatters. Like their Euro-Canadian counterparts, they wanted title to land, and were becoming discouraged and angry by the lack of government response.

In June 1884, a delegation from Saskatchewan, led by Metis hunter Gabriel Dumont, went to Montana in search of Louis Riel, who had taken American citizenship and was teaching school. They asked him to return to help prepare and present a list of grievances. Riel agreed and spent that summer conferring with local settlers and Metis.

The federal government ignored the petitions, and eventually the Metis resorted to armed rebellion. Although they won a couple of skirmishes, most notably the brief occupation of Fort Carleton, in the end they ran out of ammunition and were overwhelmed by superior technology (the Gatling gun) and a mobilized military force. After their final defeat at Batoche, Saskatchewan, Riel was captured, put on trial, convicted, and executed for treason.

The Metis in Western Canada after the Rebellion[3]

Almost immediately after suppressing the rebellion, government authorities took steps to prevent further uprisings. They developed policies intended to remove dissident elements, invariably identified as "half-breeds," from Indian bands. Steps were taken to identify metis and induce them to accept scrip, thereby removing them from the rolls of Indian bands. Most gladly did, as treaty restrictions were onerous and scrip provided

badly needed money. As a result, some Treaty No. 6 bands in northern Alberta literally disappeared by 1900.

By 1899, when negotiations for Treaty No. 8 were initiated, the government had already determined to separate the Indian and Metis populations. Scrip was not issued to Metis until Indians had identified the members of their communities and signed treaty.

While Indians had no alternative but to take the treaty, they were, in the long term, better off than Metis who opted for scrip. Unlike treaty Indians, whose hunting and fishing rights were ostensibly protected by treaty, the Metis had no such protection. By taking scrip they undermined their future access to hunting and fishing, and abrogated their rights to the annuities, education, and health benefits which were promised under treaty.

The result was that northern Metis who took scrip in 1899 saw little benefit. Many sold their scrip for a fraction of its value, believing that money was worth more than marginal agricultural land in northern Alberta. In the end, many were left indigent, forced to live on the margins of Indian reserves or deep in the bush, suffering from poverty and disease.

For the western Canadian Metis, the defeat of Riel was the end of their traditional way of life and the beginning of a transition to settled society. For those with skills valued in Euro-Canadian culture—literacy and numeracy, or the ability to farm or practise a trade—the overwhelming response was to forget the past, to deny their heritage in the face of discrimination, and to fit in.

Metis who chose to participate in Canadian economy and society used their scrip to re-establish themselves in the local economy. Some families pooled their collected scrip, and cashed it strategically—some for cash, some for land. The cash bought farm implements and other goods needed for a fresh start. Others, especially those whose ancestors had collected scrip in Manitoba, moved farther west to take up homesteads.

Metis who sold their scrip to speculators or did not have the skills needed to function successfully in the new society migrated to more isolated areas where families could still live in the bush, hunting, fishing, and trapping. This strategy was successful for the short term.

The Revival of Metis Activism

By the beginning of the twentieth century, the fortunes of western Canadian Metis were at low ebb. But in 1930 things got worse. The Natural Resources Transfer Act transferred jurisdiction over the management of natural resources, including wildlife, from the federal government to the provinces. Crown land, which the northern Metis relied upon for hunting, fishing, and gathering, was opened for homesteading. Metis hunters were now forced to purchase licences and were limited to seasonal hunts. Prior to 1930 the laws regarding hunting were either non-existent or,

like the Migratory Birds Convention Act of 1918, enforced ineffectually. Now, however, individuals who broke the law could be fined or imprisoned and have their game confiscated.

Metis people have a long history of joint action, beginning with the founding of Manitoba. In 1877, the former activists of the Riel Resistance established the Union nationale metis Saint-Joseph du Manitoba. Now, in Alberta, educated Metis versed in socialist teachings, such as Malcolm Norris and James Brady, joined forces with Metis leader Adrian Hope and a treaty Indian of mixed heritage, Joe Dion. They held meetings in the larger Metis communities to assist them in organizing to market their furs, fish, and produce more profitably. In 1932 they formed L'Association des Metis D'Alberta et des Territoires du Nord Quest (later known as the Metis Association of Alberta). In response, the provincial government in 1934 established the Ewing Commission to examine Metis social conditions and to develop strategies for assisting them. The result was the Metis Population Betterment

FIGURE 18.2 Group portrait of the Provincial Executive Committee, Alberta Metis Association, Edmonton, Alberta. (Courtesy of the Glenbow Archives PA 2218-109)

Act of 1938, establishing Alberta Metis settlements, the only land base in Canada specifically set aside for Metis.

Meanwhile, Saskatchewan Metis were dealing with similar issues, exacerbated by the federal Prairie Farm Rehabilitation Act of 1935. This legislation, developed to create community pastures out of vacant Crown lands, served to push Metis squatters off these properties—often the only refuge available to them. In 1938 the Saskatchewan Metis Association was formed to serve northern Saskatchewan, while the Saskatchewan Metis Society was established for the south.

By the 1960s, there were Metis associations active in Alberta, Saskatchewan, and Manitoba. Their major issue was whether to unite with non-status Indians to lobby governments, even though there were conflicts over priorities, not to mention cultural differences. Generally the political and social progress of the Metis during the 1960s was slow, but not much worse than that experienced by First Nations and Inuit, who also struggled with government neglect, discrimination, and erosion of Aboriginal and treaty rights.

Without constitutional recognition as Aboriginals, Metis were unlikely to get the formal recognition and Aboriginal rights enjoyed by First Nations people. In 1982 Aboriginal rights assumed new prominence, however, when the government of Pierre Trudeau set about to patriate the Canadian Constitution from Britain. Native people, concerned that Canadian politicians would exclude Aboriginal rights in a new constitution, sent delegations to Britain and to Ottawa to pressure legislators to honour their treaty commitments. Metis leaders, recognizing an opportunity to have Metis Aboriginal rights included in the constitution, lobbied persistently until they achieved their goal—official recognition as an "Aboriginal people" under the Constitution Act of 1982. This opened the way to legal challenges regarding Metis Aboriginal rights that, for the first

time, had the possibility of being won. Along with Canada's Indian and Inuit populations, they won recognition both of their existing Aboriginal rights and that those rights could not be infringed upon by the Charter of Rights and Freedoms.

After the 1982 recognition of the Metis in Canada's Constitution, the Metis National Council was established to develop and implement Metis policy across the country. Subsequently, provincial Metis organizations were established in other provinces with significant Metis populations, such as British Columbia and Ontario.

The centenary of the 1885 Northwest Rebellion provided an opportunity for the first of many Metis constitutional challenges. In 1985 the Manitoba Metis Federation sued the Canadian government, alleging fraud in the administration of scrip to Manitoba Metis in the nineteenth century. Although they were unsuccessful, Metis fortunes across Canada were changed by an event in the Ontario bush, the *Powley* case.

The *Powley* Case

On October 22, 1993, Steve and Roddy Powley shot a bull moose near Sault Ste Marie, Ontario. They tagged it with a Metis membership card and a note reading "harvesting my meat for winter." Ontario wildlife officers charged them for hunting moose without licences and unlawful possession of moose contrary to Ontario's Game and Fish Act. The Metis Nation of Ontario challenged these charges as a constitutional test case, providing financial and legal resources during the initial trial (the Metis National Council later assumed this support). In 1998, the judge ruled that the Powleys had a Metis right to hunt protected by Section 35 of the Constitution Act. The charges against the Powleys were dismissed, but the Crown appealed the decision to the Ontario Superior Court. In 2000, the Ontario Superior Court confirmed the initial trial decision and dismissed the Crown's appeal. The Crown appealed this decision to the Ontario

BOX 18.2 The *Powley* Test[4]

Because of the implications of the *Powley* decisions, the Supreme Court established a rigorous set of criteria—a "test" that individual Metis must meet in order to exercise the Aboriginal right to harvest under Section 35. The Court concluded that the appropriate way to define Metis rights in Section 35 was to modify the test used to define the Aboriginal rights of Indians (known as the *Van der Peet* test). It requires identification of the Aboriginal right in question (in this case, harvesting). It requires rights holders to identify their membership in a historic and contemporary rights-holding community in the region where the harvesting takes place, as well as confirming whether or not the harvesting is integral to the rights holder's distinctive Aboriginal cultural practice. Moreover, the onus is on the individual rights holder and the community to determine that these practices have been carried out continuously in the region, or whether the rights were infringed upon or extinguished at any time (through subsequent legislation), and whether this infringement or extinction was justified.

Court of Appeal, which unanimously upheld the earlier decisions. The Crown then appealed to the Supreme Court of Canada. On 19 September 2003 the Supreme Court unanimously affirmed that the Powleys, as members of the Sault Ste Marie Metis community, could exercise a Metis right to hunt under Section 35 of Canada's Constitution.

Consequences of *Powley* for the Metis

Because the *Powley* test requires Metis people clearly to identify their people, their communities, and their territories, Metis organizations are now obliged to identify and register individual Metis. In order for this enumeration to have any significance legally, the enumeration must follow established criteria, including individual self-identification as Metis, historical and legal proof of Metis ancestry, acceptance by a Metis community, and proof that this person is not a member of treaty Indian community or non-status Indian organization.

These stringent criteria have required Metis organizations to provide assistance in compiling this documentation, a task complicated by many Metis communities relying on oral forms of record-keeping.

A second contentious issue has been the requirement that Metis communities identify clearly demarcated "territories" where they traditionally exercised Aboriginal rights (such as hunting). Unlike First Nations communities, Metis have never been associated with clearly demarcated territories. As a people "in-between," they travelled long distances across hundreds or thousands of kilometres yearly. They lived in settlements, or wintered or summered in the back country, depending on the nature of their particular subsistence activity. Therefore, the need to demark specific Metis hunting "zones," or "areas of residence" to meet provincial legal challenges to Metis Aboriginal hunting rights has raised legitimate concerns, because what is being demanded is an arbitrary delineation of borders that did not exist historically.

An unexpected issue arising from the constitutional recognition of Metis Aboriginal status is the unusual (and initially unexplained) rise in numbers of Metis people across Canada. As Metis sociologist Chris Andersen noted, in recent years the number of people self-identifying as Metis has skyrocketed. In fact the increase in individuals self-identifying as Metis in the 2006 Canadian census has been an "astonishing and demographically improbable increase of 43 percent" (2008:347). What has happened is that a historically and culturally diverse population of Aboriginal people of mixed race has embraced the constitutional recognition of the Metis for their own particular reasons. Some may be the descendants of enfranchised First Nations people who left treaty. Some may be First Nations people without treaty status. Still others may be members of mixed-race groups such as the Inuit-European "settlers" of Labrador, or Acadians who have considerable Aboriginal ancestry but traditionally have not been recognized as Aboriginal. In all cases, the possession of biological mixed heritage appears to have been conflated with possessing the cultural and historical traditions of the western Canadian Metis and claiming the constitutional benefits that accompany that designation.

The position of the Metis National Council has been that the Metis are a largely western Canadian/Great Lakes collectivity with a common culture and heritage that had its genesis in the fur and robe trade. It is also asserted that the western Canadian Metis are a group that organized politically and socially, and were identified historically as a distinctive people. This position, however, has not prevented "small-m metis" organizations elsewhere in Canada from establishing themselves and demanding constitutional rights.

The problem with this debate over defining "who is Metis" is that provincial governments who manage the natural resources to which Metis demand Aboriginal access are reacting to the uncertainty over Metis numbers by arbitrarily restricting Metis access to hunting and constitutional rights achieved via the *Powley* ruling. In these cases, Metis organizations have been forced, repeatedly, to take provincial governments to court in order to force the provinces to honour the original Supreme Court ruling in *R. v. Powley*.

This debate over formal definition of Metis ethnic identity remains unresolved. What it emphasizes is the need for Metis organizations proactively to enumerate their members and clearly define the biological, historical, and cultural diagnostics for Metis identity.

Recent legal decisions in favour of the Metis have heightened the pressure on provincial and federal Metis organizations to get their administrative houses in order, so that they can develop and implement programs and services for a clearly identified Canadian Metis population.

For decades, Metis and non-status organizations had lobbied unsuccessfully for various forms of government assistance for their people. Because Metis and non-status Indians were not recognized as treaty Indians, the federal government denied responsibility for these groups, referring them to the provinces, who also denied fiscal responsibility. But with the patriation of the Constitution in 1982, which recognized the Metis as an Aboriginal people, the legislative foundation was laid for future legal action.

After the *R v. Powley* Supreme Court decision of 2003 served to establish legally the existence of Metis harvesting rights, a group of Metis activists, led by Harry Daniels of Saskatchewan, launched a suit against the federal government in order to legally define its constitutional responsibilities for Metis and non-status Indians. On 8 January 2013 the Federal Court delivered a landmark ruling after 12 years of procedural delays. In *Daniels et al v. Canada*, the Federal Court clearly identified the federal government's legislative jurisdiction over Metis and non-status Indians, who are identified as "Indians" under Section 91(24) of the Constitution Act, 1867. Although the nature and extent of the government's fiduciary responsibilities have yet to be defined, the ruling served to strengthen Metis constitutional rights by building on the legal precedent set by *R v. Powley* (Teillet and Madden 2013). The federal government has stated its intention to appeal the ruling (Canadian Press 2013).

A second major ruling, this time in the Supreme Court of Canada, was made in the case of *Manitoba Metis Federation Inc. v. Canada* on 8 March 2013. This case, which has been described as "a dispute nearly 150 years in the making," argued that the government of Canada failed to live up to its responsibilities to the Red River Metis when administering the distribution of lands promised to them as a result of the 1870 Manitoba Act. It is well known that the intent of the grant was to establish clear title to parcels of land for Manitoba Metis prior to the arrival of Euro-Canadian settlers. However, this did not take place. Instead, the "persistent inattention," the "repeated mistakes and inaction," and the "negative consequences following delays in allocating land grants" resulted in the dispossession and dispersion of many Manitoba Metis and their descendants (Supreme Court of Canada 2013).

The federal government has yet to respond formally to the Supreme Court decision, other than to refer it to further study.

Contemporary Metis Identity

The "markers" of a national consciousness include two important aspects of cultural identity:

> The first has to do with the content; the "what" of the "we" that which anthropologists generally call culture. The second concerns the more abstract dimension of collective identity, the question of nationality, that sense of common origin and common destiny felt even between strangers who live many miles apart. (Thomas 1985:245)

How do Metis people, scattered over thousands of kilometres, in hundreds of communities, retain that sense of "common origin and destiny" essential to nationhood without having sovereign territory, also a hallmark of nationhood?

Certainly, the reality—rather than merely the sense—of common origin has much to do with it. Commonly, modern Metis people can find relatives in almost any western Canadian community with fur-trade origins, be they Indian or non-Indian. Because of Metis marital practices, a strong underpinning of kinship unites them and provides a solid foundation for sustaining their culture.

Because of *Powley*, the importance of identifying and enumerating Metis people has new significance. The task of constructing family trees out of government, fur-trade, and religious records is now a widespread Metis pastime. What once was a hobby has become part of providing evidence required by the federal government to identify Metis families, to document their communities, and to track their movements.

Metis organizations also see the importance of recognizing the iconic leaders and events which have shaped the shared past. Louis Riel, the charismatic and controversial leader in two uprisings, and Gabriel Dumont, a famed buffalo hunter and scout and Riel's lieutenant, are honoured across Canada. A holiday recognizing Riel's contribution to Canada is observed in Manitoba. Numerous organizations, public buildings, and streets bear his name, as well as Dumont's. In Saskatchewan, the Battle of Batoche is recognized annually at a community festival and at the National Historic Site. Metis from across North America come to Batoche to remember 1885, to participate in cultural activities, to reconnect with friends and relatives, and to celebrate being Metis.

Metis cultural activities are also resurgent. Jigging and fiddling continue to be popular, along with other fine and performing arts. Beadwork and leather clothing manufacture, cookery, and other traditional home-crafts are being taught to new generations. Activities once part of daily employment—hunting, guiding, raising horses, running sled dogs, canoeing, transporting goods (activities essential to physical and cultural survival in the past) continue to be practised for subsistence, for enjoyment, and to demonstrate that Metis culture continues.

And Metis continue to occupy the role of cultural broker in Canadian communities. Metis professionals can be found in various capacities where knowledge of both Aboriginal and non-Aboriginal lifeways is required—in hospitals, schools, and universities, legislative assemblies and government departments, the military and the police forces, and the recreation and hospitality industries.

In recent years, the role of the Metis as one of Canada's founding Aboriginal peoples has been incorporated widely into school curricula. At fur-trade sites and museums and interpretive centres across Canada, in television programs, documentary motion pictures, websites and print media, the exploits of the Metis men and women who were instrumental in exploring and settling the country are presented to the public. Since 1985, there has been a florescence in scholarship devoted to Metis history and current affairs. Across Canada, Metis scholars—and scholars of the Metis—are ensuring that never again will they be "Canada's Forgotten People."

NOTES

1. This section is derived from Devine 2007.
2. This section is derived from Devine 2004.
3. This section is derived from Devine 2004.
4. Adapted from "Alberta Canada, Métis Settlements— Significant Court Decisions," The

Canadian Aboriginal Issues Database at: www.ualberta.ca/~walld/powleytest.html, accessed 22 April 2010.

REFERENCES AND RECOMMENDED READINGS

Andersen, Chris. 2008. "From Nation to Population: The Racialization of 'Metis' in the Canadian Census," *Nations and Nationalism* 14, 2: 347–68.

Axtell, James. 1979. "Ethnohistory: An Historian's Viewpoint," *Ethnohistory* 26, 1: 1–13.

Beal, Bob, and Rod Macleod. 1984. *Prairie Fire: The 1885 North-West Rebellion*. Edmonton: Hurtig Publications. The most comprehensive and even-handed account of the North-West Rebellion written for a general readership.

Binnema, Theodore, Gerhard Ens, and R.C. Macleod, eds. 2001. *From Rupert's Land to Canada: Essays in Honour of John E. Foster*. Edmonton: University of Alberta Press. Collection of essays on the fur trade and on Metis culture.

Brown, J.S.H. 1980. *Strangers in Blood: Fur Trade Families in Indian Country*. Vancouver: University of British Columbia Press. Important essay charting corporate culture and ethnic origin as shapers of fur trade society.

Canadian Press. 2013. "Government to appeal ruling that Metis, other natives are 'Indian.'" *Globe and Mail*, 6 Feb. www.theglobeandmail.com/news/national/government-to-appeal-ruling-that-mtis-other-natives-are-indian/article8304903/. Accessed 20 March 2013.

Devine, Heather. 2001. "Les Desjarlais: the Development and Dispersion of a Proto-Metis Hunting Band." In *From Rupert's Land to Canada: Essays in Honour of John E. Foster*, edited by Ted Binnema, Gerhard Enns, and *R.C. Macleod.*. Edmonton: University of Alberta Press. Describes the ethnic choices made by one fur-trade family during the period of conflict and consolidation in the northwest fur trade.

———. 2003. "Proto-Metis Community Formation and the Rise of the Metis People." Paper presented at the Metis People in the 21st Century conference, Saskatoon, University of Saskatchewan. Unpublished conference paper discussing the formal and informal marital practices of the fur trade and their influence on Metis ethnogenesis.

———. 2004. *The People Who Own Themselves: Aboriginal Ethnogenesis in a Canadian Family, 1660–1900.* Calgary: University of Calgary Press.

———. 2007. "Prosopographical Approaches in Canadian Native History." In *Prosopographia et Genealogica*, edited by K.S.B. Keats-Rohan. Linacre College, Oxford: Unit for Prosopographical Research, Occasional Paper, vol. 13.

———. 2010. "Being and Becoming Metis: A Personal Reflection." In *Gathering Places: Essays on Aboriginal Histories*, edited by Carolyn Podruchny and Laura Peers. Vancouver: UBC Press. An anthology honouring Dr Jennifer S.H. Brown.

——— and Margaret Clarke. N.d. "The History of the Metis at Buffalo Lake." Unpublished. Calgary: Metis Nation of Alberta.

Dickason, Olive. 1997. *Canada's First Nations: A History of Founding Peoples From Earliest Times*, 2nd ed. Toronto: McClelland & Stewart. Award-winning history of Canada's Aboriginal people.

Ens, Gerhard. 1988. "Dispossession or Adaptation: Migration and Persistence of the Red River Metis, 1835–1890." *Historical Papers.* Ottawa: Canadian Historical Association. Important article arguing that the Metis exodus from Red River after 1869 was an economic migration and not a forced dispossession.

———. 1992. *Louis Riel.* Ottawa: Canadian Historical Association, booklet 50. A brief survey by the current leading authority on Riel.

Flanagan, Thomas. 1983. *Riel and the Rebellion: 1885 Reconsidered.* Saskatoon: Western Producer. Provocative but influential book asserting the legality (if not the morality) of Canadian government responses to the Metis in general and to Louis Riel in particular.

Foster, John E. 2004. "The Plains Metis." In *Native Peoples: The Canadian Experience*, edited by Bruce Morrison and C. Roderick Wilson. Don Mills, ON: Oxford University Press.

Giraud, Marcel. 1945. *Le Metis Canadien.* Paris: I'Institut d'Ethnologie. Translated in 1986 by George Woodcock as *The Metis in the Canadian West*, 2 vols. Edmonton: University of Alberta Press. One of the earliest and most influential studies of the genesis and development of the Metis in western Canada.

Krech, Shepard. 1991. "The State of Ethnohistory," *Annual Review of Anthropology* 20. Palo Alto: Annual Reviews.

Macdougall, Brenda. 2006. "Wahkootowin: Family and Cultural Identity in Northern Saskatchewan Metis Communities," *Canadian Historical Review* 87, 3: 431–63.

Morris, The Honourable Alexander, PC. 1880. *The Treaties of Canada with the Indians of Manitoba and the North-West Territories.* Toronto: Bedfords, Clark, and Co.

Morton, A.S. 1928. "La Verendrye: Commandant, Fur Trader and Explorer," *Canadian Historical Review* 9, 4: 284–98. Early article documenting the early (pre-1760) French presence in western Canada.

Morton, W.L. 1956a. "Introduction." In *Alexander Begg's Red River Journal and other Documents Relating to the Red River Resistance of 1869–70*, edited by W.L. Morton. Toronto: Champlain Society. This is the best scholarly history of the transfer of HBC lands to Canada.

———. 1956b. "Introduction." In *London Correspondence Inward from Eden Colvile, 1849–1854*, edited by E.E. Rich. London: Hudson's Bay Record Society. The best scholarly history of the Red River Settlement from 1840 to 1855.

———. 1980. "Clio in Canada: The Interpretation of Canadian History." In *Contexts of Canada's Past: Selected Essays of W.L. Morton*, edited by A.B. McKillop, edited by A.B. McKillop. Toronto: Macmillan. Important article arguing that western Canada will not be able to write its own history until it becomes free of central-Canadian economic dominance.

Murray, Jeffrey S. 1993. "Metis Scrip: The Foundation of a New Beginning," *The Archivist*, 20: 12–14. © Government of Canada. Reproduced with the permission of the Minister of Public Works and Government Services Canada (2013). Source: Library and Archives Canada's website, www.collectionscanada.gc.ca

Peterson, Jacqueline, and Jennifer S.H. Brown. 1985. "Introduction." In *The New Peoples: Being and Becoming Metis in North America*, edited by Jacqueline Peterson and Jennifer *S.H. Brown*. Winnipeg: The University of Manitoba Press.

Petitot, Emile. 1891. *Travels Around Great Slave and Great Bear Lakes, 1862–1882*. Edited in 2005 by John S. Moir, Paul Laverdure, and Jacqueline Moir. Toronto: Champlain Society.

Ross, Ross.. 1972. *The Red River Settlement*. Edmonton: Hurtig Publishers.

St-Onge, Nicole, Carolyn Podruchny, and Brenda Macdougall, eds. 2010. *Contours of Metis Landscapes: Family, Mobility and History in Northwestern North America*. Norman: University of Oklahoma Press. Comprehensive collection of recent scholarship in Metis studies.

Shaw, Edward C. 1973. "La Verendrye," *Manitoba Pageant* 19, 3.

Sprague, Douglas. 1988. *Canada and the Metis, 1869–1885*. Waterloo, ON: Wilfred Laurier University Press. This volume argues that the Canadian government mismanaged the transfer of land to the Metis people after the Red River Resistance of 1868–70. The process of awarding land and money scrip to Metis claimants was lengthy (five years delayed) and open to fraud, resulting in the dispossession and dispersion of many Red River Metis, whose land ultimately went to incoming Euro-Canadian settlers.

Stanley, G.F.G. 1963. *The Birth of Western Canada: A History of the Riel Rebellions*. Toronto: University of Toronto Press.

———. 1964. *Louis Riel*. Toronto: Ryerson.

——— et al., eds. 1985. *The Collected Writings of Louis Riel/Les Ecrits complets de Louis Riel*, 5 vols. Edmonton: University of Alberta Press. Of essential importance for the period of the transfer and the Rebellion.

Supreme Court of Canada. 2013. *Manitoba Metis Federation Inc v. Canada (Attorney General)*, 2013 SCC 14. Available at: Judgements of the Supreme Court of Canada: http://scc.lexum.org/decisia-scc-csc/scc-csc/scc-csc/en/item/12888/index.do Accessed 20 March 2013.

———. 2012. *Métis Law in Canada*. Available at: www.pstlaw.ca/resources/MLIC-2012.pdf. This website, conceived, developed, and updated annually by Metis lawyer Jean Teillet, is a comprehensive summary of case law related to the Metis historically and in the present.

——— and Jason Madden. 2013. "Plainspeak on the Daniels Case (Updated Version—February 2013)," www.metisnation.ca/wp-content/uploads/2013/02/Daniels-Plainspeak-FINAL-REVISED.pdf. Accessed 20 March 2013.

Thomas, L.H. 1982. "Louis Riel," *Dictionary of Canadian Biography*. Toronto: University of Toronto Press. Authoritative discussion of Riel's life.

Thomas, R.K., 1985. "Afterword." In *The New Peoples: Being and Becoming Metis in North America*, edited by Jacqueline Peterson and Jennifer S.H. Brown. Winnipeg: University of Manitoba.

Van Kirk, Sylvia. 1980. *Many Tender Ties: Women in Fur Trade Society in Western Canada, 1670–1870*. Winnipeg: Watson and Dwyer. Important publication documenting the role of Aboriginal women in building fur-trade society.

Weinstein, John. 2007. *Quiet Revolution West: The Rebirth of Metis Nationalism*. Calgary: Fifth House. Recent history of Metis activism in western Canada from the nineteenth century to the Kelowna Accord of 2005.

CHAPTER 19

"We Must Farm to Enable Us to Live": The Plains Cree and Agriculture to 1900

Sarah Carter

Introduction

This chapter explores the topic of agriculture on Plains Cree reserves in the late nineteenth century, addressing the question of why farming failed to form the basis of a viable economy in these communities by 1900. The answer to this question is complex, but has little to do with the prevailing explanation that Plains people had no inclination or ability to farm. The Plains Cree made sustained, determined efforts to establish an economy based on agriculture, but they faced many obstacles. There were environmental and technological challenges shared by all farmers at this time. Aboriginal farmers laboured under particular disadvantages because of their unique relationship with the federal government that ought to have assisted them in this enterprise but ultimately undermined their efforts. A "peasant" farming policy imposed from 1889 to 1896 was especially damaging to Plains Cree agriculture. It is also argued in this chapter that non-Aboriginal people have persistently found it useful to insist that Aboriginal people and agriculture were incompatible, despite obvious evidence to the contrary. It was a convenient myth to sustain, because it could be claimed that people who did not farm were not in need of much land and that economic underdevelopment of the reserves was due to the indifference and neglect, not of the government, but of Aboriginal people.

Early in September 1879, at Fort Carlton, North-West Territories, Plains Cree chiefs Ahtahkakoop, Mistawasis, and Kitowehaw, with five councillors, met with Edgar Dewdney, the recently appointed Commissioner of Indian Affairs. The chiefs were frustrated that promises of agricultural assistance, made to them three years earlier in Treaty No. 6, were "not carried out in their spirit" (Anon. 1879:26). They stated that they intended to live by the cultivation of the soil, as "the buffalo were our only dependence before the transfer of the country, and this and other wild animals are disappearing, and we must farm to enable us to live." They insisted that government had not fulfilled its part of the treaty in assisting them to make a living by agriculture and that what had been given them made a mockery of the promises made in 1876. This was by no means the first effort of these chiefs to place their concerns before government officials, and there were similar expressions of dissatisfaction and disappointment throughout Manitoba and the North-West Territories.[1]

Such evidence of the strong commitment of the Plains Cree to agriculture seemed startling to me when I set out to explore why agriculture failed to provide a living for residents of arable Indian reserves in western Canada. The standard explanation, one firmly embedded in the non-Aboriginal prairie mentality, seemed compelling: that Aboriginal people of the Plains never had any inclination to settle down and farm despite concerted government efforts and assistance. I originally approached the topic with the argument in mind that agriculture was the wrong policy, for the wrong people, at the wrong time. Before I was too far along in my research, however, I found that there was little evidence of agriculture floundering because of the apathy and indifference of Aboriginal people, although it was certainly the case that this view was consistently maintained and promoted by the Department of Indian Affairs and later by many historians. Yet from the time of the treaties of the 1870s and well before, Aboriginal people were anxious to explore agriculture as an alternate economy when they began to realize the buffalo were failing them. It was not government negotiators but the Aboriginal spokesmen who insisted that terms be included in the treaties that would permit agricultural development. Aboriginal people of the western Plains were among the earliest and largest groups to attempt agriculture west of the Red River Settlement. Like most other "sodbusters," Aboriginal farmers were inclined to become commercial farmers specializing in grain. The fact that they did not had to do with government policy and intent, not with Aboriginal choice and inability.

My topic and approach are the product of a number of influences, including the work of "new" social historians who, beginning in the 1960s, argued that history should be the study not only of elites but of ordinary people as well, and of the day-to-day as well as the dramatic events. The new social history stressed that non-elites—ethnic minorities, women, the working class, and non-literate peoples— sought in various ways to transcend the limitations placed on them. They were not hopeless victims of forces beyond their control; rather, they coped creatively with changing conditions. While Arthur J. Ray, Sylvia Van Kirk, and John Milloy cast Native people in a central role as active participants in the history of the pre-1870 West, the same could not be said of the more modern era. In the dominant narrative histories of the West in the post-1870 era, Aboriginal people all but disappeared after they made treaties and settled on reserves. The story of the establishment of the rural core of the prairie West was inevitably told from the point of view of the new arrivals, with little mention of the host society, and generally a record of positive achievement was stressed and the casualties of development were downplayed. Studies of late nineteenth-century imperialisms, which increasingly drew regions into a transcontinental network, provided context for understanding that what happened in western Canada was not unique, but was part of a global pattern of Western expansion.

Aboriginal Adaptations to the Northern Plains

The Plains culture that evolved over centuries in western Canada seemed far removed from the sedentary lifestyle of farms, fields, and fences that began to alter forever the prairie landscape in the late nineteenth century. The Plains Cree, the northernmost people of the Great Plains of North America and one of the last Aboriginal groups to adopt Plains culture, developed a lifestyle that was well suited to the predominantly flat, treeless landscape and to the northern Plains climate of extremes and uncertainties. Particular habits of movement and dispersal suited the limited and specialized nature of the resources of the northern Plains. The Natives exploited the seasonal diversity of their environment by practising mobility. Plains people moved their settlements from habitat to habitat, depending on where they expected to find the greatest natural food supply. All aspects of life hinged on this mobility; their tepees, for example, were easily taken apart and moved, and their other property was kept to a strict minimum so that they would be unencumbered. As homesteaders were later to learn, basic necessities such as good soil, water, game, and fuel rarely came together in many Plains areas; this circumstance joined the great variability and uncertainty of the climate to make mobility central to the survival of the Indigenous peoples of the Plains. Many of the earliest homesteaders on the Plains found that they could not stay put either, certainly not at first; they sought off-farm jobs, especially during the "start-up" years, or they were obliged to try several localities in their search for basic necessities. External inputs in the way of seed-grain relief, subsidies, or rations were often necessary, as the resources of a fixed locality could not always sustain the inhabitants.

The buffalo was the foundation of the Plains economy, providing people not only with a crucial source of protein and vitamins but with many other necessities, including shelter, clothing, containers, and tools. Aboriginal life on the Plains followed a pattern of concentration and dispersal that to a great extent paralleled that

of the buffalo. But Plains people were not solely hunters of buffalo. To rely on one staple resource alone was risky in the Plains environment, as there were periodic shortages of buffalo, and it was mainly the gathering and preserving work of women, based on their intimate understanding of the Plains environment, that varied the subsistence base and contributed to "risk reduction," a role the immigrant women to the Plains would also acquire. Midsummer camp movements were determined not only by the buffalo but also by considerations such as the ripeness and location of saskatoon berries, the prairie turnip, and other fruits and tubers. Many of the foodstuffs women gathered were dried, pounded, or otherwise preserved and stored for the scarce times of winter. Women fished, snared small game, caught prairie chickens and migratory birds, and gathered their eggs. A high degree of mobility was essential for people effectively to draw on the varied resources of the Plains.

FIGURE 19.1 Cree camp near Saskatoon, c. 1900 (Courtesy Saskatchewan Archives Board, R–B1016)

Nineteenth-century European observers tended to see the Great Plains as a timeless land, as a place without history, its people unaffected by any outside forces and leaving no mark of their presence upon the land. Captain William Butler, who described the Plains in 1870 as a great ocean of grass, wrote that "This ocean has no past—time has been nought to it; and men have come and gone, leaving behind them no track, no vestige of their presence" (Butler [1872] 1968:317–18). European observers saw Plains people as living at the mercy of natural forces and failed to appreciate the sophisticated adaptations to the environment and the many ways in which resources were altered, managed, and controlled. Methods such as the buffalo pound, like the Huron enclosures and Beothuk drivelines for capturing deer, have been described as a form of animal management. There is evidence that people of the northern Plains were concerned with keeping up buffalo herd numbers; they periodically burned the grasslands in the autumn to keep forage levels high. This burning increased yields and encouraged earlier spring grass growth, and thus induced buffalo into favoured areas of fresh, young grass. Fire was used to influence buffalo movement—to direct a herd to a kill site and to keep buffalo away from fur-trade posts so that Europeans could not provision themselves. Fire was also used to protect valuable stands of timber.

Well before the treaties of the 1870s some Plains people, particularly the Cree and Saulteaux, had begun to raise small crops and to keep cattle to smooth out the seasonal scarcities that were increasing as the buffalo receded westward. As the homesteaders were later to learn, however—especially those who attempted farming before the development of dry-land farming techniques and early-maturing varieties of grain—yields from cultivated plants were highly unpredictable, and a more flexible economy that combined agriculture with hunting and gathering was the most feas-

ible until the disappearance of the buffalo in the late 1870s. Agriculture was a far more ancient and indigenous tradition on the Plains than the horse culture, which was a much more fleeting episode. Cree were acquainted with cultivated plant food and techniques of agriculture through several of their contacts, most notably the Mandan, Arikara, and Hidatsa, who maintained a flourishing agricultural economy on the upper Missouri. There is evidence of an agricultural village on the banks of the Red River near the present-day town of Lockport, Manitoba, that dates from between 1300 and 1500 CE (Putt 1991:64). Blackfoot were found by the earliest of European fur traders to be growing tobacco.

Aboriginal people of the Plains were not as "passive" as the landscape; their world was not static and timeless. The archaeological and historical records suggest that Plains people learned new ways regularly, that there was much adaptation and borrowing among groups, and that changes occurred constantly. The Plains Cree, for example, had a history of making dramatic adjustments to new economic and ecological circumstances, modifying the ways in which they obtained their livelihood. With the establishment of fur-trade posts on Hudson Bay after 1670, the Cree, along with their allies the Assiniboine, quickly seized the opportunity to function as middlemen to the trade. With the expansion of European fur-trade posts inland in the late eighteenth century, the Cree took advantage of a new economic opportunity and worked as provisioners of buffalo meat to the trading companies. They showed themselves to be remarkably flexible in rapidly adjusting to the rewards and demands of different environments—forest, parklands, and Plains. The branch that became the Plains Cree readily adopted many of the characteristics, techniques, and traits of Plains buffalo and horse culture. Aboriginal people such as the Cree were accustomed to making dramatic adjustments to new ecological and economic circumstances, and there is no inherent reason to believe that they could not have made adjustments to the new order of the post-1870 era by becoming full participants in the agricultural economy. The fact that they did not was due not to their own choice; rather, there was a refusal to let them do so, as they were denied access to the opportunities and resources that would have allowed them a more independent existence.

While Aboriginal people of the Plains required assistance and instruction to establish a farming economy, they had certain advantages that new arrivals did not enjoy. They had an intimate knowledge of the resources and climate of the West. They were much better informed on rainfall and frost patterns, on the availability of water and timber, and on soil varieties. They had experience with locusts, fires, and droughts. Aboriginal farmers might have had a better chance than many of the settlers from the humid east. Many of these never could accept the discomforts and conditions, and they departed, and even for those who remained acclimatization could take several years. Settlers from elsewhere might well have benefited from the knowledge Aboriginal people of the Plains had to offer. One settler in Saskatchewan, who had previously worked as a trader, consulted an Aboriginal friend named South Wind when he wanted to locate his homestead in the 1880s, and learned, for example, how to use fire to protect stands of timber and how to replenish the hay swamps. He later found local legislation regarding fire to be a "positive evil" and wrote that "our legislators should have had old South Wind at their Councils."[2] Accounts of such consultation are, however, very rare.

As early as the 1850s European travellers to the Plains reported that the Cree were concerned about the scarcity of buffalo, that many were anxious to try agriculture and wanted assistance in the way of instruction and technology. They were well aware that the buffalo hunt was no longer going to sustain them. With the demise of the fur trade,

agriculture appeared to be the only option. During the treaty negotiations of the 1870s Plains people sought government aid to make the transition to an agricultural economy. In return for their offer of an opportunity for peaceful expansion, Aboriginal people asked that they be given the instruction and technology that would allow them to farm. Aboriginal spokesmen did not see any inherent conflict between their distinctive identity and active participation in an agricultural economy. Circumstances obliged them to cease living as their ancestors had done, but they did not therefore cease to be Aboriginals. Like the Natives of the older provinces of Canada, they were in favour of agriculture, resource development, and education that would assist them to survive, but they did not intend, for example, to abandon their religious ceremonies and beliefs. Euro-Canadian observers consistently insisted on seeing Plains people as hunters, gatherers, and warriors incapable of adopting agriculture.

A Crop of Broken Promises: The 1870s

The main focus of this study is the people of the Treaty No. 4 district of southeastern Saskatchewan who settled on reserves in the Touchwood Hills, File Hills, and along the Qu'Appelle River. Most were Plains Cree, collectively known as the *Mamihkiyiniwak*, the "Downstream People," although Assiniboine, mixed Cree-Assiniboine ("Young Dogs"), and Saulteaux also settled here and were intermingled with Plains Cree bands. Although these people form the main focus, evidence was also drawn from the Treaty No. 6 district, settled primarily by Plains Cree known as the "Upstream People." In the later 1870s, the earliest years of Indian reserve settlement in present-day Saskatchewan, farming proved nearly impossible despite concerted efforts. For some bands, farming was never to be successful because of the nature of the reserve site itself. Other bands received high-quality agricultural land that was later to excite the envy of other settlers. The earliest instructions to surveyors were that care should be taken to ensure reserve lands "should not interfere with the possible requirements of future settlement, or of land for railway purposes." At that time what was seen as the "fertile belt," and the proposed route for the Canadian Pacific Railway, ran northwest along the Assiniboine and North Saskatchewan Rivers. Land further south was considered arid and unlikely ever to be wanted by settlers, so many reserves, such as those along the Qu'Appelle River, were surveyed there. But when the CPR route was changed in 1881 and rerouted through the south, many of these reserves were located near or on the railway route, in the midst of what was hoped would become the settlement belt and the heart of a prosperous agricultural economy.

Farming in the 1870s proved to be nearly impossible because the implements and livestock promised in the treaties were inadequate. Ten families, for example, were to share one plough. Bands varied in size, numbering between 17 and 50 families, but regardless of size, each was offered only one yoke of oxen, one bull, and four cows. To earn a living from the soil, every farming family required a yoke of oxen. As one Plains Cree chief pointed out in 1879, it was perfectly ridiculous to expect them to get on with so few oxen, that every farmer in the Northwest, however poor, had his own yoke of oxen, that "We are new at this kind of work, but even white men cannot get on with so few oxen" (Anon. 1879:28). In addition to the overall inadequacy of the agricultural assistance promised in the treaties, government officials were reluctant and tentative about distributing what was promised. The people prepared to farm expected their supply of implements, cattle, and seed immediately, but officials were determined to adhere strictly to the exact wording of the treaty, which stated that implements, cattle, and seed would be given to "any band . . . now actually

cultivating the soil, or who shall hereafter settle on these reserves and commence to break up the land." Aboriginal people could not settle until the surveys were complete, and in some cases this took many years. They could not cultivate until they had implements to break the land, yet these were not to be distributed until they were settled and cultivating. Government officials shared the belief that the distribution even of those items promised in the treaties could "encourage idleness," and there was concern that the implements and cattle would not be used for the purposes for which they were intended.

There were also problems with the quality and distribution of seed grain. In the earliest years the seed arrived in a damaged state and was received in midsummer when the season was far too advanced for planting. Acres sometimes lay idle because there was no seed available, and more land might have been broken had there been seed to sow. It was also learned after a number of years that people cultivating the reserves had to be supplied with some provisions in the spring during ploughing and sowing. The people of Treaty No. 6 had successfully bargained for this during their negotiations, but no such promise had been made to the people of Treaty No. 4. Although David Laird, Lieutenant-governor and Indian superintendent for the North-West Superintendency, recommended in 1877 that some provisions be distributed in the spring to Treaty No. 4 bands, this request was struck from the estimates in Ottawa. It proved impossible for more than a few to remain on their reserves and cultivate as the others were obliged to hunt and gather provisions for the group to survive. Once seeding was finished, and sometimes even before, many residents of the reserves were out on the Plains, leaving behind only a few to tend the crops.

Aboriginal farmers were hampered in their earliest efforts by the kind of ploughs they were issued. By the late 1870s, Manitoba farmers had

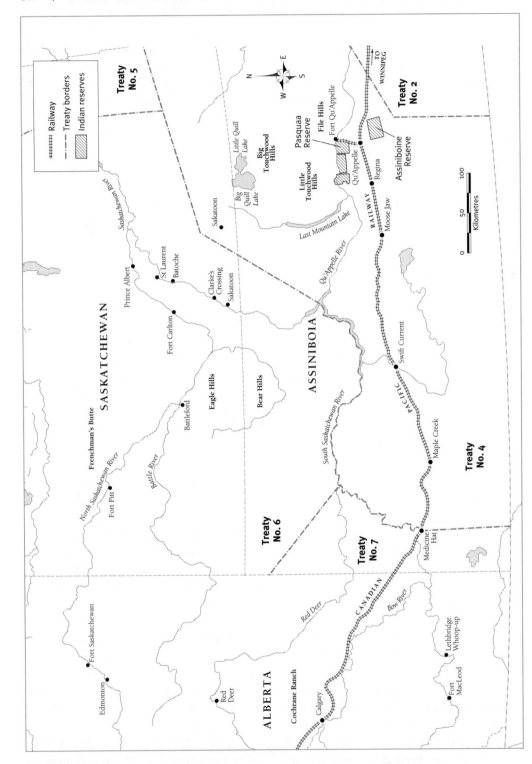

MAP 19.1 Saskatchewan and Assiniboia Districts, c. 1900

learned that American ploughs, especially the John Deere model, with its chilled-steel mould-board, were far superior for western conditions than the Ontario models. The Indian department, however, continued until 1882 to purchase only Canadian-manufactured ploughs, which proved to be unsatisfactory. There were problems keeping in good repair the implements and wagons that were distributed, as they frequently broke down, crippling operations. Wooden parts were sometimes replaced by the farmer, but the breakage of metal parts was much more serious, as reserve farmers did not have access to blacksmiths, who were also required to point, or sharpen, ploughshares. Other equipment and livestock supplied by contractors under the terms of the treaties were clearly inferior, and Aboriginal people simply refused to accept some of it. An 1878 commission of investigation found Winnipeg Indian commissioner Joseph-Alfred-Norbert Provencher guilty of fraud in the awarding of contracts and it was discovered, among other things, that it was standard practice to furnish the Indian department with "the most inferior articles" (Titley 1997:41). In 1879 one observer described the carts and wagons supplied to but refused by Treaty No. 6 people near Fort Carlton as "the poorest description of Red River carts, which have been used by freighters up to this point, and are really unfit for further use; while the wagons are literally falling to pieces." The axes, "miserably small," were also refused (Anon. 1879:29).

Perhaps the most scandalous example of corruption was in the cattle sent to a great many reserves in the late 1870s. They received wild Montana cattle, which were unaccustomed to work and could not be hitched to the plough. The milk cows given out were of the same description. The Fort Carlton bands were astounded when these cattle were brought to them from Montana, when tame cattle could have been purchased at Prince Albert or Red River. Most of the cattle died over the first winter of 1878–9. Some choked

themselves when tied in stables; others could not be fed because they did not take to the food. As one Plains Cree chief stated, "We know why these Montana cattle were given us; because they were cheaper, and the Government, thinking us a simple people, thought we would take them" (ibid.:28). He was correct. It became clear during the 1878 investigation that individuals in Winnipeg had profited by purchasing these creatures from Montana at about half the rate that they actually charged the Indian department.

Aboriginal farmers laboured under other disadvantages as well. In these earliest years there were no grist mills located near reserves, and the wheat they raised was of no use to them without milling facilities. With the disappearance of the buffalo, the main source for all their apparel also vanished. They lacked clothing and footwear, which one official described as the greatest drawback to their work. To cover their feet they cut up old leather lodges, but these too rapidly diminished. Often hungry, weak, and ill, people could not work no matter how willing.

There was little progress in agriculture in the years immediately following the treaties of the 1870s. Early on, government officials insisted that this had to do with the indifference and apathy of Aboriginal people, who willfully rejected an agricultural way of life and inflexibly and stubbornly insisted on pursuing hunting and gathering. Through idleness, it was claimed, they were creating their own problems. An explanation that belittled and deprecated the abilities of Aboriginal farmers absolved the government of any responsibility in the matter, and it was to be the favoured explanation of department officials well into the twentieth century. During these initial years of government parsimony, indifference, and outright corruption an opportunity was lost. Many of those who wished to farm found it impossible and became disheartened and discouraged. Had the government shown a genuine interest, some steps toward creating an agricultural economy might have been taken during the years before 1878–9, when the food crisis, brought on by the total disappearance of the buffalo, became severe. There was much distress, suffering, and death throughout the Northwest by 1878, although reports of starvation were systematically denied by government officials and the western press, as such news could damage the reputation of the region as a prospective home for thousands of immigrants. Once again, Aboriginal people were portrayed as chronic complainers with imaginary grievances, and they were blamed for having "not made the usual effort to help themselves."[3]

The other legacy of the years immediately following the treaties was the sense of betrayal felt by Aboriginal people who had expected government assistance in the difficult transition to an agricultural economy. As Chief Ahtahkakoop stated in 1879, "On the transfer of the country we were told that the Queen would do us all the good in the world, and that the Indians would see her bounty. With this message came presents of tobacco, and I took it at once; and I pray now that the bounty then promised may be extended to us." Three years after the treaty the chief was convinced that the "policy of the Government has been directed to its own advantage, and the Indians have not been considered so much." These chiefs had made several representations to government authorities, "but they were as if they were thrown into water" (ibid.).

Chief Pasqua, from the Pasqua Reserve in southeastern Saskatchewan, had presented Joseph Cauchon, Lieutenant-Governor of Manitoba, with similar grievances and concerns a year earlier. Pasqua had a pictograph record of his understanding of the treaty promises, and of the early years of treaty implementation.[4] His people, though willing to farm and diversify their subsistence base, had no cattle to break and work the land, no seed to sow, and no provisions to sustain them while

at work. Aboriginal people had reason to feel that they had been deceived and led along a path that ended in betrayal, that their treatment constituted a breach of faith. They were getting the clear impression that the treaties were made simply as a means of getting peaceable possession of the country without any regard to their welfare. As Aboriginal spokesmen grasped every opportunity to implore the government to assist them to make a living by agriculture, department officials reacted by increasingly blaming the Natives for their misfortunes and portraying them as troublemakers and chronic complainers, incapable of telling the truth.

The Home Farm Experiment

In the wake of alarming reports from the Northwest of destitution and starvation, an ambitious plan to both feed Aboriginal people and instruct them in farming was hastily contrived in Ottawa in the fall and winter of 1878–9. A squad of farm instructors, mainly from Ontario, was sent west in the summer of 1879. They were to establish "home farms" at 15 sites in the Northwest: six in the Treaty No. 4 district and nine in the Treaty No. 6 district. At these farms, located on or near the reserves, the instructors were to raise large quantities of provisions to support not only themselves, their families, and employees but also the neighbouring Aboriginal population. Their farms were to serve as "model farms" for Aboriginal observers, and in addition the instructors were to visit the reserve farmers from time to time to assist them in breaking, seeding, and harvesting and in building their houses, barns, and root houses. At two "supply farms" in the Treaty No. 7 district large quantities of produce were to be raised, but the farmers at these sites were not given the additional responsibility of instructing Aboriginal farmers.

The home farm plan was hastily and poorly conceived in Ottawa by people without any knowledge of Aboriginal people or of the region's soil and climate. The men chosen as instructors were unfamiliar with conditions of life in the West and knew nothing about Aboriginal people. They had to be provided with both guides and interpreters. As one Aboriginal spokesman stated, it only made sense that a farm instructor be a man "from the country, who understands the language, and with whom I could speak face to face, without an interpreter" (ibid.:2g). The official rationale for not choosing local people was that "strangers" were likely to carry out their duties more efficiently, would not have their favourites, and would treat all fairly and alike. It is also clear, however, that the position of farm instructor was a patronage appointment, and all were chosen by Sir John A. Macdonald, the Canadian prime minister, from a list furnished by Laurence Vankoughnet, deputy superintendent-general of Indian Affairs. In addition, the tasks assigned the instructors were beyond the resources and capabilities of any individual, however well acquainted he might be with conditions in the Northwest. It soon proved that the instructors had great difficulty establishing even the most modest farms. The government found itself responsible for the support of instructors, their families, and employees, who ran farms with such dismal returns that they contributed almost nothing to the expense of running them. It was also soon discovered that the farmers simply could not attend both to their own farms and to assisting on reserve farms. The instructors seldom visited the reserves and lacked even basic knowledge about the people they were to instruct. The program turned out to be an administrative nightmare. Difficulties with personnel arose early, and the program was characterized by resignations and dismissals. The instructors were angered by government decisions to charge them for the board of themselves and family even when the food they consumed had been raised by themselves.

Beset with all these difficulties, the home farm program floundered. In the House of Commons, government critics hammered away at the plan. They claimed that the instructors were incompetent carpetbaggers, but the central criticism was that there should be no such expenditure on the Aboriginal people of the Northwest, as this was encouraging idleness when they should be made to rely solely on their own resources. One Member of Parliament argued that the program was an enormous waste of money because efforts to "civilize Indians" were inevitably doomed to failure.[5] Government defenders of the program argued that the essential problem lay with Aboriginal people, who were "idlers by nature, and uncivilized." In the opinion of Prime Minister Macdonald they were not suited to agriculture, as they "have not the ox-like quality of the Anglo-Saxon; they will not put their neck to the yoke."[6]

There were many vocal critics of the home farm program in the Northwest as well. Non-Aboriginal residents viewed the program as unfair, because too much was being done to equip Aboriginal people to farm, more than was available to the true "homesteaders," upon whom it was felt the prosperity of the region depended. The home farm program ingrained the idea that Aboriginal farmers were being lavishly provided with farm equipment and other assistance that was "conducive to the destruction of self-reliance, and calculated to give them a false impression of what the Government owed them." In the wake of the food crisis in the Northwest the government had begun to provide modest rations to reserve residents. Indeed, some of the farm instructors found much of their time taken up issuing relief in the form of "musty and rusty" salt pork in exchange for assigned work. Many non-Native residents were critical of the distribution of rations, which they saw as a reward for idleness and as unfair because it gave Aboriginal farmers an advantage over other struggling farmers.

The home farm program had a very brief life in its original form. By 1884 the department had officially retired the policy, which had already

BOX 19.1 Ahtahkakoop, Mistawasis, and Kitowehaw, 1879

On 2 September 1879 a meeting took place at Fort Carlton between Indian Commissioner Edgar Dewdney and Treaty No. 6 Plains Cree leaders Ahtahkakoop, Mistawasis, and Kitowehaw. A "special correspondent" from the *Montreal Gazette* also attended and reported on the meeting in an article published in that paper on 29 September. The Hudson's Bay Company interpreter translated the words of the Plains Cree leaders beginning with Ahtahkakoop:

> We waited for you, and we see you now; we wonder if our word met you. We have often been talking of the promises we got and when we saw that they were not carried out in their spirit, we made representations to the Minister, but they were as if they were thrown into the water. We are very glad to meet you now, as you come with full authority to act. We will not touch on anything, but the promises which have not been fulfilled. . . . The cattle we got from Government all died; they were brought from Montana, and we protested that they would not do. . . . They were like the wild fowl, we saw them here, and then they disappeared; some, when tied in stables, choked themselves; some could not be fed, and to catch them was a fight, so wild were they. . . .

Mistawasis then came forward and said:

> I will tell you, as we understood the treaty made with Governor Morris. We understood from him that he was coming into the country to help us to live, and we were told how we were to get a living, and we put ourselves at work at once to settle down. . . . We expected that we would have had good cattle, but those brought were so poor that it was a mockery of the promises to give us cattle with little else than skin and bone. . . . Government is too slow in helping the Indians if they are going to help us at all. The fall before we saw [Lieutenant-] Governor [David] Laird, and wished him to give us more ample assistance in the way of farm implements and seeds. He said his powers were limited, but he would write to the Government, and let us know. To all these representations we received no answer. The country is getting so poor that it is for us either death by starvation, and such aid as will enable us to live. The buffalo was our only dependence before the transfer of the country, and this and other wild animals are disappearing, and we must farm to enable us to live. . . .

Ketawayo [Kitowehaw]:

> Every farmer, however poor, at Prince Albert has his yoke of oxen and we have tried and find that we cannot do with so few. We are new at this kind of work, but even white men cannot get on with so few oxen. . . . We know why these Montana cattle were given us; because they were cheaper, and the Government, thinking us a simple people, thought we would take them. The cattle have all died. . . . Hitherto everything we have asked has been promised to be represented to the Government, but we have never got any answer, and we want now an answer. . . .

—Anonymous (1879)

undergone much modification. Farm instructors remained and their numbers increased, but their own farms were to consist of no more than a few acres and they were to concentrate on instruction. New recruits were no longer brought from Ontario at great expense, but were men from the Northwest.

The Pioneer Experience: Agriculture in the 1880s

All who attempted farming on the Plains in the 1880s experienced frustration and failure. Crops during this decade were damaged year after year by drought and early frosts. Prairie fires became a serious hazard, consuming haystacks as well as houses, stables, and fences, and hampering the abilities of farmers not only to winter cattle but also to carry out the whole cycle of farming operations. There was a high rate of homestead cancellation, and many of the community experiments of ethnic, religious, working-class, and aristocratic groups did not survive the decade.

A major difference between the Aboriginal farmer and his neighbours was that while newcomers had the option to leave and try their luck elsewhere, reserve residents had little choice but to persevere, as under the Indian Act they were excluded from taking homesteads. Aboriginal farmers could not obtain loans because they were not regarded as the actual owners of any property, however extensive and valuable their improvements might be, and they had difficulty obtaining credit from merchants. Because of many of the technicalities and prohibitions of the Indian Act, Natives were prevented from doing business or transacting even the most ordinary daily affair. They were deprived of the right to do what they chose with nearly everything they acquired by their own personal industry. People governed by the Indian Act were prevented by a permit system from selling, exchanging, bartering, or giving away any produce grown on their reserves without the permission of department officials. A pass system, imposed initially during the 1885 Rebellion but continued well into the twentieth century, controlled and confined the movements of people off their reserves. Those who wished to leave the reserve were obliged to acquire a pass from the farm instructor or Indian agent declaring the length of and reason for their absence. The most recent arrivals to the country had far more rights, privileges, and freedom than the original inhabitants.

Despite these restrictions and the drought, frost, and prairie fires of these years, reserve farmers in some localities made significant advances in the 1880s. Several of the problems that had hampered reserve farming in the past had to some extent been ameliorated. Through a "cattle on loan" policy, for example, many bands had considerably increased their numbers of work oxen, cows, steers, heifers, and bulls. Under this system the department "loaned" a cow to an individual who was to raise a heifer, either of which had to be returned to the Indian agent. The animal became the property of the individual, although the agent's permission was required to sell or slaughter. Reserve farmers also had increased access to grist mills in the 1880s as the department initiated a program of granting bonuses to individuals who would establish mills in the Northwest. Recipients of the bonus were obliged to charge Aboriginal customers a little less than ordinary customers for a 10-year period. The department also displayed greater concern to supply the services of blacksmiths, which bolstered agricultural operations.

Reserve farmers began to acquire some of the up-to-date machinery necessary to facilitate their operations. Some reserves were fortunate in their abundant hay supplies, and a number of bands sold hay on contract to other reserves, to settlers, and to the North-West Mounted Police.

FIGURE 19.2 Native farmers, c. 1906–10. (Courtesy Archives of Manitoba, Morris, Edmund 510 (N15364))

Selling hay was one of the very few opportunities for outside employment available to reserve residents. Accordingly, mowers and rakes were the most common purchases of machinery. These were purchased with the Aboriginals' own earnings or through pooled annuities; they were not purchased for them by the department. Agents and farm instructors in the 1880s felt that access to mowers and rakes was essential for all bands, not only those that sold hay. As livestock increased on the reserves, mowers and rakes were necessary to provide enough hay. Reapers and self-binders were also acquired during this period. The self-binder lessened the danger of frost damage during a protracted harvest and it also reduced the waste produced in binding with short straw. Such machinery permitted farmers to cultivate larger areas. By the late 1880s on some reserves in the districts of Treaty Nos. 4 and 6, farmers were beginning to see some significant results of their labour,

and they had produce that they wished to sell: predominantly cattle, grain, and hay.

Like other prairie women of this period, Aboriginal women helped in the fields during peak seasons such as haying and harvest, but otherwise the business of grain farming was predominantly a male activity. Women continued to harvest wild resources such as berries, wild rhubarb, prairie turnip, and birch sap, and they hunted rabbits, gophers, and ducks. Because of increased settlement, the pass system, and calls for the restriction of Aboriginal hunting rights, these opportunities became increasingly constricted. Aboriginal women were eager to learn new skills and to adopt new technology. By the late 1880s the wives of many farm instructors acquired the title of "instructress" and they, as well as the wives of missionaries, taught skills such as milking, butter-making, bread-making, and knitting. Women adapted readily to these activities, but a chronic shortage of raw materials made it difficult to apply what they had learned. While the women knew how to make loaf bread, for example, they did not have the proper ovens, yeast, or baking tins, so they continued to make bannock, despite government attempts to abolish it from the diet, because it required more flour than loaf bread. They seldom had yarn with which to knit. There were no buttons for the dresses the women made. They were often short of milk pans, although they made their own using birchbark. One instructress reported in 1891 that the greatest drawback was "their extreme poverty, their lack of almost every article of domestic comfort in their houses, and no material to work upon."[7] They lacked basic necessities such as soap, towels, wash basins, and wash pails, and had no means with which to acquire these.

The log dwellings on reserves in this era and well into the twentieth century were invariably described as "huts" or "shacks" of one storey and one room. The roofs were constructed with logs or poles over which rows of straw or grass were laid. They were chinked inside and out with a mixture of mud and hay and had clay stoves but no flooring, and tanned hide was used for window covering. It was impossible to apply lessons of "housewifery" in such shacks. In Department of Indian Affairs publications, however, Aboriginal women were often depicted as poor housekeepers who willfully ignored instruction in modern methods. They were blamed for the poor living and health conditions on the reserves. Explanations that stressed the incapacity of Aboriginal women to change, like those that disparaged the farming abilities of the men, absolved the government of any responsibility for the poverty of the reserves.

The Pressure of Competition

As Aboriginal farmers acquired the technology required by western conditions and as they began to increase their acreages and their herds, they also began to pose a threat as competitors in the marketplace. By the late 1880s, farmers in parts of the Northwest were complaining loudly about "unfair" competition from Aboriginal people. It was widely believed that government assistance gave Aboriginal farmers an unfair advantage. Non-Aboriginal settlers mistakenly believed that reserve farmers were lavishly provided with livestock, equipment, government labour, and rations, and did not have to worry about the price at which their products were sold. There was absolutely no appreciation of the disadvantages they laboured under, or of how government regulation and Canadian laws acted to stymie their efforts. Editorials in the *Fort Macleod Gazette* regularly lamented "Indian competition," which was injuring the "true" settlers of the country. If the Siksika (Blackfoot), Kainai (Blood), Pikuni (Peigan), and Tsuu T'ina (Sarcee) were "cut loose" from the treaty, support could be given to their industries, according to the *Gazette*, but it was "pretty hard to ask the people of the country to contribute toward the support of a lot of idle paupers, and then allow them to use this very support for the purpose of taking the bread out of the settler's month [sic]."[8]

It was argued in the *Gazette* throughout the 1880s and 1890s that Aboriginal people should not be permitted to compete with the settlers in the sale of hay, potatoes, or grain. Any evidence that they were successful in securing contracts was used as proof that they had underbid non-Natives. There was no consideration that their product might be superior, as was certainly the case with the hay purchased by the North-West Mounted Police, who often noted in their reports that the best hay was bought from reserve farmers.[9] In a letter to the editor in July 1895, one local resident claimed that "it is altogether unfair to allow these Indians to enter into competition with white men who, even with hard work, find it difficult to make both ends meet and provide for their families." Evidence of unfair competition was used by the editors of the *Gazette* to bolster their larger campaign of the later 1880s to have Aboriginal people moved to one big reserve, an "Indian territory" out of the way of the Euro-Canadian settlements. It was argued that Indian policy had been a failure as Aboriginal people "had not made a single step toward becoming self-supporting."[10] There was apparently no recognition of the fact that it was impossible to become self-supporting to any degree unless they were allowed to sell their products.

Concerns about unfair "Indian competition" were echoed in other parts of the Northwest as well. The residents of Battleford and district were particularly strident in objecting to the competition of the Plains Cree in the grain, hay, and wood markets. Here, as well as in the district of southern Alberta, there was concern that reserve residents not become successful stock-raisers, as the supply of cattle to the Indian department for rations was a vital source of revenue for many settlers. On 13 October 1888 the editor of the *Saskatchewan Herald* of Battleford denounced any plan to "set the Indians up as cattle breeders, encouraging them to supply the beef that is now put in by white contractors."

Here, as in other districts, Aboriginal farmers competed with new settlers for hay land. Because of the predominantly dry years of the 1880s hay was very scarce in some seasons. Off-reserve areas where reserve farmers had customarily cut hay became the subject of heated disputes. Non-Aboriginal residents of the Battleford district successfully petitioned the Minister of the Interior in 1889 to limit the hay land available to Aboriginal farmers off the reserves, despite the fact that the Battleford agent had warned that there would be no alternative but to decrease stock on the reserves. Many influential people in the West had a direct interest in the continuation of rations and in seeing that Aboriginal people were not self-supporting. Large operations like the W.F. Cochrane ranch in southern Alberta found a sizable market for their

beef on the neighbouring reserves. In his correspondence to department officials he naturally objected to any reduction in rations, arguing that this meant that their lives, as well as their property and cattle operation, would be in danger.[11]

The Peasant Farming Policy, 1889–97

In 1889, Hayter Reed, commissioner of Indian Affairs in Regina, announced that a new "approved system of farming" was to be applied to Indian reserves in western Canada. Reserve farmers were to reduce their area under cultivation to a single acre of wheat and a garden of roots and vegetables. Along with a cow or two, this would sufficiently provide for a farmer and his family. They were to use rudimentary implements alone: to broadcast seed by hand, harvest with scythes, bind by hand with straw, thresh with flails, and grind their grain with hand mills. They were to manufacture at home any items they required, such as harrows, hayforks, carts, and yokes. This policy complemented government intentions to subdivide the reserves into small holdings of 40 acres each. Publicly, the subdivision of the reserves and the peasant farming policy were justified as an approach intended to render reserve residents self-supporting. Individual tenure, it was claimed, would implant a spirit of self-reliance and individualism, thus eroding "tribalism." Reed argued that the use of labour-saving machinery might be necessary and suitable for settlers, but Indians first had to experience farming with crude and simple implements. To do otherwise defied immutable laws of evolution and would be an "unnatural leap." In Reed's view, Aboriginal people had not reached the stage at which they were in a position to compete with white settlers.[12] Another argument forwarded against the use of labour-saving machinery was that rudimentary implements afforded useful employment for all.

Clearly, however, there were other reasons for the peasant farming formula and for allotment in severalty, reasons that were understood and appreciated by non-Aboriginal settlers. The *Saskatchewan Herald* (20 August 1887) applauded the policy for the Aboriginal farmer:

Thrown thus on himself and left to work his farm without the aid of expensive machinery, he will content himself with raising just what he needs himself, and thus, while meeting the Government's intention of becoming self-sustaining, they at the same time would come into competition with the white settler only to the extent of their own labour, and thus remove all grounds for the complaint being made in some quarters against Government aided Indians entering into competition with white settlers.

This was a policy of deliberate arrested development. The allotment of land in severalty was viewed by officials, as well as by Prime Minister Macdonald himself, as a means of defining surplus land that might be sold (Tyler 1979:114). Severalty would confine people within circumscribed boundaries, and their "surplus" land could be defined and sold. Arrested development was a certain means of ensuring that much reserve land would appear to be vacant and unused.

Despite the protests of Aboriginal farmers, Indian agents, farm instructors, and inspectors of the agencies, the peasant farming policy was implemented on Plains reserves beginning in 1889. Officials were not to authorize the purchase, hire, or use of any machinery. Even if people had purchased machinery before the policy was adopted they were still to use hand implements. Farmers with larger holdings were to use the labour of others rather than revert to the use of machinery, or they were to restrict their acreages to what they could handle with hand implements alone. Officials in the field were dismayed by the policy that robbed the farmers of any potential source of revenue. They argued that the seasons in the Northwest were simply too short for the use of hand implements, which meant a loss in yield at harvest time and resulted in a much reduced supply of hay. Agent W.S. Grant of the Assiniboine Reserve protested that "the seasons in this country are too short to harvest any quantity of grain, without much waste, with only old fashioned, and hand implements to do the work with." In his view the amount of grain lost in his agency through harvesting with hand implements would be of sufficient quantity to pay for a binder in two years.[13]

Aboriginal farmers were profoundly discouraged by the new rules. It was widely reported that many refused to work with the hand implements and gave up farming altogether. One farmer from Moose Mountain declared he would let his grain stand and never plough another acre, while another gave up his oxen, his wheat, and the reserve.[14] Other aspects of the program, such as the home manufactures idea, were unrealistic and unworkable. Homemade wooden forks, for example, were simply not strong enough for loading hay, grain, or manure. They were to make their own lanterns, but agents protested that people could not look after their cattle at night without proper lanterns. At headquarters in Ottawa it proved impossible even to acquire some of the old-fashioned implements, such as hand mills, destined for the Aboriginal farmers. But Reed was not sympathetic to or moved by the objections and complaints, and he refused to give in to the "whims of Farmers and Indians." He advised that losing some of the crop or growing less grain was preferable to the use of machinery. If grain was being lost, the solution was for farmers to confine their acreage to what they could handle. Department employees were not to convene or be present at meetings with Aboriginal farmers, as this would give "an exaggerated importance" to their requests for machinery. They risked dismissal if they refused to comply with peasant farming policy.

Effects of the Restrictive Policy

The policy of deliberate discouragement of reserve agriculture worked well. By the mid-1890s, per capita acreage under cultivation had fallen to about half of the 1889 level and many serious farmers had given up farming altogether. In 1899 a resident of Prince Albert, William Miller Sr, wrote to the Minister of the Interior that in passing through the Duck Lake and Carlton reserves, he noted "no less than five fields [which can] be seen from the trail now without a bushel of grain sown in them. . . . that previously used to be an example to the settlers around."[15] Peasant farming, severalty, and measures such as the permit system combined to undermine and atrophy agricultural development on reserves. The Canadian government acted not to promote the agriculture of the Indigenous population but to provide an optimum environment for the immigrant settler. Whatever Canada did for its "wards" was subordinate to the interests of the non-Aboriginal population. Government policy was determined by the need to maintain the viability of the immigrant community.

Aboriginal people protested policies that affected them adversely, as they had from the 1870s. They raised objections to government officials, petitioned the House of Commons, sent letters to newspapers, and visited Ottawa. But the outlets for protest were increasingly restricted. Grievances related to instructors and agents rarely went further. Agency inspectors were, as mentioned, not allowed to hold audiences with reserve residents. The published reports of agents and inspectors were to divulge only that "which it was desired the public should believe."[16] Visiting officials such as the Governor General, usually accompanied by journalists, were taken only to select agencies that would leave the best impression. Department officials, particularly those in the central office, shared the view that Aboriginal people were chronic complainers not to be believed and a people who would go to extraordinary lengths to avoid diligent work.

Hayter Reed and the peasant farming formula were disposed of the year after Wilfrid Laurier and the Liberals came to power in 1896, but the damaging legacy of the policy was to be felt for years to come. Laurier was fortunate in coming to power just at a time when a constellation of factors, including rising world wheat prices, increased rainfall on the prairies, innovations in dry-land farming techniques, and massive immigration allowed a wheat economy to prosper in western Canada. Aboriginal farmers, however, had little place in this new age of prosperity. By the turn of the century agriculture did not form the basis of a stable reserve economy, and after that date the likelihood faded even further as the new administrators of Indian Affairs promoted land surrenders that further limited the agricultural capacity of reserves. The fact that there was "vacant" and "idle" land on many reserves, to a great extent the result of the peasant farming years, conveniently played into the hands of those who argued that Aboriginal people had land far in excess of their needs and capabilities. Government policy was that it was in the best interests of all concerned to encourage reserve residents to divest themselves of land they held "beyond their possible requirements," and the policy received widespread support in the western press and from farmers and townspeople. Residents of towns near Indian reserves regularly submitted petitions claiming that these tracts retarded the

BOX 19.2 The Permit System

Edward Ahenakew used a fictional character named "Old Keyam" to convey the Plains Cree experience of life on a prairie reserve in the early twentieth century. In this passage he describes the aggravations of the permit system that discouraged interest in farming and the cattle industry:

This may be "kindly supervision" but it is most wretchedly humbling to many a worthy fellow to have to go, with assumed indifference, to ask or beg for a permit to sell one load of hay that he has cut himself, on his own reserve, with his own horses and implements. I say again, it may be right for some, but that is no reason why those who try to get on, and who do get on, should have to undergo this humiliation. . . .

For myself, I think that I would rather starve than go to beg for such a trifling thing as a permit to sell one load of hay, while I am trying to make every hour of good weather count. To sell ten loads might be different. From the standpoint of the Government it may seem good, a kind of drill or discipline. But who on earth wants this when he is busy in a hurry, and needs food for himself? I have seen with my own eyes, Indians wasting a day, even two days, trying to get a permit to sell, when they are short of food. The Agent cannot always be at home, the clerk may be away, or busy, and the Indian must wait, though he may have to drive to the Agency from another reserve. . . .

As for our cattle—there again, they are not ours. A white man, owning cattle and having no ready money, draws up a plan for himself which includes selling. An Indian may have more cattle than that white man has, but do you think that he can plan in the same way? No. He is told that the commissioner has said that no cattle are to be sold until the fall. It is useless to plan under this system, yet planning is what successful work requires. . . .

Old Keyam paused to let his words sink in, and before he could continue, a young man spoke. "I have something to add to that. Sure, we all like the farm instructor. He's good-natured, teases us, doesn't mind when we tease him. Well, we were branding cattle last week, and he asked in his joking way what we thought I D[the brand of the Indian Department] meant. Old Knife was there, and he's smart. He gave quite a speech about it, said that it stood for our chief source of light in the darkness, a sort of half-moon—only the outward curve with its full true light shone towards Ottawa in the east, the other part to the west, and that it was hollow, not giving much light, and double barred at that. Whoever planned that brand, he said, knew the whole business well."

—Ahenakew (1973:148–50)

development and progress of their districts. Such pressure resulted in the alienation of many thousands of acres of reserve land, often the best land, in the years shortly after the turn of the century. The economic viability of reserve communities was deliberately eroded by the dominant society, mainly through government policies.

Conclusion

In the post-treaty era to 1900 the Plains Cree were resolved to establish a new economy based on agriculture. They faced many impediments and frustrations in these efforts. Implements and livestock promised under treaty were inadequate, and government officials proved reluctant to distribute these. These officials insisted that people were to be settled on their reserves *and cultivating* in advance of their receiving the implements and cattle promised to them, although that which had been promised was necessary for cultivation. Seed grain arrived too late or in a damaged state and wild Montana cattle were distributed instead of domestic oxen. Workers on reserves lacked proper clothing and footwear, and they were weak because of hunger and illness. Many reserves were distant from markets and transportation and there were no milling facilities in the earliest years of reserve life.

The government attempted to address some of these problems and the food crisis in the Northwest through a "home farm" policy that was hastily devised and implemented in 1879. The plan was to have farm instructors establish model farms, raise large quantities of food for rations, and teach agriculture. It was a poorly conceived policy as these tasks were beyond the capabilities of the men appointed, most of whom had no acquaintance with Aboriginal people or with conditions in the Northwest. This policy was shelved by 1884, but farm instructors remained on many reserves, indicating an important measure of government commitment to the establishment of farming at

that time, and some advances in agriculture were made in the mid-to late 1880s. But environmental conditions were grim for all farmers at that time. There were early frosts, and drought and prairie fires caused enormous damage. Aboriginal farmers laboured under particular disadvantages. Because of the prohibitions of the Indian Act they could not expand their land base or try their luck elsewhere by taking out homesteads, and they could not take out loans or transact their own business affairs.

Despite all the challenges of the 1880s, Plains Cree farmers in some localities made significant advances, raising a surplus for sale and acquiring necessary machinery by the end of that decade. Non-Aboriginal residents of the West expressed concern about this success and the threat of competition in the limited markets. In 1889, in response to these concerns, the government introduced a "peasant" farming policy. Reserve farmers were to cultivate no more than an acre or two using only rudimentary hand implements. The central argument of this chapter is that this policy, combined with the other disadvantages and conditions that beset Plains Cree farmers, impaired the establishment of a viable economy.

Epilogue

Aboriginal farmers, who lost the opportunity to participate in commercial agriculture in the 1890s, did not regain any ground in the early twentieth century. Cree historians Edward Ahenakew and Joe Dion both describe a pattern in their communities of an initial interest in agriculture and stock-raising that was atrophied because of the weight of regulation and supervision. They fell further behind in technology as well as training, as they did not have access to either the formal or the informal agricultural education programs of the wider farming community. The reserves remained pockets of rural poverty. Twentieth-century visitors to reserves often found Aboriginal people living in the midst of farmland that was not cultivated at all, was leased to non-Natives, or was worked with obsolete methods and technology. It was generally concluded that they were a people who had been unable to adapt to farming, who stubbornly clung to the past, and who were impervious to "progressive" influences despite years of government assistance and encouragement. The initial enthusiasm of many for agriculture and the policies of deliberate discouragement have been obscured and forgotten.

A groundbreaking survey of the social, educational, and economic conditions of the Aboriginal people of Canada (Hawthorn 1966), found that some of the most depressed reserve communities in the country were in agricultural districts of the prairies where there appeared to be land for livestock or crops. According to investigators, the few farms there were marginal or sub-marginal, or the land was leased to neighbouring non-Aboriginal farmers, or farming had been abandoned altogether. From the later twentieth century there has been a variety of initiatives and programs aimed at addressing problems of reserve agriculture, with mixed results. The Saskatchewan and Manitoba Indian Agricultural Programs (SIAP and MIAP) of the 1970s and 1980s was organized to re-invigorate the involvement of First Nations in reserve agriculture, and to improve the production capacity of reserve lands (Nickels 2004). While this initiative briefly resulted in an increased number of First Nations farmers producing more crops from more land, the program suffered from a number of weaknesses, including a lack of adequate funding.

More recent developments that can enhance reserve agriculture include increased acreages as a result of treaty land entitlement and land-claims settlements. In 2007 the federal Agriculture and Agri-Food Canada department began to take steps toward developing a national Aboriginal agriculture strategy that would promote Aboriginal involvement in agriculture, support Aboriginal values of environmental stewardship and develop Aboriginal capacity through education (Agriculture and Agri-Food Canada 2007:4). The First Nations Agricultural Council of Saskatchewan has been organized to assist farmers with environmental land management and to encourage the participation of First Nations youth in the agricultural industry. The Indian Agriculture Council of Manitoba was formed in 2006; its main objective is to develop a strong, sustainable agricultural sector for First Nations producers. The University of Saskatchewan's College of Agriculture and Bioresources in 2011 introduced a post-graduate diploma in Aboriginal Agriculture and Land Management, with a generous grant from the Sprott Foundation. The latest and most innovative development is One Earth Farms Corporation, created through a 2009 agreement between Toronto-based Sprott Resource Corporation (providing $27.5 million), and 17 First Nations from Saskatchewan and Alberta that "will make them the most influential farmers in all of Canada, with a super-sized one-million-acre operation that could rival the largest corporate farms in the world" (Friesen 2009). Under the agreement, reserve land is leased at market value to the One Earth Farms Corporation, which will focus on environmentally responsible land-use strategies in cultivating grain and oilseed and in cattle ranching. Aboriginal people will be trained and employed, and First Nations will have an equity stake in the company. Blaine Favel, director of One Earth Farms, who grew up on Poundmaker Reserve in Saskatchewan and earned an MBA from Harvard, said, "I view this on a continuum of First Nations agricultural ambition. When they signed treaties, First Nations people wanted to be on the land because they had to transition away from the buffalo. When some of them had success, obstacles were put in their way by the government. But Indians have always tried to farm" (Friesen 2009).

NOTES

1. From 1870 until the creation of the provinces of Alberta and Saskatchewan in 1905, the term "North-West Territories" was used for the entire region outside of the province of Manitoba.

2. Library and Archives Canada (LAC), Saskatchewan Homesteading Experiences, MG 30 C 16, vol. 3, 790.

3. *Saskatchewan Herald* (Battleford), 26 Apr. 1879.

4. LAC, RG 10, vol. 3665, file 10094, interpreter to Joseph Cauchon, 1 June 1878. Bob Beal, "An Indian Chief, An English Tourist, A Doctor, A Reverend, and a Member of Parliament: The Journeys of Pasqua's Pictographs and the Meaning of Treaty Four," *The Canadian Journal of Native Studies* 27, 1 (2007): 109–88.

5. *House of Commons Debates*, 1884, 2:1105 (Philippe Casgrain).

6. Ibid.:1107 (John A. Macdonald).

7. LAC, RG 10, vol. 3845, file 73406–7, T.P. Wadsworth to Hayter Reed, 17 Feb. 1891.

8. *Macleod Gazette*, 16 Aug. 1887.

9. Annual Report of Commissioner L.W. Herchmer for 1889, in *The New West: Being the Official Reports to Parliament of the Activities of the Royal [sic] North-West Mounted Police Force from 1888–89* (Toronto: Coles Publishing Company, 1973), 6.

10. *Macleod Gazette*, 7 Dec. 1886.

11. LAC, Hayter Reed Papers, W.F. Cochrane to L. Vankoughnet, 6 Sept. 1893, file W.F. Cochrane.

12. LAC, RG 10, vol. 3964, file 148285, Hayter Reed to A. Forget, 24 Aug. 1896.

13. Ibid., W.S. Grant to Reed, 1 Oct. 1896.

14. Ibid., J.J. Campbell to Reed, 8 Oct. 1896, and Grant to Reed, 1 Oct. 1896.

15. LAC, RG 10, vol. 3993, file 187812, William Miller Sr, to the Minister of the Interior, 21 July 1899.

16. LAC, RG 10, Deputy-Superintendent letterbooks, vol. 1115, Reed to J. Wilson, 3 Aug. 1894.

REFERENCES AND RECOMMENDED READINGS

Agriculture and Agri-Food Canada. 2007. *Report on Aboriginal Discussion Workshops: National Report. Next Generation of Agriculture and Agri-Food Policy*. Ottawa: Agriculture and Agri-Food Canada.

Ahenakew, Edward. 1973. *Voices of the Plains Cree*, ed. Ruth M. Buck. Toronto: McClelland & Stewart. Reprinted with permission from the Bishop of the Diocese of Saskatchewan. Through his fictional character Old Keyam, Ahenakew (1885–1961) presents a vivid portrait of life on prairie reserves, especially of the crippling effects of government policies and regulations.

Anonymous. 1879. *Chronicles By the Way: A Series of Letters Addressed to the Montreal Gazette Descriptive of a Trip Through Manitoba and the North-West*. Montreal: Montreal Gazette Printing Co.

Beal, Bob. 2007. "An Indian Chief, an English Tourist, a Doctor, a Reverend, and a Member of Parliament: The Journeys of Pasqua's Pictographs and the Meaning of Treaty Four," *The Canadian Journal of Native Studies* 22, 1: 109–88.

Buckley, Helen. 1993. *From Wooden Ploughs to Welfare: Why Indian Policy Failed in the Prairie Provinces*. Montreal and Kingston: McGill–Queen's University Press. An analysis of First Nations reserve economies, including agriculture, from the treaties to the 1990s, providing understanding of poverty and unemployment on reserves.

Butler, William F. (1872) 1968. *The Great Lone Land*. Edmonton: Hurtig.

Carter, Sarah. 1990. *Lost Harvests: Prairie Indian Reserve Farmers and Government Policy*. Montreal and Kingston: McGill–Queen's University Press. An analysis of agriculture on prairie reserves from the treaties to World War I.

———. 1999. *Aboriginal People and Colonizers of Western Canada to 1900*. Toronto: University of Toronto Press. A historiographical overview of the wealth of interdisciplinary scholarship of the last three decades on the history of the Canadian prairie West with an emphasis on the multiplicity of perspectives that exist.

Christensen, Deanna. 2000. *Ahtahkakoop: The Epic Account of a Plains Cree Head Chief, His People, and Their Struggle for Survival 1816–1896*. Shell Lake, SK: Ahtahkakoop Publishing. A comprehensive biography of a prominent Plains Cree leader, as well as a rich account of the culture, society, and economy during an era of rapid change. There is a great deal of emphasis on reserve agriculture.

Dion, Joseph. 1979. *My Tribe the Crees*, ed. Hugh Dempsey. Calgary: Glenbow–Alberta Institute. An account of the early years of settlement at Onion Lake and Kehiwin.

Dyck, Noel. 1991. *What is the Indian "Problem?":* *Tutelage and Resistance in Canadian Indian Administration*. St John's: ISER books, Memorial University of Newfoundland. A critical examination of past and present relations between Aboriginal people and governments in Canada, with emphasis on prairie Canada.

Elias, Peter Douglas. 1988. *The Dakota of the Canadian Northwest: Lessons for Survival*. Winnipeg: University of Manitoba Press. A detailed analysis of the different economic strategies adopted by the Dakota, including the farming bands at Oak River, Birdtail, Oak Lake, Standing Buffalo, and White Cap.

Friesen, Joe. 2009. "Natives, Bay Street Form Country's Biggest Farm," *Globe and Mail*, 26 March, http://ctv2.theglobeandmail.com/servlet/story/RTGAM.20090326.wfarmcontains26/business/Business/businessBN/ctv-business.

Hawthorn, H.B., ed. 1966. *A Survey of Contemporary Indians of Canada: Economic, Political, Educational Needs and Policies*. Ottawa: Indian Affairs Branch.

LeRat, Harold, with Linda Ungar. 2005. *Treaty Promises, Indian Reality: Life on a Reserve*. Saskatoon: Purich Publishing. An account of life on the Cowesses First Nation in Saskatchewan in the twentieth century that provides insight into the lives of First Nations farmers, reserve agriculture, and government policies and employees.

Lux, Maureen. 2001. *Medicine That Walks: Disease, Medicine and Canadian Plains Native People, 1880–1940*. Toronto: University of Toronto Press. An account of the diseases that afflicted Aboriginal people that, along with poverty, malnutrition, and overcrowding, dramatically reduced their numbers. Lux analyzes how non-Aboriginal specialists theorized the impact of these diseases and also explores the persistence of Aboriginal healing practices.

Milloy, John S. 1988. *The Plains Cree: Trade, Diplomacy and War, 1790–1870*. Winnipeg: University of Manitoba Press. An analysis of the complex trade and military patterns of the branch of the Cree that became a Plains people. Milloy argues that the Plains Cree culture flourished in the era to 1870 and was not undermined by their contact with European fur traders.

Nickels, Bret. 2004. "A Field of Dreams: The Story of the Manitoba Indian Agricultural Program." Ph.D. diss., University of Manitoba. A study of the now defunct MIAP, including its origins and genesis, its successes and weaknesses. The implications of the demise of the MIAP are discussed, as is the contemporary situation of First Nations agriculture in Manitoba.

Putt, Neal. 1991. *Place Where the Spirit Lives: Stories from the Archaeology and History of Manitoba*. Winnipeg: Pemmican.

Ray, Arthur J. 1974. *Indians in the Fur Trade: Their Role as Hunters, Trappers, and Middlemen in the Lands Southwest of Hudson Bay, 1660–1870*. Toronto: University of Toronto Press. The first and most significant revision of fur-trade history, placing the emphasis on the role of Aboriginal people. Ray explored how the Cree and Assiniboine were involved, the extent to which they shaped the trade, and the effects of the fur trade on these societies.

Sluman, Norma, and Jean Goodwill. 1982. *John Tootoosis: Biography of a Cree Leader*. Ottawa:

Golden Dog Press. Tootoosis, from Poundmaker Reserve in Saskatchewan, gives an account of the obstacles facing reserve farmers, of government efforts to effect land surrenders, and strategies adopted to circumvent them.

Titley, E. Brian. 1997. "Unsteady Debut: J.-A.-N. Provencher and the Beginnings of Indian Administration in Manitoba," *Prairie Forum* 22, 1: 21–46.

Tobias, John L. 1983. "Canada's Subjugation of the Plains Cree, 1879–1885," *Canadian Historical Review* 64, 3: 519–48. An important revisionist analysis of Plains Cree actions and strategies in the immediate post-treaty years.

Tyler, Kenneth J. 1979. "A Tax-Eating Proposition: The History of the Passpasschase Indian Reserve." MA thesis, University of Alberta.

Van Kirk, Sylvia. 1980. *"Many Tender Ties": Women in Fur Trade Society in Western Canada, 1670–1870.* Winnipeg: Watson and Dwyer. Excellent study of the relationships between fur traders and their Native and mixed-blood wives, and the changes wrought by the arrival of white women in the middle of this period.

PART VII

The Plateau

CHAPTER 20

The Plateau: A Regional Overview

Douglas Hudson and Marianne Ignace

The Region and Its People

The Canadian portion of the Plateau culture area is essentially the same region as that defined locally in British Columbia as "the southern Interior." This area is bounded on the west by the Coast Range and on the east by the Rockies, and comprises a series of interconnected plateaus and north–south valleys that extend south into the United States. With a history of glaciation, the Interior is now environmentally diverse and includes seven biogeoclimatic zones ranging from sagebrush deserts to sub-boreal spruce forests. The resources of the Fraser and Columbia River watersheds are of key importance to the Aboriginal nations and communities of the Plateau.

The Plateau is also linguistically diverse. At the core of the Canadian Plateau are Interior Salish language communities—Okanagan, Thompson or Nlaka'pamux, Shuswap or Secwépemc, and Lillooet or St'at'imx (St'at'imc). The suffix "-mx," also spelled "-emc," "-imx," or "-imc," means "people." In the southern Plateau, in what is now the United States, are other Interior Salish and Sahaptin-speakers. At the northern end of the Plateau, transitional to the Subarctic culture area, are the Athapaskan-speaking Tsilhqot'in (Chilcotin) and Southern Carrier, who are linked both linguistically and culturally to their northern neighbours of the western Subarctic, and likely represent a southward movement of Athapaskan-speaking groups. Another Athapaskan-speaking group, the Nicola, was located in the Nicola Valley but merged with Okanagan and Nlaka'pamux communities in the 1800s. Another language, which seems to be a linguistic isolate, is the Ktunaxa or Kutenai of southeastern BC and northern Idaho and Montana.

The inclusion of the Athapaskan-speaking Tsilhqot'in and Carrier in the Plateau can be seen as problematic, if one believes that linguistic and cultural affiliation is relevant in defining culture areas. As noted in Chapter 1, all such definitions are to some extent arbitrary. In this case, early overviews of Plateau cultures included the Tsilhqot'in and Carrier, and sometimes even the Sekani. However, if one emphasizes linguistic and cultural affiliations, all these groups would be more appropriately included in the Subarctic. This is especially true of the Sekani, whose traditional territories lie outside of the Fraser and Columbia River drainages. The Tsilhqot'in and Carrier (especially the Southern Carrier around Quesnel) could, however, be seen as occupying an intermediate position between the Plateau and the Subarctic. Although the first two editions of this book included the Carrier and Tsilhqot'in in this chapter, we do not. Thus our description focuses on the Salishan-speaking groups of the Plateau. An overview of

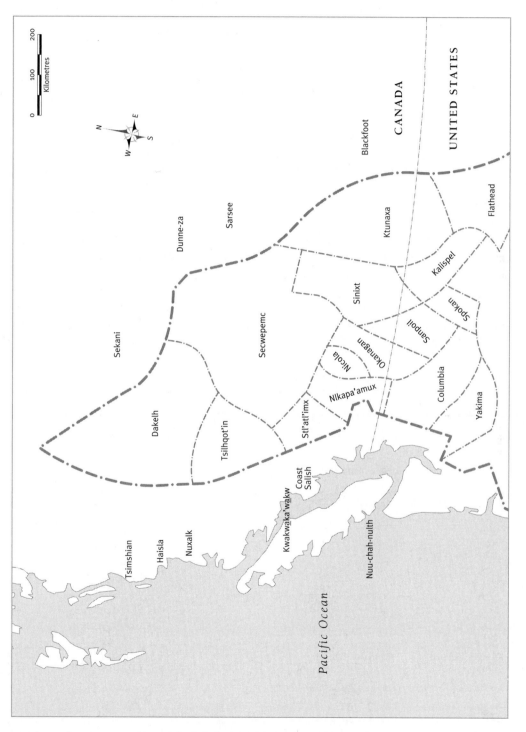

MAP 20.1 The Plateau Culture Area

the shifting boundaries of the Plateau is found in Walker (1998:1–7).

Over time, populations shifted and territorial boundaries were modified. A number of historic population shifts are directly related to European-introduced epidemics. Smallpox destroyed up to half the Sanpoil in 1782–3 and swept through the southern Plateau in both 1800 and 1832. The most devastating smallpox epidemic occurred in the early 1860s; the overall Aboriginal population of BC was reduced by anywhere from one-third to two-thirds, and among the Secwépemc alone seven bands along the Fraser River were virtually wiped out. Tsihlqot'in bands moved eastward to occupy land formerly held by Secwépemc, with subsequent population movements involving both Athapaskan and Interior Salish peoples. By the 1800s the Nicola were absorbed by the Okanagan and Nlaka'pamux (Thompson), and in the Arrow Lakes region in the West Kootenays, many of the people known as Sinixt (later known as Lakes) in the early twentieth century moved to the United States or were defined as US citizens—a consequence in part of their territory being on both sides of the new international boundary. In face of their band being eliminated by the Department of Indian Affairs, others settled among neighbouring Okanagan bands in Canada. The Aboriginal nations of the Canadian Plateau, along with their languages and subgroupings, are indicated in Table 20.1.

Plateau Cultural Patterns

The societies of the Plateau region show a high degree of cultural diversity, making it difficult to identify typical Plateau cultural patterns. One of the key features characterizing the Plateau is the availability of abundant runs of salmon. This feature can be used as a basis on which to identify

TABLE 20.1 Plateau Language Groups

LANGUAGE FAMILY	LANGUAGE (CURRENT/PAST SPELLING)	SUBGROUPING
Salish (Interior)	St'at'imx/Lillooet	Fraser River
		Lower
	Nlaka'pamux/Thompson	Upper
		Lower
	Secwépemc/Shuswap	Fraser River
		Canyon (Chilcotin R.)
		Lake (Shuswap L.)
		North Thompson
		Bonaparte
		Kamloops
	Nsilxtsín/Okanagan-Colville/Okanagan-Sylix	Okanagan
		Similkameen
		North Okanagan
		Sinixt/Lakes
Ktunaxa/Kutenai	Ktunaxa/Kutenai	Upper
		Lower
Athapaskan	Nicola (Dakelh/Carrier)	Southern
		Ulgatcho
	(Tsilqot'in/Chilcotin)	

FIGURE 20.1 Plateau Indian fishing for salmon on the Fraser River, Lillooet, BC, c. 1952. (Image HP 68625 courtesy of Royal BC Museum, BC Archives)

a common cultural pattern that distinguished Plateau groups from their neighbours. Other dominant features of Plateau culture in the 1800s were the establishment of semi-permanent winter or summer villages; the existence of kinship groups within each band that exercised stewardship over resources within the Aboriginal nation and regulated access to them by ways of kinship and **affinal** ties; and connections to the larger groups or, in a secondary sense, through inter-nation ties by way of kinship and marriage.

Plateau groups gained access to salmon through two major river systems: the Fraser and Columbia. The quantities and species of salmon, however, varied greatly among communities on the Plateau, depending on where they were situated. In addition, salmon runs fluctuate cyclically. While most Aboriginal groups on the lower Fraser had access to all five species of salmon, communities situated on the upriver watersheds depended on chinook, coho, and sockeye salmon. The size of individual sockeye runs could vary tremendously from year to year. For example, a recent four-year cycle of sockeye runs in the Stuart Lake watershed was estimated at 589,600; 35,500; 26,800; and 24,500. Plateau groups coped with these regular fluctuations in salmon availability through a system of access to resources based on **consanguinal** and affinal ties whereby, in order to obtain resources in off years, families would fish and hunt with relatives and in-laws from areas within and outside their language group. Moreover, inter-group trade in dried salmon in exchange for other foods and goods was a crucial feature of Plateau society. Dried sides of salmon were a currency among Plateau nations, and when the fur-trading companies set up posts among Plateau nations during the early nineteenth century, dried salmon obtained from the Plateau groups became the staple protein for the traders. Other Plateau groups that had fewer salmon resources relied more on game and freshwater fish. In addition to protein resources, a variety of plants played a significant role in subsistence activities and trade. Indeed, a distinguishing feature of Plateau culture was the reliance on root plants, including camas and bitterroot on the southern Plateau, and yellow avalanche lily, spring beauty, and balsam root on the northern Plateau. Plateau peoples harvested root plants through methods and regimes that are similar to techniques used in horticulture, thus blurring the distinction between hunting and gathering or foraging peoples as opposed to horticulturists.

Plateau groups followed a similar annual round of subsistence activities. In spring, people gathered at upland lakes to catch runs of trout as they were preparing to spawn in creeks running out of these lakes. During mid- to late spring, numerous green vegetables, as well as lodgepole pine cambium, were harvested. In late spring and early summer, people dug large quantities of edible roots, some of which were steamed in underground pits and then dried for winter. During the summer, families congregated along the major rivers to trap, spear, or net salmon and dry it for the winter months. One particularly important fishing location for the Lillooet was and is the confluence of the Bridge and Fraser Rivers, north of the town of Lillooet. Many different species of berries were collected and dried for winter use. In fall, families dispersed to the mountain regions to hunt large game and to prepare dry meat for winter. Deer were the most important large game animals hunted in the southern Plateau; before the twentieth century, elk and caribou were also key large game animals in the northern Plateau. The caribou range has since shrunk due to a warming trend, and moose have now become plentiful and an important source of meat in northern regions. In the winter, those groups that had access to abundant salmon resources congregated in semi-permanent villages, where stores of dried salmon sustained them through the cold months. During the winter, as people used their stored provisions, they supplemented their diet with fish caught through ice fishing and with small game caught by snaring.

Trade was also important to the Plateau economy. Networks linked the St'at'imx and Nlaka'pamux with Coastal groups, who in turn acted as intermediaries with adjacent Interior communities. Trade items from the southern Plateau entered the Interior of British Columbia via the Okanagan and Similkameen peoples, and Plains items worked their way into the Plateau through the Ktunaxa and Okanagan.

In the 1800s, Plateau groups recognized several different levels of social organization. The most important social group, in terms of day-to-day domestic activities, was the extended family, which hunted, fished, and gathered materials necessary for survival. Groups of related families that used a common territory constituted a band, which was named after the territory it occupied. Each band had from one to several villages that were occupied in the winter months. Among Plateau groups, chiefship operated mainly at the level of such large villages or clusters of interconnected small villages. Village chiefs were appointed by a council of Elders and/or community members, although in some cases there was a tendency for chiefship to be passed on from father to son. Autonomous villages within an Aboriginal nation were linked to one another through a common language and a sense of common history and custom, and especially through ties of kinship and exchange, which further served to provide mutual access for kin and in-laws to the resource-gathering locations of the diverse groups. Despite the relative economic and political autonomy of villages or bands, each Aboriginal nation had a sense of common identity and joint ownership of the resources of the entire tribe. Thus, according to oral histories and written ethnographic information from the early 1900s, the hunting grounds, plant-gathering areas, and most fishing areas were considered "tribal property." It was only in the Lillooet area that some

productive fishing rocks were considered to be owned or stewarded by particular families.

Kinship among the Plateau groups was primarily reckoned along bilateral lines—that is, it was traced through both the father's and the mother's sides. The prohibition of marriage to close kin, usually extended at least to second cousins, meant that many people were compelled to marry outside of their village group, and often outside of their band. Bilateral kinship, a tendency toward group **exogamy**, and the ethic of sharing and providing assistance to kin resulted in the creation of a network of relatives throughout the region who could be called upon to provide food, assistance, and access to hunting and fishing grounds when resources in one's own territory were scarce. Indeed, resource use and access along the entire Plateau were characterized by an inter-group and inter-nation system of primary access through immediate ties of kinship and socialization, and a supplementary system of secondary access through ties of affinity and parents' or grandparents' connections to places and groups. This brings up the third defining feature of Plateau groups: the existence of kinship groups within each band that exercised particular stewardship rights over valuable resources, with those groups most dependent on the rich salmon resources having the most formally developed and restrictive systems. Plateau societies have not remained static over time, however, and over the centuries there may well have been fluctuations in the degree to which specific ownership rights were exercised by kinship groups. The discussion here relates to Plateau cultures during the nineteenth century.

Among the St'at'imc, the most productive salmon-fishing sites were controlled—in the sense of first access and caretakership—by specific families or heads of families. Although the Plateau groups differed in the type of kinship groups that developed to restrict access to the resources, most included some dimension of restrictive, exclusive

FIGURE 20.2 Ktunaxa Indian family, c. 1914. Note the influences of neighbouring Plains groups in dress and tepee styles. (Image HP 73839 courtesy of Royal BC Museum, BC Archives)

control. On this basis Plateau groups can be distinguished from Subarctic cultures.

Plateau cultures varied also as a result of their interaction with neighbouring nations. In particular, the arrival of the horse on the Canadian Plateau during the early to mid-1700s revolutionized trade routes, travel, and some aspects of material culture. During the early 1800s, as a result of intensifying social and trade relations between the Interior and Coastal nations, the traditions of clan organization, social classes recognizing a nobility, and potlatch ceremonialism began to spread from the Northwest Coast societies to the Southern Carrier, Tsilhqot'in, and Secwépemc. These groups simultaneously incorporated and modified these trad-

itions. Clans, for example, became bilateral in order to fit the system of social organization operating in the new settings. Although the ethnographic information is limited, it appears that each dominant family within a band became associated with a clan, and by the mid-1800s northern Secwépemc families along the Fraser River were attempting to exercise ownership rights to fishing stations in the name of their clan, with other Secwépemc communities continuing to insist on the joint tribal ownership and stewardship of resources. The clan system never became fully entrenched among the Secwépemc and other Plateau groups, though, and it began to disappear after the rapid population decline brought about by the 1862 smallpox epidemic. In the southern Plateau, the Ktunaxa were greatly influenced by their associations with the Plains nations. They regularly travelled across the Rocky Mountains to hunt for buffalo, and much of their technology, such as tepee and dress styles, as well as their Sun Dance ceremonialism, bears the Plains cultural influence.

Origins

To a nation composed mainly of immigrants, questions of origins and "first arrivals" seem important. Many non-Natives, for example, enjoy studying their personal family history and tracing their roots back generations to different countries of origin. Archaeologists share these concerns with "first arrivals" and seek to answer questions regarding the origins of Native peoples in North America. To Indigenous peoples, however, these questions are irrelevant; Indigenous peoples have always been here. Plateau Indians explain origins in terms of how the earth was transformed by ancestral beings and how people separated from the rest of nature, receiving mortality as the price for guaranteed salmon runs, sunlight, and other things. Archaeological and Indigenous approaches to the issue of origins are rooted in different cultural perspectives on the past; both address the reality that Aboriginal people have occupied the Plateau for a long, long time.

Like other Interior Salish, the Okanagan narrate stories about their origin and the actions of the Creator, or the Old One. Specific features of the landscape, though, are attributed to the actions of Coyote, a character whose wanderings resulted in, among other events, the introduction of salmon to the Columbia River system. Narratives about Coyote point to his responsibility for the absence of salmon in the Similkameen River. In those accounts, Coyote was denied a woman he sought from the Similkameen people, and in retaliation he dammed the mouth of the Similkameen, forever blocking the passage of salmon. The presence today of kokanee, a landlocked salmon, in the Similkameen suggests that salmon once did ascend its waterways to spawn, but a rock slide at some unknown time forever eliminated the runs. The Coyote story is in many ways a lesson about knowing the land. The contrast between Indigenous and non-Native interpretations of the significance of landscape symbolizes the different cultural approaches that the two cultures use to conceptualize and narrate history.

Colonial Political Economy

The colonial presence in the Plateau is relatively recent. It was not until the first decade of the 1800s that trading posts were established in the northern Plateau, although European trade goods had become part of the material culture by the late 1700s. From the northern Interior posts the traders explored further south, Simon Fraser reaching the mouth of the Fraser River in 1808 and David Thompson the mouth of the Columbia in 1811. Through these explorations the fur trade gradually expanded into the Plateau and by 1821 a string of trading posts had been set up. The fur trade relied heavily on Indian participation. The forts depended on Natives not only as suppliers of furs, but also as providers of salmon, on which the forts based their subsistence. Natives also served important roles as messengers and labourers. While the fur trade did initiate some changes in technology and land tenure, its overall effect on Plateau cultures was minor and Native/trader relations were relatively balanced.

This tenuous equilibrium was shattered with a series of gold rushes in the British Columbia Interior during the 1850s and 1860s. The Cariboo gold rush alone drew thousands of miners northward into St'at'imx, Secwépemc, and—to a lesser extent—Okanagan territories. At the same time the smallpox epidemic of 1862 struck the Plateau region, wiping out entire bands and causing dramatic depopulation among the Native groups, who

FIGURE 20.3 These Tsilqot'in men in Lillooet, BC, may have been employed as ranch hands in the surrounding area. (Image HP90320 courtesy of Royal BC Museum, BC Archives)

had no natural immunity to the disease. Natives were soon outnumbered by miners and displaced from their hunting grounds, and hydraulic mining practices damaged or destroyed a number of valuable salmon spawning beds. The major gold rushes ended by the 1870s, and in their wake came colonial administrators and settlers.

The central and southern Plateau contained rich agricultural lands. By the 1880s much of the cultivatable land had been pre-empted. As farms and ranches were established and fences erected, Plateau groups lost access to some of their hunting territories and fishing stations. The 1860 Land Ordinance prohibited the pre-emption of Indian villages and fields, but even this minimal protection of Native rights was ineffectual. Due to the lax administration of the times, a number of settlers were able to pre-empt Native homesteads and cultivated fields. After 1866 the land rights extended to settlers were denied to Indians. While non-Natives could apply for free grants of land, Indians were prohibited from using the pre-emption system at all. The failure of governments to recognize Aboriginal rights to hunting or fishing grounds, and their failure to negotiate treaties to formally acquire Indian lands, further exacerbated Indian/settler land conflicts. Small reserves were established in the late 1800s, but the issue of Aboriginal title continued to be ignored by governments.

By the 1880s Indian agents had arrived and were attempting to implement the terms of the Indian Act. Government control over Indian fishing, hunting, and trapping was extended in the following decades. Fishing by means of nets, weirs, and basket traps was outlawed by federal fisheries regulations, hunting was restricted, and trapping was brought under government control. BC Native leaders continued to lobby for government recognition of Aboriginal title, and their campaign gained momentum in the 1910s and 1920s. In response, in 1927 the federal government passed legislation to make it illegal for Indians to collect or donate money for the purpose of pursuing land claims.

Plateau groups responded in a variety of ways to these forces of change. Many Natives took advantage of the economic opportunities created by the colonial economies and played an important role in the gold rushes, working as miners, guides, and freighters. As the agriculture industry developed, Natives took jobs as cowboys, farm labourers, and migrant harvesters. As well, many families incorporated small-scale cattle- and horse-raising into their round of economic activity, sold their stock on the local market, and successfully competed with non-Native ranchers. Natives also played significant roles in the transportation industry, hauling supplies by team and wagon into the Interior. Native labourers cut ties and timbers and freighted supplies during the construction of railways in the 1880s and the early 1900s. Ironically, these railways also signalled the end of Native employment in small-scale freighting; further, the railways undermined Native rights by enabling non-Native settlement and the expansion of resource industries into previously isolated regions.

The colonial economy had varying impacts in different regions of the Plateau. Secwépemc and Okanagan territories were settled early, and these groups responded by developing a mixed economy in which wage labour and stock-raising existed alongside trapping, hunting, and fishing. Other groups that occupied lands more marginal to non-Native interests were able to maintain a measure of control over their lands, continuing to follow a subsistence lifestyle based primarily on hunting, fishing, and trapping. With the rapid growth of logging, mining, and hydroelectric projects in the twentieth century, the lifestyle and cultures of all these groups changed significantly.

Contemporary Issues: Resource Conflicts

A number of resource conflicts in the Plateau emerged as significant issues in the 1980s and 1990s. North of the town of Lytton, at the conflu-ence of the Fraser and Thompson Rivers, the Stein Valley became a focal point for conflicts between the Nlaka'pamux and forestry companies. The Stein Valley is an area of much cultural significance, with pictographs, camps, trails, and other sites of historical and cultural importance to the Nlaka'pamux. The conflict was resolved by turning the Stein Valley into a park that highlights these heritage values.

Fraser River fisheries and water flows also emerged as significant issues in the late twentieth century. The Fraser River system, at the heart of the Canadian Plateau, is heavily industrialized, and a number of bands have raised more general concerns about deteriorating fisheries because of water pollution. A related issue is the twinning of rail lines along the Fraser and Thompson Rivers and the possible damage this might cause to salmon habitat. Further, many of the areas slated for expansion along the river valleys run through Indian reserves, many of which contain villages, cemeteries, and fishing stations. In response to this crisis, Indian bands from the lower Fraser Valley to the headwaters of the Thompson River formed an organization, the Alliance of Tribal Councils, to oppose what has become known as the CN Twin Tracking project. The Alliance unites people from different languages and traditional political jurisdictions. The main concerns of the Alliance centred on potential loss of reserve lands, cemeteries, and heritage sites, increased rail traffic, reduced access to traditional fishing sites, and potential loss of spawning habitats in upriver regions. In the late 1980s the Alliance (now known as the Alliance of Tribal Nations) initiated court action to prevent construction of the second rail line.

Part of the concern is that events of 1913 might be repeated. Railway construction along a stretch of the Fraser River known as Hell's Gate resulted in tonnes of rock being blasted into the river, obstructing the passage of migrating salmon. Salmon runs in the Fraser River system were almost eliminated. To many Interior Indian groups, it was a time of great deprivation.

Contemporary Social Issues

One of the most important issues discussed among Canadian Aboriginal peoples in recent years has been the impact of the Indian residential school system. Indian residential schools were a joint venture of the federal government and various religious denominations. They existed for over a century, the last ones closing only in the 1970s. The Kamloops Indian Residential School on the Kamloops Indian Reserve in the southern Secwépemc Nation at one point was the largest such school in Canada. Native children were removed from their homes and were raised in these church-run boarding schools, where they were taught Christian beliefs and morality as well as agricultural, commercial, and domestic skills, and were denied the right to speak their Native language. The explicit goal of the schools was to remove children from the cultural environment of their families so as to prevent the transmission of Aboriginal cultural knowledge, values, and beliefs.

Aboriginal people in the Plateau region are now examining the long-term psychological and social consequences to their communities of the residential schools' assimilation program. Many Native leaders today link the residential school experience to a range of social problems faced by many reserve communities, and, of course, to the loss of their Aboriginal languages.

A number of Plateau communities have taken steps to address these issues by developing their own social programs and systems of justice rather than turning to outside governmental agencies for assistance. In 1980 the Spallumcheen First Nation became the first Indian band in BC to sign a child welfare agreement with the province. In an effort to stem the apprehension of children from the community by provincial human resources workers, the Spallumcheen band council persuaded the provincial government to recognize its authority and responsibility for providing for the care of its own children and for the support and treatment of families in crisis.

Culture and Aboriginal Rights in the Courts

For many Plateau communities, though, the outstanding issue is an affirmation of Aboriginal title and rights. A number of court cases have served to raise the issue of Aboriginal rights and traditional hunting and fishing activities. In 1995, a group of Secwépemc people, in company with Aboriginal supporters from other parts of Canada, held a Sun Dance, not a traditional Plateau ceremony, on ranchland at Gustafsen Lake. The group argued that the land was a sacred place and insisted on its Aboriginal rights to the land. After a 31-day standoff, the BC government forcibly evicted them and charges were laid, resulting in the conviction of some of the participants. In the 1990s, the provincial and federal governments embarked on a treaty negotiation process, but many of the Plateau groups refused to participate, arguing that the conditions of treaty negotiation and resolution imposed by the governments, which included extinction of Aboriginal title, are contradictory to Aboriginal rights and interests. The *Delgamuukw* decision of 1997 provided a reference point for the recognition of Aboriginal title in Canadian law and also for the need to accommodate Aboriginal interests in industrial activities. As an expression of their Aboriginal rights, the Westbank band carried out logging within its traditional territory without permits from the provincial government. The Penticton band in the Okanagan erected blockades along a road leading to a ski resort to publicize their concern about such uses of traditional territories. Similar actions have been taken by members of other communities in the Lillooet and Kamloops areas to protest the expansion of ski resort facilities on traditional lands or to challenge the BC government's jurisdiction over **fee simple** title in light of a priori Aboriginal title.

Aboriginal rights in the Plateau—and elsewhere—are (re)defined in part by the Canadian legal process, in which groups asserting a claim to rights and land must show that there was an organized society that controlled identifiable territories. One such case involved a Tsilhqot'in community, the Xeni Gwet'in, or Nemiah people (the term *Xeni Gwet'in* means "people of Xeni," where "xeni" refers to a lake and valley in the Chilko Lake region west of Williams Lake, and "t'in" is a variation of the term "Dene," meaning "people." The Xeni Gwet'in sought recognition of title to (and therefore control of) a region that constituted their traditional homeland. A 2007 ruling decided that the Xeni Gwet'in had demonstrated rights to part, but not all, of the region claimed. In January 2013, the Supreme Court of Canada decided to hear this case. It is anticipated that it will produce a landmark decision, focused on the question, what land rights do First Nations still hold? The answer will be of significant importance in determining the place of First Nations within Canada.

In recent years, some Sinixt, who spoke a dialect of the Okanagan-Colville language and whose territory was identified with the Arrow Lakes area, have struggled to have their continuing existence and Aboriginal territories recognized. After the last registered Arrow Lakes Band member died in 1956, the Department of Indian Affairs declared the band, until then the sole Sinixt band in Canada, to be extinct. Most Sinixt had earlier been relocated to the Colville Reservation in Washington State, while others made associations with adjacent First Nations bands. The re-emergence of the Sinixt in Canada was in part precipitated by road construction in 1987 in the Slocan Valley that revealed burials and a village site, at a location known as Vallican. People of Sinixt ancestry set up a blockade in 1989 to halt further development of the road and sought to re-establish their presence in the region.

REFERENCE

Walker, Deward, ed. 1998. *Handbook of North American Indians*, vol. 12, *Plateau*. Washington: Smithsonian Institution.

CHAPTER 21

The Okanagan

Douglas Hudson

Introduction

This chapter describes the Aboriginal cultures of the Okanagan Valley of south-central British Columbia, home to the Okanagan people. A central theme is that the diverse relationships to the land described in early accounts continue to be a key element in contemporary discourses of identity and rights. The term "Okanagan" has several meanings. "Okanagan" originally referred not to people, but to a place. Meaning "head of the river," in reference to the farthest point upstream that salmon ascending the Okanagan River could be harvested easily: the traditionally important fishing site of Okanagan Falls. The people call themselves *skiluxw*, "people," although nowadays they also call themselves Okanagan. The term *Syilx* is used in publications of the Okanagan Nation Alliance. It refers to a language with several dialects in a dialect continuum spoken by Okanagan–Colville groups, with the term *nsyilxcen, nsilxin,* or *nsilxtsín,* "people's speech," used to refer to the Okanagan or Okanagan–Colville language. Culturally it refers to a number of communities within the larger language grouping, Geographically, it refers to a region, the Okanagan River watershed in British Columbia and Washington state.

Fieldwork: A Personal Perspective

My fieldwork in anthropology has involved working with a number of BC First Nations communities. My first research—as a student at the University of Victoria—was on Indigenous place names in the Saanich Peninsula, near Victoria. It involved Coast Salish place names and narratives, and emphasized to me the importance of the land being imbued with cultural meanings through place names and stories about topographical features. The research was an extension of a course in linguistic fieldwork, and the role of language in defining and expressing world views remains an important element of my interests. Later, I lived for a year with a Dakelh (Carrier) community in northern BC, the Tl'azt'en, carrying out ethnographic research for my Ph.D. My focus was on social organization, resource use, and social and economic change. After a stint of teaching at the University of British Columbia, I did a year's research with Okanagan and Similkameen communities on the Okanagan Indian Curriculum Project. I have also worked on landownership and occupancy studies with the Nisga'a and Taku River Tlingit in northwestern BC and on resource use with Tsay Keh Dene (Sekani) and Dunne-za communities in northeastern BC. Most recently

I worked with Stl'atl'imx, (Lillooet), communities in projects involving ethnographic fieldwork, archival research, archaeological projects, and traditional land use.

Involvement with these communities and their histories has caused me to rethink some issues in anthropology and to appreciate the different ways in which communities seek to maintain traditions and control of traditional lands—and the ways anthropology itself is in a dialectical relationship with these different histories. For example, I cite my work with the Okanagan Indian Curriculum Project.

Okanagan people were dealing with educational problems. One was a sense that their history had been reduced to meaninglessness in a region that eulogized the first non-Aboriginal settlers. For years, settler society had denied or undervalued Aboriginal history in presenting its own. Another pressing issue was ensuring that an Okanagan voice be developed, that Okanagan views of Okanagan culture and relations with Canadian society be articulated within education programs. A writing centre in Penticton, the En'owkin Centre (discussed later), grew in part out of those needs.

The picture that emerged from early accounts by fur traders and ethnographer James Teit,[1] and work by other anthropologists and historians, emphasized the importance of salmon runs in the Okanagan economy. In the contemporary picture, though, the salmon no longer come. Years of commercial fishing, irrigation agriculture, flood control, hydroelectric power, and dams had severely reduced Columbia River salmon runs. A very significant part of the material basis of Okanagan culture disappeared. Since 1954 no salmon had spawned past Vaseux Lake in the south Okanagan; but in 2003 the Okanagan Nation Alliance reintroduced sockeye salmon fry into their historic habitat at Skaha Lake near Penticton. The lament for, and anger about, the assault on salmon is an important element of contemporary writing by Aboriginal Okanagan authors.

TABLE 21.1 Okanagan-Similkameen Bands

BAND NAMES	BAND MEMBERSHIP (2007)
Okanagan (also known as Head of the Lake)	1,735
Westbank	664
Penticton	922
Osoyoos (or Inkameep/ Nk'Mip)	459
Lower Similkameen	461
Upper Similkameen	68
Upper Nicola	866

Anthropological research will increasingly involve understanding how the intellectual requirements of the discipline meet the practical needs of Indigenous people who draw on writings and research by anthropologists. One of the challenges to anthropologists will be to integrate academic and applied anthropology, merging theoretical problems with practical problems defined by Aboriginal people. In BC, the research landscape is increasingly defined by legal actions over exercises of Aboriginal rights (especially with respect to resource use) and the 1997 *Delgamuukw* decision by the Supreme Court of Canada. That decision meant that Aboriginal interests in the land and its resources had to be addressed. The following comments, then, are anthropological descriptions of Okanagan culture, mainly focused on Northern Okanagan; they do not intend to represent or appropriate the voice of the Syilx. The material is organized around a model of economic, social, and ceremonial frameworks of activities. These activities impose and create meaning on the land, and each provides an entry point into the larger cultural picture. The categories are heuristic devices; they are not necessarily the ways in which Okanagan people see their relationships to the land or to each other, a relationship articulated in a growing number of articles by Okanagan writers.

The Region

The Okanagan-speaking people lived and live in southern BC and adjacent Washington state. The international border effectively cuts across Okanagan lands and communities. While this chapter focuses on the Canadian Okanagan, the watershed extends into the United States and includes the Similkameen and Methow Rivers. Okanagan people with distinct dialects inhabit these areas. Some experts prefer the term "Okanagan–Colville" to "Okanagan." Some also note that in BC the term "Okanagan" is used in English, while in Washington "Colville" is more common. In any case, there are currently seven dialects: Northern Okanagan (Okanagan Lake and upper Okanagan River); Similkameen Okanagan (Similkameen River); Southern Okanogan (lower Okanogan River in the United States); Methow (Methow River); Sanpoil-Nespelem (Columbia River from Grand Coulee to Rogers Bar and along the Sanpoil and Spokane Rivers); Colville (Columbia River from Northport to Rogers Bar, and the Colville Valley); and Lakes (or Sinixt), spoken by people residing (or formerly residing) along the Upper Columbia River, from Northport to Revelstoke, including the Arrow Lakes, and Slocan Lake in BC. The Okanagan communities or bands in the Okanagan Valley, the Similkameen Valley, and in the upper part of the Nicola Valley are listed in Table 21.1.

Early Descriptions

Okanagan peoples are first mentioned in early fur trade records. One of the earliest descriptions was by the American fur trader Alexander Ross (1986:311–12), who in 1811 wrote:

> The Oakinackens[2] inhabit a very large
> tract of country, the boundary of which

may be said to commence at the Priest's Rapid on the south. From thence, embracing a space of upwards of one hundred miles in breadth, it runs almost due north until it reaches the She Whaps,[3] making a distance of more than five hundred miles in length. Within this line the nation branches into twelve tribes, under different names. These form, as it were, so many states belonging to the same union, and are governed by petty chiefs who are, in a manner, independent; nonetheless, all are ready to unite against a common enemy. These tribes, beginning at the southern boundary and taking each according to its locality, may be classed as follows: Skamoynumachs, Kewaughtchenunaughs, Pisscows, Incomecanetook, Tsillane, Intietook, Buttle-muleemauck, or Meathow, Inspellum, Sinpohellechach, Sinwhoyelppetook, Samilkameigh,[4] and Oakinacken, which is nearly in the center. All these tribes, or the great Oakinacken nation, speak the same language, but often differ a good deal from one another as to accent.

This description indicates that there was a named set of communities collectively known as Okanagan when the first traders arrived. Each named grouping was identified with a watershed. Today, as indicated in the list above, there are several Okanagan communities in the Okanagan and Similkameen Valleys, some on reserves adjacent to urban centres in a region that is undergoing substantial population increase. There is also a significant off-reserve population (see Table 21.1). The reserves were established from the 1860s to the 1880s, and today occupy strategically important locations in a region with substantial population, urban growth, and tourism.

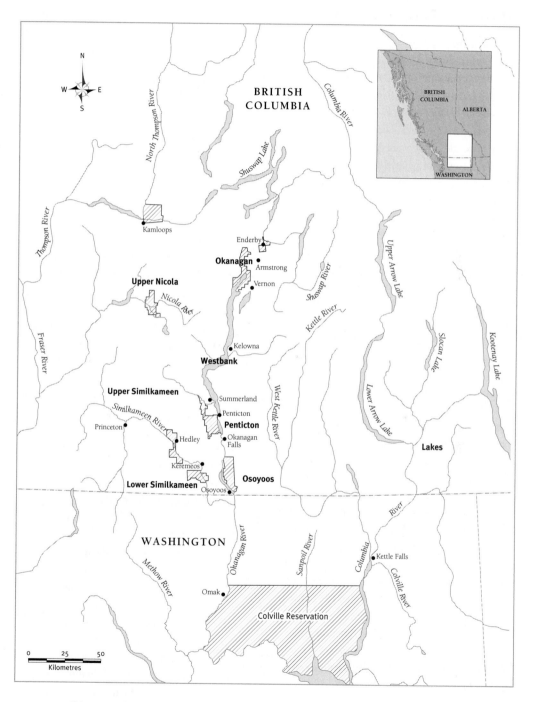

MAP 21.1 Okanagan Locations

Okanagan Society as Network

As a researcher working with seven bands, I was quickly introduced to the myriad connections between communities in the Okanagan and area. Going to rodeos became a key fieldwork activity; that is where the people were! (A fieldworker in the 1800s would have gone salmon-fishing for the same reason.) Around those events webs of connections emerged. Okanagan people interacted with each other and with neighbouring groups on the basis of social rules and traditions in a variety of activities. Three main settings, or frameworks, for interaction can be identified: (1) economic activities, (2) social and political activities, and (3) religious and ceremonial activities. These are analytic categories; in life they were not mutually exclusive. Thus, salmon-fishing was an economic activity in that fish were caught and processed; it was a social activity because the people assembled were also engaged in any number of informal activities; and it had ceremonial aspects in that a ritual specialist conducted ceremonies to celebrate the return of the salmon.

Okanagan-speaking people moved extensively throughout the region to participate in various economic, social, and ceremonial activities, utilizing a network of relatives and friends. This system ensured that people and food were redistributed, an important feature in a land characterized by seasonal and local variations in resources. It also ensured that the key fishing sites were available to numbers of people. Ultimately any speaker of the Okanagan–Colville language could be considered a potential friend. This network was a major feature of Okanagan society. To understand how it worked—and continues to operate—we need to examine its economic, social, and ceremonial basis.

Okanagan Society: Economic Activities

The traditional economic basis of Okanagan society centred on a few key locations where resources could be harvested by relatively large numbers of people at specific times of the year. The most important of these were the salmon-fishing sites in the Columbia River system, including the Okanagan. The annual subsistence cycle involved extensive movement in the summer and fall and a more sedentary life during winter, a season of important ceremonies.

Fishing

Most Plateau groups had direct access to productive fishing sites. Trout, kokanee, sturgeon (in Okanagan Lake), suckers, and other fish were taken. In late summer and fall salmon ascended rivers in the Columbia River watershed to spawn in small tributaries. The canyons through which they passed became important fishing places. The restricted number of canyons meant that people gathered at them. Two of the most important sites for Okanagan were Okanagan Falls in the southern Okanagan, and Kettle Falls, on the Columbia River. An 1865 account by Charles Wilson, a member of the Northwest Boundary Commission, outlines their importance, and the kinds of fishing technologies used:

> At the Okinagan River a weir, constructed of slight willow wands, was found, which extended right across the stream and at one end had an enclosure into which several openings were left; the remainder of the weir, being nearly, if not quite, impassable, all salmon passing up the river found their way into a sort of "cul-de-sac," where the Indians were busily engaged in spearing them. At Kettle Falls on the Columbia and Great Falls on the Spokane, salmon are caught in a large wicker basket, suspended from the rocks at one end of the falls, and projecting slightly into the water. At the foot of the rock there is an eddy, and the water coming down with less force at this point, the salmon here

make their chief effort to leap the falls,
the greater number, however, fail to clear
the rock, many leap right into the basket,
whilst others strike their noses against the
rock and fall back helplessly into the trap
below. (Wilson 1865:297)

Salmon-fishing was controlled by a salmon
chief, who directed the construction of the traps
and weirs and performed a ceremony to mark
the capture of the first salmon. The First Salmon
Ceremony symbolized the community's dependence on salmon and the need to maintain a proper
relationship with it. Under the guidance of the salmon chief, the first salmon caught was cooked and
distributed to members of the assembled community. Its bones were returned to the river to maintain
the cycle. The salmon chief also had general super-
visory powers, as the following observation from
the above source in 1865 indicates:

One blow on the head from their practised
hands settles the account of each fish,
which is then thrown out on the rocks
and carried to the general heap, from
which they are portioned out to the different families every evening by a man
known as the "salmon chief." (ibid.:298)

Prohibitions underscored the practical and
symbolic importance of salmon. Swimming was
banned upriver from the weir, and menstruating
women and recent widows and widowers could
not come near the weir or eat salmon. These
reflected Okanagan conceptions of pollution and
purity, a cultural logic that highlighted the importance of salmon and injected into resource-use
activities notions of gender and changes in status.

Information about salmon was also included
in stories about Coyote, a male transformer figure who brought salmon up the Columbia River.
The stories usually emphasized Coyote's greed as

he sought food and women. An account of why
there are no salmon in the Similkameen River
system involves Coyote going to the river and
having his advances turned down by the women
there. In frustration, Coyote erected a rock barrier
near the mouth of the river to prevent salmon
from ascending. So the Coyote story serves as an
ecological (and moral) story about the absence of
salmon in one watershed. The rock barrier exists;
the Coyote story is an Okanagan way of giving
meaning to landscape features. To obtain salmon,
Similkameen people went to Okanagan Falls, to
other places on the Okanagan River, or to groups
on the Fraser River system to the west.

The wanderings of Coyote are also reflected in
the ways that the Okanagan people describe features of the landscape. Distinctive rock formations,
for example, are referred to as Coyote's fishing place
or parts of his anatomy. Most of these formations
carry no special markings, and their meanings and
association with Coyote are embedded in oral traditions. They provide reference points for Okanagan
relationships with the land, mapping out the territory but also serving as places that evoke stories
with moral or ecological lessons.

As to division of labour, men built the weirs,
often to the accompaniment of special songs to
ensure success, but the processing of fish fell to
the women. While a weir potentially could collect thousands of fish, the availability of women's
labour to cut and dry salmon provided a limit on
the number that would be taken. Each family tried
to obtain enough salmon to last the winter; some
obtained a surplus that could be traded to neighbouring villages for other commodities. As people
from miles around gathered at major sites, these
aggregations became highly interactive scenes.
They played games (like *lehal*, "stick game"), raced
horses or on foot, traded, visited, and looked
around for potential mates. Depending on circumstances, these gatherings could last from June into
October.

BOX 21.1 Coyote, Salmon, and Dams

An Okanagan story about Coyote was brought into court hearings by a recent application to reactivate a dam originally built in 1920 at Enloe Falls, Washington, for hydroelectric power. The proposal included construction of fish ladders to enable salmon and steelhead on the Similkameen River to pass above the dam. The Similkameen and the Okanagan Nation Alliance in BC opposed the fish ladders, and brought in the Coyote account to explain why there never have been salmon in the Similkameen River above the falls.

Coyote travelled to the Similkameen and Okanagan, looking for a wife. The Similkameen, known as the mountain sheep people, rejected Coyote's advances, so he created the falls, which became a barrier to fish migration. The people in the Okanagan Valley welcomed Coyote, and in return he brought salmon there.

In 2000, the US Federal Energy Regulatory Commission rescinded a 1996 licence for hydroelectric power granted to Okanogan County, noting that no provisions had been made for fish ladders as required under the US Endangered Species Act. The issue was still a topic of discussion in 2001, as a report on the status of the dam stated: "Based on the Coyote legend, the Canadian Indian Tribes firmly believe salmon never went up the Similkameen River. The tribes adamantly oppose fish passage up the Similkameen, and have put forth a great deal of effort to make their oral history and opinion heard on this subject."[5]

While salmon were the most important fish in the Plateau, others also had their place. Kokanee (landlocked salmon) were taken at numerous creeks throughout the Okanagan watershed. The Similkameen supported abundant trout, Dolly Varden, and grayling. In spring, suckers were caught in traps as they migrated from lakes to streams. White sturgeon were caught in the major lakes and streams. Ling cod, "devil fish," were taken in winter with hand lines.

Gathering

Roots, berries, and other plant parts were collected in season from spring to fall for food, drinks, and medicine. Bitterroot (*spitlem*), one of the most important plant foods, was gathered by women in April and May in upland areas in the Okanagan and Similkameen watersheds. For example, the traditional bitterroot digging grounds of the Penticton people are located up Shingle Creek, west of Penticton (Turner 1978:27), a place I once visited in April to see what was involved. The roots are small, dug with a special digging stick of hardened wood, then dried and stored for winter use as a vegetable. April is called *spitlemtem*, "bitterroot month." A First Roots Ceremony was held in the southern Okanagan to celebrate the gift of new food and highlight the passage from winter to spring. Like fishing, harvesting bitterroot provided an opportunity for people to get together to socialize, tell stories, and exchange goods after the winter months.

The types of plant foods available to particular groups varied, but most villages had access to bitterroot in April and May, saskatoon berries in July, wild potatoes (*sxwinq'winum*) in May–June at high elevations, wild onions in June–July, black moss (*skawlip*), and a variety of other plants and berries.

A description from the early 1800s in the Okanagan region describes in a general way the cooking of plants (Ross 1986:299):

> Roots and vegetables of every description are cooked during the summer by means of furnaces in the open air; they are then baked on stones, formed into small cakes, and dried in the sun, after which the whole is carefully laid by for winter use.

The use of moss by the Southern Okanagan was highlighted by Ross:

> On the pines of this country there is a dark brown moss which collects or grows about the branches. This moss is carefully gathered every autumn, when it has the appearance of dirty, coarse wool. It is soaked in water, pressed hard together, and then cooked in an oven or furnace, from which it comes forth in large sheets like slate, but supple and pliable, resembling pieces of tarpaulin, black as ink, and tasteless; and when cut with a knife it has a spotted or marbled appearance, owing to the small number of sprigs of wood, bark, or other extraneous substances, unavoidably collected with the moss in taking it from the trees. This cake when dried in the sun, becomes as hard as flint, and must always be soaked in water before use. It is generally eaten with the raw fat of animals, as we use bread and butter. It is viscous and clammy in the mouth, with but little taste. Thus prepared it will keep for years; is much liked by the natives, and sometimes eaten by the whites. It is called squill-ape. (Ibid.)

In the southern part of the Okanagan, particularly in Washington, camas was an important plant resource and productive areas attracted people from considerable distances.

The account below indicates the complex relationship between plants, people, and ceremonies. Written in the 1930s by an Okanagan woman, Mourning Dove, it mentions going to make camp on a mountain in the southern Okanagan, Mount Baldy (*Pak-kum-kin*, "white top") at a place where there was the frame of an old sweat lodge. This was an area used to collect herbs. Mourning Dove recounted being taught at this spot about the proper uses of herbs and the association between men and women and male and female plants (Mourning Dove 1990a:86–7):

> Several different plants were used for love charms, but the rarest and strongest grew only in the high mountains on the edge of snowbanks, glaciers, or alpine springs. They were sought when in full bloom. In the forests at lower elevations, the favorite plants were red and yellow columbine. None of the plants of the low country were thought to be as powerful as those near the timberline. No herb was ever taken until the person had been thoroughly cleansed by three successive days of using the sweat lodge or taking icy baths. Clean clothing was put on after every bath. During the purification treatment, wild rose leaves and fir-bough tips were used to rub the body to remove all impurities and the human smells so repulsive to the spirits of the plants. Plants were dug only at the first light of sun or just after sunset. The body or its shadow could never block the sun from the herbs. Both sun and herbs were greeted by a song of individual invention and paid with offerings of buckskin, cloth, horsehair, beads, or, recently, coins.

Hunting

Okanagan country contained large and small game animals that were hunted or trapped. Animals hunted included deer, elk, bighorn sheep, and bear. Smaller game used for food included rabbits, marmot, and beaver. There were four great annual hunts: in spring, for deer and sheep; in late fall, for deer, sheep, elk, and bear; in midwinter, for deer; and in late winter, for sheep. Noted hunters directed collective activities. Success in hunting was seen as the outcome of knowledge and adherence to proper ritual. For example, hunts might be preceded by purification in a sweat lodge.

Division of Labour

Men and women worked together in economic endeavours in a complementary way. In general, men built weirs and hunted while women processed resources and gathered plant foods. Stored food belonged to women, giving them effective control over the household economy and the exchange of food. Both sexes were essential in functioning households.

Networks

The very nature of Okanagan social organization linked local production groups in various kinds of exchange. For example, the Ashnola area of the Similkameen watershed was an important mountain sheep habitat. The Ashnola people invited not only neighbouring Similkameen bands but also other Okanagan people as well as Nlaka'pamux (Thompson) and Nicola people to the hunt. Osoyoos (Nk'Mip) people went as far south as Kettle Falls to dig camas bulbs and traded bitterroot, hemp, and blankets to the Nlaka'pamux and Secwépemc (Shuswap) for salmon. Trading networks linked Okanagan people to the coast and the Plains, as items made their way along a vast network flowing east and west, north and south. Keremeos people, in the Similkameen, referred

to a place where Blackfoot came to trade. Based on fieldwork in the 1930s, Walters (1938:74) noted that the Southern Okanagan people went up the Methow River and crossed the Cascade Mountains to trade wild hemp (used as twine in fishnets) for seashells. Other descriptions of Inkamip trade are found in Walters (1938:77):

> Their trade relations are predominately to the north. They go up the Okanogan River beyond Lake Okanogan, about two miles from Enderby, to trade for salmon with the Shuswap. . . . The Inkamip go in August, taking about four days on horses. Since the white traders came, the Shuswap have planted potatoes for which the Inkamip also trade. The Inkamip go to the mouth of the Kamloops to trade with the Thompsons every August. They go from Lake Osoyoos to the Similkameen River, up the river on the eastside by Princeton to the head of the river, and cross to the Kamloops River. They take raw hemp, gathered in Similkameen country. . . . tanned deerskins and dried huckleberries, and bring back only salmon. . . . The Inkamip dig camas at Kettle Falls and trade for fish there.

Another example of the connections between groups is found in a description by Mourning Dove (1990a:99–100) of groups associated with Kettle Falls:

> Our camp was close to the Colvile on the west, beside our Okanagan distant relatives from Osoyoos. The west side was called La-chin (Woven kettle or Bucket) because of the many depressions made by whirlpools there. The east side was known as Scalm-achin (Dug Ground) because the ground was rough with boulders and

looked as though nature had dug it out in places. Tribes generally camped in specific areas, and Colvile hospitality saw to it that no visitor ever left without a full load of dried salmon. The Colvile camped on both sides of the falls to oversee the fishing. The east side encampment included Kalispel, Spokan, Coeur d'Alene, and Flathead, while on the west side were the Okanagan, Sanpoil, Squant, and Wenatchi.

Horses became part of Plateau culture by the mid-1700s. One result was to expand the use of traditional resources. A recurrent theme in photographs from the late 1800s and early 1900s is the use of horses to pack supplies in and food out of highland hunting and gathering areas. A second impact was to shift trade patterns. Okanagan Falls and Kettle Falls were two of the most important salmon-fishing sites (and therefore the biggest trade centres) in the region. After horses became common, trade shifted from longer water routes to overland routes, following open plateaus. In this cross-country trade between the Okanagan and the Colville, the Similkameen Valley became more important: "The great trade route to the north was now across country from Colvile to Okanagan River; then it branched off, about half of the volume of trade going up the Similkameen to the Thompson, and the rest passing on to Okanagan Lake" (Teit and Boas 1930:216).

Okanagan Society: Social and Political Activities

The basic residential unit of Okanagan society was the village, a cluster of houses containing related people who used the area's resources in common. Villages were occupied primarily during winter; the rest of the year was spent at seasonal hunting, fishing, and gathering camps. Villages were located in protected valleys, and people referred to themselves as occupants of a particular winter village.

The actual placement of the village depended on the availability of firewood, and a village might move up or down a valley as wood supplies were depleted.

Houses were either built over a circular excavation of two or three feet and covered with poles and turf or made from tule reed mats. Some of the latter resembled tepees, while others, housing several families, were oblong.

A village contained several special-use structures in addition to its dwellings. A short distance from the houses, small huts were constructed for menstruating women or girls entering puberty. Here they stayed, away from direct interaction with the main camp, as this period in one's life was considered potentially powerful, with possible detrimental impacts on resources. There were special prohibitions on eating deer meat or salmon, for example. Several sweat lodges might also be in evidence, with separate lodges for men and women. Food was stored in raised caches or pits dug into sandy ridges.

Village Organization

Local village autonomy was a feature of Plateau culture. While villages were linked through linguistic and social ties, each retained its independence. For the Northern Okanagan, several house groups, perhaps scattered in contiguous settlements, were seen as a community under the direction of a chief. The chief, usually male, derived his power from his status as a "worthy" man as a consequence of his family's high status, his knowledge of village affairs, and his ability to merit the respect of others. A chief was followed because of his attributes and did not have power to force people to do his will. Because extensive kinship ties linked most members of the community, a chief was also a person who had a large number of relatives upon whom he could call for assistance and support. The chief's status and knowledge were important in maintaining community relations and ensuring that economic and

FIGURE 21.1 Alexander Kwikweitêsket, head of the Lake band of the Okanagan. He is wearing a beaded chief's bonnet set with tail feathers of the golden eagle and hung with strips of twisted ermine skin. The robe is made of twisted hare (winter white coat). (Photo by V. Vincent, 1910. Image PN 6586 courtesy of Royal BC Museum, BC Archives)

council of Elders drawn from the community advised the chief and helped choose his successor.

If the community consisted of more than one settlement, each residential cluster also had a headman who took on some of the tasks of chief. A headman had responsibility to direct the group in successful hunting by his dream power, a power that came from a guardian spirit quest and knowledge of animals. Further, each house group in a settlement had a "house leader"—usually the eldest male—who represented the house group in dealings with the rest of the community. In parts of the southern Okanagan the chief did not give directions himself but worked through a spokesperson. However, the informality of daily living and the required seasonal movements militated against formalizing power, as individuals could relocate to other communities where there were kin.

There also were other positions referred to as chiefs, and these functioned in a variety of capacities. A salmon chief directed the construction and operation of a fish weir, and a shaman directed activities during winter dances and healing ceremonies. Thus, it may be appropriate to view chieftainship not as single fixed position, but to see chiefs and

ceremonial tasks were carried out for the benefit of the whole community. Chieftainship could be inherited; the Okanagan placed great emphasis on the order of birth, and the first-born son of a chief was a prime candidate to be named successor. A

headmen as managers of a series of specific activities—economic, social, political, and ceremonial—for which they had the required knowledge, ability, and respect.

The essence of the Okanagan political system is evident in the observations made by a fur trader in the early 1800s, in a description of southern Okanagan:

> The government, or ruling power among the Oakinackens (Sinkaietk) is simple yet effective, and is little more than an ideal system of control. The chieftainship descends from father to son: it is, however, merely a nominal superiority in most cases. Their general maxim is, that Indians were born to be free, and that no man has natural right to the obedience of another, except he be rich in horses and has many wives; yet it is wonderful how well the government works for the general good, and without any coercive power to back the will of the chief, he is seldom disobeyed: the people submit without a murmur. (Quoted in Walters 1938:94)

That chieftainship was to some extent inherited raises the question of whether, or to what extent, social classes existed. The Okanagan did not have a rigorous division into a high and low class. Rather, there were families whose members were considered to be of high status and morality, while other families had "lost their history." In other words, gaining authority was partly based on prestige, which in turn reflected proper conduct, and was partly based on institutional factors, such as being an eldest son. Those who had no history had lost, through accident or other circumstances, the respect of the community and thus lacked relatives who would attest to their character and rights to particular positions. In a sense they had lost their place in the kinship system. They were part of the community, but without the respect that they might otherwise have enjoyed.

Ownership

Okanagan communities were kinship-based, and all rights of ownership and access to resources must be seen in this light. Property could be corporeal or incorporeal. Corporeal property refers to tangibles such as land and material objects. The group—family, village, or band—owned resource areas in the sense that its members reproduced rights of access and control over them. Others could participate, but only with permission. Chiefs managed, and in that sense owned resource areas, but the extensive ties that linked Okanagan people created a social universe of friends, relatives, neighbours, and trading partners. Thus, in a sense, the region and its resources were potentially but conditionally accessible by all Okanagan collectively, with local resources controlled by various kinship and residential groups.

Incorporeal property, such as a guardian spirit, a song, or a dance, was owned by an individual, who alone had the right to perform a particular dance or song. However, there was also a social, or group, aspect to this ownership. Names were seen as the property of families, and particular names were inherited or transmitted within kin groups. Possessors of particular names, though, could confer them on others if compensated—although again the names stayed within particular families. Special songs and dances might also be transferred from a parent to a child.

Social Units

Although the nuclear family—the husband–wife pair and their unmarried children—existed in traditional Okanagan society, it was economically and socially merged into the extended family that was the basic social unit and the primary unit of production and consumption. A household was usually an extended family and might consist of two brothers and their wives and children, or of an older couple with their married children, or of "cousins" living with their families. A wealthy man of high status might establish a polygynous family (multiple wives), but this was not widespread.

The **kindred** (all one's relatives traced through the families of both parents) were important to the Okanagan. Kin provided security and protection; in neighbouring villages there would usually be at least one member of one's kindred or people who could be considered *chichops* ("relatives"). Another category of kin was the *kalh*, the descendants of a particular grandparent or great-grandparent. For example, two people descended from someone named Quinisco would consider themselves *kalh-quinisco*, with special obligations of mutual respect and support. Membership in a *kalh* is traced through both male and female lines, but does not have any corporate functions.

Kinship Terms

Okanagan kinship terms were organized on different principles from those of English. Some examples of these follow. (1) Different terms were used by male and female speakers. Therefore, the sex of the speaker was important. Males and females defined social relations in different ways, as reflected in the use of kinship terms. Not all terms differed, however—just those for very close kin. (2) Different terms were used for older and younger siblings, indicating that age was important (recall that the eldest son was most likely to inherit his father's position). (3) Sibling terms were extended to cover children of parents' siblings (people whom an English-speaker would call "cousin" were called "brother" and "sister"). This reflects the social basis of kinship terms in all societies; in Okanagan society one's parents' siblings' children are in the same kindred as oneself and therefore called by a term reflecting common membership in a social group and best translated as "person of my generation in my social group." A

detailed list of Okanagan kinship terms is found in Mattina and Jack (1990:163–5).

The determination of potential mates was another aspect of Okanagan kinship. Genealogies were the topics of extended conversations. Close cousins (first, perhaps second) were classified as brother and sister, as *skuit*. That marriages were arranged helped to ensure that they took place between families of similar social standing. The parents initiated the proceedings with a series of small exchanges, some of which predated the actual marriage, while others continued for years after. These economic exchanges gave the marriage stability by emphasizing that marriage was the concern of the group.

Life Cycle

All cultures recognize to some extent the passage of individuals from one status to another. Referred to as a life cycle, these passages often involve a social or ceremonial recognition of physiological changes (such as puberty) and social changes (such as going from unmarried to married status). The Okanagan life cycle emphasized several key events and periods in life, starting with birth. The emphasis was on being guided into, and becoming, a knowledgeable member of Okanagan society.

Birth

The birth of a child received special recognition. One of the earliest descriptions of an Okanagan birth ceremony states:

> After childbirth, the women have to live apart for about thirty days, frequently washing themselves, and, before joining the others, they have to wash all their clothes and undergo general purification. A small lodge is erected about ten or twelve paces from the large or family one, and in this the woman lives during the period of her seclusion, which is kept

with great strictness, notwithstanding the close proximity of her friends and relations. When the time of childbirth is felt to be approaching, the woman goes out and plucks a sprig of the wild rose, which she places upright in the ground of the lodge and fixes her eyes upon it during the pangs of labour, which, it is believed, are alleviated by this ceremony. The rattles of the rattlesnake are also frequently used as a medicine to procure ease in the same cases. (Wilson 1865:294)

Following their seclusion, mother and child were welcomed back into the community by the Elders. In some cases a few relatives and close friends gave an informal feast. For the next few years the baby was carried in a cradle. The infant received a temporary name during the first year, then an ancestral name was conferred, usually by a grandparent. The name had to be purchased if a person using it was still alive. The name could come from either the mother's or the father's side. Boys often received names of animals, and girls received names of plants.

Childhood

In childhood boys and girls gradually learned the distinctions between male and female roles. Education was largely informal, through observation, oral history, and comments from Elders. Tales were used to teach children, and to remind adults, about the importance of proper conduct. Parts of the physical landscape were used as reference points for information, where events were associated with natural rock formations or other features. As noted earlier, these were often tied into narratives about the activities of Coyote. These culturally defined places on the landscape served as aids in understanding Okanagan cultural history, topography, and ecology. To learn about the travels of Coyote (and the places where Coyote stopped

or transformed parts of the landscape) is to learn about the territory.

Boys learned to hunt and fight. Their first animal kill went to the Elders for redistribution, thus reinforcing the power of the group over the individual. Similarly, girls learned skills needed to perform successfully as adults—the techniques of gathering and root-digging, for example. Children's play emulated tasks and roles to be performed later as adults. For example, they might play with miniature fish weirs. Adults required children to take early morning swims in icy water and sweats in lodges to build their character and prepare them for the change from childhood to adulthood, which was signalled by puberty and the guardian spirit quest.

Guardian Spirit Quest

The transition from childhood to adulthood was an important event for males and females. Just prior to the onset of puberty, boys went into the countryside to obtain a guardian spirit, which came in a vision. This quest sought the transfer of power from the natural to the social world, and, if successful, a boy had a spirit helper for the rest of his life. Boys prepared for the quest by fasting, sweating, and physical exercise.

After preparation, a boy went to an isolated area and sought for four days the vision of a guardian spirit. This power, which was called *sumix*, had to be sought and obtained prior to or at puberty and could be drawn on later in life for assistance. After puberty it was felt the search would prove more difficult or fruitless. Not all of those who sought a guardian spirit found one and those who obtained one did not necessarily become fully aware of its power until later in life. Thus the quest of a guardian spirit, whose assistance was essential to adult success, came just at the point when boys faced manhood. The guardian spirit quest was a culturally recognized means of transferring power from the natural and supernatural worlds to the human world, where it became, in a way, social. A balance between power possessed by humans (as spirit power) and untapped power in the natural and supernatural worlds existed.

Girls also received instruction at puberty, going to a special place of retreat. These places often were the tops of large, flat rock formations that even today are marked by a circle of rocks placed around each girl in her vigil. Each rock represented a lesson learned from an Elder.

Marriage

In traditional Okanagan culture, parents arranged the marriages of their children, initiating a series of exchanges. An early exchange might feature the parents of the boy giving fish and meat (symbolic of male activities) to the parents of the girl, who in turn gave roots and berries. After marriage, a couple usually lived in the village of the husband, although the social network provided for other residential options.

It was during adulthood that the power of a personal supernatural began to be revealed, requiring a person to "dance out the power" at a winter ceremony. This is further discussed in the section on ceremonies. It seems that social maturation was paralleled by spiritual maturation. Thus marriage and participation in winter ceremonies marked the complete transition to adult status in Okanagan society.

Death

The deceased were buried in talus slopes, rock slides. Special belongings, perhaps copper pendants or dentalia,[6] were also interred. Death brought an obvious end to a person's direct participation in society, but names borne by the deceased remained in the extended family or kindred and were transferred to descendants. The birth of children who were given ancestral names maintained the family over generations; the use of previous names reinforced a world view in which the past merged with the present in a common social sphere.

Male-Female Relations

Children were born into well-defined male and female roles; by the onset of puberty, they had a good notion of their place in society. While the kinship system emphasized the importance of tracing relatives through both the father's and the mother's sides, a tendency to stress male relations existed. This "patrilateral bias" was reflected in residence patterns, the political system, and elsewhere. Women, however, did control food, giving them some economic power. Decision-making also involved the voices of both men and women. The relationship between males and females in Okanagan society was expressed as being similar to two fir trees growing up beside each other: one, a male tree; the other, a female.

Okanagan Society: The Ceremonial Framework of Action

The tension between individual rights and collective responsibilities ran as a constant theme through Okanagan society. This is perhaps best expressed in concepts and ceremonies where power (sumix) is in focus. Through the spirit quest an individual acquired power, but the community, probably through a shaman, guided the individual to use that power to benefit the community.

Although spiritual power was a dominant aspect of many Okanagan ceremonies, secular ceremonies also occurred. The following types of ceremonies can be identified. (1) Renewal ceremonies (such as the First Roots and First Salmon Ceremonies) emphasized the continuation of important food resources. (2) Redistributive ceremonies were secular and included naming ceremonies and a more elaborate distribution often called the potlatch in anthropological literature. Perhaps "potlatch" is a term best reserved for the formal exchange ceremonies among Northwest Coast groups; while the Okanagan redistributed goods and food at a number of social occasions, none are actually called potlatches. It also appears that those Okanagan who recalled potlatching saw it as something peripheral to traditional Okanagan culture but part of the culture of the Nlaka'pamux and Secwépemc. (3) Power ceremonies, including the Winter Dance and the Medicine Dance, focused on spiritual matters.

Winter Dance

An important Okanagan ceremony, one in which spiritual power was a key element, was the Winter Dance, held when people gathered in their winter villages. According to the Okanagan view of the world, the power that one acquired through the guardian spirit quest required dancing. Power itself was not equally distributed. There is the suggestion that only males obtained it, but that is unclear. It had two levels: power that could be used to protect oneself, and power that could be used for curing. The distinctions between the two main types of spiritual power are reflected in the Okanagan terms *chuchuin* and *sumix*. *Chuchuin* ("voice" or "whisper") meant that a voice came to a person during the guardian spirit quest, giving that person a supernatural helper. *Sumix* came when a person was older.

Different animals conferred different kinds of power. Most power was seen to come from grizzly bear, cougar, blue jay, rattlesnake, and eagle—all of which gave the possessor the power to cure. Blue jay also gave power to find drowned or lost people.

To perform at a Winter Dance required several steps. A neophyte had a power dream in which the guardian spirit required a dance. He then sought the service of a ritual expert (shaman, or medicine man) as master of ceremonies. A central post was erected in the dance lodge, and, in some cases, the lodge was ceremonially swept to purify it. The neophyte then danced before the assembled group and distributed gifts. Other people then expressed their power in dance.

The vocabulary of the ceremonies and formal gatherings differed from everyday speech. It was sometimes called "High Okanagan," a language of leaders and those with specialized knowledge, in contrast to the language of everyday life.[7] In the 1980s, there was concern that only a few individuals still knew the vocabulary of ceremonies and specialized knowledge. This emphasized to me the value of narratives and the coding of information. With a loss of language goes a loss of a number of levels of knowledge and ways of knowing. Not everyone was schooled in the "High Okanagan" language. So the loss of a few key people meant the loss of the equivalent of a narrative library, a class of Okanagan intellectuals whose specialized knowledge, coded in specific linguistic categories and terms, was pivotal to Okanagan culture. The role of storytellers in this society was more important than most non-Natives would think.

Okanagan Society: Summary

Okanagan society and culture required a successful and efficient technology and a flexible and workable social system that enabled people to gather in great numbers at appropriate times, yet facilitated the movement of people between different areas and villages. Traditional Okanagan society was held together in a variety of ways. Through a multitude of social ties, primarily based in kinship, most Okanagan were linked and could enlist aid from people in numerous places. Collaborative activities, such as deer hunting and salmon fishing, facilitated inter-group exchanges. Participation in ceremonies involving large groups of people reinforced mutual systems of meaning and identity.

Post-Contact Change in Okanagan Life

The earliest changes in Okanagan culture associated with European contact were in their fashion profound, but at first they were incorporated into ongoing patterns with relatively little disruption.

The fur trade did not threaten Okanagan ways of organizing social relations, using the land, or developing power. The most disruptive events of the mid-1800s were the diseases that left devastation and demoralization in their wake. For example, 13 Inkameep people died at Osoyoos from smallpox in 1883, which had initially been contracted by an Inkameep woman at the town of Hope, on the lower Fraser River, and had been brought inland.

Until the 1860s the Okanagan Valley represented a means of getting somewhere else—a route for shipping furs and trade goods to distant markets or a passageway to beckoning goldfields. But the 1860s brought prospectors and ranchers, both representing a new kind of claim on lands traditionally used by the Okanagan. A customs post to mark the US–Canada border was established at Osoyoos in 1862; a trading post and store were opened in 1866 at Penticton; and more land became pre-empted by ranchers and settlers in the 1860s and 1870s. The pressure grew on the BC and Canadian governments to restrict Aboriginal landholdings. What had been Okanagan territory became plots of land owned by Euro-Canadians. Other parcels of land were surveyed as Indian reserves, a process that took years to complete because of conflicts between the BC government and Ottawa.

Economic Changes

As the Okanagan region became incorporated into an expanding Canadian society, Indigenous labour became more important for economic activities dominated by others. These included ranching, farming, logging, sawmilling, and other activities.

It is significant that the Okanagan engaged in expanded economic activity on an ownership basis. Freighting and ranching were two such enterprises in which Okanagan people were conspicuously active. However, Okanagan cattlemen raised stock on common rangelands open to all ranchers (called a commonage) south of Vernon only until access was curtailed, largely due to pressures from non-Indian ranchers. Similarly, Similkameen cattlemen drove stock from Keremeos to Princeton for seasonal grazing until their use of "free range" was also curtailed. Some Okanagan reserves were large enough that some cattle could still be raised, but they could never become fully competitive with non-Aboriginal ranchers. In other words, attempts by the Okanagan to compete in the larger economy were systematically thwarted.

While some traditional economic activities remain important for many Okanagan, fundamental changes have taken place. Many of the key fishing places are no longer viable. Both Okanagan Falls and Kettle Falls have been lost to dams, the latter by construction in the 1930s of Grand Coulee Dam. The number of salmon reaching the Okanagan system diminished following construction of a series of dams on the Columbia. Traditional fishing technologies have also been lost. Weirs and fish traps were banned by the Canadian government around 1900 and were removed by fisheries wardens throughout the Okanagan. Urbanization and the rerouting of streams have further diminished fish production and harvesting.

Ceremonial Changes

The continuation of winter dances, guardian spirit quests, and other activities associated with spirit power was anathema to the missionaries who moved into the Okanagan Valley in the late nineteenth century. Adherents of spirit power were at one time forbidden to attend churches and winter ceremonies were condemned. This can be contextualized historically in terms of a number of pressures on BC Aboriginal cultures in the late 1800s, such as the banning of potlatches and the harsh enforcement of the Indian Act.

In recent years there has been a resurgence of cultural practices and language training that foster Okanagan identity.

Social and Political Changes

During the late nineteenth century the economic, political, and social activities of the Okanagan Indians and the Euro-Canadian immigrants became intertwined, with myriad reciprocal exchanges. For example, an 1870s account by a settler at Keremeos (Allison 1991:39) points to early economic ties:

The Indian women used to gather and dry Saskatoons, so I did the same and when they brought me trout which they caught by the hundreds in baskets they set in the One Mile Creek, I paid for them with butter and then dried and smoked the trout.

Other early writers point to close relations between Indians and non-Indians in the Okanagan, although ignoring the issue of fundamental differences of political power. A description of Penticton in the 1920s reads:

At that time we, of the town, lived much closer to our Indian neighbours than we do now. We knew each other by name, stopped to chat on the street and we played together. We depended on hay cut on the reserve or winter pasture for our horses. We bought wood and buckskin gloves from them. (Sismey 1976:19)

The Euro-Canadian settlers and their descendants have since created their own version of Okanagan history, one that talks about the material exchanges but sets aside the early social relations between the communities. The result has been a certain fabrication of social distance between the groups, one readily accepted by more recent immigrants to the Okanagan who know little or nothing of early settler history aside from the official versions.

While informal relations between Okanagan and immigrant neighbours were generally mutually beneficial, formal relations were characterized by changes over which the Okanagan had little control and to which they frequently objected. The traditional system of leadership was altered by the imposition of external political frameworks. First, Catholic missionaries introduced the Durieu system in BC Aboriginal villages about 1875, which called for church leaders in each village to be supervised by the local priest. Each village had a church chief with captains under his command. Although the ideal was to appoint already established chiefs, the church chiefs were appointed by the priest and were directed to enforce his commands concerning morality and conduct. The influence of this system seems to have largely declined by the late 1890s, but recollections of it remained with Okanagan Elders in the 1980s.

A second major change occurred when the Department of Indian Affairs established a system of elected chiefs and councillors to run band affairs. Most of the chiefs elected in this fashion were male, but in 1953 the first woman was elected[8]—to the Penticton Indian band council. All Okanagan bands now elect chiefs and councillors.

After Euro-Canadian penetration of the Okanagan, much of the responsibility for social services shifted to non-Okanagan institutions, and it became difficult to retain many cultural practices. The residential schools played an important part in undermining the teaching of traditional culture. Children began to spend most of the year in a residential school, such as at Kamloops, at some distance from their home villages. Forbidden to speak their languages and separated from siblings, the children became isolated from the teachings of their parents and Elders. Older Okanagan people retain the experiences of residential school life: cooking, washing clothes, splitting firewood, growing crops, and being taught in a foreign language (English). Perhaps with the best of intentions, albeit from a colonial perspective, the residential schools operated on the premise that the Indian child should be separated from his or her own traditions and family for most of the year.

In the 1870s, frustrated with government inaction on land rights and faced with increasing alienation of traditional lands by settlers and ranchers, some Okanagan and Secwépemc people argued for a co-operative political venture. Through armed resistance and possibly an association with Chief Joseph and the Nez Perce, then fighting the US government, a resolution to outstanding grievances would be forced. A meeting at the head of Okanagan Lake in 1877 resulted in the formation of a Secwépemc–Okanagan Confederacy. No armed resistance came, however, and the nascent confederation was effectively broken up by the Indian Reserve Commission and priests, who made agreements with individual bands and split the movement.

Okanagan involvement in political movements continued throughout the twentieth century. In 1916, several BC bands formed an organization called the Allied Tribes of British Columbia. This organization included the Okanagan. At that time, however, no resolution of land-claims issues was possible.

In the late 1960s, Okanagan people were involved in the formation of the Union of British Columbia Indian Chiefs. In the 1970s, a majority of the bands in the Okanagan Valley formed the Okanagan Tribal Council, with an office in Penticton. This in turn became part of the Central Interior Tribal Councils, representing Interior bands and tribal organizations. The political picture is more complex today; in the 1980s and 1990s a number of umbrella organizations emerged. The Okanagan communities have formed a political organization called the Okanagan Nation Alliance. The present president of the Union of BC Indian Chiefs, an important political organization that draws significant support from Interior

First Nations communities, is a former chief of the Penticton band. Okanagan women were also prominent in the development of Aboriginal women's movements in the 1960s and 1970s. The Okanagan Nation Alliance includes the following seven Canadian bands: Lower Similkameen Indian Band, Okanagan Indian Band, Osoyoos Indian Band, Penticton Indian Band, Upper Nicola Indian Band, Upper Similkameen Indian Band, and Westbank First Nation.[9]

Indian reserves were surveyed in the 1860s in the Okanagan and Similkameen. Correspondence by surveyors in 1866 points to surveys done in 1865 and earlier that were apparently deemed too extensive. At any rate, three reserves in the Okanagan were roughly laid out in 1865. As a portent of events to come, the surveyor at the time, helped by a major landholding settler in the valley, wrote that the reserve boundaries were established without the aid of survey instruments. The report also criticized the generosity of the reserves, noting that the size of one was "more than double the amount necessary to serve the Indians settled on the Okanagan" (British Columbia 1875:34–6).

The governments of BC and Canada argued for decades about the sizes of BC reserves and struck a commission in 1912 to settle the issue. It held meetings with designated Indian bands, chambers of commerce, and other parties, and presented a four-volume report in 1916, confirming the boundaries of some reserves, adding to others, and, most importantly, reducing some. In the Okanagan, of 146,428 acres of reserve land, the commission cut off 18,537 acres and added 2,600 acres.

To the federal and provincial governments, the issue of reserves was settled. To the Okanagan peoples, the process by which reserves were diminished was seen as questionable, and bands began research to substantiate claims that alienation of land occurred without the band's permission and that compensation was due. In the 1980s the federal and provincial governments agreed to settle the issue of alienated or "cut-off" lands, as they were known, and several bands have received compensation. In 1981, for example, the Penticton band received 4,880 hectares of land and $13 million to resolve their losses.

The current economic basis of Okanagan communities reflects participation in the larger economic system. Some Okanagan reserves have recreational complexes catering to tourists, others have residential housing developments on land leased from bands, and one band has extensive vineyard operations.

Contemporary Resource-Use Conflicts

Like other Indigenous groups in BC, Okanagan bands have been involved in land and resource-use issues that have gained prominence since the 1990s. Water levels are an issue throughout the Okanagan, especially to the Osoyoos band at its southern, downstream end, as irrigation plays an important role in their economy. Disputes over recreational uses of the Okanagan watershed, especially ski resorts, have resulted in road blockades, notably in areas where access is through Indian reserves. In 1994, one of the bands erected blockades along a road leading to a ski resort to publicize their concern about such uses of traditional territories.

In 2000 one of the Okanagan bands started logging in areas outside of their reserves but within their asserted traditional territory, and in doing so provoked a response from the province. The issue of Aboriginal rights as highlighted by the *Delgamuukw* decision became a key issue in the dispute. Part of the reason for the band's initiative was their concern with the treaty process and the lack of agreements while resources in their traditional territory were being harvested by non-Okanagan interests, specifically logging companies that had timber-cutting licences from the province. Years earlier, in 1971, for example, Okanagan fish-

ing rights were contested in the courts. The issue was whether or not traditional fishing rights could be exercised in a particular creek without having to seek permission from fisheries officers. At that time there was not a *Delgamuukw* decision to reach for, and in the absence of explicit treaties the judge ruled that Okanagan Indian fishing had to be subject to government fisheries regulation. In 2000, the 1997 *Delgamuukw* decision could be appealed to as one of the bases of Aboriginal activities. I say "one," because a consistent theme runs through the conflicts—that Okanagan rights flow from Okanagan culture and are not conferred by government edicts. Another band has more recently sought to reduce the timber-harvesting levels of a large forestry company on its traditional territory. Both examples show that there are parallel processes developing: first, the reassertion of Aboriginal activities that are direct continuations of visible Aboriginal activities (such as fishing), and second, the recontextualization and extension of traditional practices in a way that affirms an Aboriginal right to use traditional lands. Thus, logging is seen as both an extension of Aboriginal uses of the forest and its resources and an assertion of the right to use and manage traditional lands and resources in ways that serve the economic interests of contemporary communities.

Economic options, though, have been circumscribed by industrial transformations of the landscape. The damming of the Columbia River reduced salmon runs on the Columbia and Okanagan Rivers, with particularly severe impacts on US tribes. For the Okanagan people, the rehabilitation of salmon spawning areas is a key current issue. Many of the runs were lost or reduced not only because of Columbia River dams, but also because of extensive irrigation and water diversion projects in the Okanagan Valley itself. A whole generation of Okanagan people has grown up without direct access to what was once a crucial economic and cultural resource.

BOX 21.2 Spotted Lake

Spotted Lake, *klikuk*, is a heavily mineralized small lake about 9 kilometres west of Osoyoos, in the south Okanagan. The lake's name is derived from its appearance: mineralized circles dot the lake. It is one of the most sacred of Okanagan sites and traditionally was used for spiritual and medicinal purposes, particularly by women. Plans in 2000 by its owners to export its mineral-rich mud for commercial uses raised protests by the Okanagan Nation Alliance (ONA).

The history of Aboriginal attempts to gain control of the lake date to early in the twentieth century. In 1917 the Okanagan attempted without success to secure reserve status for Spotted Lake. Then, in 1980, they successfully opposed plans to develop a health spa at the lake. Finally, in 2000 came the proposal to export 10,000 tonnes of mineral mud for cosmetic products. Again, ONA asked the federal government to purchase the land for a reserve.

In October 2001 the federal government and the Okanagan purchased 22 hectares of land surrounding Spotted Lake. The negotiations involved the Minister of Indian Affairs and Northern Development and representatives of the Osoyoos Indian band, Okanagan band, and ONA. Spotted Lake is to be under the stewardship of the seven bands in ONA—Osoyoos, Upper Similkameen, Lower Similkameen, Okanagan, Penticton, Westbank, and Upper Nicola. The executive director of ONA at the time, a member of the Lower Similkameen band, stated: "I have always been aware of this lake, and protecting our homeland is a testament to our children. Being Okanagan is being from this place. It is part of who I am—my connection, my customs and my roots as an Okanagan woman are here" (Johnson 2001).

Education

Since the early 1980s, a number of bands and tribal councils have moved toward administering their own educational programs that now include Indigenous language and culture components. The issue of representations of Okanagan culture and history also became important. To deal with this, the En'owkin Centre was established by the six bands of the Okanagan Tribal Council in 1981 in Penticton. The En'owkin Centre developed in part out of the Okanagan Indian Curriculum Project, and its transformation from research-focused activities to the writing of curriculum material flowed from Okanagan people themselves.

An important element of the En'owkin Centre is its international school of writing, established to assist First Nations writers. They face issues of "voice," of cultural representation, and of developing literary styles. Views from within Okanagan culture are being published out of En'owkin. The term "En'owkin" itself is a statement about reclaiming voice. But as one of the writers, Jeanette Armstrong, explained (in Jensen 1995:282–99), it refers more to a conflict-resolution approach, a dialectic process of putting opposite views forward, of looking at the other side. Another goal of the En'owkin process is decolonization, of bringing representation home. Okanagan people see James Teit's classic writings, which are the basic ethnographies in the Plateau, as giving short shrift to Okanagan culture. The Nlaka'pamux were at the centre of Teit's writings, and other Plateau groups such as the Okanagan were seen as variations of a basic underlying Nlaka'pamux cultural pattern. In more recent years, a picture of Okanagan culture from within has emerged, as seen, for example, in the recent Okanagan publication *We Get Our Living Like Milk from the Land* (Armstrong et al. 1995). Increasingly the Internet is also being used as a medium to convey information from within the culture.

Post-Contact Change: Summary

Like other First Nations in BC, the Okanagan are positioning themselves in the larger Canadian society in terms of Aboriginal rights, a situation that is directed increasingly by litigation. Two factors have changed the legal landscape somewhat. One is the BC Treaty Process, and the potential for overlapping or shared First Nations' interests, in which thus far Westbank is the only Okanagan band to have participated. The other is the *Delgamuukw* decision, noted above. In the late 1980s, the establishment of a small community of people who identified themselves as Lakes or Sinixt in the West Kootenays region in southern British Columbia has focused attention on the complexities of Aboriginal identities and constitutional rights. The issue of Aboriginal rights may also be profiled in the review of the Columbia River Treaty (referring to US and BC water control and dam agreements in the Columbia River system) in 2014, and underscores the importance of the Columbia River watershed to First Nations in both countries.

Okanagan lands have become key elements in the regional economy. Reserve lands are strategically located along major transportation corridors, adjacent to urban centres that consume recreational activities and require housing. Lands outside the reserves, the traditional territories, are the same areas on which urban centres are being built or resource-harvesting activities such as logging are taking place.

The picture in the Okanagan is one of both accommodation and conflict. Aboriginal communities have had to go to court for the return of alienated reserve lands, and some are still engaged in research to document the loss of such lands. In traditional territories there is conflict over uses of the land, particularly with respect to large-scale logging by major corporations and the uses of highlands for commercial activities such as ski resorts. Paralleling the confrontational process is one that emphasizes the voice of Okanagan Aboriginal peoples, represented in writings that deal with colonialism, culture change, and continuity. An example is Okanagan author Jeanette Armstrong, whose novels *Slash* (1985) and *Enwhisteetkwa* (1982) speak of Okanagan culture in current times. She raises the issues of the environmental degradation of Okanagan land and of retaining Okanagan autonomy within an expanding industrial state. Some of her ideas are reflected in the following comments:

> The Okanagan word for "our place on the land" and "our language" is the same. We think of our language as the language of the land. This means that the land has taught us our language. The way we survived is to speak the language that the land offered us as its teachings. To know all the plants, animals, seasons, and geography is to construct language for them.
>
> We also refer to the land and our bodies with the same root syllable. This means that the flesh that is our body is pieces of the land come to us through the things that the land is. The soil, the water, the air, and all the other life forms contributed parts to be our flesh. We are our land/

place. Not to know and to celebrate this is to be without language and without land. It is to be displaced.

The Okanagan word we have for extended family is translated as "sharing one skin." The concept refers to blood ties within community and the instinct to protect our individual selves extended to all who share the same skin. I know how powerful the solidarity is of peoples bound together by land, blood, and love. This is the largest threat to those interests wanting to secure control of lands and resources that have been passed on in a healthy condition from generation to generation of families.

Land bonding is not possible in the kind of economy surrounding us, because land must be seen as real estate to be "used" and parted with if necessary. I see the separation is accelerated by the concept that "wilderness" needs to be tamed by "development" and that this is used to justify displacement of peoples and unwanted species. I know what it feels like to be an endangered species on my land, to see the land dying with us. It is my body that is being torn, deforested, and poisoned by "development." Every fish, plant, insect, bird, and animal that disappears is part of me dying. I know all their names, and I touch them with my spirit. I feel it every day, as my grandmother and my father did. (Armstrong 2001:11)

Views for the Future

As the Okanagan region continues to be "developed," issues concerning traditional Okanagan land will increasingly be contested. Access to the traditional material basis of Okanagan culture will diminish, continuing a process that started decades ago. The degree of economic integration of Okanagan communities into the nation-state will likely be an issue, perhaps highlighting differences between Okanagan Aboriginal communities that have reserve lands near urban centres and those in less urbanized regions.

I see a revitalization of Okanagan culture on another level. Writers in the En'owkin Centre will continue to stimulate a renewed interest in Okanagan culture and ideas about relations to the land and to nature. These writings will likely challenge the general direction of growth and land use in the Okanagan Valley, and will play an increasing role in political discourse about environmental issues and Aboriginal landownership and stewardship. Part of this process involves bringing back into the discourse writings by earlier Okanagan writers such as Mourning Dove. The stories of Coyote may yet again inform people about prior ecological relationships to the land.

It is difficult to predict what will happen with Aboriginal rights. Although the *Delgamuukw* decision places Aboriginal rights at the forefront of resource-use issues, each community has to prove its specific rights to traditional territories and demonstrate Aboriginal use and occupancy. As a result, litigation will likely continue to frame Aboriginal rights in ways that pit narrative histories against documentary histories. So far, the BC Treaty Process has not shown that it can bring completion to key issues of landownership and rights in a way that bridges Aboriginal and state notions of landownership and control. That the majority of Okanagan communities have yet to enter the treaty process suggests the future will bring continued discussions, disputes, and potential litigation over Aboriginal rights.

NOTES

1. A resident of the town of Spences Bridge from the late 1800s, James Teit was engaged by Franz Boas to write on Plateau cultures. His writings form the starting point for studies of Secwépemc, Stl'atl'imx, Nlaka'pamux, and Okanagan. He lived in the area for decades, was married to a Nlaka'pamux woman, and was active in Aboriginal political organizations.
2. Okanagans.
3. Shuswap, now Secwépemc.
4. Similkameen.
5. From the Minutes of the Regular Meeting of the Okanogan County Public Utility District Board of Commissioners Held in Okanogan, 19 June 2001, found at www.okanoganpud.org.
6. Cylindrical seashells used to make necklaces, etc. Prestigious trade items, their presence here indicates extensive trade networks.
7. An Elder expressed the difference as being equivalent to that between a high-school graduate and a Ph.D. He said this knowing I was working on my Ph.D.
8. By way of context, no Indians could vote in federal elections until 1960.
9. See the ONA website at www.syilx.org

REFERENCES AND RECOMMENDED READINGS

Allison, Susan. 1991. *A Pioneer Gentlewoman in British Columbia: The Recollections of Susan Allison*, ed. Margaret Ormsby. Vancouver: University of British Columbia Press.

Armstrong, Jeanette. 1982. *Enwhisteetkwa: Walk on Water*. Penticton, BC: Okanagan Tribal Council.

———. 1985. *Slash*. Penticton, BC: Theytus Books.

———. 2001. "Sharing One Skin: Okanagan Community," *Columbiana Magazine*, 5 (June).

———, Delphine Derickson, Lee Maracle, and Greg Young-Ing, eds. 1995. *We Get Our Living Like Milk from the Land*. Penticton, BC: Theytus Books. An Okanagan perspective on Okanagan land, history, and culture.

Bouchard, Randy, and Dorothy Kennedy. (2000) 2005. *First Nations' Ethnography and Ethnohistory in British Columbia's Lower Kootenay/Columbia Hydropower Region*. Castlegar, BC: Columbia Power Corporation. Comprehensive ethnographic, ethnohistoric, and linguistic research on the Lakes people; a spinoff from their BC Indian Languages Project.

British Columbia. 1875. *Papers Connected With the Indian Land Question, 1850–1875*. Victoria: Wolfenden.

British Columbia Treaty Commission. www.bctreaty.net.

Cannings, Richard J., and Eva Durance. 1998. "Human Use of Natural Resources in the South Okanagan and Lower Similkameen Valleys." In *Assessment of Species Diversity in the Montane Cordillera Ecozone*, edited by I.M. Smith and G.G.E. Scudder. Burlington, ON: Ecological Monitoring and Assessment Network. A brief but effective overview of this topic, sector by sector, for each period since 1900.

Carstens, Peter. 1991. *The Queen's People: A Study of Hegemony, Coercion, and Accommodation among the Okanagan of Canada*. Toronto: University of Toronto Press. A critical study of the social and political history of a contemporary northern Okanagan community.

Cline, Walter, et al. 1938. *The Sinkaiek or Southern Okanagan of Washington*, ed. L. Spier. General Series in Anthropology, vol. 6. Manasha, WI: G. Banta. A collection of articles on the Okanagan Indians of Washington state, based on research conducted in the 1930s.

Department of Indian Affairs. *Annual Report of the Department of Indian Affairs for 1883*. Canada, Sessional Papers.

Duff, Wilson. 1964. *The Indian History of British Columbia*, Anthropology in British Columbia, Memoir No. 5. Victoria: Provincial Museum of

British Columbia. In its time, the standard work on the topic.

Fisher, Robin. 1992 . *Contact and Conflict: Indian-European Relations in British Columbia, 1774–1890*, 2nd ed. Vancouver: University of British Columbia Press. Originally published in 1977, it continues to be an important book, both for students and for current researchers.

Jensen, Derrick. 1995. *Listening to the Land: Conversations about Nature, Culture, and Eros*. San Francisco: Sierra Club.

Johnson, Wendy. 2001. "Spotted Lake Returns to Okanagan First Nations for Safekeeping," *Oliver Chronicle*, 29 Oct.

Kennedy, Dorothy, and Randy Bouchard. 1998. "Northern Okanagan, Lakes, and Colville." In *Handbook of North American Indians*. Vol. 12, *Plateau*, edited by Deward Walke. Washington: Smithsonian Institution. A detailed overview of Okanagan culture, with additional information on Lakes and Colville.

Knight, Rolf. 1978. *Indians at Work: An Informal History of Native Labour in British Columbia, 1858–1930*. Vancouver: New Star Books. This is the authoritative work on the topic.

Lutz, Hartmut, ed. 1991. *Contemporary Challenges: Conversations with Canadian Native Authors*. Saskatoon: Fifth House. This is exactly what the title says it is: an exploration through numerous conversations about the nature, problems, purposes, and joys of Indigenous writing in Canada.

Mattina, Anthony, and Clara Jack. 1990. "Okanagan Communication and Language." In *Okanagan Sources*, edited by J. Webber and the En'owkin Centre. Penticton, BC: Theytus Books.

Mourning Dove. 1990a. *Mourning Dove: A Salishan Autobiography*, ed. Jay Miller. Lincoln: University of Nebraska Press.

———. (1933) 1990b. *Coyote Stories*. Lincoln, NE: University of Nebraska Press. Mourning Dove is the pen name of Christine Quintasket, an Okanagan author whose writings first appeared in the 1920s.

She is important in the development of Okanagan literature.

Pryce, Paula. 1999. *"Keeping the Lakes Way": Reburial and the Re-creation of a Moral World among an Invisible People*. Toronto: University of Toronto Press. The first major study of the death (they have been declared extinct) and resurrection of the Sinixt.

Ray, Verne. 1939. *Cultural Relations in the Plateau of Northwestern America*. Publications of the Frederick Webb Hodge Anniversary Publication Fund, vol. III. Los Angeles: Southwest Museum. A classic overview of the basic elements of Plateau culture.

Reyes, Lawney. 2002. *White Grizzly Bear's Legacy: Learning To Be an Indian*. Seattle: University of Washington Press. The history of a family and a people, told by a descendant of the earliest known leadership of the Sinixt.

Robinson, Harry. 1989. *Write It on Your Heart: The Epic World of an Okanagan Storyteller*, ed. Wendy Wickwire. Vancouver: Talonbooks/Theytus.

———. 1992. *Nature Power: In the Spirit of an Okanagan Storyteller*, ed. Wendy Wickwire. Vancouver: Douglas & McIntyre. Two collections of stories of Okanagan culture and history based on interviews with an Okanagan storyteller.

———. 2005. *Living by Stories: A Journey of Landscape and Memory*, ed. Wendy Wickwire. Vancouver: Talonbooks. A third, posthumous collection of stories by a master of the craft.

Roche, Judith, and Meg McHutchison, eds. 1998. *First Fish, First People: Salmon Tales of the North Pacific Rim*. Vancouver: University of British Columbia Press. Traditional perspectives on the salmon by three Asian and five North American Indigenous writers.

Ross, Alexander. 1986. *Adventures of the First Settlers on the Columbia River, 1810–1813*. Lincoln: University of Nebraska Press.

Sismey, Eric. 1976. "Okanagan Days," Okanagan Historical Society, *40th Report*. Vernon, BC.

Spencer, Robert, Jesse Jennings, et al. 1977. *The Native Americans*. New York: Harper and Row. This volume contains an overview of the Sanpoil and Nespelem of the southern US Plateau; useful for comparative purposes.

Teit, James, and Franz Boas. 1930. "The Okanagan," *The Salishan Tribes of the Western Plateaus*. Bureau of American Ethnology, 45th Annual Report. A classic account of Okanagan and Plateau culture, although with an overemphasis on Nlaka'pamux (Thompson) culture.

Thomson, Duane. 1994. "The Response of Okanagan Indians to European Settlement," *BC Studies* 101: 96–117. Summarizes the major efforts of Okanagan people to adjust to the European socio-economic order, and their ultimate failure to do so, primarily due to discriminatory legislation.

Turner, Nancy. 1978. *Plant Foods of British Columbia Indians*, Part 2, *Interior Peoples*. Victoria: British Columbia Provincial Museum.

———, Randy Bouchard, and Dorothy Kennedy. 1980. *Ethnobotany of the Okanagan–Colville Indians of British Columbia and Washington*. Victoria: Occasional Papers of the BC Provincial Museum, No. 21. An account of Okanagan plant use, with extensive ethnographic information.

Walters, L. 1938. "Social Structure." In W. Cline et al., *The Sinkaietk or Southern Okanagon of Washington*, ed. L. Spier. General Series in Anthropology, vol. 6. Manasha, WI: G. Banta.

Watkins, Marilyn. 2000. "Native Americans: Effects of Grand Coulee Dam on Native Americans in the United States," in Annex 9, "Grand Coulee Dam," in World Commission on Dams, *Dams and Development: A New Framework for Decision Making*. WCD Final Report. London: Earthscan. Describes the importance of salmon in the economy and culture of the Columbia River tribes and analyzes the consequences to them of Grand Coulee Dam.

Webber, Jean, and the En'owkin Centre, eds. 1990. *Okanagan Sources*. Penticton, BC: Theytus Books. A collection of articles on Okanagan culture and history by Okanagan community writers, anthropologists, historians, and others.

Wilson, Charles. 1865. *Report on the Tribes Inhabiting the Country in the Vicinity of the 49th Parallel. New Series*. Vol. 4, *Transactions of the Ethnological Society of London*.

CHAPTER 22

The Secwépemc: Traditional Resource Use and Rights to Land

Marianne Ignace and Ronald E. Ignace

Introduction

In late spring 1997, Marianne Ignace and two of her young children accompanied Secwépemc[1] Elder Nellie Taylor from their home on the Skeetchestn Reserve in the Secwépemc Nation into the sagebrush hills between Ashcroft and Cache Creek, British Columbia, to harvest *llekw'pin*, bitterroot. A member of the purslane family, it has been culturally and nutritionally important to the Secwépemc and other Plateau peoples for thousands of years. Its starchy taproots, harvested when the plant bursts into bright pink flowers, were widely used in a variety of dishes. Secwépemc still savour *scpet'am*, a pudding made from bitterroot, salmon eggs, saskatoon berries, and other wild fruits and roots. It can be termed one of our "national dishes." Since *llekw'pin* has always been restricted to certain soils and habitats in the southern Interior dry belt, the root was an important trade item among Secwépemc communities, and between them and other Aboriginal Nations.

MARIANNE IGNACE: After parking our car, I began digging for the precious roots with a small pickaxe, delivering my harvest to Nellie, who cleaned off the dirt and peeled the dark red skin off the shrimp-like roots. Nellie, in turn, sat with our seven-year-old daughter, showing her the difference between "male" and "female" plants, telling her about going digging llek'wpin with her grandmother long ago. Soon a rancher pulled up in his truck, telling us to get off his land and asking what we were doing on his property with a pickaxe? I explained what we were doing. He had recently bought the ranch and did not know that it was situated on llek'wpin harvesting grounds. He reluctantly tolerated us, this time.

Both co-authors have experienced such situations, with landowners telling us not to "trespass" to get to Secwépemc fishing grounds or hunting areas, and with "private property" signs and barbwire fences indicating the incompatibility of traditional resource pursuits (fishing, hunting, and plant harvesting) with settler land tenure. During the last 25 years, we have seen some of our most productive berry gathering sites turned into logging roads, tourist interpretation centres, and housing subdivisions. Our Elders' oral histories abound with memories of settlers trying to evict them from places where they had hunted, fished, gathered plants, camped, and travelled for generations. Federal fisheries policies and provincial game

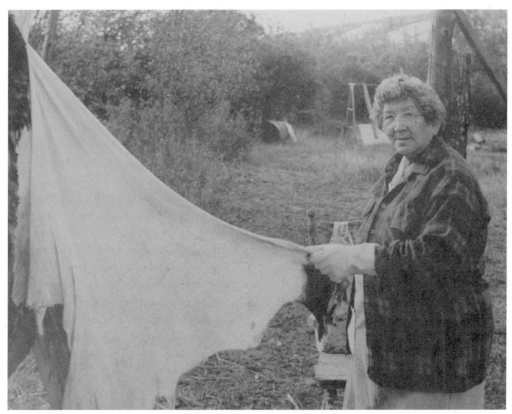

FIGURE 22.1 The late Nellie Taylor scraping a buckskin before tanning it, October 1987. (Courtesy Marianne Ignace)

regulations have criminalized traditional fishing and hunting activities across Canada.

This paper focuses on the traditional resource management and harvesting regimes of the Secwépemc and how this way of life has been affected during the past 100 years. As Secwépemc, we view using the traditional resources of our land, *Secwepemcúl'ecw*, as our collective *right*, deriving from our *Aboriginal title*. Encroachment on these rights and practices through government policies and resource development has severely challenged our ability to exercise our rights. Over generations, the combined effect of changes to the landscape produced by resource development, of government land policies and fish and game policies,

and of the assimilation policies of the Canadian government, has been to challenge the transmission of traditional knowledge about the land. It has endangered the knowledge systems, the connections between our world view and practices. As we will show, much of that connection involves our language, Secwepemctsín, which is endangered. As Secwépemc people struggle to carry out resource-harvesting, we face the connected challenges of endangered rights, endangered landscapes and biodiversity, endangered knowledge systems, and an endangered language.

As authors, we come to this topic in ways that connect Indigenous peoples, anthropology, social research, law, and politics. As co-authors, we use the term "we" when referring to the Secwépemc, because of our separate and joint connections to them through birth and marriage and as parents of Secwépemc children. At times, we choose to use the voice of one or the other.

MARIANNE IGNACE: I grew up in a Plattdeutsch-speaking area of northwestern Germany, where a different identity and language were associated with low social class and where cultural and linguistic differences were denied by the dominant society. Anthropology has provided a way to account for, and put into perspective, the experiences of peoples who have a long connection with their landscape and who have become marginalized. Coming to Canada in the mid-1970s, I already appreciated the value of collaborative research in and with Aboriginal communities in piecing together Elders' knowledge, often embedded in language, and interpreting it with their help and for the benefit of younger generations. From the 1980s, being expert witness in court cases involving the Haida and Secwépemc Nations has further shaped my work. It involved translating what Aboriginal bearers of knowledge and storytellers saw and experienced, in a language that also satisfied anthropological models and the court system. That research led to Ron and me establishing a post-secondary research and education institution operated in collaboration with Simon Fraser University, where, with academics and Elders, we train our own people in social research skills and allow them to receive their own academic credentials while staying close to their communities.

RON IGNACE: I am Secwépemc on both sides of my family. Being raised by my great-grandparents, Edward and Julienne Eneas, is what most shaped my identity. They were born in the 1870s, and followed a seasonal round of hunting, gathering, and fishing, mixed with ranching and agriculture, until near their death in the early 1960s. My great-grandfather was also chief during my early childhood, and my great-grandmother was the sister and niece of previous chiefs appointed by Secwépemc tradition, who took an active role in the Aboriginal rights movement during the early twentieth century. Their handed-down memories shaped my thinking. Unlike most of my age-mates, I was raised in our language, Secwepemctsín. After time spent at the Kamloops Indian Residential School, followed by menial labour and Vancouver's skid row, I set out to study anthropology and sociology at the University of British Columbia. Upon completing my master's degree, my community, Skeetchestn, induced me to become elected chief. They have re-elected me 10 times at this point (2002). Since the late 1980s, I have also served as chairman of the Shuswap Nation Tribal Council and as president of the Secwépemc Cultural Education Society. As part of my effort to write about the economic and cultural history of the Secwépemc, I completed a Ph.D. in anthropology with a dissertation about Secwépemc oral history and historical consciousness based on our Elders' stories about the past and written documentation by outsiders who came into our homeland.

What brought each of us to anthropology was the search for connections among Indigenous peoples and the quest for answers about how, historically, colonization took its shape. The voices of other Indigenous peoples that we hear in some anthropologists' writings have stimulated us to explain history, culture, and the underlying meanings that people give to their lives, which have too often been silenced.

We have collaborated on academic and applied research regarding Secwépemc land tenure, oral histories, political history, language, and ethnobotany. Our home, family, and lives are not separated from "the field" where we conduct research. Instead, our work pushes us to consciously consider, incorporate, and write about our lives, and the lives of our relatives, Elders, and friends. Anthropological research provides a way for us to piece together the "broken cup" of Secwépemc cultural knowledge, practices, and meanings. It also provides a way to transmit that knowledge to younger generations and those who were deprived of all but pieces of that puzzle, not as academic knowledge, but to make sense of their Secwépemc past. We thus draw on anthropological research methods, knowledge, and theory. We also question anthropological models, as our consideration of Secwépemc plant-gathering shows.

In addition, as providers for our family and community members, we have practised hunting, fishing, and plant-gathering according to Secwépemc traditions. In other words, our anthropological training has influenced the way we research, write about, and perceive the Secwépemc. Our life as or among Secwépemc people has also influenced our anthropology.

To explore Secwépemc traditional and contemporary resource use, we will begin by explaining our ancestors' system of resource use and management when their control of the land was unimpeded. We can construct this with the help of archaeological data, nineteenth-century ethnohistoric data, and ethnographic information, some of which was recorded by James A. Teit, but current and remembered practices allow us to throw further light on these data. Resource use and management, however, is more than technology and practices. There is a cognitive dimension comprising the world view, beliefs, and spiritual and social connections underlying the practices. We find that this cognitive dimension can best be understood by self-reflexively examining what one of us (Ron Ignace) knows about such connections and what the oral histories of Elders and contemporaries who hunted, fished, and gathered plants reveal about its role in their/our lives.

The second part of this chapter will examine how the processes of colonization, dispossession, and coercive tutelage have had impacts on our ability to harvest our resources and maintain control over our lands. We will thus discuss the processes of history that affected this, along with the human, social, and economic impacts on the Secwépemc.

Lastly, we will discuss contemporary Secwépemc use and control of traditional resources, including how they have become the topic of litigation, political negotiation, and practical management regimes.

Coyote's Work: Secwépemc Culture and the Seasonal Round

Secwépemc means "spread-out people." "Shuswap," widely used in the ethnographic literature and in common language to refer to us, is an anglicization of the word "Secwépemc," produced by explorers who struggled to hear some of the sounds of our language. The Secwépemc are the largest Interior Salish-speaking Aboriginal nation in Canada. Our territory encompasses some 156,000 square kilometres in the south-central area of what is now British Columbia, stretching from near the Alberta border west of Jasper to the plateau west of the Fraser River, and southeast to the Arrow Lakes and the Columbia River. Secwépemc territory is bordered by, and overlaps, that of 10 other nations, including the Salish St'at'imc, Nlaka'pamux, and

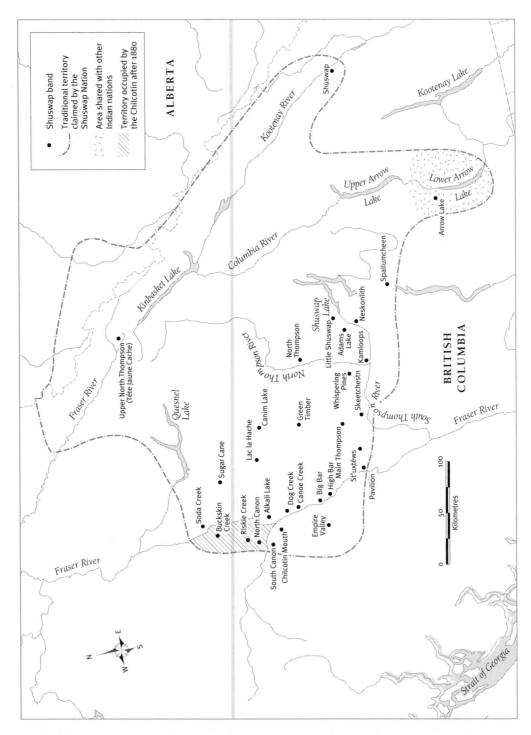

MAP 22.1 Secwépemc Territory

Okanagan, and non-Salish Tsilhqot'in, Carrier, Sekani, Cree, Blackfoot, Stony, and Ktunaxa. Secwepemcúl'ecw, our homeland, is traversed and characterized by the two major rivers of the BC Plateau, the Fraser and the Thompson. Most Secwépemc communities are and were located along these rivers and their main tributaries, although the resource-use areas encompassed all our territory (see Map 22.1).

Ancient Culture: Archaeology and Oral History

The oldest archaeological evidence of human occupation in Secwépemc territory is the headless skeleton of a young man who died in a flash flood at Gore Creek, east of Kamloops, some 8,300 years ago. Only a few years ago, his remains were repatriated to Secwépemc homeland after having been stored in a museum for decades. Like the rest of northwestern North America, the south-central Interior of BC was under a thick layer of ice during the Wisconsin glaciation until about 11,500 years ago. As the ice melted, a network of glacial lakes was established in the area of the Thompson River system and Shuswap Lakes, draining east into the Columbia River, held up by an ice dam north of what is now Lytton. The cataclysmic bursting of the ice dam shifted the drainage of the Thompson River system into the Fraser River about 10,000 years ago. Following these events, salmon runs established themselves in the Fraser and Thompson watersheds by or before 6,000 years ago. About 5,000 years ago, during what archaeologists call the Lochnore Phase, there was an influx of Salish-speaking immigrants from the coast into the Interior who introduced salmon-fishing technology among the "Coyote People"— as our ancient ancestors called themselves—of the Interior Plateau. Although our oral histories say they left to return to the coast, they brought along the Salish language, which is thought to have then merged with the language of the Coyote People.

Archaeological data conservatively suggest that the historic configuration of salmon-fishing and root-harvesting, with winter residence in underground dwellings, took shape by around 4,000 to 3,500 years ago.

Stspetékwll, our ancient oral traditions, throw a different, but complementary and even parallel, light on our origins and history. Old One, the Creator, provided humans with the arts and customs that distinguish them from animals by giving them diverse languages and showing them how to fish and to make baskets and other implements. Ancient myths also detail the travels of Tlii7sa and his brothers, and other "transformers," who travelled the ancient landscape of ice, fire, floods, and dangerous animals and monsters, defeated them, and left their marks throughout the land. Most of all, Old One sent Coyote, *sk'elep*, to finish the work of turning the land into Secwépemc land. Sk'elep broke the fishing weir of two medicine women downstream from the Secwépemc, thus enabling salmon to travel upriver into the mid-Fraser and Thompson watersheds. By impregnating the women, he connected the Secwépemc through kinship with our Nlaka'pamux neighbours on the Fraser to the south.

Stspetékwll have moral and social dimensions. The deeds of Coyote, the trickster, and of other transformers who travelled our land, challenge and affirm our values of what is appropriate behaviour and how we are socially and spiritually connected to nature and to one another. In addition, they represent the Indigenous idiom that parallels and throws light on events of geology and ancient history, cast, however, in the language of poetry between whose lines we have to read the science. In his 2008 doctoral thesis "Our Oral Histories Are Our Iron Posts: Secwépemc Stories and Historical Consciousness," Ron Ignace noted:

> The stories of my people are inextricably linked to our land, Secwépemcúl'ecw, and

to the ways in which successive generations marked the land with their deeds, named the land, showed us how to look after it, and thus deeded the land to us: we belong to it, and it belongs to us.... The ancient history of Secwépemcúl'ecw gave us the laws, what we call "yirí7 re stsq'ey's-kucw," that defined us as Secwépemc, and that gave us, what I call "equipment for living" as a people: What is traditionally marked on the land through our own history and existence of the land is mirrored in our ways of dealing with things by giving counsel to one another when issues arise that need to be dealt with and solved. Yirí7 re stsq'ey's kucw thus requires the tkw'enem7íple7ten, the ongoing advisors, to implement the ways that were set forth by our ancestors. These were literally "written in stone" by way of the t'ult ("freeze into stone") activities these ancestors carried out. Save for the destruction wrought upon our land and its markings by the newcomers, many of these landmarks exist to this day. However, the premises of these activities on the land are by no means "frozen," in that my own ancestors continually did the work to interpret them and re-interpret them. Their long-ago activities and how they related past activities to new issues provide us with good food for thought for the future.

The Traditional Seasonal Round

Secwepemcúl'ecw is subdivided geographically, the people referring to one another as follows. Tk'emlupsemc are the "people of the confluence" (of the North and South Thompson rivers). Sextsinemc, "people of the shore" (of the main Thompson River), are near the Bonaparte and Hat Creek Rivers to the west. Sét'emc, "people of the mid-Fraser River," live along the big river (the Fraser). The St'emcul'ecwemc, "people of St'emculecw" or possibly "people of cleared land," are upstream near Williams Lake. Styétemc, "inland people," live among the lakes and plateaus between the Fraser and North Thompson Rivers. Tqéqeltkemc, "people of the upper reaches," live on the mid-and upper North Thompson, although a group of them, the Kenpésq'et (Kinbasket), moved to the Upper Columbia near Ktunaxa territory during the 1800s or earlier. Sexqéltkemc, "upstream people," are on the South Thompson and eastward toward the head of Okanagan Lake. Within these divisions, there were further subgroups, centred around main villages. Each of these main villages had a chief, *kukwpi7*, appointed by custom. Disease in the mid-1800s reduced the 30 main villages to 17.

Secwepemcúl'ecw is enormously varied in topography, climate, flora, and fauna. There are nine biogeoclimatic zones. There is the interior Douglas fir zone, the wetter cedar and hemlock forests of the highland plateaus, and the dry bunchgrass, ponderosa pine, and sagebrush slopes of the interior dry belt. There are montane parklands, subalpine fir and spruce forests, lodgepole pine forests, subalpine meadows, and alpine tundras.

The annual subsistence cycle began in spring, when families gathered at highland lakes as soon as the ice broke, to net cutthroat and rainbow trout at their outlets as they prepared to spawn. These fisheries brought together large numbers of Secwépemc from different villages, facilitating social and political gatherings. April and May saw young shoots of balsamroot, fireweed, and cow parsnip harvested. People later moved to choice harvesting areas at mid- or higher elevations to dig large quantities of edible bulbs and roots, including balsamroot, avalanche lily, and spring beauties, as well as bitterroot, wild onions, biscuit root, Mariposa lily, yellowbells, chocolate tips, and tiger lily. Vast amounts were dried and stored for winter or, in some cases, prepared through a mixture of sun curing, pit-cooking, and drying. In late May, families stripped the sweet cambium of lodgepole pines. From early July to early September, numerous species of berries, including saskatoons, soapberries, three species of blueberries, huckleberries, raspberries, strawberries, blackcaps, choke cherries, gooseberries, and currents ripened at mid- to higher elevations.

As early as February, Secwépemc fished for steelhead in the Thompson River by drifting downriver in canoes at night and spearing fish attracted by their pitch torches. During late spring, the first runs of chinook or spring salmon travel up the Fraser and Thompson Rivers into their tributaries. While these salmon continue to run throughout the summer, in summer and early fall sockeye salmon return to their spawning grounds in tributaries of the mid-Fraser and Thompson river system. Although sockeye runs show great fluctuation in their four-year cycles, the different runs provided enormous quantities of food. Mid- to late fall brought runs of coho salmon. In the murky waters of the Fraser, the preferred method was dip-netting, while fishing in the clear waters of the Thompson involved harpooning, gaffing, and spearing, as well as set nets and gill nets. Before the early twentieth century, weirs and dams were an effective way to fish selectively for large numbers of salmon of a particular run.

More bulbs and roots, including chocolate lily or rice root as well as silverweed, whose stringy but fleshy roots are called "Indian spaghetti," were also harvested during this time. Late spring to early September also marked the time when Secwépemc replenished their repositories of medicinal plants, gathered especially at mid- and higher elevations. The period from August to October, when deer were fat and the fawns had matured, was the main hunting season. Task groups of related men and their parents, wives, and children would travel to base camps in or below the montane parklands.

As the men hunted mule deer, caribou, and elk higher up, the women and children lived at the base camp and set snares to trap small game. They deboned and dried the game brought in by hunters. Since early in the twentieth century, moose have replaced caribou and elk in much of Secwépemc territory. During the fall hunt, family groups would harvest black tree lichen in the Douglas fir zone, then pit-cook and dry it for winter use. Hunting also occurred throughout the year as necessary, as families gathered for a funeral or had run out of meat.

From spring to late fall, Secwépemc thus travelled to and from resource-producing locations, sometimes hundreds of kilometres from their winter villages. They camped for weeks at a time, harvested foods, and prepared them for winter, but living in camps was *as significant* a part of the way of life. Winter food was stored in cache pits near villages, but also in pits along the way to resource locations and near camps or processing locations for use next season. When horses arrived during the 1750s, they soon replaced much travel on foot or by canoe, although dugout cottonwood canoes and birchbark canoes, as well as rafts, continued to be used on the rivers and lakes.

In late October or early November, during the "entering month" when bears retired into their dens, people moved into their underground pit houses for the winter, living on preserved foods. Most of the winter villages, and thus the contemporary communities, were at or near the Fraser and Thompson valleys. Teit estimated the Secwépemc population at some 9,000 in 1850, when numerous diseases had already taken their toll. Some villages, especially those at Keatley Creek and Kelly Lake near the Fraser River, and at Clearwater on the North Thompson, had well over 100 pithouses. Other sites consisted of 2 to 4 pithouses. The first traders who arrived among the Secwépemc in 1811 noted more than 2,000 people living at the confluence of the North and South Thompson.

Fishing, hunting, and gathering involve intricate skills. They enact(ed) and transmit(ted) cultural and social principles of the division of labour by age, sex, and experience, and the social cohesion, role relationships, and economic efficiency resulting from these. As to fishing, in general (although with exceptions) men caught fish and women processed them. Older men, unable to spear fish, helped with butchering and showing younger people how to fish. Experts in making fishing gear, they passed these skills on to the younger generation. Older women supervised the gutting, filleting, and slicing of fish for drying, and tended the smoke fires and drying racks. By working alongside them, observing and copying, and sometimes being gently corrected, children and teenagers learned the important skills of slicing fish properly, hanging them, building the proper kind of fire, and so on. Learning and teaching took place by example rather than overt instruction.

Resource Management

Although Teit referred to specific "hunting grounds" associated with each of the seven Shuswap divisions, he stressed that they conceived of their land as "tribal property":

> All the land and hunting grounds were looked upon as tribal property all parts of which were open to every member of the tribe. Of course, every band had its common recognized hunting, trapping and fishing places, but members of other bands were allowed to use them whenever they desired. . . . Fishing places were also tribal property, including salmon-stations. . . . At the lakes every one had the privilege of trapping trout and erecting weirs. (Teit 1909:572; cf. Boas 1890:638)

Teit also added that "berry patches were tribal property, but picking was under tribal control. All the large and valuable berrying spots were looked after by the chief of the band in whose district they were situated" (ibid.:573). "Tribal control" here means control by the band or community since chiefship existed only at the band level. Of root-digging grounds, Teit noted that they were "common tribal property. Some people of the northern Fraser River bands laid a claim on the root-digging grounds of Quesnel Lake, where very large lily-roots grow, but these claims were not recognized by the rest of the tribe" (ibid.:582). Likewise, the chiefs of the Interior reiterated this tribal (or national) sense of land tenure to Sir Wilfrid Laurier in 1910 (see p. 431).

The collective and joint sense of ownership of Secwépemc territory and its resources continues to exist, despite the federal government's attempt to instill a sense of private property through the Indian Act and schooling. Secwépemc Elders still reveal a strong sense of their territory and its resources being owned collectively by all. In 1985, when the Skeetchestn chief and council were developing a fishing bylaw, they had recommended that all non-Skeetchestn persons had to get a permit to fish in their waters. The Elders would not approve the bylaw unless it recognized that all Secwépemc had the right to fish there without a permit. They maintained that, as Secwépemc, they had the right to fish anywhere in Secwépemc territory. Non-Secwépemc Aboriginals had to get a permit, but it must be free. Non-Secwépemc are allowed to assist their Secwépemc spouses or families in fishing, or to provide for them if their Secwépemc spouse or children are unable to do so. Should they abuse this privilege, it could be revoked. On the other hand, non-Aboriginal people were required to buy a permit and were restricted to fly-fishing. The bylaw also requires that all users of the fishing grounds keep the grounds clean and treat the fish and the place with respect. Once amended in this fashion, the band passed the bylaw. It is still in force and has not been contested.

Within Secwepemcúl'ecw, the tribal land providing equal access to resources, local regions are seen as being *stewarded* by people from interconnected communities in particular regions of the Nation. Teit used the term "division" for the seven regional groups of the Secwépemc. Our ancestors named them with descriptive geographic terms to which the suffix "-emc" ("people") was added. Thus the Sexqéltkemc or "upstream people" are the people of the eastern part of Secwepemcúl'ecw, and the St'emcúlecwemc are the "people of the cleared land" or the Cariboo region on the Fraser. Within these divisions, band territories are also described by Elders, although usually marked by considerable overlap. Particular communities, led by their chiefs and caretakers (see below), are thus collective stewards over particular tracts of Secwepemcúl'ecw. Members of all other communities within the nation are welcome at the resource-producing locations, including fishing grounds, of other communities. Elders from all parts of Secwepemcúl'ecw remember that in the past, people from all parts of Secwepemcúl'ecw would come to prolific fishing grounds such as the mouth of Deadman's Creek and High Bar, Gang Ranch, and Soda Creek on the Fraser.

Access to the resources of the nation and to a particular band was provided by kinship, descent, relations of affinity, residence, and socialization. Since residence patterns were usually patrilocal, most individuals took their primary sense of belonging to a nation and community from their father's side. In addition, a person had access to the territory of the other parent, even where that other parent was from another nation. If the other parent was from another community within the nation, an individual would get to know the hunting, fishing, and gathering areas near that community while visiting relatives and would be invited to share the harvest.

Access to other nations' territories was thus enabled by virtue of maintaining kinship ties with people from there. This gave individuals secondary affiliations with any number of other nations and communities, resulting from the out-marriage of parents, grandparents, and other ancestors. As long as kinship ties with such people were kept active, a person was welcome to fish, hunt, gather, and live in these territories. This principle of mutual access to resources by virtue of kinship and descent was common to all First Peoples of the Plateau and provided a crucial means of sharing and distributing resources. Teit also noted for the Thompson (Nlaka'pamux) people that:

> Among the Spence's Bridge and Nicola Bands any member of the Shuswap and Okanagan tribes who was related to them by blood was allowed full access to their hunting-grounds, the same as one of themselves. . . . If, however, a person who was not related to a Thompson Indian were caught hunting trapping or gathering bark or roots, within the recognized limits of the tribal territory, he was liable to forfeit his life. (Teit 1900:293)

Another way of accessing resources was through relations of affinity. A woman usually moved in with her husband's people upon marriage, but it was also customary for the new couple to live with her parents for a time, explaining the term for son-in-law, *snek'llcw*, "someone who changes house." Since a strong prohibition against marrying blood relatives existed, many people from smaller villages married outside their community. Demographic and genealogical records dating to the early 1800s show that patrilocal residence was normative, with about a third of marriages involving spouses (mostly women) from other villages.

A non-Secwépemc person married into a Secwépemc community was welcome to accompany his or her in-laws to help provide for the family. Likewise, a Secwépemc person who married a Secwépemc from another community would accompany his or her in-laws on hunting, fishing and gathering trips. For example, if a woman from Skeetchestn married a man from Alkali Lake, he would participate in the harvesting activities of Skeetchestn and become familiar with the resources there, thus providing for his family.

Resource management was thus accomplished through a system of collective ownership, sharing between communities and nations, and the stewardship of particular resources. Teit's ethnographic work notes "hunting chiefs." Our oral histories refer to the stewards over particular resources, such as game, fish, or plants, as *yucwmín'men*, "caretakers." It was their job to monitor the ripening of berries and the state of root patches, salmon runs, and game habitat and occurrence, and to let the people of their village know where and when these resources were ready or whether runs or harvests might fall short. In addition, particular individuals were also tacitly put in charge of maintaining trails to community hunting, fishing, camping, and plant-gathering areas.

Resource caretakership involves a complex set of (or dialectic relation between) resource-gathering practices and a system of knowledge and beliefs. Ethnobiologists refer to this as traditional ecological knowledge and wisdom (TEKW). At the core of the cognitive dimension of Secwépemc TEKW is our ancestors' and the present generation's relationship with the land, maintained through "storied knowledge" about the land, intimately connected to our language. All landforms and geographical features are named. These names contain roots referring to the specific nature of that place and lexical suffixes that indicate the shape or form of the place, derived from the shapes of the human body. Thus, a sidehill is *ck'emenk*, "coming together at an angle" of a belly-shape. *Pet'mémnus* is an area surrounded by wooded hills where one emerges from the woods into an open meadow

(*pet'*, "to emerge from the woods"; *men*, instrumental; *us*, "face." The additional *m* identifies the word as a place name).

In addition to the named landforms, place names commemorate the landscape. By way of ellipses and allusions, where the word merely hints at something, they can refer to the shape of landforms, natural phenomena, or animals or plants that are prominent in a location. They also commemorate past events, the oral history connected to the landscape. A subalpine area in Wells Gray Provincial Park is named *kélentem*, "he was chased," after a group of Cree invaders. A ridge on the Adams Plateau where people meditated during spirit guardian quests is called *smetúsem* (*s*, nominalizer; *met*, "to sit/live"; *us*, "face"; *em*, intransitive action). Pavilion Lake is *npétkwe7ten*, "fart in the water place" (*n*, "inside"; *p'e*, "to fart"; *-étkwe*, "water"; *-ten*, "place"), in memory of the transformer Tlli7sa killing a powerful skunk here.

In referring to places, Secwépemc speakers employ a complex system of deictics, or pointing words. They refer to landscape features as being close to the speaker, close to the listener, or away from both; absent or present; visible or invisible; coming this way or going that way; this side of the river or on the opposite side; and upstream or downstream. Together, place names, the words for landscape features, and the contexts of their use functioned like a verbal geographic positioning system which allowed detailed and accurate communication about directions and locations in an intimately known living landscape.

Secwépemc TEKW includes the relationship with all living things on the land. The act of hunting involves far more than volition and action on the part of the hunter. An animal that is killed through fishing or hunting "gives itself up," *kecmentsut*, but only if the person approaches that animal with a clean mind and body. Many stories about animals that give themselves up to be hunted during times of bereavement, or when people are in need, are handed down among Secwépemc people.

Because the animal has given itself, respect must be shown to the species and its environment. This includes a range of practices combining ritual/spiritual and practical aspects, such as ensuring physical and spiritual cleanliness before hunting through sweat bathing. The Elders do not allow fish guts to be thrown into the river, nor will they allow anyone even to spit into the river, to keep the fishing grounds clean, lest the fish stop running. Fish, of course, are known for their sense of smell, and fish guts will cause them to avoid the shore, where they can be caught. The same kind of rationale is behind women not hunting or accompanying hunters when menstruating. Respecting the harvested animal or plant also includes thanking it, not in public ceremony, but by a quiet prayer of thanks and an offering. Secwépemc raised in this tradition still make an offering of tobacco, sometimes a coin, sometimes a small food offering.

In the Secwépemc cognitive system that connects the land, living things, and humans, there are consequences for not following these norms, for not respecting the animals who give themselves. When fishers are unsuccessful despite their known skills, the reasons are not construed to be unspecified "bad luck" or lack of skill (given that they have been trained and have learned), but are related to lack of respect. The offences to animals that prevent success in hunting or fishing can also be situated in the realm of social offences against other people, especially of not sharing.

Nellie Taylor often told of how she and her partner, Cecilia Peters, went to Hi-Hium Lake to fish trout. Two young men had set up camp and were roasting the fish they had caught without offering any to the Elders. "After that, the fish just quit running for them. They never caught any more," she remarked wryly. By violating the norm of sharing (especially with Elders), they had acted inappropriately and had brought about supernatural sanction of their behaviour in that the fish stopped running for them.

The knowledge and consciousness of the spiritual and social context of harvesting were transmitted through stories that illustrated what happened to Coyote when he showed disrespect. Storied knowledge also involves the many anecdotes and stories about what happened to specific individuals that are part of the living memory of the community. A heartfelt sense of connection to the land, and the stories of the land, was also expressed in Secwépemc songs.

Practical Management Regimes

Secwépemc resource use entailed sophisticated strategies of plant propagation and habitat management developed over some 3,500 years. One of many examples involves the management and harvesting strategies around yellow avalanche lily (see Box 22.1). These included landscape burning to enrich the soil, replanting corms to ensure new growth, reseeding dug-up patches, and loosening soil with root-diggers. Lily patches managed in this way tended to produce plentiful harvests year after year. Burning, pruning, and cyclical harvesting also increased and sustained the yield of berry crops like saskatoons, soapberries, and blueberries. As Elder Mary Thomas observed, these strategies made Secwépemc plant-management regimes "just like a garden." That is, they were closely akin to horticulture, although involving "wild" plants rather than cultigens. Indeed, when Hudson's Bay Company traders introduced Secwépemc to domesticated plants (potatoes, onions, carrots, and grains) in the nineteenth century, they quickly incorporated gardening into their seasonal round. The word they coined for gardening is *kw'en'llq*, "to try out plants."

BOX 22.1 *Scwicw*—Yellow Avalanche Lily

Root crops and bulbs contributed much to Secwépemc diets well into the 1900s. Elders such as Bill Arnouse and Ike Willard reported that their families harvested several hundred pounds each season. Extended family groups would harvest *scwicw* and other roots in late spring. Adults rolled back the grassy top soil and extracted the roots, about 30–40 centimetres below the surface. In so doing, they loosened the soil, and young children would replant immature bulbs. Children would also pick the corms (the propagating part) off the bulbs and replant them. Caretakers of the *scwicw* would burn harvesting patches in early spring, in multi-year cycles. Within about two years, a burnt patch yielded large bulbs. Experiments with plant-harvesting strategies have shown that such techniques enhance crops rather than diminish them.

There is also indication that Secwépemc caretakership and management of *scwicw* went one step further: to transplanting them in a new habitat. The most prolific sites are meadows above the South Thompson River near the villages of Neskonlith and Adams Lake, about 600 metres above sea level. This area is an unusual habitat for *Erythronium grandiflorum*, which in all other locations throughout western Canada grows in subalpine meadows at around 1,500 metres.

According to Secwépemc and St'at'imc traditions, grizzly bears inspired Interior Salish people to develop processing techniques for *scwicw*. As the stories go, hunters observed grizzlies digging *scwicw*. Instead of immediately eating them, they left them exposed to the sun for some days, then returned to eat them. Chemical analysis reveals that freshly harvested bulbs contain an indigestible starch. Sun curing converts the inedible starch into fructose and edible starches. Further human intervention through pit-cooking produces a balanced combination of edible starch to satisfy hunger and fructose to satisfy the palate. Similar chemical conversions through the combination of sun curing and pit-cooking (as opposed to boiling or roasting) exist for roots that contain the starch inulin, such as balsamroot and wild onion.

Secwépemc History—the Nineteenth Century

The nineteenth century brought pervasive change. Fur traders and explorers made exploratory trips on the Fraser and Columbia Rivers in the early 1800s and established trading posts by the 1820s, notably Thompson River Post at Tk'emlups (Kamloops) in the heartland of the southern Secwépemc. Although the trade in furs fluctuated and was deemed infeasible, Thompson River Post, operated by the HBC, continued to play a major role in the Interior trade until the early 1860s. The bunchgrass hills surrounding the post provided welcome pasture for brigade horses; more importantly, the Secwépemc and neighbouring groups provided quantities of dried and fresh salmon, which became the staple of the traders. HBC records show that 12,000–20,000 salmon were bought annually from 1822 to the late 1850s.[2] The invasion of gold-seekers into the Interior in 1858 precipitated a smallpox epidemic which, during 1862–3, killed from one-third to two-thirds of the population, wiping out most Secwépemc on the west banks of the Fraser River near Chilcotin Canyon.

During the early 1860s, the BC colonial governor, James Douglas, arranged several reserves at Tk'emlups and in the Shuswap Lakes area, under a policy whereby reserves were to be allotted as "severally pointed out by the Indians themselves." Further reserves were proposed or mentioned. However, after his retirement, the colonial government rescinded them. Also, a land ordinance forbade Indians from pre-empting (claiming a homestead) or purchasing land. The 1860s also saw the arrival of Oblate missionaries at Tk'emlups and near Williams Lake.

While BC was a colony (1858–71), government policy did not explicitly interfere with Native fishing and hunting. Officials did, however, use the nomadic lifestyle of the Shuswap as an argument against them, claiming that in making a living by fishing and hunting they did not "really" utilize the land and therefore had no "real" rights to it. For example, BC colonial gold commissioner Phillip Henry Nind noted of the North Thompson Shuswap in 1865:

These Indians do nothing more with their
land than cultivate a few small patches
of potatoes here and there; they are a va-
grant people who live by fishing, hunting
and bartering skins; and the cultivation of
their ground contributes no more to their
livelihood than a few days digging of wild
roots. (British Columbia 1875:29)

These remarks foreshadow those of BC Commissioner of Lands and Works Joseph Trutch throughout the ensuing years. In 1865, Trutch wrote:

I am satisfied from my own observation
that the claims of Indians over tracts of
land, on which they assume to exercise
ownership, but of which they make no
real use, operate very materially to prevent

settlement and cultivation, in many
instances besides that to which attention has been directed by Mr. Nind, and I
should advise that these claims should be
as soon as practicable enquired into and
defined. (Ibid.:30)

Under the racist and parsimonious land policies of Trutch, reserves previously laid out by Douglas were drastically reduced or entirely eliminated. Secwépemc land title was not recognized by the institutions of the new government. In addition, the Secwépemc were prohibited from pre-empting or buying lands outside of their small reserves while large numbers of settlers were allowed to obtain, virtually free of charge, title to most of the arable land.

After British Columbia entered Confederation in 1871, the provincial and federal governments took several years to propose Indian reserves in the province. During this time, Secwépemc chiefs were considering warfare against the new government. When word of this leaked out, the governments quickly launched a Joint Reserve Commission to allocate reserves throughout BC, but with no per capita formula, as had been done in the treaty areas. The land eventually reserved for the remaining 17 Secwépemc communities amounted to about 1 per cent of Secwépemc Aboriginal territory.

The Secwépemc people, led by their chiefs, played a prominent role in the early twentieth-century Aboriginal rights movement. Through trips to Ottawa and London, and through petitions and memorials to the federal government, they tried to address our peoples' grievances regarding lands and the loss of hunting, fishing, and plant-gathering resources.

Secwépemc Traditional Resource Use, 1880s–1970s

In their presentation to Prime Minister Wilfrid Laurier when he visited their territory in 1910, in similar petitions from that time, and in their testimony before the McKenna–McBride Commission in 1913, Secwépemc chiefs complained about the loss of land and resources. Chief Andre of the North Thompson people, in his eighties at the time, said to the commissioners:

> You know how poor I am, just like as if I was tied up—therefore I am kind of poor. It seems as though I cannot help myself to better myself, like as if I were afraid all the time. Everything seems to be locked up now, different from what it used to be a long time ago. It used to be that everything was open to me, a long time ago. That is what I want. I want to be more free, so that I can get along better. I want to know whoever is the Chief that is going to help me on that point, to help me on what is good. (Royal Commission on Indian Affairs for BC Kamloops Agency 1913:56)

Joe Tomma, chief of Skeetchestn (Deadman's Creek), spoke to the commission on 29 Oct. 1913:

> The grievance of all the Indians in B.C. [is] that the white man has kind of spoilt us and locked us in. The white men have taken all the land and claimed all the water rights, and stopped us from hunting, fishing, etc. (ibid.:77)

On 25 October 1915 Chief Francois Silpahan, Little Shuswap band, declared:

> It is not on our reserve only that our hard feelings commence; it is for lands outside the reserves where the whitemen have stopped us. They stopped us from getting deer and birds, stopped us fishing. That is what we have told the Government in Ottawa. . . . When the Indians were here

a very long time ago, and able to look for their own food all over, the Indians used to increase, and they used to have good living. (ibid.:43)

As late as 1876, I.W. Powell, Indian Superintendent for BC, expressed the necessity to preserve Indian fishing in the following terms:

> There is not, of course, the same necessity to set aside extensive grants of agricultural land for Coast Indians; *but their rights to fishing stations and hunting grounds should not be interfered with, and they should receive every assurance of perfect freedom from future encroachments of every description.* (Department of the Interior 1876:32; emphasis added)

It is notable that Powell addressed the Aboriginal fishery as a right, which should be free from encroachment.

Fishing Restrictions

Until the mid- to late 1870s, the colonial and subsequent provincial governments did not interfere with Aboriginal fishing, especially for salmon. Indeed, the instructions on BC reserves, issued in 1874, noted that "Great care should be taken that the Indians . . . should not be disturbed in the enjoyment of their customary fishing grounds" (British Columbia 1875:131). Indian Superintendent Powell spoke of Indian fishing as a "right." Soon after, however, with competition for salmon from commercial fishing, especially on the lower Fraser River, the federal fisheries department began imposing restrictions on Indian fishing, asserting that Indian weirs and traps, as well as nets, were detrimental to the salmon. Antoine Gregoire, a Secwépemc from Adams Lake, was called in 1877 to give testimony as to Secwépemc fishing methods. He swore that:

BOX 22.2 Memorial to Sir Wilfrid Laurier

Presented at Kamloops by the chiefs of the Shuswap, Okanagan, and Thompson tribes by Chief Louis of Kamloops. Written by their secretary, James Teit.

We take this opportunity of your visiting Kamloops to speak a few words to you. We welcome you here, and we are glad we have met you in our country. We want you to be interested in us, and to understand more fully the conditions under which we live. . . .

When the "real whites" [seme7uw'i] first came among us there were only Indians here. They found the people of each tribe supreme in their own territory, and having tribal boundaries known and recognized by all. The country of each tribe was just the same as a very large farm or ranch (belonging to all the people of the tribe) from which they gathered their food and clothing, etc., fish which they got in plenty for food, grass and vegetation on which their horses grazed and their game lived, and much of which furnished materials for manufactures, etc., stone which furnished pipes, utensils, and tools, etc., trees which furnished firewood, materials for houses and utensils, plants, roots, seeds, nuts and berries which grew abundantly and were gathered in their season just the same as the crops on a ranch . . . and all the people had equal rights of access to everything they required. You will see the ranch of each tribe was the same as its life, and without it the people could not have lived.

They [the government officials sent by Douglas] said that a very large reservation would be staked off for us (southern interior tribes) and the tribal lands outside of this reservation the government would buy from us for white settlement. They let us think this would be done soon, and meanwhile, until this reserve was set apart, and our lands settled for, they assured us that we would have perfect freedom of traveling and camping and the same liberties as from time immemorial to hunt, fish, and gather our food supplies wherever we desired; also that all trails, land, water, timber etc., would be as free of access to us as formerly. Our Chiefs were agreeable to these propositions, so we waited for treaties to be made, and everything settled.

—Excerpted from the original in Ignace and Ignace (1999)

[the Shuswap] know, and say, that if the young fish are destroyed, the shoals returning from the sea will be proportionally diminished. That the Indians, with this fact in view, are careful not to destroy, wantonly or wastefully, the mature fish, or to impede their passage to the spawning beds. That the barriers they construct in rivers are only to retard the passage of the fish, to enable the Indians to obtain their necessary winter supply, and that these temporary obstructions are thrown open, as necessary, to give passage to the ascending fish. (Department of Indian Affairs 1877)

FIGURE 22.2 Chief Ron Ignace and his son, Joe Thomas Ignace, gaffing sockeye salmon, 2002. (Courtesy Marianne Ignace)

The near destruction of many of the Fraser and Thompson River salmon runs, due to a massive landslide at Hell's Gate on the Fraser in 1913–14 caused by CN Railway construction, further precipitated fisheries regulations. In the 1910s, the Upper Adams sockeye run, once rivalling the famous Lower Adams run, was wiped out by the construction of a log slide. Aboriginal fishers, last users of the resource, were singled out by wardens. Oral histories from this time noted fish wardens destroying weirs and fish traps and impeding fishing activity. On the North Thompson at Barriere River, a weir across the river had since time immemorial ensured a good salmon supply. The late Ida William, as affirmed by her older sister Josephine Wenlock, remembered that:

There used to be lots of people go in there and fish up there, but since the warden start bother the people. . . . They spoil everything, break all, they had some kind of little bridge where they sit down and fish, the game warden, fish warden supposed to come over and knock everything down, let it go in the water. This fish warden come around, get smart to the Indians, my mom used to say, "Geez, he's awful." This fish warden, two old ladies took him and threw him in the water. That fish warden come around, get smart to Indians, and after that kinda closed everything for Indians. They can't go out and get some fish from where they used to fish. If you want to fish in the river, you have to get a licence or something like that. (Ida William, Simpcw First Nation, Interview, 1987)

A decade after the Barriere River weir was destroyed because of the preposterous claim that it diminished the runs, the Barriere spawning grounds were all but wiped out by construction of a hydroelectric power dam by local non-Natives.

Many other memories during the first half of the twentieth century, and even into the 1980s, are about fish wardens, who in rural areas also doubled as provincial game wardens, imposing closures; destroying fishing gear, fishing platforms, and weirs; and confiscating fish.

Into the 1950s, Secwépemc carried out their traditional seasonal round of subsistence. Garden crops, however, supplemented indigenous foods. Like Aboriginal peoples elsewhere, Secwépemc of the late nineteenth and early twentieth centuries realized the usefulness of gardening, farming, and ranching. These were not conceived of as incompatible or qualitatively different activities, but as complementary ways of making a livelihood. However, the Department of Indian Affairs' "peasant farming policy" extended to the Interior of BC. Around 1900, the Department of Indian Affairs divided the arable areas of reserves into location tickets consisting of small acreages, and supplied the Indians with hand implements and seed in order to farm. The Secwépemc, for whom farming and gardening were similar to traditional plant management regimes, easily adapted to growing orchards, grain crops for their horses and cattle, and garden crops for their families, and were eager to grow surplus crops for cash. The Indian Act, however, prevented them from getting their goods to market without going through the bureaucracy of the Department of Indian Affairs. Moreover, during the early twentieth century, transport unions began to monopolize the transportation of goods and excluded Native people from membership in their unions.

At the same time, water rights were diverted away from reserves, making it increasingly impossible to irrigate crops in the dry southern Interior.

During the first half of the twentieth century many of our ancestors found seasonal employment as cowboys and ranch hands on ranches, integrating these activities into the seasonal round. Groups of Secwépemc families camped out on the margins of large settler-owned ranches such as Hat Creek, Douglas Lake, and Gang Ranch. While men engaged in farm labour, women and children gathered wild plants. Families also hunted and fished.

From the turn of the century to the 1950s, Ron Ignace's great-grandparents, Julienne and Edward Eneas, like all the 15 or so interrelated extended families of the Skeetchestn band, maintained a four-hectare location ticket on their reserve. There they grew garden crops and kept a few cows, horses, and chickens. After planting the garden in early May, the family (Julienne and Edward, their adult son and daughter, and the latter's large families) spent two weeks or longer at Xixyum Lake catching hundreds of pounds of rainbow trout, which they dried and packed home. They were joined there by families from Skeetchestn, St'uxtews (Bonaparte), Tk'emlups, and Pellteq't (Clinton). Until fall, they followed the traditional seasonal round throughout a 160-kilometre radius. As they travelled to camping, fishing, and gathering areas by horse and buggy, Julienne often packed along the family's chickens in a gunnysack, while other families took their milk cows along. At this time, most Secwépemc still relied almost entirely on country foods and gardening produce.

Elder Ida Matthew narrates her family's mixed economy during the 1930s:

Long time ago, my father, and Se7 and Maryen were all camping together at Tsqeltqéqen.

My father was clearing land at Genier's.

My mother and Maryen were picking gooseberries around the rocks, and they picked any other kinds of berries.

And when they finished work, my father and them, and Se7 and them
filled the gopher holes until they were full of water.
When the gophers came out, they clubbed them,
then they took them out, and we ate them.
And maybe some of them, my mother would dry.
And all the things they gathered, they dried . . .
And my mother was trapping groundhogs.
We were helping my mother pick whatever berries there were.
I remember we had a lot to eat,
when my mom and them picked, and when they hunted,
and when they trapped gophers. We always ate meat.
And my dad, he was setting the net in the river while he worked at Genier's.
He put a net in the river. He would spear whatever [fish] there was.
I don't remember what are all the kinds of fish called.
But I remember they were good to eat.
That's all.[3]

Despite the Department of Indian Affairs' attempts to instill and enforce a sense of private property and the nuclear family, economic production was done by co-operative labour within large extended family groups.

As noted earlier, the increasing restrictions placed on using the land by new fee simple titleholders[4] severely curtailed the ability of the people to follow their traditional seasonal round. The settlers and ranchers continually tried to oust families from what they saw as their lands. One Secwépemc Elder remembered such an incident at what had become Six Mile Ranch, situated on the grassy slopes south of Kamloops Lake. This area was called the "breadbasket" by Skeetchestn Elders: even in times of scarcity in severe winters, deer could be found there. Families used to camp at Six Mile and hunt and gather there. By the 1950s, however, landowners and their fences made this difficult:

Them *seme7s*, white people, used to kick us out of there. [Long before that] they kicked us out from Savona, where we *used* to camp, lot of people used to camp. You know the thing was, we used the place until they fenced it all along in there [during Trans Canada Highway construction in the late 1950]. We used to go down by M's there. Dad would park the old wagon. We'd walk down the rest of the way. . . . We'd go down there, maybe camp the night, and then from there, dad would hobble the horses, and we'd camp. . . . They always ask us, "Why did we give up our rights?" We had no choice; we were chased out. We were told we were trespassing.

Another Elder remembered:

[In the 1950s] I had a car, so I'd take my brother and my dad, take them out there to go hunt, and we already had to open gates to get to hunt. So we had to open farmers' gates. So I told my dad, "Why should we not use our land to hunt in?" I said, "I'll go knock on [the farmer's] door and let him know that we are hunting on our land here." So I go down there and knock on his door, and [he said], "Go ahead, let your brother and dad hunt." He calls it his field now, but that was all our hunting areas. So there, we are slowly getting fenced out. Fences are really getting us. (Translated from Secwepemctsín by the authors)

Since the 1951 revisions to the Indian Act, "provincial laws of general application" came to apply to Indians on reserves, and the provincial Department of Fish and Game began prosecuting Indians hunting off reserve. Evading game wardens thus became an ongoing aspect of hunting. As Skeetchestn hunter Terry Deneault remembered, during the 1960s and 1970s the "*séme7s* [white people] didn't allow us to hunt, so just like the deer, we used to have to hide away." Other Secwépemc who hunted then noted that the nature of hunting changed. Hunters often carried out clandestine hunting trips, quickly making a kill and taking the carcass home before the game warden could catch them. This had an impact on people's ability to learn the ritual practices and the many storied discourses surrounding hunting. One person remembered about this time:

In the sixties to the seventies, [game wardens] were pretty nasty. They were always on our case about hunting out of season. They were after us because we used to hunt all year long, because we needed to take care of our families. . . . They really enjoyed chasing us around. They were always trying to catch us. . . . At the same time you had to get the deer. So you found them real quick, shoot them, clean them, skinned them,

gutted them and run, and you're back out of there. . . . I think that's eroded our culture with hunting and fishing. When I was hunting here in the sixties with my uncles and in the seventies with my brothers, we never took time to even say a prayer after we shot a deer. It was like, "Get that thing done and let's get out of here!" I find now, when I go hunting with my family members . . . when we catch the deer or moose, we'll take the time to say the appropriate prayer and thank-you's, and take time to teach the children how to properly take care of the animal, what they should be watching for, how they should be doing it, so then the knowledge begins to be passed on in the proper manner. That did not really happen here in the late sixties and seventies. There was only one purpose, that was to get a deer and to get out of there as quick as you could. (M. Ignace 2001:50)

Enforced attendance at residential school for virtually all Secwépemc children between about 1930 and 1970 also had consequences for the transmission of skills, knowledge, and the spiritual connections related to resource pursuits. Children would spend only a few weeks at home during July and August, thus having little chance to engage in resource-harvesting with their elders.

Changes to the Environment

In the Interior of BC, cattle grazing has produced severe impacts on forests and grasslands. As noted earlier, ranching has been a facet of Secwépemc economics for a century. Early in the twentieth century, however, provincial grazing permits allocated virtually all non–fee simple lands in the Interior of BC as private grazing leases to non-Aboriginal ranchers. As foresters concur, cattle ranching has wreaked havoc with many indigenous plant species. For decades, cows have browsed on and trampled root plants like spring beauties or "Indian potatoes," bitterroot, yellow avalanche lily, and others. The habitats of these plants have been further reduced by the spread of non-indigenous species such as dandelion, mullein, introduced grasses, thistle, and knapweed.

Since the 1960s, logging activity has intensified, resulting in a continuous patchwork of cut blocks throughout the plateaus and mountains of the area. While the succession of growth in clear-cuts supports the regeneration of some berry species and supports continuing habitat for ungulates, logging has had a devastating impact on numerous food and medicinal plants whose habitats are wetlands or moist areas, which were drained and eroded through logging activity. A vast network of logging roads, some established on the ancient horse and foot trails used by Secwépemc hunters, now extends throughout the region. Other roads criss-cross them and have destroyed the old trails.

In recent decades, urban development put further pressures on people's ability to use traditional resources. The urban and suburban population of the south-central Interior, centred around Kamloops, increased tenfold. Sprawling subdivisions now stand where families used to camp, gather berries, and hunt. Competition from sport hunters and fishers has increased. Secwépemc hunters, in general, are reluctant to hunt during the fall hunting season, as the forests become populated with sport hunters.

Secwépemc plant-harvesting has declined notably in recent decades. Some families continue to gather large quantities of berries, including blueberries, huckleberries, chokecherries, and especially soapberries, highly valued as the main ingredient for a beverage and whipped up into "Indian ice cream." The vicious cycle of the effects described above, including habitat loss, knowledge loss, the availability of market foods, and threats from settlers, have resulted in indigenous root crops and green vegetables being replaced in the diets of most Secwépemc. In recent years, however, younger generations of Secwépemc have begun recapturing the knowledge and skills to harvest these plants. Some have begun to reintegrate them into their diets.[5]

Legal Issues

Aboriginal fishing for food and ceremonial purposes has been recognized as an Aboriginal right in law since the 1990 Supreme Court of Canada *Sparrow* decision, supported by Section 35 of the Constitution Act, 1982. *Sparrow*, however, has not improved Secwépemc ability to catch fish. Commercial overfishing on the coast, as well as environmental conditions, caused Pacific salmon stocks to reach all-time historic lows. As last users of the resource, the Secwépemc have had few fish available. Declining fish stocks, in turn, resulted in charges being pressed against numerous Secwépemc fishers. In 1994, Daniel Gaspard of the St'uxtews band was criminally charged for selling about a dozen salmon. As noted earlier, the trade in *scwik'* (dried sides of salmon) is an ancient activity among Interior Aboriginal peoples. The judge, however, could not (or would not) grasp the traditional rules of access to the fishery and trade in fish, and chose to accept expert evidence presented by the Crown that, unsupported by data, denied the existence of the St'uxtewsemc, denied the importance of fishing, and asserted that Secwépemc trade in fish was insignificant, involving "exchanges like trades of desserts at church picnics."[6] Daniel Gaspard was eventually acquitted on appeal.

In another case from 2000 (*R. v. Deneault and R. v. Lebourdais*), fishers from two Secwépemc communities were criminally charged as they returned from the Secwépemc fishing grounds at High

Bar on the Fraser. The Crown asserted that the Secwépemc Aboriginal right to fish did not extend to all fishing grounds within the nation but only to stations near one's own reserve, in complete conflict with traditional protocols of access. Upon Marianne Ignace's presentation of anthropological expert evidence for the defence, as well as Elders' and witnesses' testimony, the Crown dropped the charges. Several years later, some of the same individuals from Neskonlith, near Chase, were charged with illegal fishing on the Fraser River, based again on the Crown's assertion that the Aboriginal right to fish did not extend to fishing grounds not near the fishers' reserve. This time, the judge somehow believed the Crown's argument that prehistorically Secwépemc would not and could not have travelled 100 kilometres or more to fish!

Given the *Delgamuukw* decision, some Secwépemc communities have engaged in court action over specific tracts of land scheduled to be logged or to be developed into resorts or golf courses. They argue Aboriginal title to the land, supported by past and ongoing traditional use of the land. The Six Mile land dispute involved the Skeetchestn band's opposition to real-estate development, including a golf course, resort hotel, and housing, on what had become fee simple land as well as on a parcel of Crown land on Kamloops Lake. The Stk'emlupsemc, as stewards within the Secwépemc Nation over this area, argued that its inherent title to this land and its fundamental economic interest in the land were being violated by impending development. The bands sought to have its Aboriginal title registered on par with the developer's title, thus questioning the provincial land registry system. In the end, a settlement was negotiated. The province compensated the bands for loss of hunting areas, created some protected areas involving heritage and spiritual sites, supported alternate economic opportunities through eco-tourism, and agreed to put the Secwépemc Nation's Aboriginal rights and title in abeyance.

Members of the eastern Secwépemc communities also launched blockades and protests at Sun Peaks ski resort near Chase, arguing for unextinguished Secwépemc Aboriginal rights and title to the area and against destruction of the landscape and resources due to resort development.

On the political level involving the Secwépemc as an Aboriginal nation, the legacy of having suffered the "divide-and-conquer" strategies imposed by federal and provincial governments—including splitting our nation into several agencies and the legal status that bands as "First Nations" versus Aboriginal nations enjoy—has made joint action difficult.[7] In the last three decades, the Secwépemc have been represented through a variety of tribal councils, including the Shuswap Nation Tribal Council, which represents nine of the southern bands, and the Northern Shuswap Tribal Council, which includes four northern bands. One band, Ts'kw'aylaxw or Pavilion, is part Secwépemc and part St'at'imc (Lillooet) and is affiliated with the Lillooet Tribal Council; the Kinbasket (Kenpésq'et or Shuswap) Indian Band in the far east was at one time affiliated with the Ktunaxa, although it joined the Shuswap Nation Tribal Council in recent years. The remaining communities, High Bar, Little Shuswap, and Esk'et, are independent. The Northern Shuswap Tribal Council (formerly Cariboo Tribal Council), and the Esk'et (Alkali Lake) First Nation joined the troubled BC Treaty Process; the Shuswap Nation Tribal Council did not join it because of the enormous debt load taken on by First Nations in the process of negotiations and the continuing stipulation that treaties must *extinguish* Aboriginal title. Despite these obstacles, all Secwépemc communities continue to hold unity meetings and maintain dialogue on joint initiatives as a nation.

What the Future Holds

In light of over a century of shrinking access to resources and government policies that criminalize traditional resource activity, why do Secwépemc continue to fish, hunt, and gather and to insist that these activities are inextinguishable *rights*?

Throughout the period we described, our chiefs, Elders, and community members have continued to exercise, and to insist on, our rights. The "Memorial to Laurier," court testimonies, and oral histories all bear witness to that. Secwépemc people continue to see hunting, fishing, and plant-harvesting as activities that express who we are. Most of us who pursue hunting or fishing do so on weekends, but that does not mean that, economically and culturally, their significance has waned. In many Secwépemc households, game and fish constitute an important part of the diet. The cycles of redistributing game, fish, and wild plants allow us to maintain our ancient values of sharing. As one younger Secwépemc observed:

> It's still a very important part of our diet yet. The people still rely on it this every day, [to feed] big families. It's a necessity, as a matter of fact. Most people, they look at it as a part of not only our diet, but as a traditional thing we've done for many years, and we continue to do them, it's our right there, and we're going to hang onto it. (M. Ignace 2001:51)

In times of life-crisis a people's deepest values are immanent. So it is with Secwépemc traditional resource use. When a person has died, during the four days of the wake and at the feast following the interment, relatives and friends of the bereaved family prepare salmon, trout, deer meat, and moose meat, all from animals who gave themselves up, taking pity on those in grief. Hunters, without needing requests or instructions, go out to hunt in honour of the deceased and to comfort the family. They bring back food and stories of animals that turned up at unusual places, giving themselves for the occasion, or that carried messages from the deceased, witnessing the power of those who have departed.

Conclusion

And this brings us back to the beginning. Sadly, the trip to gather *llekw'pin* in 1997 was Nellie Taylor's last. Until weeks before her death in July 1998, she asked for the plant medicines that sustained her for so many years, although the "White man's disease" (lupus) that ravaged her body had no final Secwépemc remedy. However, in the months before she died, she took comfort in eating *llekw'pin*, soapberries and other berries, Indian rhubarb, and root plants, drinking teas, and continuing to speak Secwepemctsín. We know that she took comfort in the feast of country foods that honoured her, where one last plateful was sent to her through the fire. As survivors, we also take comfort in her teachings, which validate our rights, our knowledge, and our practices of traditional resource use.

ACKNOWLEDGEMENTS

This paper represents a portion of our collaborative research in and with Secwépemc communities since the mid-1980s. In 1990–3, 1994–7, and 1999–2002, some of our work was funded by the Social Sciences and Humanities Research Council of Canada through various Strategic Research Grants in which we collaborated with Dr Nancy Turner (University of Victoria) and Dr Hari Sharma (Simon Fraser University). Other parts of our research were supported by the Shuswap Nation Tribal Council and by the Skeetchestn and North Thompson (Simpcw) First Nations/bands. We would like to thank the many Secwépemc Elders, relatives, friends, and colleagues who have shared their knowledge with us. *Yiri7 re skukwstsetselp!* This paper is dedicated to the memory of Nellie Taylor.

NOTES

1. We use the practical orthography for writing Secwepemctsín developed by linguist Aert Kuipers and Secwepemctsín speakers in the 1970s and 1980s. It enables one to represent all six vowels and 43 consonants on a standard keyboard, but some sounds need explanation. A "c" is a hissed sound made by putting the tongue against the roof of the mouth, as in the German "ich." An "r" is made in the same position in the mouth, but is voiced. The "ll" (equivalent to the linguist's "barred l") is a kind of hissed "hl" sound. The "q" is a uvular stop or "throat k," and the "x" is produced in the same part of the throat, but with friction, like the German "ach." The "g" is a hummed throat sound made in the pharynx, a bit further back in the throat than the French "r." Letters followed by an apostrophe indicate glottalized sounds, plosives, made with a catch in the throat. The "t" actually sounds like a popped "tl." Finally, the "7" denotes a glottal stop, or a "catch in the throat," and can occur in the middle or at the end of a word. In addition, to help pronunciation, stressed syllables of words are indicated with an ´ accent mark, as in "Secwépemc." For a detailed description of Secwepemctsín phonetics and orthography, see Palmer (2005) and Marianne Ignace (1998).

2. For details on the extent of fishing for the Hudson's Bay Company post, see Archibald McDonald Dispatch to HBC Governor George Simpson, 1827, John McLeod's Journal, Thompson River Post (TRP), 1822–3; Archibald McDonald Journal, TRP, 1826–7, and diary of trip with G. Simpson; John Tod Journal, TRP, 1841–3; Paul Fraser, TRP, 1850–2, 1854–5; William Manson, TRP Journal 1860–4; John Moffat, TRP Journal; John Tait, TRP Correspondence 1873–5. All the above are situated at the Kamloops Museum and Archives, as well as in the Hudson's Bay Company Archives at the Manitoba Provincial Archives.

3. This narrative is part of a larger body of Secwépemc texts recorded, transcribed, and translated by Marianne Ignace, Ron Ignace, and Mona Jules. To reflect the way of speaking in the Secwépemc language, and the poetry of their speech, these narratives are rendered in verse form.

4. Fee simple is the ordinary form of landholding in Canada.

5. Of importance in this endeavour has been our collaborative ethnobotany research since 1990, which has involved more than 40 Secwépemc Elders from all our communities, as well as ourselves, Dr Nancy Turner (University of Victoria), Dr Harriet Kuehnlein (McGill University), and Secwépemc and non-Aboriginal research assistants. This multidisciplinary work has led to numerous publications and to courses in ethnobotany through Secwépemc Education Institute, in collaboration with Simon Fraser University. In these courses, we have convened Elders and younger Secwépemc to teach, learn, and practise plant-harvesting and processing techniques, and to share the traditional knowledge behind these practices. Many of our students and Elders in turn have reintegrated traditional plant-harvesting and processing, including pit-cooking, into activities in their own communities.

6. The Crown's anthropological expert witness in *R. v. Gaspard, R. v. Lebourdais,* and *R. v. Deneault,* was Sheila Robertson, a geographer who has acted widely in this capacity for the Crown, most notoriously in *Delgamuukw v. R.* See Culhane (1998) for a scathing critique of Robertson's evidence.

7. We use the term "Aboriginal Nation" as "a sizeable body of Aboriginal people with a shared sense of national identity that constitutes the predominant population in a certain territory or collection of territories. Aboriginal Nations usually contain numerous First Nation communities within the same nation" (Canada 1996, vol. 1: xiv). By contrast, the term "First Nation" by and large is a euphemism for an Indian band under the Indian Act, reflecting merely a single community rather than the larger political, linguistic, and cultural entity.

REFERENCES AND RECOMMENDED READINGS

Anastasio, Angelo. 1972. "The Southern Plateau: An Ecological Analysis of Intergroup Relations," *Northwest Anthropological Research Notes* 6, 2: 109–229. This article notes that communities and nations on the Columbia Plateau maintained relations through sharing resources. This was facilitated through kinship-based protocols of access.

Boas, Franz. 1890. "The Shuswap," *Second General Report on the Indians of British Columbia*, Sixtieth Annual Report of the British Association for the Advancement of Science for 1890, London.

British Columbia. 1875. *Papers Connected to the Indian Land Question, 1850–1875.* Victoria: Wolfenden Government Printer.

Canada. 1913–16. Royal Commission on Indian Affairs for BC (McKenna–McBride Commission), Kamloops Agency 1913, Transcript of Testimony. Vancouver: Union of BC Indian Chiefs.

———. 1996. *Report of the Royal Commission on Aboriginal Peoples*, 5 vols. Ottawa.

Culhane, Dara. 1998. *The Pleasure of the Crown.* Vancouver: Talonbooks.

Dawson, George Mercer. 1891. "Notes on the Shuswap People of B.C.," *Transactions of the Royal Society of Canada* Section II, part 1: 3–44. A significant early report on the Secwépemc, written by the head of the geological survey of Canada, an avid amateur ethnographer.

———. 1892. "Notes on the Shuswap People of British Columbia," *Proceedings and Transactions of the Royal Society of Canada for the Year 1891*, series 1, vol. 9.

Department of Indian Affairs. 1877. RG 10 Series, 24 Sept.

Department of the Interior. 1876. *Annual Report of the Department of the Interior for the Year Ended 30th June, 1876.*

Fladmark, Knut R. 1986. *British Columbia Prehistory.* Ottawa: Canadian Museum of Civilization. Written by a notable scholar, this is a standard work on the topic.

Hayden, Brian, ed. 1992. *A Complex Culture of the British Columbia Plateau.* Vancouver: University of British Columbia Press. This book, based on data collected in the early 1970s, presents articles on St'at'imc (Fraser River Lillooet) resource use. Since the Upper St'at'imc are closely connected to the Western Secwépemc, they are of interest. Articles by Steven Romanoff, Michael Kew, and Randy Bouchard with Dorothy Kennedy are especially relevant to our discussion of fishing and resource use among the Secwépemc.

Ignace, Marianne. 1998. "The Shuswap (Secwépemc)." In *Handbook of North American Indians.* Vol.12, *The Plateau*, edited by Deward E. Walker. Washington: Smithsonian Institution. Summarizes and evaluates early ethnographic information and provides a history since the early 1800s. It also throws light on Secwépemc place names and names for groups as rendered in multiple orthographies.

———. 1999. "Guardian Spirit Questing in the 90s: A Mother's View." In Peter Murphy, George Nicholas, and Marianne Ignace, eds, *Coyote U: Stories from Secwépemc Education Institute*, edited by Peter Murphy, George Nicholas, and Marianne Ignace. Penticton, BC: Theytus Press. Written from a personal perspective, this essay details the difficulties contemporary Secwépemc parents and teenagers face in following traditional practices like guardian spirit questing.

———. 2001. Report on Oral History Information from Skeetchestn Band Members, Six Mile Area. Prepared for Skeetchestn Indian Band.

——— and Ron Ignace. 1999. "The Memorial to Sir Wilfrid Laurier: A Commentary." In *Coyote U*, edited by Peter Murphy, George Nicholas, and Marianne Ignace. This is the text of the memorial, with historic and cultural commentary.

Ignace, Ronald. 2008. "Our Oral Histories Are Our Iron Posts: Secwépemc Stories and Historical Consciousness." Ph.D. diss., Simon Fraser

University,Department of Sociology and
Anthropology.

Palmer, Andie Diane. 2005. *Maps of Experience:
The Anchoring of Land to Story in
Secwépemc Discourse*. Toronto: University of
Toronto Press.

Peacock, Sandra, and Nancy J. Turner. 1998. "Just Like
a Garden: Traditional Plant Resource Management
and Biodiversity Conservation on the B.C. Plateau."
In *Biodiversity and Native North America*, edited
by P. Minnis and W. Elisens. Norman: University of
Oklahoma Press. This article discusses the detailed
plant management and propagation regimes of the
Secwépemc and other Interior peoples.

Teit, James. 1900. *The Thompson Indians of British
Columbia*. New York: American Museum of
Natural History, Memoir No. 2.

———. 1909. *The Shuswap*. Memoir of the American
Museum of Natural History. New York. This is the
most detailed source on nineteenth-century and pre-
contact Secwépemc culture. It should be read in conjunction with his *The Thompson Indians, The Lillooet,*
and *The Salishan Tribes of the Western Plateau.*

Turner, Nancy J., Marianne Ignace, and Ron Ignace.
2000. "Traditional Ecological Knowledge and
Wisdom of Aboriginal Peoples of British Columbia,"
Ecological Applications 10, 5: 1275–87. This article
summarizes some of our TEKW research, particularly on Secwépemc root-plant gathering and
management.

Union of British Columbia Indian Chiefs, n.d. Royal
Commission on Indian Affairs for BC, Kamloops
Agency 1913. Transcripts of Hearings.

Walker, Deward E., ed. 1998. *Handbook of North
American Indians*, vol. 12, *The Plateau*.
Washington: Smithsonian Institution. The volume
features encyclopedic coverage on all Canadian and
US Plateau peoples.

PART VIII

The Northwest Coast

CHAPTER 23

The Northwest Coast: A Regional Overview

Margaret Seguin Anderson

The Aboriginal cultures of the Pacific coast of Canada developed in a rich natural environment. Villages and seasonal camps in sheltered harbours close to rich salmon spawning routes allowed access to shores and shoals that also yielded halibut, cod, herring, oolichan, shellfish, and marine mammals in abundance. Unique localized resources were recognized and exploited by each tribe, and even by each village, but frequent contacts between neighbouring groups along the coast stimulated sharing of ideas, techniques, and institutions throughout the area, creating the patterns that outsiders have designated as Northwest Coast culture. This cultural complexity developed in situ over several millennia. By about 2,000 years ago the cultures of the region had developed most of the features that were associated with Northwest Coast culture at the time of contact.

The evolution of knowledge, tools, and techniques permitted an effective adaptation to the maritime zone; the Aboriginal patterns of such items as halibut hooks have never been bettered. The permanent villages of large red-cedar plank houses located in protected sites throughout the area were built by skilled carpenters and embellished with carvings that have received recognition as masterworks of a great artistic tradition. Well-built canoes 18 metres and more in length carried the people to their fishing sites, to collecting terri-tories for shellfish, berries, bark, and roots, to hunting areas for land and sea animals, and to other villages for purposes such as trade, weddings, feasts, and occasionally raiding. A few trails, such as the famous grease trails in the North, penetrated the thick rain forests that barred movement past the beach rocks up the steep mountain slopes that plunged into the fjords.

Cultures along the entire Northwest Coast display a number of common cultural features: permanent winter villages; elaborate ceremonial activities, including property distributions; sophisticated traditions of rhetoric; and even similarities in the sound systems of the languages throughout the region. For example, even though there are four distinct and apparently unrelated language families represented along the British Columbia portion of the Northwest Coast (Haida, Tsimshianic, Wakashan, and Salishan), all of them share the fairly unusual features of glottalized consonants, a uvular series of stops, and lateral fricatives; neighbouring Northwest Coast nations in Alaska and Washington state display the same features. Archaeologists have found evidence of trade dating back thousands of years, including obsidian that can be traced hundreds of kilometres to a few source deposits. The evidence is strong that this is an area in which there has been intensive cultural interaction for thousands of years. In fact, these cultures evolved as trading nations, and their distinctive cultures could not have developed without trade.

Salmon has been for thousands of years the staple food and cultural foundation of all the groups on the Northwest Coast, and also of their neighbours in the adjacent Interior. Coastal cultures had access to an array of resources, and the number of runs that they could intercept meant that their salmon stocks very rarely failed them; the Interior groups, on the other hand, were reliant on fewer stocks upriver, close to the spawning grounds, and these were subject to huge fluctuations and frequent failures. The development of the technology to dry, store, and transport salmon (and its essential condiment, oil from fish or sea mammals) was the prerequisite allowing for the development of the complex cultures of this entire region. This technology provided the base on which the Coastal groups built elaborate cultures founded on wealth accrued through the harvest and trade of food from the productive territories owned by extended groups of kin. While there was extensive use of the other plant and animal resources, the most important resource, and the foundation of the distinctive culture of the Northwest Coast, was salmon. It is no wonder that the people of this entire region have been dubbed "salmon people." The per capita consumption of salmon by the Northwest Coast peoples reached 220 kilograms of fresh, edible salmon each year (Newell 1997:29).

Huge quantities of salmon, fish oil, berries, and other products were normally preserved and traded by Coastal and Interior groups each year. Here is an account of one Interior group's smokehouses:

An inspector visiting Babine Lake and the headwaters of the Skeena River in 1904 gives an interesting description of the operations of the Indians: "The banks of the Babine river have a lovely appearance at this place and a most wonderful sight met our eyes when we beheld the immense array of dried salmon. On either side there were no less than 16 houses 30 x 27 x 8 feet filled with salmon from the top down so low that one had to stoop to get into them, and also an immense quantity of racks, filled up outside. If the latter had stood close together they would have covered acres and acres of ground, and though it was impossible to form an estimate, we judged it to be nearly three-quarters of a million fish at those two barricades, all killed before they had spawned, and though the whole tribe had been working for six weeks and a half it was a wonder that so much salmon could be massed together in that time. It was estimated that each Indian family used about one thousand salmon per year; a total for the Indian population of that district alone of about one million fish. Fish was the principal food of the multitude of dogs. Salmon were used as an article of commerce and formed a sort of legal tender, ten salmon being equivalent to a dollar. Dried salmon were sold to miners, merchants, and packers operating dog sleighs. It has been estimated that the average consumption of fish by Indians in British Columbia amounted to about twenty million pounds per year: about seventeen and one-half million pounds of salmon, three million pounds of halibut, and one-quarter million pounds of sturgeon, herring, trout and other fish as well as eighty thousand gallons of fish oil valued at $4,885,000 in 1879, and at $3,257,000 in 1885. (Carrothers 1941:5–6 n. 2)

Two years after this scene was described, the government forced the destruction of the weirs at

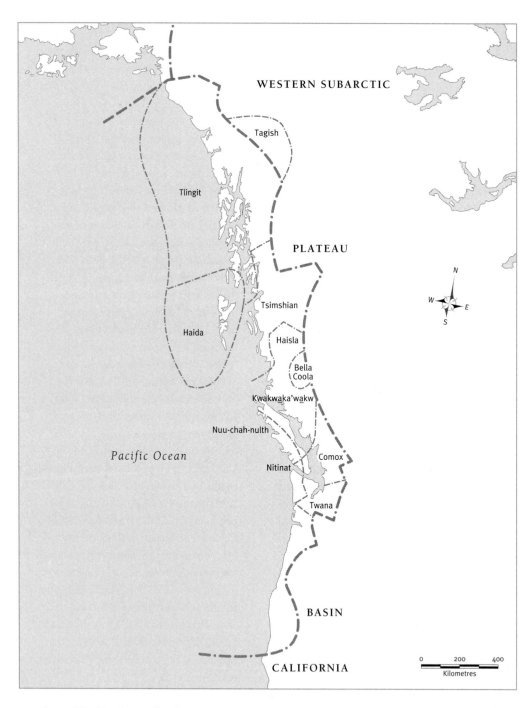

WESTERN SUBARCTIC

Tagish

Tlingit

PLATEAU

Tsimshian

Haida

Haisla

Bella Coola

Kwakwaka'wakw

Nuu-chah-nulth

Comox

Nitinat

Twana

Pacific Ocean

BASIN

CALIFORNIA

N
W   E
S

0   200   400
Kilometres

MAP 23.1 The Northwest Coast

Babine, despite warnings by their own agents that this would cause starvation in the Interior. The large number of fish taken by Aboriginal people had become an issue as soon as canneries appeared on the coast, and a campaign to wrest fish from Aboriginal fisheries was mounted through political manoeuvring and media hysteria such as the following headline story from a Victoria newspaper of a century ago:

> Indians Wiping Out Sockeye
>
> A report in detail concerning the manner in which Indians at the head-waters of the Skeena and other northern rivers are striking at the very root of the life of the salmon-fishing industry in British Columbia, one of the greatest sources of the people's wealth, has been received. . . . no less than 2,000,000 salmon. . . . were killed in the Indian traps this year. That number of fish, if canned, would make about 142,857 cases. (Newell 1997:91)

In fact, the Aboriginal fisheries were not a danger to the stocks; long-standing Aboriginal fisheries management practices ensured that there would be sufficient escapement for spawning, even in years of scarcity and looming famine. But the campaign to appropriate salmon and other resources for commercial exploitation impacted the Coastal nations heavily.

The large quantity of salmon observed at Babine Lake in 1904 was needed by communities in the Interior for their winter food supply; it was the staple food and the largest source of calories—the core of a diet that was supplemented by other local foods and oil-rich seafoods traded from the coast. This supply was not always reliable, however; each salmon run has a four-year cycle in which abundance varies 1,000 per cent and more from the dominant year to the low year

in the cycle. Babine Lake is a terminal fishery, and the stocks available there are limited to those that spawn in the lake and its source creeks. If these stocks were in a low-cycle year; if a landslide blocked an important part of the river system during the period when the juvenile fish for a given run were moving out to sea; if extremely high water—or water that was too warm, too cold, or too loaded with silt—caused high mortality among the returning spawners; or if any of a number of other crucial variables were unfavourable, then the numbers could be so reduced that the Babine Lake runs were a small fraction of their normal abundance and the local people would be unable to dry sufficient salmon for their needs. In such a situation, fish for trade, on which other Interior groups depended, was unavailable from the Babine. The same scenario applied to Interior groups who relied on salmon from the upper reaches of the Fraser watershed, including the Nechako. In some years other Interior groups had surplus available for trade. The long-established trade networks within the Interior were crucial to the survival of all the communities in the region, and the area near the divide between the watersheds of the Skeena and Fraser was central to this. However, occasionally there was a year when none of the Interior groups had sufficient fish to supply their needs and trade to other communities for the essential winter supply. When this occurred, the Coastal groups could reap huge profits by trading dried salmon for valuable furs, moose and caribou hides, wild sheep or mountain goat wool and horns, obsidian, copper, amber, jade, slaves, and other valuable goods. This opportunistic profit was facilitated by the fact that Interior and Coastal traders made regular trading trips and Coastal traders were constantly aware of the state of the fish runs on which various Interior groups relied. Dried eulachon, oils from eulachon and other vertebrates, and foods preserved in oil were staples of the regular trading excursions, but traders also offered smoked seal meat, dried

FIGURE 23.1 Of all the Northwest Coast populations, the Haida were the most devastated by diseases introduced by Europeans. Ninstints on Anthony Island was already abandoned by 1901 as a result of population depletion from epidemics, the forest beginning to reclaim the site. (Image PN 837 courtesy of Royal BC Museum, BC Archives)

first Europeans arrived at Fraser Lake to establish Fort Fraser, they anticipated being able to purchase their winter supply of dried salmon from the Aboriginal traders there; however, there was a shortage that year due to a failure of the Stuart River run and they had to turn to other sources of supply. When the runs that Interior people relied on were inadequate to supply all the communities, there was no choice but to turn to Coastal groups for salmon and other seafoods.

In addition to filling the demand caused by shortfalls in the Interior in poor years, Coastal traders regularly supplied Interior groups with fish and sea-mammal oils and other Coastal products. Salmon dried in the Interior is oil-poor because the fish have depleted their stores of fat during their lengthy migration upriver. For example, it is more than 1,100 kilometres up the Fraser to the spawning grounds in the northern Interior. These lean fish dry and store exceptionally well but lack nutrients needed to sustain people during the cold Subarctic winters. Interior game is also extremely lean and nutritionally inadequate for winter survival—it is literally possible to starve on a diet of such lean meats. Coastal salmon, on the other hand, is richer in oil, and even when caught in the river mouths or lower river courses (as most Aboriginal fisheries were), the product was relatively rich. This meant that it would not dry as well or last as long in storage, but it provided

halibut, half-dried salmon and (full-dried) salmon *wooks*, smoked cockles, seaweed, dentalia shells, and manufactured items such as rattles and kerfed boxes so perfectly constructed of single cedar planks bent to shape and pegged at the corner and bottom that the resulting box could hold water—or grease!

When Europeans entered the region they benefited from the Aboriginal trade and tried without success to take control of it. When the

more calories and essential nutrients. A supply of nutrient-rich oils from the coast formed an essential component of the Interior Aboriginal winter diet. The river corridors and grease trails were busy every year supplying this need, and traffic intensified in times of scarcity in the Interior.

The trade between the coast and Interior has gone on for millennia, and it was an essential factor in the cultural development of both Coastal and Interior peoples, who sustained relatively densely settled populations and complex cultural practices more common among agriculturalists while living as hunter–gatherers. Trade with Interior communities was a key part of the context in which Coastal cultures developed and flourished, elaborating their distinctive emphasis on ownership of territories and resources validated and dramatized through art, ceremony, and lavish distributions of wealth obtained through trade.

The complex cultural pattern of the Northwest Coast was developed only after salmon became established in the rivers, and the peoples of this region recognize and affirm the importance of these fish. People spoke of salmon respectfully, treated them with care as the source of well-being and wealth, and saw themselves as people whose entire lives were intertwined with the salmon. The territories of the Coastal nations yielded abundant harvests of many types of foods and materials used to manufacture such items as boxes, bowls, canoes, luxury goods, and tools. But the key resource, and the foundation of the wealth of the entire region, was salmon.

Ownership of the territories was vested in local corporate groups of kin; control of territories and access to resources was gained by inheritance of a ranked name/title among all the groups, and in some could also be obtained through marriage, as a gift, or as a prize of war. Inherited differences of rank associated with economic and supernatural privileges were substantial among all the groups. Chiefs, acting on behalf of their kin groups, had the power to allocate resources, command labour, make alliances, and even to take the life of a slave.

Shamans used both an extensive natural pharmacopoeia and supernatural abilities to cure illness. The natural remedies were potent, and the social cohesiveness created for a patient by the dramatic shamanic performances healed illness of the spirit as well.

The religious beliefs of all the groups emphasized contact with supernatural beings who controlled wealth, health, and life itself. Humans endeavoured to establish relationships with supernatural powers through ceremonial activities, notably ritual purifications, feasts, potlatches, and winter dance ceremonies. Ritual occasions drew on the power of the artistic traditions to create lavish events in which setting, costume, oral literature, drama, song, and dance expressed the profound spirituality that pervaded the cultures. Gift-giving feasts called potlatches manifested the wealth and power of the great chiefs, who had the ability to mediate with the supernatural powers. Winter ceremonial dances, often lasting months at a time, represented the supernatural forces that created order, brought wealth, and ensured the continuity of the group.

The intrusion of Europeans into the Northwest Coast brought few changes for the first 100 years from initial contact in the late eighteenth century. The early maritime explorers exchanged iron tools and other European goods for furs, foods, and Native artifacts, but did not seek to alter the pattern of Native cultures—indeed, the traders were heavily reliant on the Indigenous people for their own provisions as well as for furs. The first European goods obtained were integrated into the traditional cultures as prestige items and useful tools in Native technologies. But the explorers set the stage for more radical changes by demonstrating the potential profit to be made from the furs traded by the Coastal Natives, especially the fur of the sea otter, which could be sold for huge profits in China. A very busy maritime fur trade was quickly established, reaching its greatest magnitude in the decades around the beginning of the nineteenth century. The early nineteenth century saw the establishment of permanent trading posts along the coast, but the sea otter population was depleted by the 1830s. The trade shifted to other furs, many obtained from Interior groups, and the coast chiefs reaped large profits as shrewd middlemen. Though the profits of the trade were high, the cost was also great. A number of Old World diseases were introduced, taking a huge toll among the Native population. Smallpox, measles, venereal diseases, tuberculosis, and influenza swept through whole tribes, sometimes reducing the population to a small fraction of its former level. Unscrupulous traders anxious to obtain scarce furs traded alcohol and firearms, which made hostilities between traditional enemy groups much more lethal.

Even greater changes occurred as missionaries, adventurers, gold miners, and settlers entered the area in large numbers in the mid-nineteenth century. Many of the intruders had an exaggerated sense of the glories of "civilization" and little understanding of or tolerance for the complex cultures of Native people. Rights in land were not acknowledged, and resources were appropriated without apology. British Columbia entered Confederation in 1871, placing the Native population under the existing accretion of statutes relating to Indians, which in 1876 became the Indian Act, and small reserves were provided for each local group. In most cases the allocation was unilateral, involving little consultation and no agreement by the Native group. Though Native title had not been extinguished by any treaties or agreements (except for a few groups in the southern part of Vancouver Island), the province refused to enter negotiations to do so. A few groups pressed their claims repeatedly, notably the Nisga'a in the North. In 1973, the Nisga'a case was finally heard by the Supreme Court of Canada. Although the

decision was split, the federal government was forced by the narrowness of this decision, and by the implications of the case presented around the same time by the James Bay Cree, to recognize a continuing Native title. The *Delgamuukw* decision in 1997 clarified crucial questions, affirming that Aboriginal title, where it can be established in fact, is a living right that must be reconciled with Crown sovereignty. Most of the First Nations of BC have spent over a decade attempting to negotiate treaties based on Aboriginal claims to their traditional lands through the BC Treaty Process. The province is quite inflexible, however, and the process may prove extremely lengthy.

The extravagance of potlatches during the nineteenth century was often viewed with astonishment and dismay by outsiders, particularly those bent on fitting Native people into the mould of Victorian civilization. The disruption of traditional, established rank relationships among chiefs and the huge surplus of wealth that entered Native economies during the fur trade are now thought to have created stresses and imbalances in the traditional system, leading to lavish competitive potlatching as a way of re-establishing social order. Late in the nineteenth century the potlatch was outlawed by the Canadian government, causing it to go underground and curtailing the scale of the events. Masks and paraphernalia associated with the potlatches and winter ceremonials were confiscated, and fines and prison confinement were sometimes levied in an attempt to enforce the law. Despite almost universal conversion to various Christian denominations, the traditional functions of the feasts were continued by many groups through this period, and, with the dropping of the prohibition during the 1950s, the feasts and dances are once again public celebrations in many Native communities.

Native languages were vigorously suppressed by the agents of Dominion authority as well. Until the 1940s and even later in some areas, standard policy in many schools was to administer corporal punishment to pupils who spoke in their Native tongues. Inevitably, the policy succeeded, to the extent that there are now very few Native speakers under age 40 in any Northwest Coast language. Official policies and public attitudes have reversed, but unless the language programs now offered in schools are given much higher priority the languages will not long survive.

As the fur trade declined in significance and the economy of BC began to focus on the lumber industry and the commercial fishery, Native people on the coast continued to fish, hunt, trap, and engage in other traditional activities, but they also entered the new industries in substantial numbers. Native men fished commercially during the salmon runs while Native women worked long hours in the canneries scattered along the coast, to which entire families moved for several months of the year. The economic cycle of the developing resource industries was frequently boom/bust; labour shortages during the boom periods made entry into wage labour both easy and attractive for Natives, who made up a large proportion of the population of the province. The centralization of many industries and the rapid expansion of the immigrant settler population have pushed Natives out and decreased the significance of their participation in all industries.

The absolute number of Indians in BC fell during most of the nineteenth century, reaching a low point of under 25,000 in 1929. Though the Indian population is now greater than it was before initial contact, it constitutes less than 3 per cent of the population of the province. There are close to 200 bands in BC, most with memberships under 500 persons. The greatest proportion of the population is along the coast, as it was in Aboriginal times. About 50 per cent of registered Indians reside on reserves, which are the smallest in area per capita of any province. Each band is governed autonomously, with funding for some programs provided through the federal Department of Indian Affairs. In the last two decades, tribal associations have been formed in a number of areas on the coast, bringing together tribal or regional associations of bands to lobby and to provide a link in the administrative chain as the federal government attempts to devolve service delivery to local communities as well as to attempt to negotiate treaties. Economic development, improved facilities and educational opportunities, and the settlement of the land claims remain the primary focuses, as they have been for the past several decades.

REFERENCES

Carrothers, W.A. 1941. *The British Columbia Fisheries.* Political Economy Series 10. Toronto: University of Toronto Press.

Newell, D. 1997. *Tangled Webs of History: Indians and the Law in Canada's Pacific Coast Fisheries.* Toronto: University of Toronto Press.

CHAPTER 24

Understanding Tsimshian Potlatch

Margaret Seguin Anderson

Introduction

This chapter will focus on the Tsimshian feasts, which, with the feasts of the other Northwest Coast groups, are referred to as "potlatch."[1] Gift-giving feasts were widespread on the Northwest Coast at the time of contact and were sometimes very elaborate and lengthy during the nineteenth century. They continue to be an important focus and in the past three decades have increased in frequency and prominence. Although there have been numerous descriptions and analyses of such feasts, none seemed to provide an integrated account that "made sense" of either the traditional or the current Tsimshian feasts that I read about and saw. In particular, the literature gives little insight into the symbolic value of the actual events to the Tsimshian.

Accounts of traditional Tsimshian feasts have emphasized their importance in structuring social and economic relations, but have given little insight into the significance of details of the feasts, displays, and orations involved, into the logic or pattern of the symbols as selected and ordered in time and space, or into connections with the symbolic value of elements in other aspects of Tsimshian culture. I refer to these aspects of the feasts when I speak of the symbolic value of the actual events to the Tsimshian. I will attempt here to interpret Tsimshian feasts by tracing connections between

elements found in the feasts and other aspects of the culture. I focus on the relationships among Tsimshian belief in reincarnation, traditional attitudes toward other realms of power—including spirits, animals, and supernatural beings—and, most significantly, the relationship between an individual and his father's clan. The appreciation of these relationships makes the traditional potlatch of the Tsimshian understandable not only as a means of perpetuating a social structure but also as a viable economic system. Furthermore, the shape of the modern feast system and the significance of its continuity for over 200 years are clarified when seen in this context.

A Personal Note

The reader of an ethnographic essay may not always be aware that it is an intensely personal account, not an impersonal presentation of objective "facts." It is sometimes equally difficult for an author to convey effectively the extent to which her background, interests, and the history of her particular research effort have shaped the final presentation. The following personal information seems relevant here. I am not Tsimshian. I am a linguist by training. I taught in a department of anthropology for 19 years and then became the first chair of First Nations Studies at the newly established University of Northern British

Columbia. There I was able to help create a space in the curriculum for First Nations to develop an Indigenous scholarship, including courses on languages of the region (Haida, Tsimshian, Nisga'a, Gitksan, Haisla, Wetsuwet'en, Carrier, Ts'ilqot'in, and Cree). I began work on Tsimshian culture in the village of Hartley Bay, at the invitation of members of the community, to work with a local language program, and six years later married a man from the community; we were married for 20 years until his death in 2005. I recently retired as a professor at UNBC, living and working in Prince Rupert (where my late husband fished commercially). I work with language programs among the Tsimshian, Nisga'a, and Gitksan, and help coordinate a cohort of students who are preparing to teach Tsimshian culture and the Sm'algyax language.

As a linguist, I am concerned always with language, and most particularly with *meaning* in language; as a linguist who taught for many years in an anthropology department, I am concerned with meaningfulness of *cultural* phenomena. My approach to understanding the feast system starts from the assumption that the Tsimshian are not just "doing something" in the feasts, but that they are also "saying something." Trying to understand how the Tsimshian interpret the messages of feasts implies building a Tsimshian "cultural philology." One way to do this is to "deconstruct" meaning from context and exegesis, and then to "reconstruct" an enriched interpretation. Successive layers of such an interpretation act to focus understanding of the parts and the whole. Each fragment of information provides part of the interpretation for the others. This sort of approach is sometimes referred to as **hermeneutic**. It is an instance of a trend in the social sciences that Geertz describes: "many social scientists have turned away from the laws and instances ideal of explanation toward a cases and interpretation one, looking less for the sort of thing that connects planets and pendulums

and more for the sort that connects chrysanthemums and swords" (1980:19).

Constantly probing for meaning in the activities of anyone is occasionally disconcerting. The difficulties have been ameliorated in my work in Hartley Bay because the feast system is viewed as important and interesting there, and because I first met people in the village while I was working on their language program. Though I am not Tsimshian, being in a Tsimshian village feels comfortable, intellectually and practically. Sometimes, as a woman, I felt more at home in a place where women are relatively potent than I did in "my own" milieu at the university in the 1970s, where the power structure was generally overwhelmingly male. A past president (2000–2) of the Tsimshian Tribal Council is a woman, Deborah Jeffrey, who in 2011 was named to a national panel on Aboriginal education. The CEO of the Wilp Wilx̱o'oskwhl Nisga'a is also a woman, Deanna Nyce, with whom I have worked for 15 years developing programs and co-authoring several papers. In every Aboriginal community in this region, women hold positions of responsibility in education and social services and maintain strong roles in family and community activities. Tsimshian traditional practices that fostered strong matriarchs are being undermined steadily, however. Residence in nuclear families, band membership rules that long recognized links through males only for several generations, submersion as minorities in urban communities, and the imposition of education and religious institutions that denigrated matrilineal descent and succession have led to a lack of understanding of these institutions among many Tsimshian people, eroding the foundation of this aspect of the culture.

The research for this work included 5 years of intermittent residence in Hartley Bay over 15 years. During that time I sought an understanding of the nature of current feasts in that community and discussed oral traditions with many Elders, a number of whom have died in this time. I have also assembled recollections of activities in the community over the past 70 years. Textual material collected in Hartley Bay by William Beynon has provided some independent documentation from the 1940s and 1950s. Texts and descriptions of feasting traditions from other areas, especially Viola Garfield's ethnographic work at Port Simpson, have been consulted and discussed with community members, but most of the materials from other locales are considered foreign; similarities are seen as interesting, but do not compel integration.

The interpretation that follows is intensely local, in that the material from Hartley Bay vastly outweighs that from other communities and sources. Paradoxically, much of the locally derived interpretations should prove to hold in their general contours for other Tsimshian groups, as well as for the linguistically related Gitksan and Nisga'a. The material reveals patterns grounded in conventions of discourse and linguistic structure that were shared by all speakers of the Tsimshianic languages. These patterns constituted the process by which Tsimshian people defined "otherness" and "us-ness." They produced unique practices and the existing context in each locale, but I hope that the patterns themselves express some of the shared understandings that constitute the unique genius of Tsimshian culture.

The Context of the Study: The Tsimshian

Traditional Tsimshian chiefs conducted themselves with the formality and concern for protocol now associated with international diplomacy. Each territory was held to be a world apart, distinct in history, custom, and law; to enter the territory of another village (or even of another lineage segment) was to enter a foreign land. The inhabitants of each domain figured as reciprocal, symbolic "others," providing an important component of a view of the universe as a place of many worlds.

The people of each village emphasized the foreignness of outsiders by epithets (both polite and pejorative) and by descriptions of the exotic practices of each. Actual and classificatory kinship relationships penetrated the insularity of each village. Knowledge of other groups was often intimate and detailed. Ideas, customs, and objects moved easily between groups, but adoption of foreign customs was framed by the premise that, once adopted, the customs were no longer foreign; they were placed within the local meaning system. If a chief received a privilege such as a dance from a neighbouring chief, the privilege and the story of its acquisition became a part of the interpretative context for his own group—part of their story. If the other group understood it differently, that was the natural result of the foreignness. As long as each chief had a legitimate claim to use the privilege, interpretations were correct for respective worlds, and this would be affirmed at performances. The external form was shared, as was the understanding that allowed the local interpretations to coexist. Foreigners might be seen as capricious, and potentially dangerous, but not as wrong in being foreign.

Generalizations became broader as distance increased, and all the groups beyond the Northern Kwakiutl were merged as *didoo* ("people down south"). Details of shared kinship and history were known, but had to be constantly revitalized in order to continue to hold force in structuring interactions.

People who arrived late on the coast, and who seemed to live in ships rather than houses, became known as 'amsiwah, or "driftwood people"; their peculiarities became known far and wide, most notably the absence of women among them. The Tsimshian have come to know a great deal about the 'amsiwah, of course, and we have become a very significant "other" group for them; yet only occasionally have we 'amsiwah understood the Tsimshian in the context of the local meaning systems in which they continue to live.

The Tsimshianic Groups

The Tsimshianic-speaking peoples occupied territories along the Nass and Skeena rivers and their tributaries and estuaries, extending to the islands and coast to the south. There were four major linguistic divisions: the Nisga'a on the Nass; the Gitksan on the upper Skeena, above the canyon at Kitselas; the Coast Tsimshian on the lower reaches of the Skeena and the adjacent coast; and the Southern Tsimshian, who extended Tsimshian culture as far south as modern-day Klemtu.

The four Tsimshianic divisions were united by closely related languages. Boundaries between the divisions were marked by the linguistic patterns themselves, by distinctive ecological contexts in each division's territories and the annual cycles attuned to those contexts, by different emphases in ritual activities, and by the political context and relationships to foreign groups maintained by each. The boundaries were bridged by long-established travel and trade relations, intermarriage, feasting exchanges between certain chiefs, and occasional conflict.

There were up to four exogamous clans in each village, designated by the primary totemic crests of each: blackfish and grizzly bear, raven and frog, eagle and beaver, and wolf and bear.[2] A clan might include several distinct lines that traced origin to separate ancestors whose exploits were recounted in the lineage history; these lines maintained mutual exogamy but did not consider themselves directly related, and they sometimes hosted each other at feasts and in various ways interacted as mutual "others." The local segments of these lineages were the groups that held territories and feasted as units. Depending on the size of the local segment there might be one or more houses headed by chiefs who had inherited names carrying economic and ritual privileges. The chiefs had established relative ranks, which determined their right to precedence in political interactions.

The territories belonging to a local segment of a clan were administered by the chiefs, each of whom inherited control over a specific territory when he succeeded to the name of his maternal uncle. Women also held names of high rank, inherited from their own mothers and maternal aunts, but it was unusual for a woman to hold a territory-controlling name, though she might hold the privilege of managing certain resources such as berry-picking grounds. Generally, each clan represented in a village had control over sites for each type of available resources in the area, but one local lineage segment often held the highest-ranked names and controlled the bulk of the territory.

Large red-cedar plank dwellings housed each of the local lineage segments; if the group was large and several chiefs were of high rank there might be several such houses for a segment. The residents of each house were usually a group of men closely related through their mothers, with their wives, children, dependants, and slaves; such a group was the unit of production and consumption. The man bearing the highest-ranked name was deemed to be the owner of the house, but he took counsel with the holders of the other ranked names in making decisions about matters that bore implications for the power and prestige of the house. Matters of mutual interest, such as defence, were discussed with the chiefs of the other houses in the village as well. Succession to the highest-ranked names was a matter of concern to chiefs in other villages, and was validated by guests assembled from a wide area. Individuals who did not hold high-ranked names associated with territories could join one of the houses to which they were related.

All changes in social relationships were declared and legitimated by property distributions and feasts. The major focus of feasting among Tsimshian groups was the cycle that began with the death of a chief and culminated with the installation of his heir, usually the eldest son of his eldest

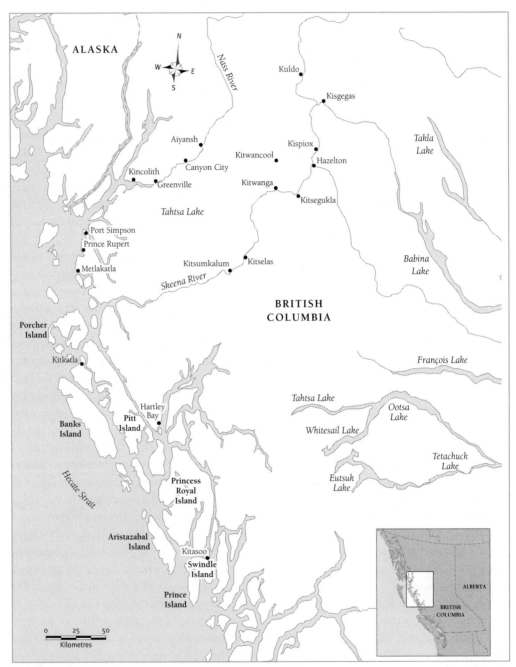

MAP 24.1 Tsimshian Communities (data from Duff 1959)

sister. The cycle typically included a memorial feast, the feasts associated with the erection of a memorial pole and the building of a new house, and the final feast of name assumption. When the deceased was the head of a local lineage, guests were generally invited from all groups with which political relationships were maintained. The prestige of the local lineage and the maintenance of its economic and political power were dependent on the success of events, including distribution of sufficient wealth to demonstrate control over territories.

Chiefs were responsible for relationships with other villages and with foreign tribes such as the Haida, Tlingit, and Haisla. They also bore responsibility for keeping their group in balance with the supernatural beings who controlled the continuation of food and wealth. Each lineage had inherited relationships to supernatural beings encountered by the original holders of their names. Animal species such as bear, salmon, seal, and mountain goat were governed by their own chiefs, who demanded proper respect. Named locations were also occupied by powerful supernatural beings who controlled the continuation of the wealth of an area and the safety and success of those who visited. Accounts of ancestral interactions with supernatural beings were an integral part of the assumption of a ranked name. Such events were depicted by the crests that were carved and painted on houses, poles, and specific household goods of each chief; some powers might also be dramatized in performances, which involved masks, costumes, songs, and dances exclusively owned by the lineage. Some of these crest privileges were common to all members of a lineage; others were restricted to those holding a particular, highly ranked name.

Winter ceremonial performances and dances brought supernatural powers into the Tsimshian worlds. The old Tsimshian form of winter ceremonial was the *halayt*, which was firmly integrated into the rank structure. Chiefs controlled supernatural power for the people, manifesting their abilities in dramatizations of a special set of names. A series of four winter ceremonial dances had apparently been entering the Tsimshian system via the Northern Kwakiutl connections at Kitimat and Bella Bella in the late pre-contact period. Two of these were open to all ranks, but two were restricted to particular chiefs.

Another form of relationship with supernatural power was the province of the ritual specialists known as shamans, some of whom were also chiefs. Shamans practised several sorts of healing based on the Tsimshian understandings of the nature of illness. Part of the responsibility was to combat the effects of witchcraft, which was surreptitiously practised by disaffected individuals.

The material culture of the Tsimshian was a magnificent manifestation of this intricate, coherent, symbolic vision. The privilege of owning and displaying many treasures was restricted to those with sufficient rank to respect them properly by distributing property; other items were limited to those with supernatural powers, such as shamans and members of secret societies. The large houses were carved and painted with designs representing the crests of the house owner, fronted with complex poles erected in honour of past chiefs. Everyday objects such as clothing, baskets, canoes, fish hooks, and storage boxes were finely made, frequently displaying complex symbolic decoration. The sculptural style of Tsimshian carvers has been acclaimed, and their creations were sought by other groups during traditional times as avidly as by modern collectors.

The relationships of the Tsimshian to the land, to their neighbours, to supernatural beings, and even to themselves were ultimately radically transformed by the intrusion of Europeans and Euro-Canadians. Initial contacts with explorers and maritime traders did not undermine the traditional patterns; the goods received in trade were incorporated into cultures as useful items in traditional technologies or as prestige items in the system of crest privileges. But sea otter furs proved to be tremendously valuable and led to the rapid development of a maritime trade. The sea otter was brought to the edge of extinction within five decades. The trade shifted to land furs, which the Tsimshian acquired by direct trapping and by controlling the trade of Interior groups, reaping large profits as middlemen.

A land-based trading post was established by the Hudson's Bay Company in Tsimshian territory at the mouth of the Nass River in 1831 and moved in 1834 to Fort Simpson (later Port Simpson, now Lax Kw'alaams). The chiefs who controlled the trade became even wealthier, and the nineteenth century was probably the period of greatest opulence for the Tsimshian. Huge amounts of wealth entered the Native economy and a ready supply of iron tools allowed the carvers to reach even higher standards and greater productivity. At the same time, established relationships of rank were destabilized by new aggregations around the trading post, which brought together chiefs who had not previously had stable political relationships through the feast system. There were extraordinary mortality rates because of diseases such as smallpox, measles, influenza, and venereal infections. Frequent deaths encouraged the promotion of multiple claims as names became vacant, leading to some competitive potlatching.

Other influences entered the area. In 1857 a lay preacher for the Church Missionary Society named William Duncan came to Fort Simpson. He began by learning the language of the Coast Tsimshian; he was ultimately to convert most of the Coast Tsimshian people and to build a new community

FIGURE 24.1 Metlakatla, BC, showing the eastern portion of Metlakatla with cannery buildings on the left. (Image HP 55799 courtesy of Royal BC Museum, BC Archives)

with them at Metlakatla, a traditional Coast Tsimshian site. Metlakatla was a great success, and nearby groups actively sought missionization.

Duncan fought the *halayt*, but awarded various badges and the insignia of new power that replaced it, so that the Tsimshian church became in effect a Tsimshian institution. Church activities, hymn singing, participation in brass bands, sports days, village offices, and clubs were all enthusiastically embraced by the Tsimshian who joined Duncan. Shamanic healing was denounced, but Duncan made available substitute services, and the use of traditional medicines not accompanied by ritual performance was not prohibited. Duncan did not forbid the telling of stories, and he was of the opinion that several demonstrated knowledge of the Flood and other biblical events. Property distributions for display were denounced, but Duncan himself obliged the same rank system by granting positions of authority to chiefs in the new community structure and by collecting property and redistributing some of it through the chiefs. Duncan did assign English-type last names, which were transmitted patrilineally, but did not forbid the remembrance and transmission of Tsimshian names, nor apparently of feasts at which they were bestowed, as long as the format included Christian prayers and distribution of presents only as payments. The chiefs also had leading roles as public speakers and as Duncan's counsellors. Duncan's intransigence was difficult for many of the church workers who came to work with him, but it was quite consonant with the behaviour the Tsimshian expected of a chief. A Christian Tsimshian social pattern was forged from the desire of the Tsimshian to retain their territories and power and from Duncan's visionary Christianity.

Duncan stayed at Metlakatla for 25 years, drawing increasing numbers to the village and the Christian Tsimshian life. Duncan became hugely influential because of his great success, but he never lost his intransigence in the face of what he saw as error. This led him into difficulties with authorities in the church; in 1887 he left to start a New Metlakatla in Alaska, with more than 800 Tsimshian people. The land to which they moved was far from traditional territories they had continued to use for hunting or fishing, and many firm converts chose to remain in BC. Old Metlakatla reverted to a small village, and the populations of other villages were restored.

During the late nineteenth century the Tsimshian saw an influx of gold-seekers, adventurers, and a few settlers. By then the Aboriginal nations were no longer treated as sovereign. When British Columbia entered Confederation, small reserves were allocated to each village, and the Tsimshian groups came under the provisions of the Indian Act without ever having signed treaties; none of the groups have abandoned claims to their traditional territories. The Nisga'a pressed their Aboriginal claim with tenacity, leading the government at one point to pass a law forbidding the raising of funds to finance such activities. The Nisga'a claim was finally heard by the Supreme Court of Canada. Despite an ambiguous decision issued in 1973, the case was one of the major factors that set the stage for serious negotiations between the federal and provincial governments and the First Nations of British Columbia. The current British Columbia Treaty Process has roots in these events, and in 2000 the Nisga'a at last achieved their Final Agreement, which included land, cash compensation, and extensive self-government powers.

The Tsimshianic languages were used during initial missionization but were suppressed by later missionaries, educators, and administrators. Southern Tsimshian is now extinct. There are few speakers of the other Tsimshianic languages under the age of 40. Official suppression of the languages has been abandoned, but they are unlikely to continue as living systems unless they are given substantial artificial support. While positive steps have been initiated, the revitalization of these languages is not yet a policy priority and few resources have been allocated.

The Tsimshian participated actively in the development of the modern economy of their homeland. Their success in the commercial fishery is particularly notable, but the Tsimshian people also made contributions in areas such as logging, transportation, and commerce.

The Symbolic Structure of the Traditional Tsimshian *Yaawk*

The preceding section has established a context. In this section I weave threads between some traditional Tsimshian religious premises and symbolic association and the traditional *yaawk* as the central Tsimshian social institution. The model of symbolic analysis has its roots in philology, as discussed above. Because of constraints on length, three sections of the argument are presented in précis; the fourth section is presented in greater detail to illustrate the sort of evidence available.

1. The Symbolism of the House

The Tsimshian local matriclan, which was the functioning feast group, was a *waap* ("house"). A house is symbolically a box, a container. Persons were not *in* a *waap*, they *were* the *waap*.

The matrilineage is imaged as a house, which is a container motif, like a box containing preserved food and/or wealth. The participants in

---

BOX 24.1 First Nations Language Revitalization

The 28 First Nations languages indigenous to BC represent six distinct language families. All are seriously endangered, and some languages have already been extirpated. The federal and provincial governments have spent well over $3 billion building and maintaining beautiful museums such as the Canadian Museum of Civilization and the Royal British Columbia Museum to store and display artifacts from Aboriginal cultures. During 2007, funding for First Nations language retention and revitalization programs in BC from all sources amounted to less than one-tenth of 1 per cent of that. The Assembly of First Nations is seeking support from government for new legislation that would provide protection and support for the languages of the First Nations, including official language status and stable funding for documentation, development of curricula, and a range of language learning programs. There have been some positive initiatives spearheaded by local First Nations. They include immersion schools, such as a short-lived one at Gitwangak. Language and culture adult immersion programs are offered through the Secwépemc Cultural Education Society (SCES). A new Developmental Standard Term Certificate in First Nations Language and Culture program for language teachers was approved by the BC College of Teachers, and several groups have pursued this route to prepare certified teachers of their languages. University courses in 14 languages are offered for credit by the University of Northern British Columbia, and in 6 languages through the SCES program partnership with Simon Fraser University. Despite all these efforts, however, the erosion of Indigenous languages seems inexorable, and will only be reversed through a determined—and well-funded—long-term struggle.

a feast are assigned places within the house. The feast "empties" the house. Houses are much like persons; built by father's clan, named at a potlatch after the building, and carved and painted with the crests of the lineage (Garfield 1939:276). In fact, the significant "members" of the lineage are not particular individuals but the "social persons" of the ranked names. Individuals are required to carry the names, but the structure of the lineage is the structure of the names. From this perspective individuals are indeed contained, *in* a name. This interpretation of the significance of containers is quite different from that in work developed from a psychoanalytic perspective (Dundes 1979; Fleisher 1981), which suggested that the potlatch on the Northwest Coast was a manifestation of "anal erotic character traits."

The Tsimshian see themselves as forming the container, rather than as being inside it; their concern is not with excretion per se, but with the restoration of real beings to their proper worlds and with the preparation of an "empty container" ready to receive new wealth.

2. "Real" People

A *waap* includes individuals who were more or less "real." A "real" person (*Sm'ooygit*, "chief") held a high name, passed to him or her matrilineally; each name was associated with an origin story, crests, songs, dances, and economic powers. Becoming "real" depended on lifelong participation in the property distributions at *yaawk*. Relations between groups, whether human villages or different species, were mediated by their respective real people.

That *Sm'ooygit* literally translated as "real person" has often been noted. "Reality" in this sense means "exemplary," but this is not an absolute quality. It should be seen as a cline: slaves are outside the cline; commoners are less real than chiefs; chiefs can be ranked from less to more real. Real animals can appear in human form in the human world. Occasions are also more and less real; real occasions are those in which real beings interact, altering the world. Real people were those who had been "shown to the people" and "pushed up" since childhood; who had "fed the people" by giving feasts and distributing property; who had "put

FIGURE 24.2 High-ranking Gitksan women dressed in ceremonial regalia that includes frontlets, Chilkat blankets, and dance aprons, 1910. (Image PN 3929 courtesy of Royal BC Museum, BC Archives)

on a name" entitling them to social and economic prerogatives; who "could talk to people"; and those whose conduct, particularly on "real" occasions, affected the entire lineage.

Communication and negotiation within and among human groups was channelled through these real people. Decisions within a *waap* were made by the ranking name-holder with the support and advice of his councillors. If there were several houses in a local clan, the ranking members of each, led by the highest-ranking name-holder, managed the affairs of the local clan. Relations between local clans were arranged by the highest-ranking persons in the village, in consultation with advisors and with the consent of the ranking name-holders from the other local clans. Consent was given by participating in public feasts and ceremonies at which decisions, particularly concerning successions to names, were announced. Relations with other Tsimshian groups, including trade, marriage, and settlement of disagreements, were similarly channelled through the real people, usually the highest-ranked name-holder(s). Relations with non-Tsimshian, including notably the Nisga'a and the Gitksan (speakers of Tsimshianic languages, but not called Tsimshian), Haida, Tlingit, and Northern Kwakiutl groups, were essentially "royal affairs." These interactions were particularly delicate, even potentially violent if mishandled. Apparently the early missionaries and traders were also thought to be "real." Collison (1915:9) mentions that "in the spring (April) of 1860, Mr. Duncan first visited the Nass River. He was well received at the lower villages, where several of the chiefs feasted him and gave him presents of furs."

Since the real people were responsible for dealing with other groups for the entire constituency (house, lineage, village), their conduct was important to the group. Failure of any sort was an indication that standards were not being maintained. Failure in fishing or hunting demonstrated that real people among the animals were not prepared to acknowledge the claims of the human group. A wound or an accident signalled a loss of prestige and potency—if relations with other powers were correct then the accident would not have occurred. Generally, when an accident happened to a real person, distributions of property served to inform other real beings that any defect had been remedied and were a part of a cure, along with increased self-discipline. The person was said to "wash" by making these distributions. Failure to be treated appropriately at a feast (being called later than appropriate, or given less than proper in relation to others) also had to be answered—otherwise it was evident that the individual or group belonged to the level accorded them, and the prestige of the person slighted was actually diminished. Since such a loss of power would affect the individual's influence with all other real beings and reflect on *all* members of the lineage, demands for rightful recognition were not mere self-aggrandizement.

Individuals with more reality were more potent. Relations with beings in all worlds were required, and these were mediated by the real beings. Interaction of a real being entailed simultaneous effects on the less real beings under his sway—for example, if the chief of the spring salmon willingly entered a river where fishermen were waiting, so would his tribe.

3. Animal People

In addition to the Tsimshian tribes and other human groups they were acquainted with, Tsimshian recognized other societies. Each animal species had its own village, with "real people," commoners, and slaves, similar to Tsimshian villages. Food animals came to the Tsimshian by the animals' own consent, directed by their chiefs. There were also villages for human ghosts, with similar social structure. However, spirits of both animals and humans were subject to reincarnation.

Actions taken on animal bodies in human villages influenced the animals in their own villages. Complete, respectful consumption of animal bodies was required to ensure the health of the animals. Proper reincarnation among humans was dependent on human feasting. The consequences of actions in one domain could be observed in the others. Real animals in their villages were aware of actions taken by humans; human shamans were especially adept at perceiving other worlds.

Whether we interpret them as literal or metaphoric statements, their myths indicate that traditional Tsimshian did not view the universe anthropocentrically: They were aware of parallel worlds, some inhabited by animal people and some by supernatural powers, as exemplified in the story of "The Prince Who Was Taken Away by the Salmon People" (Boas 1916:192 et seq.), which also shows the way in which actions in one world had consequences in the others. The story tells us that a young prince who had taken a bit of dried salmon from his mother's box to feed a slave during a famine was taken by the salmon to their village. The salmon village had houses carved with figures of spring salmon, the largest inhabited by the old chief of the spring salmon, who had been ill with palsy for two years:

The sick chief ordered his attendants to spread mats at one side of a large fire. They did so. Then the Prince went and seated himself on the mats which had been spread for him by the chief's attendants. As soon as he was seated on a mat, behold! An old woman came to his side, who touched him, and said, "My dear Prince!" Then she questioned him. "Do you know who brought you here?" The prince replied, "No"—"The Spring Salmon have brought you here, for their chief has been sick with palsy for over two years.

When you unfolded the salmon the other day, the chief got a little better because you did so."

Though the other worlds were very like the world of the Tsimshian, there were also clear refractions of structure. In their domain, animals perceived themselves as human and perceived humans as powers or foreigners (never, apparently, as food animals). The salmon come to the world of the Tsimshian to fish for their own salmon, which are to us the leaves of the cottonwood tree, and while there, their salmon bodies are food in turn for the Tsimshian. As long as the proper respect was shown to the salmon caught, as long as the fish was completely consumed (and any bones, etc. burned afterward, or returned to the water), the salmon would return.

Each world (each village) was as "real" as the others. Relations between each village/world were the particular responsibility of the real people and the real beings, and also shamans, who were especially adept at discerning the state of affairs of other worlds and at negotiating with them, frequently being given tokens of supernatural power from other worlds. A real person who put on a high name was connected to other worlds through the tokens of contacts with real beings made by his predecessors in that name—tokens such as songs, dances, crests, and power. These treasures and potent connections were maintained in perpetuity by the feast system.

Among these other worlds were villages of ghosts. Although the details of the traditional understanding of reincarnation are no longer clear, the concept is still firmly held in Hartley Bay, and evidence from the Gitksan suggests that in Aboriginal times the parallel to the worlds of the animal people was close. That is, a baa'lx (person reincarnated) also preferred to come back to a person who is generous at feasts.

4. Fathers, Feasts, and Naming Ceremonies

Tsimshian saw symbolic associations between fathers, foreigners, animals, and the supernatural. A father contributed food to his wife and children, members of a *waap* different from his own, as animals fed their bodies to humans, who lived in a world other than their own. Just as the real animal remained in its own village, the reality of a father remained a part of his own *waap*. Members of the father's clan had special ritual duties to a child and were paid by the child's matriclan for these duties at feasts.

Though the most significant category of kinship relations for Tsimshian was the matrilineal clan to which an individual belonged, the *ksi'waatk* ("where you come from," your father's side) was extremely significant in an individual's life as well. The name given to a child was supposed to have been selected from a set of names belonging to the matrilineage, but it should also have reference to the side of the father. Throughout life, services were performed by "father's side," or "father's sisters," including the naming of the child, piercing of ears, birthing, mourning, and all medical treatment. Services such as house-building and pole- and canoe-carving were also to be purchased from the father's clan. In turn, an individual returned respect to the father's side—"paying" when a crest of the father's side was displayed, giving food to a member of the father's clan who returned blankets or other goods to the giver, being supported by a member of the father's side in some dances, and paying for the many services provided. By a careful comparative analysis of kin terminologies from Tsimshian, Haida, and Tlingit, Dunn (1984:5) established several symbolic associations:

> From the Tsimshian perspective a set of binary opposition serves to set the Haida and the Tlingit apart. . . . The Haida are symbolic male, while the Tlingit are symbolic female. The Haida are elder, the Tlingit younger. The Haida are animal, supernatural, and unfamiliar, while the Tlingit are human and "known," i.e. related. For the Tsimshian the Haida are "father" while the Tlingit are "little sister."

The association of fathers with supernaturals, animals, and foreigners (Haida especially) allowed the Tsimshian to maintain reciprocal relations with supernaturals and animals in their own world through feasts and payments made to the father's side. Powers, good relations with animal real people, and success were gifts from the supernatural—first received from a supernatural father, then passed on matrilineally. The father/benefactor is inevitably located by the end of the story in a different world/village than the child/receiver, who has a token of the gift embodied in a name, story episode, song, dance, crest object, and so on. (There are few Tsimshian tales of human males marrying supernatural women, and none that I know of resulted in children; in a matrilineal system, children of such a union would not, of course, be Tsimshian anyway.) The continued potency of the gift from the supernatural father was contingent on a continued relationship with the benefactor in the other world.

The establishment of payments and services also allowed for clear delineation of rights in persons, despite mixed residence patterns. Since any service performed by a member of a person's father's lineage was promptly and publicly paid for by members of the mother's lineage, there was a clear statement of group affiliation. Each residence unit necessarily included members of other clans, but even a long-term resident belonging to another clan was an outsider, while a visitor from an allied house/clan from a distant village was immediately accorded a place fitting his or her status.

The traditional feast system was central as the context for keeping and building relations of power. The names were an incarnation of powers that were socially manipulable. One interesting possibility is that the guests at a *yaawk* might have been receiving food and gifts in an inversion of the bestowal of gifts by non-human real beings, in fact, instead of those beings. Gifts from the non-human real beings included food, wealth, and crests. Since gifts must be publicly acknowledged, and eventually the giver should become a receiver, by their participation in feasts the hosts (real human beings) keep relations of power and dependence valid with the other real beings (represented by real human beings who were guests, instead of real beings from other worlds).

As animal food had to be consumed for animals in their villages to be reincarnated and healthy, humans had to "eat" the wealth held in a lineage for more wealth to return. This was particularly important at death, which was the centre of Tsimshian feast activity. By feasting, in which one's father's clan received wealth, the integrity of power in other worlds was ensured and future wealth for the clan was possible. Wealth was returned to enable future wealth, as animal food was consumed to ensure future reincarnated animals. One effect of the feast, then, was to return substance accumulated in a *waap* to the fathers, reuniting the fathers' substance with their own reality, which is part of their own matrilineal *waap*.

Payments for services and gifts were given throughout life. The great potlatches were generally given at the time of assumption of a name at the death of one's predecessor (usually mother's brother). Contributions to this endeavour were collected from all members of one's group. The guests were persons of sufficient reality from other clans in the same village, other Tsimshian villages, and foreign groups. Property was distributed according to the rank of the guests as payment for specific services performed (burial, putting on a name, carv-

ing a pole, etc.) and for validating the *yaawk* by attending. The clan was in fact emptying its wealth to its fathers, since the services were performed by the members of father's clan, and since classificatory kinship terminology made brothers and sisters of clan members; each of the guests was *ksi'waatk* to the host or his siblings, all of whom contributed to the feast. By giving to fathers the clan is simultaneously giving to the supernatural animals with whom fathers are symbolically associated, thus restoring their (the supernatural animals') worlds by reuniting substance with reality.

If the *yaawk* centred on emptying a clan after the death of a name-holder, it simultaneously was involved with the filling of the name by the incarnation of a new name-holder, who had the responsibility to "bury" his predecessor in the name and was thus generally the host of the event. It is by understanding this that we can understand why the clan had to be emptied. Just as a hunter had to be clean—to fast and purge himself—before hoping to encounter animals, a new name-holder came to the supernatural full of things acquired by his predecessor through his connection to the same supernatural, holding part of the substance of the supernatural that had never been restored; the feast restored this substance so it could be re-acquired.

If the term "incarnation" for the elevation of the new name-holder is taken seriously, it may be useful to see the assumption of the name as the final stage in the reincarnation that was begun at birth. The services of naming performed by the father's clan make it likely that this is appropriate, as does the comparison with the closely related Gitksan, who make it explicit that a person should take the name of his or her *baa'lx*. If this was indeed the final step in reincarnation, it is interesting to recall the story of "The Princess Who Rejected Her Cousin" (Boas 1916:185 et seq.). The relevant material is too long for quotation, but a general summary with a few quotations is necessary to show its significance for the argument to be developed (my summary notes are in square brackets):

A very long time ago there was a great village with many people. They had only one chief. There was also his sister. They were the only two chiefs in the large town. The chief also had a beautiful daughter, and the chief's sister had a fine son. . . . they expected that these two would soon marry. . . . the girl rejected the proposal. . . . but the young prince loved her very much, and still she refused him. . . . the princess wanted to make a fool of her cousin. . . . [she led him on, and asked him to show his love, first by cutting his cheeks, and by cutting off his hair—which was dishonourable as a mark of a slave. He did as she wished, but then she rejected him and mocked him]. . . . "Tell him that I do not want to marry a bad-looking person like him, ugly as he is;" and she gave him the nickname Mountain with Two Rock Slides, as he had a scar down each cheek. . . . the prince was so ashamed and left his village with a companion. . . . he came to a narrow trail and went along it, finally meeting an old woman in a hut who knew him and his story. She told him he would come to the house of Chief Pestilence, and told him how to behave so that Chief Pestilence would make him beautiful. The prince did as she told him and became as beautiful as a supernatural being. . . . when he came back his companion was just bones, but he took him to Chief Pestilence and he was also made beautiful. . . . they returned to their own village. . . . the princess wanted to marry him. . . . he then mocked her. . . . she went with a companion. . . . they met a man who asked them which way they

intended to go, and the princess told him they were going to see Chief Pestilence. . . . She passed by him, and did not look at him, for she was ashamed to let anyone look at her. . . . [They got to Chief Pestilence's house, but with no counsel such as the young man had received, she went to all the maimed people in the house who called her, and was maimed and bruised they eventually returned to their own village, where the princess lay in bed, and finally died.]

This story may be interpreted as a story of two types of death and reincarnation, one proper and the other socially censured. If the relationship between the prince and the princess is remembered, it will be apparent that the young man who "went away" (died) had behaved properly in life, and we may assume that the old woman whom he encountered on his path represented his father's clan aiding him in the other world. The young woman, on the other hand, had humiliated the prince, *the son of her father's sister* (who was the person who would ordinarily help at the burial, mourn, and participate in a mortuary feast as a guest). She met with no helpful guide on her travels; she did encounter a man, who may have been a representative of her father's side, but he offered no counsel because she was too ashamed to talk to him. If this interpretation is accurate, it establishes the central symbolic nexus or rationale for the feasting of the Coast Tsimshian, which primarily centred on the mortuary feast and the elevation of an heir: *to make it possible for the lineage members to be reincarnated properly.*

Several expressions and customs in current use are clarified in the context of this interpretation. First, people who are more real are *ksi'waatk* to a wider group of people. "Big" people thus provide services to and receive gifts and payments from more people. This was apparently also true in the past; Boas indicated rules for the "support" of dancers (1916:512) that show a much wider group of people treated a person with a big name as *ksi'waatk*. In certain dances it was (and is) necessary for onlookers to hold up dancers. Each dancer is supported by a noble who is of the same clan as the father of the dancer—so that during an encounter with the supernatural in this world, one is supported by one's *ksi'waatk*, who also supported one in such an encounter in other worlds, helping one to be properly restored to this world. The more real a person, the more potent was the connection with supernatural.

Another example of a current usage both is clarified in this context and contributes to an understanding of the traditional symbolism: if a person makes a gift of food to another and then eats from the gift, it is said that "You'll get sores." The process of "incarnation" may have been continuous, requiring constant good relations with supernaturals. This would explain the emphasis put on "washing" if a real person had an accident or made a mistake, and the expectation that real people should be physically without defect. One washed away shame by distributing property, usually to *ksi'waatk*. The vilest insult that could be hurled by a traditional Tsimshian was that a person was *wah'a'yin*, or "his scabs don't heal" (the literal translation is "without healing"). In English texts this is glossed as "without origin" or "having no relatives." These two glosses may imply that such a person had no *ksi'waatk* to provide treatment for injuries in return for payment, and, perhaps in the light of the argument above, that there was also no supernatural connection to give potency to the person's name—that, in fact, the person was not real.

The Tsimshian knew that they were real and that their villages were real. No place was at the centre of the Tsimshian universe, but all places are equally centres. The Tsimshian also knew that they had a duty to partake of the gifts received from other worlds and to return gifts to those worlds through their fathers, who connected them to those other worlds.

Modern Feasts

Although one of the most significant functions of the inter-tribal feasts was the protection of territories, the real threat to Tsimshian territorial sovereignty after the middle of the nineteenth century did not come from other Tsimshian or Native groups but from the encroachment of white resource appropriation and settlement and the failure of the province to acknowledge the validity of the original ownership. The set of "others" to be considered in the world has shifted so that the most significant rival is Canadian society at large. The patterns of asserting claims vis-à-vis the new power remained within the Tsimshian tradition. Councils of chiefs drew from all tribes, forming organizations to press land claims and other crucial issues. One of the most significant organizations was the Native Brotherhood of British Columbia, which held its first meeting in Port Simpson on 15 December 1931. Delegations from Masset, Hartley Bay, Kitkatla, Port Essington, and Metlakatla attended. By 1936 the efforts of such active organizers as Chief Heber Clifton of Hartley Bay and Chief Edward Gamble of Kitkatla had brought in branches from Vanarsdale, Klemtu, Bella Bella, Kitimat, Kispiox, Kitwanga, Skeena Crossing, and Hazelton.

The Local Context: The Gitga'ata

The modern Tsimshian village of Hartley Bay is located at the entrance of the Douglas Channel in the southern portion of Tsimshian territory. The village was established in 1887 by a small group of people who had their traditional territories in the same general region, centring on their winter village, about 19 kilometres north of the present village.

From the 1860s to the 1880s the Gitga'ata joined the mission village of Metlakatla, probably residing there in the winter and travelling to their own territories for the balance of the annual cycle. When Duncan left Metlakatla to begin his community again in Alaska, the founders of Hartley Bay established a new permanent village in their own territories. This village was strict, as Duncan might have wished. From the beginning the community defined itself as a progressive, Christian, Tsimshian village, with equal emphasis on each aspect of the definition. A council of chiefs wielded a firm hand over all aspects of daily life in Hartley Bay during its early decades, and all Duncan's rules were enforced until the middle of the twentieth century, when curfews and Sunday work prohibitions were relaxed.

The first reserves for the village were allocated in 1889, with additional allocations by the Royal Commission on Indian Affairs in 1916. The chiefs at Hartley Bay steadfastly refused to participate in the process, insisting instead on a settlement of their title to their entire traditional territory, which the commission would not discuss. At the present time the village of Hartley Bay is engaged in the land-claims process with the other Coast and Southern Tsimshian villages.

Feasting was apparently continued without interruption. Recollections of Elders from Hartley Bay indicate a firmly ensconced modern feast tradition early in this century. The feasts were of the sort considered respectable by Duncan; they still begin with prayers. The feasts given were solemn at funerals and had a lighter tone when the occasion was not so serious. The person who was to inherit a name generally "buried" his uncle, including sponsoring the memorial feast and paying the members of the father's side who had prepared the body and supplied the coffin. Marriages were arranged by families, in some cases as late as the 1960s, and generally they still maintain clan exogamy or include a clan-adoption process to maintain the formal structure of exogamy.

Traditionally, the names within a clan were ranked; the relative rank was displayed most prominently at feasts, when guests were seated in positions according to rank. The convention of recognizing the highest-ranked chief in the strongest clan in a tribe as the chief of the village was shared by all the Coast Tsimshian villages and is followed at Hartley Bay at the present time; the hereditary chief of the Gitga'ata is Wah'modm, the highest name of the Blackfish. Within each clan there is a recognition that lesser names were also traditionally ranked among themselves, but little regular use is now made of these relative rankings.

The interpretation of traditional feasts offered above was that they were a mode of discourse, a way of creating messages and expressing the social order to members of the group and to other groups. The organization of the feast discourse conforms to conventions of discourse structure observed in some conversations at the present time in Hartley Bay. Very briefly, the convention is that the event (conversation or feast) cannot end until consensus is reached and overtly expressed. In the conversations to which it applies, this means that a listener can subtly compel modifications in a statement by declining to provide a supportive closure to the conversation; in feasts, it means that the appropriate guest must be present and participate for the feast to fulfill its function.

The discourse convention includes the understanding that it is inappropriate to hold discussions with persons who do not have a proper authority to speak on a matter. It was manifested in the dealings of the Gitga'ata with the Royal Commission on Indian Affairs, which visited Hartley Bay in 1913. "The Indians were asked to give testimony as to the character of the reserve, population, etc., but they flatly refused to do so" (Campbell 1984:27). Eventually, a request for lands was submitted by a missionary in the village.

The current feasts at Hartley Bay continue to function as discourses, following the traditional

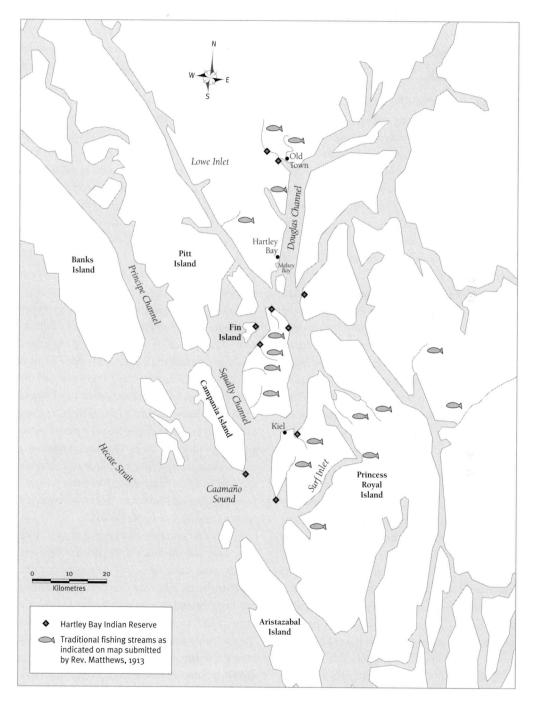

MAP 24.2 Fishing Sites in the Territory of the Gitga'ata

patterns. However, the discourse currently gains interpretation in the historical and structural context in which the Tsimshian are now placed.

A Unique Feast

The Raven Feast of Chief Billy Clifton, on 2 January 1980, was in many ways typical of current feasts at Hartley Bay, but in a few respects it was a unique event. The feast was hosted by the late Billy Clifton, who was ranked as the highest resident chief of the Raven clan in Hartley Bay. The most unusual feature of this event was the adoption by Mr Clifton of his uncle, Chief John Clifton, as a member of the Raven clan.

Ordinary feasts are based on a well-understood pattern in which the guests ratify the acts of hosts. Their presence is an acknowledgement of the right of the host clan to present their claims. Implicit in the Raven Feast of Chief Billy Clifton was a violation of these expectations. It was not an ordinary right of the Ravens to take a member of the Eagle or Blackfish clan as a member (and Chief John Clifton was already a member of both these clans, having been born an Eagle and adopted by his own father to be a Blackfish). This adoption was extraordinary and required explicit affirmation to be successful.

The process of adopting Chief John Clifton and putting a Raven name on him was marked by several modifications of ordinary feast procedures. The primary orator for the Raven clan, the late Ernest Hill Sr, delivered a prologue speech, which "made sense" of the adoption. He addressed the concerns of the Ravens, indicating that the new Raven would help their clan, and he made explicit claim that the adoption would make all the clans work together and was good for the entire village, including the Blackfish and Eagles.

The adoption allows Ravens to put claims on John Clifton, thus potentially infringing on the exclusive claims of the Eagles and the Blackfish. In ordinary feasts, the clan of the father is asked to put the name on the individual. The namers are then paid off, which gives the father's clan restitution for the service, as well as for raising the child. The adoption of Chief John Clifton as a Raven, and the putting on of his Raven name, was performed by members of both the Eagle and Blackfish clans. They thus showed that they were willing to share rights in him with the Ravens. The involvement of both clans in this adoption makes it clear that the namers are *ksi'waatk*, not only in the sense of the father's clan but in the more general sense of "where you come from." Chief John Clifton was being taken from both the Eagle and the Blackfish clans, and members of both ratified the adoption by participating.

This feast, then, presented a new kind of claim couched in a traditional form; a "new tradition" has been forged. This new tradition celebrates the unity among members of the village and it is incarnate in the person of the chief who participated in all three clans. Symbolically, three have become one, and low has become high. I have couched the process in these terms deliberately because I would argue that the symbolism is distinctly Christian, not as a replacement of traditional symbols but as an interpretation of them. Christian symbols are the sensible interpreters of traditional Tsimshian symbols in this village, which has never wavered from the Christian Tsimshian course set when the people came back from Metlakatla.

The new structure has appeal at this time, particularly for members of the Hartley Bay community who were not tightly integrated into the traditional rank hierarchy. The privilege of names has been extended to most members of the village, but the stock of ranked names is running out. The late Chief John Clifton was perhaps the only member of the community who could have creatively re-formed symbolic structures in this way. The political context of the village now is a united one, confronting the next round in the struggle to retain their territories not from rival chiefs but from a non-Tsimshian government. This feast may be a manifestation of the context within one village, in which a chief and the united people are "One Step Higher," which is the English translation of the Raven name given to Chief John Clifton.

Current Issues and Future Challenges

In this new millennium, the community of Hartley Bay faces many of the issues confronting other First Nations: effective governance, access to economic opportunities and management of resources in their territories, local control over education, and the urgent concerns of ensuring cultural and linguistic vitality for future generations. In the area of governance, Hartley Bay is exploring forms of internal and external political organization that will meet the aspirations of the community. At present the community still relies on a chief and council system for internal governance, elected under the "band-custom" provisions of the Indian Act. Subsequent to a court decision, members of the band who are not resident on reserve participate in community governance by voting and running as elected chief and council; the relationship between the on-reserve membership of the band (about 160 people) and the off-reserve membership (about 500 people) remains a focus of considerable tension at present. The growing proportion of members resident off reserve due to the addition of members under Bill C-31 has added pressure. However, a number of local factors are also involved, including a shrinking absolute number of on-reserve residents due to increasingly constricted economic opportunities; whereas the Hartley Bay School had 78 children enrolled in grades K–10 in the late 1970s, in 2002 it has fewer than 50. For a time there was a move to involve the hereditary chiefs in decision-making through the Tsimshian Tribal Council, and to represent through them the unity of the Tsimshian Nation in negotiations with governments. This

was never effected consistently, and the Tsimshian Tribal Council is now defunct (a treaty society has assumed some of its functions, especially negotiation of treaty through the BC Treaty Process). One of the continuing difficulties has been that the long-term suppression of the feast system has made identification of the currently entitled nameholders difficult in some communities, and the traditions of generosity, respect, and authority that underpinned the system have been considerably eroded. Since the Tsimshian system was repressed for so long there is a great deal of "straightening out" to be done. Band membership rules relied on patrilineal descent for several generations, and there are now many situations in which none of the matrilineally descended members of a house are resident in its home community. In some cases there have been wholesale adoptions, some legitimated by feasts and others self-styled and clearly illegitimate. Some ambitious and unscrupulous people are rumoured to have "gotten a name from a tombstone"—a reference to attempts by interlopers to usurp the rights of succession. The Gitksan and Nisga'a have organized processes to empower the hereditary chiefs to address such violations, but the Coast Tsimshian have not yet found a means to address this, and it is causing serious disruption in some communities.

Shifting management priorities and the downward spiral of employment and income in both the forestry industry and the fisheries have been difficult to combat. For example, Area Six, the fisheries management area closest to Hartley Bay, has been almost entirely closed to commercial fishing in recent years, which local people attribute to favouritism toward sports fishing interests from Kitimat and fly-in lodges. This has made it uneconomic for fishing vessel owners to reside in the community. At the same time there is pressure to decrease the number of days for commercial fishing in nearby areas such as the mouth of the Skeena River. One reason is that while there are large available stocks of some species such as sockeye (millions of these fish return to the Skeena River each year), other stocks that migrate at the same time are small (some runs number under 2,000), and the current technology available to the commercial industry makes it expensive to harvest selectively. It is ironic that a century ago the federal government destroyed weirs and traps that had been used for millennia on the grounds that they were a threat to conservation. These same technologies are now being touted as remedies to the problems confronting the mixed-stock fisheries. However, individuals and groups with extensive investment in the current fishing industry are deeply concerned about the impact of such schemes on their futures. Commercial fishers have also suffered through several rounds of government "solutions" that have cut back the privileges of fishing licences (commercial licence holders used to be able to fish the entire coast, but now must purchase three separate area licences to do so; they used to be able to switch from trolling to gill-netting and now can use only a single gear type on a licence). The Aboriginal Fisheries Strategy and community rather than individual licences are being used to reorient harvesting away from the current industrial mode. Hartley Bay received a community licence for harvesting herring roe-on-kelp several years ago, and this is one of the economic projects that offers some potential; when the Tsimshian Tribal Council was active it employed fisheries guardians and trained community members in fisheries management, but none of them have achieved a real role in the management process. The future of this key economic sector is likely to be very turbulent. Two Tsimshian communities have accepted commercial salmon aquaculture operations in their territories, though vocal segments of these communities are vehemently opposed to this industry on the grounds that it is a danger to wild stocks and pollutes shellfish beds in the area. Meanwhile, prices

paid for sockeye salmon—the "money fish" of the commercial fishery—have dropped from over $5 per pound in the mid-1990s to $1 per pound in 2008. The Allied Tsimshian Tribes filed suit claiming an Aboriginal right to a commercial fishery, but the court found that while the Tsimshian were traders, there was not sufficient evidence that trade in salmon was a distinctive part of their culture at the time of contact. At the same time, environmental organizations are seeking to partner with Tsimshian communities to help them build sustainable futures in their territories—or to manipulate First Nations as their puppet spokespersons to take control of the coast, rename it the "Great Bear Rainforest," and close it to all commercial activities. Which interpretation one accepts depends in large part on prior assumptions. The pressures on communities are intense.

Logging reserve lands and developing a tourism business at a former village site are other current projects that Hartley Bay is pursuing to establish a more diversified economy, though recent downturns in the coastal forestry industry have been devastating. The Tsimshian Treaty Society is working on issues such as land rights, management of fisheries, and forestry in their territories. Other issues, including repatriation of Tsimshian cultural objects from museums and the development of educational programs, including Tsimshian language and cultural programs have been led by the First Nations Education Council of School District 52 and the Ts'msyen Sm'algyax Authority. Social control within the communities has broken down drastically—with unemployment rates up to 90 per cent, high-school graduation rates below 30 per cent, and bleak opportunities for progress at the treaty table, the rates of substance abuse, family violence, and suicide have multiplied. The greatest certainty as the Tsimshian community moves into the twenty-first century is that many of the issues they confront will remain unsettled for a long time.

Conclusion

This chapter has focused on the Tsimshian feast complex. The interpretation presented offers some insights into the meaning system that gave coherence to the traditional Tsimshian feasts and to the adaptations that have been made in changing circumstances over the past century. The Tsimshian people continue to seek a future in which they can maintain their identity and manage their own affairs on the lands where their culture developed over several thousand years, and where it can continue to flourish.

BOX 24.2 Looking for Justice

In 1997 the Supreme Court of Canada issued its decision in the *Delgamuukw* case, named after a Gitksan Sm'oogit who was one of the plaintiffs. The Court clarified a number of issues in this ruling (quotes here are from the majority opinion).

1. Where it can be established in fact, Aboriginal title is a living right protected by the Canadian Constitution and must be reconciled with Crown sovereignty.

   "Aboriginal title encompasses the right to exclusive use and occupation of the land held pursuant to that title for a variety of purposes, which need not be aspects of those aboriginal practices, customs and traditions which are integral to distinctive aboriginal cultures. . . . Section 91(24) of the Constitution Act, 1867 (the federal power to legislate in respect of Indians) carries with it the jurisdiction to legislate in relation to aboriginal title, and by implication, the jurisdiction to extinguish it. . . . A provincial law of general application cannot extinguish aboriginal rights."

2. Oral histories are admissible in court and must be given independent weight.

   "The factual findings made at trial could not stand because the trial judge's treatment of the various kinds of oral histories did not satisfy the principles laid down in *R. v. Van der Peet*. The oral histories were used in an attempt to establish occupation and use of the disputed territory which is an essential requirement for aboriginal title. The trial judge refused to admit or gave no independent weight to these oral histories and then concluded that the appellants had not demonstrated the requisite degree of occupation for "ownership." Had the oral histories been correctly assessed, the conclusions on these issues of fact might have been very different."

3. Aboriginal rights may be infringed, but not without consultation and compensation.

   "Constitutionally recognized aboriginal rights are not absolute and may be infringed by the federal and provincial governments if the infringement (1) furthers a compelling and substantial legislative objective and (2) is consistent with the special fiduciary relationship between the Crown and the aboriginal peoples. The development of agriculture, forestry, mining, hydroelectric power, general economic development, protection of the environment or

Continued

endangered species, and the building of infrastructure and the settlement of foreign populations to support those aims, are objectives consistent with this purpose. Three aspects of aboriginal title are relevant to the second part of the test. First, the right to exclusive use and occupation of land is relevant to the degree of scrutiny of the infringing measure or action. Second, the right to choose to what uses land can be put, subject to the ultimate limit that those uses cannot destroy the ability of the land to sustain future generations of aboriginal peoples, suggests that the fiduciary relationship between the Crown and aboriginal peoples may be satisfied by the involvement of aboriginal peoples in decisions taken with respect to their lands. There is always a duty of consultation and, in most cases, the duty will be significantly deeper than mere consultation. And third, lands held pursuant to aboriginal title have an inescapable economic component which suggests that compensation is relevant to the question of justification as well. Fair compensation will ordinarily be required when aboriginal title is infringed."

The *Delgamuukw* case and other recent court decisions, such as the reaffirmation of the treaty right of Mi'kmaq Indians to a "moderate livelihood" from their resources, have been widely discussed and it has been anticipated that these judgments would lead to a breakthrough at last in the treaty-making process in BC. Ten years after the *Delgamuukw* decision there has been little real progress at the treaty table, though a number of economic deals between the province and various bands have provided some access to resources. When it was first elected, the provincial government insisted on a province-wide referendum on the treaty-making process that was condemned by Aboriginal leaders. The questions in this referendum were simplistic and biased. The government declared that the results of the referendum vindicated its positions. Several court cases have been brought to force consultation on logging plans on Tsimshian territories as well as the development of the second phase of the container port at Prince Rupert. Other BC First Nations are also looking to the courts for justice. There is widespread frustration that court decisions are being ignored by the provincial government.

NOTES

1. This chapter summarizes my monographs on feasts. My field research was supported by grants from the Contract Ethnology Program of the National Museum of Man and the Social Sciences and Humanities Research Council of Canada. While aspects of the interpretation presented here have been discussed with members of the community of Hartley Bay and a copy has been submitted to the band council of the village, the interpretation, and any errors, are my responsibility.

   Spellings of Tsimshian terms follow the system in Dunn's *Practical Dictionary of the Coast Tsimshian Language*. Original spellings are retained in quotations from other authors.

2. Nisga'a educator Dr Bert McKay (d. 2003) noted that crest animals are those that can eat the same foods as do humans (personal communication). This seems to be an apt observation for all except the frog, but the frog is a complex symbol everywhere on the Northwest Coast.

REFERENCES AND RECOMMENDED READINGS

Adams, John W. 1973. *The Gitksan Potlatch: Population Flux, Resource Ownership and Reciprocity.* Montreal: Holt, Rinehart and Winston. A cultural ecological analysis based on 1960s fieldwork. Adams argues that the Gitksan redistributed people to territories and resources by assigning individuals to groups through the feast system. The description of current feasts is detailed.

Anderson, Margaret Seguin, and Marjorie Halpin. 2000. *Potlatch at Gitsegukla: The 1945 Field Notebooks of William Beynon.* Vancouver: University of British Columbia Press. In 1945 there was a 10-day cycle of feasts, *halayt* performances, and totem-pole raisings attended by William Beynon in his role as a Laxkibu Sm'oogyit. His field notebooks are the best account of feasting during the twentieth century, shaped by his insider perspective and knowledge of the language and culture. Anderson and Halpin provide a lengthy introduction.

Barbeau, Marius. 1929. *Totem Poles of the Gitksan, Upper Skeena River, British Columbia.* Ottawa: National Museum of Canada, Anthropological Series no. 12, bulletin 61. Along with *Totem Poles* (1951), this is one of Barbeau's longer and more enduring contributions.

Berger, Thomas R. 1981. "The Nisga'a Land Case," in Berger, *Fragile Freedoms: Human Rights and Dissent in Canada.* Toronto: Clarke, Irwin. A clear presentation of the struggle for recognition of the Nisga'a claim to hereditary lands. Berger represented the Nisga'a before the Supreme Court; although the panel split, the case helped set the stage for serious land-claims negotiations in Canada.

Boas, Franz. 1916. *Tsimshian Mythology.* Washington: Bureau of American Ethnology, Thirty-first Annual Report. A rich collection by the Tsimshian Henry W. Tate. Boas provides extensive annotation and a description of traditional cultures based on information in the myths.

Campbell, Ken. 1984. "Hartley Bay: A History," in Seguin (1984).

Collison, W.H. 1915. *In the Wake of the War Canoe: A Stirring Record of Forty Years' Successful Labour, Peril and Adventure amongst the Savage Indian Tribes of the Pacific Coast, and the Piratical Head-Hunting Haida of the Queen Charlotte Islands, British Columbia.* Toronto: Musson Book Company. Reprinted by Sono Nis Press, Victoria, BC (ed. Charles Lillard), 1981.

Duff, Wilson. 1959. *Histories, Territories and Laws of the Kitwancool.* Victoria: British Columbia Provincial Museum, Anthropology in BC, Memoir no. 4. A record of the information considered significant by the people of a Gitksan village, significant because of the collaboration involved in producing it as well as for the information presented.

Dundes, Alan. 1979. "Heads or Tails: A Psychoanalytical Study of the Potlatch," *Journal of Psychological Anthropology* 2, 4:395–424.

Dunn, John Asher. 1984. "International Matrimoieties: The North Pacific Maritime Province of the North Pacific Coast," in Seguin (1984).

Fleisher, Mark. 1981. "The Potlatch: A Symbolic and Psychoanalytical View," *Current Anthropology* 22, 1:69–71.

Geertz, Clifford. 1980. "Blurred Genres: The Reconfiguration of Social Thought," *American Scholar* 49, 2:165–79.

Garfield, Viola. 1939. *Tsimshian Clan and Society.* Seattle: University of Washington Press. An extremely valuable discussion of traditional and developing social organization by an important contributor to the area.

Robinson, Will, and Walter Wright. 1962. *Men of Medeek.* Kitimat, BC: Northern Sentinel Press. House history from a Tsimshian Sm'oogyit who died in 1949; considerable material of interest in understanding world view and social organization.

Seguin, Margaret, ed. 1984. *The Tsimshian: Images of the Past, Views for the Present.* Vancouver: University of British Columbia Press. A collection of recent scholarship from diverse perspectives focused on a single group; includes material on feasts, shamanism, history, and culture change.

Usher, Jean. 1973. *William Duncan of Metlakatla: A Victorian Missionary in British Columbia.* Ottawa: National Museum of Canada, Publications in History 5. A scholarly analysis of the activities of this intriguing missionary.

CHAPTER 25

The Coast Salish: Transnational Identities in the Land of the Transformer

Michael Marker

The Coast Salish people represent one of the most powerful cases of cultural survival and renewal in the Indigenous world. Although these communities have faced powerful forces of assimilation and dislocation, they have both resisted and adapted to modernity, maintaining their languages, ceremonies, and core traditional values. Despite colonization and urbanization, the Coast Salish world of interconnected villages has remained in many ways a vital and separate reality from the mainstream, dominant societies that surround them. Families experience the geography of the region based on their connections to traditional ways of life, ceremonies, and cultural relationships to other families and communities across borders and waters. It is through the intricate regional connections of families, villages, and ceremonies that traditional knowledge has been protected and nourished.

Two factors of Coast Salish history and living patterns that are presently receiving attention from scholars have to do with: (1) ways that the border between Canada and the United States divided a common people who resisted the policies of separation, continuing to pattern their lives around traditional relationships to place; and (2) the effects of arguably having been engulfed by urbanization more than any other Indigenous group in North America. The border divided extended family groups while the booming cities pushed Coast Salish cultural life into private and protected spaces. Understanding the Aboriginal people of the Strait of Georgia and Puget Sound means both comparing and contrasting histories and policies across the border and, at the same time, recognizing the permeability and even invisibility of the border in the Coast Salish world.

While academics have tended to research and write about the Coast Salish in a way that reflects one or the other side of the border, some ethnographers have followed Native people's stories back and forth between communities on both sides of the line. People often live for a time in one community and then move across the border to live with relatives in another community. While, in one sense, the border has been fairly invisible to the Coast Salish, it has also been a powerful signifier of differences between government policies and national cultures. Recently, environmental groups have joined with Aboriginal communities in renaming the entire ecosystem the "Salish Sea." Such alliances between environmentalists and Aboriginal leaders are part of a movement beyond the immobilizing politics of modern nation-states to a consideration of Indigenous knowledge as a framework for reconceptualizing the deep interconnections between human economies and the natural ecosystems.

I learned about Coast Salish place-based educational values when I moved to the Lummi reservation in western Washington in the 1970s. I became a teacher of Lummi high-school students in 1988. In 1996 I started a teacher education program at the tribal college. Throughout this time I made friends and listened to Elders talk about community life in the past and their experiences with schooling. My own family history and my Arapaho ancestry helped me to understand some aspects of the narratives from community members. My Ph.D. dissertation was a history of Lummi education with a focus on the stories from Lummi people who survived racist public schools during the 1970s, when backlash against Indian fishing rights victories was so explosive in Puget Sound. Later, as I began teaching at the University of British Columbia (UBC), I visited Coast Salish communities in the Fraser Valley and listened to Elders and Aboriginal leaders discuss history and the challenges of revitalizing the economies and traditional values of the people of S'ólh Téméxw (Sto:lo territory). Travelling back and forth across the Canada–US border to participate in events in Coast Salish communities, I began to see some of what Aboriginal people experienced in their connections to each other in a zone divided by powerful nation-states.

Anthropologist Bruce G. Miller emphasizes that "both the academic and popular literatures have commonly split the Coast Salish world in two, treating those living in Puget Sound and adjacent lands as constituting one world and those in British Columbia as constituting another. This practice fails to conform to the prior Aboriginal reality, before contact with non-Indians and before treaties and borders" (2008:6). Anthropologists, historians, and Aboriginal community leaders such as Tom Sampson, former chief of the Tsartlip First Nation, have recently put more emphasis on the reality of the border: the sometimes shared and sometimes separate experiences of Coast Salish

people in this transnational region (Boxberger 2007; Harmon 1998; Raibmon 2005).

During the time I was teacher education director at Northwest Indian College at Lummi, I recruited students for the program from both sides of the border. My program coordinator in the Bachelor of Education program was both Musqueam and Lummi. As we drove together back and forth between the two reserve communities, he often talked about how permeable the border was for him and his family. His family, like so many other Coast Salish people, travelled throughout the region for fishing, ceremonies, and jobs in resource industries. He had a whole set of commitments and responsibilities to his extended relations that required travelling and visiting communities on both sides of the border frequently. Working with him and getting to know his family, I saw how Coast Salish people had mental maps of the territory that were still connected to pre-contact understandings of place. As I developed the teacher education curriculum working with Elders and cultural specialists, we negotiated the tension between emphasizing local knowledge and responding to the expectations of accreditation agencies for more universalized and standardized kinds of learning outcomes.

One of the goals of the teacher education program was to have the curriculum reflect and respect the culture of the local Aboriginal people. Naming is important. I talked with Bill James, retired director of Lummi language at Northwest Indian College. He provided us with the name "Oksale" (*aahksaaluh*), meaning "teacher" in Lummi Straits Salish. First Nations control of education has evolved to re-insert the local into both program and curriculum development. This Indigenous educational movement toward a more place-based curriculum is occurring at the same time that globalizing forces are pressuring public schools to prepare students for participation in competitive international contexts. While mainstream schools may be giving students the message that they have no stake in the local, Aboriginal education must take the opposite stance. Self-government and community sustainability requires an education that supports traditional cultural values and a collective commitment to the land. Youth must be prepared to take up the challenge of connecting the Salish understanding of past to the goals of healing, community development, and positive transformation of their communities.

In working with students and community members at Lummi, we began to use local stories and history as the central element of curriculum development. Integrating local knowledge into the teacher education curriculum was already a core element of the Native Indian Teacher Education Program (NITEP) at UBC where I taught courses and received advice from Coast Salish Elders. NITEP began in 1974 and has been the leading model for Indigenous teacher education in Canada. The program has a Coast Salish emphasis since the university is located on the territory of the Musqueam nation. At the First Nations House of Learning at UBC events are begun by Musqueam Elders who offer both prayers and welcome words in the Hun'qumi'num' language. I took many ideas from NITEP and introduced them into the Oksale Teacher Education Program. Because many of the students at the tribal college were Coast Salish and attached to communities on both sides of the border, we developed courses and curricula that emphasized both a borderless geography and a comparative approach to policies of colonization and Indigenous resistance. My work in educational anthropology has emphasized how place-based pedagogy activates and formulates an Indigenous critical consciousness guiding the work of decolonization.

The comparative approach to understanding the ethnohistory of the region is messy and, at times, confusing, since the colonizing conditions for Coast Salish people look more similar across the border than different. However, when we see differences across the border we must avoid the tendency to "find out which country had the better Indian policy, or the most positive relationship with its Aboriginal population, but should instead seek to understand the reasons for the similarities and differences in Aboriginal history, and Aboriginal–non-Aboriginal relations, and Indian policies in the two countries" (Binnema 2006:35). Thinking of the Coast Salish region as an international zone of cross-cultural negotiations comes closer, I think, to the ways that Native communities have experienced the two surrounding dominant societies that have occupied their world rather than speaking of Canadian Coast Salish and American Coast Salish as separate entities. The Coast Salish people have had categories and borders imposed upon their world. The borders of the reserves and the international border between Canada and the United States are the borders of colonization and empire. Meanwhile, the borders drawn by anthropologists of their cultures, languages, and communities were also inventions of powerful, outside Others. Governments and academics continue to constrict and classify Aboriginal experience in ways that chop up the profound holism of place-based readings of history and culture.

Anthropologists, until the 1940s, tended to describe the Coast Salish as simply a variation of the larger Northwest Coast culture region, although more affected by settlement and urbanization than their northern neighbours. Because Boasian salvage ethnographers were less interested in studying adaptive culture change than in reconstructing pre-contact pasts, they missed opportunities to observe the resilience of Coast Salish communities that were resisting assimilation in the midst of accelerating non-Indian immigration. Many of the early ethnographers, such as George Gibbs, who served on the US Boundary Commission from 1857 to 1862 surveying the forty-ninth parallel, were employed by government agencies. The reports prepared by these individuals reflected the assimilationist agendas of the governments of the times. Gibbs, like others of his time, saw Coast Salish Indians as a vanishing race. In the first half of the twentieth century many ethnographers considered Coast Salish, surrounded by cities, to have lost their culture rather than having revised cultural forms in dynamic and resilient ways. Both the ethnographers and the government agents who were employed in the larger colonial project of categorizing Indigenous peoples did not understand the nature of Coast Salish space and patterns of living.

In the pre-contact world and in the nineteenth-century Coast Salish world, families travelled by canoe from village to village for ceremonies, trading, and just to visit friends and relatives. There was a tendency for people to marry outside their own village, creating an extended network of kinships and social connections that knitted the communities together. Annual canoe journeys were necessary to maintain relations or advance social status through ceremonies and exchanges of goods and people. The Coast Salish world is a set of multi-village communities. The relationship of families and individuals within this multi-village reality is affirmed by inter-group gatherings.

Hereditary privileges, such as the claims to ancestral names and the authority to tell certain stories were reaffirmed by ceremonies and seasonal visits. Such privileges were passed down in families but required public recognition at ceremonies and traditional events. Moreover, the potlatch, central to the Coast Salish economic and social system, required that families travel throughout the region as wealth and status were distributed and redistributed at potlatches that could last days or even weeks. The canoe journeys connected the villages as components of a social and ecological consciousness, a universe in constant motion.

The European-based cultures that arrived to colonize carried belief systems rooted in the social assumptions of the nineteenth century. European ideas about land, law, history, progress, and racial hierarchies formed patterns of engagement and rationalizations for conquest. The effects of government policies that divided up land were parallel to the problems created by dividing Coast Salish people at the border. At the Lummi reservation, nineteenth-century US government policies of assignment and allotment created a checkerboard pattern of small parcel land ownership. Indians who met the standards of "civility" were then declared "competent" to sell their individual allotments to settlers and speculators who found both legal and illegal means to acquire reservation land.

As in the pre-contact world, people now are intermarried between villages and land is owned by individuals and families from both sides of the border. The borderless Coast Salish world has been difficult for federal officials to divide and administer since Aboriginal people have continued to maintain aspects of old inter-village affiliations that are often more influential than modern nation-state identities of being Canadian or American. For example, a road-improvement project protecting a bluff at Lummi has recently been delayed because the land is owned by families from both Lummi and Saanich. The US Bureau of Indian Affairs (BIA), needing to acquire right-of-way, has not been able to accommodate the legal complexity of this cross-border land-ownership condition. The BIA recognizes only tribes within the boundaries of the United States. The Saanich families have no official Aboriginal status on the Lummi reservation—even though they are connected by marriage, history, and culture. Meanwhile, for the Coast Salish people, the modern bureaucratic problems of divided land are simply a continuation of colonialism's efforts to separate families based on the imposed laws of unnatural borders. The contours of life for Coast Salish communities are still connected to pre-contact values and continued patterns of family relations between villages across the border.

Both the British and the American treaties of the mid-1800s reflect the attitudes, values, and pressures of the negotiators and the different understandings of space, resources, and religion. The pressure to secure land from the Indians for settlement was well underway in the 1850s. As agriculture, logging, and mining brought thousands of settlers and speculators into the region, Coast Salish people participated in the wage economies of the region on both sides of the border and were entrepreneurs who provided building supplies and food for the growing cities. They also played a vital role in early transportation, carrying passengers and cargo on canoes up and down the region's rivers. While Indian labour was important in the early development of fishing and logging industries, Chinese immigration provided a cheaper and more efficient workforce, displacing Aboriginal workers.

By the early twentieth century, Coast Salish families were travelling to eastern Washington to harvest hops in the Yakima area. These migrations had become part of the extended network of community gatherings and were more than simply economic ventures. In many ways these fall hop-picking sojourns, just after the salmon season, fulfilled some of the same cultural goals and purposes as earlier canoe journeys. People from both sides of the border shared family news of marriages, births, and deaths. Dances and healing ceremonies were part of the social reality of these annual convergences of interrelated people.

Coast Salish people often define their world differently from the ways academics have divided for the culture region. Saanich Elder Dave Elliot, for example, made distinctions between communities based on whether a people's village was located where a river brought salmon every year or whether they had to devise technologies such as reef netting to get the fish out in the tidal salt water. In reef netting, a salmon run would swim over the net slung between two or more canoes. With expert timing, fishermen would lift the net and haul the fish into the canoes. Dave Elliot also explained how the Canada–US border had divided the Coast Salish people and kept some from fishing on the US side of the boundary. Saanich people lost reef net locations on the US side of the border and fell into poverty as a result. On the Washington state side of the border, Lummi Elder Al Charles, during an oral history interview in 1973, explained how the border divided Lummi and Saanich families: "Our people lived right in the Islands across the boundary line. There was no boundary line between your people and other people. They put a boundary line and split us in half, and got us all balled up here" (Charles 1973). He told a traditional story of Si'malh, a powerful young man who had raided villages and violated the laws. In the story, a group of warriors pursue him to Vancouver Island, where they decide to turn back. On the return trip, storms disperse the group to different islands and beaches, where they form the customary villages of the San Juan and Gulf Islands. Listening to the recording, it becomes obvious that Al Charles is trying to get the interviewer to understand that the Lummi world is seamlessly connected to other Coast Salish communities across the border. His people are the people of the islands and the border has little meaning in this context. His traditional story of Si'malh is told in an effort to establish, in the mind of the listener, that the border is a conceptual impediment for understanding the Coast Salish sense of place.

Languages and Place-Based Knowledge

One of most widely recognized ways of dividing Indigenous peoples into groups and categories has been based on language groupings. The Coast Salish region in the 1800s had more linguistic diversity than any other region in North America. Coast Salish individuals often spoke four or five mutually unintelligible languages as well as Chinook Jargon, the common trading language, rooted in the Chinookan languages of the Columbia River system and with English and French words added as the language evolved after contact. Chinook Jargon was a simplified trading language that contained as many as 800 words. The Jargon was an essential vernacular for both settlers and Indians throughout the nineteenth century and emerged from the unique conditions of linguistic diversity and widespread travel and trade in the Pacific Northwest. In many ways, as John Lutz points out, "Chinook jargon is part of a regional identity that is neither fully Aboriginal nor fully European" (2008:297). While the trading language was commonly heard in the streets of the booming cities of Victoria and Seattle throughout the nineteenth century, it was considered a kind of slang and not useful for describing the intimate details of land, animals, spirits, and relationships. The limits to the Chinook Jargon became evident when Washington territorial governor Isaac Stevens insisted on negotiating treaties from 1854 to 1856 in the trading language. In hindsight, it seems clear that it was impossible to explain the conditions of the treaties to the tribal leaders in the Chinook Jargon. The multiplicity of perspectives from the different heads of villages that came to sign the treaties were reduced to a one-dimensional, and mostly one-sided, conversation about commodities. Even among linguistically similar communities people had different social and economic orientations. The ways that the languages and stories explained the peoples' contexts and histories on the land was rendered invisible or irrelevant to the treaty-making process. This is, of course, but one specific example of a general principle, of language being a powerful element of colonial control. Later, the residential schools would attempt to eradicate Indigenous languages in children as a more consolidated form of state control.

The Coast Salish languages are connected to the larger Salishan language family, which contains 23 languages. Sixteen of these languages are spoken in the Northwest Coast culture area while the others belong to Interior Salish peoples. Bella Coola is geographically far to the north of the Coast Salish region, yet, because the language is a Salish family language, Bella Coola is regarded as a Coast Salish enclave community. In the northern portion of the Coast Salish region, the most widely spoken languages are Sechelt, Squamish, and a diversity of dialects of Halkomelem along the Fraser River system. Straits Salish is spoken at Saanich, Sooke, Songhees, and Lummi. On the Olympic Peninsula and Hood Canal, Clallam, Twana, and Quinault were some of the foremost languages with Chehalis and Cowlitz spoken in the south. Lushootseed is the most widespread language group in the Puget Sound region. Tillamook is considered the southernmost Salishan language. All these language sets have many separate dialects and spoken variations. Because people travelled so much throughout the region, individuals not only became multilingual, they also were multicultural in their extensive knowledge of each other's oral traditions and the creation stories associated with mountains, rivers, and sacred sites. Successful canoe journeys required knowing the history of each place and the languages and traditions of the villages as family groups travelled throughout the region.

To be familiar with languages in the Coast Salish world has always meant being able to interpret the stories and the geography that each language referenced. Many Coast Salish people make strong connections between their languages and the spiritual life of the people such that language, spirit, and landscape are inextricably connected. The languages flow from the **cosmology** that includes both practical knowledge and moral/religious understandings; Indigenous people tend not to separate these realms. For Indigenous peoples of North America, it was never as important to know *when* an event occurred as *where* it occurred. The languages, like the religions, are place-based and

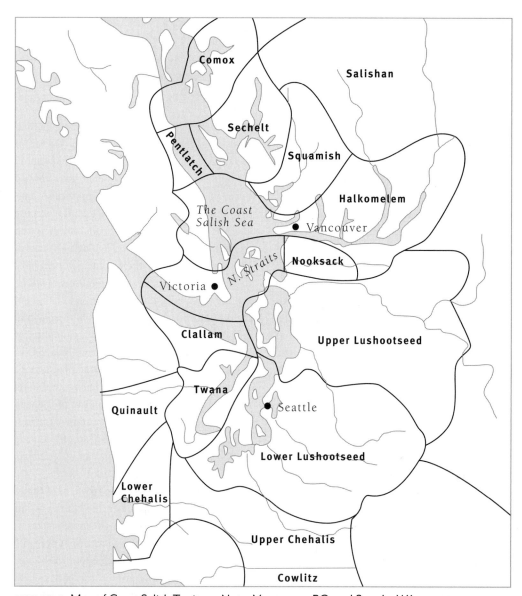

MAP 25.1 Map of Coast Salish Territory. Note: Vancouver, BC, and Seattle, WA, are 225 kilometres apart. (Source: Patrick J. Twohy, *Beginnings: a Meditation on Coast Salish Lifeways*. Self-published. Used by permission of the author.)

directly connected to the accumulated experience of ancestors.

Settlement, Treaties, and Divisions in the Coast Salish World

In many respects, there is no comprehensive or unified way to view the Coast Salish. Many of the divisions and definitions of the Coast Salish world have come from anthropologists who were trying to describe a diverse group of people who shared kinship and broad socio-economic relationships. British and American concepts of space and social relations were entirely different from the ways that Coast Salish communities were structured. Coast Salish societies were aggregates of collective households rather than unified political, civic villages. They were tied by kinship and ceremonial bonds to other Coast Salish communities. Land ownership in the traditional Coast Salish world was connected to family privileges and to traditions of resource management responding to a web of relationships that included plants and animals. The settler societies that took over Native space in the mid-1800s viewed land as possession and commodity. Both British and American cultural values emphasized agriculture and industrial development. Coast Salish spiritual beliefs about places, power, and oral tradition were disregarded by the newcomers.

The Coast Salish had two distinct economies, a subsistence economy and what has been called a prestige economy. The subsistence economy was primarily organized around the acquisition and circulation of food. The prestige or wealth economy, formalized by the potlatch complex, maintained the social order, affirmed rights and privileges for prominent individuals, and fortified relationships between villages in the region. Individuals from influential families would accumulate goods and then host a potlatch, giving away all the wealth to ensure and advance status among their own and other communities. Potlatches were hosted by families who invited both their own community and distinguished families from other villages. These events, which lasted several days or even weeks, featured feasting, dances, speeches, and the gambling game Slahal.[1] While these two economies of Coast Salish life operated in a separate cultural ethos from the capitalist economy of the settler society, Native people began to utilize wage labour to supplement their own economic goals toward the acquisition of status. In the Coast Salish prestige economy, wealth was acquired for the purpose of advancing status, not for personal consumption and increased sustenance. The Potlatch Law of 1884 was an effort by the Canadian government to force Native people into capitalist individualism and to expedite their assimilation into modern society. Because the potlatch was both a form of economic distribution as well as a validation of social relations, the stability of the Coast Salish world was threatened by its removal. People broke the law and risked being sent to jail by continuing to host and attend potlatches in out-of-the-way valleys or islands away from government and missionary surveillance. Aboriginal people recognized that without the social economy of the potlatch, their world would fall into chaos.

In the 1850s both Britain and the United States were eager to open up the Pacific Northwest for settlement. A gold rush brought miners, settlers, and speculators into the region throughout the 1850s. After the Treaty of Washington was signed in 1846, both nations pushed forward to deal with the Native people of the region to advance the interests of each nation-state and accommodate the movement of settlers who were eager to establish farming, logging, and mining. In Victoria, James Douglas, chief factor for the Hudson's Bay Company and colonial governor, negotiated 14 agreements and set aside small reserves for Coast Salish people. On the US side of the border, Washington territorial governor Isaac Stevens took a more heavy-handed approach to the treaty process. Stevens pushed a policy of consolidating different tribes and villages, crowding together on reservations people who sometimes had mutual hostilities.

The Douglas approach created smaller pieces of land than did the American process, but the Aboriginal people were generally able to remain in their traditional homelands, albeit confined to a tiny portion of their original land base. The reserve lands were later reduced by Joseph Trutch, Douglas' successor, who thought Aboriginal people were an impediment to the necessary development of the colony. He reduced the lands for Sto:lo communities and supported the settlers against the Indians. His view, common at the time, was that the Indians had no use for large tracts of land since they were not clearing or farming the land (although some clearly were). Trutch's policies led to Sto:lo protests to the government and to the threat of an Indian war along the Fraser.

Isaac Stevens used intimidation and threats to force Indians to sign the treaties. He was unwilling to consider Aboriginal perspectives and was in a hurry to get the treaties ratified. His brutal approach to the treaty process led to an Indian war in Washington territory. Many Coast Salish groups were dissatisfied by the terms of the treaties and the inadequate amount of reservation land that was allocated. Nisqually leader Leschi was the most recognized opponent of the treaties. He led an attack against the city of Seattle and for the day of 26 January 1856 the city was under siege. A naval sloop and artillery fire drove off the warriors. The 1854–6 war against the settlers in Puget Sound was brief, but had the effect of dividing the region into Indian and non-Indian worlds both geographically and mentally. At least, the differences between the two were stressed by settlers who wanted Aboriginal people confined and out of the way of development. The war made clear to Coast Salish leaders the power of American military technol-

ogy as they encountered exploding cannon shells for the first time. Leschi was captured and hanged in 1858 for murder. He admitted to having killed soldiers in open combat, not to murder, but many of the settlers thought Leschi started the war and they wanted revenge. The trial provoked protest from a group of progressive territorial citizens who saw Leschi as innocent and Stevens as wanting to make a show of governmental authority to control Indians. Interestingly, James Douglas was successful in negotiating treaties with Coast Salish bands in part because the British settlers on Vancouver Island, even though eager for land, knew of the war south of the border and were cautious about pushing Aboriginal groups too far.

The differences in treaties and settler states across the invisible border created somewhat divergent environments for Aboriginal people who also found themselves subject to the borders of reserves in Canada and reservations in the United States. The Douglas treaties were template documents based on the Treaty of Waitangi in New Zealand. They were essentially land-sales agreements. The Stevens treaties in Washington territory between 1854 and 1856 went beyond simply establishing reservations and included wording that protected fishing rights and provided for medical access and education. Both the text on sharing the fish "in common" with the settlers and the provision for education would become important points for protecting economic and cultural resources in the future for US Coast Salish communities.

While the Stevens treaties were plagued by the use of Chinook Jargon for crude translations, the Douglas treaties were not clearly understood by Coast Salish people either. It is quite probable that Aboriginal leaders, not understanding Western approaches to legal text, simply viewed the documents as general agreements, or rather as acknowledgements, that they were to share resources with the settlers and to live in peace. They may have been viewed as ceremonies of affirmation of evolving conditions, rather than a relinquishing of so much of what Aboriginal people could not have imagined owning in the Western sense, let alone selling. In many ways these tensions and confusions about treaty language continue to be troublesome, contributing to disputes about history and meaning in the modern context of unresolved land claims.

From our vantage point in history, it is easy to forget how incredibly unsettled life had become for the Coast Salish. Cole Harris has noted that the effects of disease had killed 20 per cent of the Aboriginal population of Vancouver Island a year or two before the first treaties. Moreover, the Native world was overwhelmed with turmoil from inter-tribal warfare brought about by the reorientation of trading patterns and the general destructive effects of colonization. It was a chaotic moment of uncertainty in the social reality of the Coast Salish people. Harris concludes that "it is not even certain that all the Native groups in question understood that they were selling their land" (2002:25). The treaties were essentially, for the Native groups, oral agreements.

Even the idea of a permanent village was not the same in the Coast Salish world as in the framework of European notions about place and sedentary living patterns. Coast Salish peoples had large cedar plank houses that they lived in for four winter months. These are sometimes referred to as permanent winter villages. In the spring people set out for fishing camps, reef net sites, and seasonal villages for harvesting the salmon, berries, camas, and some wapato. Both camas and wapato were starchy plants that were staple foods on the west coast. Camas beds were owned by families and their care involved practices for increasing the yield of crops by burning and by covering the beds with seaweed. While the harvesting sites, winter village sites, and fishing locations could be regarded as owned by extended family groups, concepts of ownership, as well as principles of resource

management, were founded on relationships to animals, plants, and the oral traditions that defined the proper ethical and ecological conduct with regard to fish and other resources. Coast Salish Elders have explained to me that primary differences between European and Indian approaches to land and resources can be found in the contrast between the Western emphasis on individual rights versus the Indigenous stress on responsibilities. Of course, the practices regarding ownership of land and resources are complex and cannot be reduced to simple dichotomies between Native and non-Native worldviews. For example, communal land rights are still widely found in Europe.

Meanwhile, the differences in concepts of property and ownership—particularly ownership of land—between Aboriginal and European cultures were at the heart of the confusion about what exactly was agreed upon in both the Douglas and the Stevens treaties. Coast Salish communities had a complex system for dwelling in and responding to the land. These treaties were made across a vast linguistic divide where ideas of land, space, spirit, and human responsibilities to the natural world were located in different universes. A thoughtful examination of Salish oral traditions shows how both moral and ecological conduct is outlined in the stories and mythology. The Indigenous perspective that individuals belong to the land contrasts with the European belief that land belongs to individuals.

In the 1855 Point Elliott Treaty, Stevens made a prohibition against Indians travelling to Victoria. He wanted to limit the influence of the British and reinforce the concept of the border in the minds of Native people. The US government also wanted to keep Coast Salish people on the reservations and impede their ability to maintain family and kinship alliances across international borders. Besides confining Indians on land away from the path of civilization and development, the reservations were supposed to keep a boundary between Native communities and lawless, avaricious settlers. Aboriginal people, for the most part, did not remain on the reservations and reserves, but continued travelling throughout the region and generally ignored the border. The laws intended to keep Coast Salish people on one side of the border or the other were essentially unenforceable because the largest canoes were faster than anything else on the water in the nineteenth century; they eluded the pursuit of government authorities. Moreover, in the Coast Salish world, a reality in constant motion, there were too many canoes travelling between too many villages for government agents and militia to keep track of, much less control.

Cultures are largely defined by the forms of transportation and the ways that mobility factors into the sense of space and territory. Coast Salish groups usually had both permanent village sites and seasonal villages for fishing and other harvesting activities, but the people did not experience a sedentary way of life in these fixed locations. Canoe travel was fundamental to the culture and connected people and resources, spaces, and relationships.

The treaties, especially the Douglas treaties, were vague about delineations of land areas and Douglas had problems understanding exactly which extended family groups he was making agreements with. The Stevens treaties in Washington territory created problems because incompatible tribes were crowded into common reservations. Douglas, on the British side of the border, had an opposite problem. He tried to make separate reserves, but did not understand how people were connected across the categories the non-Natives had invented. For example, he attempted to make a territory for the "South Saanich," but did not understand that the land was neither exclusively Saanich nor Songhees. People belonged to both groups and shared the space based on customary family privileges.

Throughout the latter half of the nineteenth century, the Coast Salish communities closest to urban centres were most overcome by the effects of alcohol and the predations of criminals from the cities. Missionaries and government agents, witnessing an alarming death rate, were convinced that the Coast Salish people were fated for extinction. The churches advocated for mission schools, industrial schools, and eventually residential schools. Myron Eels, a missionary and ethnologist who worked at the Skokomish reservation from the 1870s through the 1890s, noted the extreme numbers of Coast Salish people ravaged by alcoholism, disease, and poverty. He saw that proximity to cities and towns in Puget Sound caused these problems and he blamed unprincipled settlers for profiting from the misery of Aboriginal communities.

Traditional Education and Schooling for Assimilation

Coast Salish communities maintained languages, traditions, stories, and ceremonies in the midst of the dramatic changes making their world disappear. At the same time, missionaries and government officials were working to unravel Native social space by banning the potlatches and winter dances. In traditional education, adolescents were prepared by designated adults not only to learn skills associated with subsistence and survival, but to find spirit helpers and visions for connecting practical knowledge to supernatural powers. Learning had stages of development, but was part of a lifelong journey of identity discovery. Sto:lo Elder Sonny McHalsie puts it this way:

> One of the teachings of the elders is that we're always learning; we never quit learning from the day we're born to the day we die. It seems like that was one of the teachings of the past. You're told to do things. You're never told why. You're just

told to do it. And that's because that's how we do it! And it isn't until later on that you start putting things together, you start realizing why (McHalsie 2007:85).

Young people would be told stories as a way to learn both moral and ecological concepts together. These Coast Salish stories often featured the triumphs of X:als, the transformer who changes the forms of reality to bring order out of chaos.

Coast Salish people on both sides of the border were sent to residential schools (called Indian boarding schools in the United States) and the government policies for assimilation and the eradication of languages and traditional cultural practices were comparable across the border until the 1920s. In the 1930s however, the course of action in Washington, DC, began to take a new direction. As a result of the Indian Reorganization Act of 1934 and the policies of Indian affairs commissioner John Collier, most of the Indian boarding schools were closed. Coast Salish students in Washington state were integrated into local public schools. The two best-known schools in western Washington,

---

BOX 25.1 X:als[2] the Transformer

The stories of X:als, the changer, are known throughout the Coast Salish world. X:als is both a creator and a transformer of the landscape which was, at an earlier time, unstable and populated by creatures that were distorted versions of the animals of the present era. X:als arrives and gives people and animals their present forms. The stories are part of what Sto:lo people call sxwoxwiyam, tellings of ancient knowledge that explain the formation of the world.

Often the stories are about X:als' many travels throughout the region and how he would change people who had acted badly into stones. Others, who acted wisely and generously, were turned into resources for human beings, such as cedar or beaver. Because X:als has a presence and moral authority that is so similar to themes in Christianity, there have been many questions about whether the stories were influenced by missionaries or whether they predate Christian influences in the Coast Salish region. It is probable that, while the there was much mixing of religious traditions and ideas, the concept of a prophet descended from the Creator is older than missionary influences. In any case, it is sublimely and uniquely Coast Salish.

The X:als stories happened in physical spaces and created a map with both geographical references and moral instruction. X:als puts marks on the landscape in this way. The point to be made here is that the physical landscape connected with the traditional knowledge of the old people holds the prospect for developing meaningful understanding of the Coast Salish cosmology. Nanaimo Elder and storyteller Ellen White has utilized the X:als stories to help Aboriginal youth struggling with difficult questions of identity and ethics in a modern, often culturally hostile, world. She has emphasized the traditional way of being able to speak to objects respectfully: "Xeel's teaches the importance of respecting all things, both living and non-living. The people were taught to 'speak to' the tree and honour it if they were going to take bark from it or cut it down to make a canoe" (White 2006:40).

Cushman in Puyallup and Tulalip in Everett, were closed by the end of the 1930s. As some Coast Salish students lived in communities in both BC and Washington, they encountered the differences in educational contexts.

The conditions in the public schools that Coast Salish families encountered on the US side of the border were not necessarily an improvement over the harsh environment of the residential schools in British Columbia. Racism and the denigration of Native culture were entrenched in the public schools of western Washington. During the 1960s and 1970s, the heightened political tensions from the backlash against Indian fishing rights victories spilled over into the classrooms and Coast Salish students in public schools were targets of violence from students and teachers. The centrepiece for the controversy was the 1974 *Boldt* decision which determined that Coast Salish tribes had reserved for them 50 per cent of the salmon fishery, based on the 1855 Point Elliott Treaty. A storm of protest erupted from commercial fishers and others resentful of what they viewed as special Indian rights. Many Coast Salish parents decided to send their children to Chemawa Indian Boarding School in Salem, Oregon, as a way to escape the racism and violence of the local public schools. Thus, a boarding school that had been used by the US government for assimilation and the eradication of Salish culture and languages during the late nineteenth and early twentieth centuries actually became a safe haven from the racism in public schools during the 1960s and 1970s. The continuation of residential schooling in BC is contrasted with the experiences for Lummi, Nooksack, Swinomish, and other Coast Salish groups in public schools in Washington state.

In British Columbia, the residential schools were the primary vehicle for the loss of Coast Salish languages and traditional values. For Sto:lo people, Coqualeetza residential school is a focus for a mixture of stories about how the residential schools devastated Aboriginal families, but then became a site for the development of self-determination and cultural restoration. Coqualeetza, in Sardis, was a Methodist institution. Sto:lo people attended both Coqualeetza and the Roman Catholic St Mary's School in Mission. Both schools were built to assimilate Aboriginal people into the dominant society, but only at the margins of that society. In many ways the history of these two schools shows the evolution of the ways Coast Salish people have reclaimed colonial educational sites to become cultural revival spaces and offices for First Nations governments. These former residential schools are now centres for research and have played an important role in Halq'eméylem language revival and curriculum development projects. In the 1970s linguist Brent Galloway worked with Elders at the Coqualeetza Education Training Centre to develop a Halq'eméylem writing system. This orthography has been a powerful tool for the revival of Halq'eméylem, the upriver dialect of the broader language group of Halkomelem.

One of the most important publications to come from the former residential schools, now cultural revival sites, is the *Sto:lo–Coast Salish Historical Atlas*. It is a collaborative effort between the Sto:lo Aboriginal Rights and Title department and a selected group of anthropologists and historians. The atlas gives important information on Sto:lo history, place names, traditional knowledge, identity themes, environmental issues, social structure, and sacred sites. It is replete with photographs, maps, and elaborate graphics. This production represents the evolution of Indigenous education. A few decades ago the prevailing ideas were that Native people should abandon their languages and cultural values to assimilate into Western modernity. Presently, the revival and retrieval of Indigenous place-based knowledge is considered by progressive educators, Aboriginal and non-Aboriginal, to be an essential component of ecological education for all students. The Sto:lo have now carefully decided to publish aspects of their traditional knowledge in order to educate the dominant Canadian society. Keith Thor Carlson's preface explains that the atlas is "a powerful educational tool with application to ongoing Sto:lo Nation treaty negotiations" (Carlson and McHalsie 2001:xv). While the goal of the atlas is to educate Aboriginal and non-Aboriginal audiences alike about S'ólh Téméxw (Sto:lo territory), it is a problem for Coast Salish communities to publish information about sacred sites and traditional knowledge. It is especially a problem to publish information about ceremonies and private understandings regarding such things as winter spirit dancing. There is a spiritual danger associated with speaking about personal knowledge and sacred rituals in a public context. Coast Salish families who participate in private longhouse ceremonies are taught not to discuss what goes on during these rituals.

Coast Salish communities are surrounded by urban populations; they have, to a certain extent, been very visible and accessible to the dominant societies. At the same time, they have developed complex systems to protect access to traditional knowledge. Coast Salish communities in BC are using publications and media to increase their visibility toward goals of acceptance and negotiation with the dominant society.

In Washington, however, tribes have taken a distinctly more protectionist stance on issues of access to place names, language, and aspects of

---

BOX 25.2 The *Sparrow* Decision, the *Boldt* Decision, and Coast Salish Fishing Rights

For Coast Salish people on both sides of the border, the most pressing concerns have to do with protecting Aboriginal rights and self-determination. Because Coast Salish life is based on fishing, the right to fish has been the major emphasis for communities on both sides of the border. Different histories of colonization have produced different conditions for fishing rights struggles. In *R. v. Sparrow* (the *Sparrow* decision), the Supreme Court of Canada recognized and affirmed Aboriginal fishing rights as a core part of the unique cultural rights possessed by First Nations. Musqueam fisherman Edward Sparrow was arrested for fishing with a net that was longer than allowed by the band's food fishing licence. He argued that he had an Aboriginal right to catch fish. The 1990 decision determined that Musqueam fishing practices, continuous since pre-contact times, must receive constitutional protection. Although the *Sparrow* decision is only an acknowledgement of Aboriginal rights to fish rather than an allocation of salmon, it has been foundational in securing Coast Salish traditional economies. While there is no treaty for these fishing rights, there is recognition of pre-existing rights along with the Canadian government's responsibility to protect Aboriginal cultures. In this case, Aboriginal cultural difference is protected by the Constitution. That cultural difference is maintained by the combination of tradition and community economic structures related to fishing.

On the US side of the border, the 1974 *Boldt* decision (*United States v. Washington*), named for federal judge George H. Boldt who heard the case, was not about cultural difference, but rather about how the nineteenth-

the traditional culture (Rasmus 2002). There is a prevailing sense that, as one Lummi Elder told me, "anything we share will be snatched up and we will find out that somebody is teaching a version of it [at the local university]." For the Lummi and other US Coast Salish groups, there is an uncertain benefit in educating the public about their histories and ways of life. Unlike their Canadian cousins, there is no opportunity to make claims for increased land and resources through a treaty process. Treaty-making in the United States was stopped by Congress in 1871. Tribes in Washington state continue to press not for new treaties, but rather for the federal government to honour the ones already made. By making traditional knowledge more accessible to the public, Coast Salish com-

munities in Washington think they would risk having their ceremonies and languages appropriated, commodified, and sold as cultural entertainments for an urban and suburban American population that produces and consumes stereotyped Indian images.

The two different Indigenous strategies for dealing with traditional knowledge have come from engaging with different kinds of nation-state policies and from different experiences with schooling. Groups such as the Sto:lo have cautiously decided that Canadian society is sufficiently open to the sharing of Indigenous knowledge within an advancing movement toward decolonization for both Aboriginal and non-Aboriginal societies. For US communities such

century treaties intended the settlers to share the fish "in common" with Indians. The *Boldt* decision did not grant fishing rights to Coast Salish communities. Instead, the court established that the treaty language of "in common" meant that Aboriginal leaders who signed the treaty had agreed to share 50 per cent of the salmon with the settlers. The ethnographic research for the decision concluded that the Indians had intended to have some control of the fishing practices of the territorial citizens. The court decided that treaty tribes should be able to harvest 50 per cent of the fish. The outcome transformed Coast Salish communities by re-allocating the salmon fishery, providing an economic boost to impoverished reservations. The decision also produced a backlash from resentful non-Indian fishers and their supporters. Much of the backlash spilled over into local schools where Indian students experienced racism and violence from students and teachers alike.

Phase II of the *Boldt* decision determined that the tribes had the right to have fish protected from environmental degradation. Coast Salish communities became important legal factors in the region's environmental policies and issues related to growth and development. The protection of salmon habitat is a focus for much of the environmental research now being done by Coast Salish communities. The survival of the Coast Salish people has always depended on a respectful relationship with the salmon people. The First Salmon Ceremony is a traditional event that celebrates the relationship between salmon and human beings, but it is also an assertion of self-determination since the Coast Salish economy and culture is dependent on salmon. The Coast Salish on both sides of the border are combining Western scientific knowledge and traditional ecological knowledge for salmon enhancement and management. Aboriginal sovereignty and the protections of treaty rights are inextricably linked to the protection of salmon.

as the Lummi, there is persistent suspicion about the motives of academics and others who would exploit and publish Indigenous knowledge to advance careers and profit economically. Because education is one of the most influential encounters with the dominant society, Coast Salish peoples have developed some ideas about how their cultural knowledge will be received by the public from their experience of attending school. Education has been a volatile and culturally dangerous zone for the maintenance and renewal of identity. When that identity is expressed in ways that trouble and contradict the narratives of progress and civilization, the schools act to crush the challenge to their authority to define social reality.

US Coast Salish communities have struggled against visible and invisible pressures by public schools and non-Indian expectations to perform versions of "Indianness" that conform to the public misunderstandings about both history and culture. In these communities, Coast Salish Elders and cultural committees have seen cultural information distorted and carelessly displayed. They have decided to control, as much as possible, access to information about traditional knowledge and ceremonial reality. These Elders regard the dangers from distortions of knowledge to be a threat to self-determination, since powerful outsiders can misinterpret the complexity and intricacy of cultural life. Coast Salish communities must do a delicate dance with the surrounding dominant societies. They must continue to communicate their cultural values and histories to the mainstream public, but they must also protect the knowledge from misappropriation and erosion by those who have incomplete understanding of the culture. In the Internet age, cultural privacy will be difficult to maintain for these communities. The sanctity of the traditions and ceremonies is at stake in these debates about which traditional knowledge to make public.

Travel and Transformation

While Coast Salish communities experience differences between the dominant societies that surround them, they continue to think of themselves as a common people with the border as a manifestation of their common and divided experiences with colonization. People continue to cross the border for events and ceremonies. Canoe pulling (paddling) and canoe racing have been two of the most enduring features of Coast Salish life, especially since they bring people together across the border. Annual war-canoe races at Cultus Lake in Chilliwack, BC, and at the Lummi Stommish festival in Bellingham, Washington, attract thousands of Coast Salish people from both sides of the border. The canoe races are traditional events that bring families and communities together to fulfill some of the same functions as did gatherings hundreds of years ago. Canoes and canoe names are passed on in families. Stories are told about particular canoes and the spiritual powers of both canoes and pullers. Social networks are fortified and identities and genealogies are recited. There is a sense that the past is alive and present in all that occurs at these events.

FIGURE 25.1 Twelve men posing for their portrait with *Saanich #5* racing canoe in West Saanich, BC, c. 1925–35. (PN 11779 (AA-00256) Courtesy of Royal BC Museum, BC Archives)

Coast Salish canoes and canoe pulling are a part of a common identity that connects people across the border. The Swinomish community in La Conner, Washington, used canoe racing to gain public attention and acceptance in the 1940s, when many local non-Indians were opposed to self-governance and treaty rights (Miller 1998). A Saanich traditional knowledge specialist told me about how his father used to travel by canoe alone and often at night from Vancouver Island to the San Juan Islands to visit Lummi relatives. He told me that people knew the tides so well "they called them just like people's names. They would ride the tide to San Juan Island. 'It was just like a bus,' he used to say. You could see San Juan coming up closer, very fast." The stories of canoes and canoe journeys are essential parts of the oral history that continue to inspire Coast Salish imagery.

Recently, there has been a revival of traditional canoe travel throughout the Coast Salish region, and in July 2007 the Lummi Nation hosted a *tl'aneq* or potlatch/feast gathering of 68 canoe families from communities up and down the west coast. It was the first potlatch hosted at Lummi since 1937. At these gatherings, clan crests are displayed, family privileges are noted, and names are passed down from ancestors in complex protocols. All this is done in the presence of witnesses and honoured guests. The role of witnesses is a highly specific part of all ceremonies in Coast Salish life. Witnesses are invited from different communities and are expected to pay close attention to all the speeches and events of the ceremony. They then return to their own communities and must give a validation of the formal aspects of names and any changes in social status that occur in these contexts. They give their support for the legitimacy of all the transactions and affirmations. In return they are provided with food and gifts. The inter-village canoe journeys were essential to preserve the complex social fabric of Coast Salish life; the revival of the journeys help maintain these connections in spite of the dramatic social and environmental changes that have occurred over time in the region. While the international border has made seasonal travels difficult because of increased border security, there is presently a growing awareness that the revival of summer canoe journeys can be an effective way to restore the sense of a Coast Salish eco-region that is not divided by the border.

The canoes are participating in an emerging partnership with the United States Geologic Survey helping with scientific research on the

FIGURE 25.2 Lummi, July 2007, where over 100 canoes have gathered. Here a canoe family that has just gone through the cultural protocols of receiving permission to land at the reservation beach is now carrying their canoe to their camping spot. (Photograph by the author)

water quality changes in the "Salish Sea." Canoe skippers are given water quality probes and global positioning system devices to carry on board during summer canoe journeys. The canoes are well suited for research on water quality because they move at a slow speed that is ideal for the use of the probes. And, because the journeys cross the border frequently, they can help give environmental scientists an important snapshot of the region that could parallel the way Aboriginal people see a borderless world (Grossman and Gibbons 2008). The nature of traditional ecological knowledge in the Coast Salish region is also a consideration for scientists as they begin to develop new/old forms of understanding "place" to interpret the interconnectedness of what is, after all, a single ecosystem.

Place-based pedagogy, directly connected to the memories and knowledge of Elders, holds both the promise and the problem for developing culturally responsive education for Indigenous peoples. The mainstream educational institutions that Coast Salish people must attend to receive degrees and job training are culturally oriented toward conditions of advancing globalization. The long-sustained presence on the land which was required for Indigenous knowledge becomes clouded by modernist education practices. Coast Salish communities are developing projects to provide a more place-based education for youth who can become dangerously disoriented from their own identities. The X:als stories are being used in Coast Salish language courses and in other aspects of studies that emphasize knowledge of the cultural region as a primary focus for education.

For the Lummi Nation, the word *Shelangen*, "the way of the people," has become part of the mission for the community's schools. This word, from the Northern Straits Salish language, has a powerful animating force for linking education to cultural renewal and identity fortification. *Shelangen* begins with the stories of X:als

and other traditional forms of knowledge. The emphasis on traditional values and respect for Elder knowledge creates a communal context that is helping youth and families heal through education. Canoe pulling and traditional teachings that fortify identity are vital in reviving community life and reorienting youth toward their role as stewards of the bioregion. In this sense, traditional knowledge can provide a template for educational reform toward a broader societal change that centres ecological knowledge and regional, rather than national, citizenship as a way to a more sustainable human future.

Conclusion

In this essay I have pointed to some emerging themes both in the scholarship and in the lived reality of Coast Salish people. The region is one of the most studied and elusively complex zones for both anthropology and history. Boundaries that are assigned to people and territories seem to shift and lose meaning depending on who is interpreting the borders. One of the understated pieces of Coast Salish experience is the way that the Canada–US border has created colonial divisions that have been problematic both for the life of the people and for a meaningful understanding of Coast Salish cognitive geography. How the border is imprinted in peoples' conceptions of space and self is a process deeply embedded in history. Narratives from Elders such as Dave Elliot and Al Charles make the border invisible at one moment, but a powerful denotation of colonialism's effects in the next. I have endeavoured to show how borders imposed by colonialism parallel the ways scholars have tried to devise categories in order to explain the interconnected and shape-shifting nature of the Coast Salish world. In many ways it is a world of continual motion requiring people to make annual inter-village canoe journeys to affirm and sustain the holism of the social and natural ecosystem.

The history of contact and settlement shows commonalities and differences across the border. The stories about both James Douglas and Isaac Stevens, who made treaties in the region, are well known by Elders and other community members, but these histories are hardly recognized by the surging urban populations that surround the small reserves. It is both the divided/undivided borderland's condition and the ways Coast Salish people have protected traditional knowledges in the midst of overwhelming surveillance that set the region apart from other Indigenous spaces globally. The Coast Salish people experienced devastating effects from unceasing settler settlement and from the disorienting assimilationist forces of being in such close proximity to large cities.

The schools continued the invasion of Coast Salish lands by taking children away from learning on the land. Both Canada and the United States sent Native children away to residential schools and pursued similar policies toward assimilation until the 1930s when Bureau of Indian Affairs Commissioner John Collier established a new federal direction toward integration and cultural revitalization. In the United States, most of the boarding schools were closed by the 1940s. In Canada, church-run residential schools continued to operate until the 1980s; while Coast Salish people in BC point to these institutions as containing a dark legacy of abuse and educational

marginalization, the conditions for Coast Salish families in Washington who attended racist public schools could be as bad or worse.

Presently, with the advancement of self-governance on both sides of the border, Coast Salish communities are making their traditional knowledge, including the lessons from X:als, the Creator/Transformer, the centre of educational mission statements. Teacher education programs such as Oksale at Northwest Indian College at Lummi and NITEP at UBC have emphasized local Coast Salish community knowledge and the reinforcement of Indigenous identity among the students. Aboriginal educators and community leaders are combining traditional knowledge with Western science, providing a more Indigenized learning environment for Coast Salish youth. The merging of traditional ecological knowledge (TEK) and environmental science is an advancing interdisciplinary approach to environmental policy in this borderlands region. The oral traditions are regional ways of making sense of what the land is trying to teach people about how to live. The revival of the canoe journeys that re-establish some of the traditional patterns of inter-village travel has opened a space for modifying thought about the ecology of the region and how it is connected to the stories of humans and animals from an ancient way of understanding the land.

NOTES

1. Slahal is often called the bone game, or sometimes the stick game. It is a gambling game where players guess the pattern of marked and unmarked cylindrical bones concealed in the hands of their opponents. Players face each other in teams and the game is accompanied by singing and drumming. Some of the songs are owned by families as a form of property.

2. There are many different spellings of this name based on phonetic systems and Coast Salish languages. In the Coast Salish world, the Transformer is a universally accepted creator and teacher who transforms people and animals into stone or places them as landmarks to show locally based universal truths. The word is pronounced with a backward "x" and then dropping the strong "h" sound in the word "halls," "hulls," or other variations depending on the dialect.

REFERENCES AND RECOMMENDED READINGS

Barman, Jean. 1986. "Separate and Unequal; Indian and White Girls at All Hallow School, 1884–1920." In *Indian Education in Canada, Volume 1: The Legacy*, edited by J. Barman, Y. Hébert, and D. McCaskill. Vancouver: University of British Columbia Press. Examines the conditions of a school at Yale, BC, that provided different educational environments for Native and non-Native girls. Explores the experience of both Coast Salish students and the then general attitudes in the Fraser Valley.

Binnema, Theodore. 2006. "The Case for Cross-National and Comparative History: The Northwestern Plains as a Bioregion," in S. Evans, ed., *The Borderlands of the American and Canadian Wests: Essays on Regional History of the Forty-ninth Parallel*. Lincoln: University of Nebraska Press.

Boxberger, Daniel. 1989. *To Fish in Common: The Ethnohistory of Lummi Indian Salmon Fishing*. Lincoln: University of Nebraska Press. Explores the history of both fishing technology and the dynamics of Lummi negotiations with the dominant society over fishing rights. Shows how Coast Salish communities are linked across the border through their fishing economies.

———. 2007. "The Not So Common." In *Be of Good Mind: Essays on the Coast Salish*, edited by Bruce G. Miller. Vancouver: University of British Columbia Press.

Carlson, Keith Thor, ed. 1996. *You Are Asked to Witness: The Stó:lō in Canada's Pacific Coast History*. Chilliwack, BC: Stó:lō Heritage Trust. A collaborative work with Elders and traditional knowledge specialists. Provides detailed cultural and historical information from a Coast Salish perspective. Began as a curriculum project to provide accurate information for BC schools.

——— and McHalsie, Albert, eds. 2001. *A Sto:lo Coast Salish Historical Atlas*. Vancouver: Douglas & McIntyre.

Charles, Al. 1973. Interview by Jeff Wilner, College of Ethnic Studies, 26 April, tape #23, Northwest Tribal Indian Oral History Collection, Western Regional Archives, Bellingham, WA.

Deloria, Vine Jr. 1977. *Indians of the Pacific Northwest: From the Coming of the White Man to the Present Day*. Garden City, NY: Doubleday & Company. A historian and Indian fishing rights activist, Deloria is an Indigenous scholar here writing on Coast Salish history.

Grossman, Eric, and Helen Gibbons. 2008. "USGS Will Collaborate with Coast Salish Indigenous Peoples to Measure Water Quality in the Salish Sea," US Geological Survey. Available at: http://soundwaves.usgs.gov/2008/05.

Harmon, Alexandra. 1998. *Indians in the Making: Ethnic Relations and Indian Identities around Puget Sound*. Berkeley: University of California Press.

Harris, Cole. 2002. *Making Native Space: Colonialism, Resistance, and Reserves in British Columbia*. Vancouver: University of British Columbia Press.

Keddie, Grant. 2002. *Songhees Pictorial: A History of the Songhees People as Seen by Outsiders, 1790–1912*. Victoria: Royal BC Museum. A thorough documentation of the role of the Songhees in the life of Fort Victoria (their village was in the Inner Harbour) through photos, maps, paintings, etc.

Lutz, John Sutton. 2008. *Makúk: A New History of Aboriginal-White Relations*. Vancouver: University of British Columbia Press.

McHalsie, Albert. 2007. "We Have to Take Care of Everything That Belongs to Us." In *Be of Good Mind: Essays on the Coast Salish*, edited by Bruce G. Miller. Vancouver: University of British Columbia Press.

Miller, Bruce G. 1998. "The Great Race of 1941: A Coast Salish Public Relations Coup," *Pacific Northwest Quarterly* 89, 3:127–35.

———. 2001. *The Problem of Justice: Tradition and Law in the Coast Salish World*. Lincoln: University of Nebraska Press. A leading advocate for a comparative, cross-border approach to the Coast Salish, Miller examines the differences and commonalities between forms of traditional justice and the challenges presented by different cross-border policies.

———. 2008. "Conceptual and Practical Boundaries: West Coast Indians/First Nations on the Border of Contagion in the Post-9/11 Era." In *The Borderlands of the American and Canadian Wests,* edited by Sterling Evans. Lincoln: University of Nebraska Press.

Poth, Janet, ed. 1983. *Saltwater People, as told by Dave Elliot Sr.* Victoria, BC: Saanich School District 63. Poth here presents us with the teachings of Saanich Elder Dave Elliot Sr, on the history and the ways of knowing and living of his people.

Rasmus, M. Stacy. 2002. "Repatriating Words: Local Knowledge in a Global Context," *American Indian Quarterly* 26, 2:286–307.

Raibmon, Paige. 2005. *Authentic Indians: Episodes of Encounter from the Late-Nineteenth-Century Northwest Coast.* Durham: Duke University Press.

Ruby, Robert H., and John A. Brown. 1976. *Myron Eels and the Puget Sound Indians.* Seattle: Superior Publishing Company. A pictorial record of the material culture, including implements, tools, and weapons, of the Indians in Washington state's Puget Sound in the late nineteenth century.

Smith, Marian W., ed. 1949. *Indians of the Urban Northwest.* New York: AMS Press. Essays by anthropologists working in the Boasian tradition. Important for understanding emerging ideas about a distinct Coast Salish history and experience apart from the larger Northwest Coast region.

Suttles, Wayne. 1987. *Coast Salish Essays.* Seattle: University of Washington Press. The foremost ethnographer of the Coast Salish, Suttles presents a wide range of subjects, including religious and ceremonial matters and hunting and fishing practices. His ecological approach connects the effects of contact with Aboriginal and non-Aboriginal groups on changes in Coast Salish life.

Thompson, Laurence C., and M. Dale Kinkade. 1990. "Languages." In *Handbook of North American Indians.* Vol. 7: *Northwest Coast,* edited by Wayne Suttles. Washington: Smithsonian Institution. Highly regarded survey of North American Indian languages. Kinkade was a specialist in Salish linguistics.

White, Ellen R. 2006. *Legends and Teachings of Xeel's, The Creator.* Vancouver: University of British Columbia Press.

PART IX

Conclusion

CHAPTER 26

Taking Stock: Legacies and Prospects

C. Roderick Wilson, R. Bruce Morrison, and Christopher Fletcher

In the early twenty-first century, what can be said about the place of Inuit, Metis, and First Nations people in Canadian society and beyond? In exploring the question, we will briefly review where we have been, consider the contours of current life, and give some thought to what lies ahead.

In the early decades of the last century it was generally believed that Native people were dying, both literally and culturally. In earlier centuries disease had swept through most populations on the continent, laying waste whole communities. By 1900 the worst killers, particularly smallpox, were abating, but Native populations generally continued to decline through the 1920s. In both Canada and the United States the so-called Indian wars were over. Indians and Metis, defeated militarily, seemed literally to be at "the end of the trail," as a popular sculpture of the period expressed it.

Reserves were established across southern Canada, and, under the authority of the Indian Act, agents decided which Natives were Indians and controlled where those defined as Indians could live and travel, what crops they could plant, to whom they could sell their produce, whether or not they could butcher their own animals for their own consumption, and myriad other details of daily life. The Act explicitly prohibited various activities, such as alcohol consumption and voting, taken for granted by most Canadians. It also outlawed participation in ceremonies that were central to many Indians—the Sun Dance of the Plains and the potlatch of the Northwest Coast. This is analogous to passing a Catholic Act to regulate the lives of Canadian Catholics that prohibits them from attending Mass, or passing a Baptist Act banning baptism.

To put it simply, Indians were now administered as a colonized people. The common assumption was that those who managed to survive physically would in time become members of Canadian society virtually indistinguishable from others. To that end the Act provided that any Indians acquiring an education, economic independence, or a non-Indian husband would automatically cease to be Indians. They had acquired the means to participate in society as Canadians and, it was assumed, had already become separated from their natal communities.

The Metis, whether Red River Metis or simply Natives who for one reason or another did not have legal status as Indians, were generally left to whatever fate they might find. Various schemes designed to extinguish any Aboriginal claim were introduced; these usually took the form of scrip entitling the bearer to land. Many Metis did not receive scrip, and most who did were not in a position to take advantage of its potential (for a number of cultural, technological, and economic reasons). As a result, most Metis have had no special status; legally, many were seen as squatters on Crown land. Until the Constitution Act was passed in 1982, Alberta was the exception, having passed in 1938 a Metis Population Betterment Act establishing "colonies" on the model of the federal reserves. Although the Act provides a significant opportunity for some Alberta Metis to find land that is legally secure, this protection entails a substantial loss of local control and subjection to an external bureaucratic structure. Other provinces also have developed programs specifically to alleviate social problems associated with the Metis. On the one hand, these programs are mute testimony to the unrealistic nature of the federal government's assumptions about the circumstances under which it considers itself to have fulfilled its obligations to Canadian Natives. On the other hand, the provincial agencies administering these programs tend to put their clients into a limited version of the same kind of dependent, controlled status as the federal government has historically placed status Indians.

Although the Inuit have a long history of contact with outsiders, the harshness of their environment and the lack of resources that would bring significant numbers of Euro-Canadians to the Arctic have until relatively recently inhibited the development of a colonial administration. That changed in the early 1950s as the government felt it necessary for national security purposes to create a northern presence and because, on humanitarian grounds, it felt obligated to provide educational and health services. In the late 1950s the trend further accelerated when for many Inuit both the caribou and the fish failed and people starved. One consequence of increased services was an increased governmental presence that is colonial in character. The nature of this colonialism is illustrated through a small event almost lost to memory: In late 1984, as Inuit heard of widespread famine in Ethiopia, they responded with great generosity—famine and

sharing are things they know about. The town of Spence Bay, in addition to money collected from individuals, sent the entire surplus from the town budget, some $48,000. Their gift was disallowed on the grounds that all expenditures by the town in excess of $200 need government approval. One of the ironies of this case is that by then the centre of colonial control for northern settlements was no longer Ottawa but Yellowknife.

As each chapter has indicated, however, Canada's Aboriginal peoples have, by and large, survived their colonial experiences. Admittedly, there have been substantial losses, both demographic and cultural, but Canadian Native societies have demonstrated the capacity and will to make major accommodative changes to their new circumstances, to attempt to change some of those circumstances, and to maintain their unique identities. Given the desperate conditions of many of these societies 100 or even 50 years ago and the strength of the social forces working for their assimilation, their continued presence as functioning societies is a considerable feat.

Some "Hard" Data

How many Natives have survived a century and more of colonialism and what are their characteristics? Let us start by making a few demographic generalizations, based on the 2006 census. First, they are a growing population. The census counted 1,172,790 Indian, Métis, and Inuit people —3.8 per cent of Canada's total population. This was an increase from 3.3 per cent in 2001 and 2.8 per cent in 1996, with the Aboriginal population growing six times faster than the non-Aboriginal population. Fewer than 800,000 people called themselves Aboriginal in the 1996 census. On the other hand, one must note that these particular comparisons are problematic in that these numbers are now based on self-reporting, and the general climate in the country means that families that formerly did not regard themselves as Aboriginal now claim to be.

Second, they are a young population; the median age is 27 years (as opposed to 40 for the general population). Another way of saying the same thing is that they are growing rapidly, with a birth rate about 1.5 times the national average (although a few decades ago it was four times the average). Only 5 per cent are seniors (65 or older) compared to 13 per cent in the general population.

Third, they are disproportionately a northern and rural population. Aboriginal people constitute 77 per cent of the population in Nunavut, 48 per cent in the Northwest Territories, 23 per cent in Yukon Territory, 14 per cent in Saskatchewan and Manitoba, around 5 per cent each in Alberta and BC, and no more than 2 per cent in Ontario and those provinces to the east, except Newfoundland and Labrador, at 4 per cent. But at the same time, Ontario has more Aboriginal people than any other province or territory. Perhaps we should rephrase the first sentence of this paragraph: Aboriginal people still are spread more evenly across the whole country than is the general population.

Finally, they are an urban population: 54 per cent live in areas loosely defined as urban, up from 50 per cent in 1996 (on the other hand, 81 per cent of non-Aboriginal people were urban in 2006). Table 26.1 indicates the 10 largest urban concentrations of Aboriginal peoples. At the same time, urbanization among Indigenous people is to a surprising extent a western phenomenon. The numbers of Aboriginal people in Toronto, Ottawa, and Montreal are far lower than one might expect. Regina and Montreal have roughly the same number of Aboriginal inhabitants—but Montreal is 20 times as large! And consider Prince Albert, where one person in three is Aboriginal. The sense of community and the distance physically and socially from one's home community are likely to be very different in such a location. In addition, status Indians moving to the city are moving into an administrative limbo: the federal government has historically seen its responsibility as having to do with reserves, while provincial and municipal governments have tended to see the federal government as being entirely responsible for all Native people. Only belatedly is this problem being specifically addressed by all three levels of government.

Now, let us look at some more specifics. According to the recently (June 2011) constituted Aboriginal Affairs and Northern Development

TABLE 26.1 Urban Aboriginal Populations, 2006

CITY	ABORIGINAL POPULATION	PERCENTAGE OF TOTAL POPULATION	INDIAN	METIS	INUIT
Winnipeg	63,385	10.0	25,900	40,980	350
Edmonton	52,100	5.1	22,440	27,740	590
Vancouver	40,310	1.9	23,515	15,075	210
Toronto	26,575	0.5	17,270	7,580	315
Calgary	26,575	2.5	10,875	14,770	250
Saskatoon	21,535	9.3	11,510	9,610	65
Ottawa–Gatineau	20,590	1.8	10,790	7,990	730
Montreal	17,865	0.5	10,135	6,010	570
Regina	17,105	8.9	9,495	7,185	25
Prince Albert	13,570	34.1	6,715	6,680	10

2006 Census, Statistics Canada

Canada, formerly Indian and Northern Affairs Canada (INAC—formerly and sometimes still known as the Department of Indian Affairs and Northern Development [DIAND]), as of 2006 there were 698,025 Indians in Canada. This apparently straightforward statistic, however, becomes amazingly complicated upon scrutiny. Like other statistics published by Indian Affairs, it refers only to those registered by the federal government—status Indians and Inuit. This population of "Indians" may vary significantly, both in total numbers and in other ways, from populations defined by other criteria. In the Canadian census, for instance, people are asked to self-designate their ethnicity. In 2006 Statistics Canada came up with 564,870 registered Indians, compared to 558,175 in 2001. In the 1991 and 1981 censuses, the INAC and Statistics Canada numbers varied by 10 and 13 per cent, but in different directions! With regard to its 1996 figures, Statistics Canada noted that they were low because 77 Indian reserves and communities had "incomplete enumerations." In 2006, only 22 reserves had incomplete enumerations. This is an improvement, but still leaves us with not fully comparable data. While the INAC count is based on precise criteria as to who exactly is legally an Indian, and that is a question of importance, the point is that there are other legitimate terms in which one can phrase the question of who is an Indian.

The term "non-status Indian" designates individuals who may think of themselves as Indian and so be regarded by others, but who are excluded from government lists. In government statistics they are usually lumped together with Metis people, both being "unofficial" Indians (at one time both groups frequently were referred to as "half-breeds"; this may or may not have been appropriate in particular instances). In the 2006 census, some 389,785 Canadians designated themselves as Metis, up significantly from 292,000 in 2001; 204,000 in 1996; 135,000 in 1991; and 98,000

in 1981. A 91 per cent increase in 10 years is far beyond any natural increase. Clearly, a far higher percentage of the population who could claim Metis status are now doing so. This is nevertheless a very low number that probably indicates more about the unsatisfactory nature of the census question or about the current usefulness of the term than about how many people it could properly be applied to. By way of contrast, note that the Ontario Metis Aboriginal Association (one of two Metis associations in Ontario) claims a membership of over 200,000. Depending on the criteria employed, estimates of the non-status and Metis population for the country as a whole range from a low of some 400,000 to more than 2 million. The largest Metis populations are found in Alberta, Manitoba, and Ontario.

The Inuit have been administered, and counted, separately from Indians. In the 2004 edition of this text, we stated that because their bureaucratic history has been briefer and less subject to efforts to exclude community members from official lists, there is less disagreement about how many there are. That situation no longer seems clear. INAC counted only 49,115 Inuit in 2006, while they had 56,190 in 2001, up from 36,215 in 1991 and 25,370 in 1981. These figures contrast with Statistics Canada's list of 50,485 in 2006 and 45,070 in 2001.

The federal government has kept count only of status Indians and Inuit. The Constitution recognizes Indians (undefined), Inuit, and Metis as Aboriginal people. Accordingly, we can only state that they number somewhere between 1 million and 3 million.

As Table 26.2 indicates, Ontario has the largest status Indian population in the country, followed by British Columbia. BC stands out for its high number of bands. Yukon (at 514 people per band) has the smallest average band size, followed by the NWT at 646. BC has the smallest average band size of any province (626) and Alberta (at 2,299) has the largest. While the NWT and Yukon have the fewest people living "off reserve," they also have few people actually living on reserves because few were ever established (again, note the non-comparability of many statistics). While the category "off reserve" is not quite the same as "urban," the statistics in this column are indicative of the extensive and ongoing urbanization of Canada's Indian population. The national average of 44 per cent living off reserve is up dramatically from 29 per cent 25 years ago. Even the NWT, at 29 per cent living off reserve being the least urban region, exhibits a major shift from its 7 per cent figure of 25 years ago.

A somewhat different perspective on residential patterns is provided by another set of INAC statistics involving the characterization of communities as urban, rural, remote, or "special access." Using these criteria, the Atlantic region, Alberta, and Saskatchewan have their status Indian populations most concentrated in urban and rural areas (at over 90 per cent), while the most remote is Manitoba (at almost 50 per cent), followed by Yukon and NWT.

As noted above, Canada's Native population is younger than the non-Native population and is growing at a faster rate. Among the general

TABLE 26.2 Status Indian Residence by Region, 2007

REGION OR PROVINCE	NUMBER OF BANDS	POPULATION (% OF NATIONAL)	ON RESERVE (% OF PROVINCE)	CROWN LAND (% OF PROVINCE)	OFF RESERVE (% OF PROVINCE)
Atlantic	33	32,219 (4.1%)	19,475 (60.5%)	27 (0.1%)	12,717 (39.5%)
Quebec	39	70,946 (9.1%)	48,218 (68.0%)	1,588 (2.2%)	21,140 (29.8%)
Ontario	126	171,953 (22.1%)	81,901 (46.4%)	1,645 (1.0%)	88,407 (51.4%)
Manitoba	63	127,159 (16.3%)	78,747 (60.9%)	951 (0.7%)	47,461 (38.1%)
Saskatchewan	70	125,666 (16.1%)	60,729 (48.1%)	1,833 (1.5%)	63,104 (50.1%)
Alberta	44	101,161 (13.0%)	62,013 (61.4%)	2,779 (2.8%)	36,369 (36.0%)
British Columbia	198	123,927 (16.0%)	59,009 (47.6%)	315 (0.3%)	64,603 (51.3%)
Yukon	16	8,221 (1.1%)	502 (6.1%)	3,400 (41.5%)	4,319 (52.5%)
Northwest Territories	26	16,798 (2.2%)	295 (1.7%)	11,159 (66.4%)	5,344 (31.8%)
Canada	615	778,050	410,889 (52.8%)	23,697 (3.0%)	343,464 (44.1%)

SOURCE: *INAC (2008).*

population, 18 per cent are under 15 years old; the corresponding figure for Aboriginals is 30 per cent. Such differences have consequences. The present Indian population (and that of Aboriginals generally) is characterized by an unusually large number of young, economically dependent people. This has created a high demand for educational and social services. In the coming decades, however, as this group matures, they will generate new demands for employment opportunities, frequently in regions now having few jobs. A second consequence is more internal to the Indian community. What kinds of pressures for change are created by a situation in which, quite suddenly, the majority of the population is very young but very few are elderly?

While a population that is growing instead of declining suggests a social turnaround of more than simply demographic consequence, it does not mean that all is well for Canadian Indians. Although mortality rates continue to drop, they are still high; for people under 45 they are typically 3 times the national average. The death rate for children under one year of age declined dramatically in recent decades, but it is still twice the national average. Violent deaths generally are 3 times the national average and among the young may be 10 times the national rate. Suicides among young Indian adults are very high; for those aged 15–24 the rate is 6 times the national average. Rates for women are lower, but for young adult Indian women they are 7 times the national average. For Inuit, suicide rates are 11 times the national average. Conversely, middle-aged and elderly Indians have suicide rates close to or below those of the general population. Further, non-Indians are about 3 times more likely to die from cancer or diseases of the circulatory system than are Indians. Indians are thus at higher risk in many, but not all, categories of mortality.

The most clearly disproportionate statistics involve incarceration in provincial prisons (which involve sentences of less than two years). In 2006 Natives constituted 4 per cent of Canadians but 24 per cent of those in provincial custody. The Prairie provinces had the most disproportionate numbers: in Saskatchewan, where 15 per cent of the population is Native, 79 per cent of the prison population was Native; in Manitoba the numbers were 16 per cent and 71 per cent.

Such statistics could be cited almost endlessly, but it is necessary to ask questions about what they mean. Usually they are presented much as they have been here, with an explicit contrast between Indian and non-Indian. It seems obvious that Indians are in most respects severely disadvantaged in comparison to other Canadians. Unfortunately, the data frequently do not allow for meaningful comparison, because in critical ways the populations being compared are so different. Comparing, for example, the case of deaths by fire, it is clear that even though the numbers have generally declined in recent decades, mortality rates in First Nations communities run about four to eight times the various provincial rates. However, comparing northern remote reserves, where wood stoves are commonly the only source of heat and winters even longer than in the rest of the country, with southern suburbanites would be placing the causality on ethnicity instead of geography. Given that in some regions a very large number of Natives live in areas of difficult access, would the incidence of death by fire in correspondingly remote non-Native communities be any lower? Perhaps, but we do not know, so we are left comparing apples and oranges. Thus, although the data do not really provide a sound basis for social action, agencies must act on the available information. While presumably no one argues that there should be a fire hydrant next to each trapper's cabin, the argument is frequently made that all Canadians should have the same level of social services. This noble ideal, ostensibly redressing apparently scandalous social inequity, fails to take account of the diverse real-world conditions in which people live and often becomes a rationale for moving Indians to places where there are fire hydrants or for bringing urban amenities, through industrial development, to rural and remote people. Neither solution is necessarily beneficial. That is, "comparative" statistics can buttress arguments for providing services that Native communities desire, or they can be used to justify programs that would undercut their social or economic foundations (note Chapters 7 and 11 for examples). In other words, the attempt to create equal living conditions for Indians, buttressed by non-comparable data, confuses general equality with specific identity and results in socially undesirable consequences.

There are always interpretive problems. Media in recent years have run a number of stories about high rates of tuberculosis among First Nations and Inuit people. Often these stories focus on outbreaks in individual communities. While these indeed may be devastating, it is more telling to examine the larger picture. Infection rates can also vary dramatically on a yearly basis; again, average rates over time tell a more accurate story. Infection rates are highest in isolated communities, those with no road access. How many non-Natives live in such places? But even so, it is inescapably true that Aboriginal rates are high; nationally they have been running about eight times higher than for non-Natives. Overcrowded living conditions are clearly a critical factor, and one in which the federal government has responsibility. Nevertheless, it is also the case that infection rates have been coming down and currently all agencies have made reducing rates further a high priority.

Indians are much less likely than other Canadians to have a legally sanctioned marriage. This in some part reflects the failure of the government to recognize traditional forms of marriage. More importantly, it indicates the impact of legislation on choices about legal marriage. Unmarried mothers receive much higher welfare payments than do separated or divorced mothers. Until 1985 the Indian Act, Section 12(1)b, stripped Indian status from women, and from the children of women, who married men who were not legally Indian. For decades many Indian women found it not in their interest to be formally married. This may well have implications for family stability and social attitudes, but the statistics cannot reasonably be interpreted simply as they might be for non-Indian populations.

As a last example, consider that although the "sixties scoop" of Native children by social services workers is long over, there are still five times as many Indian children as non-Indian in the "care" of the government. While the Indian population has almost doubled in the last 25 years, the percentage of Indian children being taken into care has also doubled. In the same period, the number of adoptions of Indian children has grown by a factor of five, while the proportion being adopted by non-Indians has grown from about 50 per cent to about 80 per cent; put another way, eight times as many Indian children are now lost to the Indian community as formerly. This has been explained largely on the basis that these children are now living in better material and social conditions. That claim would of course be difficult to substantiate in many cases, but even if it were true, would the pattern be justified? By what standards does one judge—is the number of toilets per household an appropriate measure? Does a *community* have a right to its children even where parental care undeniably has broken down?

Finally, to return to an earlier point, however inadequately the INAC statistics indicate conditions for Aboriginal people generally, and however misleading they may be when interpreted out of their cultural and social context, the fact that these statistics have been generated about one segment only of the Canadian population, in order to facilitate their administration, is in itself a dramatic statement about the nature of the relationship.

Renewal

Optimism is increasing in many Native communities today. That is not to say that all is well. Even the average non-Indian is aware of at least some aspects of the negative statistical profile as it is generally presented: inadequate housing, over-representation in prisons, high mortality rates, etc. Nevertheless, the negative picture is much less than the whole story. The main story has to do with the renewed vitality of Native society.

The reader will remember that reference has been made from time to time throughout this book to the impact of images and ideas on our thinking. A dominant image in Canadian thinking is that Native people are best considered as part of the past: their social structures and economies are antiquated; they may have a legitimate or even honoured place in history, but their traditions are a hindrance to them and the country; that they might have a viable future as Natives is almost unthinkable. This pervasive stereotype, when reinforced by the generally held negative statistical profile of contemporary Native people, has profoundly damaging consequences. These negative effects may be seen at work in the general population, in school textbooks, among public policy planners, and at times among Native people themselves.

To counter the notion that Native society is moribund, we have three observations. Several chapters have demonstrated that changes in the lifeways of Aboriginal peoples have been substantially less than commonly supposed. People living in remote and northern communities continue to engage in traditional economic activity while also interacting with broader economic flows. Often the fruits of traditional food production are incorporated into social networks that include people living far from traditional homelands. For example,

Dorval, Quebec, has a substantial Inuit population. Friends and relatives flying in often bring caribou, char, ptarmigan, and whale meat, just as they do when visiting northern communities. Urban living is thus structured on the traditional principles. A second observation is that, although traditional activities may have been substantially modified, there are important continuities in meaning, purpose, and function. That is, rather than seeing change as indicating a decline of "genuine" Native culture, change is viewed as normal and universal. Aboriginal society, like all others, incorporates new ideas, technologies, and practices within existing cultural schema. Novelty is not damaging; it is the very substance of human life. Our final observation is that active resistance to assimilation has marked the Canadian Aboriginal experience. For example, despite the devastating effects of residential schools over generations, the policy of cultural displacement through education failed. Aboriginals emerge from this episode determined to retake power over their lives. As the highlights of the report of the Royal Commission on Aboriginal Peoples (RCAP) declared, they "have an enduring sense of themselves as peoples with a unique heritage and the right to cultural continuity"(RCAP 1996:x). Our assessment of these findings is that the Native community, even in those areas where there is less continuity with the past, has persisted and is experiencing renewal.

Renewal, as used here, takes many forms and includes all aspects of life—economic, social, political, educational, political, and religious. Most of all, it has to do with identity. For increasing numbers of Canada's Aboriginal people, to be Native (whether Inuit, Metis, or Indian) is to have pride, in the sense of self-esteem. One of the most important areas of Native renewal is growing success in controlling alcohol abuse. This combats the dominance in Euro-Canadian society of the image of the drunken Indian. More importantly, it is a fact that largely through their own efforts this major social problem is being controlled. The point is best made by reviewing some specific cases.

Alkali Lake in central BC is part of the Secwepemc (Shuswap) Nation and home to about 400 people. In 1972 the chief and his wife felt almost alone in being sober and were desperate to do something to alleviate the terrible problems they saw associated with drinking. They had no particular expertise or resources. Starting with one person, a band councillor in whom they saw potential, they worked on him, even to the extent of following him into the bar and just sitting there as he drank. In time he responded to their intensive attention (shaming is a powerful traditional technique of inducing socially approved behaviour), and they turned to others. After four years they had recruited only a handful of non-drinkers, but it was a start. The chief learned to exert other kinds of pressure, also. People who committed alcohol-related offences on the reserve were presented with the options of choosing to enter treatment or of being dealt with by the law. He learned that bootleggers could be charged under the Indian Act, and went himself with the RCMP to collect evidence to convict the five bootleggers on the reserve, one of whom was his mother. Minimal fines were levied, but the point was clear that he meant business and that subsequent charges would be made under the Criminal Code. Welfare and family allowance cheques were converted into groceries and clothing before people could drink them. By 1979, 98 per cent of the adults were abstainers. As these efforts took hold, other areas of life changed. A number of families pooled their resources to start a grocery store. Several families pooled their funds to buy a house in town for their high-school students to use. A piggery and a co-operative farm were started. Seeing the positive changes, DIAND provided funds to start a sawmill. In short, the entire social and economic fabric of the community was revitalized. Although at this point in time the economic aspects of the case described, written in 1985, seem overly optimistic due to the cessation of short-term DIAND funding, this does nothing to diminish the almost miraculous social transformation that was accomplished. Nor does it diminish the continuing impact that the "Alkali Lake story" has had on other Native communities seeking sobriety.

What needs to be said about Alkali Lake at this point? Well, some 25 per cent of the people now drink, virtually all of them young people. Each individual and each generation has its own battle. It continues to be the case that all who want work are able to find it. But decades ago it also became apparent that alcoholism was only the most obvious problem in the community. Virtually all adults had suffered sexual abuse, at school and in their families. That, like alcoholism, had to be specifically addressed. The main weakness of the summary above is that it emphasizes the economic and political aspects of Alkali's success. At least as important was the effort of the community to work together and to rely on their cultural and spiritual foundations.[1]

On a more formal level, the groundbreaking work of the Nechi Training, Research and Health Promotions Institute at Edmonton is noteworthy. Founded in 1974, it created a new model for addictions counselling and treatment. It was one of the first formally constituted programs of its kind to be conceived and operated by Native people. The central purpose of the Institute was to train addictions counsellors, but the diverse group of people who participated in the program during the early years began working in many other fields, especially health care, education, social work, and business development. Nechi's mission, although always focused on addictions counselling, quickly involved a broad range of community development activities. This broad scope reflects Nechi's ideal of basing its work on traditional values and traditional knowledge. That is, the holistic perspective Nechi adopted saw addictions as symptoms of a much larger problem. Nechi's work in developing

BOX 26.1 Arrows to Freedom Drum and Dance Society: A Twenty-Fifth Anniversary (1985–2010)

In 1985, addicted to alcohol and drugs on Vancouver's Skid Row, a 27-year-old Plains Cree residential school survivor made a desperate decision. Wallace James Awasis (originally from Thunderchild Reserve, Saskatchewan) voluntarily had himself committed to the Round Lake Treatment Centre near Vernon, BC. As he tells it, it was either that or suicide. At Round Lake, Elders such as Alden Pompana (Dakota) introduced Wally to Plains-style ways: drumming and singing, sweat lodge, powwow, and Sun Dance. They taught him that "culture is healing." An Aboriginal person can be healed (emotionally, spiritually, psychologically, and perhaps even physically) using the values, pride, ceremonies, rituals, and knowledge inherent in Aboriginal cultures. A person can be whole, strong, and free from addictions and suffering (the legacy of colonialism) through the reclamation of traditional teachings, philosophies, and sacred ceremonies. Almost simultaneously, three of Wally's brothers—Kenny, Dale, and Duncan—who had endured the same types of government and church abuses, also voluntarily sobered up after years of their own hard struggles with alcohol and despair.

Soon after he returned to Vancouver from Round Lake, Wally took it upon himself to establish the Arrows to Freedom (ATF) Drum and Dance Society in an attempt to stay sober and to pass on the teachings from Round Lake to urban Indians who were suffering in the same ways he had. In an era when one of the only meeting places for Aboriginal people living in cities were the skid row "Indian bars," the Awasis brothers, through ATF, designed and promoted what would become an ongoing phenomenon of sobriety and cultural healing. They created alcohol-and-drug-free social and spiritual spaces for all urban Indians, no matter what Nation of origin, in Vancouver and environs; they initiated Plains-style powwows, Native family nights, and sweat lodge and other ceremonies; they instituted the Red Road Warriors Support Group (an Indian-style Alcoholics Anonymous); they taught cultural awareness in schools and workshops; they patrolled the streets helping out other Native people; they drummed, sang, counselled, and inspired. Recently, Wally described that pivotal time in his life:

> I remember those days when I took back my Cree cultural ways and helped to transform a city of lost Aboriginal spirits that needed something to instill hope in their lives. It was like a cultural revolution that captured the hearts and minds of the young people and gave them recognition as a viable thriving community living within the heart of an otherwise desolate place. I wanted to let people know that not all Aboriginal people were/are alcoholics, drunks, bums, drug addicts, prostitutes, gang members, jailbirds and other typical stereotypes. We were like the weeds that find a way to survive, grow, and flower between the cracks of cement in an otherwise overwhelming sea of a concrete jungle. As we flourished, the city soon realized that we . . . existed and that we were not going away. They had to deal with us in a positive way because we were not a threat to them and it was

Continued

difficult for them to oppress a people that had no intention of causing anyone harm. . . . We never asked for anything from the city: no money, no help, no handouts. We were a movement that took our own healing seriously and needed no help from anyone but ourselves.

The life stories of the Awasis brothers indicate to me that for many urban Indians, a return to one's home reserve (as either a permanent move or a lifetime of extended visits) may be a vital component in their personal healing journeys. This return (or series of returns) might also be prompted by a wish to pass on to their own people, especially youth, the skills and teachings they learned in the city. Dale and Duncan left Vancouver a few years after ATF was formed, continuing their cultural healing work back on the prairies and in northern Alberta. In 2004, Wally graduated with a B.Ed. degree from the University of British Columbia. In autumn 2005, he returned to his home reserve to teach at Peyesiw Awasis (Thunderchild) Community School. Three years later, he was appointed principal. Duncan Awasis served as the school's cultural advisor and elder, but also dedicated many years to conducting traditional Cree ceremonies and counselling Native prisoners at Prince Albert penitentiary. Wally moved to Saskatoon in 2011 to begin a Master's program. Sadly, he soon passed away. Dale Awasis, who earned a B.Ed. in the 1980s from the University of

Saskatchewan, has taught Native children on reserves in three western provinces. In 2007, he earned a Master's degree from Gonzaga University and was elected Chief of Thunderchild First Nation. In 2010, he travelled to the United Nations in Geneva to promote the rights of Native people in Canada. He became Director of Education for the Treaty No. 8 First Nations of Alberta in 2011. Kenny Awasis continues to organize cultural and spiritual events and programs in and around Vancouver and elsewhere in Canada. Like his brothers, he also teaches Cree.

For over 28 years, these hard-working role models have steadfastly maintained the principles of their original motto: "Arrows to Freedom. Freedom from Alcohol and Drugs. Sobriety in Action." They have taught *hundreds* of Native children, youth, and adults to drum, sing, dance, reject alcohol and drugs, take pride in their identity, and participate in traditional ceremonies and activities. Countless Aboriginal people across western Canada have become part of the ATF Drum and are now lifetime members. Many have also earned the right to become healers, drum-keepers, ceremonial leaders, and *cultural* teachers themselves. As always, the official "Arrows to Freedom Drum and Dance Society" name, as well as the drum itself, remained with Wally wherever he lived or travelled and are *activated as needed*. Arrows to Freedom lives on in the twenty-first century and the cultural healing continues!

—Lindy-Lou Flynn, Edmonton, Alberta.

formal training models based on Native traditional knowledge was a truly innovative idea in the 1970s. It is now part of the predominant treatment and intervention paradigm.

An encouraging recent example is the news that the Nakota and some other Alberta reserves

have adopted into their school curricula for grades three to six an alcohol-prevention program. The program was developed by academics and Elders working together. The lessons are tailored to Aboriginal values, beliefs, and customs. A module on tobacco explains the difference between

FIGURE 26.1 Wally (at back), Raven, and Thunder Eagle Awasis take the Arrows to Freedom drum into Carnegie Hall at Hastings and Main, the heart of Skid Row in the Downtown Eastside of Vancouver. ATF established Native Family Night here in 1986. "The Carnegie" is an alcohol- and drug-free community centre for people of this most destitute urban neighbourhood in Canada. In the words of Kenny Awasis, "This is where the people needed it the most . . . so that they could come in one day a week out their lives and share a little bit about these ways" of drumming, singing, dancing, and spirituality, to help them in their own recovery. (Courtesy Lindy-Lou Flynn)

good tobacco and poison tobacco. A self-esteem module teaches an understanding of the inner spirit. Important as programs such as that offered by Nechi are, preventative programs are even more vital.

A final example comes from the federal government and the Canadian Institutes for Health Research. At the end of the 1990s the Medical Research Council was reorganized into a collection of 13 virtual health institutes, each addressing specific significant Canadian health issues. The Institute of Aboriginal Peoples' Health (IAPH) was created to address the considerable health disparities between Aboriginal and other Canadians. A critical need is rigorous health research that demonstrates not only what problems exist but what solutions may be. The IAPH has invested heavily in a series of initiatives designed to foster health research careers for Aboriginal people and to encourage research reflecting Aboriginal needs and perspectives. The IAPH example is important for what it says about normalizing the Aboriginal presence within our knowledge and power structures.

Conclusions to be drawn from these examples include: (1) although we can discuss alcoholism and its treatment as isolated matters, in the real world, for both the individual and the community, life demonstrates interconnectedness; (2) although Nechi and other organizations may work closely with non-Native organizations such as Alcoholics Anonymous, the active leadership of local Native people is imperative; (3) although professional expertise may be useful when available, it is probably more important that plans be locally devised and implemented; and (4) it may be that for many problems—particularly if they are chronic—technical answers are less important than social ones, for resolution will likely involve concepts such as respect, dignity, and control. To put these comments another way, the examples cited illustrate the attempts of Canadian Native people to create an appropriate Native milieu for themselves.

The reader will not be surprised to learn that there are also increasing numbers of Native-run businesses. So much is this the case that some major banks now have Native financial services divisions. There are also Native-owned trust companies, landholding corporations, and other agencies with considerable capital to manage. These moves represent explicit, self-interested decisions to invest resources in Native communities and Native people because they are recognized as having profit-generating potential. As a banker noted when the trend started, "The thing that held native people back has been lack of capital and no structure for capital formation. . . . They're starting to hire the kind of talent that's necessary to do it. When you put together the people, resources, land and dollars, you get an explosive situation. I think this will be one of the big stories in finance and development" (O'Malley 1980). Many difficulties that Aboriginal people experience in entering business flow from the reserve system, in which land is held by the Crown. People are unable to capitalize their businesses with the value of the land base since it cannot be converted to cash. While this has preserved the Aboriginal land base from exploitation by unscrupulous profiteers, it has slowed the movement of capital into Native hands and kept Aboriginal people outside the business mainstream. In its 2009 *Federal Framework for Aboriginal Economic Development,* the Harper government proposed to change this; at the time of writing, this plan was in the early stages of implementation. In the meantime, examples of successful Native-owned and controlled businesses exist, and these can be expected to accelerate as resources are collected and financial management skills developed.

The Sawridge band near Slave Lake, Alberta, is a prime example of the trend. It opened the first Native-owned hotel in Canada in 1973. It has since enlarged the hotel, opened others in Jasper and Edmonton, built a shopping centre in Slave Lake, formed two trust companies, and with four other regional bands created a very successful management services company. The band was fortunate in having modest oil revenues to initiate these ventures and also in having capable management. While traditional government development structures often discouraged responsible management, many contemporary leaders recognize it as a key to achieving their goals.

It is also clear that Native leaders recognize the importance of linkages between sectors: economic development is not solely economic in its purposes or effects. In Saskatchewan the Meadow Lake Tribal Council (MLTC) was created to pool the resources of nine reserves and to implement a broad range of development activities. They successfully took over a school system, partly to promote their long-range plans for developing local leadership. Their lumbering operation, NorSask Forest Products, continues to lead the industry in percentage return on assets, return on equity, and return on capital employed (and runs the only major Canadian sawmill that is wholly paid for). From 30 years of transformative successes, MLTC has learned: (1) the road to prosperity is through healthy people leading healthy lives; (2) it is imperative to get the best advisors and technicians you can, and to listen to them; (3) petty differences must be put aside for the common good; and (4) corporate business growth is the vital ingredient in vibrant community development.

Where is this leading? In 1994 it led to Nicaragua. Contigo International, MLTC's non-governmental organization, took its integrated approach to economic and social development to the Miskito Indians of eastern Nicaragua. Based on their own experience, Contigo attempted to help the Miskito harvest 400,000 hectares of pine forest and develop specific projects for each of the 14 villages involved. One way of thinking about how

this worked is to state that they soon realized that Nicaragua is not Saskatchewan, and that while Cree and Miskito people share world views, their social, economic, and political realities are very different. The logging operation was soon cancelled and in 2008 the social program was also halted due to lack of co-operation by the Nicaraguan government. Nevertheless, we would suggest that this project constituted a very significant statement about the way the MLTC and its people view their world.

The contemporary projects we have mentioned contrast sharply with the historic past in which reserve economies usually had little impact on regional economies except as a raison d'être for government services. A good example of the new potential has occurred at Wendake, a Huron reserve near Quebec City. Under the leadership of Chief Max Gros Louis, 14 businesses were organized. The band is now the largest employer in the area, while the reserve is now home to about 120 businesses. When the companies were organized 52 families were on welfare. Now all able-bodied persons, as well as 125 non-Aboriginals, are employed. Another comes from First Air, the country's third-largest airline. First Air is owned by the Inuit of Nunavik and has developed a comprehensive routing that links northern and southern communities from the Atlantic to the Arctic to the Pacific. First Air was purchased with compensation that flowed to Inuit from the James Bay and Northern Quebec Agreement. It is an example of how Native-run business can serve home communities and be profitable.

Let us end this topic of economic development with two notes of caution. The first is that many reserves have extremely limited potential for economic development. The second is that even where there is economic potential, external constraints may exist. As a case in point we note the Squamish First Nation's plans to develop their Kitsilano reserve, at the southern end of Vancouver's Burrard

BOX 26.2 Iisaak

Iisaak. Among the Nuu-chah-nulth people of Vancouver Island, the word (pronounced E-sock) means "respect." These days it also refers to Iisaak Forest Resources, a forest services company jointly owned by the Nuu-chah-nulth. The reference, of course, is to the philosophy of the company, rooted in traditional values. Another key concept is *hishuk-ish ts'awalk*, "everything is one." That is, the company seeks to respect the limits of what is extracted from the forest and the interconnectedness of all things.

Iisaak operates in the Clayoquot Sound area. In part it owes its existence to the massive civil disobedience that took place there in 1993, with the arrest of more than 800 people for blockading logging operations. They were protesting the "business as usual" clear-cut logging of one of the last stands of old-growth forest on the coast, in an area of exceptional natural beauty. As it happens, the protests were within an area the Nuu-chah-nulth First Nations had claimed as traditional territory in 1980. This claim had been accepted for negotiation by the federal government. Various attempts were made throughout the 1980s to reconcile the competing interests of Aboriginals, environmentalists, forest companies, governments, and local communities. The failure of these attempts led to the well-known blockade.

Eventually, in 1999 Iisaak was created as a partnership between the Nuu-chah-nulth and MacMillan Bloedel (later bought out by Weyerhaeuser). Later in the year agreements were also signed with an environmentalist consortium and then with a local association of displaced non-Native forest workers. Since 2005 the Central Region Nuu-chah-nulth First Nations are sole owners of Iisaak.

Iisaak manages a forest of some 91,200 hectares. It is concerned with sustainability, but it also pursues collaborative approaches involving all local communities, value-added products, and the utilization of techniques fostering biodiversity, forest complexity, and quality of product. In 2011 Iisaak harvested some 85,00 cubic metres. Since its inception, it has restored over 78 kilometres of stream, rehabilitated 66 hectares of riparian habitat, stabilized 48 hectares of landslide area, and deactivated 247 kilometres of forestry road.

Iisaak is very much a project in progress, but the prospects are encouraging. Its forest was certified in 2001 by the Forest Stewardship Council, an international non-governmental certification body stressing "best practices" policies and high conservation value forests. Later in the year it received the prestigious Gift to the Earth award from the World Wildlife Foundation. Iisaak not only is showing respect, it is receiving it.

Bridge. The plan, announced in 2010, is to develop four hectares intensively; the problem is that this will contravene Vancouver's stringent land-use policy. The Squamish, of course, are correct in noting that they are not subject to Vancouver's regulations. They are, however, dependent on the city for access to power, water, and other services. At this point the issue is unresolved, but both sides have publicly recognized the importance to both of real dialogue continuing.

Educational innovation was alluded to above in the context of economic change; it needs to be

considered in its own right. One of the most significant changes of the past three decades is the
growth of Native-controlled schools and school
systems. This is not an automatic panacea, but it
has been of vital importance in restoring a sense
of community and personal identity that goes far
beyond learning the "three R's." That schools can
teach both computer programming and traditional
languages, that functionally monolingual students
(and they still exist) learn to read French or English
better if they are first literate in their own language,
that children have the inherent right to appropriate role models in their schools: these are ideas
that need to be accepted widely and to be pon-
dered at length. The residential schools of the past
may indeed not have been intentionally villain-
ous, but we all, and especially Native people, are
still paying for the psychological and social havoc
they created.

That the number of Native students in the
post-secondary educational systems has increased
exponentially in recent years is in part an aspect of
generalized Native renewal. That the growth is so
impressive is also a function of the base being so
low; in absolute terms the numbers are still small.
That there are now some Native medical doctors
in Canada is a matter of pride, but also of shame
in that there are so few. Nevertheless, students
in these and other programs are important. It is
critical that Native communities have functioning
in them educated people, including professionals
(the current number of Native medical doctors in
Canada is about 200; that is about 10 per cent of
what it should be proportionally).

There have always been Native intellectuals.
There have been Native academics, including
anthropologists, but their numbers historically
have been few, although in recent decades that has
changed. One also needs to remember that some
of the early Native anthropologists were not called
that, but rather were referred to as informants. That,
hopefully, has changed. Among the changes is the

number of Native people, trained in anthropology
and other disciplines, who are using that training to analyze productively aspects of their own
situations. As anthropologists we find this especially exciting because, while there are difficulties
in studying one's own society and culture (partly
because one of the universal features of culture
is the creation of generally accepted fictions), the
insights of an insider are nevertheless frequently
of a nature virtually inaccessible to an outsider.
The Canadian Journal of Native Education is a
good source of some of this material, much of it
done by graduate students. Likewise the *Canadian
Journal of Native Studies*; *Pimatisiwin: A Journal of
Aboriginal and Indigenous Community Health*; and
the recently launched *Aboriginal Policy Studies*
provide high-quality outlets for academic research
by and about Canadian Aboriginals.

We will in no way do it justice, but we must
mention not merely academic writing by Natives,
but writing of all sorts—life stories, poetry, plays,
songs, novels, and opera. The list of performance, creative, and literary works grows each
year. Renewal in Aboriginal society is also an
expressive phenomenon through which the past
and the future are re-imagined in the present. In
2008, Metis writer Joseph Boyden was awarded
the Giller Prize for the best English-language
Canadian novel, *Three Day Road*. In 2002, we had
Atanarjuat (*The Fast Runner*), medal winner at
Cannes and at or near the top of everyone's list of
the best films of the year—not the best Aboriginal
film, but the best film.

There is a virtual explosion in Native arts, and
it has been coming on for decades. The continuing
development of computer, video, and sound technology coupled with the reduced price of software
and broad penetration of the Internet throughout
the country mean that a sound and video production studio are within the reach of every community. In two Inuit examples we see the breadth of
success of Aboriginal music. Susan Aglukark, an

Inuk from Arviat Nunavut, has blended Inuit language with country and gospel influences in a way that garnered her international accolades, Juno awards, and massive sales. Equally successful, Tanya Tagaq is a well-known throat singer who collaborated with Iceland's iconic multimedia artist Björk on *Medúlla*, a remarkable album almost entirely composed of human-made sounds. She has also worked with the experimental classical musicians Kronos Quartet. And we can make similar observations for acting, painting, carving, dancing, and other arts, both within Aboriginal communities and across the world. It is all significant simply because it is there; Native people are expressing their joys and sorrows through the arts as do other people who have the resources.

Possibly the best indicator of the outburst of Canadian Indigenous productive activity generally might be the National Aboriginal Achievement Awards, presented annually since 1993. In 14 different categories they recognize achievement by people who have made significant contributions to their communities and to the whole nation. And it seems appropriate here to mention that the education award in 2004 went to one of our authors, Dr Carl Urion.

A final point in this section is that economic development, operas, and alcohol treatment centres are important not only in their own right, and as examples of a general renewal, but are inextricably linked with renewal as a spiritual phenomenon. Anthropologists have analyzed the series of Indian attempts early in the colonial era to regain control of their lives by religio-political means as a series of revitalization movements. The Longhouse Religion of the Iroquois, the Ghost Dance of the Sioux, the Native American Church, and the Shakers of the west coast are historical examples that are still current. Recent movements are more diffuse, so we have spoken only of renewal, but there are linkages. North American Natives have consistently responded to crises essentially as

spiritual problems, of which the specific workings out are related to a core of meaning.

Traditional religious forms were long repressed in much of Canada, forcing many of them underground. Increasingly, the meaning of these forms is being rediscovered or more openly acknowledged. Some of the momentum is legislative (e.g., the "Potlatch Law" was dropped in 1951; Elders may now conduct services in federal prisons), but the larger factor is a resurgent nativism. Traditional ceremonies such as the sweat, pipe, fast, and Sun Dance are now widely practised. It is important to note that this trend is not merely the repetition of something that the grandfathers did, but a revival or even a reinvention of living traditions. For many Native people it is also true that Christianity has become at least part of their spirituality.

Today, as in the past, activities that are primarily ceremonial are an important part of Native calendars. Possibly the best example is the former Indian Ecumenical Conference at Morley, Alberta, in the 1970s drawing up to 10,000 participants from across the continent. Since 1987 it has continued locally and through its sister organization, the Centre for Indian Scholars. On a smaller scale, Native people attend personal or regional rites in growing numbers.

The outcomes of this renewed spiritual heritage are many. They include such diverse and related activities on the west coast as constructing longhouses, erecting totem poles, carving ceremonial regalia, making prints and paintings, taking potlatch names, and joining traditional societies. They include such varied "political" acts as Chief Robert Smallboy leading his band into the wilderness to escape contamination by Euro-Canadian society, the American Indian Movement occupying DIAND offices in the 1970s, and traditional chiefs lobbying the British House of Lords to prevent the patriation of the Canadian Constitution. They include economic acts as apparently separate as remote James Bay Cree hunters accepting as gift the lives of moose that give themselves to the hunters, and Metis architect Doug Cardinal winning an international competition to design a new building for the National Museum of Civilization in Ottawa.

The formation of Canada constituted a massive, sustained shock to Aboriginal society. Contrary to Euro-Canadian expectations, Native people have survived. It is yet too early to say that they are everywhere flourishing, and they are still threatened, but the evidence of renewed vigour is there for those who will see it.

We noted that although the Indian and Inuit populations continue to experience rapid growth, it is the Metis population that has experienced the most explosive growth— up 91 per cent from 1996 to 2006. Most of that growth is not due to Metis children being born, but rather results from adults who formerly did not report themselves as Metis deciding to do so. In this connection we would note that the census also provides opportunity for people who do not identify themselves as Aboriginal to nevertheless declare themselves as having Aboriginal ancestry. Some 500,000 non-Aboriginal Canadians in 2006 chose to do so. We suggest that this is, at least in part, a sign that they think of having Aboriginal ancestry as a good thing. Native renewal is first of all a good thing for Native people. That it is good for the whole country is worth thinking about.

The Need for Structural Change

In spite of the positive signs of renewal in Canada's Native communities, for these developments to come to fruition there must be basic change in the structural arrangements whereby Aboriginal peoples are governed as part of Canadian society. The failures of the past and the present are not merely the result of such factors as inadequate health-care services, inappropriate textbooks, or restricted access to capital, important though these matters are. While failures of health, education, and economic growth must be addressed in their own right, and while it is important to be aware that Native people are experiencing some success in resolving these social problems, it is essential to recognize that the subordinate legal status of Native peoples will continue to manifest itself in various forms of social malaise if the status quo is maintained. To a greater or lesser extent Native problems are rooted in the fundamental fact of Canadian Native history and contemporary life, that is, they are subjugated peoples without control over the defining facts of their lives.

Native people are quite aware of their colonial status, although all might not put it in these terms. The various forms of renewal—artistic expression, religious rites, political activism, even Native businesses—have in common a strong sense of identity, in being Native. Hence, Native leaders have a long tradition of attempting to create conditions whereby Native communities can function as polities within Canada, or, in the current phrase, can achieve some form of self-government.

The facts of life on the reserves have changed considerably in recent decades, but the fundamental nature of the Indian–government relationship has changed not one whit. Indians have been granted the right to vote and to drink, agents no longer live on the reserves, and many bands have control over expenditures; many harsh and arbitrary features of the reserve system have been moderated. "Consultation" and "development" have become bywords of the new era. Unfortunately, it is still possible to argue that nothing much has been altered: assimilation (first officially repudiated in 1946) remains the overall goal, and Ottawa, however benign its intentions and practices, retains ultimate power.

The Indian Act was last rewritten in 1951. A number of the previous Act's most odious features were repealed at that time. Among other changes, the clause making the potlatch and Sun Dance illegal was dropped. While in a sense this was a victory for all Native people, it is more significant that the change was unilateral: there was no consultation, no apology, no compensation, and no return of confiscated property. The changes were made and Indian people found out about the changes after the fact, just like the rest of us.

Indian Affairs was reorganized in 1964 to provide increased responsibility to personnel working at the community level. Much the same impetus that gave rise to this reorganization led to the commissioning of a landmark investigation by anthropologists to analyze data collected nationally on the educational, social, and economic conditions of Indians and on this basis to make policy recommendations. Commonly called the Hawthorn Report, its release in 1966–7 touched the national consciousness with its detailed inventory of the disadvantaged conditions of most Indians. Amid promises from Ottawa of increased consultation, the reserves were almost flooded with community and economic development workers. Two facts are relevant: (1) government action to correct long-standing problems resulted from studies by non-Indian academics, not as a result of the needs themselves or of the petitions of Native people; and (2) while DIAND sent many fine people to work on various projects, many failed because the local community did not have the power to make key decisions. Such failures left some communities worse off than before.

Shortly thereafter, the now infamous 1969 White Paper on Indian Policy was released. At the stroke of a pen it proposed to abrogate federal responsibility for Indians. That this occurred during a period when DIAND was trumpeting its new, consultative approach is more than ironic. Appearances to the contrary, the White Paper was actually well-intentioned, but was based on assimilationist assumptions. Three characteristics of its chief promoters (Prime Minister Pierre Trudeau and Indian Affairs Minister Jean Chrétien) stand

out as symptomatic of general problems in Indian–government relations: (1) they had no understanding of Indian culture or history; (2) their genuine concern for the rights of individuals left no place for the concept of group rights; and (3) as politicians they tended to judge questions of Indian rights from the perspective of their dominant concern—how alternative responses would affect the struggle to keep Quebec in Confederation. The proposals were totally and emphatically rejected by Indians, primarily through the activity of provincial and national Indian associations. This in a sense marked their coming of age as bodies created by Indians in response to the necessity of acting corporately when attempting to negotiate with the government. Nevertheless, it took a sustained, national effort to block a government initiative that was disastrously ill-conceived.

In 1974 the government established the Office of Native Claims. Typical of its work was resolving a claim by Treaty No. 7 Indians that they had never received the annual funds for ammunition stipulated by the treaty. A simple contractual obligation a century old could be settled only through the creation of a special agency by the government.

When writing the first version of this chapter in 1985, we stated, "At this moment the government continues to propose, as it has for several years, immanent change in Section 12(1)b of the Indian Act, which strips Indian status from women who marry non-status men. While the present legislation clearly produces inequity, whatever change is made in this clause merely changes the formula whereby winners and losers in the 'Indian game' are determined. It will not address the basic problem of Ottawa's defining who can be an Indian." When rewriting this paragraph in 1994 and 2003, we saw no reason to change that assessment, nor is there now. The legislation, Bill C-31, was passed in 1985. It has had enormous impact; almost 120,000 people have received status as Indians under this change to the Indian Act, with some

10,000 waiting for their applications to be acted on. For many, being reinstated has been a profoundly significant event; for others, it has meant that not much has changed. The legislation has continued to be very controversial, partly because of its inequity in denying some grandchildren Indian status, depending on who their grandparents were, a federal failure to provide funding, and partly because the process was not negotiated, but imposed unilaterally by Parliament.

The inequity issue has been resolved. In *McIvor v. Canada*, Sharon McIvor and her son, who had gained status under Bill C-31, asserted that the Indian Act discriminated against them on the basis of sex. In particular, they alleged that they were unable to transmit status to any grandsons, but would have been able to do so if McIvor were male. The government lost the case and two appeals, finally deciding to appeal no further. Bill C-3, Gender Equity in Indian Registration Act, came into effect in January 2011. It is of immediate practical significance because under the old legislation status families were already having about one child in five lose status, and the trend would have accelerated.

The courts, while generally protecting treaty rights, have not held them sacrosanct. In a series of cases concerning hunting rights (starting with *Regina v. White and Bob*, two BC Indians accused of hunting deer on a reserve contrary to provincial game regulations), the courts have held that treaties take precedence over provincial law. However, in *Regina v. Sikyea* (where a Treaty No. 11 Indian shot a goose for subsistence purposes out of season), the court ruled that the federal Migratory Birds Convention Act unilaterally invalidated that aspect of the treaties. This is quite consistent with the nature of a parliamentary democracy, wherein any government "promise" is subject to change by a simple majority vote. The decision is, of course, contrary to the Indian view that a treaty can be changed only by mutual consent and that the necessity of mutual consent further implies that Indians exist and have rights independent of any act of Parliament.

Here again, however, recent events force some amendment of the argument. In a case involving the Musqueam of BC, *R. v. Sparrow* (1990), the Supreme Court decided that federal regulations on fishing did not apply to the Musqueam because their right to fish was, in the language of the Constitution Act, an "existing aboriginal right." This was the first time the court addressed the issue of what the language of Section 35(1) of the Act actually meant. It was a significant and historic reversal of much of the trend noted above. However, as Asch and Macklem (1991) note, the judgment was made not on the basis of inherent Aboriginal rights but of contingent rights, of rights ultimately deriving from the action of the state.

With this thumbnail sketch of the last half-century in mind, one can see why First Nations people and leaders are more than a little skeptical about offers of consultation. Historically, federal offers of consultation have not meant much. In the case of Bill C-7, the First Nations Governance Act, proposed in 2002 as a major revision of the Indian Act, the bill was already framed when the call for consultation went out. Is consultation after the fact worth bothering with? It is not to be wondered at that opposition to this bill was so deep and widespread that it was, in the end, simply dropped.

Interestingly, at the moment, in 2012, the shoe is, in a sense, on the other foot. Shawn Atleo, National Chief of the Assembly of First Nations, wants to "push the reset button," to scrap the existing Indian Act and the whole bureaucracy built around it and to start over in a new relationship based on mutual respect, autonomy, and responsibility. It is a hopeful vision, but one that will certainly face strong opposition from entrenched forces on both sides of the relationship.

A Basis for Change

George Manuel, Indian elder statesman, developed the concept of the Fourth World in a seminal book of that title. The idea refers to tribal peoples who have become incorporated into modern nation-states, but it rejects the notions associated with the Third World concept. An image that Manuel uses to express his central idea is the Two Row Wampum Belt, an Iroquois record of an early treaty in which two parallel rows run the whole length of the belt. It symbolizes the continued, undiminished existence of two independent yet intimately connected realities. It represents his vision (and, it must be noted, the current vision of Shawn Atleo) of what Canada must become if Aboriginal peoples are to participate fully in the nation.

Manuel's vision is at odds with the picture of Indian–government relations elucidated above. Perhaps the clearest expression of the assimilationist–unilateralist position was articulated by then Prime Minister Trudeau: "we won't recognize aboriginal rights. . . . It's inconceivable . . . that in a given society one section of the society have a treaty with the other section of the society" (1969:331). Fortunately for Canada's Native people, their own efforts, rulings by the courts, and public opinion have shifted the political realities.

Historically, intense lobbying by Native organizations, particularly in response to the 1969 White Paper and around the Constitution Act of 1982, has been central in reducing the federal drive for accelerated assimilation and in enlarging the non-Native constituency that believes new legislative alternatives for Native governance are possible.

Recent court decisions have had a profound effect on government policy. British colonial policy, most clearly enunciated in the Royal Proclamation of 1763, recognized Aboriginal rights; this eventually led to treaties and the reserve system. The government's theory was that treaties extinguished Aboriginal title; one consequence was the view that even reserves were owned by the Crown and held "at the good will of the sovereign" in trust for his or her Indian wards. Court decisions involving Aboriginal rights tended to be incredibly ethnocentric by modern standards, reserving full rights to those Natives who, by European standards, were civilized.

The 1973 Supreme Court judgment in the Nisga'a case (*Calder v. Attorney General*) was a turning point. Since they had never signed a treaty, the Nisga'a claimed still to possess Aboriginal rights. They also used anthropological testimony to demonstrate that they had exercised a sophisticated form of land tenure prior to European contact and subsequently. Although the Nisga'a lost the case on a technicality, all six judges giving substantive decisions recognized that the Nisga'a had possessed rights of a kind that the Court could recognize; they split evenly on the question of whether these rights persisted. The prime minister was forced to acknowledge that perhaps Aboriginal peoples had more rights than he had thought.

Subsequent initial judgments in cases involving James Bay Cree and Dene claims reinforced the idea of continuing rights. In the Dene case the claimants were signatories to a treaty (No. 11), but the universal testimony of those then present was that it had not been conveyed as something that would lessen, let alone terminate, their rights. Court recognition, or near recognition, of persisting Aboriginal rights encouraged both the government and Native groups to negotiate agreements rather than risk all in court, where neither side could be sure of winning. The court decisions allowed Natives negotiating comprehensive agreements (the Inuit, Dene, and James Bay Cree) to press for recognition of continuing decision-making rights, and not mere public consultation.

The Mackenzie Valley Pipeline Inquiry and the 1977 report by Justice Berger are noteworthy not only because they showed that an eminent jurist thought the Dene had continuing social and political rights and because ordinary Dene successfully communicated their views to the inquiry and to the public, but because the inquiry demonstrated widespread public support for the notion of treating the Dene fairly, that is, of recognizing continuing Aboriginal rights. This and similar cases also deeply involved anthropologists and other scientists in such support roles as gathering and analyzing data and refuting the assimilationist arguments of the developers. In fact, the demands for solid evidence regarding such matters as historical and contemporary land-use patterns have led to the development of more sophisticated research techniques.

The 1982 decision of the Supreme Court in favour of the Musqueam band of Vancouver was another turning point. It recognized that: (1) Aboriginal title still exists; (2) bands own reserve land; (3) verbal promises by federal officials are legally binding; and (4) DIAND must transact Indian business only with the permission of the band council and in its best interest.

The *Sparrow* case, as noted above, while in several regards a significant step in recognizing the continuing nature of Aboriginal rights, makes those rights contingent on state action and hence lessens the likelihood of government or judicial recognition of inherent rights to self-government.

The 1997 *Delgamuukw* decision has been mentioned by several of our authors, notably Anderson. It was clearly a gain for Aboriginal peoples, establishing that Aboriginal title continues and that oral history relating to ownership must be given equal weight with documentary history by the courts. One of the ironies here is that the ruling was made by way of overturning a lower court decision that was couched in what most anthropologists would regard as ethnocentric language disparaging societies that had not developed writing and a "civilized" way of life. Developing satisfactory ways of evaluating oral history (as we already do written history) will not be easy, but the Court has at least

opened the door. While at this writing there have been no further landmark cases focused on this issue, scholarship on it has been active. The most recent and probably the most important appears to be Miller (2011).

Important though the *Delgamuukw* affirmation of oral history was, its greater importance is with respect to Aboriginal title. It affirms that Aboriginal title is inalienable except to the Crown, is communal, includes the right of both traditional and modern forms of economic exploitation, and is protected by the Constitution. On the other hand, *Delgamuukw* also affirmed that Aboriginal title is not absolute, but may be infringed upon by both federal and provincial governments if there are "compelling and substantial reasons" to do so and if the special fiduciary (trustee) relationship between the Crown and Aboriginal peoples is maintained. As is always the case, it will take time to sort out the practical implications of all this, but it is clearly part of a long-term trend of the courts being forced to spell out the ongoing nature of Aboriginal rights to governments that, to varying degrees, had tended to assume that they would go away.

Reference was made above to the testimony of Treaty No. 11 signers, that they had not understood the treaty to involve a transfer of land title, regardless of the written text. The logic of that testimony has now had some 20 years to develop, and literally scores of land-claims cases involving treaty are coming before the courts, for, of course, the oral history in the earlier treaty areas is of the same nature: the treaties were seen as establishing a reciprocal relationship with the Crown, not as "selling land." Parenthetically, one might comment that it is hard to imagine that a person knowing a Native community in any kind of depth could imagine them knowingly agreeing to a transfer of land title. In any case, Indians in treaty areas are anticipating that the courts will recognize that they have some continuing rights in their traditional lands outside of the reserves.

Toward Self-Government

What, then, are the practical prospects for Native self-government in Canada? In many respects the answer to this depends on where one is. Self-governance in an immense territory such as Nunavut is vastly different than in a small reserve, as commonly exists. In the former case, control over broad aspects of jurisdiction like justice, education, and health is accorded to an Inuit-led government. In the latter, relatively few can be granted as a reserve is typically heavily dependent on the surrounding non-Aboriginal territory for services.

Let us expand on the complexity of Aboriginal governance. The Inuit of the former eastern Northwest Territories achieved self-governance in 1999. By virtue of geographic and historic vagaries, they remain a substantial majority (85 per cent) in their region, and so Nunavut became a reality. This is an unprecedented degree of self-determination within a public government, that is not dependent on ethnic identity. Thus Nunavut is both a federal territory, like the Yukon and Northwest Territories, *and* an essentially Inuit political and administrative domain.

In contrast, the political evolution of the Inuit of Nunavik (Northern Quebec) has been remarkably successful, yet of very different character. In the years after World War II Nunavik was largely administered by the federal government despite being provincial territory. With the rise of a distinctly Québécois political consciousness in the 1960s, Northern Quebec was re-appropriated by the province, progressively displacing the federal government from areas of provincial jurisdiction. In the 1970s Nunavik Inuit signed the James Bay and Northern Quebec Agreement, formalizing the Inuit place within many areas of northern governance. Nunavik cannot be a territory like Nunavut, yet through persistent negotiation over many years new forms of Aboriginal administrative autonomy and competence were developed.

In 1999 the Nunavik Political Accord, setting that part of Quebec north of 55 degrees on the road to self-government, was signed by Inuit (represented by the Makivik Corporation), provincial, and federal officials. The three parties agreed in December 2007 to work toward establishing new self-government powers in Nunavik, with the goal of empowering Inuit in the region to govern themselves. A negotiated proposal was put to the people of Nunavik in a referendum in April 2011, but strongly rejected. Negotiations are continuing.

The success of the Inuit in achieving considerable degrees of self-determination is in part at least a reflection of how Inuit society has always organized itself. A strong sense of collective identity and objective coupled with traditional leadership has been translated into broad-ranging and inclusive political agreements that include many compromises. In contrast it is unlikely that there will be a parallel Dene political realm in the western NWT (Denendah) despite the fact that there is strong cultural and linguistic affinity over a broad territory. We posit that, in part, this is because of the value that the Dene place on individual autonomy and family as organizing structures for production. Despite the remarkable achievements of the Dene Nation and other collective political organizations over the past two generations, at this point only three groups have signed self-government agreements: the Gwich'in in 1992, the Sahtu in 1993, and the Tlicho in 2003. For all the rest, the Deh Cho, Deline, Norman Wells, Tulita, Akaitcho, and the Northwest Territories Metis, negotiations are slowly progressing (see Chapter 11 for detail on the Deh Cho case).

The Yukon is also a patchwork, but of a different complexion. From 1995 to 2006, 11 of their 14 First Nations have become self-governing. White River, Ross River, and Liard are not in active negotiations and remain Indian Bands under the Indian Act.

Newfoundland and Labrador present interesting internal contrasts, with the Natives of

Labrador pursuing self-government and those of Newfoundland recognition as status Indians.

In 2005 the Labrador Inuit Land Claims Agreement came into force, creating the Nunatsiavut government, a self-governing body. There are no reserves involved, but there are two forms of Inuit ownership of land recognized. The specific arrangements are very complex; for instance, the existing rights of non-Natives in the area, of both individuals and corporations, are also recognized.

The Innu Nation of Labrador presented a land claim for about 70 per cent of Labrador to the federal government in 1978. A tripartite agreement between the Innu and the provincial and federal governments determining how negotiations would proceed was signed in 1996, and the Tshash Petapen Agreement ("New Dawn Agreement") between the province and the Innu was signed in 2008. Negotiations continue to bring the federal government into the agreement.

The Labrador Metis Nation, comprising Inuit Metis living in southern Labrador, was formed in the early 1980s. In 2010 they presented the federal and provincial governments with their NunatuKavut Land Claims Document. There will be years of negotiation ahead.

On Newfoundland itself things have moved in a different direction. Starting in the 1600s, Mi'kmaq moved onto the island, where they were treated by the colonial government simply as settlers. But with Confederation came the possibility of recognition as status Indians. In 1972 the people of Conne River formed an elected band council, and in 1973 the Federation of Newfoundland Indians (FNI) was formed. In 1984 the federal government recognized the Conne River Mi'kmaq as status Indians under the Indian Act, and in 1987 Conne River was recognized as a status Indian reserve. In 2008 the FNI signed an agreement with the federal and provincial governments, and in 2010 the Qalipu Mi'kmaq First Nation Band was created. It

will not have reserves but will be a vehicle for providing services to the Mi'kmaq of Newfoundland.

In any case, some forms of self-government are being developed across the country without recourse to the Constitution. As noted earlier, many Natives see the process of renewal as being, in a broad sense, a path to self-government. That is, through various means of self-help, by running their own schools, health facilities, businesses, and the like, they are actively taking increased control over their own destinies, regardless of external support or opposition. For status Indians, however, despite the extent of internal renewal generated, there remain the formal, unilateral mechanisms of federal power, even under the current proposed changes to the Indian Act. As previously noted, although renewal is requisite to dignity, sustained renewal requires an end to dependence.

British Columbia is a special case because almost none of it was covered by treaty. Not until after 1973 did any of its governments recognize the need for treaties. A treaty process has been instituted to both remedy this deficiency and to move ahead into significant self-government, but not yet with much success. The first resolved case was that of the Nisga'a, and it has become controversial. Following the 1973 Supreme Court decision, serious negotiations did not occur until 1991 and an agreement did not emerge until 1998 (111 years after Nisga'a chiefs first petitioned for recognition of their land rights). It was formally signed in May 1999. The agreement allowed the Nisga'a to retain 1,992 square kilometres of their traditional land (note that most media reports had it that they were given the land!), it compensated them for lost land and revenues, and it recognized them as a distinct polity within BC. The least one can say about the aftermath is that it was filled with political rhetoric, most of it premised on the dubious propositions that in a democracy everyone should have a say, even in government-to-government negotiations, and that if the other First Nations follow suit, BC could end up with 50 independent governments. In 2011, the BC Supreme Court dismissed the legal challenge to the treaty. Possibly it could still end up in the Supreme Court of Canada.

Only one other such treaty has been negotiated in BC, that of Vancouver Island's Nuu-chah-nulth people, in April 2011.

In Alberta, negotiations between the Lubicon Cree First Nation and the federal government about a reserve, "only" 70 years after it was first promised to them, and an economic, social, and political package that would allow them to move forward have not moved at all since they broke down in 2003. In the meantime, over 2,600 oil and gas wells have been drilled on Lubicon land. It is worth noting at this juncture that the failure of governments to honour agreements is not merely a feature of some distant past; current examples can still be found. For instance, in October 2011, officials of the Pimicikamak Cree First Nation at Cross Lake in northern Manitoba closed their school because roads accessing the school were unsafe due to artificial flooding as a result of activity carried out under the Northern Flood Agreement (NFA). The NFA had been signed in 1977, to help the Pimicikamak and neighbouring Aboriginal communities adjust to a major hydro-electric dam, which has dramatically impacted the local ecosystem. It has never been fully implemented.

Nevertheless, in spite of far more failures than we would like to see, the federal government has publicly committed itself to proceeding toward self-government and is working on a piecemeal basis to that end. Substantive negotiations are painfully slow—at the present rate the process will take a century or more—and the current federal government continues to resist the idea of an inherent right to self-government. But a start has been made. In the meantime, numerous bands are taking control of at least part of their system, on the basis that they must do what they can.

In 1969, when the White Paper was presented, it would have seemed ludicrous to suggest that in 45 years some Canadian Native people would have achieved meaningful self-government and that for many the possibility could seriously be discussed. The Two Row Wampum Belt may yet become a meaningful symbol of the Canadian experience.

Reconciliation

As a nation Canada was built by the collective efforts of its Indigenous peoples, and the French, English, and subsequent settlers. Our human geography is resolutely plural. The often disgraceful treatment of Aboriginals since colonization is a repudiation of the generosity and commitment to shared destiny that marked so many early interactions between Europeans and Natives. We believe that this state of affairs is inconsistent with the general ethos of the country, including a considerable openness to cultural diversity. Canada's treatment of Aboriginal peoples and the relatively weak efforts to address these injustices undermine our legitimacy and position among nations.

It is astonishing to us as educators to encounter in the classroom the same stereotypes, falsehoods, and wildly inaccurate portrayals of Aboriginal peoples year after year. We are not disparaging students here, but take this situation to indicate a broad social and cultural malaise. Canada has yet to construct a factual national narrative of the place of First Peoples in the country. We hope this book provides some encouragement toward this goal. In describing the Canadian experience, we have tried to avoid offering a litany of past injustices. Rather, we sought an acknowledgement of the harsh realities that Aboriginal peoples faced in the process of building this country and a proper incorporation of that history into the way we understand the past and envision the future. The seemingly endless process of negotiating new agreements between Aboriginal peoples and governments will not resituate Aboriginal peoples.

For this, a more profound integration of Canada's Aboriginal reality must occur. Since Confederation, we have exceptionalized the Native presence by delimiting little pockets of tolerated existence. As a result of denying rights extended to all others, Canada has been obliged continuously to create legislation and policy to mitigate failure. Never quite catching up to its own agenda, the country seems mired in problems of its own making. Throughout the nearly 150 years of Confederation, Aboriginal peoples have sought new and respectful forms of engagement with the country while facing harsh realities of the effects of marginalization. Is there any hope to move beyond this state of affairs? While we cannot say for sure, in closing we return to the RCAP recommendations and explore the issue of reconciliation.

In 1996, after five years of hearings, research, and deliberation, the report of the commission called for recognition of the effects of injustice on Aboriginal peoples today and reconciliation between the Aboriginal and non-Aboriginal peoples of the country. Central to its recommendations is the need for Aboriginal and non-Aboriginal Canadians to rediscover the spirit of sharing and partnership that marked their initial relations. To do so requires a new understanding of how history and culture intersect the lives of all Canadians today, not just of Aboriginal peoples, and it asks that the country at large reconcile themselves with the past in a new partnership. There is an open, embracing quality to the RCAP report that speaks to the continuity of the vision of Aboriginal hopes in this country. To enact such an ethos, however, requires reshaping the landscape of Aboriginal presence in the country's schools, public spaces, institutions, and neighbourhoods. It means a normalization of the Aboriginal presence in all our lives; it would require an equal and sustained embrace to be possible.

The government response to RCAP has been muted at best. We are now seven Parliaments removed from its tabling, making it political ancient history, yet the moral imperative that initiated the commission remains. Several ideas like an Aboriginal Parliament are simply dead, and it is fair to ask if there is any evidence that RCAP has a sustained effect. It is not that no efforts have been made. There have been a number of tangential responses, like the establishment of the Aboriginal Healing Foundation (AHF) and ongoing acknowledgement of and compensation for those who suffered residential school abuse. A final element intended to come to terms with residential schools is a Truth and Reconciliation Commission (TRC), which has begun. TRCs are formal processes through which conflicts and injustices between governments and/or groups of people can be acknowledged, recorded, and resolved, in theory permitting new, more just, and constructive ways of interacting to emerge. The most widely known TRC is that of post-apartheid South Africa, where an entire society organized around racial segregation had to renew itself on egalitarian terms. How to reconcile the historical injustice with the pressing need to move forward is a major cultural challenge in South Africa, and Canada is faced with an analogous challenge. Our TRC is meant to bring attention the residential school era and its effects on people today. Among its objectives are permitting those affected by the schools to be heard in a safe and culturally appropriate setting, fully documenting the residential school era, raising public awareness of the era, and finding appropriate means to commemorate the experience. Healing is an absolute necessity for those who suffer now and to make a coherent future for the next generations. Yet healing is one step among many, and it is important to keep in mind the original spirit of the RCAP recommendations on the need for a national reconciliation. Adopting a victim-centred approach, while needed, will not address the broader questions of how to remake the partnership in light of historical reality. Can the country emerge from the past and make a new and equitable future, or will we simply continue to stumble along finding good paths at times, becoming lost at others? A more just and positive Canadian Aboriginal experience requires sustained vision from all of us.

NOTE

1. The best overview of their history can be found at the Four Worlds International website at www.4worlds.org/4w/ssr/Partiv.htm.

REFERENCES AND RECOMMENDED READINGS

Akiwenzie-Damm, Kateri. 1998. *Residential School Update.* First Nations Health Secretariat. Ottawa: Assembly of First Nations. Broad coverage of perhaps the most critical Aboriginal social issue of our time.

Asch, Michael, ed. 1997. *Aboriginal and Treaty Rights in Canada: Essays on Law, Equality, and Respect for Difference.* Vancouver: University of British Columbia Press. A collection of essays exploring a number of contemporary legal issues as they impact Canadian Native peoples. It is in effect a plea for broader, more anthropological rulings from courts.

———— and Patrick Macklem. 1991. "Aboriginal Rights and Canadian Sovereignty: An Essay on *R. v. Sparrow,*" *Alberta Law Review* 29: 498–517.

Dickason, Olive P. and David T. McNab. 2009. *Canada's First Nations: A History of Founding Peoples from Earliest Times,* 4th ed. Toronto: Oxford University Press. Currently the standard text, taking a very broad perspective and touching on most contemporary issues.

Dyck, Noel. 1991. *What is the "Indian Problem": Tutelage and Resistance in Canadian Indian Administration.* St John's: ISER Books, Institute of Social and Economic Research, Memorial University of Newfoundland. A careful analysis of the fundamental contradictions in Canada's Indian policy, with thoughtful recommendations for the future.

Francis, Daniel. 1992. *The Imaginary Indian: The Image of the Indian in Canadian Culture.* Vancouver: Arsenal Pulp Press. An exploration of the roots of our images about Native people and the current realities flowing from those ideas.

Frideres, James S., and Rene R. Gadacz. 2007. *Aboriginal Peoples in Canada: Contemporary Conflicts,* 8th ed. Don Mills, ON: Pearson. A historical and sociological analysis of the legal, demographic, and social status of Canadian Native people.

Goddard, John. 1991. *Last Stand of the Lubicon Cree.* Vancouver: Douglas & McIntyre. A detailed account of Canada's best-known case of failure to come to agreement on a land-claims settlement. In a sense it is now dated, but then, nothing much has changed since it was written.

INAC. 2008. *Registered Indian Population by Sex and Residence, 2001.* Ottawa: Minister of Public Works and Government Services Canada.

Lobo, Susan, and Steve Talbot. 2001. *Native American Voices: A Reader,* 2nd ed. Upper Saddle River, NJ: Prentice-Hall. Although largely American in content, this very broad-ranging book by Aboriginal authors does present Canadian and joint perspectives as well.

Long, David, and Olive P. Dickason. 2011. *Visions of the Heart: Canadian Aboriginal Issues,* 3rd ed. Toronto: Harcourt Brace. Covers a broad range of issues with insight, and often written in a powerful voice.

McFarlane, Peter. 1993. *Brotherhood to Nationhood: George Manuel and the Making of the Modern Indian Movement.* Toronto: Between the Lines.

A study of the life of George Manuel and his impact on the Canadian Indian movement.

McKee, Christopher. 2000. *Treaty Talks in British Columbia: Negotiating a Mutually Beneficial Future*, 2nd ed. Vancouver: University of British Columbia Press. Historically, BC has been the most intransigent province with respect to treaties. This volume analyzes the current complexities.

Malloy, Tom. 2000. *The World Is Our Witness: The Historic Journey of the Nisga'a into Canada*. Calgary: Fifth House. Broad coverage of the first modern treaty in BC and a focal point for recent debate.

Manuel, George, and Michael Posluns. 1974. *The Fourth World: An Indian Reality*. Don Mills, ON: Collier-Macmillan. A profound, simple, and influential combination of political philosophy and personal narrative. Essential reading for the serious student and a marvellous starting point for the novice.

Miller, Bruce Granville. 2011. *Oral History on Trial: Recognizing Aboriginal Narratives in the Courts*. Vancouver: UBC Press.

Newhouse, David R. 2000. "From the Tribal to the Modern: The Development of Modern Aboriginal Societies." In *Expressions in Canadian Native Studies*, edited by Ron F. Laliberte. Saskatoon: University of Saskatchewan Extension Press.

O'Malley, Martin. 1980. "Without Reservation," *Canadian Business* 53, 4: 37–41.

Perpetual, Jeanne, and Sylvia Vance. 1993. *Writing the Circle: Native Women of Western Canada— An Anthology*. Edmonton: NeWest. Mor 50 Indian and Metis women write about their lives, to great effect.

Ross, Rupert. 1996. *Returning to the Teachings: Exploring Aboriginal Justice*. Toronto: Penguin Books Canada. Ross displays more cultural understanding than anyone else writing on this difficult subject.

Royal Commission on Aboriginal Peoples (RCAP). 1996. *People to People, Nation to Nation: Highlights from the Report of the Royal Commission on Aboriginal Peoples*. Ottawa: Minister of Supply and Services Canada.

———. 1996. *Report of the Royal Commission on Aboriginal Peoples*, 5 vols. Ottawa: Government of Canada. The most thorough analysis and recommendations concerning Aboriginal conditions in Canada.

Statistics Canada. 2003. *Aboriginal Peoples of Canada: A Demographic Profile*. Ottawa: Minister of Public Works and Government Services Canada.

Tennant, Paul. 1990. *Aboriginal Peoples and Politics: The Indian Land Question in British Columbia, 1849– 1989*. Vancouver: University of British Columbia Press. A detailed political history of the treatment of Indian lands in a complex jurisdiction.

Tester, Frank James, and Peter Kulchyski. 1994. *Tammarnit (Mistakes): Inuit Relocation in the Eastern Arctic, 1939–63*. Vancouver: University of British Columbia Press. A broad examination of the evolution of Canadian Aboriginal policy in the North during the formative stage of the modern era.

Trudeau, P.E. 1969. "Remarks on Aboriginal and Treaty Rights." In *Native Rights in Canada*, 2nd ed., edited by P.A. Cumming and N.H. Mickenberg. Toronto: General Publishing, 1972.

Waldram, James B. 1988. *As Long as the Rivers Run: Hydroelectric Development and Native Communities in Western Canada*. Winnipeg: University of Manitoba Press. Modern economic development projects are examined in the context of the historical relationship between the Crown and the colonized.

Weaver, S.M. 1981. *Making Canadian Indian Policy: The Hidden Agenda 1968–1970*. Toronto: University of Toronto Press. The definitive study of how the 1969 White Paper came to be; reveals the government's internal debate over policy formation.

Wiebe, Rudy, and Yvonne Johnson. 1996. *Stolen Life: The Journey of a Cree Woman*. Toronto: Knopf Canada. A moving, in-depth analysis of a single case involving our "justice" systems.

GLOSSARY

Aboriginal Pertaining to the original inhabitants of a particular territory and their contemporary descendants; in Canada, the First Nations, Inuit, and Metis peoples.

acculturation The process of learning a second or subsequent culture.

affinal Related by marriage.

allotment by severalty A form of landholding in which single pieces of land are owned by individuals, as opposed to various forms of communal ownership.

Amerindian A person indigenous to North or South America.

anadromous fish Species of fish that spend most of their life in the sea and migrate to fresh water to breed.

assimilation The process whereby an individual or group no longer identifies with their primary culture and becomes part of another group.

babiche Thin, dehaired strips of rawhide used in the manufacture of various artifacts, such as snowshoes and fish nets.

bast The inner bark of trees, or fibre obtained therefrom.

clan A kin group whose members believe themselves to be descended from a common ancestor so distant in time that not all connecting links can be specified.

cognatic Descent rules and groups formed by the operation of such rules, in which descent is reckoned through both male and female links, most commonly in the form of either bilateral descent (reckoned through equal affiliation with the relatives of one's father and mother) or of ambilineal descent (reckoned through either female or male links).

consanguine A "blood" relative.

cosmology A "map" of the social and natural world for a culture that explains what kinds of beings there are, where they are, and how they interact.

cultural broker Someone who acts as an intermediary between two cultures, usually helping members of the subordinate culture learn to operate in a dominant culture.

culture The set of learned behaviours, beliefs, values, and attitudes characteristic of a social group.

dual economy The idea that a traditional economy based on reciprocity and a modern economy based on the market can coexist, especially in "developing" regions.

economic man The idea that human behaviour can be explained by economic self-interest.

endogamy Marriage within one's social group.

epistemology The philosophical study of the grounds of knowing, especially with regard to the limits and validity of knowledge.

ethnography 1. The fieldwork method of cultural anthropology in which a specific group is intensively studied through participation in their daily lives. 2. A study reporting the results of such fieldwork.

ethnology The theoretical method of cultural anthropology; the study of human behaviour generally through cross-cultural comparisons.

exogamy Marriage outside of one's social group, typically a clan or lineage.

extended family A social group consisting of near relatives in addition to the central conjugal unit and their offspring.

factor A person who carries on business transactions for another; specifically, a senior field rank in the Hudson's Bay Company.

fee simple Land that is owned and may be passed on to heirs without restrictions, i.e., the ordinary form of landholding in Canada.

fiduciary A relationship that involves one party (such as DIAND) acting as trustee for another (such as the various Indian bands).

Fourth World A concept developed by George Manuel to describe the internal colonialization of Indigenous peoples within nation-states formed by settler societies; includes Aboriginal people around the world who have been incorporated into contemporary states.

hermeneutics The perspective that explains human behaviour by understanding actions as parts of systems of meaning.

holophrastic The condition of a word being so densely packed with complex meaning that a simple translation is not possible. Some linguists claim that entire languages can be so characterized; other linguists reject the claim. In any case, it is a characteristic found to some degree in all languages.

horticulture Food production from temporary fields using human labour and relatively simple tools.

household The social group living together as a domestic unit.

hunting and gathering Refers to subsistence by means of hunting and fishing and by collecting vegetal material in a way that involves less tending of plants than actual gardening; also called foraging.

Indigenous people The original inhabitants of a particular territory and their contemporary descendants; in Canada, the First Nations, Inuit, and Metis peoples.

kindred The totality of one's relatives, counting bilaterally.

leister A barbed, three-pronged fish spear.

lineage A set of kin whose members trace descent from a common ancestor through known links, usually forming a matrilineage (with female links) or a patrilineage (with male links).

market economy A system of exchange in which goods are moved through the mechanism of buying and selling them for money.

materialism The perspective that explains human behaviour primarily by recourse to the material conditions of life, such as economic advantage.

matrilineal Having descent through the female line; children of both sexes are assigned membership in the kin group of the mother.

matrilocal Post-marital residence with the family of the wife's mother.

moiety A unilineal descent group that is one of a pair; i.e., each person or clan in the society is a member of one or the other moiety.

Native people The original inhabitants of a particular territory and their contemporary descendants; in Canada, the First Nations, Inuit, and Metis peoples.

non-status Indian A person who self-identifies as Indian, but is not entitled to be registered as such under the Indian Act.

nuclear family A domestic group consisting of a wife, husband, and their unmarried children.

ontology The branch of philosophy concerned with the nature and essential properties of being.

ossuary A place where bones of the dead are deposited.

pan-Indian 1. Something characteristic of Indian peoples in general. 2. The modern trend for Indian peoples to borrow cultural traits from each other and so, in at least some ways, become more alike.

participant observation Learning by doing; the primary field method of anthropology, whereby living within a community provides the primary means for learning about it.

patrilineal Descent through the male line; children belong to the father's kin group.

patrilocal A couple living with or near the husband's father.

patronym 1. Loosely, a surname passed down patrilineally. 2. Strictly, a child taking a name formed from the father's name plus a prefix or suffix, as in *Johnson*, son of John.

phratry A unilineal descent group composed of two or more clans. Members of the phratry will be considered to be closely connected in some regard.

polygyny That form of plural marriage (polygamy) in which one man marries two or more women.

potlatch Major ceremonial feast found on the Northwest Coast and to a lesser extent in the intermontane West; for a time outlawed by the Indian Act.

reciprocity A system of exchange in which gifts are given to people who then have an obligation to offer other gifts.

resistance In anthropology, the notion that Aboriginal responses to external forces are partially shaped by the desire for and necessity of opposition.

sarvice berry Old-timer's rendition of "service berry," more generally known in Canada as saskatoons.

shaman A religio-medical practitioner whose powers to heal, find game, and/or divine the future come from spiritual helpers.

sinodont A term applied by Christy Turner to a dental pattern encompassing the prehistoric and contemporary peoples of China, northeastern Asia, and the New World.

structuralism A perspective that attempts to discover orderly patterns common to languages, myths, kinship systems, and other aspects of culture.

totem Derived from an Ojibway word referring to relatives, primarily refers to animist notions linking contemporary kinship groups to animals, natural objects, or natural phenomena from whom various rights and obligations are derived through descent.

value A conception of the desirable or the valuable; by extension, the moral and aesthetic aspects of culture.

weir A fence-like structure placed across a stream or inlet; in conjunction with fish traps, it facilitates the efficient harvesting of fish.

world view The overall framework through which a person views life; how people think the world is. An opposition is frequently posited between sacred and secular world views.

INDEX

Page numbers in **Bold** indicate maps and illustrations.